The

Bibliographical Society

of

America

1904–79

A Retrospective Collection

The
Bibliographical Society
of
America
1904-79

A Retrospective Collection

Published for the Bibliographical Society of America
by the University Press of Virginia
Charlottesville

THE UNIVERSITY PRESS OF VIRGINIA
Copyright © 1980 by the Bibliographical Society of America

First published 1980

Library of Congress Cataloging in Publication Data
Main entry under title:

The Bibliographical Society of America, 1904–79.

1. Bibliography—United States—History—Addresses,
essays, lectures. 2. Bibliographical Society of America—Addresses,
essays, lectures. I. Bibliographical Society of America.
Z1216.B52   016.973   80-14334
ISBN 0-8139-0863-9

Published with assistance from the Lathrop Colgate Harper Litt. D. Trust Fund

Printed in the United States of America

Contents

Foreword

In January 1979, our membership at large were asked to nominate articles for inclusion in this collection. We asked for recommendations of contributions to our *Papers* which were thought to have demonstrated "the highest degree of excellence, articles of critical importance which have moved forward the art of bibliography."

From this beginning the anthology began to take on its own character. As we collated the assorted recommendations and scanned the *Papers* ourselves, the nature of the volume grew beyond the original concept. The result is a retrospective collection which seeks to represent, in the broadest possible way, the diverse contributions of the members of our Society to its *Papers* over a long period of time.

We hope that the result has achieved a proper balance between scholars and collectors, technical bibliography and bibliophily and that it accurately reflects the concerns and accomplishments of our membership in the general field of bibliography. Mr. Tanselle's paper, delivered at the January 1979 annual meeting, thus appropriately concludes the volume.

Without the cooperation of countless members and the prompt and able assistance of the officers of the Society, this book could not have been initiated, gathered, ordered, and published within the short space of eighteen months. I am most grateful to all who were drafted into service at one time or another by the Publications Committee. The timely gift of a long run of the *Papers* from Miss Geraldine Beard greatly facilitated reproduction of most of the articles gathered in this volume.

Stephen Parks
Chairman, Publications Committee

Introduction

The decision to publish a volume commemorating the seventy-fifth anniversary of the founding of the Bibliographical Society of America involved, at first, plans for a volume of original essays on various aspects of bibliography in America today. The committee appointed to carry out the project ultimately came to the conclusion that the state of bibliography in this country made such a formalistic approach inappropriate. This feeling was reinforced by the effective survey presented by G. Thomas Tanselle at our seventy-fifth annual meeting in 1979, "The State of Bibliography Today." Instead, the committee adopted the proposal put forward by Lola Szladits to reprint a selection of articles drawn from our *Papers*, and to use the Tanselle paper, not as an introduction as originally planned, but as a summation at the end.

The diversity of the thirty-nine pieces chosen strongly suggests that bibliography as it has been practiced in America during the past three quarters of a century does not present itself as a neat arrangement. Instead, the articles range over the whole face of the world of books. An interesting characteristic of the selection is the preponderance of articles concerned with the relationship between books and people — in particular collectors, as opposed to those concerned with the more technical aspects of bibliography. One thing which is apparent is a continued concern about the quality of bibliographical work done in America. George Watson Cole in 1920 issued a plea for rigorous standards, a plea which was echoed in Tanselle's talk in 1979. In 1922 Pierce Butler called attention to inadequate bibliographical practices among scholars, and in 1957 Curt Bühler felt compelled to do the same.

If the volume contains a fair sampling of our past, it also suggests a varied prospect for the future, both in terms of the directions open to bibliographers and in terms of the kind of men and women who will be carrying the work of bibliography forward. It is to be hoped, however, that they will not lose sight of their common denominator — the book.

Thomas R. Adams
President

The
Bibliographical Society
of
America
1904-79

A Retrospective Collection

A PLEA FOR AN ANATOMICAL METHOD IN BIBLIOGRAPHY

By Victor Hugo Paltsits of New York Public Library

HAVING been asked by our President to present a short account on bibliographical methods, so far as illustrated by my own work, I have set down the following notes and criteria.

During the past ten years I have put into print bibliographies of the Jesuit Relations of New France, the "Lettres édifiantes," the Lewis and Clark Expedition, the works of Father Louis Hennepin, the voyages of Baron Lahontan, and the writings of Philip Freneau, as well as other smaller studies. In their preparation I have relied upon the original sources, extant in widely scattered libraries or private collections, and have even imported editions that were otherwise inaccessible. I have always familiarized myself with the bibliographical attempts of predecessors in any given subject, but have invariably found them persistent in error and unskilled in method. This has obliged me to ignore them and to work independently from original sources. These things are a matter of record in my introductions, and I quote from my Lahontan Bibliography, because I have there enunciated my bibliographical doctrines with particular emphasis, as follows: "The present bibliography differs from all its predecessors, in that it gives an analysis of each volume by its component parts, by its pagination, by its signatures, and by the location of its plates and maps. This is, to coin a new

1

term, anatomical bibliography, and follows an idea which I have sought, in several similar monographic studies, to introduce as a more scholarly method in American bibliography. Only by such means can the librarian, scholar, or collector ascertain whether his books are perfect, or wherein they lack completeness. The mere lumping of pagination or plates falls far short of usefulness; it is, indeed, a source of irritation and annoyance."

The term "bibliography" has a certain amount of dignity about it, which accounts for its being made to cover a multitude of sins. Hence we see lists of authorities appended to the works of authors, or catalogues or classed lists on a given subject, masquerading under that dignified term. But a list is only a list, and a catalogue is merely a catalogue—neither is a bibliography. Any one can compile a list, many can make a catalogue, but very few persons can agonize to bring forth a bibliography.

BIBLIOGRAPHICAL ACTIVITIES OF HISTORICAL SOCIETIES OF THE UNITED STATES

By Reuben G. Thwaites

THE present assigned survey is confined, with a few minor exceptions, to the published bibliographies of historical societies proper—those embodied in the list made by a committee of the American Historical Association, printed in the latter's Report for 1905, pp. 249-325. Such general institutions of learning as the Carnegie Institution of Washington, the Library of Congress, the American Philosophical Society, and the Smithsonian Institution are eliminated, as well as the publications of colleges and universities, for to include these would lead us too far afield. Genealogical and patriotic hereditary societies are also excluded, for their field of interest is, as a rule, strictly bibliographical, along the line of their own membership; although occasionally they have issued publications of considerable value to the general student of American history.

The American Historical Association has quite naturally been the chief agent among us, in promoting bibliographical effort in the field of history, as well as in otherwise stimulating scientific methods of historical work. Numerous large enterprises have been undertaken under its auspices—notably bibliographies of the writings of the several members of the Association; of the publications on American history for special periods; and, emanating from its own Public Archives and Historical Manuscripts commissions, lists of manuscripts and reports on the availability of these sources for purposes of research. Special bibliographies are included in many of

3

the formal papers published by the Association, notably several for the Southern States; while the authors of the Winsor and Adams prize essays have also appended to their papers reasonably complete bibliographies. Thus the publications of this Association contain a considerable body of exceptionally valuable bibliographical material.

Among the State and local societies of the country, bibliographical activity has been more desultory, both in method and in character. The inspiration for such undertakings has usually come from some few of the individual members, who appreciate the usefulness of what is nevertheless a somewhat thankless task. For example, the Southern History Association is apparently indebted in large measure to A. S. Salley, Jr.; that of Maine to the work of Joseph Williamson; and the Buffalo Society to that of its secretary, Frank H. Severance.

The material prepared by members or officers of local societies is not infrequently published under other auspices than that of the societies themselves. Credit, therefore, cannot be given to the society, save in those obvious instances where the author's connection therewith is known. Among those of such character may be noted Bates's Bibliography of Connecticut Laws; the Bibliography of the District of Columbia, inspired by the Columbia Historical Society, although issued from the Government Printing Office; a bibliography of Maryland, appearing in the Historical Magazine for 1870; that of New York, prepared by A. P. C. Griffin, and published in Boston, 1887; that of Ohio, issued by Peter G. Thomson, at Cincinnati, in 1881; and that of Rhode Island (1864), inspired by the now defunct Narragansett Club.

A number of the general and state societies have published seriatim bibliographies concerning their especial localities or fields of study. Thus the Archaeological Institute of America from time to time publishes in its *Journal* valuable bibliographies on archaeology; the Jewish Publication Society in similar manner keeps abreast of works on Jewish history and polity; the Iowa Historical Society publishes an annual list of books concerned with that State; while the Wisconsin Society occasionally issues revised reading lists on Wisconsin and early Western history in general.

I. Manuscript lists. Among the earlier enterprises of the historical societies of the original thirteen colonies, were catalogues and calendars of such manuscript material relating to their respective colonies as was to be found in European, especially in English, archives. New York made a fairly complete publication of transcripts of documents of this character. Other societies were content to furnish more or less detailed descriptions of these important sources. Such are New Hampshire's List of Documents in the Public Record Office, London, relating to New Hampshire; Stevens's similar list for New Jersey (published in 1858); that of Pennsylvania and Delaware, issued by the Historical Society of the former colony; and that for South Carolina, occupying the first three volumes of its society's Collections. Recent work in this line, inspired largely by the Historical Manuscripts Commission, has appeared in the Reports of that Commission; and a descriptive catalogue of both public and private manuscript collections of the Old Northwest and adjoining commonwealths, recently appeared from the press of the Wisconsin Historical Society.

While not an historical society, and thus beyond the pale of the present inquiry, one cannot forbear speaking of the important bibliographical work of the Bureau of Historical Research in the Carnegie Institution of Washington. Several of its publications in this field have been of the highest merit, and of great value to students of American history. The recently-issued Bibliography of Writings on American History for 1903 is an eminently useful undertaking, worthy of being continued from year to year. The Institution finds itself unable to continue this enterprise, but it is hoped that the historical societies of the country may be induced to co-operate in its future publication.

II. Descriptions of Archives. These have largely appeared under the auspices of the Public Archives Commission, and for some states embrace almost a complete generalized list of available public documents, still in manuscript form. Some earlier reports of the Commission gave useful summaries of the archival collections at Washington, in the Library of Congress and the several departments; while recent attention to the Spanish-American archives of Texas and the Southwest has been fruitful.

III. Public Documents. Among the local societies, bibliographies of colonial laws, and of early series of public documents, have been found useful. The work of Gen. A. W. Greeley, for the documents of the early congresses, has placed all students of American history under obligations to his patience and industry.

IV. Book Lists. The subjects of the bibliographies published by historical societies, concern either the local history or the literature of their respective localities. Several of the various nationalistic and denominational societies have furnished useful lists for their respective subjects, such as the Schwenkfelders in America, the Scotch-Irish bibliography of Pennsylvania, and German-American hymnology. In addition to state bibliographies already referred to, some attention has here and there been given to early American imprints. Episodes of American history, and publications of

American writers and travellers, are also among the subjects scanned.

Quite naturally, a large proportion of the subject matter already published by the societies has related to American history and biography. Notable exceptions to this rule are, however, Thatcher's account of the Latin sources of the First Crusade, Johnson's Edward III as King of France, several lists on English history, and R. P. Roosevelt's Bibliography of Hugo Grotius.

V. Newspapers. The New Jersey society has made a considerable catalogue of early American newspapers. Published lists for Illinois and Nebraska embrace early journals of their respective states; while those of New York and Wisconsin furnish annotated accounts of their entire collections to date.

We have seen that much excellent bibliographical work has, on the whole, been done by American historical societies; but it has been both spasmodic and sporadic in character. Efforts should be made to induce a more general spread of such enterprises on their part, and if possible more systematic treatment. Publication of the sources, in extenso, is of first importance to historical scholarship. It is almost equally necessary, however, occasionally to make record not only of the issues of the press concerning the field in which the society works, but of the location of unpublished material for its study.

Historical societies have, as a rule, specialized fields of investigation; their own collections of books and manuscripts furnish opportunity for careful, exact, and scholarly bibliographical work, and they have ready access to other collections; while their office as public servants would seem to make them especially responsible for producing the tools of research. In the case of societies not individually rich in such collections, nevertheless solicitous to help, co-operation is always possible. Bibliographical undertakings of considerable importance might well be carried on between societies of the same state or section. Such co-operation would doubtless prove one of the most fruitful methods for carrying on well-considered enterprises of this character, so essential to students of our history and institutions. ([1])

(1). See "Report of Committee on Methods of Organization and Work on the part of the State and Local Historical Societies," in *Annual Report* of American Historical Association, 1905, vol. 1, p. 249-325—especially p. 268-272.

LUTHER S. LIVINGSTON

A BIOGRAPHICAL SKETCH

BY GEORGE PARKER WINSHIP

An American scholar died on December 24, 1914. Self-made, the doors of opportunity opened to him but a few months before this, and with many misgivings he passed through them. To his surprise, he found himself among men of recognized attainments, who welcomed him to their assembly and conducted him to a seat beside the most honored. While he was still wondering how best he could show his appreciation of their recognition, he died.

Luther Samuel Livingston was born at Grand Rapids, Michigan, on July 7, 1864. His mother's father, Luther Lincoln, was a nature-loving wanderer who transmitted an abiding fondness for the deep woods and the lofty pines. From the neighborhood of Taunton, Massachusetts, he took his young wife to Michigan. They were pioneers on the outskirts of what is now Detroit, and then moved on to the river bank beside the rapids, where they were among the first to claim a home-site. Their daughter Keziah married Benjamin Livingston. His father, Samuel, left Ireland at the beginning of the nineteenth century, and the son reached the Michigan settlement by way of western New York and Canada.

9

The first money Luther Livingston earned, by vacation work sweeping after the laborers on a street-paving contract undertaken by his father, was spent for a pair of heavy tramping shoes and for a set of Chambers' *Cyclopaedia of English Literature*. When he left the high school in 1881, he went to work in a local bookshop. Four years later he was obliged by ill health to give up regular indoor employment, and spent the summer months collecting butterflies and wild flowers in the fields and swamps near Grand Rapids. In the autumn he secured a position in another bookstore, where he stayed until 1887, when he went to New York and became the shipping clerk for Dodd, Mead & Co.

Livingston never liked city ways, and in 1888 he took up a plot of government land at Melbourne, near the head of navigation on the St. John's River in Florida. The inspiration for this venture came from the books of Thoreau. He was ambitious to emulate the simple life as expounded by the Concord seer. Unluckily the Florida glades concealed no motherly neighbors from whose pantry shelves pockets could be stuffed with doughnuts, and the life proved too simple. After a year of unremunerative grubbing at palmetto roots, Livingston returned to the New York bookstore.

In 1891 he was invited by a friend who had discovered his fondness for flowers to visit the greenhouses of Pitcher & Manda at Short Hills, New Jersey. His familiarity with the technical names of the different plants and his accurate information about unusual varieties attracted

the attention of one of the partners, who forthwith
offered him a place on their staff. He was assigned to
the task of compiling catalogues. In this work his
aptitude for precise statement and for the clear differentiation of peculiarities found ample scope. The
printed catalogues compiled by him have become classics
among horticulturists. His descriptions set a standard
which rival establishments were unable to attain, and
they have been copied extensively by other firms, who
thereby contributed to the spread of his unrecognized
influence upon American gardening.

He was just beginning to realize the opportunities for
original investigation which the making of catalogues
offered, when his employers sent him to Colombia to
collect orchids. During the eighteen months he was in
South America, he made three trips to the head of navigation on the Magdalena River, a distance of nine
hundred miles, and brought out a thousand cases of
Cattleya trianae. An equal number of cases, containing some of the rarest and most beautiful orchids ever
collected, were transported in canoes from Arauca down
the Orinoco River to Bolivar, about two thousand miles,
where they were shipped to the United States. He also
made an important collection of butterflies and bird
skins for his own amusement while he was in the interior.
The systematic notebooks in which the record of this
trip is preserved and the delightful gossipy letters to his
mother furnish an abundant store of general ethnological
and geographical as well as special botanical information.

The financial disturbance of 1893 affected the market for orchids, and before the end of the year Livingston was once more in the book business. A few months with Walter R. Benjamin enabled him to become familiar with the trade in autographs, and then he went back to Dodd, Mead & Co., with whom he was identified until his physical disaster in 1912.

In 1898 he married Flora V. Milner of Deer Lodge, Montana, a friend of his boyhood. Mr. and Mrs. Livingston made their home at Scarsdale, nineteen miles north of New York City. There he found three acres of woods, cliffs, swamp, and proper soil for the garden into which he put the happiest part of every week. Under his wizard touch, this little country home lot became a botanical museum. Month by month he added to his treasures until he was nearing the consummation of his ambition to possess a healthy growing specimen of every variety of flowering plant that could be induced to take root in the latitude and longitude of New York City. There were iris from March to July, oriental poppies of all colors by the thousand, rock plants from all over the world covering the cliffs and ledges, tulips in profusion of species. Matilija poppies from southern California and Japanese anemones running wild were only two of the attractions which drew to this little garden on every Sunday a steadily widening group of friends. The flowering shrubs were overshadowed by pines and evergreens from the far corners of the globe; the *Sequoia gigantea* from the Coast Ranges of the Pacific,

Torreya from Florida, *Banksiana* from Hudson Bay,
Deodars from India. The parting from that garden
within sight of the reflected lights of Broadway was not
least among the tragedies of Livingston's last year.

When the members of the firm of Dodd, Mead & Co.
in 1910 decided to devote their energies to the wholesale
publishing business, Robert H. Dodd entered into a
separate partnership with Livingston under the firm
name of Dodd & Livingston. Livingston's remarkable
memory for minute details and his ability to recognize
peculiarities in volumes with which he was unfamiliar
had long been an important asset which did much to
give the house its pre-eminent position among American
dealers in rare old books. These qualities combined with
the instinctive confidence which everyone who dealt
with him felt in his frankness and sincerity gave the new
firm an unassailable position. His visit to London in
1911 strengthened personal friendships with nearly every
British collector of consequence, and put him on the
way to become the best-known bookseller on either side
of the Atlantic.

By a curious fatality, it was on the day the "Titanic"
sank, April 14, 1912, that Livingston collapsed under
his own weight, with a broken thigh, at his home in
Scarsdale. Six months before he had slipped on wet leaves
in the garden and broken a leg and arm, which healed
unsatisfactorily. After the second accident, the doctors
sought for an explanation. They found that through
some vagary of his physical system, which had been

anaemic from childhood, the organs had ceased to send lime to the bones. The medical people have their own names for the things that ailed him, and no one who saw him during the months that followed this discovery is likely to forget the brave, wistful smile with which he remarked that he was assured of lasting fame, not because of anything that he had written, but as an extraordinary medical phenomenon. He was of sufficient importance, from that point of view, to be transferred to the Rockefeller Institute for Medical Research. There, for four months, Dr. McCrudden and his collaborators experimented with him. At last a line of treatment was found that proved helpful. The bones showed stronger in the X-ray prints, and the doctors told him that some day he might walk again. When his improvement was assured, Mrs. George D. Widener asked him to become the first librarian of the Harry Elkins Widener collection, in charge of the Memorial rooms which are the center of the great library building at Harvard, which perpetuates the memory of what she and Harvard and booklovers everywhere lost when the "Titanic" went down.

The appointment was recognized by everyone as the best that could have been made. The business acquaintanceship between the bookseller and the collector began soon after Harry Widener graduated from Harvard, and quickly ripened into warm personal friendship. "He loved you, Mr. Livingston, and has talked to me so often of your knowledge and the help you were to him in advising him about books," wrote the mother, in her first letter referring to the plans for the Memorial. "Hundreds of times he has told me, that when he could afford it, he would love to have you for his private librarian. You were so congenial with him and he loved working with you."

The knowledge that the doctors expected him to live, and that for the first time in his life he was to have leisure and opportunity to do the things which he knew, as well as anyone, that he could do better than anybody else, gave Livingston the interest in living which was worth more than all the medicines. He planned to spend the summer of 1914 on the Massachusetts North Shore, and stopped in Boston on the way, to break the journey and to visit the half-finished Widener Memorial building. He chanced to be in Cambridge during Commencement week, and Mr. Lane invited him to attend the Phi Beta Kappa dinner. He went in his wheeled chair, and to his surprise—consternation almost—for he knew of Harvard mostly by tradition, he found that he was the only person present who was surprised at his being placed among the guests at the speakers' table. This was the first of many incidents which made the closing months of his life happier than he had imagined possible. He found himself more than welcomed by people whose names he knew and honored. As these men and women came to see him, at first through neighborly sympathy, their respect for his ability rapidly developed into admiration for his bravery and love for one of the sweetest natures this world has ever known.

During the summer at Pigeon Cove, it became evident
that the doctors, in fighting to restore the strength to
his bones, had drawn too heavily upon the rest of his
weakened system.   He did not die, because of an unalter-
able determination to live until he had justified the faith
and repaid the kindnesses of his old and new friends.
He went to a Boston hospital for observation, and then
settled in his bed at Cambridge to prolong the fight, on
his nerve, with a superb courage, after the physical
machine was ready to stop.   The doctors did what they
could, and he did more, but the odds were all against him.
Life went out on the morning of December 24, 1914.

The corporation of Harvard University appointed
him the librarian of the Harry Elkins Widener Collection, upon Mrs. Widener's nomination, at its meeting
on November 30, 1914.   Four weeks later he was buried
from Appleton Chapel, by the College Preacher.   The
body rests at Mount Auburn, under a beautiful pine tree.

Livingston's first publication was an anonymous
pamphlet entitled *Chrysanthemums*, which was issued by
his employers, Pitcher & Manda, at Short Hills, in 1893.
It was a separate reprint of a portion of their regular
catalogue for the autumn of that year.   This brochure
attracted considerable attention at the time among
horticulturists, and it has provided the substance and
much of the phraseology for articles on that plant printed
since its appearance.

Most of his bibliographical work was done with books
which were in his hands pending their sale by Dodd,

Mead & Co.   The unusual value of the catalogues issued by that house was recognized widely for some time before bookmen who were not conversant with the New York trade gossip became aware of Livingston's part in them. The extent to which his notes on rare volumes and peculiar editions has been copied by other booksellers and by the editors of catalogues is the convincing tribute to the thoroughness with which he exhausted each subject that he undertook to examine.

A number of his trade catalogues developed into regular bibliographies.   It was thoroughly characteristic of his attitude toward his work that when he described any set of books for sale, he pointed out the titles which were not included with the same care that he gave to describing the choicest treasures in the offering.

Livingston's name first appeared on a title-page on the first volume of *American Book Prices Current*, which was published in 1895.   The work of compiling the material for this volume was done entirely by him.   He was assisted in the work for the succeeding volumes by Miss Ida Stewart, and by Miss C. E. Dyett, who gradually took almost entire charge of the routine compilation and the preparation of copy for the printer.

The mass of information contained in the first ten volumes of this series was sifted together, rearranged in alphabetical order, and combined with the important part of the English publication with the same title, in the four volumes of *Auction Prices of Books*, published in 1905.

From 1898 to 1901 he was a regular contributor to
The Bookman. Most of his articles appeared under the
separate headings, "The Book Hunter" and "The Book
Mart." He also wrote two series on *The First Books of
Some American Authors* and *The First Books of Some
English Authors.* A few of these were reprinted in
separate form. Stevenson's *An Object of Pity or the
Man Haggard* was prepared for publication in this magazine, but a change in the editorial policy led to the decision
not to use it, after it was in type, and so it was issued
independently in a limited edition.

He was an active member of the group that tried to
establish *The Bibliographer* as the American organ for
those interested in bookish technicalities. During 1902
and 1903 he prepared for it facsimile reprints of two
important early American tracts and of the first edition
of Milton's *Comus.* Each of these was reissued in
separate form. He also edited facsimiles of a rare
German edition of the *Vespucius Voyages* and of the first
edition of Bacon's *Essaies.* He planned to republish a
number of other books of this sort, in connection with
his work at Harvard. The first of these was in type
before he died and is the last number in the list of his
publications.

In 1905 he began to contribute regularly to the *New
York Evening Post* and *The Nation,* under the heading
"News for Bibliophiles." A few articles of the same
character were written for "The Bibliographer" column
of the *Boston Evening Transcript.* The *Nation* articles

on "The Robert Hoe Library," "Beverly Chew and His Books," and "The Harry Elkins Widener Stevenson Collection" were reprinted in pamphlet form.

The trade catalogues of sets of Kipling and Tennyson proved so helpful to collectors that he was induced to prepare similar descriptions of the first editions of the writings of Pope, Mark Twain, Meredith, and Swinburne. These were privately printed for the owners of sets of the works by these authors, which Livingston had been largely instrumental in enlarging. These led naturally to his assuming the task of completing *The Chamberlain Bibliographies* of Longfellow and Lowell, which were based on the researches and notes of Jacob Chester Chamberlain of New York City, and printed by Mrs. Chamberlain as a memorial of his absorbing interest in American authors.

Livingston's appreciation of the point of view of scholars as well as book collectors had a chance for expression in the *Bibliography of Charles and Mary Lamb*, printed in 1903 for A. J. Spoor of Chicago. This volume also demonstrated his ability to treat the driest details of bibliography in such a way as to bring out their importance to the history of literature, and his skill in making a readable presentation of such minutiae. These characteristics, the marks of genuine scholarship, developed rapidly during the ensuing decade. Self-educated, and always a student, he wrote carefully, as to expression as well as facts, and his style as he came to write more easily reflected the accuracy

of his instincts, lightened by the buoyancy of his
nature.

The altogether satisfactory appearance of Livingston's last and most important publication gladdened the
final month of his life. This volume grew out of a plan
to write a description of a single volume belonging to one
of his best friends. Under the incentive of a request
from the publication committee of the Grolier Club of
New York, it was expanded into an exhaustive study of
Franklin's Passy Press. The instinct for the meaning
of the half-hidden evidence of the physical make-up of
a pamphlet worked just as surely when applied to the
interpretation of written documents. His ingrained
habit of refusing to form an opinion or to state his conclusions as long as the evidence seemed incomplete
maintained his interest in researches long after all his
associates had decided that there was nothing left to be
discovered. He would not begin to write until he knew
what he wanted to say. The consequence was that when
he wrote he expressed himself confidently and readably.
The volume on Franklin and the printing press at Passy
will long stand as the entirely adequate example of what
a bibliographical investigation ought to produce.

BIBLIOGRAPHY—A FORECAST

BY GEORGE WATSON COLE, L.H.D.

THE sale in December, 1919, of the Christie-Miller copy of the 1599 edition of Shakespeare's *Venus and Adonis* for £15,000 called out numerous comments. Much surprise has been expressed at the high prices that have been realized for other rare books. Those familiar with the records of book auctions during the past twenty or thirty years are well aware that the price of rare books has been steadily mounting, and that those sold, for what were at the time considered high prices, would if now placed in the market bring very much more.

The question is naturally asked, Why do these books bring such amazingly high prices? It may be said, to begin with, that the increasingly high prices realized on many rare books that have come into the market during the last decade or two are largely due to the character of the books themselves. A number of wealthy collectors have been attracted by them, and not without cause, for never, in the history of bookselling, has such a large number of superlatively rare books been offered for sale within such a limited period.

As long as a book continues to be privately owned, there is a possibility that it may again come into the market. But it is a well-known fact that rare books have a tendency to find their way into public institutions. Once there, they are permanently removed from the

market.   Every book so locked up reduces the number of
tuose that can again be offered for sale.   Consequently
this fact, when known, creates a desire on the part of
any collector who knows of it to secure a copy.   The law
of supply and demand comes in and hence the ever increasing prices that are realized.

In the case of the *Venus and Adonis* just mentioned,
though it was but the Fourth Edition, it was the only
copy known of the earliest edition still remaining in
private hands.   Its appearance, therefore, presented the
only possible opportunity that a private collector could
ever have of adding it to his collection.   Is it then at all
surprising that in a competition between two gentlemen
possessing the finest collections of Shakespeare's works in
the world, outside of the British Museum, a battle royal
took place for its possession?   And what more could be
desired than that this same rarity should find a place
on the shelves of a library in this country where it can
at any time be consulted by a student of Shakespeare?

These high prices are not an unmixed evil.   They
stimulate owners to search their libraries and place
their rare books in the market in order that they may
profit by these high prices.   The recent Mostyn, Christie-
Miller, and Newdigate-Newdegate sales, to name but a
few, no doubt owe their origin to this cause.

High prices are inevitable where wealthy collectors
compete for the possession of rarities, especially where
most of the known copies have already found their way
into public collections.   The Henry E. Huntington

Library, as is now well known, is no longer a private collection, and the rarities absorbed by it will never again come into the market. Mr. Huntington is still actively engaged in rounding out and strengthening it and will doubtless continue to interest himself in its growth in the future as in the past.

That high prices are not entirely due to his competition is shown by the fact that at the Huntington duplicate sales, from which Mr. Huntington himself was removed as a competitor, surprisingly high figures were uniformly maintained. This was no doubt due to the high character and extreme rarity of the items offered, many of which then appeared at public sale for the first time.

Another important fact should not be overlooked. The rush of owners to place their collections in the market and take advantage of the prevailing high prices now being realized is bringing to light not only copies of acknowledged rarity, but is even revealing many whose very existence has in some cases been questioned; while, in not a few instances, those have appeared that heretofore have been absolutely unknown to bibliographers.

A few of these cases are so striking and are of such importance in literary history that we may be pardoned in calling attention to one or two.

In the Christie-Miller sale advertised to take place November 28, 1919, but postponed until the following month, occurred a copy of Robert Greene's *A Quip for an Upstart Courtier* (no. 50), the earliest of the three editions known to have been printed in 1592. This work was published posthumously and, as originally printed, contained a scurrilous attack upon Gabriel Harvey and his two brothers. In the later editions this attack was suppressed, the only part retained being a reference to the father of the Harveys whose calling was that of a rope-maker. This allusion to the calling of the father (as modified) naturally seemed to writers on the controversy as wholly inadequate to account for the vitriolic bitterness displayed by Gabriel Harvey and his brothers in the progress of the controversy, there being nothing about the calling of a rope-maker to merit such a revengeful attitude.

All writers on the subject have therefore thought that there must have been something more than this mere innuendo to account for the bitterness excited in the mind of Gabriel Harvey and to have caused him to open the vials of his wrath and vilify the memory of Robert Greene, then dead, and of Thomas Nash, his defender. What are we to think of one, no matter what the provocation, who vents himself in the following sonnet which Gabriel Harvey included in his *Foure Letters and Certaine Sonnets*, 1592, where he says:

> Come fellow Greene, come to thy gaping graue:
>   Bidd Vanity, and Foolery farewell:
> Thou ouer-long ha∫t plaid the madbrain'd knaue:
>   And ouer-lowd ha∫t rung the bawdy bell.
> Vermine to Vermine mu∫t repaire at la∫t:
> No fitter hou∫e for bu∫y folke to dwell:
> Thy Conny-catching Pageants are pa∫t:

Some other muſt thoſe arrant Stories tell.
Theſe hungry wormes thinke long for their repaſt:
Come on: I pardon thy offence to me:
It was thy liuing: be no ſo aghaſt:
A Foole, and Phiſition may agree.
　　　And for my Brothers, neuer vex thy ſelfe:
　　　Thy are not to diſeaſe a buried Elfe.

How unlike this is William Basse's sonnet on the death of Shakespeare:

On Mr. William Shakeſpeare

Renowned Spencer lie a thought more nigh
To learned Beaumont, and rare Beaumont ly
A little nearer Chaucer, to make rome
For Shakeſpeare in your threfold, fourfold tombe.
To lodge all fouer in one bed make a ſhifte
Until Domes day, for heardly will (a) fifte
Betwixt this day and that by fate bee ſlaine,
For whom the curtains ſhal bee drawne againe.
But if Precedencie in death doe barre
A fourth place in your ſacred Sepulcher,
In this uncarved marble of thy owne,
Sleepe, brave Tragedian, Shakeſpeare, ſleepe alone;
Thy unmoleſted reſt, unſhared cave,
Poſſeſſe as lord, not tenant, to thy grave,
　　　That unto others it may counted bee
　　　Honour hereafter to bee layed by thee.

So completely had the original edition of Greene's *Quip for an Upstart Courtier* dropped out of sight that all writers on this controversy in their attempts to discover the cause of Harvey's animosity settled upon a short passage where Harvey's father had been described as a rope-maker.   The copy which has now come to light formerly belonged to Richard Heber and was sold in the first sale of his library (no. 3132) in 1834 for £1 15s. It, together with many other of Heber's treasures, was bought by Mr. Christie-Miller and its location lost sight of.   Only upon its reappearance at the recent sale has its importance as a piece of contemporary literary evidence been fully realized.

The *Quip for an Upstart Courtier*, the occasion of Harvey's outburst of spleen, though the fact was unknown to him, has since been found to be plagiarized from a much older work by Francis Thynne, entitled *The Debate betweene Pride and Lowlines*.   This was published about 1570 and the only known copy of it, formerly in the Bridgewater House Library, is now in the Huntington Library.   The *Quip* takes the form of a dispute between a courtier (Velvet-Breeches) and a tradesman (Cloth-Breeches) as to which of them is entitled to the greater respect.   It is determined to leave the final decision to a jury.   As the dispute takes place in a highway, wayfarers, as they approach, are halted to form the panel from which the jury is selected.   People representing many callings as they approach are accosted and examined as to their qualifications to serve on this jury.   Among them is a rope-maker.   This gives Greene an opportunity to reflect upon the calling of the father of the Harveys and upon his three sons, which he does, as follows:

I both wondred and laught to heare Clothbreeches make this diſcourſe, when I ſaw two in the vallye together by the eares, the one in leather, the other as blacke as the Deuill: I ſtept to them to part the fraie, and queſtioned what they were, and wherefore they brawled: Marry quoth hee, that lookt like Lucifer, though I am blacke, I am not the Deuill, but indeed a Colyer of Croyden, and one ſir that haue ſolde many a man a falſe ſacke of coales, that booth wanted meaſure, and was halfe full of duſt and droſſe.   Indeed I haue beene a Lieger in my time in London, and haue played many madde pranckes, for which cauſe, you may apparantly ſee I am made a curtall, for the Pillory (in the ſight of a great many good and ſufficient witneſſes,) hath eaten off booth my eares, and now ſir this Ropemaker hunteth me heere with his halters, I geſſe him to be ſome euill ſpirite, that in the likeneſſe of a manne, would ſince I haue paſt the Pillory, perſwade me to hange my ſelfe for my olde offenſes, and therefore ſith I cannot bleſſe me from him with *Nomine patris*, I lay *spiritus Sanctus* about his ſhoulders with a good crabe tree cudgell, that hee may get out of my company.   The Ropemaker replied, that honeſtly iourneying by the way, hee acquainted himſelfe with the Collyer, and for no other cauſe pretended.   Honeſt with the Deuill, quoth the Colliar, how can he be honeſt, whoſe mother I geſſe was a witch, for I haue herde them ſay, that witches ſay their praiers backeward, and ſo dooth the Ropemaker yearne his liuing by going backward, and the knaues cheefe liuing is by making fatall inſtrumentes, as halters and ropes, which diuers deſperat men hang themſelues with Well quoth I, what ſay you to theſe, ſhall they be on the Jurie?   Veluet breeches ſaid nothing, but Cloth breeches ſaid, in the Ropemaker he found no great falſehood in him, therefore hee was willing hee ſhould be one, but for the Coliyer, hee thought it neceſſary, that as he came ſo he ſhould depart, ſo then I had the Ropemaker ſtand by till more came, which was not longe.

The rope-maker's response, as here given, is wholly unlike that in the First Edition, which reads as follows:

The ropemaker replied, that honeſtly iourneyeng by the way, he acquainted himſelfe with the Colliar, & for no other cauſe pretended.

And whether are you a going qd. I?   Marry ſir qd. he, firſt to abſolue
your question, I dwel in Saffron Waldon, and am going to Cambridge
to three ſons that I keep there at ſchoole, ſuch apt children ſir as few
women haue groned for, and yet they haue ill lucke.   The one ſir
[Richard Harvey] is a Deuine to comfort my ſoule, & he indeed though
he be a vaine glorious aſſe, as diuers youths of his age bee, is well giuen
to the ſhew of the world, and writte a late the lambe of God, and yet
his pariſhioners ſay he is the limb of the deuill, and kiſſeth their wiues
with holy kiſſes, but they had rather he ſhould keep his lips for madge
his mare.   The ſecond ſir [John Harvey] is a Phyſitian or a foole, but
indeed a phyſitian, & had proued a proper man if he had not ſpoiled
himſelfe with his Aſtrological diſcourſe of the terrible coniunction of
Saturne and Jupiter.   For the eldeſt [Gabriel Harvey] he is a Ciuilian,
a wondrous witted fellow, ſir reuerence ſir, he is a Doctor, and as
Tubalcain was the firſt inuenter of Muſick, ſo he Gods beniſon light
vpon him, was the firſt that inuented Engliſhe Hexamiter: but ſee
how in theſe daies learning is little eſteemed, for that and other familiar
letters and proper treatiſes he was orderly clapt in the Fleet, but ſir
a Hawk and a Kite may bring forth a coyſtrell, and honeſt parents
may haue bad children.   Honeſt with the deuil qd. the Colliar, [etc.].

The discovery of this copy of the unexpurgated edition now for the first time brings to light the real cause
of the bitterness and vituperation of Harvey against
the character of Greene.   Critics and literary scholars
have been misled from reading the later editions into
believing that Harvey took umbrage because he and his
two brothers were called the sons of a rope-maker.   The
original passage (also reproduced in facsimile in the
Britwell-Court sale catalogue) shows that the Harveys
had a real cause of grievance and that their family had
been held up to contempt.

This discovery of a long-lost edition of a well-known
work reminds us of the discovery of another whose
very existence had been hitherto unsuspected. The
Newdigate-Newdegate collection was advertised to be
sold at Sotheby's, January 22, 1920, but previous to
that date was sold *en-bloc* to the late George D. Smith.
In this sale appeared a copy of Robert Greene's *Pandosto;*
The Triumph of Time, 1595. Bibliographies of English
literature give the dates of many non-existent editions
which have crept into them by mistake. The discovery
of editions hitherto unknown is of less frequent occurrence.
This was just what happened in the latter case. Early
editions of this work, from which Shakespeare borrowed
the plot of *The Winter's Tale*, are by no means of frequent
occurrence. Of the First Edition (1588) there is only an
imperfect copy in the British Museum; while of the
Second Edition (1592) the only copy at present known is
in the Library of Mr. William Augustus White, of Brooklyn. Then comes the Third Edition (1595), the Newdigate-Newdegate copy hitherto unrecorded, which has
come to this country and found a resting-place in the
Huntington Library.

Pandosto was a popular romance and ran through
nine editions. Its title was then changed to *The Pleasant*
Historie of Dorastus and Fawnia, under which name it
appeared some fifteen times or more.

Such new discoveries, together with the fact that so
many rare books are being brought to this country, raises

some very interesting questions regarding the present
status of the records of English literature. The bibliographies of the past when critically examined are found to
be far from satisfactory. The information they impart
is of varying degrees of fullness and reliability. Those
compiled in the past contain information gathered from
many sources, much of it copied from previous works of
a similar kind and not, to any great extent, from the books
themselves. In the early bibliographies the information
given is scanty as regards titles and descriptions, and on
investigation it is too often found unsatisfactory. Frequently they serve only as hints that such and such books
exist, and that fuller information should be sought for
elsewhere. These old bibliographies are valuable in a
way, but modern requirements call for fuller information
derived from the books themselves.

The term "scientific bibliography" has been suggested
as a proper one to be applied to modern bibliographical
methods as distinguished from those of the past. The
question naturally arises, Is the term "scientific" a
proper one to use in this connection? The word "scientific," as defined by the *Century Dictionary*, is "concerned
with the acquisition of accurate and systematic knowledge
of principles by observation and deduction: as scientific
investigation." If it be true that the knowledge acquired
by bibliographers is based upon observation and that
deductions are made from such observation, and, furthermore, that this all leads to a more accurate and systematic
knowledge of books, the term "scientific bibliography"

would seem to be properly applied to work in this field of research.

The term "anatomical bibliography" has also been suggested as a proper one to apply to the work of the bibliographer as at present carried on. May not this expression also be properly applied to such work? This term, we also think, may with propriety be applied to the work of the modern bibliographer. For, not being satisfied to consider a book as an entity, he anatomizes or examines it minutely, and considers it point by point in order to discover the relations that each part bears to the whole. For a book, as is well known, is made up of separate sheets, each of which bears an important relation to the whole.

Bibliography, itself, has been defined to be a science that treats of books, their materials, authors, typography, editions, dates, subjects, classifications, history, etc.

The writer has made a somewhat critical study of the books of the Elizabethan and Jacobean printers, not only of single copies, but, in numerous cases, of several copies of the same book. In this work he has found it of the utmost importance to examine and compare them not only sheet by sheet, but leaf by leaf. The structural parts of the book have therefore been critically examined. As a result he has come to feel that there is such a thing as anatomical bibliography, and that no satisfactory study of books can be carried on which does not take into careful consideration the relations of their different parts. Only by keeping this feature firmly in mind and applying it can we arrive at a thorough and scientific study of bibliography. Little, so far as we have observed, has been written upon this phase of the work.

It is evident, then, that the materials that go into the composition of a book and the processes employed in transferring a manuscript into a finished and marketable book should each be considered in its natural order. These are: (1) paper and paper-making; (2) types, typesetting, and printing; and (3) binding and binders.

The bibliography of the past was to a great extent a work of paste-pot and scissors, of inkhorn and goose-quill. That phase has had its day, and a new era has arisen. The old style of bibliography was not without its value. To it the bibliographer of today owes an infinite debt of gratitude, for the records thus prepared serve as a foundation upon which to construct better work. Like all work based upon the compilations of one's predecessors, it copied both good and bad. While in the main it is good, it lacks the accuracy and authority required at the present day, which insists upon a full and unerring description based upon an actual examination of a book, and, whenever possible, upon a comparison of several copies.

The importance of such a comparison, when it can be made, is strikingly shown by the following example. The Hoe copy of Goodall's *Poems and Translations*, London, 1689 (sale catalogue, 2:1474), on examination was found to contain four leaves in the first sheet or half-sheet and appeared to be perfect. These leaves consisted of a title-page and three leaves containing "The Table" of contents.

From all appearances, when seen alone, this copy seemed absolutely perfect. On comparing it with another, the Chew copy, the latter was found to contain eight preliminary leaves instead of four. The four additional leaves, not in the Hoe copy, were found to contain the license, two leaves of dedication, and a leaf of errata. As the leaves in the Hoe copy bore no signature-marks and the printed matter was complete as far as it went, no suspicion of lacking leaves was aroused. The dedicatory leaves of the Chew copy had two signature-marks, A3 and A4. An examination of the paper in the Chew copy disclosed the fact that the eight preliminary leaves were printed on a single sheet with portions of the watermark on the first, fourth, fifth, and eighth leaves. At the end of the Table is the catchword "ERRA-" over which, in the Hoe copy, a slip of paper had been neatly pasted. A portion of a watermark also appears on the first leaf of the Table in the Hoe copy. A perfect copy of this book therefore contains the following leaves:

> 1 license
> 1 title-page
> 1 dedication to the Countess of Clarendon
> 1 dedication to Mr. Roderick (in verse)
> 3 "The Table"
> 1 Errata verso
> —

Total: 8 leaves.

Only by such a critical method can the errors that have crept into the old bibliographies and which have been handed on by more recent writers be eliminated. Only by such a method can bibliography be built up on a scientific basis.

Records made after a thorough examination of the book itself may be termed "descriptive bibliography." The records of books contained in the old bibliographies may be defined according to the fulness of the information or lack of it, which they give. Where author, full title, size, number of volumes, place, printer, date, and signature-marks are given, the book may be said to be *described*. If only author, title, place, and date are given, it may be said to be *recorded*. If all that is given reads, for instance, "another edition, 1662," it is merely *noted*.

In referring to catalogues and bibliographies, it is much to be desired that the character or amount of information given concerning a book should be differentiated by the use of some such or similar terms. If this were systematically done, the expressions, "Hazlitt *describes* a copy," "Lowndes *records* a copy," or "Herbert *notes* a copy," would at once indicate the amount and character of the information to be expected when the reference is looked up.

The modern bibliographer is no more content to base his statements on a superficial examination of a book than the medical man is to base his upon a hasty inspection of his patient. The latter tests, probes, and amputates if need be. Sir William Osler himself would no more have thought of practicing medicine without a thorough knowledge of the science of anatomy in all its branches than the

present-day bibliographer would of following his profession without a theoretical and practical knowledge of
the component parts of a book and their relation to each
other.

The modern bibliographer may properly be called the
anatomist of the book. If he would be successful in his
vocation he must be thoroughly familiar with all that is to
be known about the paper on which a book is printed,
its quality, method of manufacture, and through what
processes it goes in order to become a part of a book. He
must similarly be acquainted with the methods employed
by the printer in turning a manuscript into a printed book.
He must understand the art of printing and be able to
detect in every instance the points in which the printer
has mistaken the ideas of the author (in so far as typographical essentials are concerned, and in a lesser degree
the changes involved in textual matters). And, no
less important, he must be able to detect the places
where the binder has mistaken the order in which the
printer intended the various parts of the book to be
bound.

The bibliographer of the present day, therefore, has
ceased to consider a book as an entity, and, instead,
regards it as a series of fragments or parts combined or
assembled by the binder, sometimes as the printer
intended it to be put together and sometimes not.

The modern bibliographer, therefore, is not and cannot
be satisfied with the examination of a single copy of a
book, especially if it seems to contain any abnormal or

unnatural features.   His object primarily is to describe a
perfect copy.   In the various vicissitudes through which
old books have come down to us they have often undergone many and varied changes, and, in many cases, it is
with difficulty that a copy can be found that is in its
original binding or is still in its pristine condition.   It may
even be made up of parts of two or more editions, and it
is incumbent on the bibliographer to determine from
which editions they have been taken.   The indignities
which book-collectors and binders have perpetrated on
some copies of books would make an interesting and long
story.

Hence, modern bibliography becomes comparative
as well as anatomical, and the analogy between it and
medicine, that has just been made, becomes still closer,
for we have not only to consider bibliography ana-
tomically, but comparatively.   A book should not only
be considered by itself, but the processes of the author,
copyists, compositors, pressmen, and binders of different
periods, to say nothing of the jugglings of book-sellers
and collectors in their endeavor to perfect copies, should
all be taken into account.   The methods of the past are
no longer a criterion by which to judge those of the
present day.

In the remarks which follow an attempt will be made
to give the reasons and to show why bibliography has at
last come to stand upon a scientific basis.

1. We have first bibliographies which give abundant
titles, but are weak in descriptions.   They often merely

give dates. Such entries are simply *notes* which the
compilers never had the time, opportunity, or inclination
to expand. A characteristic example of this class of
bibliographies is to be found in Watt's *Bibliotheca Britannica*, published in 1824.

2. The next class of bibliographies is of a mixed nature
the best feature of which consists of full and exact descriptions made by their compilers from the books themselves.
To these, however, are often added information derived
from the owners of the books and that gleaned from previous publications covering the same field. Confining ourselves to bibliography of English literature, such are
Ames and Herbert's *Typographical Antiquities* and
Hazlitt's *Hand-Book* and his series of *Bibliographical
Collections and Notes*, extending from 1876 to 1903.

3. We come lastly to bibliographies covering a more
limited field, the best examples of which, perhaps, are to be
found in those prepared by Thomas J. Wise in which
the bibliographical history of each work is fully given.

We believe the time has come for a change in bibliographical methods. It would be folly, were it possible,
to discard what has already been done. It represents
too much research and labor and is too valuable in suggestions to be dispensed with. The work of the future
must consist more and more in collecting, classifying,
and digesting the mass of information to be found in the
bibliographies of the past, and in the location, if possible,
of copies of every edition through which any given work

has passed.   This, so far as we are aware, has not, as yet,
been systematically done.

It is never safe to accept uncorroborated statements
made in any bibliography.   Check-lists ought to be prepared and sent out broadcast for the purpose of locating
copies of editions about which information is desired.
When this is once thoroughly done, questionable details
can be settled by the use of photostat copies.   In the
Huntington Library this method is being tried and the
Check-List that has been issued is intended as a step in
this direction.

We recently worked out from the best information we
possessed the bibliographical history of two works,
Pandosto and *A Quip for an Upstart Courtier*.   The discovery of the Newdigate and Britwell copies, therefore,
came to us as a not unwelcome surprise, as it enabled us
to take one more step toward completing the bibliographical history of those two works.   Now that these
copies have been added to our collection we shall be able
more satisfactorily to complete our records.

So I believe the work of "comparative bibliography"
is that which we must now take up in order that old
ghosts may be laid and that our stock of information may
be greatly increased by new discoveries.

Our friends of the English Bibliographical Society have
in hand a work exactly in this line, the compilation of a
short-title list of all works by English authors, printed in
England or abroad before 1640, giving the location of a
copy of every title recorded.   It is estimated that this

work will take three or more years to complete and that it will comprise about 30,000 titles. The *Check-List* of the Huntington Library it is hoped will be of some slight service in enabling the Society to trace a considerable number of unique copies in this country. A similar work ought to be undertaken here so that we may learn definitely what was done by the early presses in our own country, and where copies of each work can be found.

When this preliminary field work is completed, then will come the work of tabulation and recording. This work lies before us, and at no time in the world's history could it be taken up with more surety of success.

The photostat, invented and perfected within the past decade, has provided an inexpensive medium of reproduction. By its use we are virtually enabled to place side by side copies scattered from one end of the earth to the other. By its means we are able to compare different copies and compel them to yield up their secrets as effectively as if they were under our very eyes. With these aids questions as to editions, issues, title-pages, use of old sheets, etc., can be for once and for all settled and information imparted to the scholar or textual critic which will enable him to perform his work more easily and with greater certainty. Numerous instances might be cited in which we have been enabled by the photostat to thus settle questions which could not have been solved in any other way.

BIBLIOGRAPHY AND SCHOLARSHIP
BY PIERCE BUTLER

MOST of the members of this Society know that reputable scholars are habitually indifferent to the usages of scientific bibliography; many are conscious of distressing consequences which result from that indifference; and quite a few, it is altogether probable, have definite opinions of just what ought to be done in remedy. It is therefore a hazardous undertaking to attempt to speak of these matters, for I shall be in constant danger of wearying the reader with commonplaces and platitudes. Yet the impulse to speak of them is so strong that I cannot but make the venture. For one thing my work at the Newberry Library, in the Department of Book Selection, keeps me always conscious of how frequent and how disastrous are the bibliographical shortcomings of standard authorities. But there is another reason. I am myself a product of the present standard educational system turned out according to blue-print specifications by high school, college, professional school, and university. I am quite certain that if instead of entering upon librarianship as I did six years ago, I had gone on to teach, I should have cited authorities to my pupils, or to my readers, in exactly the same careless hit-or-miss style which the ordinary scholar follows. Thus my own experience prevents my looking at bibliographical errors, lapses, indiscretions—call them what you like—without wanting to parody John Bradford's cry when he saw the criminal going to execution.

A large part of bibliographical labor, and that perhaps the most important part, is performed not by professional bibliographers but by scholars whose main interest is focused upon altogether different matters. It is no doubt unavoidable that this should be so. Indeed, I suspect it is a very fortunate state of affairs; a specialist has resources which the most industrious layman may fail to discover. We professional bibliographers need feel no pangs of jealousy nor begrudge to scholars in other fields than the one we have chosen, pre-eminence as the bibliographical authorities upon their particular subjects. Yet on the other hand we must feel ourselves vastly concerned if those who do that work fail to do it well. Professionals cannot but find themselves disquieted and moved to protest if amateurs are allowed to establish low standards in their science. Now it will require no elaborate argument from me, I am quite certain, to persuade you that this is just what has happened in the field of modern bibliography. Low standards have been set, so low that we who must look upon them from a professional point of view are often made to blush with shame when the irreverent deride our boasted science.

My first plan for presenting this subject was to offer you a demonstration of how low these standards are, by means of statistical analyses of the errors contained in sample sections of the bibliographies of such works of undeniable scholarship as, *The Cambridge Modern History*,

The Cambridge History of English Literature, and the like.
But upon second thought I decided that although the
resultant figures might be very interesting and even
exciting they would not be very illuminating. After I
had presented them, about all I should be able to say
would be "Cheer up! Things are a whole lot worse than
you realize. . . . ." Because I am bold enough to aim
somewhat beyond this, I looked farther for an example
which would show, not only how disastrous it may be
for a scholar to neglect bibliographical exactness, but
also for one of which I could venture to say how and
why he habitually does so. An examination of my book
shelves, with these particular needs in mind, led me to
select a book which seems to fulfil somewhat adequately
every possible requirement as a terrible example. It is a
little volume entitled *Social Psychology,* published in 1908,
and since, frequently reprinted. For the book itself I
have only respect and admiration. Its bibliographical
usage is a fair example of modern work of the kind, being
if anything above rather than below the average. The
academic experience of the author, according to the
record of *Who's Who in America,* is typical of that of
hundreds of contemporary scholars. Moreover I believe
the book is one of great significance bibliographically, for
I feel certain that its footnotes must have been consulted
any number of times during the past dozen years. The
author, who has evidently been a great reader, has the
happy faculty of quoting passages of such striking interest
that one is inspired with the desire to look up the writings

quoted and read more of them.   Finally, this book was put forth under the imprint of a publishing house which values so highly the decencies of formal "style" that it has issued a pamphlet guide to authors in the preparation of their manuscripts.

Taking this book then, as a fair and satisfactory sample, I tested its bibliographical citations to determine just how far they would carry a reader who attempted to use them.   I copied off on slips, just as they were given, its citations of eighty works quoted by the author.   In nearly every instance he keeps close to the formula used in his first reference.   Here he says:

> . . . . Thus Cooley observes: "The more thoroughly American a man is, the less he can perceive Americanism." [And so on for five lines.]

Against the word Cooley there is a superscript "1," and the corresponding footnote reads

> "Human Nature and the Social Order" 30.

So I wrote on my slip all a reader would have,

> Cooley
> Human Nature and the Social Order, p. 30,

and so on for the eighty works quoted.

A reader might conceivably take his reference in this form to a book dealer, but my imagination shrinks from attempting to picture what the result would be.   More probably he would go to a library, so that is what I did in his place.   I went to the public catalogue of the Newberry Library to look up the books, limiting myself strictly to use of the information contained on the slips. Now the Newberry cards for works by persons whose family name is Cooley are not very numerous so I had to read through only five cards before I found the reference and discovered that the author's name was Charles Horton Cooley. But other citations were not so easily identified. Had I not known that "Ellis" meant "Havelock Ellis" in reference to the title *Man and Woman,* I should have had to read 144 cards before finding the title, or on a similar supposition, 205 cards for James, *Principles of Psychology.* I did not know that "Roberts" meant "Peter Roberts" for the title *Anthracite Coal Communities* and that "Thomas" meant "William Isaac Thomas" for the title *Sex and Society,* so there was no pretense about my reading 212 and 347 cards before finding these two entries.

In short, so far as this author's citations would carry him, to find the 67 titles which are in the Newberry Library a reader must examine 2,640 cards, and to be sure that the other 13 titles are not in the library he must read 636 more, a total of 3,276 cards for 80 titles.

There are also other faults in these citations. In four instances the author's family name or the title is incorrectly given and two of these ($2\frac{1}{2}$ per cent) I have never been able to identify. Nine of the works (11 per cent) have been published in more than one edition, so that the pagination may vary.

I am quite certain that anyone who cares to spend the time can find, without searching far, a score of works for

which he can compile figures equal to or worse than those
I have cited, but, unless his temper be under perfect control, the wiser course is not to do so.   After giving the
matter careful consideration, I have decided that scholarship is not promoted to any marked degree by our flying
into a rage and calling names.   If we are to win any
headway we must do more than vociferate to high heaven,
and attempt first of all to understand just how it is and
why the situation is what it is.   But such an understanding is just what we usually lack.   Here for example
is a quotation from a paper, "For Better Bibliographies,"
by Martha Hale Shackford, of Wellesley, in the May,
1919, number of the *Educational Review*, LVII, 434 ff.
She says: "How preposterous it is to waste the time of
busy people by a foolish idea of saving space through the
omission of vital details!   Or does the naïf creator of the
bibliography think there are no authors in the card catalogue save those he mentions?"   Miss Shackford's is an
excellent paper except for this: she attributes false motives
where in reality no motive exists.   I am certain that the
author whose book I cited, for example, when he fails to
give his author's initials has no mistaken idea of saving
space, or any illusions concerning the size of the library
catalogue.   His bibliographical shortcomings are due
solely to his failure to think of such matters at all.

I speak thus positively not through charitable unwil-
lingness to attribute base motives but because I know
that is the reason why I should have committed the same
faults had I not drifted into librarianship.   I venture to

interpret by my own experience.   My author is, as I have
already said, a fair example of the modern scholar and I
myself am a product of the same educational machine
that manufactured him.   Therefore, I believe I do him
no injustice when I suppose that his academic experience,
so far as bibliographical matters are concerned, was not
greatly dissimilar to my own.   Let me describe that.

For fourteen years, from 1901 to 1915, I was a student
and a frequenter of libraries.   To find the books I wished
to read I had to use bibliographical processes.   For fourteen years I used library catalogues, footnotes, lists of
authorities, readers' guides, bibliographical manuals, and
yet at the end of all that time I had no conception
of the how and the why of scientific bibliography.   If I
had had occasion to refer to an integral formula in Percy
F. Smith's *"Elementary Calculus*, New York, 1902," I
should probably have written "See Smith, p. 79."   If
Queen Victoria's *Letters* had been one of my sources, in
giving the list of authorities I should have been as likely
to put it under "Q" as under "V."

Yet I had not only experience to teach me better but
formal instruction from as far back as high school.   There
Mr. H. H. Ballard, of the Berkshire Athenaeum, used to
visit us once or twice a year, urge us to use his library,
explain the bibliographical key to it, and offer us all sorts
of assistance.   He would describe the reference-room
service and its commoner equipment such as the
Encyclopaedia Britannica and *Poole's Index*.   And we
did use them.   Mr. Ballard's unfailing interest in our

schoolboy readings and his unflagging efforts to stimulate
our interest in the world of books was a valuable educational factor and one for which I am very grateful. Then
I went to college. Down at Dickinson we had no extensive library and the librarian was anyone at all. But
there were two of our teachers, both modern language men,
who used to give informal talks on how to use what was
there. They described the catalogue and also laid stress
on the reference rule that the first places to look were
always the *Encyclopaedia Britannica* and *Poole's Index*.
I was a great reader. Every summer I carried home
with me a notebook listing volumes I was anxious to
consult which were not in the college library, and I
always spent a few days of my journey visiting bookshops
and libraries of Philadelphia, New York, and Albany.
During the summer I usually managed to reach Spring-
field and Boston, where my favorite guidebook was still
that grubby list of volumes that I wished to examine.
The whole summer after my graduation I spent, unma-
triculated, reading at the University of Pennsylvania.

Now I usually failed in all these wanderings to find
some of the books I was most anxious to see simply
because my citations were imperfect bibliographically.
Yet that taught me nothing. I remember vividly how
disappointed I was that summer in Philadelphia when,
after searching the twelve volumes of Waller and Glover's
magnificent edition of William Hazlitt, I failed to find a
passage which I discovered several years later was from
the pen of his grandson, William Carew Hazlitt. My

notebook said only Hazlitt, and though I remembered that
the reference came from the *Contemporary Review*, lacking
record of year and page, I could not verify it. This, of
course, is only a sample of my bibliographical misadven-
tures; there were plenty of others. As I look back at
them now they amaze me, not only for my stupidity
in learning nothing from them, but also for the more
astonishing failure of every one of the professional librarians I met to take advantage of the concrete example my
difficulty offered them and turn my attention to the
practical necessity of a complete citation.

But to resume my narrative. I next registered at
Union Theological Seminary and Columbia University.
At Union, Dr. Gillett and Professor Rockwell were librarians in my time. Both of them described to us the
requirements of scientific bibliography but in such
abstract and general terms that it failed to leave any
impression. I suspect that both of them told us about
the *Encyclopaedia Britannica* and *Poole's Index*. At
Columbia, I took a course in historical bibliography
under Professor Shotwell. One afternoon he called in an
expert cataloguer to set us on the right bibliographical
path. I remember distinctly that she told us a whole
lot about the *Encyclopaedia Britannica* and *Poole's Index*
and then as if remembering that we were advanced
historical students she described the *Dictionary of National
Biography*, and the *New Oxford Dictionary*. After that
I went to Hartford Seminary. Professor Thayer, the
librarian there, gave a course in bibliographical method

but I never took it. It may have been an excellent course, the very instruction I ought to have received 'way back as an undergraduate at Dickinson, but I suspect it was largely concerned with two reference works whose names I shall not mention.

Such was my academic experience. So far as bibliography is concerned, I suppose it was no different from that of hundreds of my contemporaries. Let me attempt to sum it up: on my side I was so entirely interested in the contents of books that I had no attention to spare for the points of their title-pages. I knew there were people interested in such things, but I classed them with those others who were interested in postage stamps or old coins. I thought no more of the bibliographical points of a volume I read than I do today of the date and inscription on a coin when I spend it. That was my side of it. On the other hand there were those whose duty it was to teach me better, but they, without exception, failed to express themselves in a vocabulary which a layman might understand. If they avoided technical terms they spoke in generalities. Librarians are not gifted with the teaching faculty; if they were, not all of us would be librarians.

Or to look at that experience from another side; does it not teach that certain practical measures might have cured me of my bibliographical blindness? Here are four propositions:

1. In the larger colleges and universities the library staff should include at least one teacher of bibliography.

2. In the smaller institutions where that would be impracticable, librarians should be supplied with a manual of bibliographical pedagogy, sample lessons, and a syllabus of a normal course.

3. Examinations in formal bibliography should be prerequisite to every higher degree just as ability to use foreign languages now is.

4. Occasional bibliographical criticisms of standard works in various learned journals, and personal letters of protest addressed to individual authors, might also be worth while.

WHAT BIBLIOGRAPHY
OWES TO PRIVATE BOOK CLUBS

By Ruth S. Granniss

IT WAS London in the season of 1812, and a notable assembly might be found daily in the dining-room of the Duke of Roxburghe, which had been appropriated to the vendition of his books. There for two and forty successive days, with the exception only of Sundays, were the voice and the hammer of Mr. Evans heard, with equal efficacy, and there "were such deeds of valour performed, and such feats of book-heroism achieved as had never been previously beheld; and of which 'the like,'" says Dr. Dibdin, "will probably never be seen again. The shouts of the victors and the groans of the vanquished stunned and appalled you as you entered." June 17 was reached, the day of the sale of the Valdarfer Boccaccio of 1471, perhaps at the time (we are told) the most notorious volume in existence, concerning which Mr. Nicol, in his Preface to the catalogue had "not a little provoked the bibliomaniacal appetites" of his readers, telling them that it was one of the scarcest if not the very scarcest book that existed, having preserved its uniquity for upward of three hundred years. Sir Egerton Bridges and two other collector-friends had done Dr. Dibdin the honor of breakfasting with him that morning, and upon the conclusion of the repast Sir Egerton's carriage conveyed the party from Kensington to St. James's Square through a torrential downpour, and the sudden darkness which came across the crowded room as they entered gave additional interest to the scene of the combat. At length, the moment of the sale arrived. After some preliminary sparring a thousand guineas were bid by Earl Spencer—to which the Marquis of Blandford added "ten."

51

You might have heard a pin drop. [It must be told in the doctor's own words.[1]] All eyes were turned—all breathing well nigh stopped, every sword was put home within its scabbard—and not a piece of steel was seen to move or glitter save that which each of these champions brandished in his valorous hand. See, see!—they parry, they lunge, they hit; yet their strength is undiminished and no thought of yielding is entertained by either. Two thousand pounds are offered by the Marquis . . . . "two thousand two hundred and fifty pounds," said Lord Spencer. The spectators are now absolutely electrified. The Marquis quietly adds his usual "ten" and there is an end of the contest . . . . down dropt the hammer, and the echo of the sound of that fallen hammer was heard in the libraries of Rome, of Milan, and St. Mark. . . . . The price [proceeds the doctor] may be truly said to have astonished the whole Book-World. Not a living creature could have anticipated it: but this might be called the grand era of Bibliomania.

'Tis an old story to you all, and the frequenters of modern book auctions smile at Dr. Dibdin's naïve amazement over the monstrous price (nearly $12,000 for one book), but, as he wisely remarked, his was a grand era and not only of bibliomania, but also of bibliophily and of bibliographical enthusiasm, as one result of the sale well demonstrates. For, on that very evening, at a dinner in a "fair tavern" prearranged in honor of the sale of the Boccaccio by Dr. Dibdin, who "little apprehended the results of that dinner," the famous Roxburghe Club was formed by eighteen bibliophiles, among them Lord Spencer himself, not appearing to have suffered the least from his recent contest. The event is thus noted in the *Gentleman's magazine:*

As a Pillar, or other similar memorial could not be conveniently erected to mark the spot where so many Bibliographical Champions fought and conquered, another method was adopted, to record their fame, and perpetuate this brilliant epoch in literary annals. Accordingly a phalanx of the most hardy veterans has been enrolled, under the banner of the far-famed Valdarfer's Boccaccio of 1471, bearing the title of the Roxburghe Club.

So began the long line of private book clubs and printing societies, with their countless services to literature and to scholarship, to our familiarity with the sources of history, to varied phases of bibliography, and to the arts of the book.

[1] *The bibliographical decameron*, by Thomas Frognall Dibdin (London, 1817), III, 65.

The story of their usefulness has been told by Abraham Hume in his *Learned societies and printing clubs of the United Kingdom*, in John Hill Burton's *Book hunter*, in the Appendix of Lowndes' *Bibliographer's manual* (1864), in Adolf Growoll's *American book clubs*, and elsewhere. Within a few months the First Edition Club of London has brought out a comprehensive work on the subject by Harold Williams, who describes with charm many societies of specific or limited interests, which we shall be obliged regretfully to pass over, since there are two appalling questions which we have to consider at the outset:

What is Bibliography?
What is a Book Club?

I do not make bold to answer either, nor yet to contradict my friend who explained, on hearing the title of this paper, "But, all book-club publications serve bibliography in one way or another." Properly speaking, of course, he is right. Every worth-while manuscript rescued from oblivion and put into print, every reprint of a scarce work, every book over which skilled pains are exercised in any portion of its production, is a service to bibliography; and book clubs have produced many such. It is not of these that I wish to speak, however, imposing as their record would be, but rather of the more obvious things —books dealing with the physical making or makers of books, detailed lists of authors' works, written or printed; facsimiles showing the exact form in which great works first saw the light; catalogues and other useful tools for bookworkers.

As to the second question, the societies to be considered are, for the most part, made up of limited numbers of book-lovers, who care both for the contents and the clothing of their volumes, and their clubs usually partake of a certain social nature; to a greater extent, that is to say, than the technically bibliographical, antiquarian, scientific, literary, and historical societies, whose professed business it is to publish works, each of its own kind, whose great services are everywhere recognized, and to which we would now pay proper tribute. If my reasoning does not always seem sound, I fall back upon the unquestioned understanding of an audience of this character, and upon the comforting statement of the first historian of the subject who, after frankly confessing the difficulties of determining what societies are professional and what are not, and exactly what is meant by the term "learned society," washes his hands of the responsibility with the sentence, "In general, however these forms of expression are sufficiently understood in society, without the formality of definition."

I am pleading for a little more recognition on the part of the average librarian or bibliographer of the many useful contributions made to his working apparatus by clubs or societies formed for the promotion of the book arts and kindred subjects. Far too often, it has seemed, in bibliographical reference books, a publication of such a society is entirely ignored or receives scant mention, scholarly though it may be; while a bare list of books on a popular subject is acclaimed for its usefulness. Of course, such lists are useful, and of course, too, the equally useful publication of a book club may have been issued in too small a number for general reading, but, to one who will really look for it, a copy is nearly always available and pays for the search; sometimes, indeed, it contains the last word on its subject. The *Union list of serials* will help to find it.

Oftentimes it is a work which the general publisher would not have undertaken, and which is issued by a club for its members because there are enough people among the membership who are willing to pay the large price per copy necessary to insure the printing of the book at all.

To return to our Roxburghe Club, the first parent of them all, the Club did not for many years even issue its own publications, but each member in turn was supposed to print "at his own expense some rare old tract, or composition, and present every fellow-member with a copy." The Club still to a great extent follows this rule, but has produced some important works at the joint expense of the members—notably a magnificent reproduction of a manuscript *Apocalypse* in the Library of Trinity College, Cambridge, with Preface and description by Dr. Montague Rhodes James, probably the greatest living authority on the subject. Some half-dozen other great manuscripts have been produced under the editorship of Dr. James, reproductions in facsimile of complete manuscripts having become a most important feature of the Club's activities. The other specialty of the Roxburghe Club (observed almost entirely in its earlier years) is the reprinting of the texts of rare English works from early editions, and the printing of valuable old papers and documents. Among the editors of its nearly two hundred publications are Sir Frederic Madden, Frederick J. Furnivall, George F. Warner, Alfred W. Pollard, Falconer Madan, and many other distinguished scholars and bibliographers.

As applying especially to our chosen field, we should mention the *Transcript of the registers of the Worshipful Company of Stationers, 1640–1708*, in three volumes, presented to the Club in 1913–14 by George Edward Briscoe Eyre. Certainly there is much that is intriguing in the titles of *A Roxburghe garland*, presented in 1817 by James Boswell, son of the biographer; and *The book of life; a bibliographical melody*, dedicated to the Roxburghe Club by Richard Thomson, in 1820—little as those volumes may add to the sum of the knowledge of bibliography today.

A late publication of the Roxburghe Club is *A book of Old Testament illustrations of the middle of the thirteenth century sent by Cardinal Bernard Maciljowski to Shah Abbas the Great, king of Persia; now in the Pierpont Morgan Library at New York; described by Sydney C. Cockerell, director of the Fitzwilliam Museum, Cambridge, with an Introduction by Montague Rhodes James, provost of Eton*, with ninety-two facsimiles of pages, many of them magnificently done in color. This was presented to the Club and its members in 1927, by Mr. J. Pierpont Morgan, who ten years previously had presented another facsimile of an illuminated manuscript (*Gospels of Matilda of Tuscany*) in behalf of his father, whose death occurred shortly after his admission to the Club.

In this connection it may not be out of place to quote from the history of the Club a brief résumé of the types of persons who are its members, as with certain substitutions, the addition of a goodly number of physicians and a somewhat larger proportion of business men, I fancy that about the same statistics would be found true of American book clubs.

The average age of members at their election has been forty-five, though one member, Mr. J. Pierpont Morgan, joined the Club at seventy-five, and one, the third Earl of Powis, at twenty-one. Seventy-three have been peers and seventy-six members of Parliament: four-and-twenty have been clergymen and the same number have been called to the bar: about twenty have been professors, fifteen librarians of public institutions, twenty soldiers, and twenty men of business: three have been famous writers and about fifty have written books: three have been Prime Minister.

Other American members of the Club, besides the Morgans, father and son, were James Russell Lowell and Whitelaw Reid. The United States is also represented by A. Chester Beatty, whose collection of Oriental and Western manuscripts is housed in his London home.

A history of the Club, with descriptions of its members and its publications, was published in 1927 and is in itself a very interesting bibliography and a mine of information concerning the great private libraries of England and their owners during the last century and a quarter. In the Preface the Club makes a twofold claim for itself, as the oldest existing society of bibliophiles in Great Britain and probably in the world, and also as the "parent of those publishing societies which have done so much in this country for history, letters, antiquity and other branches of literature and art."

It is rather in its second phase that it has fathered such important associations as the Percy Society, named in 1840 for the accomplished editor of the *Reliques*, which during its lifetime of some dozen years rescued from oblivion countless ballads, chapbooks, and other fugitive pieces of literature. In this category, too, may be named the Hakluyt Society (1846), for the publication of rare and valuable voyages, and geographical works; the Early English Text Society, founded by F. J. Furnivall in 1864, the object designated by its name having been splendidly carried out through a long series of books; and, founded at a much later date (1907), the Malone Society, for faithfully reprinting Elizabethan and Jacobean plays, most of them having been brought out under the editorial care of a brilliant bibliographer, Dr. W. W. Greg. The distinguished work in facsimile-reproductions of the New Paleographical Society and of the Type Facsimile Society should be noted with gratitude.

Invaluable to scholarship as these publications are, however, we may seem to be wandering afield into the realm of the Learned Society, and away from book clubs, used in our chosen, narrow sense of the word, although, in passing, it is pleasant to note the close relationship.

The earliest follower of the Roxburghe Club was the Bannatyne, founded by Sir Walter Scott in protest against the smallness and exclusiveness of the earlier club, and with the object of printing rare works connected with Scotland. It would not fall within our limits, had it not, in the midst of its many historical publications, been presented with a *Catalogue of the library at Abbotsford*, which, as almost always is the case with the catalogue of an author's library, reflects the character of its owner. In this instance, the compiler assures us, "The reader has before him a faithful inventory of the materials with which the national Poet and Novelist had stored his mind before he began his public career."

Sir Walter was a member of the Roxburghe Club when he founded the other, having been elected, as "the author of 'Waverley,'" in 1823. In the early records it is narrated that on the only occasion when he dined with the Club (it was at the Freemason's Tavern) "Mr. Cuff gave a three course dinner off plate to include turtle and desert at a guinea a head, at which everyone appeared gratified and satisfied."

One point of interest about the Bannatyne Club is that it printed more copies of its publications than were needed for its members, selling the remainder. Of its successors, the Maitland, the Camden, the Spalding, the Chetham, and several others followed its historical trend, but it must not be forgotten that the New Spalding Society published a *Bibliography of the shires of Aberdeen, &c*, and that it is to the Chetham Society that we owe *Collectanea Anglo-poetica*, the extensive catalogue of Thomas Corser's library (1860–83).

Toward the middle of the century various clubs arose, some of which strayed far from the bookishness that marked the prototype of them all. That quality was somewhat restored in the Philobiblon Society, founded in 1853; and received a joyous reincarnation in Ye Sette of Odd Volumes, which "for half a century," writes Harold Williams "has dined, read papers, criticized and jested." Scattered through its long list of *Opuscula, Miscellanies*, and *Year-bokes* are many valuable bibliographical aids, such as *Pens, ink and paper*, by D. W. Kettle (1885); *Books for children of the last century* and *Coloured books for children*, by Charles Welsh (1886 and 1887); *A short sketch of liturgical literature*, by Bernard Quaritch (1887); *Odd volumes and their book-plates*, by Walter Hamilton (1899); *University magazines and their makers*, by H. C. Marillier (1902); and *Decorative bookbinding in Ireland*, by Sir Edward Sullivan (1914). A list of the small volumes published by the Sette from 1878 to 1924 may be found in *An odd bibliography*, compiled by Ralph Straus (1925).

To return for a moment to the Philobiblon Society, it should be noted that in its fifteen volumes of handsomely printed *Bibliographical miscellanies* (1854–84) there are various notes of considerable value on libraries, public and private, by Beriah Botfield and others, a lecture on *The origin and progress of printing*, by Henry G. Bohn, and other articles on printing and presses (especially valuable for early private presses), on rare books and on early manuscripts.

In writing his book on *American book clubs*, the first one, so called, of which Mr. Growoll could trace the record, was the Seventy-six Society, founded in Philadelphia in 1854, its interests being purely historical; but in a preliminary chapter he notes, among other progenitors, Benjamin Franklin's Junto, a literary society formed by Franklin, with his companions in the employ of Samuel Keimer, in 1726, from which humble beginnings resulted, among other things, the founding of the first lending library in Pennsylvania (now the Library Company of Philadelphia), and the plan for the first magazine conceived in this country, the *General magazine*, forestalled by only three days by its short-lived rival, the *American magazine*. In Boston, early in the nineteenth century, an association of literary men called the Anthology Club performed a like service by establishing a reading-room and library, which eventually became the Boston Athenaeum. Good services, these, to the science of books!

Most of the earlier book clubs of America were founded with the avowed objects of reprinting, or printing from manuscript, rare works of historical interest. In New York there were "The Club" and the Bradford Club, both short-lived, with memberships limited, the first to seven, and the second to four (later five) bibliophiles. Again we must pass over the historical services performed, and note the "extra volume" of the Bradford Club—Evert A. Duyckinck's *Memorial of John Allan* (1864), one of the most delightful accounts which has been written of a genuine collector and his books. Similarly, with the Prince Society of Boston, named for a great collector whose books and manuscripts are preserved in the Boston Public Library, we select the *Letters from New England, A.D. 1686*, by that eccentric London bookseller, John Dunton, whose *Life and errors* and *Religio bibliopolae* make such entertaining reading. It was surely an adventurous soul who, to collect a bill of £500 and in the hope of selling a few books, would essay the four months' voyage from Gravesend to Boston in 1685! The letters, printed from the original manuscript in the Bodleian Library, in 1867, were edited by William Henry Whitmore, the scholarly editor of the Society's *Hutchinson papers*. A late useful publication of the Prince Society is *The New England Company of 1649 and John Eliot* (1920), with Introduction by George Parker Winship, giving descriptive and bibliographical details of Eliot's Indian Bible.

In 1864 Francis S. Hoffman, of New York, organized the Club of Odd Sticks, which would doubtless have been forgotten long since had it not produced one volume (its only publication), which was a complete departure from the work of its American predecessors. This was a reprint of no less a work than Thomas Frognall Dibdin's *Bibliomania; or book-madness*, seemingly the first American edition of this rich stimulant for the book-lover. It had first seen the light as a slender volume in 1809, eight years before the founding of the Roxburghe Club, described by its author (the originator of the Club) in his *Bibliographical decameron*.

Two short-lived groups bearing the names of printers, Zenger and Rivington, from which we might expect something essentially bibliographical, devoted themselves to historical studies, while the objects of clubs with such names as Knickerbocker, Narragansett, Hamilton, and Washington are too evident to need comment. Most of these, however, had a common origin in the desire of small numbers of book-collectors and scholars to preserve in worthy form the records of the past, often at great cost and personal effort. Some went to ridiculous lengths, it is true, to preserve secrecy as to the identity of their members and to insure the scarcity of their publications, but most benefactors of mankind have their foibles. Two of the especially mysterious societies, the U.Q. (Unknown Quantity) and the Agathynian clubs (the secret of the latter's name has never, I believe, been fathomed), deserve mention for their particular efforts to produce handsomely made volumes. Indeed, one of the professed objects of the Agathynian was "to stimulate the development of the typographical art in this country to its utmost perfec-

tion." It seems also to have been the first American club to attempt to issue reproductions of early printed books. But a fire
in the Bradstreet Bindery consumed practically the entire
Agathynian edition of the *Proverbs of Erasmus*, with a bibliography of G. P. Philes, and put an end to the brief existence of
the Club in 1867.

Chicago has the honor of being the home of the first book club
formed in the West (it was the West in the sixties, was it not?),
though perhaps its Franklin Society, founded in 1869 for "mutual improvement and social enjoyment," may be more properly
classed among professional clubs, as its members were chiefly
printers. At all events, it seems to have been the first American
association of the kind to possess a library of books on book-
making—perhaps any kind of library—and it did pioneer bibliographical service in its day, with a publication on *Early newspapers in Illinois*, by Henry R. Boss, and its periodical called
the *Printing press*, to which the Great Fire unfortunately put
an end after seven numbers had been issued. Fires seem to have
been particularly hard on bibliography at that period!

With the Historical Printing Club, founded by Gordon L.
Ford, of Brooklyn, and his two sons, Worthington Chauncey
and Paul Leicester, all men of literary distinction aside from
their fame as bibliophiles and bibliographers, we reach the great
days of American book clubs. "Originating in a desire," writes
Mr. Growoll, "to put into print certain historical and bibliographical material which no publisher could be induced to publish at his own risk, its first publications were merely 'privately
printed' but so many requests for copies reached the originators
of this Club that it was decided to assume a club name for imprint, and to put a price on the publications." This is a little
involved, but I shall follow Mr. Growoll's lead and mention the
publications indiscriminately, whether they bear the imprint
"privately printed" or that of the Historical Printing Club. The
list makes an imposing array, even bereft of the Club's valuable
historical contributions, for the most part edited by Worthington C. Ford.

In bibliography we have *Websteriana: a catalogue of books by Noah Webster, collated from the library of Gordon L. Ford* (1882; 6 copies); *Bibliotheca Chaunciana* (1884; 10 copies); and, between 1886 and 1889, bibliographies of Alexander Hamilton and Benjamin Franklin, and reference lists on *The federalist; Treasury reports and circulars issued by Alexander Hamilton, Pamphlets on the Constitution of the United States, 1787–8, History and literature relating to the adoption of the Constitution, The official publications of the Continental Congress*, and *American magazines printed in the eighteenth century*, as well as a *Check list of bibliographies, catalogues, reference-lists, and lists of authorities of American books and subjects.*

All of these, as well as much initial work on the notable bibliography of *Parson Weems*, lately completed in memory of her brother by Mrs. Emily Ford Skeel, are the work of Paul Leicester Ford. *The Press of North Carolina in the eighteenth century*, with a bibliography of the issues (1891), was prepared for the Club by Stephen B. Weeks, and the *Burr bibliography* by Hamilton Tompkins, in 1892.

In a newspaper article preserved by Beverly Chew in his copy of Frederick Locker-Lampson's *London lyrics*, published in 1883 by the Book Fellows' Club, we read that Mr. Valentin Blacque, one fine day, invited to dine with him two fellow-book-collectors, William Loring Andrews and A. Duprat, and delivered to them a speech which may be reconstructed from the memory of the two guests as follows:

That he [Valentin Blacque] was founder and only member of a club called The Book Fellows, which at its first meeting had made him President, as was his due; Treasurer, as was his penalty, and Secretary, executive, membership, and publication committees, as was his pleasure. If they desired to become members he would pass upon their application at once. No initiation fee was required, but they were expected to share proportionally in the expense of the publication of the first book, which would be Locker's "London Lyrics."

It should be stated that at the time Mr. Andrews had not begun his series of beautifully made books about books and bookmen, and that it was ten years before Mr. Duprat, the bookseller, issued his first *Booklover's almanac*, which ran for several years and contained, by the way, many a choice morsel of bibliographical lore. Both gentlemen fell in with Mr. Blacque's plan with enthusiasm, but, after the publication of two books, some question as to the advisability of extending the membership beyond the original three led to the idea of a club of broader scope, and the result was the Grolier Club.

An initial meeting of the nine founders was held at the home of Robert Hoe on January 23, 1884, Mr. Andrews being again a leading figure, along with Theodore Low DeVinne, master-printer, Alexander W. Drake, who did so much for the art of illustration in this country, and other distinguished bookmen.

The object of the new Club was, and still is,

the literary study and promotion of the arts pertaining to the production of books including the occasional publication of books designed to illustrate, promote and encourage those arts; and the acquisition . . . . of a suitable Club building for the safekeeping of its property, wherein meetings, lectures and exhibitions shall take place from time to time, likewise designed to illustrate, promote and encourage those arts.

Of the 84 regular publications of the Grolier Club, 19 are about printing and printers, 17 are bibliographies and catalogues, 12 are on illustrations and engraving, 3 deal with the love of books and their collecting (bibliophily, I suppose would describe them in a word), 2 with bookbinding, and 1 each, with bookplates and illuminated manuscripts. Of the remaining, 14 are works of literature, printed or reprinted in such manner as to exemplify some special phase of printing or illustration, or simply as fine pieces of bookmaking; 5 are volumes of transactions and lists of the Club's publications, and 7 are engravings and bronze medallions, which also illustrate the interests of the Club.

A brief résumé of works under the principal subjects with which we are concerning ourselves shows, on printing and printers, a reprint of the first edition of *A decree of Star Chamber concerning printing* (1637), the first publication of the Club, issued late in 1884; four works by Theodore Low DeVinne; *A descrip-*

tion of the early printed books owned by the Grolier Club (1895); works on *The Charles Whittinghams, printers*, by Arthur Warren (1896); on *Franklin and his press at Passy*, by Luther S. Livingston (1914); on the Gilliss and the DeVinne presses (1926 and 1929); *The American press at the end of the eighteenth century*, by Bernard Fay (1927); translations into English of two great treatises on the alphabet (Albrecht Dürer's *On the just shaping of letters* [1917], and Geofroy Tory's *Champfleury* [1927]); and several reprints and facsimiles of early works on printing and of rare volumes.

In its four volumes of collations and notes on *Original and early editions . . . . of English writers from Langland to Wither*, and *from Wither to Prior* (1893 and 1905), and in its facsimiles of and bibliographical notes (by H. W. Kent) upon *One hundred books famous in English literature*, the Club has made valuable contributions to the bibliography of English literature, while many of the catalogues of its exhibitions, issued as Club publications, partake of the nature of bibliographies. The subjects of these catalogues extend from *Early editions of Italian books* to *The poets laureate of England*, from Pope and Dryden to Dickens, Stevenson, and books illustrated by Leech and Rowlandson.

An authoritative *Bibliography of William Blake*, by Geoffrey Keynes (1921), takes its place in both classes already named, as well as in that of book illustration and engraving, wherein fall many important publications of the Grolier Club, such as *American engravings upon copper and steel*, by D. McN. Stauffer (1907), and others, which relate more closely to art than to bibliography.

The three books which we have classed under the heading of bibliophily are: an elaborate edition of the greatest of them all, Richard de Bury's *Philobiblon*, and translations from the French of the lives of those two great book-lovers, Charles Henry, Count Hoym, and Jean Grolier de Servier, Viscount d'Aquisy—whose name the Club bears.

Some of these publications, as we have said, are elaborated catalogues of exhibitions which have been held. In addition, the Club has issued seventy small hand-catalogues of exhibitions on varied subjects.

The exhibitions, not only of the Grolier, but also of similar clubs, both in America and England, have, themselves, been a tremendous stimulus to bibliography and to interest in its study. The sight of a long array of first editions of our favorite author, of the only known copy of a book, of the gorgeous Golden Gospels, or of the original manuscript of a great work, may turn a casual student into one of those special investigators or great collectors who provide the resources whereby libraries of the future may be filled with the results of present researches and the relics of the past. You will remember that it was John Hill Burton who stood up for the proposition that, if there be no other respectable function in life fulfilled by the book-hunter, "he is the feeder, provided by nature for the preservation of literature from age to age, by the accumulation and preservation of libraries, public and private."

Two highly specialized book clubs which began life in the mid-eighties are the Filson Club, for preserving data concerning Kentucky and its neighbors; and the Dunlap Society, founded by Professor Brander Matthews for the preservation of the literature and portraiture of the American stage. To the former we owe W. H. Perrin's work on *The pioneer press of Kentucky* (1888), and to the latter, bibliographies of William Dunlap and Dion Boucicault (included in lives of these dramatists), as well as lists of *Early American plays* and *Later American plays*, compiled respectively by Oscar Wegelin and Robert Roden—both published in 1900.

In 1886 the Club of Odd Volumes was founded in Boston, with James F. Hunnewell as president. Its objects, as set forth in its constitution, are almost identical with those of the Grolier Club, and its publications and exhibitions are along similar lines. In addition to contributions to literature and its series of reprints of *Early American poetry*, it has published, with direct bearing on bibliography: George Littlefield's works on *Early Boston booksellers* (1900); *Early schools and schoolbooks of New England* (1904); and *The early Massachusetts press* (1907); James F. Hunnewell's essays on *The triumphs of early printing* (1902); and *Collectors* (1908); papers on Walpole, Caxton, and Isaiah Thomas by E. Percival Merrett, George Parker Winship, and Charles L. Nichols; *Notes from a country library*, by Harold Murdock (1911); and *The Boston book market, 1679–1700*, by Worthington C. Ford (1917).

In addition to many valuable catalogues, the Club has issued of late years brochures containing running descriptions of its exhibitions—the story of the subject entertainingly told, with special references to works shown. For examples we cite: *Catalogue of an exhibition illustrating the varied interests of book buyers, 1450–1600*, published in 1922; and *The ways of authorship; an introduction to an exhibition of literary manuscripts* (1927).

Like the Grolier Club and the Club of Odd Volumes, the Rowfant Club of Cleveland, founded in 1892, rejoices in a clubhouse of its own, wherein are held its weekly discussions of bookish matters, its exhibitions, and its annual ceremonies on Candlemas Day. Its principal contributions to our subject are: bibliographies of Thoreau and Hawthorne by Samuel Arthur Jones (1894) and W. H. Cathcart (1905); an edition of Franklin's *Autobiography* (1898); an Appendix to the *Rowfant Library of Frederick Locker-Lampson* (1900); *Auction prices of American book-club publications*, compiled by Robert F. Roden (1904); and *Bibliographical notes on Puckle's Club* (1899). Among the Club's "Rowfantia" are several delightful contributions. An excellent account of the Rowfant Club forms very suitably the last chapter of Augustine Birrell's *Character sketch of Frederick Locker-Lampson*, from whose library the Club derives its name.

The Caxton Club of Chicago began its useful career in 1895, also with the object of studying and promoting the arts pertaining to the production of books, and it has been especially wise and fortunate in that it has gone straight to the fountainhead of knowledge—the British Museum—for its authors, and has produced authoritative works, in its series on the great English bookbinders by Cyril J. H. Davenport; in Alfred W. Pollard's *Essay on colophons* (1905); and in *Ancient books and modern discoveries*, by Sir Frederick G. Kenyon (1927). Among other good books issued by the Caxton Club are *The French bookbinders of the eighteenth century*, by Octave Uzanne (1904); *William Caxton*, by E. Gordon Duff (1905); and a translation of Henri Estienne's *Frankfort book fair* (1911).

Catalogues of noteworthy exhibitions and addresses of bibliographical interest have been issued by both the Rowfant and the Caxton clubs, as well as by the Franklin Club of St. Louis, founded about 1909.

Other American clubs with like objects are the Philobiblon of Philadelphia, which published a facsimile edition of the first American edition of *Magna Charta*, printed by William Bradford in 1687, and whose long list of exhibitions and addresses (unprinted) is impressive; and the Dibdin Club of New York, formed in 1897 by a small number of men "interested in publishing bibliographical material for which a publisher might not readily be found."

The latter has given us a *Descriptive catalogue of the library of Charles Lamb* (1897), with the romantic and pathetic story of the library described by Charles Welford and G. L. D. Duyckinck, and the very useful works of Adolf Growoll on book-trade bibliography in the United States and in England (1898 and 1903), the later work containing Wilberforce Eames's *List of catalogues, etc., published for the English booktrade from 1595 to 1902.*

The Bibliophile Society of Boston has brought out many interesting literary and historical works from original manuscripts, largely those in the collection of William K. Bixby, several of them being in facsimile, and has published a handsome edition in four volumes of Dibdin's *Bibliomania* (1903). Its yearbooks, too, contain bibliographical material.

In 1912 the western coast came into the field, with the formation of the Book Club of California, of which you will hear at length at your next meeting. Among its handsomely printed publications are some which apply here, but we leave them to their next historian. California has three recently formed clubs, the Los Angeles and the Zamorano, which have put out lists of books printed by John Henry Nash and by William Morris, and the brand-new Roxburghe Club of San Francisco, from which, if names are significant, we may expect much.

Two interesting book societies, closely allied with colleges, are the Elizabethan Club of Yale and the John Barnard Associates of Harvard. Both have published books on their activities, and the former has printed a list of the rare books in its library, presented by Alexander Smith Cochran (1912); as well as a facsimile of its copy of *Common conditions*, edited by Tucker Brooke in 1915. These clubs owe much to the guiding hands of Dr. Keogh and Dr. Winship, and one cannot refrain from an appreciative word of the work of these gentlemen, and of a few other librarians in universities, in arousing students to a sense of the fineness of such interests.

A recent recruit to the cause is the Quarto Club of New York, whose *Papers* (two volumes have been published) include such useful articles as Lois C. Levison's on *A maker of books* (Dard Hunter).

Returning to England for a glance at its modern clubs, we find the Baskerville, founded in Cambridge in 1903; the Walpole Society, which in 1924 collaborated with the Malone Society in the publication of *Designs by Inigo Jones for masques and plays at court*, with much bibliographical material gathered from the great Chatsworth Collection and elsewhere; and the First Edition Club, founded in 1922, "to promote the study of book-collecting, bibliography, the classification and preservation of books; to assist in improving the standard of book-production."

The Baskerville Club, according to Mr. Williams, "hesitated on the borderline of the book club, printing society or bibliographical society," being entirely without recognizable organization. It published two bibliographical works of distinction in its *Handlists* of imprints of the Baskerville Press (1904), and *Bibliography of the works of John Donne* (1914), by Geoffrey Keynes.

Like the more fortunate of the modern American clubs, the First Edition Club has a delightful clubhouse where its exhibitions and bibliographical and social activities are carried on. It has already a noteworthy list of bibliographical contributions to its credit, besides several publications chiefly of literary interest. In the former class are bibliographies of William Butler Yeats and of Austin Dobson, compiled respectively by A. J. A. Symons and William Dobson; *Catalogue of an exhibition of the works of Lord Byron; Thirty bindings described by A. D. Hobson; Bibliography of the principal modern presses in Great Britain and Ireland*, by G. S. Tomkinson; and, lastly, *Book clubs and printing societies of Great Britain and Ireland*, by Harold Williams, to whom this paper is greatly indebted.

The First Edition Club is following the lead of the American Institute of Graphic Arts in exhibiting, yearly, fifty books representative of the bookmaking of the year in their respective countries, and the interest aroused by these traveling collections is a great stimulus to the arts of the book and their study.

Several of the clubs which we have been considering have their own libraries, in which the study of their special subjects may be carried on with ease and dispatch—not the least of the services which they perform. The only one of these libraries of which I can speak with authority is that of the Grolier Club, which contains some twenty thousand books about books, and which is open freely to the public in general and to students of bibliography in particular, under the regulations of the Club.

It has seemed expedient within the limits of this paper to confine our investigation to book clubs of Great Britain and the
United States, but there exist Continental clubs which well
repay investigation, and there is at least one book club in the
Orient.

Bibliography is indebted to private book clubs for the books
about books which they publish, for the exhibitions which they
hold, for the libraries which they form, and for the love of books
which they foster. Foremost among the objects of many of the
clubs which we have been considering is the emphasis on typography and all that goes into making a book physically sound,
beautiful, and enduring, and herein may lie one of their greatest
services to bibliography. For the consciousness of these things,
once awakened, almost inevitably leads to research into the
history of all literature as it has been transmitted from age to
age in manuscripts and in printed books.

GLEANINGS FROM INCUNABULA
OF SCIENCE AND MEDICINE

By ARNOLD C. KLEBS

I N MODERN times the name of "science" is applied to manifold human activities. This indicates that the process of specialistic grouping of efforts still continues and that the application of the successful methods of natural science within such groups holds out the greatest promise of progress. Sometimes we resent the intrusion of newcomers in fields which we have long tilled with care and have come to regard as a privileged possession. To allow, however, the title of "science" only to disinterested pursuits of knowledge by certain approved methods and without reference to any practical application would be a futile and unpopular gesture. We are certainly still far from an ideal science which, inspired by Terence's famous words, "homo sum, humani nihil a me alienum puto," would embrace the whole range of all that is knowable and at the same time beneficial to mankind. We have accumulated and stored so much that we are simply forced to specialize.[1] Despite the fact, often pointed out, that in the evolution of living beings, plants and animals, extreme specialization stops progress, that only the generalized types produce higher forms, and that in human history in Alexandria and Rome the same took place, we see nevertheless no way by which the modern tendency can be stopped, and we are even convinced that only by specialistic research can really notable advances be made.

Medicine occupies a unique and persistent position in all these canalizing activities. Somehow its function escapes every attempt at a sharp delimitation and definition. It is characteristic that Sarton in his admirable *Introduction* finds it easy to indicate for every branch of science which he enumerates its object and scope, except for medicine, which he leaves undefined.[2] But perhaps by saying "medical sciences" and not "medicine" he thought he had given all necessary definition, leaving the details to the text of his third series, for which he gives only the outline here. When he reaches this stage of his work he will doubtless have become aware of the fact that the principal actors in the human drama he unfolds before us are almost all physicians. There were three professions, it must be admitted, that clamored for the honor of having been the original specialties, that of the priest, of the magician, and of the physician. They all professed in common to possess special knowledge with which they could help their fellow-beings and their tribe. We need not examine here why and how they did it; we shall only note that in every primitive society of man, one or more of these craftsmen had segregated themselves from the common herd in order to minister to obvious needs. All three have come down to us, borrowing from one another, proud of their knowledge and their calling, except the magician, who has to use various disguises, for he is much misunderstood these days.

No doubt, therefore, the physician—we shall not consider the other two just now—was an early if not the earliest man of science. But merely to profess his knowledge was not enough, for he had to show how he could provide for definite needs of his tribe. Strongly desirous to help, feeling in himself the power that he could help, he went to acquire knowledge. And in this ardent striving he scanned the skies and trod the earth searching for remedies, above and below, to alleviate suffering. The knowledge he acquired he registered and passed on with guiding words to his son, and he to his son, and so on. And here he still is and he can boast, as Osler said, of the same unbroken continuity of methods and ideals.[3] He is still the craftsman of old, but he has learned much, and his skill has become greater;

he has taken from the sciences that sprang from his craft all they could give him for his needs; some of them he has built and adapted to these needs. With his hand on the pulse of suffering man, his eyes fixed on the hidden sores and miseries of civilization, his ears open to the plaints of sick and shattered existences, he found he needed so much more than these sciences could provide. He even found that sometimes they tempted him away from his principal task to glorious adventures in promising bypaths of search and circumscribed effort. He tried these narrow paths but never lost the broader outlook. Did not Dante, that divine bard of all human aspirations, ask for admittance at the door of the physicians' guild in Florence, and with him and after him all the wisest and best thinkers of the times, and the great painters? So today do they need a better label than that of medicine? Rightly a national homage was paid to one of their leaders, and the president of this republic said before him, "Dr. Welch is our greatest statesman in the field of public health." Yes, public health, a great ideal and a wide field; the maintenance of that vigor and well-being without which nothing is possible; in comparison with it what is that science that provides salable mechanical gadgets, elaborate classifications and formulas of so-called positive knowledge, unless constructive and sympathetic thought is given to the wider problems of mankind? It is notable that Dr. Welch should now head an entirely new institution which, by the study of history, attempts, and no doubt will succeed, to integrate the multiple specialties into which modern medicine has become divided.

Scientific Thought and Action

The simple experience which teaches us that the effectiveness of a bodily action is proportionally increased by its repetition so that it becomes a habit, a more or less unconscious automatism, is at the bottom of all successful craftsmanship. It establishes a rule that holds good for both the "skilled" and "learned" crafts. Whether or not these aptitudes of body and mind are inheritable is still a moot question, but historically the fact seems corroborated that crafts run in families. One thing seems clear, and that is that in their evolution they do not run parallel courses. The more delicate and complex a technical action becomes in the naturally restrained field, the more should one expect the mind to expand to ever wider fields of new activities. But this is not so, and one observes almost invariably that the action habit also entails a thought habit that forces the mind into the field of action from which it can extricate itself only in the rare cases of great intellectual elasticity. The technical evolution has outrun somatic evolution. The effect on materialistic science is inevitable. Our instrumental facilities as to accuracy have been enormously perfected, so that everything of former ages seems incredibly crude to us; and still there are no indications that our mental powers, of discernment, of judgment, have correspondingly grown. Nay, we find sometimes among the older authors infinitely simpler, saner approaches to and judgments of problems for which sometimes fantastic solutions are proposed by modern experimentalists. A time seems to have come when it would appear to be profitable to slow up the rhythm of instrumental and experimental subtilization, and turn to the problems imposed by the broader human needs and not merely by a successful methodology.

The Printing Machine

A striving for machine-like precision underlies most modern scientific and medical aspirations. It is well to recognize this and to realize its advantages and shortcomings. As in a real machine, the mechanization of thought increases the scope and effectiveness of action, but only inside of restrained fields. A modern machine is a complex affair, an assembly of machines. Improvement of component parts can increase its efficiency up to a certain extent, but a time comes when this does not pay any more and the machine has to be scrapped and a new one built. Human thought inhibited by tradition and age-old habits resists, even when mechanized, this scrapping and rebuilding. It makes its improvements inside of the old structure. We express this when we say that the machine is getting the better of us, and we try to improve the machine by making it foolproof, to simplify its operation. This interplay and mutual adaptation of the mental and the material machine dominate all modern scientific striving, and if we look through the annals of history for the origin of this evolutionary element, we are forced to find it at that moment when the machine enters the realm of thought, that is, when the printing press made the results of individual intellectual and technical labor utilizable by an ever increasing number of pupils. Thus for the turn that science has taken, the advent of the printed book is of fundamental importance; modern scientific progress is simply unthinkable, impossible, without it. In the approach to an ultimate science based on ideal truth we have deliberately chosen the machine as our helpmate. It has given us excellent service in the limited field of material experience and we have good hopes of gradually transcending the self-imposed boundaries by a better understanding of the interplay of matter and energy, and its effect on wider human aspiration. There is much work for laboratories still ahead, and they will have to widen their scope so as to embrace also that practically untapped field of research, human thought itself, in recognition of the fact that thought of all ages is equivalent, deserving scientific consideration like any other fact of nature. We have learned to preserve an objective and dignified attitude when we are facing nature. We no more speak of her whims and fancies; we simply approach them unmoved. But when facing thought we become uneasy and emotional; what does not fit into the thought habits acquired in a bad school we call all sorts of names: superstitious, credulous, infantile, etc. We are indignant and arrogant when we find somebody attacking our favorite ideas, especially all the "-isms" from Darwinism to behaviorism. If we want to preserve our scientific self-respect we have to relearn many things, and especially attain a dignified respect for the thoughts of others and especially for the thought of earlier workers who, while lacking some of our advantages, had none of our prejudices. We have the most unscientific conviction that we are the end and the top of evolution, when we ought to know that our age is but a phase in a long process and that five hundred years from now our work and thought will be judged as we judge now the work and thought of the men who for the first time printed it on paper so as to exchange it with others. And as water is always clearest at its source, any study of modern scientific thought can suitably begin with that of the incunabula literature, which, as I shall try to show, links the thoughts not of one but of a hundred ages.

Incunabula

It is not necessary here to discuss the many points of interest which the incunabula have for the bibliographer, the archaeologist, and the collector. In the past twenty years this interest has grown to a remarkable extent, and justly so, for it would be difficult to find another object of antiquarian interest which marks so sharply and so precisely a decided turn in human affairs. It is natural that incunabula have mainly been studied as the artistic products of the first printers rather than as to their contents. There was so much to do in the clearing of the often obscure origin of unsigned incunabula, in the following-up of the complex wanderings of some printers, in the studying of their types and their practices of composition. This part of the work goes on persistently though slowly. The exact description and determination of some forty thousand single items, some of them extant only in unique copies and often widely separated in different corners of the world, is a very difficult undertaking, especially since there are comparatively few workers in the field who have reached the necessary degree of competence for making descriptions and determinations. Nevertheless, the accumulation of reliable material has augmented to such an extent that the analysis of the contents of these books, and with that the dissemination of ideas during the period under consideration, can now be undertaken with a fair promise of profit. Why this has not been done before explains itself, not only because of the inaccessibility and insufficient preparation of the material, but also because of a bias in favor of manuscripts as offering better source material for literary studies than the incunabula or early printed books. It is perhaps incorrect to speak of a bias, because the student of the manuscript literature as a rule leaves the printed material *ipso facto* out of consideration, and takes a special interest in those manuscripts which were not printed at all. The objection to incunabula because they reproduce badly the manuscript texts, or because they are based on inferior texts, is occasionally heard, but is rarely based on a systematic examination and comparison of various editions.

I have given to the study of incunabula of medicine and science the better part of the past fifteen years after having been introduced to them in the Surgeon General's Library by Colonel Fielding H. Garrison. I am now engaged with the final revision of a general bibliography of the incunabula of science and medicine, a work which, with the welcome assistance of the New York Academy of Medicine, I hope to bring to an early termination. I have extracted from my records data which I believe can throw a clearer light than hitherto obtainable, on the extent, on the various aspects, and on the paths of dissemination of the earliest scientific literature as it issued from the first European presses.

The Printers

We know very little about the individual lives of the earliest printers. For information we have to depend mostly on inferences we can draw from their work. These suggest that they were by no means only journeymen or specialized craftsmen, such as they were soon to become, but often academically trained men with a good knowledge of the works they were handling and printing, guided by the advice and help of the learned with whom they naturally associated. As the promoters of a new art they were probably less mechanized and specialized than, for instance, the professional scriveners.[5] They were the true descendants of the *vagantes*, the wandering scholars of the early Middle Ages, unknown, poor, but cheerful carriers of progressive, because living, thought.[6] When the early printer rises out of the usual anonymity by attaining material prosperity we get to know him better. Most often he becomes a powerful head of a great press in continuous contact with the intellectual work of the day like Schöffer at Mainz and Koberger at Nuremberg, some creating around their press a little academy of their own like Aldus Manutius at Venice, others mainly shrewd business men like Vérard in Paris, and only a very few like Müller Regiomontanus, who uses his press for his scientific work just as today we would use the typewriter.

Of the channels by which manuscripts, as "copy," reached the earliest presses we have no comprehensive account; we learn about them only by casual references in the books themselves, to patrons, correctors, and others associated in the publishing work, also from accounts, contracts, and correspondence of printers in often rather inaccessible documents. The printers evidently were too busy doing things, the others too busy furnishing copy; nobody had time to talk about it, less to write of it. It is characteristic of this intense preoccupation that we have no single incunable in which the method of printing is explained. But from documentary and other evidence we can infer that with certain rather typical exceptions, the scientific men of the day took a very active interest in the promotion of printing. I have elsewhere gone into this evidence in detail.[7] It seems to show that especially medical men furthered with great energy and sacrifices the new art. Those who did not share the interest in the new art were the ones, occurring in every age, who on general principles object to innovation.

The reaction against the printing machine was an ephemeral one, but it is interesting to fix our attention on it, because it illustrates already at that time the deep-seated antipathy against all mechanical, machine-like performance. Man is an animal distinguished from others by his ability to make and use tools so as to free himself in order to master his surroundings, but when once his tool, by his efforts, has reached a certain degree of complexity, he begins to fear it; he longs for and perhaps attains simplicity once more, to begin over again. It is the same in the intellectual as in the mechanical realm. The Greeks began building with their philosophical tools the Alexandrian machine, the Christian thinkers with Arab and other helpers in similar striving produced the scholastic machine, and parallel with them out of medieval craftsmanship came the printing machine. And the humanists who heralded the new freedom patterned on Greek models in that movement which *they* called Renaissance turned against both scholasticism and printing, little aware that they themselves were playing a part in the scientific evolution which inevitably would lead again to greater complexity, to the huge machine which *we* call "modern science." It was not against the essence of scholasticism that the man of the Renaissance turned, for that was based on the very Greek ideals which he thought to have rediscovered; he merely turned against its complexity and machine-like precision. In his rather artificial, pagan joyousness and motility, he felt hemmed in by the tyranny of the syllogism and bored by too finely spun subtleties; the sonorous rhythm of Ciceronian dia-

lectics and Virgilian lyrics suited him better. Also could he see
nothing of the deep feeling and spiritual elevation in medieval
sculpture or painting or building; all seemed futile and rather
mechanical symbolisms vastly surpassed by the beautiful realism of the art of Phidias and Praxiteles. We cannot help but
see in this Renaissance, just as in the Reformation, that grew
out of it, a revolutionary movement which ruffles the surface
but does not touch the deeper substance of the stream of human
destiny. The machine had come into the world, and it had
come to stay.

If formal rather than substantial, our debt to the Renaissance
is nevertheless great. Undoubtedly it has improved language,
not only Latin but the vulgar tongues equally. Many of the
better texts that came under the new presses we owe to the
labor of the humanists. Ruskin exaggerates when he rages
against the soullessness of Renaissance architecture, but there
is much truth in his contention that only great genius in art
can proceed by means of mathematical and scientific precise-
ness to harmonious creation. Beautiful work was done by the
painters, and the scientific book owes much to the surer and
truer delineation of the artist and the fine craftsmanship of the
woodcutter. By blending the simple forms of the Carolingian
minuscule with those of the sober Roman majuscules the hu-
manistic penman gave us the script we still use, but which had
reached the acme of its perfection in the types of Jenson's Venetian press and some of its successful imitators. It was expressive
of the reaction against the complexity of the monastic script
which the Italian classicists had dubbed "Gothic," viz., "barbaric," in their unreasoning contempt for all that had come to
them from that age. They thought it an intruder between antiquity and themselves and so coined the derogatory epithet
"Middle Ages." But curiously, the Gothic script held out for
long in printing, against the Roman, especially in scientific literature. Of its forms the majestic *textura*, created by Guten-

berg's craftsmanship for his Bible, prevailed as "black letter" in many Dutch, English, and other presses; the *lettera veneta*, a fine Gothic *rotunda*, improved by Jenson, had a wide sway in all Europe; the lively "bastard" forms held the vogue in France, and as *Schwabacher* or *Fractura* still compete with the Roman in Germanic lands. It is an earmark of confidence in "scholasticism," which to the humanists spelled futile speculation and pedantry; but to others confidence in solid, disciplined thought, confidence in that thought which had found its highest expression in an all-embracing synthesis of knowing faith, in the *Summa* of a Thomas Aquinas.[8] Like the Gothic cathedral, a harmonious creation of many thoughtful minds and skilful hands, it stood there in glorious grandeur, holding out to suffering mankind the promises of salvation.

Now, as little as then, have we any accurate means of ascertaining what kind of literature and which books were most read and so exerted a determinable cultural influence. For incunabula we cannot even calculate, as we can for books today, which were the best sellers. We can, however, say with fair accuracy which authors and which books were most frequently reprinted. (Here we are ahead of today, when the first edition can appear simultaneously with, say, the two-hundredth.) The determination is of great interest even if we do not know, or at least rarely know, the exact number of copies per edition (varying from three hundred to three thousand). We can also estimate further, by the number of editions, the relative degree of interest in definite subjects. Of course in such comparison the fact must always be taken into consideration that a broadsheet or a small pamphlet can more easily be reprinted than a large volume, but naturally the greatest difficulty is experienced when one tries to classify the various books according to subjects. To take our classification of the modern sciences as the basis of such a subject list would necessitate a violent disturbance of the intellectual atmosphere of the time we wish to study.

For it is necessary to remember always that even when we are
able to separate certain disciplines from the broad subject of
science as then understood, this separate subject never stands
by itself in the sense of a modern specialty; the author's mind
will invariably oscillate between his subject and others and
consider applications which we would strictly avoid. Hence a
certain amount of arbitrariness has to prevail in the selection
of subjects, and in general it may be said that the ideal of perfect consistency can never be reached in this matter.[9]

Authors

Rows of names head as authors our incunabula. They hail from
many countries, and from every age, from Hippocrates to Sebas-
tian Brant. Evidently they must have inspired confidence in
their worth in those that selected them for the press. Some
proved to be "successes" and were passed on as such to the
next century. Others could not stand the strong light of the
new publicity; though popular enough in script, they looked
old and decrepit on the printed page. Soon they were dropped,
to fall into oblivion. Thus we have in incunabula an admirably accurate barometer with which to gauge the pressure of
scientific thought. But whence came the pressure? Who were
the authors? The quattrocento humanists (those of the twelfth
were not so cocksure) thought they lacked freedom and originality. Faithfully this was repeated by the later ages, copying
each other. But Taylor, to whom we do well to listen on everything touching the Middle Ages, thinks differently:

From the Carolingian period onward the men interested in knowledge
learned the patristic theology, and, in gradually expanding compass, acquired
antique logic and metaphysics, mathematics, natural science and jurispru-
dence. . . . . Their comprehension of it became part of their intellectual faculties, they could think for themselves in its terms, think almost originally and
creatively, and could present as their own the matter of their thoughts in
restatements, that is in forms, essentially new.[10]

The originality, the novelty, in this creative realization, therefore, was in the form and not in the substance; in concepts, in words, not things. Who does better? We think we have something more tangible, fascinated as we are by the seemingly unlimited range of power we can extract from our instruments or effect by our machines. Is this "substantial" contribution so original? Have we not also only changed one form into another form when we successfully attacked matter? By what magic should the material field convey upon its fruit a light of originality of which the mental field is barren? In substance man worked only once originally, and that was when he made a fire. That was the great outstanding deed in all his evolution. And this elementary creation made that upper organ, his brain, with which he could make concepts, words, and handle them like things. But they were words only, convenient approaches to a few "facts" in an immense universe, and with them he was enabled to make all those mental, but also those material, constructions that fascinate us now. No, we have not invented a "new" originality, which those "authors" lacked. Better, perhaps, should we speak of both in the etymological sense of "augmenters."

The Earliest "Authors"

The history which follows the prejudiced Renaissance tradition usually places Pliny, Galen, and Ptolemy in the forefront as the scientific teachers of a benighted humanity. In the incunabula period we have them of course in full force. But in that earliest age which we call "dark" because the records are so scant, when in the monastery schools the fires of learning were kept burning, in wild regions of what is now Italy, Spain, France, Germany, Switzerland, Ireland, England, they had not yet arrived. Priscian provided the juvenile terror, Ovid and Virgil the adult joy, of language. Diligent monks had copied them in portable compendia, and soon they were known by heart. With

them came similarly Boethius, Cassiodorus, and Martianus
Capella. They were the three pillars of the bridge that carried
antique learning through troubled times. Their names still vi-
brate inspiringly in incunabula times, Boethius' immortal work
being called for in numerous editions in Latin and the vulgar
tongues. Martianus Capella, the African, in his immensely popular work introduced generations to the charms of the seven
liberal arts, which he figured as bridesmaids at the wedding of
Philology and Mercury. And Cassiodor the senator, Boethius'
young admirer and with him in high places under Theodorich,
did effective spadework, also for scientific culture, in his monastery the Vivarium in Calabria, even more than his famous contemporary, St. Benedict of Nursia, at Monte Cassino, by stimulating his monks to literary occupation, to the copying and extracting of authors on natural science which he named and
showed in the library. His and Martianus' work had been pro-
grammatical and encyclopedic; it inspired and guided the
studies of the monastic and cathedral schools, and in Carolingian times it was fully adopted. Boethius' contribution was
of different stuff and scope. Few books had a wider and deeper
popularity than his *Consolation of philosophy*. The form of dialogue, intermixed with verse, made a great appeal. Not a scientific book, it made innumerable proselytes for science. As a
cosmogony in great style it offered inspiration to a Dante. But
he also wrote as a teacher of scientific subjects. Important is his
mathematical work derived from Nicomachus. But fundamental for all times to come was his translation of Aristotle's
Logics. Long before "the philosopher" was to appear again in
Arabic garb to a more sophisticated people, his rules of disciplined thought were learned and applied over and over again.
Already the crucial questions put by Porphyry in his *Isagoge
to the logics* were revolved and considered: "Genera and species,
have they substantial existence or are they bare intellectual
concepts; if substantial are they corporeal or incorporeal; are

they separable from sensible properties of the things?" "These questions," he concluded, "require a longer investigation." Realists and nominalists carried it on for centuries, and if we listen to our physicists today we realize that they are still occupied with the investigation of this problem. Posited as it was, its scientific importance consists in that it stimulated powerfully, and from these earliest times steadily on, the gathering of data that might help in its solution.

"Popular" Science

There is another literature to be considered that held its own from very early medieval times to the incunabula period and beyond. It reproduces thoughts and strivings of this childhood phase of European culture which I think just for this reason merits closest attention, for we have learned to realize the powerful effect which early memories and early habits have on later destiny. It is mostly anonymous or pseudonymous, mainly didactic, and sometimes in metric form and therefore often classed as "pseudo-science" or "popular science," and variously evaluated. Thus Manitius[11] states that medieval man, lacking the sense for exact observation necessary for natural science and philosophy, was little helped by the Roman *compendia* he had, as they were only "dilettante and superstitious writings." To the average clerk, he thinks, mathematics and the science dependent on it were a closed book, the *computus* and *compendia* on theoretical music answering merely practical needs. Olschki discusses the same point in connection with somewhat later books, and especially those in the vulgar tongues.[12] He distinguishes two classes of these books, the ones intended purely for edification such as the French *Roman de la rose* or the *Divina commedia*, and schoolbooks such as Brunetto Latini's *Trésor*, Ristoro d'Arezzo's *Composizione del mondo*, Megenberg's *Buch der Natur*. According to him the former class, though dwelling on natural and realistic phenomena, has no influence whatever (or a bad one, leading to a magical or pseudo-scientific attitude) on scientific evolution, while the latter serve as a useful introduction. In this view he turns decidedly against that of Alexander von Humboldt, who insisted on the useful interplay of "serious knowledge and the delicate inspiration of fantasy" in advancing culture. A feeling for nature, poetical description of natural events, landscape painting, he thought, were means of stimulating the more serious search. I sympathize with this "romantic" view, though I am well aware that the emotional contemplation of nature will more easily lead to artistic creation than to logical and critical analysis, but then again we cannot possibly think of an epoch as scientifically sterile in which a *Roman de la rose* or a *Divine comedy* could have been written. They might have led, or as some have it misled, the general intellectual evolution into other fields than those of exact scientific thought (as has happened in most oriental civilizations), but the point that matters is that they mark vividly the existence of a decided interest in the objects of natural science. History cannot afford to ignore the fact of this interest.

Regimen of Health

Man's prime interest is in himself and his likes. Hence it would follow that when he gives expression of this interest in the tangible domain it will occupy itself with the welfare of his body, with his health. Even if for some reason or other he reverts to intangible domains, the interest in the body still prevails though it becomes negative and is expressed in asceticism and self-castigation. So whichever way he turns, he will formulate a *regimen sanitatis*. Earthbound and carnally minded, it will assume an orderly procedure, scientific in our sense, because naturally striving for accuracy. *Fons* and *origo* of all science and all the sciences, the literary expressions of this egotistical tendency merit always attention. In the incunable literature we find two *regimina sanitatis*, enormously popular then and for centuries after. Their age has not yet been satisfactorily determined. One is in prose in the form of an admonitory letter from Aristotle to his young pupil Alexander, not only on health but also on rules appropriate for a budding prince; the other, in verses, purports to be the joint expression of the famous School of Salerno. The Aristotle letter is, according to Sudhoff, the older of the two. He found traces of it in Sicily and Toledo already in the twelfth century, while there are no definite traces of the Salernitan *opus* much before Arnaldus de Villanova wrote his commentary to it at the end of the thirteenth or beginning of the fourteenth century; Sudhoff does not even exclude the possibility of Arnaldus having written the verses himself. There can be no question about the relative popularity of the two works, the second being one of the most frequently reissued books in the world, while the Aristotle letter survived mainly because it found a German translator in the fifteenth century who procured for it great local favor.[13]

The Salernitan poem as it has come down to us contains numerous interpolations and additions. Such were made probably from its beginning, and one can only guess that those dealing with diet were the original verses. No author is named in it, but its Salernitan origin cannot well be doubted, neither the authenticity of its dedication to a king of England, probably William II, whose brother Robert, Duke of Normandy, underwent treatment at Salerno on his return from a crusade in 1099. We have no clear record about a co-operative medical activity in Salerno until the middle of the eleventh century, that is, at least a generation before the advent of Constantine the African and the first European universities of Bologna and Paris. But we have many reasons that allow us to suspect that there was one for many generations before this date, and there is internal evidence in the *Regimen* which makes one feel that its origins fall into this older period. As Daremberg has well said:

It is the work of everybody, and it is the work of nobody; or rather it is the true echo of the good sense of a people in matters of hygiene; it has all the characteristics of a popular writing; the precision, a certain naïveté, happy turns of expression, and I don't know what, something living and what one would not expect to find in a school poem.[14]

Salerno, it must not be forgotten, was a great health resort in Roman imperial times. It also belonged to Magna Graecia, whose language and customs survived for long under Byzantine, Lombard, Norman, Sawbian, and Moslem rule. The earliest masters of the school testify to the vitality of the Graeco-Latin tradition, before the arrival of Constantine the African and his Greek and Latin science from Arabic sources, and before Frederick II regularized the study and practice of medicine— all of which meant the end of that tradition, though in some ways the fame of the school was spread more than before.

It is a slender thread, this *Regimen*, with which to tie the bulky structure of the future science to a dim past. There were others, of course, spun in Roman and Visigothic Spain, in Egypt, Syria, and the Byzantine Empire, but the subtle, pervasive, and persistent influence of the *Regimen* and the literature directly related to it in many ways illustrates better the continuous flux of events than the highlights reached at intervals. The knowledge of healing herbs was naturally embodied in the *Regimen*. It also was a very ancient science, this of rhizotomists that furnished material for a Theophrastos and Dioscorides. Many of the verses on this in the *Regimen* are also found in the famous *Macer floridus, de viribus herbarum*. Therefore, it was thought, they must have been taken from this earlier poem. But who knows that it was earlier? The name of the author points to Aemilius, of whose herb lore we read in Ovid's *Tristia*, but philologists will allow no resemblance to his authentic works. Imperial Rome knew nothing of it, just as little as of the *Herbarium* and the *De re coquinaria*, sailing respectively under the classic names of Apuleius and Apicius until they reached the port of incunable presses. I have no proofs, only little indications here and there that make me feel that all this pseudonymous literature on diet, hygiene, food, and herbs are echoes of Salernitan or pre-Salernitan activities. We also have the old *Physiologus*, perhaps scientifically unimportant, because allegorically versifying animal lore. It points to Monte Cassino, where Theobaldus, its presumed author, once was abbot. Then we have the poem on the virtues of Pozzuoli's mineral springs; Puteoli, that later rival of Salerno, close to Naples where Frederick II had transferred the university, artificially, and none too successfully. Early traces of an occupation with astronomical subjects as we find them in the fables of Hyginus, in Solinus, the abbreviated *Quadripartitum* of Ptolemy in the form of the popular *Centiloquium* make us think of a beginning of pure science, but then already and for times to come the interest was astrological, that is, again in relation to human health and welfare and the art of divination.

Illustration

Curious is the fate of the *Herbarium Apulei*, referred to above. We have some ancient manuscripts of it, mostly with plant pictures, some of which Singer has finely reproduced.[15] One of the best dates from the early seventh century and is now at Leyden, and an Anglo-Saxon version of it was made already in the eleventh century. Its origin is earlier, however, though not as early as the time of Lucius Apuleius of Madaura, who wrote the *Golden ass*. Renowned as a great magician throughout the Middle Ages from the third century on, his name was probably appended to this book in memory of his scientific powers. It is merely a list of medicinal plants, giving briefly indications of their virtues and synonyms of their names with corresponding though rather crude pictures. It represents a purely practical abridgment of the more elaborate and more realistic herbals of Byzantine craftsmanship, of which a very fine specimen, the Dioscorides Codex, dedicated to the Emperor's daughter, Juliana Anicia, is still extant. The Apuleius herbal, copied and recopied through centuries, testifies to a remarkable continuity of tradition, and undoubtedly fulfilled an expressed demand for this sort of book. When the first presses began printing in Rome, the owner of one, Lignamine, finding one of these manuscripts in Monte Cassino, decided to print it. It appeared about 1480 with illustrations, but never again in that form. Nevertheless in 1484 it was re-formed by the famous press of Schöffer in Mainz as the *Herbarius*. Not a copy by any means, only the adoption of the principle of the herbal with more realistic pictures, and as such it became the starting-point of a long line of herbals, continually improving in precision of text and illustration, through the famous works of the "fathers of botany" in the sixteenth century, to our "truly" scientific textbooks of botany. The printing press did in one century what the thousand years before could not possibly have done.[16]

With the beginning of the great schools of translators in Southern Italy, where Constantine the African is the most prominent representative, and in Spain, where Gerard of Cremona holds a similar place, the Latin scientific literature becomes at once abundant and complex. While Europe was struggling with elementary difficulties of existence, Moslem civilization had already reached a high degree of material prosperity and devoted itself to manifold cultural aims. Most important among these was the preservation of the scientific literature which had been gathered from Alexandrian Greek as well as from Persian and Indian sources. Arabic was the scientific language of that movement, and it is yet one of the tasks for the history of science, to discern how much Arabic science has contributed of her own to the bulk taken over from other sources. That the contribution was readily absorbed by a Europe thirsting for knowledge, and well prepared for it in those centuries following the dissolution of the imperial power of Rome, is evident in a massive manuscript literature of which the most popular representatives came under the early presses. In the space at my disposal it would be impossible to give anything approaching an adequate outline of this literature, and I shall therefore limit myself to describing what were the most popular books printed at the end of the fifteenth century, feeling that whatever our present judgment might be of the worth of these books, they fulfilled without doubt their mission in those days.

ALBERTUS MAGNUS: *Liber aggregationis. De mirabilibus mundi*

The erudite of many lands and tempers have called this little book by bad names, and have considered it an insult to the lofty scientific reputation of the Great Albert, who, they say, could not possibly have written it. I know only one, an American, who kept his temper and showed his sense of humor when he refused to listen to all these learned vituperations of a book which he found in innumerable manuscript and printed editions and which therefore must have made a decided appeal to the reading public through many centuries. For him as a scientific observer of past thought there was only one thing to do, to analyze the contents. This American, L. Thorndike, I shall follow in the not always easy task of scrutinizing this kind of scientific literature.[17] In the incunable editions, of which we count from about 1477 on more than sixty, the book is called mostly by the foregoing title, or *Book of secrets*, or *Of the virtues of herbs, stones and animals*. In the manuscripts it is often entitled *Experimenta*. The treatise on *The wonders of the worlds* is sometimes added to the *Aggregator*. Both these works profess a belief in magic and in wonders, just as Albert does in his so-called genuine works, so that this element, which enrages most the erudite critics, cannot speak against this authorship. In the *mirabilia* he states clearly: "It is the wise man's business to make an end of marvels" and "a thing is marvelous and wonderful (pet expressions of our advanced civilization) only as long as most people cannot detect its cause . . . . when philosophers realized that everything was wonderful, they began to experiment and bring forth what there was in things." The only reproach that can be made to the author is that he is too satisfied to reveal the sensational features of the various wonderful virtues of things and marvelous occurrences in nature without a more serious attempt to explain them. Evidently the experimental school of the Dominicans in Cologne, which the author mentions and with which we know Albert to have been connected, had not yet been able to find adequate solutions. Notable is a critical attitude toward contemporary attempts to explain everything in terms of the hot, cold, dry, moist, following Galen, also against similar explanations from the course of the stars, but of course "one must be prepared to believe what reason cannot confirm." Some of the chemical recipes for making gunpowder, fireworks, etc., are interesting if they date from the thirteenth century, but they may be later interpolations.

The next book in the order of popularity is also attributed to the same author, with more than fifty incunable editions:

ALBERTUS MAGNUS: *Secreta mulierum*

This again, some say, cannot be by Albert the Great; it probably is by his pupil, Henry of Saxony, or by an Albert of Saxony —all unhelpful conjectures, owing to a too serious consideration of the whims and fancies of scribes and printers who liked to increase the interest in their products by altering the headlines. Again here, as with the *Aggregator*, we can only say that the views expressed on processes of generation, birth and care of infants, are not incompatible with similar views expressed in Albert's admittedly genuine works. It was put on the Index because of its alleged obscenity, and therefore had to be handled like other products of prohibition with circumspection, with the natural result that its popularity was increased. In the history of obstetrical thought and practice the little book has an entirely honorable place.

A great part of Albert's scientific as well as theological con-

tributions were printed by the incunable presses. We have a
dozen or more titles of scientific interest. His immense literary
activity consisted mainly in paraphrasing the work of Aristotle,
from Latin translations of Arabic versions, and in close contact
with the work of Avicenna. A full estimation of his addition to
the traditional knowledge becomes possible only through advancing research, but already we can fathom that it was very
considerable.

AVICENNA: *Canon medicinae*

That after five hundred years the name of the great Persian
physician and his system of medical theory and practice should
have maintained their incredible popularity, and that it should
have continued for at least another hundred years, are sufficient
reasons to regard the book as one of the most significant intellectual phenomena of all times. In the Arab world of today he
is still as he was then, the "prince of philosophers." To the
modern scientific physician who tends more and more to retire
from active practice into the quiet of pure laboratory research,
Avicenna should make a special appeal, for he held that it was
infinitely more important for a physician to know one hundred
books than to see a single patient. In an immense range of
subjects which engaged his inquiring scientific mind, medicine
seemed rather simple. But this simplicity must have seemed
rather complex to the poor student who had to work his way
through the bulky and ponderous volumes. Rigid order
with a clear classification after a definite system being then, as
now, the basis of a scientific textbook, Avicenna's *Canon* answered admirably to the demands for a comprehensive guide to
clinical teaching. Being difficult to understand in part, intrinsi-
cally and also because of blundering renderings of Arabic terms
in barbaric jargon by careless translators, many men thought
it necessary to expound and elucidate the words of the master.
Thus the commentation of Avicenna provided material for spe-

cial-research students. So it comes that the canonic literature
of medicine called for a great number of editions. We do not
know the exact proportion of Avicenna's original additions to
the evident borrowings from Greek sources. His theories, and
the classification of phenomena based thereupon, naturally differ from ours, but the careful reader, even today, can find—
often hidden, alas, in what seems to us useless verbiage—very
shrewd observations of a scientifically trained man of the world,
clear descriptions of rare diseases, and some conceptions about
the etiology of disease which have a curiously modern flavor.
Avicenna is not the first but the last of the many great Persian
and Arabic systematizers of medicine, but the comprehensive-
ness of the *Canon* gave it unique distinction as a schoolbook for
long generations.

The next of incunabula "best sellers" which I now have to
present in the order of popular evaluation offers again some of
those features that send shivers down the backs of the really
erudite historian.

Lucidarius

Among the starving intellects there were some that asked:
"How is this big world divided? What are those islands peo-
pled with Indians? What those strange folk of different color
and shapes in Syria and Africa? What are the elements, the
winds, the seas? How do our minds work, the planets move,
the stars sparkle, the moon shine, and the comets dart through
the skies? How are babies made, born, cared for? What do the
wise say about all that?" Perfectly legitimate questions, and
they are interestingly answered in this little book and often
nicely illustrated by appropriate and striking pictures. It pre-
tends to be no more than a catechism of science for the educated
layman who liked to read about these things in his vulgar
tongue. Nearly fifty incunable editions of this book appeared,
in German, Italian, and Czech. There is another *Elucidarius* or

Lucidaire in Latin and French, probably somehow connected originally with this book, but different in context as it is rather a dogmatic manual for clerics. It has been attributed to Honoré d'Autun or to another Honoré le Solitaire, not very convincingly. But it seems certain from the evidence of manuscripts that it is the product of a literary movement which set in after the crusade of the Guelph Duke Henry the Lion, on his return to his faithful spouse Mathilde in Brunswick, then Saxony, in the second half of the twelfth century. Somehow this Mathilde, daughter of Henry II of England and Eleanor of Poitou, seems to have been the center of this movement out of which issued, with this little book, other renowned books such as the *Song of Roland* and *Tristan and Iseult*. The title of the book, as so often, came to be taken as the name of the author and as "Meister Elucidarius" enlightened countless generations until it became more presentable to the sophisticated nineteenth century under the name of *Little Cosmography*.

There are two popular works of the twelfth century, the *Image du monde* of the above-mentioned Honoré d'Autun and the *Philosophia mundi* of Guillaume de Conches (both of which found a feeble reflection on incunabula pages, the first by itself, the other in the great encyclopedia of Vincent of Beauvais, the *Speculum naturale*), which seem to have some relationship with our *Lucidarius*. Schorbach, who studied the *Lucidarius* in great detail, has not been able to decide the matter.[18]

Next in popular appreciation come the incunable *Herbals* already discussed above; they are immediately followed by the *Somnia Danielis*, the most read of the dreambooks and probably of very ancient lineage. The book has been studied carefully by Maurice Helin with particular reference to the incunabula editions, of which he lists thirty-seven editions with excellent facsimiles.[19] I have not studied the book, but from what I hear of it, it might well offer scientific material to work upon, especially to the psychoanalytically-minded.

The *Auctoritates Aristotelis*, which occupy the next place, giving merely brief sentences from Aristotelian and other philosophic works, may be mentioned here only as a measure of the immense popular appeal which the name of the "philosopher" made to that generation, as to many before and after. Very few understood him then as afterward, but they tried to understand him, and that fact alone is significant. The mass of young people who clamored for entrance into the Museum of Natural History in New York, to hear an exposition of Einstein's theory of relativity, signifies a similar interest today.

ARISTOTELES: *Problemata*

From 1473 on, as many editions as those of the preceding books were called for of these *Problems*. They belong to the class of minor writings of Aristotle on natural history, which competent philologists from Renaissance times to ours have considered as spurious. Their transmission came via Sicily, where Graeco-Latin translators were working for King Manfred (1258–66), just as they had done for his father, Frederick II, and his grandfather, the Norman Duke Roger in Palermo, those great patrons of early science. The book, about whose translation Manfred is known to have reported to the University of Paris in 1263, is very similar to some of the works of Michael Scot and of Adelard of Bath, who also were connected with the Sicilian *Curia* at an earlier epoch, and whose works were suitably recorded by the incunabula presses.[20] It is frankly a compilation from Aristotelian and other allied works, and as such it was described by Manfred. Why we should not be able to remember this without prefixing "pseudo" to the great name is difficult to see. The book is most interesting and no doubt was very stimulating, and for that Aristotle would gladly have lent his name. Galen, Seneca, Genesis, Ipocras, Avicenna, Averroes, Albertus Magnus, and the *Regimen sanitatis* of Salerno are cited in it, as in many of the *florilegia* of the time.

Peter of Abano, the great physician and philosopher of the school of Padua of the thirteenth century, is connected with the work, though not as its translator, as sometimes stated, but as its expositor. The press also reproduced this work. The book attempts to explain a number of physical peculiarities of the human body. Such questions as why men grow bald and women not; why hair is sometimes soft, sometimes hard; why fright could raise the hair; why the brain is partly white, partly gray; why it is cold; why man has one nose and two eyes; and many more about various regions and parts of the body—all these questions we are likely to call absurd, probably having answered them satisfactorily.

John of Holywood: *Sphaera mundi*

Nobody will dispute the scientific standing of this *magnum opus* of the learned Yorkshireman who usually goes by the name of Sacro Bosco. In this domain of cosmic beatitude there is no strife; as soon as one fixes the orbits of the stars and speaks of them in mathematical terms, one is friend with everyone else who uses the same methods, whether near or far, in space or time. Sacro Bosco was buried anno 1256 at the Mathurins in Paris, and his *Sphaera* rolled on peacefully, leaving traces on the paper of numerous scribes and commentators, and between 1472 and 1647 in some seventy and more editions. We are told that he only restated what Ptolemy and several Arabs had found. At any rate, distinguished men such as Michael Scot, Cecco d'Ascoli, Pierre d'Ailly, Regiomontanus, Le Fèbvre d'Etaples, and many others found it worthy of further commentaries. Not having read the book, or studied its sources, I cannot judge its originality, and am content to note its immense popularity, while I admire the beautiful *editio princeps* of Ferrara (1472) and that other one (1482) of the master-printer of Venice, Ratdolt, who specialized in mathematical and astronomical literature, using even a three-color process for some of his astronomical diagrams.

ANIANUS: *Compotus manualis*

Rivaling with the *Sphaera* of Sacro Bosco in the number of editions, though probably not in the matter of scientific importance, this book has been most interestingly studied by David Eugene Smith,[21] based on the examination of extant manuscripts and a series of some sixty editions printed between 1488 and 1529 (thirty-three incunabula). This little book deals with the ancient concept of time which modern science allows us to dispense with, having recognized that our clocks are nothing but terrestrial speedometers indicating progress in space only. The determination of solar and lunar time, and from that the adjustment in the Christian calendar of the movable and fixed feast days, is done by the clever expedient of using the knuckles of the fingers of both hands as a sort of counters, the meaning of which is indicated on woodcut diagrams of hands. The *Compotus* consists of a text in verse and a commentary in prose. The verse has the familiar leonine jingle of the Salernitan *Regimen sanitatis* which we considered above, also of those didactic medical poems in which Gilles de Corbeil deplored the decadence of medical art in Montpellier under the Arabs and sang of the glory of Salerno. I should suspect its origin in this direction. Smith does not want to decide; he does not know manuscripts earlier than the thirteenth century, but he does not exclude the possibility of some connection with the famous monastery at Aniane founded in Carlovingian times near Montpellier, which, having belonged to the Benedictine order, naturally suggests an influence from Monte Cassino. One thing is certain, that the author was not Alsatian, as some have suggested, merely because the first dated edition of 1488 was printed in Strasburg.

For Haskins "one of the clearest indications of intellectual revival in the early twelfth century is the large number of manuscripts of that period and shortly before which deal with the elements of arithmetical and astronomical reckoning." I should suspect that in that survival rather than revival of the Latino-

Greek tradition the medical production would run a close parallel course with the arithmetical and astronomical, but the great importance of the latter for the evolution of scientific thought must be readily conceded.

The remarkably tenacious hold on the public mind which these primitive but eminently practical treatises exhibit by reappearing in full vigor after centuries in the new presses is a very interesting historical phenomenon. In arithmetic and in astronomy, as well as in medicine, it recalls the humble origin of the sciences, in the practical popular needs. To this field belong also the numerous almanacs, calendars, prognostications, and *judicia* which appeared on broadsheets and in little booklets. Only of almanacs we have more than three hundred different editions. They all offer interesting historical material which has been very little studied.

Regimen sanitatis Salernitanum

Belonging here in the order of popularity, I record it once more because it gives me a chance to say something about the Arabic phase of the great school, whose influence is reflected in the incunabula with emphasis, though in quantity it does not approach the *Regimen*. Constantine the African, who belongs rather to Monte Cassino than to Salerno, by his translations and appropriations, became the great propagator of Greek science, mainly medical, from Arab sources. His name heads no incunable entry (his main work was printed first with Isaac Judaeus in Lyons, 1515), but the *Articella*, a bunch of minor Greek (mainly Galenic and Hippocratic) works, was gathered by him. Then there is the Salernitan *Nicolaus' antidotarium*, which no self-respecting edition of Mesue's pharmaceutical work could afford to omit; not to forget the medical *pandectae* of Matthaeus Silvaticus (10 edd.). Then the very important *Circa instans* of Platearius, whose text in numerous, especially French, manuscripts brought plant illustrations, and became the textual basis of a long series of printed herbals already referred to. Very important also is the stimulating effect on surgical practice of Salernitan writers, though in the incunabula their works are hidden under the great name of the Frenchman Guy de Chauliac.

PLINY: *Historia naturalis*

Of larger works this is by far the most popular of scientific incunabula, and some of the editions are of the most beautiful of the whole time. Even the humanists, who looked askance on most scientific writing, inclined to damn it as "scholastic" rubbish, took warmly to the *Historia*, though many of them wrote works pointing out Pliny's errors. The book is so well known that I need not go into it here, especially since Thorndike has done it so well in his *History of magic*. I am struck particularly with one remark he made when noting the rambling and discursive, rather than logical and systematic, mode of Pliny's presentation. He said: "I have often thought that the scholastic centuries did mankind at least one service, that of teaching lecturers and writers how to arrange their material." This was indeed a great step and of fundamental importance in the material orientation science was taking, and in this the possibility of a still more lucid and surveyable[22] arrangement, such as the press could provide, no doubt made printing the indispensable vehicle of the scientific thought of the future. On the other hand, it seems true that for the verbal projection of living events the narrative, which *relates*, is more suitable than description, which *dissects*, cutting living relations, and in this Pliny's presentation may have an advantage over our mode.

BARTHOLOMAEUS ANGLICUS: *De rerum proprietate*

With more than seventy editions extending into the sixteenth century, twenty-five incunabula—twelve in Latin, eight in French, two each in Dutch and Spanish (these latter non-Latin ones most interestingly illustrated), and one in English—must make one think that Bartholomew the Englishman must have led the interests of many people in the direction of natural knowledge. As Thorndike suggests, "Such elementary and popular works are more likely to have survived the stagnant and destructive period of the Black Death and Hundred Years' War and to have come down to us than are the more advanced, original, and elaborate works of the thirteenth century." And Bartholomew in the version of Trevisa says:

> Spryngynge tyme is the tyme of gladness and of love . . . . thynge that seemed deed in wynter and widdered, ben renewed in springing time . . . . and water in spryngynge time is unholesome to drynke . . . . it is infect with frogges and other wormes that then brede. And therefore, if it be nedefull to drynke water that tyme, Constantyne counseyleeth to seeth it first, that it may be clensed and pourged by boyllynge.

I think if I were not allowed any other books, I could be quite happy with Pliny and Bartholomew alone.[23]

MESUE: *Opera medicinalia*

We do not seem to know who Mesue was, for no Arabic manuscripts of his work have been found. It may be that like the medieval founder of chemistry, "Geber," who cannot be identified with the ninth- or tenth-century Jabir, or the "Apuleius" of the *Herbarium*, who cannot be the African mystic, "Mesue" stands also as an eponymic reminder of the collective scientific activities of just those early medieval epochs when craftsmen were uniting their own and others' experiences. Mesue is the pharmacological Bible of many long generations. It was indispensable as a guide to the many new drugs and compounding manipulations to which the Arabs were introducing the Western world. Even the humanists who scoffed at the oriental *filoso-fandi aviditas* had to accept the odoriferous gift, and it is interesting that the two *editiones principes*, for there are two, were printed in a matchless Roman *humanistica* type, from presses that are still puzzling bibliographers. One evidently belongs to the Venetian printing sphere, though probably not to Venice itself, to which it is traditionally assigned. No one knows much about the indicated printer, the "good priest Clemens of Padua," to whom we are introduced in the prefatory letter of Niccolò Gupalatini to the Veronese physician Peregrino Caval-cabovi (who had printing relatives in Verona) under date of "Venetiis 1471," the fifteenth calends of June. Patriotic Italians have hailed him *unbekannterweise* as the first native printer. It being his only book, it would seem that three towns might claim to be its press place. Then the other *princeps:* It is fully dated but without indication of place: 1471, the fifth ides of June, and of no personalities whatever. Close-running and puzzling, indeed: Scholderer in Osler, *Incunabula medica*, No. 10, put it to Venice or Florence with two marks of interrogation, but just lately he has decided to assign it definitely to Florence (*British Museum catalogue*, VI [1930], 615), where it heads the list of books printed in the fifteenth century, and where I have put it intuitively long ago, for with its special type of *humanistica* it could not have gone anywhere else. But these are details and the main question remains unsolved, open to all bibliographers: Who printed this, the earliest, the most important specialistic and therefore most modern scientific incunable? The question embraces both *editiones principes*. As regards the claim that Clemens was the first native Italian printer, we cannot allow it, for Lignamine the Messenian at Rome printed his Sueton in 1470 *mense sextili*.

HIPPOCRATES: *Aphorismi, etc.*

He comes rather late in our list of "best sellers" and not even with the *Opera omnia*, which in Greek Aldus brought out only in 1526, and in Greek-Latin the Junta only in 1588. But the true Hippocratic spirit, that essence of medical common sense which is of all ages, we have already found in that inconspicuous literature beginning with Salerno. Scholars knew it by heart in the easy cadence of rhymes they loved; it was the medical craftsman's conscience that kept him straight when complex problems came in bewildering multiplicity. So we have to go with a microscope through the incunabula pages to find the learned taking notice of him. Jacob of Forli, who at the high school of Padua about 1380 had been as *alter Hyppocras* in charge of the matutinal *lectura* on the aphorisms, is the first, with the *expositiones* developed then, to appear on the penultimate day of October, 1473, in the fine Roman script of an unknown press in an unknown place, similar in form to those of Jenson's but not his—another puzzle for bibliographers to solve.

Other of the Hippocratean incunabula deal, *horribile dictu*, with dreams, the nature of man, the physician's astrology, of prognostics, the "ivory capsule"—trifles perhaps for the one who prefers his Hippocrates in Littré's fine edition of 1839 in ten volumes, gems to some others who like to read what part of the thought of a great man had enduring validity in the eyes of the many. But of course there is nothing in the whole literature of science like the wise words of the aphorisms, with its sonorous *incipit* that still vibrates through the world: "Life is short and art is long"; "Occasion is fleeting, experience fallacious, judgment difficult."

RHASIS: *Liber IX ad Almansorem, etc.*

Medicine and science will have to be always grateful to the Arabs for having brought down to us this great Persian. He could not compete with his great textbook-writing compatriot, Avicenna, in the massiveness of production and appeal to school men, but for truly scientific method and insight it would be difficult to find his better. Sarton is quite right to label his chapter on the second half of the ninth century "The time of Al-Razi," for there was surely nowhere in the world so universal a scientific thinker as Rhasis at that time. And still we do not know yet with any amount of precision in what field lay his greatest contribution. It looks as if the chemists had more claim on him than any other scientists, and since it is in this field that Arabic science probably made its most important and most original contribution to the West, we ought perhaps not to insist too much on his reputation as a clinician. But this he was undoubtedly, and as such he appears in the incunable literature, as fresh, clear, and wise as he was five hundred years before. He is always called a Galenist, and theoretically of course he was, but with erudition carried so lightly and wisdom shared so freely he resembled little the cantankerous high-brow who kicked every colleague passing his shop on the Via sacra.

Rhasis' first commentator was Gianmatteo Ferrari da Grado of Pavia, grand-ducal archiater and great light of medical scholasticism of the complex brand. Osler, who had a manuscript consultation by him, after reading it thought it must have been a "formidable thing" to fall into the hands of a medieval physician. But one great merit Ferrari had—he was the first physician of whom we have record who personally arranged for the printing of his *opus*, and we even know what it cost him. It saw the light of day, as I have shown elsewhere, before October 29, 1472.

It is often said that the Arabs, on the whole, stopped scientific progress. How much they really contributed to the education of our forbears is well illustrated by the case of the undisputed medical reformer, the great Vesalius. As he tells himself, one of his distant ancestors, Peter, wrote a commentary on one of the fens of Avicenna, his grandfather did the same for Rhasis, and he himself for his scientific début wrote a paraphrase on the same book (1537), using Eberhard's text to help him.

GALEN: *Ars parva* (*microtechne*)

Last but not least in my list of public favorites is the great Galen. Neuburger writes about him and I translate freely: "In him Greek medicine reaches not only its second apogee, but its epistemological conclusion, and, fundamentally, the whole preceding development has no other significance than that of a gi-

gantic intellectual process, which transformed the Hippocratic
art into the Galenic *science*."[24] This sums up poignantly what
I took long to extract from the incunabula, from those first
machine-made products of a collective mentality, striving toward machine-like precision and toward that materialistic perfection which our science seems about to have attained.

Thus I see the past and the present. But is this present perhaps already the past? A few days ago Sir James Jeans in his
Rede Lecture on "The mysterious universe" said at Cambridge:
"To-day there is a wide measure of agreement, which on the
physical side of science approaches almost to unanimity, that
the stream of knowledge is heading towards a non-mechanical
reality; the universe begins to look more like a great thought
than like a great machine."[25]

Notes

1. As I write this, an interesting page in *Science*, LXXII (1930), 318, catches my
eye. In the left column a scientist from Iowa says, among other things, "The end of all
science is classification . . . . ," and to this, in the right column, another correspondent
from North Carolina, speaking from a viewpoint unconnected with the subject discussed by his confrère, seems to make an unwitting answer when he reports that he has
collected from the literature on insects of the order Homoptera about 150,000 references to about 30,000 species distributed in 5,000 genera. And he adds, presumably
with a sigh, that one hundred and seventy-two years ago Linné had described 1 genus
and 42 species of this same group of insects.

2. George Sarton, *Introduction to the history of science* (Washington, 1927), p. 34.

3. William Osler, "Chauvinism in medicine," in *Aequanimitas and other addresses*
(Philadelphia, 1904), p. 280.

4. It is impossible to make a quantitative comparison of the entire scientific pro-
ductivity in incunabula times and in ours. But a juxtaposition of some figures available from allied scientific fields to those from incunabula literature is impressive. For
approximately the same length of time (thirty-five years) the Concilium Bibliographicum at Zurich (director, Professor J. Strohl) has collected up to 1929 for six specified
fields of scientific research a half-million titles of works by about half the number of
authors.

FIFTEENTH-CENTURY PRESSES		CONTEMPORARY PRESSES	
	TITLES		TITLES
Natural philosophy....more than	215	Paleontology.............	39,900
Astronomy, astrology...........	185	Biology....................	7,345
Medicine.....................	410	Micrology, etc.............	4,186
Technology...................	120	Zoölogy...................	356,350
		Anatomy..................	37,641
		Physiology................	68,924

This gives a very small fragment of modern scientific thought in juxtaposition to the totality of what may be called scientific thought at the end of the fifteenth century.

5. Those engaged in scientific work know the great stimulating effect they receive from every improved instrument. Each seems to enlarge the world, and we have faith that our knowledge will increase in proportion to the enlarging power of our microscopes or the farther reach of our telescopes. There may be limits, but at any rate we do not anticipate them.

6. Though dwelling mostly on the lyrical side of their activities, Miss Helen Wadell has recently discussed them in a most attractive book, *The wandering scholars*. London: Constable, 1927.

7. A. C. Klebs, "Gianmatteo Ferrari da Gradi and the *editio princeps* of his *Practica*," *Essays presented to Sudhoff* (Zurich, 1924), pp. 211–36, and Klebs-Sudhoff, *Die ersten gedruckten Pestschriften* (München, 1926), pp. 85 ff.

8. Whitehead has lately (*Vanuxem Foundation lectures* [Princeton, 1929], p. 33) drawn attention most interestingly to the fact that until the most recent period it would be difficult to discern any influence of speculative reason upon the evident progress technology has made during the last three thousand years. He sees in the enormous advance of technology in the past one hundred and fifty years the final contact made by speculative reason with practical reason. "The speculative reason has lent its theoretic activity, and the practical reason has lent its methodologies for dealing with the various types of facts. Both functions of reason have gained in power. The speculative reason has acquired content, that is to say, material for its theoretic activity to work upon, and the methodic reason has acquired theoretic insight transcending its immediate limits. We should be on the threshold of an advance in all the values of human life."

9. Even in a relatively unimportant matter like the spelling of proper names of authors and printers, and of towns and countries, a great deal of trouble is experienced when one tries to be consistent. My beau ideal is to spell all these names the way they would be spelled by those most concerned in their vulgar tongue and not in Latin or any other language. It corresponds to the desire of the best scholars in the various lands, but it simply cannot be carried through with absolute consistency. All we can do is to follow as far as possible the direction indicated, without upsetting too much very old and deeply fixed habits. Quattrocento people were not as particular about spelling as we are, and for that reason alone a certain amount of arbitrary choice has to be used. As regards town and country names I have on the whole adhered to the English usage, although I always feel that Proctor's adoption of local forms was much the fairer way. Somehow *Padua* comes easier than *Padova*, and *Cologne* easier than *Köln*, but since not even the *British Museum catalogue*, the chef d'œuvre of incunabula bibliography, follows Proctor's lead, I follow sheepishly its example.

10. Henry Osborn Taylor, *The mediaeval mind* (Macmillan, 1911), I, 14–15.

11. *Geschichte der lateinischen Literatur des Mittelalters*, II (1923), 726.

12. Leonardo Olschki, *Die Literatur der Technik und der angewandten Wissenschaften vom Mittelalter bis zur Rennaissance*, I (Leipzig, etc., 1919), 13.

13. Ten incunable editions mostly from Augsburg between 1472 and 1495: Hain 13736, etc.

14. Charles Daremberg, *Introduction: L'école de Salerne en vers français* (Paris, 1861), p. lvi.

15. Charles Singer, *Studies in the history and method of science* (Oxford, 1921).

16. In "Herbals of the fifteenth century," *Papers of the Bibliographical Society of America*, Vols. XI–XII (1917–18), I have studied in detail the incunable series of the

various illustrated herbals. The list which I established then comprises some forty editions, and it has since not needed any important revision.

17. *A history of magic and experimental science.* 2 vols. London: Macmillan, 1923.

18. Karl Schorbach, *Studien über das deutsche Volksbuch Lucidarius und seine Bearbeitungen in fremden Sprachen.* Strassburg: Trübner, 1894.

19. Helin, *La clef des songes,* forming Tome III of *Documents scientifiques du XVe siècle.* Paris: E. Droz, 1925.

20. About these important contributors to early science see also Thorndike in the work cited and especially the masterly introduction by C. H. Haskins to this epoch, in his *Studies in the history of mediaeval science* (Cambridge, 1924; 2d ed., 1927).

21. D. E. Smith, *Le comput manuel de Magister Anianus,* forming Tome IV of *Documents scientifiques du XVe siècle.* Paris: E. Droz, 1928.

22. I see that there is no other but this mongrel word to express the much-needed sense of the German *übersichtlich.* Apparently only Carlyle found it necessary.

23. Thorndike's account of the book is admirable (Vol. II, chap. liv), and the abstracts from it in *Social life in Britain from the Conquest to the Reformation* (compiled by G. G. Coulton; Cambridge University Press, 1919) provide an excellent introduction to this remarkable book.

24. Neuburger, *Geschichte der Medizin* (Stuttgart, 1906), I, 354.

25. *London Times,* November 5, 1930, p. 15.

PRINTER'S COPY IN
THE EIGHTEENTH CENTURY

By FREDERICK A. POTTLE

I T IS unnecessary, I trust, to enumerate to members of a
bibliographical society the values to be derived from a
study of printer's copy. Even when we have pushed a text
back to its first printed edition, there is still a great deal that
we do not know and cannot know about it until we have seen
the author's copy and the corrected proofs. Of course it almost
never happens in books printed before 1800 that we are so
fortunate as to possess both copy and proofs; when we recover
even fragments of either, we are justified in making the most of
them. But we are not always certain what it is that we do have.
About proofs there can be but little question, but the identification of printer's copy is by no means so simple a matter as dealers in manuscripts have been prone to assume. Whenever a
manuscript for a printed book turns up, the dealer is likely to
catalogue it as printer's copy, and few purchasers are in a position to gainsay him. Printer's copy of old books is, in the nature
of things, excessively scarce. And there have hitherto been very
few studies setting forth the criteria by which it can be in-
fallibly detected.

That is to say, I know of very few. There may be, scattered
in various unlikely places, several trustworthy descriptions of
English manuscripts which passed through the hands of a
printer before 1800. But I have come upon only two and they
are both for the Elizabethan period: "An Elizabethan printer
and his copy," by W. W. Greg, in *Library*, IV (4th ser.), 102–18,

and "Proof-reading by English authors of the sixteenth and seventeenth centuries," by Percy Simpson, in *Oxford Bibliographical Society proceedings and papers*, II, Part I, 5–24. For the period in question one could not ask for better. Dr. Greg has investigated the autograph manuscript of Cantos XIV–XLVI of Sir John Harington's translation of *Orlando furioso*, now in the British Museum, a portion of the copy from which Richard Field in 1591 set the printed book; and Mr. Simpson has performed the same service for the Bodleian manuscript of the fifth book of Hooker's *Ecclesiasticall politie* which served as copy for John Windet in 1597. These two fine manuscripts show with gratifying completeness how an author prepared copy at the end of the sixteenth century and how a printer treated it. If they are at all unrepresentative, it is because the authors were more careful and the printers more painstaking than usual.

The conclusions reached by Dr. Greg and Mr. Simpson may be briefly summarized for our purposes as follows:

1. In Elizabethan times copy could be written on both sides of the paper. Both these manuscripts are written book-fashion in pages, though numbered in folios.[1] Corrections and additions were made between the lines and in the margins, which were purposely left generous for that purpose.

2. The proofreader made occasional notes and queries in the copy, just as today. But the only certain and invariable sign of his activities is the marking of the beginnings of the type pages. There were as yet no long galleys; each page was a galley. The beginning of each page is indicated in the copy by a long square bracket opening toward the right, and opposite in the margin is entered the signature letter and the number of the page *in the gathering*.[2] Thus the marginal notation "D3" does not mean, as

---

[1] I suppose so, though Greg's facsimile shows no folio number. (The manuscript has been severely trimmed.) He refers to the page from which the facsimile was made as "119a." Mr. Simpson says that Hooker's folios are numbered, though his facsimile happens to be of a verso.

[2] Harington's copy being in stanzas, the bracket would in general not have been nec-

in a printed book, the third *leaf* of signature D; it means the third *page* of that signature, or that which in the book bears the notation D2.

3. The printer normalized punctuation, capitalization, spelling, italics, etc., according to the practice of the printing-house in which he worked, and without any previous editing of the manuscript. Field's compositor paid very little attention to Harington's spelling or his punctuation. Hooker's manuscript was prepared more in accordance with Windet's standards, but even here the printer asserted his own preferences in spelling and punctuation.

It has been correctly assumed that we cannot, without verification, set up these same tests for eighteenth-century copy. But what the tests for that period are has not hitherto been made clear. The recovery among the Malahide papers of a very large portion of the printer's copy of James Boswell's *Journal of a tour to the Hebrides* and a long, continuous fragment of the copy of the *Life of Johnson* makes it possible to investigate the problem with a sufficient quantity of authentic material.

The manuscript of the *Journal of a tour to the Hebrides* (which, with the rest of the Malahide manuscripts, is now in the possession of Lieutenant Colonel Ralph H. Isham) consists of 314 octavo leaves, roughly $4\frac{1}{2}$ by 7 inches, the great majority of which are written on both sides. These leaves were paged continuously from 1 to (probably) 676, but one leaf is now missing at the beginning, thirty-eight leaves have disappeared at various places in the interior, and at least one leaf is missing at the end.[3] The manuscript is not, in its present form, the

---

essary. To judge from Dr. Greg's facsimile, the proofreader merely drew a short straight line in the margin between the stanzas where the breaks came. Field's proofreader entered the page of the printed book as well as the signature notation $\left(\text{e.g., } \frac{\text{T.5}}{215}\right)$; Windet's was content to record only the signature and the page within the *gathering*.

[3] For a full collation see No. 33 of *The private papers of James Boswell . . . . in the collection of Lt.-Colonel Ralph Heyward Isham: a catalogue by Frederick A. Pottle and Marion S. Pottle* (Oxford University Press, 1931).

entire copy sent to the printer; it is Boswell's original manuscript journal, edited for publication in a way later to be described, and reassembled as a journal after having served as printer's copy.

From various references scattered through Boswell's later journals, we know that the record which he kept while on the tour with Johnson was contained in three bound notebooks. It began on August 18, 1773, the day on which the pair left Edinburgh, and was probably continued down to the middle of October 22, 1773, when they were at Lochbuy in Mull. (Pages 641 of the manuscript and 343 of Hill's edition of the *Tour*. The point of division is the paragraph in which Lady Lochbuy angers Johnson by offering him cold sheep's head.) The entries for August 18, 19, and 20 were in Boswell's "short-hand" style: "a method of my own of writing half words, and leaving out some altogether so as yet to keep the substance and language of any discourse which I had heard so much in view, that I could give it very completely soon after I had taken it down."[4] With August 21 the style became more full, and finally ended by being almost that of a printed book, though there are some standard abbreviations throughout. For Dr. Johnson's stay in Edinburgh before starting on the tour, Boswell had only rough notes on loose pieces of paper, which have been preserved. From October 22 to November 11 he seems to have had the same kind of memorials, though they are now lost. At various dates during 1780, 1781, and 1782 he continued the full journal from these notes down through the first two paragraphs of October 26, 1773; at least he says in a footnote to the printed book (Hill, p. 360) that this was the last paragraph which Johnson read, and as Johnson certainly saw the journal in June, 1784, it was probably the last Boswell had written until he prepared the text for publication.

This manuscript, while still in its bound notebooks, was read by Sir William Forbes, Mrs. Thrale, and Dr. Johnson. Bos-

[4] *Life of Johnson*, ed. Hill, III, 270.

well had it with him at Oxford in June 1784, and persuaded Johnson to write on the blank verso of page 667 the paragraph concerning the Honorable Archibald Campbell which duly appeared in the printed text.[5]

In the spring of 1785 Boswell came down to London to put the *Tour* to the press. He plunged, however, into a whirl of dissipation and got little or nothing done until Edmond Malone, who, as the story goes, had seen a specimen sheet at Baldwin's, took charge of this wayward genius and saw to it that he applied himself steadily to his task.[6] The two worked together over the entire copy. At least half the revision is in Malone's hand, though in passages of any length he appears to be writing from Boswell's dictation. It is not too much to conclude that it was he who taught Boswell the method of preparing copy which was followed for both the *Tour* and the *Life of Johnson*.

The procedure they adopted is difficult to explain clearly, though perfectly easy to understand when one has the manuscript before him. For the portion up to August 19, for which Boswell had only rough notes, fresh copy was prepared. But beginning with the eighth page of the manuscript, it was decided that the original record would serve. The leaves were torn from their covers and prepared for publication by expanding the contractions and making additions and substitutions between the lines and in the margins. Where the changes were too extensive to be managed in this fashion, the passage in the original was scored out and the new paragraph written on a separate piece of paper, the connection of the new matter to the text being indi-

---

[5] Hill, p. 357. The printer had trouble with Johnson's difficult script and printed the last sentence, "He lived in 1743, or 44, about 75 years old." Hill is quite right in saying, "This must be a mistake for *He died*." Johnson also wrote "Hickes" instead of "Hicks." In the *Life of Johnson* Boswell appears to give the date June 9 to this paragraph, but his own note in the Hebrides manuscript, apparently written on the spot, is dated June 15.

[6] The younger James Boswell said that his father and Malone first met on this occasion, but he was certainly mistaken. As Professor Tinker points out (*Letters of Boswell*, II, 349, n. 3), Malone had been a member of the Literary Club since 1782. Boswell's 'ournal shows that they first met at a dinner at Sir Joshua Reynolds', April 14, 1781.

cated by a system of reference signs. As these supplementary
leaves have all disappeared, it is not possible to say definitely
just how they were associated with the original manuscript.
Since the foliation makes no account of them, one's natural
assumption would be that they were kept in a pile by themselves, and never inserted in the main bulk of the copy at all.
But surely the easiest way, for both author and printer, would
have been to interleave the original manuscript, where necessary, with blank pieces of paper of the same size as the original
leaves, giving the interleavings page numbers to correspond
with the pages which they faced: thus, facing page 16 (a verso)
of the journal would be page 16 (a recto) of an interleaving; facing page 17 (a recto) of the journal would be page 17 (a verso)
of the interleaving. Then as the printer turned over a page, he
would have all the copy for the next before him at a glance, the
leaf with the additions being on his left when he was working on
a recto page of the original manuscript, and on his right when
he was working on a verso. He would have to glance from side
to side, but he would not ordinarily have to go from the front
of a leaf to the back and then return to the front again. (In a
few instances Boswell's printer was asked to do even that.)

It will perhaps have occurred to the reader that there is a
simpler and better way, provided one makes his first draft with
the intention of editing it for printer's copy. If you write on
only one side of your leaves, you can make your additions and
corrections on the blank versos, those for any leaf being written
on the verso of the preceding. The concluding portion of the
journal (p. 645 to the end), being written only on one side, was
in fact handled in this way. Here, when the (originally blank)
versos have been paged, they bear the numbers of the pages they
face.

The insertions on separate leaves and blank versos were not
all the printer was expected to make. When Boswell had letters
or other documents, such as Johnson's Aberdeen burgess-ticket,
to introduce, the printer was directed by a note to "take it in,"

or to "take in leaf C," or "take in letter marked D." Such documents were pretty certainly not intercalated but sent in a parcel by themselves. It must be remembered that the eighteenth-century printer worked with small portions of copy at a time, and so was less likely to be confused than he would have been if he had been given in one lot the entire copy for the book prepared in this manner.

The copy, however, is at best very untidy and complicated in appearance; it does not look to twentieth-century eyes like printer's copy at all. And when one compares a few pages with the printed book and finds wide divergences in spelling, punctuation, capitalization, italics, not infrequently in phraseology, his first impression would certainly be that this was not printer's copy but a revised draft, to be transcribed and normalized by an amanuensis. But he would be wrong. That is *was* printer's copy is shown by the triumphant marking of signatures at places exactly corresponding to the signature division of the printed book. The *pages* are no longer marked off as in Elizabethan times; we have merely the appropriate signature letter and the number of the page that begins the signature (F65, G81, H97, etc.). Beyond these unobtrusive symbols, I do not think that there is another note or jotting by the printer in the entire manuscript. In particular, there was no editing of the manuscript in the printing-shop. The printer had to decide on capitals, punctuation, italics, etc., as he went along.

Of the manuscript of the *Life of Johnson*, 120 quarto leaves survive, 111 of them being continuous. The outside dates are March 15, 1776—March 31, 1778 (roughly, Hill, II, 432—III, 230). But, as in the case of the *Tour*, a good deal of the actual copy is missing. I quote from my description in the *Catalogue* (No. 303):

Boswell first wrote out a rough draft on one side of quarto leaves of uniform size. He did not, however, transcribe the many letters and other documents which he wished to include, but associated them in some way with the draft, indicating either in the draft or on the documents themselves what portions

were to be "taken in." Wherever necessary, documents in a series were connected by links, probably on separate pieces of paper. Quotations from books,
if they ran to any length, were handled in the same way; the printer was given
a page reference, and the beginning and ending of the quotation indicated.
More than this, when Boswell found portions of his original Journals which
could be included with only minor revision, he frequently tore them out of
their covers and directed the printer to "take them in." The Ashbourne Journal of September 1777 was one of these portions, falling between pp. 619 and
620 of the draft. . . . . This rough draft, though containing occasional hiatuses
and notes for expansion or revision, was carefully and fully written, and was
in general capable of publication as it stood. Having finished it, Boswell sub-
jected the whole to "nice correction." This revision was minute and extensive,
and gives evidence of a great deal more of anxious thought and patient labor
than one would infer from the constant accusations of idleness and impotence
with which he was filling his Journals during the period that he was at work
on the MS. Phraseology was altered, passages were transposed, some omissions were made, and a good deal was added. . . . . Some verbal correction
was made between the lines and some revision indicated in the margins, but as
the margins of this copy were narrow, Boswell usually resorted to the blank
versos of his leaves for most of his additions and corrections. The changes for
any leaf were invariably made on the verso of the *preceding* leaf, so that as the
printer turned over the leaves, he might always have the entire copy for any
given portion before him at once. The various corrections and additions were
connected with the text by an elaborate system of reference signs, but sometimes the additions are (to use Mr. Scott's phrase) of such "labyrinthine complexity" that, on the evidence of such leaves alone, one would doubt whether
a printer could ever have followed such copy. That this MS, however, *was* the
printer's copy is established beyond doubt by the presence of all the signature
marks (D, E, F, G, I, L, M, N, and Q of Vol. II of the first edition) which
would have fallen within this copy, most of them agreeing exactly with the
signature division of the printed book; and in those cases where they do not
agree, we can account for the variation by an addition or deletion made in
the proofs.

To summarize:

1. In spite of the story related by Johnson to Boswell
"that a large portion of [the *Dictionary*] having by mistake
been written upon both sides of the paper, so as to be inconvenient for the compositor, it cost him twenty pounds to have
it transcribed upon one side only," these manuscripts make it
amply certain that printer's copy *could* be written on both
sides. One should, however, expect to find such copy so ar-

ranged that the compositor would not have to turn a leaf backward and forward.

2. Printer's copy may be very untidy and confused in appearance. But if one sees additions and corrections connected with the text by a consistent system of reference signs, he should suspect that they were intended for a printer rather than for an amanuensis. At this period printers expected to do the work that is now performed by stenographers; if the copy was not radically ambiguous, they would decipher almost anything and reduce it to order.

3. A divergence in spelling, capitalization, italics, even of phraseology, means little. The printer normalized as he went along, and the author (if Boswell was a typical example) was lavish of proof correction.

4. Though in a long manuscript one would be pretty sure to find notes by author or proofreader that would identify it as printer's copy, the one infallible test is the marking of the signatures. These are often inconspicuous and may be missed unless one hunts up, by the aid of the printed book, the exact spots where they should occur. If no signature appears, one should search a little on either side; something may have been added or deleted in the proofs. But if the signature markings are consistently absent from the places where they ought to be, one may be certain that the manuscript is not printer's copy.

SABIN'S *DICTIONARY**

By ROBERT W. G. VAIL

O N THE day before the Fourth of July in the year 1848 the ship "West Point" sailed into New York harbor, and among her passengers was a young Englishman of twenty-seven who had come with his wife and two small sons to seek their fortunes in the New World. His name was Joseph Sabin, and he came from Oxford, where he had been trained as a bookbinder, but his employer, recognizing his special aptitude as a salesman, soon transferred him to his bookstore, where he shortly became the valued adviser of the scholars of the old university town who frequented the shop. Later, in partnership with another young man, he opened a store and book-auction business of his own, married his partner's sister, learned a great deal more about rare books and their values, but failed to make much of a success of his venture.

And so the year 1848 found him established in America, where his remarkable knowledge of books and prices made him immediately valuable to the booksellers of Philadelphia and New York. Working at first for others, he later established his own bookshop and auction business, met various reverses because of the panic of 1857 and the outbreak of the Civil War, but finally became firmly established in New York.

In the course of time he was recognized as the foremost American authority on rare books and the most successful book auctioneer in the country. He became the valued and trusted friend of the leading collectors and soon developed a special

* Read, December 31, 1936, at a meeting of the Society held in Providence, R.I.

interest in the literature of American history, a field in which
his knowledge was extensive and his judgment unquestioned.
Within a comparatively few years he had compiled over one
hundred and fifty catalogues, edited and published a series of
reprints of rare books in the field of American history, and published a journal for booklovers.

Joseph Sabin was a man of positive opinions and a great admirer of genuine learning, but he would put on a brusque manner and make short work of a literary charlatan or a mere pre-
tender to historical scholarship. He was a vigorous writer with
a terse and sometimes caustic style, and, though a forceful
speaker in the cause of temperance, he was never temperate in
the amount of work he was willing to undertake. He was, however, never too busy to talk to a real booklover and was always
happier in singing the historical and bibliographical praises of
a rare volume than in trying to find a purchaser for it.

Having established his New York business on a permanent
footing, he turned it over to his sons and devoted the rest of his
life to the compilation of his great work: *A dictionary of books
relating to America, from its discovery to the present time*, an
undertaking which had its inception in 1856 and the first part
of which appeared in January, 1867. When he died on the fifth
of June, 1881, at the age of sixty, Sabin had printed eighty
parts of his *Dictionary* and was a third through the fourteenth
volume. The double number containing Parts 81 and 82, on
which he was at work when he died, was published the following
year.

Then the work was taken over by a quiet, modest, studious
young Brooklyn bookseller of twenty-six named Wilberforce
Eames, who, like his predecessor and his later collaborator, had
received much of his most valuable training for this new task
through the compiling of book-auction catalogues. He began
where Sabin had left off, with the word "Pennsylvania," and
in 1884 published the double number 83–84. Working single-

handed and without thought of other remuneration than the knowledge he would gain in the process, Mr. Eames devoted most of his spare time and many hours when other good citizens were asleep to his self-appointed task. Thus he carried the *Dictionary* along with him while he grew in bibliographical stature until he became, what he still is at the age of eighty-one, the greatest American bibliographer who ever lived.[1]

When Joseph Sabin published his *Bibliography of bibliography* in 1877, he predicted that his *Dictionary* would "probably be completed in 1880." But he found, as we have who came after him, that it is exceedingly difficult to estimate the speed of compilation of so vast an undertaking. From 1884, when Volume XIV was finally completed, until 1892 when the first double number of Volume XX came from the press, Mr. Eames worked steadily on this great task. Then came a long pause in the progress of the *Dictionary*. As Mr. Eames, by this time librarian of the Lenox Library, wrote in 1894, "Other duties have hindered me from continuing the work, but I hope to resume it some day."

Not until 1906 was it possible to make a new beginning, and then the two-year grant of the Carnegie Institution of Washington was only sufficient to help prepare a small part of the waiting copy for the press. Once more the project slumbered until a committee of the American Library Association brought it back to life in 1924. The enterprise was then taken over by the Bibliographical Society of America, and, with the aid of a grant from the Carnegie Corporation and the contributions of a group of nine friends, Parts 117 through 121 were completed between 1927 and 1929 under the watchful eye of Mr. Eames, now Dr. Eames, bibliographer of the New York Public Library. Again an untimely end threatened the *Dictionary*, for it was once more left without funds and unfinished in the midst of the seemingly endless Smith family.

[1] [Dr. Eames died December 6, 1937.—EDITOR.]

So the Bibliographical Society, working through the friendly mediation of the American Council of Learned Societies, made another successful appeal to the Carnegie Corporation in 1930. A further grant was secured, and (beginning with "William Smith" in Part 122 of Vol. XXI) the work put in charge of its third editor, so that the burden which had rested for so many years on the willing shoulders of Dr. Eames might be made lighter.

With the new grant came a larger staff, now totaling six, and the *Dictionary* began to take longer strides so that by the beginning of the current year the end was at last in sight. Though the final grant was exhausted and the staff disbanded by the middle of the year, with the work from "WO" to the end still unfinished, it was finally possible to bring the great undertaking to an end in this month of December, 1936, eighty years after Joseph Sabin, in his bookstore on Canal Street, first began collecting titles for his *Dictionary*.

No great scholarly enterprise such as "Sabin" can hope to be self-supporting, and so we cannot be sufficiently grateful to those who made its continuance possible from the point where it languished among the Smiths in 1892. Our sincere thanks must go out to the Carnegie Institution, to the group of friends who came to the rescue in 1927, to the American Council of Learned Societies (and its permanent secretary, Dr. Waldo G. Leland) which lent its prestige to our plea for funds, and especially to the Carnegie Corporation, which supplied the larger grants and so insured the completion of the work.

To the Bibliographical Society of America and its Sabin Committee all praise is due for energetically and persistently standing back of the *Dictionary* in spite of embarrassing delays and unforeseen difficulties. Most of all, we should be grateful to the one who acted as liaison officer between "Sabin" and its financial backers. It was largely through his individual appeals that the necessary funds were raised; he it was who carried our apologies for delays and our requests for further grants to our backers; and it was because of his personal promise that the work would be finished this year that the final grant was secured. We are, therefore, especially grateful to the chairman of the Sabin Committee and director of the New York Public Library, Dr. Harry Miller Lydenberg.

The twenty-ninth and final volume of "Sabin" ends with serial number 106413, but thousands of these serial numbers represent not one but many titles or editions; in some cases dozens of editions appear in the main entries or the notes of a single number. It is, therefore, probable that well over a quarter of a million different publications appear in the *Dictionary*, as well as the location in the world's great libraries of not far from a million copies.

Those who have not attempted a similar task will hardly realize the great amount of patient labor which has gone into the compilation of some of the groups of material here described. Dr. Eames' studies of the writings of Captain John Smith and Amerigo Vespucci are each of them, in the scholarly difficulty of their compilation and in their value to the historian, easily the equivalent of a doctorial dissertation. And such important groups as Miss Elizabeth G. Greene's South Carolina, Tennessee, Texas, Vermont, and Virginia bibliographies and Miss Marjorie Watkins' "Treaties" are of the highest type of bibliographical scholarship.

The very difficult work done by the staff of the John Carter Brown Library in the letters *U* and *V*, with their preponderance of complicated seventeenth-century Latin, Spanish, and Dutch titles, and the fine work of Mr. Willard O. Waters in compiling the George Washington titles merit the highest praise. These are but random illustrations of the scholarly usefulness of the *Dictionary* and of the great service performed by its contributors. Surely the tool-makers are worthy of praise as well as the skilled workmen who later erect enduring, scholarly edifices through the use of such tools as this.

The story of the growth and development of American bibliography may be clearly traced by a careful examination of the twenty-nine volumes of "Sabin." When, eighty years ago, Joseph Sabin began his ambitious and well-nigh foolhardy task of recording the entire literature of American history, he was working under a fearful handicap. Of course, he had a phenomenal memory for bibliographical details and had undoubtedly handled more rare and important American titles than anyone else of his generation. But there were not a half-dozen really good public collections of American historical books in the whole country in 1856, and most of the rare Americana was in a dozen or two private libraries, for the collecting of Americana had only begun. There were comparatively few bibliographical reference works for Sabin to use, and many of them were poorly arranged, woefully incomplete and inaccurate, and almost none of them gave the locations of copies. There were virtually no published catalogues of the great national libraries, and only a few author, subject, or regional bibliographies of any value.

The Sabin staff of recent years has been more fortunate. There have been dozens of co-operating libraries; many skilled librarians, bibliographers, and collectors have come to the rescue; and there are hundreds of valuable bibliographies to help locate and describe elusive rarities and supply necessary footnotes. The very richness of our resources has at times been an embarrassment, for a simple "Sabin" entry of two or three lines has sometimes been evolved only after many hours among scores of bibliographies, catalogues, and source books.

In compiling the recent volumes of "Sabin," we began with the 3 × 8-inch author and title slips inherited from Mr. Sabin and Dr. Eames. Many of them were clippings from unidentified auction, dealers', or library catalogues, some were actual title-pages taken from imperfect books, others were manuscript notes of volumes examined in days gone by, and still others were mere cryptic references of a word or two which took much ingenuity to interpret. In many cases these titles were incomplete and had to be verified from actual copies of the books, if such copies could be found. And it must be remembered that these original Sabin entries represented only a fraction of the titles eventually included in the *Dictionary*.

The next step was a thorough search of the catalogues of the New York Public Library, the Library of Congress, and the British Museum. Then the brief check lists sent by the many co-operating libraries were examined in order to find new titles and editions, and letters were written for complete descriptions of these new titles. If these sources failed, bibliographies, histories, and other reference works were consulted, and more letters had to be written to those who owned or might be expected to own such material. When full authors' names had been secured (no small task), the entries were typed in duplicate on $5\frac{1}{2} \times 8\frac{1}{2}$-inch slips and filed.

While three of the staff were compiling a given block of material in the quarters generously provided for them by the New York Public Library, two other assistants were at work on a later part of the alphabet at the American Antiquarian Society, Harvard, or in the Boston libraries, with headquarters in the former library and later at Harvard. Their completed titles were then sent to the staff in New York for further addition and revision. In the meantime other paid or volunteer assistants were at work in Philadelphia and Washington, and a constant correspondence was necessary with libraries throughout this country and occasionally with those in Europe.

When the titles, collations, and notes were completed, the locations of copies were added from library check lists and bibliographies. Then the work of each assistant was twice checked by the assistant editors, and the titles sent to the editor

for final revision. He made many changes and additions and
not infrequently discarded unimportant titles. Then he added
the page numbers and the serial numbers and sent the copy to
the printer in batches of several hundred titles at a time.

When the titles were in type, the galley proofs were read by
the printer, the editor, and the assistant editor, and last-minute
entries inserted from the letters and check lists of belated
correspondents. In some cases, additional sets of galley
proofs were sent for further revision to individual libraries or
specialists, as in the case of the Yale College entries, which
were generously proofread by the catalogue department of the
University library and by the honorary curator of the special
collection of Yale memorabilia. Finally, the page proofs were
read by the printer and by the editor, who added the caption
titles, supplied the copy for title-pages, dedications, and other
preliminary leaves, and shortly thereafter another part was
delivered to the subscribers.

This brief summary gives very little idea of the intricate detail of the task of compiling and editing "Sabin." The typed
instructions prepared for the use of the staff fill fifteen single-
spaced pages, but even a perusal of this outline of Sabin practice is inadequate to the proper understanding of the many
difficulties.

The patience, accuracy, and devotion of the "Sabin" staff,
always working under pressure and at top speed in order to
finish the task before the appropriation should run out, is
beyond praise. Of course, there are many mistakes in the *Dictionary*, for our sources of information were often incomplete
and inaccurate, and we were frequently compelled to rely on
the work of others when we could not examine the books ourselves. But all who use the *Dictionary* should remember with
gratitude not only the wonderful work of Joseph Sabin and
Dr. Wilberforce Eames who, between them, did more than half
of the *Dictionary* almost singlehanded, but also the splendid

services of Elizabeth Grosvenor Greene, Marjorie Watkins, and the others who have spent devoted years of patient work behind the scenes so that historians, librarians, bibliographers, collectors, and booksellers might have available a reasonably accurate description of the more important books relating to America.

And we should not forget our patient and accurate printers, the printing-house of William Edwin Rudge and, later, the Southworth-Anthoensen Press, or the hundreds of librarians, cataloguers, scholars, and collectors who have searched their shelves and their notes in order to make our records more complete. "Sabin" is not the work of two or three individuals but is a great co-operative enterprise which never could have reached its present usefulness without the aid of hundreds of persons whose names and services were known only to the editorial staff.

Sabin is finished, and, as did the monks writing in their scriptoria during the Middle Ages, we have placed after the last entry of our manuscript a fervent "Laus Deo." On the title-page of each volume of "Sabin" you will find the following quotation from the Preface of Anthony à Wood's *History of Oxford* of 1674:

A painfull work it is I'll assure you, and more than difficult, wherein what toyle hath been taken, as no man thinketh so no man believeth, but he hath made the triall.

And to those who find inconsistencies, errors, and omissions in the pages of this work of ours, I would quote a phrase from Foulkes Robartes' all-but-forgotten treatise: *The revenue of the Gospel is tythes* (Cambridge, 1613):

Who faulteth not, liueth not; who mendeth faults is commended: The Printer hath faulted a little: it may be the author oversighted more. Thy paine (Reader) is the least; then erre not thou most by misconstruing or sharpe censuring; least thou be more vncharitable, then either of them hath been heedlesse: God amend and guide vs all.

PROBLEMS IN NINETEENTH-CENTURY AMERICAN BIBLIOGRAPHY

By ROLLO G. SILVER

IN the course of a paper prepared for this Society precisely twenty years ago, Dr. George Watson Cole reminded us that

> The modern bibliographer may properly be called the anatomist of the book. If he would be successful in his vocation he must be thoroughly familiar with all that is to be known about the paper on which a book is printed, its quality, method of manufacture, and through what processes it goes in order to become a part of a book. . . . He must understand the art of printing. . . .

We have seen these principles applied with evident success to bibliography of the Colonial period. In the nineteenth-century field, however, we have been so occupied with the necessary ground-work of listing and locating texts that we have not had time to consider the perplexities inherent in them. If we are to progress from simple classification to knowledge about the processes of nineteenth-century American book-making, we must first answer the host of technical questions which have arisen. Our problem at the outset is to evaluate particular technological advances, with reference to their relationship and evolution at definite stages in the century. This problem initiates the need for a complete report on the materials used in book-making and the men who used them. Furthermore, it is necessary to trace the emergence of mass production as a power in altering the physical appearance of a book. What is peculiar and new to the nineteenth century is the rapid and conscious change of method in making a book. The student must not be satisfied with simply cataloguing inventions without reference to the periods of experimental design which lie between. He must bridge the gap between the inventive idea and its product, and he must do so before his source material further diminishes. In this situation we can take advantage of two helpful factors. Because of the temporary closing of European collections students interested in bibliographical research will find it more convenient to work with American subjects. In our universities there are students trained in pure scholarship who could be a mine of effective collaboration if the problems could be presented to them.

This paper points to some of the problems which confront us and suggests the first step towards solution.[1]

Our major need is the accumulation of detail on which rests our understanding of the processes of printing. At the beginning of the century the printer worked with equipment as cumbrous as his neighbor's ox-cart; at the end of the century he was the servant of a machine as slick and impersonal as an airplane. The interim between the two epochs is filled with confusion and discrepancy for the bibliographer, who must piece out the story between successive differences in rates of speed. To some extent the difference in speed accounts for the difference in the quality of the book.

The excellence of our early American bed-and-platen presses is shown by Joel Munsell's statement that importation had almost ceased by 1800. One of these, the Ramage press, was made of Honduras mahogany and later of iron. Ramage enlarged the diameter of the screw, faced the platens with brass, and imported and improved the Ruthven press. By 1837 he had manufactured over twelve hundred presses. Information about the Ramage

[1] A copy of this paper with notes on its source material has been deposited with the Permanent Secretary. The author wishes to thank Messrs. William A. Jackson, Hellmut Lehmann-Haupt and Lawrence C. Wroth for their aid in clarifying the problems discussed.

press is too widely scattered for reference. Mr. Milton W. Hamilton of Albright College has been assembling material about Ramage, but he writes me he is not yet ready to project a paper.

The transition from the screw to the lever was made by George Clymer's Columbian press, a development about which we know comparatively little. Every history of printing mentions Clymer's introduction of the lever. We know certain externals of his fame: most New York newspapers were printed on a Clymer press, it was used in the King of England's printing office, the Emperor of Russia enthusiastically presented Clymer with six thousand rubles, and the King of Holland and the King of Spain patronized him. But bibliographers await the answers to their questions: what inventions or ideas stimulated Clymer to introduce the lever? How did he arrive at the aptness of method which helped quicken the pace of printing in the early part of the century? We await a complete study of the life and work of this early expatriate.

A particular instance of our lack of certainty about simple facts is the mystery of the toggle-joint. Who made this next contribution to printing? Hoe implies that Peter Smith invented it in 1822; Oswald declares that it was invented by John J. Wells. However, there is a patent for a press granted Otis Tufts in 1813 which mentions a toggle-joint.

The orderly progress of printing bears within itself, as does all scientific invention, both change and permanence. It is probable that the most popular of bed-and-platen presses, the Washington press of Samuel Rust (later purchased by the Hoes), incorporated the latest devices to the extent that it suited the business needs of the book-trade of the eighteen-thirties. This cast iron and wrought iron press suited the environment so well that it was still being used for proofs almost a hundred years later. Many of the books we collate must have been printed on the Washington press. It is no exaggeration to say that until we know more about its sizes, operation, and distribution we can know little about the

American printing industry of the first half of the nineteenth century.

Even as the hand press flourished, printers occupied themselves with the obsession of the century — energy — and experimented with the rudimentary power press. According to the *American Dictionary of Printing and Bookmaking*, Jonas Booth of New York printed an edition of *Murray's Grammar* in 1823 on a machine press constructed after the principles of one he had seen in England. Booth, by the way, was one of the first Americans to use composition rollers. An historically early power press was the one-horse-power contraption built by Phineas Dow for Daniel Treadwell and set up in Boston in 1827. One must note here that while the energy for Boston's first power press was supplied by a stalwart Canadian horse, New York was, as usual, behind New England in culture and refinement. The energy for New York's first power press was, it seems, supplied by a mule.

In 1830 two of Dow's employees, Seth and Isaac Adams, began the manufacture of the most popular of early power presses. Over one thousand Adams presses in fifty-seven sizes were produced. Their decline in popularity emphasizes two important bibliographical points: as soon as printers found that press work could be saved by imposing twelves as sixteens and twenty-fours as thirty-twos, they looked for a press which could fulfill this requirement. The Adams press could not; and, moreover, electrotyping had provided a plate strong enough for use in cylinder presses.

This broad view of the spread of printing must not obscure the fact that there is a distinction between the date of invention of a press and the date of its general use in printing houses. We must emphasize the point that there was a modifying period of preparation to be undergone before the novel appliance could be accepted. We know that power presses were used in 1827. Yet ten years later Harper & Brothers possessed thirty-seven hand presses and only one power press. The first power press in Chicago was set up in 1843, yet in 1852 the city contained only one more such press.

The cylinder press was even slower in becoming generally employed. 1796 is the earliest date for a patent for a cylinder press in America, but whether Apollos Kinsley's press was ever used is still in doubt. Patents for cylinder presses were also filed in 1811 and 1829. America's adaptation of the cylinder press actually began when Major Mordecai Noah imported a Napier from England in 1829. The freight charges and duty were so high that the Major was forced to leave the machinery in bond. Another editor bought it, and Robert Hoe was called in to assemble it. The Hoes, with their customary habit of imaginative adaptation, produced cylinder press after cylinder press, improvement after improvement. Yet the cylinder press was not in general use in the book-trade until the middle of the century.

I do not need to say that the trend of the development of printing in nineteenth-century America was regulated by the House of Hoe. In the hands of Hoe's brother-in-law, Peter Smith, Sereno Newton, and others of the firm, the self-evolving process of invention was given a direction which infected many admirers. The value of their achievement necessitates an authoritative history, for which a beginning has been made by Stephen D. Tucker. Unfortunately this history exists only in typewritten copies. In our study of the Hoes we are confronted with a situation which will become more prevalent the longer we wait. Most of the business records of the firm were destroyed; only those from 1870 still exist. Here we may perhaps find out who bought the presses, the price, terms of sale, and dates of installation. Such is the stuff of bibliography.

There remain the other manufacturers of cylinder presses — Campbell, Taylor, Cottrell, Potter, and the inventor of the rotary perfecting press, William Bullock. Will the time come when their contributions will be evaluated?

Stereotyping is another technique of which the date of introduction in America is vague. John Watts's edition of *The Larger*

Catechism, New York, 1813, is probably, as the title-page states, "the first book ever stereotyped in America." Traditional histories tell us that David Bruce introduced the art when he returned from London in 1812 or 1813. But in the *Typographical Miscellany,* Joel Munsell quotes an article from *The Long Island Star* of October, 1811. This article announces the establishment of a manufactory of printing presses in New York by Mr. Francis Shield of London. "Mr. Shield," the article states, "is also in possession of the art of taking stereotype plates, and has specimens in his possession." Further investigation may corroborate what seems to be a new date for stereotyping in America and Mr. Shield may finally receive the credit for its introduction. Still, we owe to David Bruce's invention of the planing machine the rapid and full development of the profession. There was a decided lag in the use of stereotyping in the small cities. While New York had five stereotypers in 1820, and eight or nine in 1830, there were no foundries in Syracuse, Troy, or Utica before the Civil War and only one in Rochester. In New York plates were freely used for books and advertisements in 1840, but the first stereotyping plant in Providence was established in 1881.

Dr. George A. Kubler of New York is preparing a history of stereotyping for which he has searched libraries all over the world. This history which will contain the results of twenty-five years of research will, however, be written for professional stereotypers and will be limited in its scope.

Many of us who have attempted to collate a nineteenth-century book have often wished that some enthusiastic electrotyper might follow Dr. Kubler's example. At present the bibliographer who tries to find out about electrotyping history and methods becomes lost in a maze of technical formulas. And such terms as Smee battery, resistence board, and Voltaic battery conquer our bibliographical curiosity. A collaboration between a technical expert and a bibliographer might tell us what we want to know about electrotype plates: how and when they were used in book production, the cost of preparing them, storage facilities for the plates, the relationship of electrotyper and publisher, and, of course, electrotyping and imposition.

The unusually large number of signatures which are found in some American books must be accounted for. If this was due to the fact that the book was first printed, then stereotyped and then electrotyped, information must be made available.

Then, still more important to the bibliographer is the study of type-setting and type-founding. It is to be hoped that Dr. Wroth will continue his study of the work of Dr. William Church. There are other unmonographed men, like William Mitchell, the inventor of the first practical type-setting machine, who deserve our attention. Before 1900 over two hundred and eighteen American patents for type-setting machines were issued and our skill made New York City the first in the world in which type was set by machinery. The acceleration of invention, of course, came during the final half of the century. Thus the impetus given to printing by a small group of pioneers resulted in a steady and expected advance in ratio with the growing social need.

Characteristic of a century which permanently substituted mass production for individual effort is the story of the type-founding industry. We are aware of the huge combine which overshadows the names of the individual type-founders. These men, who worked in such cities as St. Louis, Albany, Baltimore, Buffalo, Pittsburgh, Cleveland, Chicago, and Cincinnati, will in time become anonymous if they are not soon rescued from oblivion. There is the enterprising Elihu White, who began founding type in Hartford in 1804 and in 1810 was the only type-founder in New York City. As far as we know, White ran an independent business, but later men like him were forced by the price war of 1885 to form the American Type Founders Company. An analysis of this organization would reveal the widespread geographical distribution of the industry.

Let me carry one more coal to Newcastle and suggest an ex-

amination of nineteenth-century book illustration. Here again
the need is not only an analysis, but a study of the antecedents and
results of a fast moving and revolutionary subject. Investigations
in this field are beginning. Professor Lehmann-Haupt writes:

> Three of my students in the Library School, independent of each other, have
> chosen a subject in the field of photo-mechanical reproduction. One of them is
> making a bibliographical study of facsimile editions of books; another one is in-
> terested in the use of photographs as book illustrations in the first hundred years
> since the invention of photography; a third one is considering an evaluation of
> the comparative merits of photographic reproductions used in art books. As a re-
> sult of these three converging interests, we are also trying to tackle some solution
> of that ticklish and complicated question: In what order have the various photo-
> mechanical processes been developed and in what order have they been applied
> in book production and illustration?

When we leave technology and come to materials, we find, as
we are beginning to expect, that the materials which go into the
book have been similarly ignored. Within its limitations the study
of paper can strengthen the direction of bibliography by giving
us a constant inductive tool. The foregoing discussion has been
centered on some of the modifications of the printing process. In
its essence the expansion of paper-making is analogous to nineteenth-century printing. Early in the century the printer had at
his command a handsome and sturdy American paper. But soon
the demand far outran the supply. Before long the force of mass
education and mass production started the degeneration of rag
paper into the thin and sleazy pulp. The rise in the scale of education brought with it the familiar evils of competition and cheap-
ening of product.

Our factual information about paper-making consists of the
cursory history by Weeks and several published studies of individual mills such as the Willcox Mill and the mills at Newton
Lower Falls. Miss Marie Dickoré of Cincinnati who is studying
the mills of the Little Miami Valley has located the site and the
year of the first paper mill in Ohio and has found some of its
water-marked paper and much of its regular paper. This paper,

Miss Dickoré says, "was used in printing some of the laws of the Northwest Territory and the newspapers of that period besides some of the well-known books of that time." Mr. John Anderson of the Queens Borough Public Library, New York City, is making a study of paper-making on Long Island; and Mr. Marvin A. Miller is preparing a work on the whole subject of paper-making in the United States.

Nineteenth-century American bookbinding has at present but one acolyte. Mr. J. W. Rogers is enlarging his article, *The Industrialization of American Bookbinding*, to include his new findings. This will appear in the spring as part two of a volume on bookbinding. The first part is a thorough survey of bookbinding by hand in Colonial America and the young Republic by Miss Hannah Dustin French of the Wellesley College Library. The third part, by Professor Lehmann-Haupt, deals with the rebinding of old volumes. Apart from the bibliographical importance of cloth the study of bookbinding could be expanded to include antiquarian aspects. Mr. Jackson has pointed to the fascinating field of shingle-board bindings. Perhaps some of the more romantic of us may set out to find an actual instance of a man who took a shingle from his house to bind a book. But the realist must forego such a luxury until he has made coherent a subject still so discrete and fragmentary.

In this paper I have assumed that we must believe that the investigation of any method and material used in making a book can be of help to bibliography. Might not the study of ink help us in identifying reprinted signatures or in dating an inscription? This might seem exaggeration to most of us, but at present very little knowledge of nineteenth-century ink has been organized for the bibliographer. The discovery of coal-tar colors in the middle of the century introduced new features into the printing trade. Gamble's *List of References on the Chemistry and Manufacture of Writing and Printing Inks* is, of course, our starting point.

Any consideration of printing must include, happily enough,

the men who laid the foundation for its development. The nineteenth-century American printers were practical men whose lives were significant to the community as well as to the craft. Information on these men and the atmosphere in which they lived is becoming available. Joel Munsell, the printer-historian, is being studied by Mr. David Edelstein of New York. Here, for the first time, we shall have the complete story of Munsell's week in jail where he went rather than disclose the authorship of a supposedly libelous pamphlet which he had published. Much information about nineteenth-century printers is turning up in a check-list of books illustrated by Alexander Anderson which is now being prepared by Miss Helen Knubel and Mr. Lawrance Thompson. Is anyone studying Daniel Fanshaw, who installed some of the earliest power presses in his book office, printing most of the books of the American Bible Society? Fanshaw, by the way, was one of the few printers who ever accumulated a million dollars. Other enterprising men were C. A. Alvord, in his day unsurpassed for handling the wood-cut, Isaac Ashmead who introduced the power press in Philadelphia, John F. Trow who introduced the Mitchell type-setting machine, and, of course, Theodore De Vinne. Then there is the mystery of the autobiography of T. H. Carter, the Boston printer. Several books have mentioned and quoted from this autobiography, but I have found no one who can locate a copy. I have cited only a few names; any thorough study of the nineteenth century will have to be based on such contributions as Mr. George McKay's *Register of Artists, Booksellers, Printers and Publishers in New York City 1801-1820*, an example which, we hope, will be copied in other cities.

Before 1840 more than twenty different cities had organizations of printers, yet we know about only a few of these organizations. The records of an organization give an excellent picture of the trade (see, for example, *Book and Job Printing in Chicago*, and *Printers and Printing in Providence*), by showing the struggles over wages, over the separation of the crafts, the problems of hours, and the entrance of women into the industry. Organizations of employing printers must also be studied. The only recent work in this field has been *The Origin and History of the New York Employing Printers' Association* by Charlotte E. Morgan.

I have sketched rapidly what seems to be the haphazard state of the technological history of the last century. This dominant tone is repeated in the histories of the publishing houses of the time. They are usually nothing but a poor compromise between a pedigree and an advertisement, often having been issued for an anniversary celebration. Their extreme subjectivity blurs the character and intentions of the publishing house. If we are to throw light on the prevalent methods of commercial printing on a large scale we must strive for the complete and impartial history of each individual firm. One of our needs is a list of the successive imprints of each house with the devices used at the time. A step in this direction is being taken by Professor Anne M. Boyd of the University of Illinois, who is preparing a list of American publishers with historical data. As this list is intended as an aid to book selection only, no attempt is made to list every imprint, or to describe the devices.

Another opportunity to increase our technical knowledge is offered by one incident in the history of Harpers. When they were burned out in 1853, they built a new plant the following year. A study of this plant would afford a complete picture of the latest equipment available to the publisher of 1854.

The small town publisher has been a fruitful subject for the researches of Barrows Mussey and Milton W. Hamilton, whose *Country-Printer New York 1785-1830* will be followed by a study of Vermont journalism now being prepared.

There is one topic which is entirely dependent on information gathered from the files of the publishers themselves, namely the relationship between author and publisher. But lack of co-operation has hindered the student in his search. Requests for information usually bring replies such as: "Our records are rather intimate and cannot be seen," or "They are only available for accounting purposes." Perhaps the publisher uses these reasons to avoid saying what he really means. If he would tell the truth, he probably would write: "We realize that records one hundred years old should be made available to accredited students. However, to get at the records is very expensive in time and trouble. We have had so many requests about various authors that we are sick and tired of being bothered." One cannot blame the publisher; he is quite right. But if bibliographers are to know the complete story of the nineteenth-century book-trade, they must have some of the information which is in the files. The longer bibliographers wait, the fewer will be available records.

I should like to suggest a method by which an accredited investigator, under conditions established with the individual publisher, would be allowed to see relevant records. Would it not be a good idea for the Society to act as the medium? Such a course would have two advantages: the publisher would only be requested to do this for worthy projects and the Society would have the benefit of competent investigation.

The most feasible plan might be to have a small committee at the service of scholars who are attempting to secure bibliographical information. By its very existence the committee would stimulate investigation of the problems discussed in this paper, and might act as a clearing-house to integrate information for nineteenth-century bibliographers. The concentrated effort of a group ready to give an impetus to the student will facilitate preparing the many particular articles which have to be written before a general study can be made.

In this paper, in order to select apposite references to the impact of science upon the making of a book, I have stressed the factual-historical bias. But I realize that we cannot think in terms of infinite detail alone. Let us wait patiently, but not too long, for a general definition of the principles of nineteenth-century bibliography.

On the reference shelf next to our desks McKerrow's *Introduction* and Wroth's *Colonial Printer* stand side by side. Next to these two volumes there is an empty space which seems to grow wider every time we look for the book which ought to be there. Members of The Bibliographical Society, is it not time that we begin to think about a manual of nineteenth-century bibliography?

THE BIBLIOGRAPHICAL SOCIETY OF AMERICA–ITS LEADERS AND ACTIVITIES, 1904-1939

By HENRY B. VAN HOESEN

HE Bibliographical Society of America is neither a section nor an affiliate of the American Library Association, but deserves a place in Dr. Frank P. Hill's projected history of the A. L. A.* for a variety of reasons. Librarians were the prime movers in the organization of its parent society, the Bibliographical Society of Chicago (1899-1904); the development of this into a national society was discussed at several meetings of the American Library Association and effected in the formation of the Bibliographical Society of America at the St. Louis Conference of the A. L. A.; and this close association with the A. L. A. has been maintained ever since by annual

---

* Dr. Hill's work was unhappily interrupted by illness and this chapter, shortly before his death, was relinquished to the Bibliographical Society of America. The paper is published approximately as it was written late in the year 1939. Attention is called to the increase in membership from some 600 at the end of 1939 to about 840 (September, 1941), which might alter to some extent the writer's analyses of the residence and professional interests of the membership. — Editor.

and other meetings, joint bibliographical undertakings and other common interests. The first by-law of the Bibliographical Society of America required that "the time and place of the annual meeting of the Society shall correspond with the date and place of the meeting of the American Library Association, unless otherwise determined by vote of the council," and the omission of this requirement in the revised Constitution and By-Laws of 1927 (when the Society was incorporated) has not altered the practice.

So far as any one person may be designated as founder, the honor belongs to Aksel G. S. Josephson, who acted as chairman of the committee formed to organize the Bibliographical Society of Chicago, arranged several preliminary meetings in the spring of 1899, and at the organization meeting in October of that year expressed the hope that "the organization of this society may lead to the founding of a national bibliographical society." Mr. Josephson was at the time in the fourth year of his long service as Chief Cataloguer of the John Crerar Library and his published bibliographical work had already begun in 1892, just a year before he came to the United States; his bibliographies of Swedish dissertations (1892-97), on the history of science (1911-15) and the history of industry (1915), and his *Bibliographies of Bibliographies* (1901, second ed. 1910-13) are merely the best known and most used of his many bibliographical contributions. He served as Secretary of the Chicago society 1899-1903 and then as President 1903-04, was for thirty years almost constantly either an officer, editor, or member of Council of the Bibliographical Society of America; his contributions to the Society's papers and discussions were many and varied, e. g. *Efficiency and Bibliographical Research, Plan for a Complete Bibliography of American Literature and for a Bibliographical Institute, Literature of the Invention of Printing, Fifteenth-Century Editions of Fasciculus Temporum in American Libraries*, etc. Though now retired, he still maintains a keen and active interest in the Society.

The first President of the Bibliographical Society of Chicago (1899-1901) was Charles H. Hastings, then connected with the Library of the University of Chicago. Joining the Library of Congress staff in 1901, he has rendered conspicuous world wide service to bibliography through the expert service of the Card Division of which he is chief. Professor Camillo von Klenze, of the German faculty of the University of Chicago, succeeded Hastings (1901-03) and was succeeded by Josephson (1903-04). Josephson thus played the leading role both in founding the Chicago society and in organizing the Bibliographical Society of America with the Chicago group as a local chapter. The continuance of this Chicago chapter is significant of the strength of such local organizations, as its demise, in 1912, is significant of some of the weaknesses of a national society.

The Organization Committee of the Bibliographical Society of America, which took over, with slight modification, the Constitution proposed by the Chicago group, consisted of John Thomson, Wilberforce Eames and William Coolidge Lane. Thomson was at once librarian of a public library (the Free Library of Philadelphia) and bibliographer of rare works of literature. The Society's census of fifteenth-century books owned in America was undertaken, almost with the beginning of the Society, upon his initiative and was carried on with his labor down to the time of his death in 1916. Eames was, and even after his death two years ago, still remains the Society's most distinguished bibliographer. His editing of Sabin's *Dictionary of Books Relating to America* began in 1885 and his work and advice were continued until its completion by the Society under the editorship of R. W. G. Vail (1930-36). Lane was Librarian of Harvard College Library from 1898 till his retirement in 1929, was the author of several of Harvard's *Bibliographical Contributions*, and was the president of the Bibliographical Society of America during the first five years of its existence.

After its organization, the affairs of the Bibliographical Society of America lay in the hands of the Council as provided in the Constitution: "A president, two vice-presidents, a secretary, a treasurer and a librarian ... the last ex-president, and four councilors. The officers shall be elected annually by the members of the society and shall serve until the election of their successors. Of the councilors one shall be elected each year." In 1916 an amendment was passed substituting *editor* for *librarian*, but the former wording was adopted in the Constitution drafted in 1927, in connection with the incorporation of the Society, and approved by the Society in 1928. Ten years later a new amendment deleted the word *librarian*. In 1938, in view of the increased amount of routine work in the offices of the Secretary, Treasurer, and Chairman of the Publication Committee, the Council appointed a Permanent Secretary, with nominal stipend, to serve as the executive officer of the Society in all routine matters, as managing editor of the Society's publications (*cf. News Sheet* 50), and as collector and custodian of the Society's archives.

Before the appointment of a Permanent Secretary, it should occasion no great suprise to find that there were periods of rather casual attention to routine business of other than financial import. Thus elections were sometimes held in haste, sometimes forgotten, and sometimes unrecorded in the Society's publications. However, such circumstances are not unnatural in a small and academic group of people possessing a high degree of mutual confidence, and not possessing a paid secretariat. The case of a councillor elected to succeed a man whose term had not expired and the leaving in office of one whose term had expired may serve as examples of the difficulty of compiling the following lists, in which it is hoped that the successions are pretty well established.

The lists given in the front of each volume of the *Papers* fairly regularly down to volume 18 (1924) show some inaccuracies (e. g. the list given in volume 7, page 6, for the year 1911-12 is the list elected for 1913-14), and accordingly the "authentic" list based on these and published in *News Sheet* 12 is also incorrect.

The accompanying table is based, in the first place, on the records of elections as reported in minutes of meetings, etc. (place of publication indicated at foot of column), and the names of those reported elected or appointed by the Council are italicized. Names not so marked are carried over from preceding columns for the duration of the terms for which they had been elected (in case of members of the Council) or until their successors were elected. This scheme works out very satisfactorily until a series of years (1929-1932) for which no elections to the Council are reported. From this time on the succession seems again clear and authenticated. In years when no elections are reported, the method of determining terms apparently varied; in 1905 all the councillors' terms were lengthened by one year; similarly, sometime between 1929 and 1933, the four councillor terms seem to have been extended to five years; in other years, e. g. 1916, the election of councillors was for the remainders of the regular four-year terms. To supplement the printed sources, the writer has consulted the Society's archives and corresponded with most of the former officers and councillors who are still living.

Presidents

1904-09   William Coolidge Lane

1909-10   Azariah Smith Root, Librarian of Oberlin University, 1887-
          1928, honored with the title "Professor of Bibliography" early
          in his career (1890). He made important contributions to the
          Society in its organization period, in his papers on the origin of
          printing, etc., and in his two presidencies, 1909-10 and 1923-
          26.

1910-12   William Dawson Johnston, at the time Librarian of Columbia
          University, later of the St. Paul Public Library and (1921-25)
          of the American Library in Paris. In the early discussions of the
          Society his chief interest seems to have been in the proposed in-
          ternational catalogue of the current literature of the social
          sciences.

1912-13   Charles Henry Gould, Librarian of McGill University from
          1892 until his death in 1919, and founder of the first library
          school in Canada (1904).

1913-14   Andrew Keogh, at the time Reference Librarian of Yale Uni-
          versity, later Librarian (1916-38) and Sterling Professor of
          Bibliography (1924-38). His *Some General Bibliographical
          Works of Value to the Student of English,* 1901, is an early speci-
          men of the range of his interest and distinction in bibliography.
          He served the Society also at various times as councillor, mem-
          ber of Publication Committee, and delegate to the American
          Council of Learned Societies.

1914-16   Carl Bismarck Roden, at the time Assistant Librarian, later
          (1918-   ) Librarian of the Chicago Public Library. He
          served as Treasurer of the Bibliographical Society of Chicago
          and of the Bibliographical Society of America till 1912, and
          was on the Society's Publication Committee for some twenty-
          five years.

1916-21   George Watson Cole, Librarian of the Henry E. Huntington
          Library (1915-24). Most famous for his catalogues of the E.
          Dwight Church Library, the list of his other important works
          fills nearly half a column of *Who's Who in America.* The So-
          ciety's publications include a number of his essays on biblio-
          graphical method, book collectors, etc., and his eager interest
          in a proposed series of monographs, to which he also contri-
          buted financially, continued up to his final illness in 1939.*

1921-23   William Warner Bishop, Librarian of the University of
          Michigan since 1915. His conspicuous contributions in the field
          of librarianship have included the promotion of standard bib-
          liographies (e. g. for college libraries) although they have
          thrown into the background his more recondite bibliographi-
          cal interests.

1923-26   Azariah Smith Root.

1926-29   Herman Henry Bernard Meyer, then director of the Legisla-
          tive Reference Service of the Library of Congress, with which

---

* The Society is one of the beneficiaries of a trust established by Dr. Cole. The income from the property assigned to the Society (the George Watson Cole Publication
Fund) is to be used to pay for some of the publications of the Society, including the
issue of the *Papers* in which this study is printed. —Editor.

he was connected from 1905 till his retirement in 1935. The numerous practical subject bibliographies which he compiled in his work as Chief Bibliographer (1908-23) did not in the least dull his literary appreciation or his interest in his own collection of poetry, books printed by Bruce Rogers, etc. His *Bibliography in Relation to Business and the Affairs of Life* (B. S. A. *Papers*, vol. 10) contrasts "bibliography, the servant of the muses, and bibliography, the servant of the planner and doer of the world's work;" and his collection of over a hundred thousand cards toward a bibliography of American imprints 1800 to 1876 is characteristic of his vision and industry. He served on the Publication Committee for six years; was a member of the Council almost continuously from his presidency until his death in 1937; and during this latter period was active as a committee man in most of the Society's projects. First elected a delegate to the American Council of Learned Societies in 1928, he was its Secretary-Treasurer from 1935 until his death.

1929-31   Harry Miller Lydenberg, then Assistant Director and since 1934 Director of The New York Public Library. He has been one of the Society's delegates to the American Council of Learned Societies since 1928, succeeding Dr. Meyer as Secretary-Treasurer in 1937, has been a member of the Society's Council ever since his presidency, and has been indispensable to every important committee and project such as "Sabin," *Union List of Newspapers*, *Union List of International Congresses and Conferences*, *Incunabula in American Libraries a Second Census*, etc.

1931-33   Lawrence Counselman Wroth, Librarian of the John Carter Brown Library since 1923 and Research Professor of American History in Brown University since 1932, author of many significant books on early American printing, and American books and historical documents. He is chairman of the Society's Publication Committee (since 1936) and of the Committee on the Second Census of Incunabula. His *The Bibliographical Way* (read before the Society in 1936 and published in the *Colophon*, n.s. vol. 3, no. 2) is a classic contribution to the discussions of bibliographical method.

1933-36   Augustus Hunt Shearer, Librarian of the Grosvenor Library
           since 1917, an editor of the *Guide to Historical Literature*, 1931,
           and author in bibliography and in history, the field of study
           from which he entered library work. During his presidency and,
           preceding that, his fourteen years as Secretary, the member-
           ship of the Society greatly increased, and the *News Sheet* de-
           veloped from an ephemeral mimeographed circular in 1926 to
           a well-printed leaflet containing detailed proceedings of meet-
           ings and other "Notes and Queries" of permanent record
           value. Prevented by ill health from completing the third term
           of his presidency, he was able in his fortunate recovery to re-
           sume an active part in the Society's affairs as a member of the
           Council.

1936-37   Leonard Leopold Mackall, editor and literary historian of
           Goethe, and noted among bibliographers particularly for his
           contributions to the catalogue of the Osler Medical Library,
           1929, his preparation of material for the catalogue of the
           W. J. De Renne Georgia Library, 1931, and his "Notes for
           Bibliophiles" column in the *New York Herald-Tribune Books*.
           The meetings over which he presided had a unique atmosphere
           of bibliographical learning blended with merry humor never
           to be forgotten by the audiences.

1937-38   Earl Gregg Swem, Librarian of William and Mary College,
           editor of the *William and Mary College Quarterly Historical
           Magazine*, and further distinguished for his bibliographies of
           Virginia and the Confederacy—particularly the *Virginia His-
           torical Index*, which reviews have described as "beyond price,"
           "altogether . . . a model of what such an index should be."

1938-39   Victor Hugo Paltsits, Keeper of Manuscripts and Chief of the
           American History Division of The New York Public Library,
           editor and author of numerous important historical and bib-
           liographical works in the field of Americana. He had served
           the Society as a member of its Publication Committee, 1906-
           09, and as Vice-President, 1921-23; noteworthy among his
           contributions to the Society's papers and discussions is his *Plea
           for an Anatomical Method in Bibliography* (*Papers*, vol. 1).

1940   Randolph Greenfield Adams, Director of the William L.
                Clements Library of American History at the University of
                Michigan, a distinguished teacher and scholar in American
                History and Bibliography, a champion of the librarian's rights
                and duties as bibliographer, and a presiding officer, conversa-
                tionalist, and, if need be, controversialist, of liveliness, origi-
                nality and humor.

First Vice-Presidents

1904-06   Herbert Putnam, Librarian of Congress from 1890 until his
                retirement in 1939.
1906-09   Reuben Gould Thwaites, Secretary of the State Historical So-
                ciety of Wisconsin until his death in 1913.
1909-12   William Warner Bishop, then Superintendent of the Reading
                Room of the Library of Congress.
1912-13   Herman Henry Bernard Meyer, then Chief Bibliographer of
                the Library of Congress.
1913-14   Charles Homer Haskins, then Professor of History and Politi-
                cal Science and Dean of the Graduate School of Arts and Sci-
                ences at Harvard University.
1914-16   James Christian Meinich Hanson, then Associate Director of
                Libraries of the University of Chicago.
1916-17   Frederick Warren Jenkins, then Librarian of the Russell Sage
                Foundation.
1917-19   Herman Henry Bernard Meyer.
1919-20   George Parker Winship, then Librarian of the Harry Elkins
                Widener Collection of Harvard University.
1920-21   William Warner Bishop.
1921-22   Herman Henry Bernard Meyer.
1922-23   Lucius Lee Hubbard, Regent of the University of Michigan,
                bibliographer of *Gulliver's Travels*.
1923-26   Harry Miller Lydenberg.
1926-28   Charles Martel, then Chief of the Catalogue Division of the
                Library of Congress.
1928-29   Harry Miller Lydenberg.
1929-33   James Christian Meinich Hanson.

1933-35   George Burwell Utley, Librarian of the Newberry Library.

1935-36   Leonard Leopold Mackall.

1936-37   Earl Gregg Swem.

1937-38   Robert William Glenroie Vail, then Librarian of the American Antiquarian Society.

1938-39   Randolph Greenfield Adams.

1940   Henry Raup Wagner, historian and bibliographer of early discoveries and the West.

Second Vice-Presidents

1904-06   Reuben Gould Thwaites.

1906-09   Ernest Cushing Richardson, then Librarian of Princeton University.

1909-10   William Dawson Johnston.

1910-11   Worthington Chauncey Ford, then Editor of the Massachusetts Historical Society.

1912   Charles Henry Gould.

1912-13   Clark Sutherland Northup, Professor of English in Cornell University.

1913-14   Byron Alfred Finney, then Reference Librarian of the University of Michigan.

1914-16   William John James, then Librarian of Wesleyan University.

1916-18   Clarence Saunders Brigham, then Librarian of the American Antiquarian Society.

1918-21   James Christian Meinich Hanson.

1921-23   Victor Hugo Paltsits.

1923-26   Charles Martel.

1926-28   Theodore Wesley Koch, Librarian of Northwestern University.

1928-29   James Christian Meinich Hanson.

1929-33   Phineas Lawrence Windsor, Librarian and Director of the Library School of the University of Illinois.

1933-35   Leonard Leopold Mackall.

1935-36   Earl Gregg Swem.

1936-37   Margaret Bingham Stillwell, Curator and Librarian of the Annmary Brown Memorial.

1937-38   Randolph Greenfield Adams.

1939   Henry Raup Wagner.

1940   William Alexander Jackson, Assistant Librarian in Charge of the Treasure Room and Associate Professor of Bibliography, Harvard University.

Secretaries

1904-06   Charles Alexander Nelson, then Reference Librarian of Columbia University.

1906-09   William Dawson Johnston.

1909-12   Aksel Gustav Salomon Josephson.

1912-14   Adolf Carl von Noé, then Professor of German Literature in the University of Chicago.

1914   Willard Otis Waters, then In Charge of the American History Section in the Catalogue Division of the Library of Congress.

1914-19   Henry Ormal Severance, then Librarian of the University of Missouri.

1919-33   Augustus Hunt Shearer.

1933-40   Henry Bartlett Van Hoesen, Librarian and John Hay Professor of Bibliography, Brown University.

Permanent Secretaries

1938-39   Robert William Glenroie Vail.

1940-   George Leslie McKay, Curator of The Grolier Club, New York.

Treasurers

1904-13   Carl Bismarck Roden.

1913-36   Frederick Winthrop Faxon, bibliographer, publisher and bookseller, Boston, Mass.

1936-37   Mary E. Bates, Secretary to Mr. Faxon, Acting Treasurer after Mr. Faxon's death.

1937-   Charles Eliot Goodspeed, author and bookseller, Boston.

Librarians

1904-09   Wilberforce Eames.

1909-12   William Newnham Chattin Carlton, then Librarian of the
           Newberry Library.

1912-13   Andrew Keogh.

1913-16   Carl Bismarck Roden.

1916-28   Office lapsed.*

1928-38   Charles Clarence Williamson, Director of Libraries and Dean
           of the School of Library Service, Columbia University.

1938   Office abolished.

Members of Council appear in the table appended to this article.

Delegates to the American Council of Learned Societies

1928-   Harry Miller Lydenberg, Secretary-Treasurer of the A. C.
           L. S., 1937-.

1928-36   Herman Henry Bernard Meyer, Secretary-Treasurer of the
           A. C. L. S., 1935-36.

1937-38   Andrew Keogh.

1938-   Henry Bartlett Van Hoesen.

Delegates to the American Documentation Institute

1937-39   James Thayer Gerould, then Librarian of Princeton Univer-
           sity.

1940   Eugene B. Power, University Microfilms, Ann Arbor, Mich.

* The Library, including that of the Bibliographical Society of Chicago, consisted of such books as had been presented by authors, editors and publishers, and had
been stored in boxes, at the Newberry Library, from 1909 until 1917 when it was
deposited with the New York State Library School at Albany, the office of Librarian
of the Society having been abolished in 1916 in anticipation of this. A list of the
books was published in the Thirty-Eighth Annual Report of the School (1924), p.
25-37. After the transfer of the School to Columbia University in 1926, such books
as came to the Society were deposited there, Dr. Williamson being considered as Librarian. In December, 1938, the Council resolved "that the Library of the Society be
discontinued and that the Council recognize the absorption of the Society's library
by the New York State Library in 1926 and authorize the Columbia University
School of Library Service to keep as part of its library any of the Society's books
which the School had acquired since that date." The office of Librarian of the Society was abolished by amendment of Article 3 of the Constitution at the annual
meeting of the Society, June 21, 1939.

Publication Committee

The *Papers*. This Committee either as a whole or in the person of the Chairman or Editor has had fully as great responsibility as the Society's officers and Council in determining the scope and character of the Society's contributions to learning. The chairmen and editors have been:

1904-09   Wilberforce Eames.

1909-19   Carl Bismarck Roden, with Aksel Gustav Salomon Josephson as Editor, 1916-18.

1919-25   George Parker Winship.

1925-36   James Bennett Childs, Chief of the Division of Documents of the Library of Congress.

1936-   Lawrence Counselman Wroth.

The *Bulletin* of the Society was edited by a special committee, of which W. Dawson Johnston was chairman in 1907-08 (vol. 1, nos. 1-4), A. G. S. Josephson in 1909-11 (vol. 1, no. 4-vol. 3), and Adolf C. von Noé in 1912 (vol. 4).

The *News Sheet*, begun in 1926, was issued from the office of Augustus H. Shearer, first as Secretary of the Society and then as President, until 1936; in 1937-38 (nos. 43-48) Henry B. Van Hoesen acted as editor; subsequent issues have been the work of the Permanent Secretary.

The various special publications, each with its own editor, are listed below.

Membership

The scope and activities of a society are obviously closely related to its membership, and as one varies so does the other. The Bibliographical Society of Chicago in its first year gained a membership of 99 (78 Chicago members and 21 non-resident); in 1903, as it was on the verge of becoming a national organization, the total membership increased by nine, but the Chicago membership dropped from 78 to 61. The realization of the national society further increased the total membership (147 in 1905, 202 in 1907, and so on) but further reduced the Chicago membership, to 24; and, now with a total membership of some 600,* the Chicago membership is only a dozen. This loss is significant of the weakness of a national organization in getting and keeping the interest and support of colleagues who cannot or will not follow the conventions from place to place or whose interest in the organization is dissipated with the loss of the personal and social atmosphere of the local club.

A change in the character of the membership is also apparent. Root's paper before the Bibliographical Society of Chicago in 1902 described the likely membership of a national bibliographical society in three groups:

(1) Librarians, "not . . . any large percentage of the members of the American Library Association," but, "In all the great libraries of the country . . . the university and college libraries . . . ⌊and in⌋ public libraries of what I may venture to call the second grade," librarians "who are attracted by the wealth of material at their hand towards investigation and scholarly discussion."

(2) "what I will venture to designate as the student class of America . . . university and college professors, professional bibliographers and private investigators."

(3) "the class which I will designate as the amateurs in bibliography, the collectors and book-hunters."

These classes were not mutually exclusive at the time and are less so today, so that any statement of their relative number in the membership of the Bibliographical Society of America can be no better than approximate and may be open to the accusation of arbitrariness. Classes 2 and 3 are more easily distinguished as professorial and collector. However, even with these qualifications, one may be fairly sure of certain tendencies:

* The membership is now about 840 (September, 1941). — Editor.

(1) The relative increase and later decrease in the librarian class (50 per cent in the Bibliographical Society of Chicago, 1902-03, 60 per cent in the Bibliographical Society of America, 1904-05, and 45 or 50 per cent in recent years, although the actual number has nearly trebled).

(2) The relative decrease in the "student" or professorial class (in the Chicago group, 20 per cent in 1900 and 15 per cent in 1903, in the national society about 10 per cent from 1905 on).

(3) The relative stability in the collector, bibliophile and literary class (about 20 to perhaps 25 per cent).

(4) The development of the institutional membership (one in 1900, four in 1903, nine in 1905, and 160, i.e., more than 25 per cent, in 1940).

On the whole, Root's remarks were prophetic—some 250 or 300 is certainly *not* many of the American Library Association membership of 14,000 and can hardly be considered even a fair representation of "all the great libraries of the country." It is not clear to the writer where Root would have drawn the line between the student class and the amateurs, collectors, etc., but limiting the former to the professional student, generally connected with some institution of learning, the Society seems to have gained only a dozen or so in thirty years and, relatively speaking, to have lost. The third group, made to include the independent collector, bibliophile and literateur, has grown in number proportionately with the growth of the membership as a whole and, what is even more significant, its contributions in the way of bibliographical research have been too substantial to be grouped under Root's designation of "amateur." It is the lack of this type of contribution from institutional members that makes one inclined to deplore, not the large number of institutional members, but the fact that they form so large a portion of the membership —in other words, deplore the fact that the individual membership is not much larger. It is surprising that there are not 600 instead of 150 institutional library members and at least double that number of individual librarian members.

The Bibliographical Society of America can hardly launch a general campaign for members, since it is a learned society with admission to membership not automatic on payment of dues but subject to the approval of the Society's Council. However, inferences from the observations above and from the 50 per cent increase in membership during the past five years lead to the expectation of further growth of the Society through closer contact with the members of other learned societies of the American Council of Learned Societies, more contacts with collectors and independent scholars, and growing interest of librarians and professional scholars interested in practical and subject bibliographies as chronicled in the *News Sheet*.

The great advantages of a local chapter organization over a national is its ability to hold together these three groups of members with diverse interests even in the field of bibliography, by virtue of the personal interest which local colleagues maintain in each other's work and by means of more frequent meetings with greater opportunity for discussion of diverse topics. However, the Chicago chapter, though it had thriven as an independent Bibliographical Society of Chicago, seems to have languished gradually into inactivity and, in 1912, dissolution, and there has been no serious attempt to organize other chapters, although other learned societies, notably the Archaeological Institute of America, have done this very successfully. Neither has there been an attempt at the sort of affiliation of state and local societies in which the American Library Association has been fairly successful. Further, in hopeful speculating as to the future membership of the Bibliographical Society of America, it seems most likely that, with the growing interest in bibliography and book collecting, the growth of independent local societies and book clubs and the increase in the membership of the national society will go along together and react upon each other.

Activities

This sketch of the history of the organization and its personnel is consistent with the history of its activities. The objects of the Bibliographical Society of Chicago as formulated by Josephson's committee had been (By-Law II): "To encourage and promote bibliographical study and research. -2. To compile and publish special bibliographies. -3. To arouse interest in the history of books and libraries." As to what should be understood by the word *bibliographical*, Josephson said in his "Introductory Remarks" at the organization meeting: "Our work should cover the whole range of the history of the book—printing, illustration and binding, publishing and bookselling, history and management of libraries, and last, but not least, bibliography proper, the registry of printed books and the recording of their contents." Again in a paper before the Society in 1902 on *Some Bibliographical Desiderata and the Ways and Means to Carry Them Out*, he said, "The function of bibliography, I take it, is the recording, classification, and evaluation of printed literature."

In the same year, in a paper on *The Scope of an American Bibliographical Society*, Azariah S. Root, a future president of the Society, quoted from the *New English Dictionary* the two variant definitions of *Bibliography* ("the description and history of books" etc., and the "list of books") and said "it seems to me certain that a national bibliographical society can only hope to succeed by taking . . . for its field the broadest possible idea of bibliography." This advice, to the end of bringing together three groups—"librarians," the "student class of America," and "the amateurs in bibliography, the collectors and book-hunters"—was probably wise and was certainly prophetic. Dr. Root himself preferred the first definition, leaving the preparation of "guides for readers" to the "long-contemplated Bibliography Section of the American Library Association," but this section of the American Library Association was never organized, and if it had been, one may well doubt whether the Bibliographical Society of America would ever have obtained the membership support it now has.

The Constitution of the Bibliographical Society of America—in 1904 as now—stated the Society's object as "to promote bibliographical research and to issue bibliographical publications," still without attempt at definition of terms. The word *Bibliography* is, therefore, still as moot a term as, say, *Library Science*. The two definitions quoted by Root still remain two definitions uncombined and unreconciled except that the division of opinion nowadays is not squarely between the historical (description and history) and the enumerative (lists of books). The historical school will approve of lists which constitute the registry or record of the books' existence, particularly if the books are rare or historically significant, while the enumerative school would include the recording of books by subject and critical scholarly selective subject-lists, but both schools will share Root's hesitation to include in the scope of the Society the ephemeral "popular aids," the ordinary routine "lists of references," etc., and both occasionally accept, presumably for the sake of interesting presentation, a sort of literary history or "book-talk" that is not strictly bibliography under either definition.

The varying inclusiveness and exclusiveness of these various points of view appear from a glance through the volumes of *Papers* and the list of projects undertaken or sponsored by the Society.

The papers published in the *Year-Book* and special publications of the Bibliographical Society of Chicago were for the most part in the practical, enumerative field, both general—like *Bibliographies of Bibliographies, General and National Bibliographies, Indexing of Bibliographical Periodicals*—and in special subjects, e. g. statements of bibliographical accomplishments, methods and needs in History, English Literature, Physics, History of Philosophy, Mathematics, *Italian Communal History*, Oliver Cromwell, *Travels in Italy in the Eighteenth Century*, etc.

Papers such as *On Some American Bookmakers, The Beginnings of the Book* and one or two others, with the record of a complaint that there were not more such, indicate the other direction of the Society's interests.

The Bibliographical Society of Chicago further discussed various projects which, like their papers, deserve mention here as indications of what was to follow in the next forty years: English Books before 1640 in Chicago Libraries; Incunabula in Chicago Libraries (John Thomson, of the Free Public Library of Philadelphia, was compiling a list of incunabula in the United States); Privately Printed Books in the United States; First Editions óf American Authors; Serials.

The Bibliographical Society of America, in the main, inherited from the Bibliographical Society of Chicago its membership, its Constitution, its projects, and the same variety of papers, but gradually there developed a trend away from the "practical" enumerative subject list, never decisive but nevertheless significant.

The discussion at the meetings in 1904 emphasized the activities, in the field of subject bibliography, of the Carnegie Institution (American history and *Index Medicus*), the American Library Association Publishing Board (guides to reading, etc.), the American Historical Association, etc. Projects discussed were: A bibliographical institute, a bibliographical periodical, indexing of bibliographical periodicals, a list of bibliographical periodicals, a list of incunabula in American libraries, the continuation of Sabin, a bibliographical handbook, a new list of special collections in American libraries. The papers published in the first volume of *Proceedings and Papers*, 1904-1907, were concerned with subject bibliography, *The Need of Bibliographies in Literary History, Contributions to the Theory and History of Botanical Bibliography, Material in the Library of Congress for a Study of United States Naval History, European Historians of the Turks in the Sixteenth and Seventeenth Centuries, Bibliographical Activities of Historical Societies, An*

International Catalogue of Current Literature of the Social Sciences, and the bibliography of Economic Science, Commerce, Sociology, Political Science, Municipal Government, Colonial Government, and International Law.

But the same volume also contained Paltsits's *Plea for an Anatomical Method in Bibliography, The Bibliography of American Music,* and *The "1546" Edition of Gaddesden's Rosa Angelica;* with reports on the Incunabula and Americana projects, and (new projects) *The Need of a Bibliography of American Colonial Newspapers,* and *Plans for a Union Catalogue of American Colonial Laws.*

The volume for 1907-08 is about evenly divided between early printing in the South and Connecticut bibliography on the one hand and the bibliography of science on the other.

Thereafter subject bibliography very nearly but never quite disappears, as the following list will indicate: Vol. 4 (1909), two papers on the bibliography of economics; Vol. 5 (1910), Modern Philology; Vol. 8 (1914), Social Work; Vol. 10 (1916), Shakespeare, and *Bibliography in Relation to Business and the Affairs of Life;* Vol. 11 (1917), The Literature of the Great War; Vol. 16 (1922), American History Sources and Library Collections; Vol. 17 (1923), Guide to Historical Literature; Vol. 22 (1928), Canadian History, Balearic Islands; Vol. 24 (1930), Medical Literature of Mexico and Central America; Vol. 25 (1931), Russian Expansion to America, English language. This list of subject bibliographies omits those of early books (incunabula and Americana) since the Society's interest in these has been enlisted rather from the historical than from the subject point of view.

Further evidence that subject bibliography was never deliberately excluded from the scope of the Society appears in the attention paid to it in the *Bulletin,* of which four volumes were published in 1908-12. The recording of "Any serious bibliographical work undertaken in America . . . is included in its scope." The list in the first number was arranged under "Manuscripts,"

"Printing," "Bookselling and Collecting," "Americana," and "Miscellaneous" (from "Architecture" to "Whale Fisheries"). After the decision to combine *Bulletin* and *Papers* in one serial, in 1913, "Preference was expressed for subjects of actual practical interest, rather than of purely bibliographic or historic value." However, "practical" should not be taken to imply subject bibliography, for the very next sentence in the Proceedings of the meeting (June 25, 1913) reports "It was voted to recommend, to the Publication Committee, that a series of monographs with preference for bibliographies of American authors be issued on a subscription basis," and, in 1914, it was announced that the Publication Committee "intends to lay emphasis on American bibliography and American printing."

The systematic listing of bibliographies dropped with the end of the *Bulletin* in 1912 (although there is a page or two of Notes in each volume of *Papers*) and has never been fully resumed. The *News Sheet* has, however, carried "Notes and Queries" of this sort and, since 1937, has made a special feature of "Bibliographies in Preparation" (in which it has enjoyed the collaboration of the American Library Association's Bibliography Committee). Published bibliographies are occasionally mentioned or discussed but the tendency has been to leave such listing and reviewing to other agencies—the review section of the *Papers*, of the *Library Quarterly*, of *College and Research Libraries*, and listing in the *Library Journal*, the *Bibliographic Index*, etc.

Equally significant with the published papers, though often less conspicuous, are the topics and projects discussed and encouraged in one way or another, e. g., in addition to those mentioned above: Union List of serials, Bibliography of manuscript codices, Early American literary periodicals, Bibliography of English fiction in the eighteenth century, Bibliography of William Blake, Bibliography of English philology, Record of photostatically reproduced books and manuscripts, Reprint or new edition of the British Museum catalogue of books, Scandinavian-

American bibliography, Bibliography of American statute laws, Rag paper for government publications, Bibliography of American travel, Continuation of the Bibliothèque Nationale catalogue, Bibliographical guide to English periodical literature before 1800, Collective catalogue of railroad economics, Sponsorship of the *Library Quarterly*, Support of the *Gesamtkatalog der Wiegendrucke* and of the *Gesamtkatalog der preussischen Bibliotheken*, Cole's Index to the (British) Bibliographical Society publications, Bibliography of international congresses and conferences, Author catalogue of American books 1801-1866, Bibliography of cathedrals, Library of Congress repository of cards for bibliographies in print or manuscript, Desirability and practicability of publication of selective English translations from the continental European literature of librarianship, Co-operative catalogue of eighteenth-century Americana, Bibliographical instruction in colleges and library schools.

The conspicuous achievements of the Bibliographical Society of America, aside from its part in the general promotion of bibliographical research within its own membership and in co-operation with other learned societies, are its publications: *Papers*, vol. 1-33 (1904-39), with an *Index* to vol. 1-25; *Bulletin*, vol. 1-4 (1907-12); *News Sheet*, no. 1-55 (1926-40); *Census of Fifteenth Century Books Owned in America* (1919, reprinted from *Bulletin of the New York Public Library* of April-December 1918) edited by George Parker Winship; *Index to Bibliographical Papers Published by the Bibliographical Society and the Library Association 1877-1932*, by George Watson Cole, 1933; *Bibliotheca Americana, Dictionary of Books Relating to America from its Discovery to the Present Time, Begun by Joseph Sabin* . . . vol. 20 pt. 3 - vol. 21 pt. 1, edited by Wilberforce Eames and vol. 21 pt. 2 - vol. 29 by R. W. G. Vail, with Dr. Lydenberg as chairman of the "Sabin Committee"; *American Newspapers 1821-1936, a Union List of Files Available in the United States and Canada*, edited by Winifred Gregory, with Dr. Gerould as chairman of the Society's Committee; *International Congresses, a Union List of their Publications Available in Libraries of the United States and Canada*, edited by Winifred Gregory, 1938, with Dr. Gerould as chairman of the Committee; *Incunabula in American Libraries a Second Census*,* edited by Margaret Bingham Stillwell, with Dr. Wroth as chairman of the "Second Census" Committee.

COMPLETE LIST OF OFFICERS AND COUNCILLORS

Adams, Randolph Greenfield	President, 1940-; Vice-President, 1938-39; 2nd Vice-President, 1937-38
Bain, James	Councillor, 1904-08
Bates, Mary E.	Acting Treasurer, 1936-37
Bishop, William Warner	President, 1921-23; Vice-President, 1909-12, 1920-21
Boyd, Julian Parks	Councillor, 1940-
Brigham, Clarence Saunders	2nd Vice-President, 1916-18
Brigham, Johnson	Councillor, 1913-17
Carlton, William Newnham Chattin	Librarian, 1909-12
Childs, James Bennett	Councillor, 1937-38; Chairman of Publication Committee, 1925-36
Cole, George Watson	President, 1916-21; Councillor, 1921-26 (ex-President)
Cole, Theodore Lee	Councillor, 1907-16
Eames, Wilberforce	Librarian, 1904-09; Chairman of Publication Committee, 1904-09
Faxon, Frederick Winthrop	Treasurer, 1913-36
Finney, Byron Alfred	2nd Vice-President, 1913-14
Ford, Worthington Chauncey	2nd Vice-President, 1910-12; Councillor, 1919-23
Gerould, James Thayer	Councillor, 1935-38; Delegate to American Documentation Institute, 1937-39
Goodspeed, Charles Eliot	Treasurer, 1937-
Gould, Charles Henry	President, 1912-13; 2nd Vice-President, 1912; Councillor, 1913-14 (ex-President)

* Published in November, 1940. — Editor.

Hanson, James Christian Meinich   Vice-President, 1914-16, 1929-33; 2nd Vice-President, 1918-21, 1928-29; Councillor, 1908-13, 1923-28

Harris, George William   Councillor, 1904-06

Haskins, Charles Homer   Vice-President, 1913-14

Hubbard, Lucius Lee   Vice-President, 1922-23

Jackson, William Alexander   2nd Vice-President, 1940-; Councillor, 1938-39

James, William John   2nd Vice-President, 1914-16

Jenkins, Frederick Warren   Vice-President, 1916-17

Johnston, William Dawson   President, 1910-12; 2nd Vice-President, 1909-10; Secretary, 1906-09; Councillor, 1912-13 (ex-President)

Josephson, Aksel Gustav Salomon   Secretary, 1909-12; Councillor (as ex-President BSC) 1904-09; Councillor, 1912-16, 1918-35; Editor, 1916-18

Keogh, Andrew   President, 1913-14; Librarian, 1912-13; Councillor, 1914-16 (ex-President), 1928-33; Delegate to American Council of Learned Societies, 1937-38

Koch, Theodore Wesley   2nd Vice-President, 1926-28; Councillor, 1910-14, 1925-26

Lane, William Coolidge   President, 1904-09; Councillor, 1909-10 (ex-President)

Legler, Henry Eduard   Councillor, 1904-07

Livingston, Luther Samuel   Councillor, 1914

Lydenberg, Harry Miller   President, 1929-31; Vice-President, 1923-26, 1928-29; Councillor, 1931-33 (ex-President), 1933-; Delegate to American Council of Learned Societies, 1928-

Mackall, Leonard Leopold   President, 1936-37; Vice-President, 1935-36; 2nd Vice-President, 1933-35

McKay, George Leslie   Permanent Secretary, 1940-

Martel, Charles   Vice-President, 1926-28; 2nd Vice-President, 1923-26; Councillor, 1916-19

Meyer, Herman Henry Bernard   President, 1926-29; Vice-President, 1923-26, 1928-29; Councillor, 1931-33 (ex-President), 1933-; Delegate to American Council of Learned Societies, 1928-

Nelson, Charles Alexander   Secretary, 1904-06; Councillor, 1906-10

Northup, Clark Sutherland   2nd Vice-President, 1912-13

Paltsits, Victor Hugo   President, 1938-39; 2nd Vice-President, 1921-23; Councillor, 1940- (ex-President)

Plimpton, George Arthur   Councillor, 1919-25

Power, Eugene B.   Delegate to American Documentation Institute, 1940-

Putnam, Herbert   Vice-President, 1904-06

Richardson, Ernest Cushing   2nd Vice-President, 1906-09; Councillor, 1917-37

Roden, Carl Bismarck   President, 1914-16; Treasurer, 1904-13; Librarian, 1913-16; Councillor, 1916-21 (ex-President); Chairman of Publication Committee, 1909-19

Root, Azariah Smith   President, 1909-10, 1923-26; Councillor, 1910-12 (ex-President), 1926-27

Severance, Henry Ormal   Secretary, 1914-19

Shearer, Augustus Hunt   President, 1933-36; Secretary, 1919-33; Councillor, 1936-37 (ex-President), 1937-40

Stephens, Henry Morse   Councillor, 1916-19

Stillwell, Margaret Bingham   2nd Vice-President, 1936-37

Swem, Earl Gregg   President, 1937-38; Vice-President, 1936-37; 2nd Vice-President, 1935-36; Councillor, 1938-39 (ex-President)

Thomson, John   Councillor, 1904-12

Thwaites, Reuben Gould   Vice-President, 1906-09; 2nd Vice-President, 1904-06

Utley, George Burwell   Vice-President, 1933-35

Vail, Robert William Glenroie   Vice-President, 1937-38; Permanent Secretary, 1938-39

Vance, John Thomas   Councillor, 1928-32

Van Hoesen, Henry Bartlett   Secretary, 1933-40; Delegate to American Council of Learned Societies, 1938-

von Noé, Adolf Carl   Secretary, 1912-14

Wagner, Henry Raup   Vice-President, 1940-; 2nd Vice-President, 1939

Wall, Alexander James   Councillor, 1938-
Waters, Willard Otis   Secretary, 1914
Williamson, Charles Clarence   Librarian, 1928-38
Windsor, Phineas Lawrence   2nd Vice-President, 1929-33
Winship, George Parker   Vice-President, 1919-20; Councillor,
                                    1916-18; Chairman of Publication
                                    Committee, 1919-25
Wroth, Lawrence Counselman   President, 1931-33; Councillor, 1933-
                                    36 (ex-President); Chairman of Pub-
                                    lication Comittee, 1936-

A CORRECTION

In *The Papers*, Volume 35, Second Quarter 1941, p. 172, it is errone-
ously stated that the late Augustus H. Shearer became Secretary of our Society in 1912. Dr. Shearer was first elected Secretary at the Society's annual meeting on June 25, 1919.

EDITOR.

Officers and Councillors

of the

Bibliographical Society

of America

	1904-05	1905-06	1906-07	1907-08	1908-09
President	*Lane*	Lane	*Lane*	*Lane*	*Lane*
Vice-President	*Putnam*	Putnam	*Thwaites*	*Thwaites*	*Thwaites*
2nd Vice-President	*Thwaites*	Thwaites	*Richardson*	*Richardson*	*Richardson*
Secretary	*Nelson*	Nelson	*Johnston*	*Johnston*	*Johnston*
Treasurer	*Roden*	Roden	*Roden*	*Roden*	*Roden*
Librarian	*Eames*	Eames	*Eames*	*Eames*	*Eames*
Editor					
Permanent Secretary					
Councillor (Ex-Pres.)	*Josephson*	Josephson	Josephson	Josephson	Josephson
Councillors	*Harris*	Harris			
	Legler	Legler	Legler		
	Thomson	Thomson	Thomson	Thomson	
	Bain	Bain	Bain	Bain*	*Hanson*
			Nelson	Nelson	Nelson
				Cole, T. L.	Cole
					Thomson

| (Note: Italic shows record of election) | Papers 1:25 Printed Ballot | | Papers 1:111, 116 | ALA Bull. 1:294 *d.May1908 | Papers 3:11 |

1909-10	1910-11	1911-12	1912-13	1913-14	1914-15
Root	*Johnston*	Johnston	*Gould*	*Keogh*	*Roden*
Bishop	*Bishop*	Bishop	*Meyer*	*Haskins, C. H.**	*Hanson*
Johnston	*Ford*	*Ford*-Gould*	*Northup*	*Finney*	*James*
Josephson	*Josephson*	Josephson	*von Noé*	*von Noé*	*Waters*-Severance*
Roden	*Roden*	Roden	*Roden*	*Faxon*	Faxon
Eames*-Carlton	*Carlton*	Carlton	*Keogh*	*Roden*	Roden
Lane	Root	Root	Johnston	Gould	Keogh
Nelson					
Cole	Cole				
Thomson	Thomson	Thomson			
Hanson	Hanson	Hanson	Hanson		
	Koch	Koch	Koch	Koch	
		Cole	Cole	Cole	Cole
			Josephson	Josephson	Josephson
				Brigham, J.	Brigham, J.
					Livingston **

Bull.	Bull.	Bull.	Bull.	Papers	Papers
1:54	2:38	4:36	4:34	7:126	8:97
*Resigned July 1909		*Resigned Jan. 1912		*Papers, 7, and Bull. 4:34, read C. S. Haskins	*Resigned (Letter from Mr. Waters) **d. Dec. 1914

	1915-16	1916-17	1917-18	1918-19	1919-20	1920-21
President	Roden	Cole, G.W.	Cole	Cole	Cole	Cole
Vice-President	Hanson	Jenkins	Meyer	Meyer	Winship	Bishop
2nd Vice-President	James	Brigham, C.	Brigham, C.	Hanson	Hanson	Hanson
Secretary	Severance	Severance	Severance	Severance	Shearer	Shearer
Treasurer	Faxon	Faxon	Faxon	Faxon	Faxon	Faxon
Librarian	Roden					
Editor		Josephson	Josephson			
Permanent Secretary						
Councillor (Ex.-Pres.)	Keogh	Roden	Roden	Roden	Roden	Roden

Councillors	1915-16	1916-17	1917-18	1918-19	1919-20	1920-21
	Josephson	Brigham, J.				
	Brigham, J.	Winship	Winship			
	Cole	Martel	Martel	Martel		
		Stephens	Stephens	Stephens*	Plimpton	
			Richardson	Richardson	Richardson	Richardson
				Josephson	Josephson	Josephson
				Ford	Ford	Ford
						Plimpton

	Papers	Papers	Papers	Papers	Papers
	10:168	11:141	12:134	13:152	14:39

* d. 1919

1921-22	1922-23	1923-24	1924-25	1925-26	1926-27	1927-28
Bishop	*Bishop*	*Root*	*Root*	*Root*	Meyer	Meyer
Meyer	*Hubbard*	*Lydenberg*	*Lydenberg*	*Lydenberg*	Martel*	*Martel***
Paltsits	*Paltsits*	*Martel*	*Martel*	*Martel*	Koch	Koch
Shearer	*Shearer*	*Shearer*	*Shearer*	*Shearer*	Shearer	Shearer
Faxon	*Faxon*	*Faxon*	*Faxon*	*Faxon*	Faxon	Faxon
Cole	Cole	Cole*	Cole	Cole		

1921-22	1922-23	1923-24	1924-25	1925-26	1926-27	1927-28
Josephson						
Ford	Ford					
Plimpton	Plimpton	Plimpton				
Richardson	Richardson	Richardson	Richardson			
	Josephson	Josephson	Josephson	Josephson		
		Hanson	Hanson	Hanson	Hanson	
			Plimpton	*Koch*	*Root*	Root*
				Richardson	Richardson	Richardson
					Josephson	Josephson
						Hanson

1921-22	1922-23	1923-24	1924-25	1925-26	1926-27	1927-28
Papers	Papers	Papers	Papers	Papers	LJ	NS 8
15:51	16:65	17:71	18:64	19:78	51:980	*d.Oct.1927
		*Instead of Bishop			*Official Stationery	**Official Stationery

	1928-29	1929-30	1930-31	1931-32	1932-33	1933-34
President	Meyer	Lydenberg	Lydenberg	Wroth	Wroth	Shearer
Vice-President	Lydenberg	Hanson	Hanson	Hanson	Hanson	Utley
2nd Vice-President	Hanson	Windsor*	Windsor	Windsor	Windsor	Mackall
Secretary	Shearer	Shearer	Shearer	Shearer	Shearer	Van Hoesen
Treasurer	Faxon	Faxon	Faxon	Faxon	Faxon	Faxon
Librarian	Williamson	Williamson	Williamson	Williamson	Williamson	Williamson
Editor						
Permanent Secretary						
Councillor (Ex.-Pres.)		Meyer	Meyer	Lydenberg	Lydenberg	Wroth
Councillors	Richardson					
	Josephson	Josephson				
	Vance*	Vance	Vance	Vance		
	Keogh	Keogh	Keogh	Keogh	Keogh	
		Richardson	Richardson	Richardson	Richardson	Richardson
			Josephson	Josephson	Josephson	Josephson
					Meyer	Meyer
						Lydenberg
	NS 11 & 12	NS 16		NS 22	NS 25	NS 30
	*NS has Benz (cf. Archives)	*NS has Williamson. Official Stationery of this year has Windsor.				

1934-35	1935-36	1936-37	1937-38	1938-39	1940	1941
Shearer	*Shearer**	*Mackall**	*Swem*	*Paltsits*	*Adams*	*Adams*
Utley	*Mackall*	*Swem*	*Vail*	*Vail-Adams*	*Wagner*	*Wagner*
Mackall	*Swem*	*Stillwell*	*Adams*	*Adams-Wagner*	*Jackson*	*Jackson*
Van Hoesen	*Van Hoesen*	*Van Hoesen*	*Van Hoesen*	Van Hoesen	*Van Hoesen*	*Vail*
Faxon	*Faxon*	*Faxon**-Bates*(acting)	*Goodspeed*	Goodspeed	*Goodspeed*	*Goodspeed*
Williamson	Williamson	Williamson	Williamson			
				Vail	*McKay*	McKay
Wroth	Wroth	Shearer		Swem	Paltsits	Paltsits

1934-35	1935-36	1936-37	1937-38	1938-39	1940	1941
osephson						
Meyer	Meyer					
ydenberg	Lydenberg	Lydenberg				
Richardson	Richardson	Richardson***	*Childs*			
	Gerould	Gerould	Gerould	Gerould*-*Wall*		
		Meyer****	*Shearer*	Shearer	Shearer	
			Lydenberg	Lydenberg	Lydenberg	Lydenberg
				Jackson	*Wall*	Wall
					Boyd	Boyd
						C. A. Wilson
NS 33	NS 37 & 41	NS 41, 42 & 44	NS 45	NS 49, 50 & 51-52	NS 55	NS 57

*Resigned May 1936

*d. May 1937
**d. Aug. 1936
***Resigned
****d. Jan. 1937

*Resigned

EARLY COPYRIGHT LITIGATION AND ITS BIBLIOGRAPHICAL INTEREST

By R. C. BALD

T HE early history of the Stationers' Company is frequently cited as an illustration of the Tudor genius for compromise, for governmental control of the press was successfully combined with a measure of industrial self-government. During the second half of the sixteenth century and the early part of the seventeenth century the Company exercised a threefold authority: (1) it regulated conditions of production and labor within the trade; (2) it protected the rights of its members in their property; and (3) it acted as the intermediary by which the government controlled the press. But if the seventeenth century is interesting to the political historian for the breakdown of the Tudor compromise it is likewise interesting to the historian of the press for the decline of the Stationers' Company. All three functions just enumerated were either lost or drastically curtailed, and of them the last was the first to go.

During most of the period of the Civil War, Parliament ex-

172

ercised direct control over the press, and after the Restoration it continued to do so by means of the Licensing Act of 1662 which, except for one interval, remained in force until 1693. It is true that even after 1693 the real battle for the freedom of the press had still to be won, but when it was fought out in the eighteenth century the Company had no part in the struggle. The protagonists were Parliament on the one side and a few obstreperous individuals on the other.

The decline of the Company is also to be seen in its Registers, which in the latter part of the seventeenth century record only a fraction of the output of the press. A. W. Pollard has shown that several attempts were made to compel stationers to enter their publications, but without any lasting effect.[1] The trade clearly felt that an entry had lost some of the significance it once possessed, and that it was more important to comply with the regulations about licensing which Parliament had imposed. When the Licensing Act lapsed the stationers, as we shall see, soon found that their Company was incapable of protecting their rights, and the Copyright Act of 1709 was passed by Parliament in response to their repeated petitions.

Still further evidence shows how the Company's control of the trade was relaxing. The careers of Francis Kirkman and Richard Head, co-authors of *The English Rogue*, are instructive. Kirkman, who was active as bookseller and publisher between 1658 and 1680, was never a member of the Stationers' Company. He was a Blacksmith by patrimony, but, as a citizen of London claiming the right to trade freely within the City, he could set up shop and sell books or any other form of merchandise he chose. It is true that he could not enter books in the Stationers' Register, but he could always get his printer to do this if he thought it necessary. On the other hand, Head was a freeman of the Company,[2] and,

[1] *Some Notes on the History of Copyright in England, 1662-1774*. In: *The Library*, III, 1922-23, pp. 97-114.

[2] According to the Freemen's Book he was admitted on June 4, 1660.

though his activities as bookseller and publisher were of the slightest, he sometimes found it useful to be able to enter the books he had written. Clearly, the old guild system was fast breaking down.

During the first century of its existence, however, the Stationers' Company was the main arbiter of disputes as to the "right of copy," the phrase used in Milton's *Aereopagitica* and generally by the stationers. It settled cases arising between its members and enforced its own rights in the "common stock."[3] But there were certain restricted but highly important books, such as Bibles, prayer-books, and statutes, over the printing of which the Company had no control. The right of copy in these had been reserved to the Crown and the printing of them had been vested in a few privileged individuals, such as the King's Printer, by royal patent.[4]

In all these provisions an author had no share. He, of course, made his bargain with a printer, and if he parted with his manuscript for a price he surrendered all further rights in it. Government was concerned only with the control of the printing trade, not with the rewards of authorship. No system of royalties had yet been thought of, but it did occur to an occasional author in the seventeenth century that it might be possible to obtain exclusive rights in his work by means similar to those by which some of the printers had obtained special privileges. In 1618, for instance, the dramatist Thomas Middleton secured a patent conferring on his nominee William Alley the right of sole printing for his tract *The Peacemaker or Great Britain's Blessing* (sometimes ascribed to James I himself), and in the following year it appeared with the phrase "cum privilegio" at the foot of the title-page.[5] Similar patents

[3] W. W. Greg and E. Boswell. *Records of the Court of the Stationers' Company, 1576 to 1602*, pp. xlvi-xlviii and lxiv-lxix. See further C. B. Judge. *Elizabethan Book-Pirates, passim*, and H. R. Hoppe. *John Wolfe, Printer and Publisher*. In: *The Library*, XIV, 1933-34, pp. 241-288.

[4] Greg, *op. cit.*, pp. lxiv-lxv, lists the principal patents in force during the period 1576-1602.

[5] *The Works of Thomas Middleton*, ed. A. H. Bullen, I, pp. xliv-xlvi.

for varying terms of years were secured by Samuel Daniel for his *Collection of the Historie of England*, 1618, by George Sandys for his translation of Ovid's *Metamorphoses*, 1626, and by Sir William Alexander for his *Psalms of King David*, 1628.[6] Historically and legally author's copyright was a monopoly, and it was secured by the same means as any other monopoly.

There is nothing to suggest that any seventeenth-century authors had recourse to the law-courts over the violation of such privileges. In cases of dispute or piracy, all that was usually necessary was that the patentee should present himself and his patent before the Court of the Stationers' Company. Sandys's *Ovid*, for instance, was pirated in 1628 and apparently again in 1631, but on both occasions he obtained speedy redress by appealing to the Court.[7] Even when no patent was involved, it was possible in certain circumstances for an author, or the owner of an unpublished manuscript, if he were sufficiently notable or powerful, to assert his rights. On several occasions the King's Men were successful in preventing the publication of their plays,[8] and the Court Book of the Stationers' Company contains the following minute under the date December 3, 1660:

The Lord Powess haueing heretofore compiled a Romance Entituled & imployed Mr. Griffin at the said Lordships proper charge to print an impression thereof, & haueing lately made some adicions thereto with intent to reprint it at his like chardg came this day to the Court & complained that the widow of Mr. Griffin aforesaid layd claime (by entrance) to the Originall Copie, soe that his Lordship could not proceed in his designe, withall affirming on his Honour (& offering alsoe his Oath) that he never contracted with Mr. Griffin for, or gave him a right in the said Originall, & Mrs. Griffin (now attending) haueing only the entrance of the said booke to offer in behalfe of her title, the Court willing to doe Justice to both partys referred to the whole (by their consent alsoe) to

[6] R. B. Davis. *Early Editions of George Sandys's "Ovid": the Circumstances of Production.* In: *Papers of the Bibliographical Society of America*, XXXV, 1941, pp. 255-76 at p. 267.

[7] *Ibid.*, at pp. 270-71.

[8] *Variorum Shakespeare*, 1821, III, p. 159, and *Malone Society Collections*, I, pp. 364-69.

our Master who was desired to put such finall & speedy issue thereto, as shalbe Just.[9]

But in this case the author was a peer; furthermore, he had not sold his manuscript but had himself defrayed the costs of printing.

It is symptomatic of the decline of the Stationers' Company that after the Restoration lawsuits over books and rights in their publication began to come fairly frequently before the English courts. The Company was apparently no longer capable of settling such disputes by its own authority.[10] Between 1660 and 1709, when the first Copyright Act was passed, at least sixteen suits were brought,[11] and nearly all of them were based on privileges conferred by royal patent.[12] But the patents involved were of much larger scope than those which had been granted to individual authors. The Company itself owed its own privileges to patents; other

[9] Court Book D, fo. 63 a. Manuscript contractions here and elsewhere in this article have been silently expanded.

It is unfortunate that the clerk did not catch the name of the book. The only known work of Percy Herbert, second Baron Powis, is *Certaine Conceptions or Considerations of Sir Percy Herbert upon the strange change of Peoples dispositions and actions in these latter times. Directed to his sonne.* This does not sound like a romance (unless the clerk was being ironical), but it was entered in the Stationers' Register by Edward Griffin on March 27, 1652, and printed by him in the same year. It is quite possibly the book at issue, even though no later edition of it is known.

[10] Greg, *op. cit.*, pp. xlvii and xlviii, mentions several lawsuits between 1576 and 1602 in which both individual stationers and the Company were engaged, but it is clear that this method of settling disputes was exceptional.

[11] *Stationers* v. *Law Patentees*, 1664-67, Carter, p. 89; *Roper* v. *Streater*, 1670, *cit.* 2 Chan. Cases, p. 67, and Skinner, p. 234; *Mayo* v. *Hill*, 1673, *cit.* 2 Show. K. B., p. 260; *Stationers* v. *Seymour*, 1677, 1 Mod., p. 256; *Ponder* v. *Braddill*, 1679, Lilly's Modern Entries, I, p. 67; *Stationers* v. *Marlowe*, 1680, Lilly's Modern Entries, p. 63, and *cit.* 2 Show. K. B., p. 261; *Stationers* v. *Gayne*, 1681, *cit.* 10 Mod., p. 107, and H. R. Plomer's *Dictionary of Printers and Booksellers from 1668 to 1725, sub* Gayne; *Stationers* v. *Lee*, 1681-83, 2 Chan. Cases, pp. 66, 76, 93 and 2 Show. K. B., p. 258; *Stationers* v. *Wright*, 1681-83, *cit.* Skinner, p. 234; *Hill* v. *University of Oxford*, 1684, 1 Vern., p. 275; *Stationers* v. *Parker*, 1685, Skinner, p. 233; *Stationers* v. *Skinner*, 2 Inst., p. 47; *Stationers* v. *Edwards*, 1696, Plomer, *op. cit.*; *Stationers* v. *Wellington*, 1703, Plomer, *op. cit.*; *Stationers* v. *Gwillim*, 1706, Plomer, *op. cit.*; *Stationers* v. *Partridge*, 1712, 10 Mod., p. 105.

[12] "Letters patents or grants of privilege heretofore made or hereafter to be made of, for, or concerning printing" had been specially exempted from the operation of the Statute of Monopolies of 1624 (21 Jac. I, cap. 3, sec. 10).

important grants were held by the two universities, by the King's Printer, and by a certain Colonel Atkins, who had succeeded to the right of printing law books. At one time or another the privileges conferred in all these patents were challenged. But in twelve of the sixteen cases the Stationers' Company brought the action, and in nine out of the twelve they took proceedings against printers and booksellers who had infringed their right to the sole printing of such permanent best sellers as primers, psalms, and almanacs. Thus a large proportion of these suits represent the attempts of the Company to buttress its crumbling authority. Most of them, however, are barren of literary interest, and only two merit further mention.

The Company of Stationers v. *Partridge*[13] is in many respects a typical example of the litigation of the first period, though it dragged on until three years after the passing of the Copyright Act. However, it deserves singling out for two reasons. First, there was the notoriety of the defendant, who had survived the mockery of Swift's attack in *The Bickerstaff Papers* but now had to suffer the humiliation of being charged in his posthumous existence that his prognostications had violated the Company's monopoly of almanacs. Secondly, Partridge fought back harder than many previous defendants had done, for, in spite of earlier decisions, he challenged the legality of the Company's rights. He must have had a good lawyer, since the court was persuaded to say some hard things about monopolies which restricted the liberty of the subject. But no final decision was handed down, and the Stationers, finding that their lucrative privileges were in danger, apparently decided to withdraw their action. The pendulum was swinging so far against them that they could not be sure that the courts would uphold their ancient rights, though, it must be added, it was not till 1775 that a definite decision was given against them on this point.[14]

[13] 10 Mod., p. 105.
[14] *Stationers' Company* v. *Carnan*, 2 Black. Rep., p. 1004.

The earlier case of *Ponder* v. *Braddill*, 1678,[15] is quite exceptional for its time since it is, as far as I know, the only one of its
period in which an individual stationer went to law to assert his
rights in a book he had published in the normal manner. The book
at issue was *The Pilgrim's Progress*. It had been duly licensed and
entered in the Stationers' Register, but Braddill had pirated it
within three months of its publication. Owing to Parliament's
temporary failure to renew the Licensing Act Ponder found that
he could get no redress and was forced to abandon his action. The
Stationers' Company either could not, or would not, help him,
otherwise the action would not have been brought; but, in spite of
the obvious justice of his case, his appeal to the law only seemed
to show that pirates could operate with impunity. The situation
was one that urgently needed a remedy, yet thirty years later
(and fifteen after the Licensing Act had finally lapsed) it was
still so bad that stolen versions of *The Predictions of Isaac Bickerstaff* appeared on the streets a few days after their publication,[16]
and Gay's *Wine* was twice pirated within a year of its appearance.[17]
It is easy to see why the stationers petitioned Parliament to intervene.

The preamble of the Act of 1709 states that "Printers, Booksellers and other Persons have of late frequently taken the Liberty of printing, reprinting and publishing . . . Books and other
Writings, without the Consent of the Authors and Proprietors . . .
to their very great Detriment," and therefore that it is necessary
to prevent "such Practices for the future." Accordingly, the Act
granted twenty-one years' copyright to the owners of works already in print, but only fourteen years to books published after it
came into force, though if the author were still alive at the expiration of the term his right reverted to him and he could dis-

---

[15] Lilly's *Modern Entries*, I, p. 67, and F. M. Harrison. *Nathaniel Ponder: the
Publisher of The Pilgrim's Progress*. In: *The Library*, XV, 1934-35, pp. 257-94, at
p. 270.

[16] *The Prose Works of Jonathan Swift*, ed. H. Davis, II, pp. xii-xiii.

[17] W. H. Irving. *John Gay, Favorite of the Wits*, pp. 32-33.

pose of it for another fourteen years. Piracy was to be punished by the confiscation of all the unauthorized copies and by a penalty at the rate of a penny for each sheet seized. The copyright was granted, of course, to the author or his assigns, but a book was almost invariably assigned before publication. Thus the main effect of the Act, in spite of its being called an Act for the Encouragement of Learning, was to establish the rights of the booksellers.[18]

Not unnaturally, the number of lawsuits died down for some years after 1709, but when the copyright periods had expired they began to multiply again. The second of the two periods of litigation with which this paper deals extended to 1774, when the famous case of *Donaldson* v. *Becket* decided that the common-law right of perpetual copyright which the booksellers still claimed had, if it ever existed, been abolished by the specific provisions of the Act. There were, of course, numerous books in which rights had passed by assignment from one stationer to another for the better part of a century before 1709,[19] and the trade seems to have

[18] According to tradition Swift was mainly responsible for the drafting of this Act (though it was amended in committee), and Addison is also said to have had a hand in it. See A. Birrell. *Seven Lectures on Copyright*, pp. 20, 93, 128.

If Swift were in any way responsible for the Act he was soon to find that he was far from having provided adequate protection for all an author's rights. In 1710 Edmund Curll published *The Complete Key to the Tale of a Tub*, attributing it to Swift and his cousin Thomas; Swift wrote bitterly, "It is strange that there can be no satisfaction against a bookseller for publishing names in so bold a manner. I wish some lawyer could advise you how I might have satisfaction; for at this rate there is no book, however vile, which may not be fastened on me." In the following year, when Curll published his unauthorized edition of Swift's *Miscellanies*, Swift again wrote, this time to Stella, "That villain Curll has scraped up some trash, and calls it Dr. Swift's Miscellanies, with the name at large, and I can get no satisfaction of him. Nay, Mr. Harley told me he had read it, and only laughed at me before Lord-Keeper and the rest." (Quoted by R. Straus. *The Unspeakable Curll*, p. 35.)

[19] The extent of these claims is well illustrated by an incident which occurred late in the seventeenth century. In 1693 Sir Roger L'Estrange proposed to bring out a new translation of Josephus, but a group of booksellers who owned the rights in an earlier translation advertised as follows: "This is to caution all *Booksellers* and *Printers* from being concern'd therein; it being the Resolution of the Proprietors of the present *English Copy*, to use all lawful Means to vindicate their Right, and recover Satisfaction for the Damages they shall sustain by this New Undertaking; they and their Predecessors having been in just and quiet Possession of the same for near One Hundred Years." See A. W. Pollard. *Copyright in Josephus.* In: *The Library*, 3rd series, VII, 1917, pp. 134-35.

assumed in all good faith that it could continue this practice. For a time, too, the courts accepted this assumption, though without actually giving a definite ruling, until the protests of the "have-nots" eventually forced a decision. Meanwhile, it is important to note that the litigants of the second period were individuals—authors as well as publishers—with definite statutory rights. They did not go any longer for protection to the Company, but to the courts, and the Company was not concerned with such disputes except in so far as entry in its Register constituted formal notification of copyright under the Act.

Lawsuits became frequent again in the 20's and 30's of the century. Piracy was still common, and the success of the Dublin booksellers, who were beyond the reach of English law and could pilfer at will,[20] acted as an incentive to the less scrupulous of their English rivals. The machinery provided by the Copyright Act for dealing with piracy proved cumbrous and inefficient. As a result, remedies were sought not in the courts of law, which could only administer the provisions of the Act, but in Chancery. The Court of Chancery had much wider discretionary powers. If the plaintiff could show that a presumptive right existed and that it was being injured, or was likely to be injured, the Court would immediately issue an interim injunction against the defendant. This injunction remained in force until the case came on for hearing, and only then could the plaintiff's right be challenged. However, the hearing might not occur till several years later, and there was the further possibility that points of law would be sent to one of the common-law courts for argument and decision before the Chancellor would give judgment. Usually an interim injunction was enough to quell a pirate. Quite apart from the legal costs involved, the case was not worth fighting out; to-day's best

[20] It should be added that the English booksellers retaliated by appropriating books published in Dublin. In his preface to his reprint of the Dublin edition of Swift's *Literary Correspondence*, 1741, Curll wrote: "As to the present Case, it is well known, that the Dublin Edition of these Letters is Lawful-Prize here, and whatever we print is the same there." (Quoted by Straus, *op. cit.*, p. 193.)

seller is likely to be a drug on the market in five years' time.

Many of the cases of this second period have no interest whatever for the lawyer; they added nothing to the interpretation of the law, because they never got further than the preliminary injunction. Where the piracy was a blatant infringement of the copyright term, there was usually no reason why the case should go any further. But when the period granted by the Act had expired the situation was different. At first defendants submitted to the interim injunctions, but eventually the subject of perpetual copyright became a topic of widespread public debate, and it was really a series of mishaps that prevented it from being settled by the courts until 1774. However, many of the cases have an interest quite apart from their legal significance, since the proportion of important literary works that were the subject of litigation is surprisingly large. Proceedings against unauthorized printing soon after the original publication were taken on behalf of Steele's *Conscious Lovers*,[21] Pope and Swift's *Miscellanies*,[22] Pope's *Dunciad*,[23] Johnson's *Rasselas*,[24] Richardson's *Pamela*,[25] and Fielding's *Joseph Andrews*,[26] while among the books fought over after the copyright period had expired were *Paradise Lost* (twice),[27] *The Spectator*,[28] and Thomson's *Seasons*.[29]

In another group of cases the author or his heirs appeared as plaintiffs, usually seeking to restrain a publisher from printing manuscripts without their consent. In the earliest of these cases[30]

[21] *Tonson* v. *Clifton*, 1722, *cit.* 2 Brown, p. 138.

[22] *Motte* v. *Faulkner*, 1735, *cit.* 4 Burr., p. 2325.

[23] *Gilliver* v. *Snaggs*, 1729, Viner's Abridgement, p. 278.

[24] *Dodsley* v. *Kinnersley*, 1761, Amb., p. 403.

[25] *Richardson's case*, 1740, *cit.* 2 Eq. Cas. Abr., p. 523.

[26] *Millar* v. *Lynch*, 1742, *cit.* 2 Eq. Cas. Abr., p. 523.

[27] *Tonson* v. *Walker*, 1739, *cit.* 4 Burr., p. 2325; *Tonson* v. *Walker*, 1752, 3 Swans., p. 762.

[28] *Tonson* v. *Collins*, 1760, 1 Black., pp. 301, 321.

[29] *Millar* v. *Taylor*, 1769, 4 Burr., p. 2303;. *Donaldson* v. *Becket*, 1774, 2 Brown, p. 129.

[30] *Burnet* v. *Chetwood*, 1720, 2 Mer., p. 441.

the book concerned was Thomas Burnet's *Archaeologia Philosophica*, a book still remembered because it supplied Coleridge with the motto for *The Ancient Mariner*. George Burnet, executor of the author, obtained an injunction against an English translation that had been announced. Pope, as is well known, sued Curll over the publication of his letters, and secured an injunction against the parts of the volume he had written, but not against those written to him by others.[31] Gay's nephew and executor, Joseph Baller, inherited a whole batch of suits arising out of the piracy of *Polly*.[32] The trouble here arose partly out of the fact that Gay's original subscription edition, "printed for the author," had never been entered in the Stationers' Register as provided for by the Act, but the courts had the liberality to decide that failure to enter did not destroy the author's copyright. The Duke of Queensberry went to law over the unauthorized publication of Clarendon's *Life*,[33] and in 1770 the actor-dramatist Charles Macklin tried to stop the publication of his successful farce *Love a-la-Mode*.[34]

Three cases have been selected for fuller description in order to illustrate as many as possible of the characteristics already mentioned. Each of them also contributes a certain amount of information which students of eighteenth-century literature seem not to have been aware of, and each of them puts the bibliographer on his mettle to identify the editions to which they refer.

In *Tonson* v. *Tooke* (sometimes called *Tonson* v. *Clifton*) Jacob Tonson the younger, in a bill filed on December 7, 1722,[35] stated that by deed poll dated October 20 last Sir Richard Steele had agreed, in consideration of the sum of £40, to assign him all the rights to *The Conscious Lovers*. This is interesting, for we know that as early as March 1 Lintot had advanced Tonson £25 for

[31] *Pope* v. *Curll*, 1741, 2 Atk., p. 342.
[32] *Baller* v. *Walker*, 1737, *cit.* 2 Atk., p. 93.
[33] *Duke of Queensberry* v. *Shebbeare*, 1758, 2 Eden, p. 329.
[34] *Macklin* v. *Richardson*, 1770, Ambl., p. 694.
[35] P. R. O., Chancery Bills, C. 11, 690/21.

"half of Sir Richard Steele's play that was to be published," and on October 26, six days after Tonson actually acquired the play, agreed to pay him £70 for "the half of the Conscious Lovers." [36] Tonson had thus made a handsome profit even before the presses started to work. The bill goes on to recite that Tonson duly entered the play in the Stationers' Register, proceeded to print "many Thousand Copys" of it, and had since sold a good part of them. However, Francis Clifton, Robert Tooke, John Lightbody, and Susanna Collins (the second and third names are later insertions wherever they occur) had bought a copy of Tonson's printed edition, had printed several hundred copies of it, and had given notice of publication on Monday next. If, as is asserted,[37] the original publication took place on December 1, six days before Tonson's bill was filed, this was quick work. The only answer was from Tooke, who made a complete denial of everything alleged against him, and was perhaps wrongly brought into the case. Tonson secured his injunction on December 11,[38] and thus the matter ended.

The bill in the first case of *Tonson* v. *Walker*[39] alleges that in March, 1739, various advertisements appeared announcing the publication in twelve weekly parts, at 2d. a part, of a new edition of *Paradise Lost*, with a Life of Milton and a set of plates. In most of the advertisements interested persons were invited to apply to "J. Stanton Distiller and Printer in Fleet Lane London," but an advertisement in *The Kentish Post* for April 4 revealed to the anxious Tonsons the true identity of the pirate: "The printer of the above work," it stated, "is R. Walker in Fleet Lane London, and such persons as are inclinable to take this in are desired to speak to J. Abree in Canterbury or his Newsmen who serve the History of the Bible and other Books published Weekly in Numbers." By

[36] J. Nichols. *Literary Anecdotes*, VIII, p. 303.
[37] G. A. Aitken. *The Life of Richard Steele*, II, p. 276.
[38] 2 Brown, p. 138.
[39] C. 12, 1214/66.

April 12 the Tonsons and their partners had launched their action;[40] their long and elaborate bill was filed on the 17th; and on May 5, after four numbers of Walker's publication had appeared, the Lord Chancellor ordered that

> an Injunction be awarded against the said Defendant Robert Walker otherwise James Stanton his Servants Agents or Workmen from printing publishing selling or disposing of the said book or poem intitled paradise Lost or the life of the said John Milton composed by the said Elijah Fenton untill the said Defendant shall fully answer the plaintiff's bill and this Court take order to the Contrary.[41]

Tonson's rights to *The Conscious Lovers* were clearly unchallengeable, and Walker made no attempt in 1739 to test further the legality of the firm's claim to *Paradise Lost*. In 1751, however, he printed *Paradise Lost* once more; another action was brought, and this time the case came up for hearing. But Walker had been ill-advised enough to print, besides the text of the poem, the introduction and notes from the latest Tonson edition; since these last were unquestionably within the statute, Walker quite properly lost the case, and the Court was relieved of the responsibility of deciding the major issue.[42]

I have not been able to make certain whether any copies of the edition of *The Conscious Lovers* that was complained of escaped the net cast about it by the injunction, but the British Museum certainly possesses Walker's 1739 edition of *Paradise Lost*; what is more, instead of containing a mere four parts, it is complete. Walker may have come to terms with the Tonsons by agreeing to pay them a share of his profits, but he is just as likely to have gone ahead surreptitiously in defiance of the injunction. A number of ornaments which frequently occur in Walker's other publications are to be found in this edition,[43] which can easily be recognized by

[40] *Chancery Register of Affadavits*, C. 41/50, no. 1094.

[41] *Register of Chancery Decrees and Orders*, C. 33/372, fo. 208 *b*.

[42] *Tonson* v. *Walker*, 1752, 3 Swans., p. 672.

[43] This statement is made on the authority of Mr. G. E. Dawson, of the Folger Shakespeare Library, who has made a special study of Walker and his Shakespearian piracies.

its evasive imprint: "London: Printed for a Company of Stationers. MDCCXXXIX."

Walker's imprint seems to have been imitated from an earlier one used on the same work, for there is an edition of *Paradise Lost* with the imprint "London, Printed for the Company, MDCC-XXX." Its title-page also bears a scroll-work device in which the design is based on the intertwined letters T and J, and in the British Museum there is an edition of Steele's *Conscious Lovers*, dated 1723, on which the same monogram appears, though here the imprint is "London, Printed for T. Johnson." This cannot be the edition complained of in *Tonson* v. *Tooke*, since Thomas Johnson was an English bookseller at The Hague (not Amsterdam, as Plomer's *Dictionary* asserts), where he had been active since 1710. Johnson's London imprints suggest a specific intent to deceive; in Holland he was beyond the reach of English legal processes, and his editions were doubtless designed for smuggling into England as well as for lawful sale on the Continent.

It is impossible to leave consideration of *Paradise Lost* without mentioning that the bill in the first case of *Tonson* v. *Walker* contains a complete history of the rights in the poem from the original assignment on April 27, 1667, down to the time when the action was begun. From Symonds, the original assignee, they passed in 1680 to Brabazon Aylmer; from him Jacob Tonson the elder secured first one half, and then the other; but in 1704 he parted with a quarter to Richard Wellington. By 1739 this quarter-share had been divided up amongst no less than ten booksellers, who were all joined to the action as plaintiffs. John New and James Hutton each had an interest of one 36th; Samuel Birt, Edward Wickstead, and Richard Chandler one 72nd each; Richard Wellington Jr. and Bethell Wellington five 108ths each; Aaron Ward eleven 432nds; John Brindley five 216ths; and John Oswald five 432nds! The copyright of *Paradise Lost* was evidently of considerable value if such small shares of it were held, and one recalls that old Jacob Tonson, on being asked what poem he ever got the most by, immediately replied, "*Paradise Lost.*" [44]

The third case is *Macklin* v. *Richardson.*[45] Macklin wrote his successful farce *Love a-la-Mode* in 1759, but he refused to authorize its publication until 1793, in his extreme old age, when he could no longer act in it. Nevertheless, the first act was printed in *The Court Miscellany or Gentlemen and Lady's New Magazine* for April, 1766, with a statement that the second act would appear next month. Macklin promptly obtained an injunction, with the result that some copies of the magazine contain a cancel where the play should be, and when the case came on for hearing four years later the injunction was made perpetual. The bill tells how the text of the play was secured. The defendants, Richardson and Urquhart, had "employed one Gurney to go to the playhouse and take down the words of the farce from the mouths of the actors, for which they paid him a guinea. Having so done, and corrected his notes from the memory of the defendant Urquhart, they published the first Act." The shorthand writer was either Thomas Gurney (1705-70), the first official shorthand writer in England to be appointed to Parliament and the law courts, or Joseph Gurney (1744-1815), who was first assistant and then successor to his father. Nevertheless, the text produced by Gurney with Urquhart's assistance is markedly inferior to that put out by the author in 1793.

Love a-la-Mode was published on various occasions before 1793 both in London and Dublin, the earliest edition apparently being that of 1779. Such editions as I have seen give substantially the same text of the first act as *The Court Miscellany* had done, and their second act is by no means identical with that afterwards published by Macklin. In spite of the Court of Chancery and its injunctions, Richardson and Urquhart evidently waited quietly for a while before disposing of their text, and it was in print for at

[44] *Spence's Anecdotes*, ed. S. W. Singer, p. 344.
[45] Ambl., p. 694.

least fourteen years before the author consented to the publication of the play.[46]

It seems certain that Chancery proceedings such as have been described were only partially successful in stopping piracy. Copies of pirated editions will never, of course, be as numerous as those of authorized ones, but it is usually possible to find and identify them. I admit that I do not know of a copy of the pirated *Joseph Andrews* of 1742, and only one copy of the pirated *Pamela* of 1740 has been recorded.[47] Nor have bibliographers yet been able to identify Braddill's editions of *Pilgrim's Progress*, in spite of Ponder's very precise description of the differences between the true and the false ones. Yet a glance through the list of translations of Burnet's works shows that the injunction in *Burnet* v. *Chetwood* had very little effect, and every eighteenth-century bibliographer knows of the existence of the pirated editions of *The Dunciad* and *Polly*. It is true that a piracy of *Paradise Lost* in 1739 or 1751 is utterly irrelevant to an editor of Milton, and it may seem to have nothing even for the bibliographer except the fun of identifying it. Yet every imprint, every ornament, or every type face may reveal something of a pirate's methods and activities, and it is essential to the preparation of accurate texts of a number of important eighteenth-century works that piracies should be identified and eliminated. No other source of information helps to do this so much as the lawsuits to which some of them gave rise.

[46] The view expressed here as to the relations of the texts of *Love a-la-Mode* differs somewhat from that held by W. Matthews in *The Piracies of Macklin's Love a-la-Mode*, in *R. E. S.*, X, 1934, pp. 311-18. Since the earliest authorized version of the play has disappeared (for it is not to be found in the Larpent Collection), it is probable that the question will always remain an open one.

[47] W. M. Sale, Jr. *Samuel Richardson*, p. 16. It is worth recording that another famous novel of the period was also pirated. A recent English bookseller's catalogue contained the following item: "Goldsmith, O. *The Vicar of Wakefield*, possibly a pirated edition . . . 2 vols. in 1, 12mo., old calf. 'London' (no printer's name), 'Printed in the Year 1766.'" I was unable to secure the book, and do not know whether it was the cause of legal proceedings.

PROBLEMS IN THE BIBLIOGRAPHICAL DESCRIPTION OF NINETEENTH-CENTURY AMERICAN BOOKS*

By Jacob Blanck

WHEN it was suggested that I make some remarks on the problems involved in the bibliographical description of nineteenth-century American books, I was at first inclined to dismiss the idea with the statement that the existing problems were so few and so trivial that they were hardly worth discussion. But that first inclination, like most snap judgments in bibliography, failed to stand up in the face of examination. In fact, the more consideration I gave the subject, the more I became convinced that one who attempts a bibliography of almost any nineteenth-century American author has embarked on a task that may prove endless.

Compared with such riddles as *The Vicar of Wakefield*, with its many textual points; or compared with *The Pickwick Papers* or *Vanity Fair*, this may seem a somewhat exaggerated statement. Nevertheless, if one wishes to pair these problems of English publications with American, it would not be inappropriate to compare Washington Irving's *Sketch Book*, in the original seven paper-covered parts, with *Pickwick*. And, as bibligraphical puzzles, *The Vicar of Wakefield* and *Huckleberry Finn* make good companions. Also, we may compare the problem of nineteenth-century American books with that offered by incunabula, for in both of these fields the bibliographer encounters difficulties that are

* Read at the Society's meeting held in Chicago, December 30, 1941.

worth the attention of a Hain or of any of the gentlemen who were the founding members of the Roxburghe Club.

And so after some thought, I came to the conclusion that there were two special problems that confront the bibliographer of nineteenth-century American books: first, changes in manufacturing methods; second, scarcity of large collections of American first editions due to the indifference of collectors and institutions. I hasten to add that this latter condition has changed considerably during the past twenty years.

Let us consider the first of these problems and see how it affects the technical description of books. First, we must agree that it is not sufficient to translate the physical form of a book into familiar bibliographical symbols. One may describe to perfection a pamphlet of seven leaves, but until the bibliographer can explain that seventh leaf the collation is incomplete. Is the seventh leaf the result of its excised conjugate? Or is it the result of an insert? In order to answer the question there must be some knowledge of the conditions under which the pamphlet in question was produced. As R. F. Roberts wrote recently, the mere fact of having square brackets on your typewriter doesn't make you a bibliographer.

The nineteenth century began with the birth of the industrial era. Steam, after long experimentation, had been harnessed; electricity was becoming the study of practical men rather than the toy of the philosophic. The individual artisan was engaged in a losing struggle with the mill and the factory. In short, the industrial era was at the beginning of flood tide, and fantastic predictions were made and believed. The turn of the century was witnessing the birth of an era that would eventually boast its ability to produce a million intricate machines, one differing by not the slightest from the other. Mass production, with all its connotations, not the least of which is uniformity, was the inevitable, if not the conscious, goal. The craftsman was to be finally submerged, and in his place the machine was to appear. Theoretically, our productions were to be manufactured like so many cookies cut by the same form, but whether or not this happened we shall see presently.

If this condition, this striving after mass uniformity, affected life in general, the book was not to escape the change. And here we have the first problem of the bibliographer who approaches nineteenth-century American books.

While the bibliographer who works with the earlier books has but the product of movable types with which to contend, the research worker who attempts nineteenth-century American bibliography must take into account the processes of stereotyping and electrotyping and, later, of linotype, monotype and the other mechanical devices that were introduced during the nineteenth century. By the time that century ended it had become possible to manufacture a book in which every step in production, from typesetting to binding, could be done by machine. Mechanization of book production was carried to its logical end; certain publishers established what may be properly called factories for the purpose of writing the romances that the presses so copiously produced. Staffs, working on a weekly basis, produced dozens of novels which were issued under a common pseudonym. It has been rumored that Jack London and Sir James M. Barrie, at one time or another, were workers in such factories, but thus far no evidence, pro or con, has been produced. It has been definitely established, however, that Upton Sinclair did such work.[1]

A not unrelated problem is that of pseudonyms. The late Edmund Lester Pearson once wrote that "it was an age when a fictitious name was part of the equipment of half the authors. And a room in the psychopathic ward awaits anyone who tries to unravel

---

[1] Upton Sinclair wrote several juvenile thrillers for Street & Smith. As *Ensign Clarke Fitch* he wrote *A Soldier Monk*, New York [1899]; *Clif: The Naval Cadet*, New York [1903], both appearing in the "Columbia Library Series." As *Lieut. Frederick Garrison* he wrote *Off For West Point*, New York [1903], published as part of the "Boys' Own Library Series."

their mystifications." [2] All these factors, the mechanization of printing, typesetting, binding and writing, *must* be recognized when one considers the bibliography of the nineteenth century. These are problems, with the exception of the pseudonym, that in no way affect the bibliographer who concerns himself with the preceding centuries. And thus it is that the industrialism of the nineteenth century, with all its pride in assembly line uniformity, increased, rather than decreased, the problems of the bibliographer.

The printer of the preceding centuries had a limited supply of type, so limited, in fact, that more often than not, in the event he had undertaken a book of some size, it was necessary to print the first few gatherings, distribute the type, reset, and then print the succeeding gatherings; the process was repeated until the entire book was printed. Moreover, if the book was unusually large — the 1647 folio of Beaumont and Fletcher provides an excellent example — the publisher might break the text down into several comparatively small takes and give each to a different printer. In this manner several printers working independently would turn out their allotted portions, and eventually all the sheets would be brought together as a bound unit.

The important point here is that, under either circumstance, once a book was printed the printers could not afford to keep their types standing in the hope of a second printing. To have done so might conceivably have meant that there would have been no types available for whatever other work was forthcoming. In the case of the printer who was obliged to distribute his type after printing but a few gatherings, the picture is even clearer. What we have in his case is a single printing with no changes save those inevitable corrections and alterations that so often occurred, and still occur, during the course of printing. Thus when the available stock of a book was exhausted and the market required additional copies, the latter had to be printed from completely reset types;

[2] *Dime Novels* . . . , Boston, 1929, pp. 21-22.

and such new editions were readily distinguishable from the old ones.

The nineteenth-century printer, on the other hand, was seldom exposed to the same set of circumstances. The greater portion of the books that concern this discussion were printed and published in the great centers of the Eastern seaboard: Boston, Philadelphia and New York, cities where the printing press had been in operation before the end of the 1600's. By the time the industrial era of the nineteenth century steamed into existence, these centers not only had enough type for normal production but, and this is important, by 1815 they had adopted the newly introduced method of stereotyping and could thus release their types for other jobs.[3] The stereotype plates remained and from them thousands of books were reprinted during the course of months or years. The machine age had arrived. Uniformity had come to book manufacture. And so, while the student of early books may very often turn to his colophon, with its explicit statement as to time of printing, and thus establish priorities of issue, or secure the same information from the title-page, how is the bibliographer to distinguish the reprints of the nineteenth-century American publisher if the latter merely reprinted from plates without so much as a reprint notice? Unfortunately that is just what too often happened.

Let us jump to the latter part of the century and take a horrible example of nineteenth-century publishing—let us take, for example, Daniel Lothrop of Boston, who, under the original firm

[3] "Stereotyping by plaster was brought to . . . [the United States] . . . by David Bruce in 1813."—*The New International Encyclopaedia*, Second Edition, New York, 1935, Vol. 19, p. 217.

"School editions of the New Testament in bourgeois, and the Bible in nonpareil (1814-15) were their [David and George Bruce's] first stereotype works; and subsequently the earlier issues of the American Bible Society, as well as a series of Latin classics, were also produced."—*The National Cyclopaedia of American Biography*, New York, 1909, Vol. 11, p. 274.

"In America, stereotyping was introduced by David Bruce (1813) who served his apprenticeship in Edinburgh. The first book stereotyped in the United States was the Westminster Catechism, printed by John Watts in 1813."—*The Encyclopaedia Britannica*, Fourteenth Edition, Vol. 18, p. 504.

name of D. Lothrop & Company, was probably the worst offender in a century noted for cheap paper and shoddy printing. Lothrop, as the publisher of a magazine for juveniles, hit upon the happy device of so printing his magazine from plates that, once the plates had been used for the purposes of his magazine, they could be broken down into book-page size and used for the manufacture of books. It was his almost invariable practice not to date title-pages, which sly trick was presumed to conceal the age of the book from the unsuspecting. Under these circumstances he issued in 1881 his most successful book, *Five Little Peppers and How They Grew*, published soon after his marriage to the author.* During the first fifteen years of the book's existence an average of a thousand copies a week were sold, a total of 1,090,000 copies; and during the first few months of this period the book was issued with no readily apparent change in format and imprint.

Here, then, is a typical example of the possibilities of book manufacture during the nineteenth century, and it presents a fairly common problem that is totally unknown to the bibliographer of the earlier days of handset type. Because of certain changes we have been able to identify the first printing of *Five Little Peppers*,[4] and but for these it would be difficult indeed to describe the first printing in accepted bibliographical form. Thus, we are obliged to go back to the point mentioned earlier: It is not a question of merely describing what we see; it is rather the problem of interpreting the physical facts of the book. To do this requires some knowledge of the conditions under which the book

* The book was received at the Copyright Office Otcober 13, 1881; Daniel Lothrop and Harriet Mulford Stone ("Margaret Sidney") were married October 4, 1881.

[4] The text of the reprints was revised extensively. Italics, which are quite frequent in the first printing are, more often than not, changed to roman in the reprints. For ready identification the following points are given: 1st printing: p. 7 (being the first page of text), last line ends: " . . . little Pep-"; p. 231, the caption reads: ". . . said Polly." Later printings read (at points indicated): ". . . and the little"; ". . . said Phronsie." The first printing carries an 1880 copyright notice, later changed to 1881 and still later 1880! As late as 1902 the book was issued from the original unrevised plates with an 1880 copyright notice. The latter bears the imprint of one of the successor firms and can, therefore, be identified as a reprint.

was produced; requires some acquaintance with the methods and shortcuts attempted by the nineteenth-century printer or publisher.

At this time I would like to make brief mention of an important contribution to bibliography that has been of immeasurable help in cutting through the confusion caused by printing methods similar to Lothrop's. I refer to what is commonly called "the broken-type theory," a system so revealing and so simple that it must, eventually, be generally accepted. Its great exponent was the late Merle Johnson,[5] and, as one who has made an attempt to continue his research, I can state that many of his conclusions, based wholly on the examination of type, have since been proved correct by the discovery of less tenuous points. Briefly, the theory is this: that as type or plates are used in the printing of a book, certain wear must of necessity occur. In the ordinary course of printing, quite often the metal becomes chipped or broken due to any number of possible causes. If it is suspected that a book exists in two or more states it becomes fairly obvious that copies with unbroken type, or the copies showing evidence of least wear, preceded those copies with type defects—or the evidence of continued printing. The theory does not assert, as some allege, that broken or worn type is proof positive of a reprint. We know that some books were first printed from battered type, *Huckleberry Finn* being an example. The study of the printed page can and does reveal much to the trained eye, and any bibliographer who is instinctively certain that two books under observation are of two different printings will do well to consult a practical printer who can point out evidences of wear if they are not sufficiently apparent to the bibliographical eye. Among the books whose status has been clarified by this method is Louisa M. Alcott's *An Old-*

---

[5] Prior to his death in 1935, Merle Johnson discussed the theory at length and with anyone willing to listen. So far as I know Johnson mentioned his theory in print but twice: in the introductions to *American First Editions* (revised edition), New York, 1932, and to *High Spots of American Literature*, New York, 1929.

Fashioned Girl, and Stephen Crane's *The Red Badge of Courage.* It is worth mentioning that this same method of detection is an accepted fact, and not a theory, in print collecting and philately. It is one of the tools that the bibliographer of nineteenth-century American books will do well to study—especially if he is to unravel the typographical antics of such publishers as Daniel Lothrop.

The second obstacle that has impeded the fuller development of nineteenth-century American bibliography is indifference. Obviously one cannot describe a book unless it can be located. Like Dame Hannah Glasse's recipe for rabbit pasty: first catch your rabbit. The bibliographer who ventures into the earlier period has a tremendous body of information on which he may build. The bibliographers who preceded him have cleared a path which, while it may not be a broad highway, is something more than a footpath in the wilderness. Nineteenth-century American first editions, until quite recently, were the stepchildren of bibliophily, and cross-eyed stepchildren at that.

It was not until P. K. Foley published his epochal *American Authors* in 1897 that the collecting of American first editions started to come into its own. Some years before Foley, in 1885, the mysterious Leon brothers issued the first catalogue to be devoted in its entirety to American first editions, as opposed to Americana. The publication was such an event that the publishers issued the catalogue not only in an ordinary edition but also in a de luxe large-paper edition printed on Whatman paper. In a sense, this catalogue was the first bibliography of American first editions, for the compilers listed all the known works of their chosen authors whether or not the titles were in the shop's stock. The Leons, so far as we know, issued no other catalogue, and vanished. Eight years later, in 1893, Herbert S. Stone published his *First Editions of American Authors,* and in the introduction to that book Eugene Field, one of the earliest collectors of nineteenth-century American authors, mentions eighty collectors by name, of which number but three or four were collecting nineteenth-century American first editions.

But Foley was the great milestone. And he came decades ahead of his time, for American first editions were not actively collected until the 1920's. True, Foote had appeared,[6] and Arnold[7] and Chamberlain and Maier,[8] but they were solitary voices among bibliophiles. It was in 1910-20 that collectors in more generality began to discover American first editions—and also discovered that for the most part they were totally or inadequately described. True, Sabin and Evans were partially available, but Sabin was not to be completed until 1936, and Evans, to this day, has not progressed in its chronological arrangement into the nineteenth century. Furthermore, these were not, essentially, tools for the collector of first editions in general, but designed primarily as aids to the collector of pure Americana. There were the trade catalogues compiled by Roorbach, Kelly and Leypoldt, but these were trade publications, of tremendous value to the research worker, but not manuals for the collector. There were some few single-author bibliographies, a few exhibition catalogues, and little else. On the other hand, there were hundreds of tools devoted to early printed books and to British and Continental authors.

To demonstrate the small esteem in which the average collector held American first editions, let us consider Seymour de Ricci's *The Book Collector's Guide*, published twenty years ago by The Rosenbach Company.[9] This compilation, subtitled "a practical handbook of British and American bibliography," was advertised as a list of books "which fashion and the verdict of bibliophiles have decided to be the most desirable for an enlightened

---

[6] Sale, Nov. 23, 1894.

[7] Sale, Jan. 30-31, 1901.

[8] Chamberlain sale, Feb. 16-17, 1909. A second sale, of duplicates and lesser authors, on Nov. 4-5, 1909, should not be overlooked. The Maier sale, Nov. 16-17, 1909, marked the nadir of values of first editions of American books.

[9] Philadelphia and New York: The Rosenbach Company, 1921.

collector." An enlightened collector . . . . ! The book consists of 649 pages, of which a scant thirty—about five per cent of the whole—are devoted to American first editions. It may be argued, with some reason, that since American literature was but a youngster, the disparity was natural. But that argument, valid though it may be, does not explain why the *total* space allotted to Mark Twain, James Fenimore Cooper, Walt Whitman, John Greenleaf Whittier and Edgar Allan Poe should have been about five pages in the aggregate—less than one per cent of the whole book —while at least that much space was given to George Meredith, a like amount to Oscar Wilde, and 11 and 14 pages to Robert Louis Stevenson and Algernon Charles Swinburne, respectively. Of even greater significance is the fact that the list makes no mention of the earlier American authors, such as Charles Brockden Brown, Susanna Rowson or the author of *The Power of Sympathy*. The nineteenth-century authors who are not mentioned at all make an impressive list, including Louisa May Alcott, Thomas Holley Chivers, Richard Henry Dana, Jr., Henry William Herbert, Francis Parkman, Emily Dickinson and—Herman Melville.

It is not my intention—especially in these days—to suggest that this condition was the result of an anti-American conspiracy, but I do offer the fact as evidence that the indifference to American first editions and the consequent absence of collections devoted to them constitute a problem that only time and the activities of the collector can remedy. Without benefit of numerous collections, or the observations of collectors, the bibliographer must start from scratch—a joyous enough undertaking but somewhat tempered when it is discovered that certain books must remain undescribed because they cannot be located. The situation has changed, but the change has been made, in the main, within the past twenty years. Collections such as those assembled by Walter T. Wallace, Stephen H. Wakeman (the greatest of all), Carroll A. Wilson, Parkman D. Howe, Frank J. Hogan, Owen

Aldis, J. K. Lilly, Jr., Owen D. Young and W. T. H. Howe are rare.

Thus these two factors, manufacturing methods and indifference, make nineteenth-century American bibliography something apart from all other bibliography. The language is the same whether one is concerned with Gutenberg or Mark Twain, but the backgrounds differ, and the student of the later period, while he should and must know something of what preceded his chosen era, cannot apply the same rules. The methods of manufacture differ no less than the collecting habits, and these two differences must be respected for what they are, for what they represent.

We are beginning to build a great body of American bibliographical knowledge. To-day in the city of Chicago there is an index of about seven million cards representing the present status of the Historical Imprints Inventory. These seven million cards represent but a fraction of the work that is yet to be done. We must, among other things, formulate a set system of bibliographical description and must create that system now, while we are in the first stages of the construction. The tools and the language of bibliography are available; it is simply a question of how best to apply them. The desire and the ability exist—the fact of the Bibliographical Society of America proves that. If further proof is wanting we can point to the dozens of bibliographies of American authors—good, bad and indifferent—that have come forth during the past twenty years.

I believe it possible to establish a more or less uniform method, one that will be completely understandable, concise and definitive. In 1937 Thomas Franklin Currier published what is probably the best single-author bibliography ever done in the United States, his bibliography of John Greenleaf Whittier.[10] It has everything that most bibliographers would call for except the customary lining off of the title-pages. Mr. Currier explains that after examining large numbers of a single title, and finding no

[10] Harvard University Press.

differences on the title-pages, it is needless to line off since it may be assumed that all copies are alike. Yet, with others, I believe that the bibliographer ought to leave a record of what he considers the normal title-page, for it is obvious that the variant, if it exists, might pass unremarked unless an observer had some basis for comparison. If it were possible I should like to see the libraries of the United States catalogue their books in such manner that the cards could be used as permanent and definite bibliographical records. As matters now stand most libraries, following the method of the Library of Congress, disregard upper-case letters except when used at the beginning of a title or in a proper name. This certainly is not good bibliography. I also believe that we should abandon the use of the metric system, because to the average American collector fifteen centimeters is an unknown quantity while eight inches presents a very definite picture. If we are to improve American bibliography, and I think we shall, then we must so define our terms that they cannot be misunderstood by any person who wishes to use them. Possibly the most misused and misunderstood words in all bibliography are the words state, issue, and edition.

Shortly before *The Colophon* suspended publication, one of its editors, Frederick B. Adams, Jr., suggested that a group of ten or a dozen bibliographers undertake the task of collating the same book; and that, after the collations had been completed, they meet and discuss the individual results with a view to arriving at a universally acceptable collation. The plan unfortunately was interrupted by the war, but its merit remains.

The obstacle of form can be overcome. The indifference to all American authors with the exception of a certain few, such as the great New England group, is disappearing. Private collectors, in this, have led the way, with the libraries, too often, a quarter of a century behind them. There are certain exceptions: Harvard, Yale, Middlebury College, the American Antiquarian Society, to mention but a few, where the collecting and the preservation of

American first editions goes on with more than a little enthusiasm. But there are certain libraries, unfortunately, where this indifference to nineteenth-century American authors continues to survive as a curious contradiction.

On the whole, the problem of the description of nineteenth-century American books is being solved. We are learning how the books were produced; there is every indication that we shall arrive at something resembling a standard method of description; tools such as the Historical Imprints Inventories and Rollo G. Silver's projected directory of nineteenth-century American publishers, will not be the least important contributions. The dealers in rare books, and in particular the dealers of the younger generation, are bringing a fresh curiosity to their work that has already resulted in some remarkably large contributions. Of no little significance is the fact that the membership of the Bibliographical Society of America has almost doubled within the past few years. And if one may judge by these portents, American bibliography has attained its majority.

Mechanized Collation:
A Preliminary Report*

By Charlton Hinman

AMONG the major labors of critical bibliography are at least two kinds of detailed textual comparison, or collation: the comparison of different *editions* of a given work and the comparison of different *copies* of the same edition. We shall here be concerned only with the second of these two kinds.

The importance of the very detailed collation of different copies of the same edition is now widely recognized: such collation is our sole means of obtaining the fullest possible record of the variant readings which, particularly in books of the sixteenth and seventeenth centuries, different copies of the same edition so frequently contain. These variants, and especially the variants which are the result of systematic stop-press correction (of changes deliberately introduced, that is, during the course of the printing), have two primary values as bibliographical evidence, a

---

* Read at the Society's meeting held at the Pierpont Morgan Library, New York, on 3 January 1947, where Dr. Hinman illustrated his paper by a demonstration of the "machine" herein discussed, showing collations of corresponding (but variant) pages from different Folger copies of the First Folio of Shakespeare. A similar report was made before the Bibliographical Evidence Section of the Modern Language Association of America at its recent meeting in Washington.

general value and a particular. They have much to tell us about early printing-house methods and techniques generally; and they *may*, at least, have a great deal to teach us about the specific text under scrutiny in particular. Even when merely negative, evidence from collation is likely to be useful in textual studies; and sometimes it is excitingly positive. Exciting or not, however, the collation of different copies of the same edition is now acknowledged to be an absolutely essential step in innumerable editorial projects; and it sometimes has very considerable value quite apart from the light that it may be able to throw upon particular texts. Dr. Greg's monograph on the variants in the Pide Bull *Lear*[1] provides an almost perfect illustration of both the particular and the general values of collation of this sort.

At present, however, collation is one of the most arduous and time-consuming of all possible bibliographical activities — and often, although fortunately by no means always, one of the dullest. Hence it will surely be agreed that a mechanical device which would make accurate, high-speed collation possible would scarcely be unwelcome to bibliographers. It would be useful, first of all, in hosts of relatively small-scale collation tasks: in making it the work of a day or two rather than of a month or two to collate the eight extant first quartos of this work or the six surviving copies of that. And perhaps even more important, such a device would for the first time bring large-scale collation within the realm of practical possibility. The collation of a large number of the 230-odd surviving First Folios of Shakespeare, for example, has long been contemplated. The results of such a collation would inevitably be of very great interest both generally, to all students of critical bibliography, and specifically, to students and to editors of the text of Shakespeare. The time and labor required for collation on so large a scale have hitherto, of course, rendered

[1] W. W. Greg, *The Variants in the First Quarto of 'King Lear': A Bibliographical and Critical Inquiry* (London, 1940).

it impracticable; but given a satisfactory mechanical aid, large-scale collations of this sort could at last be undertaken.

Such a device would almost certainly have numerous other values to bibliographical investigation as well. It would be useful in the detection of cancels and of resettings and of various kinds of faking and forgery; and it would greatly simplify the study of other bibliographical problems, such as the peculiarities of the headlines in a given book — problems not necessarily involving the detailed collation of texts. Possibly, indeed, such a device would have considerable utility entirely outside the bibliographical world; but probably to most of us the device now in question would be most useful simply as a collation aid — as my instrument has so far been to me.

It should be said at once that the device now in question is not yet entirely perfected; and hence that these remarks must be regarded rather as a preliminary report than as a final statement. Last summer, through the courtesy and with the constant and generous coöperation of the Director and of the Staff of the Folger Shakespeare Library (to say nothing of various kinds of help furnished by a number of private individuals as well as by the Veterans' Administration, the Navy, the Bureau of Standards, and numerous other government agencies), I finally managed, after many false starts, to set up in the Folger Library an instrument by means of which I could actually collate corresponding pages of different copies of the First Folio of Shakespeare at something like fifty times the speed at which I could collate the same pages without mechanical aid.[2] But before I could actually collate at this speed I had to microfilm, with special apparatus and with great care, the pages to be compared, and then to mount the microfilm in slides; and thereafter, during the actual collation process, I had to spend considerable time making mechanical adjustments of a very exact kind. The photographic process, since it is more or less independent of the collation process proper,

[2] Patent on this instrument was applied for during the summer of 1946.

need not be considered at the moment; but I should like to say a word or two here, if only by way of disclaimer, about the time required for mechanical adjustments. My machine is made of a pair of ordinary microfilm projectors (borrowed from the Navy), some pieces of a wooden apple box (abstracted from a trash pile), some heavy cardboard (begged from the Folger bindery), and parts of a rusty Erector set (more or less hi-jacked from the small son of a close personal friend). With such materials, and with an almost complete innocence of even the most elementary knowledge either of optics or of mechanical engineering, I was not able to construct a very finished instrument. The gadget that I finally managed to set up — and actually to do some collating with — is really very crude indeed. Much awkward tinkering and countless little experiments have convinced me, however, that even my rough experimental instrument is capable of *indicating*, at least, the way in which really efficient high-speed collation is eventually to be realized; and reliable optical instrument manufacturers have assured me that a suitable instrument for this purpose *can* be made — a relatively simple but finished instrument with which all required adjustments can quickly and easily be effected (as, with my crude trial instrument, they cannot all be).

I can perhaps best give an idea of what, essentially, this instrument is and how it works by telling the story that finally put me on what I believe is the right track. I have since learned that the story itself is not true; but the underlying optical principles, happily, remain sound.

According to the story it was one of our common wartime practices to send a plane out to photograph a given target area soon after an attack on that area; and then, shortly before a new attack, to send out another plane to photograph the same area from the same position — or at least from as nearly the same position as possible. The problem was that of discovering any changes in the enemy's fortifications (gun emplacements and the like) since the time of the first photograph; and this problem was said to have been solved in the following manner. The two pictures were thrown upon a single large screen. They were not thrown upon this screen simultaneously, however, but alternately: first one picture for a fraction of a second, then the other picture for the same brief period, then the first picture again, and so on. The result was — or at any rate was supposed to be — that wherever there had been no change in the target area since it had first been photographed the screen showed only a single, perfectly motionless picture of that area; but that wherever there had been a change the picture on the screen flickered or wobbled, more or less violently depending upon the extent of the difference recorded by the two cameras.

Although there are several good reasons why this procedure would not be likely to succeed in aerial reconnaissance of the kind described, these reasons do not apply to the process of collating books by the utilization of the same fundamental principles — or, in general, of rapidly comparing any largely similar *flat* surfaces which can easily be placed, *without tilt*, at *exactly the same distance* from the lens of a camera. And the instrument now in question is based on precisely these principles. Microfilm images of the two pages to be collated are projected to the same screen from each of two projectors, and the two images are exactly superimposed. Superimposition having been achieved, the alternation of the two pages is begun. This is accomplished by setting in motion an extremely simple subordinate mechanism by which the projection lenses of the two projectors are alternately covered and uncovered — at any desired speed, since the occulting mechanism is controlled by a rheostat. The result of this process is, of course, that the screen shows a single, motionless picture of the page in question wherever the two exemplars being compared are identical, but that variants produce very prominent wobbles or flickers.

And thus, almost at a glance, differences are strikingly apparent. Needless to say, even the finally perfected collation instrument will not tell us what the variants mean. It will, however, permit us to discover their existence and their positions far more rapidly than heretofore — and, with certain qualifications which are associated with the preliminary photographic process, quite as surely and as accurately.

It will perhaps have been noticed that I passed rather quickly, in the foregoing account, over the superimposition step. It is here, of course, that the need for rapid, easy, and precise adjustment arises. For although slight departures from perfect register can be tolerated, the superimposition must be fairly exact. With crude equipment it is not always possible to get sufficiently exact register *quickly*; but experiments have indicated that, given the adjustment devices that can be expected in a finished instrument, this difficulty will be largely resolved. And it may be worth observing here that even pages which are in fact distinctly wedge-shaped in relation to each other, by reason of paper shrinkage or stretching, can be brought into perfect register on a screen; and that, although some kinds of shrinkage or stretching cannot be optically rectified, such extreme irregularities as would render mechanized collation impossible appear to be very rare.

Since we shall eventually have, I believe, a somewhat different and far more efficient instrument, I shall not attempt a detailed description of the merely experimental form. But I should like to say a few words here about the relation of the photographic process to mechanized collation; for even a finished instrument of the kind we have so far been discussing will require the microfilming of the books to be collated by its aid.

It may be observed in passing, first of all, that photographic reproductions are simply not always *wholly* reliable at best. But assuming that, as a general rule, they are sufficiently reliable for use in ordinary collation projects, the fact yet remains that the time required to microfilm a book for the purposes of mechanized collation is almost as great as the time required for the actual collation. If, therefore, mechanized collation could be effected without the need for a preliminary photographic process, both a great deal of time and a considerable amount of expense could be avoided. Why, then, must we use microfilm? The answer is, I believe, that we need not — *always*. But collation machines are not likely to be easily portable; and whenever we are obliged to collate books that cannot be brought together, the only solution may well be, still, the use of reproductions. And when perfected collation instruments using such reproductions are readily available to bibliographers it may be possible so to standardize rare-book microfilming procedures that it will be relatively easy to collate, with mechanical aid and at high speed, the often very widely scattered copies of the books that we study as critical bibliographers. The collation device of which we have been speaking was made with this end in view.

Nevertheless, there is certainly also a great deal of collating to be done that does not require the use of microfilm reproductions — because the originals themselves are readily available. Hence what we really need is two different collation instruments: one for work with originals, to be used whenever possible in preference to the other, the one which works with reproductions.

It once seemed clear that any device which would permit the projection of such large objects as folio pages would require light, and therefore heat, of an intensity so great as to endanger the pages themselves. It now seems almost certain, however, that a collation device which works directly with originals, and even with very large originals, need not subject these originals to any more risk of damage than microfilming does. Such a device would utilize the same fundamental principles as the other, but would project images of opaque objects rather than of films. President Jackson tells me, indeed, that just such a device was nearly perfected at Harvard several years ago. Wartime shortages stopped work on it before it could be put into operation; yet there is little doubt but that a finished instrument of this kind is now possible too.

I believe, therefore, that we shall eventually be able to collate different copies of the same edition far more easily than at present, whether these copies are already at hand in one place or are scattered over a large part of the world; — and to collate as many copies in one year as would now take fifty. What we need first, of course, is a few of the *perfected* tools.

Aldis, Foley, and the Collection of American Literature at Yale*

By Donald C. Gallup

IN November, 1911, Mr. Owen Franklin Aldis, a graduate of Yale in the class of 1874, gave to the University Library some six thousand volumes of first and important editions of American belles-lettres "as a nucleus for a thorough and complete collection for the advanced study of American literature, its History and Bibliography." Mr. Aldis had maintained an interest in books from his undergraduate days as Chairman of the *Yale Literary Magazine*. He had gone from Yale to the Columbia Law School and the practice of law, and eventually founded the real estate firm of Aldis and Company in Chicago. Serious trouble with his eyes forced him in 1911 to curtail both his business and collecting activities, and the gift of his collection to Yale followed. On January 12, 1912, he wrote to the Yale Librarian, Mr. Schwab:

> During the last twenty years I have bought largely from P. K. Foley, among others. He is a little careless at times, and may sell very cheap or at very high prices. He is, also, not careful about the condition of a book. But in certain directions I believe him to know more than any other man in America.
>
> I think it will be wise & expedient for you to let him know early, that he is now dealing with the *Yale Library* (& *not* me) and that you cannot and must not buy at very high prices! Also, that you doubt the advisability of buying *any* book which may not be *perfect* & in fine condition. It will be well to start well with him. No one picks up so many nuggets as he, though some are found in pretty rough and unrefined shape.

This letter establishes the beginning of the Aldis collection as

* Read at the meeting of the Society in New York, January 23, 1948. This paper is based principally upon the letters of P. K. Foley to Owen F. Aldis, preserved in the Yale Library and quoted with the Library's kind permission.

in the early 1890's. But it is probable that Mr. Aldis bought only incidentally from Foley until 1903, for the earliest of Foley's letters to Aldis preserved at Yale is dated January 13, 1903, and on April 3, 1908, we find Foley referring to "those lists from which we have worked during the past five years." Certainly from 1903 until 1909, the bulk of Aldis' accessions came from Foley.

The kind of collection which he wished to build up was from the first clear in Mr. Aldis' mind. It was to contain American literary first editions in "as perfect a form as possible," with especial emphasis upon association books, particularly of those he referred to as "all the little, poor, crawling authors." He drew up and sent to Foley long lists of desiderata, and Foley kept a drawer in his shop reserved exclusively for Aldis books, shipping them off periodically. These shipments seem to have averaged, at the height of the Aldis-Foley association, as many as a hundred books a month, not including autograph letters and occasional manuscripts; and they indicate that the collection must still have been in its comparative infancy at this time. Aldis examined each shipment, keeping the books of which he had either no other copies or copies in inferior condition, and returning the remainder to Foley for credit. This system was applied to the manuscript material as well. Mr. Aldis wished to have in each book a letter from its author referring specifically to it, and Foley frequently supplied letters containing such references in exchange for others without them.

By 1906, Foley had obviously come to regard Aldis as his star customer, and almost every shipment included a bibliographical discovery. The amount of material he turned up is little short of miraculous, and his letters shed considerable light on the methods he used. Although his first large purchases for Aldis seem to have been in the sales of C. F. Libbie & Company of Boston, he relied as a rule not so much upon auctions as on scouts, advertisements (particularly in country newspapers), and the descendants of authors and their publishers. He wrote to Aldis on July 12, 1909:

I have already compiled new lists of the books still wanted, and have forwarded them to trusty hands. Wholesale advertising has not proved successful, and the communication forwarded direct to him whom we look upon as likely to supply our wants is far more affective [*sic*] than such information, should it reach him in a more general way, and as if *he* were only one of many. I am hopeful of some results within a week—and within a month shall be greatly disappointed if the results will not amount to something. . . .

I have used such means as I thought most affective [*sic*] to reach survivors of Roberts Bros., and other old-time publishing houses, but am met by the information that very little importance was attached to an author's work, soon as it passed through the printer's hands. I believe Mr. Ticknor the only survivor of the old publishers who had the literary instinct sufficiently developed to preserve such things. However, I still have some hope of reaching members of the families—members who were not connected with the *business*, and therefore all the more likely to appreciate letters etc.

Certainly Aldis had no reason to complain of Foley's endeavors in his behalf, and the prices seem on the whole to have been reasonable. When Aldis returned to Foley a Poe letter as too expensive at $77.50, Foley replied that it had cost him $65.00 plus commission, "so you can perceive," he wrote, "that my advance was modest." Aldis had on the same occasion returned a manuscript volume containing poems by Whittier, Bryant, and Halleck, priced at $127.50. Of this, Foley admitted: "I fear that's a case in which I let my desire to acquire run away with my rules of thrift and careful purchase."

The question of condition was a thornier one, and, as might be expected with Foley's sources of supply, this was not his strong point.

Regarding the repairing of books, in an artistic manner [*he wrote to Aldis on September 4, 1906*], I have seen some which were treated by Bradstreet, of New York, and I do not believe that they could be improved upon, no matter where or by whom. One item was a copy of "The Celestial Railroad," which I sold for a mere song owing to its dilapidated condition; but when I next saw it, in a slip case, it looked almost perfect, and had I not suspected that it was the copy which I had sold, I think it would have passed without my detecting the faint outlines remaining of rents in leaves and wrapper. I understood from the gentleman who had that done that Bradstreets are very exacting, and unless one has other work of a more remunerative nature done by them they decline any surgical cases, such as those I have alluded to. When in New York it may be well for you to have an interview with the manager.

Another reference to Bradstreet occurred three weeks later:

The copy which I sent is the only one which I could procure of Wallace's "Boyhood of Christ"; I have struggled hard to get a perfect copy, but the fragile condition makes it almost impossible. I fancy that Bradstreet can make the thing look presentable, although it would seem to be a rather hard task, as it did not look so at first.

Occasionally, Foley's advice to Aldis was more reprehensible. These passages are from 1906:

Butler's "Parnassus," as you will perceive, is water-stained, but the paper is good and will bear cleansing, so as to leave it as clean as issued; I do not recommend cleansing as a rule, but this little thing has proved such a will-o'-the-wisp that I thought it better to secure the copy. . . .

[Mrs.] Sigourney's "Whisper [to a Bride]" came in second-edition form and, considering its fine condition, I thought it perhaps better to attach it; should an unsatisfactory copy of the first appear, the binding will be worth having. "Richard Hurdis" (Simms) was in rather unsatisfactory state, so I sent an odd Volume 1 which I happened to have, that your binder may substitute the concluding leaves for those which are stained in the other.

And this from 1908:

. . . Longfellow's "Evangeline" is a third edition, but if I remember rightly your first was not quite satisfactory, and the text of the third being the same as the first, except the advertisements, perhaps the cover etc. of that which I send may be of great aid.

But I am being perhaps unfair to both men in pointing out these few survivals of nineteenth-century collecting ethics. As a matter of fact only one of Foley's five suggestions appears to have been carried out by Aldis, and the exhaustive campaign which both collector and book-seller waged for the improvement of copies resulted in a relatively high standard of condition for the period during which the collection was assembled; the number of books in original boards or wrappers is considerable, and the dozens of unique and out-of-the-way items which Foley supplied are extremely impressive.

Foley's *American Authors, 1795-1895*,[1] was published in 1897, only a year after its author had established himself in business in Boston. Although it contains errors, it is still today in many ways an indispensable tool. Had it been published at the end instead of at the beginning of Foley's book-selling career, it would have approached much closer a model bibliography. We are told that he himself preferred not to discuss the book. Certainly he was well aware of its shortcomings. On August 4, 1906, he wrote Aldis of a discovery he had just made concerning the first editions of William Dean Howells and added: "Just imagine how little people know who base their faith on bibliographies!" And his letters are filled with corrections of his publication. On July 12, 1909, he wrote:

Regarding the "wants," you may cancel "William Guthrie," 1796, by Dunlap . . . I thought the crime of placing the little load on Dunlaps's shoulders was mine—but on examination find that Sabin's Dictionary was at fault, and that I merely borrowed the fault therefrom. You can also strike out Julia Ward Howe's "Golden Eagle," 1876, which was written by J. B. Howe, and her "Hyppolytus," 1858, which is believed to have been acted *from manuscript* and never printed. Halpine's two Dublin titles, 1870, also take rank among the books which were projected, but never assumed tangible shape.

I have done considerable prowling after some of those waifs and strays and believe, in time, I shall assume the form of a point of interrogation! Besides wrestling with references in American libraries, colleges, etc., I have sprinkled similar enquiries through sources of information in England, Ireland and Scotland—and some of my correspondents begin to show signs of weariness. If I could divorce myself from the grind for a whole year, and go into the thing regardless of cost (time, labor, currency, etc.), I think much might be accomplished in gleaning hidden facts—but that is a task which I dream of, rather than expect to accomplish.

A letter from Aldis which must have made a complimentary reference to the bibliography occasioned one of Foley's most revealing replies. It is dated August 28, 1909:

I thank you, sincerely and gratefully, for your kind words, whilst feeling conscious—there is none more so—that neither my performance nor self merit them.

[1] Patrick Kevin Foley (1856-1937), *American Authors, 1795-1895. A Bibliography of First and Notable Editions Chronologically Arranged With Notes.* Boston, Printed for Subscribers [The Publishers' Printing Co.], 1897. 350 pp.

The twelve years which have passed since the appearance of that magnum opus (bless the mark!) have convinced me of how ill prepared I was for the task. But travelling a road unexplored, except by travellers whose suggestions were so often worse than useless, because misleading, and with no real guide save instinct one only wonders that the performance was not even worse. . . .

Yes—first editions must, I suppose, be acknowledged dull, but not entirely separated from the glow of romance. . . .

I have followed the old fellows of the Revolutionary period and since through newspaper, periodical, tract and elsewhere, until a certain affection for each and all of them remains—even peculiarities of phrase and thought have grown more and more familiar, until I seem to have met with the grave and reverend sirs (and some entirely the reverse) in another existence.

This and many others of Foley's letters to Aldis, incidentally, attest the truth of Charles T. Goodspeed's observation that "they are an asset to any collection." Even the unpromising subject of the weather produces this passage:

I trust the mild climate of Washington proves enjoyable after our snappish apology for one; to-day brought forth a little frozen breath, sharp as a serpent's tooth. Yet—with all faults of temper and temperature there be some of us who love New England as another Eden—the growling old subscriber hereof among others.

If Aldis and Foley had had another five years in which to work on the collection, one wonders what the result might have been. As early as June 8, 1909—before Mr. Aldis' important purchases (through Walter M. Hill of Chicago) in the Chamberlain (Part II) and Maier sales later in that year—when Aldis had made his decision to present the collection to Yale, Foley (who, next to its owner, probably knew the collection best) could write:

Yale College Library will possess the best representative collection of American literature, in its first published form, in the land—this is no figure or flower of speech, either. Many of the items are not duplicated elsewhere, without mentioning the unique feature which is formed by the addition of letters and manuscripts relating to the authors' works, and in so many cases to the volume which shelters the manuscript or the letter itself. It will, indeed, form a princely gift, and in what form could one prefer to be remembered than in connection with a gift which will endear him to generation and generation!

Mr. Aldis was from the first insistent that the Collection at

Yale be called by some name not his own in order that others might be more willing to add to it, and the conditions which he laid down were those under which he believed its growth might be most rapid. A separate room with accommodations for students was to be provided; a special custodian was to be appointed; and no stamp or mark or writing of any kind was to be made in or upon any of the books.

Being pretty well acquainted with the peculiarities of book collectors [*he wrote to Professor Lounsbury on November 27, 1911*], it . . . seemed to me important to impress upon their minds that the collection would be carefully cased, guarded and preserved, in a scrupulously clean and perfect condition; and therefore, I inserted certain conditions about such matters into the gift, so that the University Library could get all the collectors and book worms on its side!

He outlined even more concrete plans for the growth of the Collection in a letter to Mr. Schwab on December 28:

My intention was . . . to try to make this collection bibliographically complete, and one containing not only the rare books but all books,—that is, first editions and collected editions, so as to make it useful . . . and perhaps indispensible [*sic*] to bibliographers, biographers, historians and students of American literature; to protect it thoroughly, and to so shelve it that it might be used with the utmost possible convenience. . . .

An earlier letter, of December 20, had pointed out that

At the present moment bibliographies of James Russell Lowell, of Charles Brockden Browne [*sic*] and of Bret Harte are being prepared; the compilers have to run all over the country . . . . In five years from now it would not be necessary to do this. Profssr. Lounsbury for instance had to go to a dozen places to write a short life of Cooper. Another gentleman finds it all but impossible to write the life of Charles Brockden Browne [*sic*] . . . for the same reason. Now many of these books are not expensive or rare and yet I think they ought to be in this collection. In a word I should be glad to see the Library add . . . whatever proper material it has in good condition of American Belles Lettres of first editions from the earliest period down to and including the Authors living and writing in the year 1900. The fact that such books may be cheap or not valuable from a money point of view has little or nothing to do with their value for the scholarly study of American Literature.[2]

[2] This letter is in the hand of an amanuensis, who was presumably responsible for the misspellings.

Mr. Aldis therefore proposed first that all books not already protected be cased *at his expense* and the whole collection arranged chronologically under author. Then, that an exact list be made of all titles, including such as could be added from the Yale Library. When this work was completed, he would send to Yale "a reasonably intelligent person of some bibliographical experience" who would go over the principal authors with the latest and best bibliographies, and make careful lists of all gaps to be filled. With such lists, proper advertising, and the aid of Foley and other book-sellers, Mr. Aldis expected to continue the work of collecting even though he could (because of eye-trouble) give the matter very little personal attention. "It seems to me foolish," he wrote to Mr. Schwab, "to go on without a clear and definite plan in the expenditure of money at random on rare books. I never have collected in this way and do not wish to begin now. . . . We shall doubtless lose some . . . books by this delay, but in the end will more than make up . . . by having a systematic plan for buying and filling gaps in an orderly way."

It was in the matter of the proposed transfer of books to the Collection that the plans came to grief. The Library simply did not have sufficient funds to replace volumes transferred and did not feel that these could be withdrawn from circulation—particularly in the undergraduate library. But Mr. Aldis became insistent on this point, and eventually refused to continue buying for the Collection until a list of books transferred was sent him. This was never done, and as a result several hundred titles which were being held by Foley and other dealers pending the consolidation of the Collection at Yale were never purchased. One of these was a copy of Bryant's *Embargo* (1808) which Foley had turned up and offered to Aldis for the Collection at twenty-five hundred dollars. Although Mr. Aldis was tempted, he felt that he did not wish to make even an offer to Foley until his preliminary conditions were accomplished at Yale. Had not the First World War intervened, they might have been, but from 1918 until his death in Paris in 1925, Mr. Aldis spent most of his time in France and was no longer actively in touch with the Collection.

Even now, more than thirty-six years after their arrival at Yale, Aldis' books (although the Collection of which they are the nucleus has been increased approximately four-fold) are still not completely catalogued—a situation which has resulted in the Collection's not being adequately known among bookmen and scholars generally. Aldis' plan for a collection which would be bibliographically complete is still very far from realization. (How much simpler an undertaking this Society's project for a bibliography of American literature would be had his dream become a reality!) But although the general development has not been so rapid as Mr. Aldis had hoped it would be, additions to collections of individual authors, such as Clemens, Cooper, and Whitman—to mention only three of the most important—have caused those sections to take their place among the most distinguished in the world.

Even now, five years seem too short a time even to approach the impossible goal of bibliographical completeness. But, as the cataloguing of Aldis' books proceeds, it becomes increasingly evident that the most difficult part of the task of collecting had already been finished in 1911. The Collection is in effect a memorial not only to its founder but also to the Boston book-seller who contributed so substantially to its accumulation. If Foley did not publish the revision of his bibliography which his friends and associates urged him to undertake, one of the principal reasons is here. It is fitting that future bibliographers, biographers, and historians, coming to appreciate the resources of this collection of books and manuscript material, should apply not only to Aldis but to Foley himself those words from his letter already quoted: ". . . in what form could one prefer to be remembered than in connection with a gift which will endear him to generation and generation!"

Casting Off Copy by
Elizabethan Printers: A Theory*

By WILLIAM H. BOND

WE are accustomed to the idea that in the sixteenth century, as today, the text of a book was normally set up consecutively. Thus, if we consider a quarto in fours, we assume that the compositor began by setting the first page of the outer forme of a certain gathering, then set the first two pages of the inner forme, then the second and third pages of the outer forme, then the third and fourth of the inner, and last the fourth page of the outer forme; and so on through the book. Or, if the book were split among two or more compositors, each would set his portion consecutively. Exceptions will come to mind—for example, a paginary reprint might easily be set up forme by forme from the sheets of an earlier edition—but consecutive composition is generally accepted as virtually axiomatic.[1]

The corollaries are sufficiently familiar. The inner forme will be completely in type before the outer, and hence may go to the press first; conversely, all but the last page of a one-sheet gathering must be in type before any of it can be printed. Perhaps the most interesting corollary was stated by Dr. McKerrow: "When we come across a clear case of the same material (initial letters, ornaments, &c.) being used more than once in a gathering, we may infer, with little or no risk of error, that we are dealing with a page-for-page reprint of an earlier edition." Dr. McKerrow's

---

* Read at the meeting of the Society in Philadelphia, June 5, 1948.

[1] The standard (and also the clearest) account of the problems of composition and imposition as they bear on the matter at hand is to be found in R. B. McKerrow, *An Introduction to Bibliography*, 2nd impression (Oxford, Clarendon Press, 1928), pp. 29-34 and also p. 18, n. 2.

discussion, which I cite not to contradict but because, as usual, his is the definitive statement of the matter, closes with a quotation from Moxon:

> But no wise *Compositer*, except he work on *Printed Copy* that runs *Sheet* for *Sheet*, will be willing to *Compose* more *Sheets* to a *Quire* than he shall have a *Fount* of *Letter* large enough to set out, unless he will take upon him the trouble of *Counting off* his *Copy*, because he cannot *Impose* till he has *Set* to the last *Page* of that *Quire*; all the other *Sheets* being *Quired* within the first *Sheet*, and the last *Page* of the *Quire* comes in the first *Sheet*.

Not all of Moxon's statement is germane to the problem we have to consider, but it contains one phrase to which insufficient attention has been directed: "unless he will take upon him the trouble of *Counting off* his *Copy*." The compositor could set and impose one forme at a time if he counted off or cast off—that is, *estimated*—the amount of copy for the pages of the *other* forme of the gathering occupying his attention. On the face of it this would appear to be a cumbersome method, to be used only in exceptional cases. Yet there exists evidence which I believe demonstrates its employment in a fair number of publications by three different printers whose combined careers extend over more than fifty years of the Elizabethan and Jacobean period. Most of the cases I can cite were observed in the course of a systematic examination of the earlier publications of Thomas Marshe, who printed from 1554 to 1587;[2] two additional examples from the presses of Thomas Creede and of Henry Bynneman were discovered entirely by accident. I have not studied the other work of Creede and Bynneman, nor have I attempted any proper survey of their contemporaries. This is admittedly in the nature of a preliminary report. But I have no doubt that evidence of the type I shall describe is to be found in the work of still other printers. At

[2] The study of Marshe was begun at the Folger Shakespeare Library under the grant of a research fellowship; this work was prematurely terminated by the war and has not yet been resumed on any considerable scale. My debt of gratitude is none the less great to the late director of the Folger, Dr. Joseph Quincy Adams, for the opportunity to begin the project.

any rate, its incidence is sufficiently great to remove it from the class of mere freaks. And if my interpretation of this evidence is correct, we shall have to revise some of our notions of Elizabethan printing-house practice and state some of our theoretical rules concerning it in less dogmatic terms.

The demonstration begins with a convention older than printing itself: that (barring variations in the size of the handwriting or the type, or other similar factors) there should be a fixed number of lines to the page throughout a normally and properly made manuscript or printed book. Variations from the norm are a familiar phenomenon in printing of all periods. They arise from deletions or insertions, or simply from careless mistakes. Whether caused by alterations in the text or by errors, we might expect them to appear pretty much at random. That is, in a carelessly printed book we should find overset and underset pages scattered throughout, with a roughly equivalent distribution of irregular pages in the outer and the inner formes of the respective gatherings. But in the books which I am about to cite, pages with too few or too many lines do *not* appear at random. There is a striking regularity about their occurrence which we may well examine more closely and attempt to explain on grounds other than careless error.

The simplest and perhaps the most striking example is the first edition of John Dolman's translation, *Those fyue Questions, which Marke Tullye Cicero, disputed in his Manor of Tusculanum*, printed by Thomas Marshe in 1561.[3] This is an octavo of 224 leaves, signed ¶[8], B-Z[8], A-E[8]. The text runs from B1 to the second E6[v], and is normally set 27 lines to the page. But excluding the beginnings and endings of the five sections, where headings necessitate a certain irregularity, and also sigs. K1[v]-K4[v], which contain verse set three stanzas to the page, no fewer than 92 pages have either more or fewer than 27 lines. The variation runs from 24 to 29.

[3] *S.T.C.* 5317. I have examined the Lockton-Morris (perfect) and Farmer (imperfect) copies at the Folger, and the perfect Aldenham copy at Harvard.

Of the 27 gatherings of text, 23 include at least one irregular page.[4]

In only one case do irregularities occur in *both* formes of a single gathering; and except for four pages in sig. I, five in S, one in Y, three in A, and one in the second D, every instance of wrong lineation occurs in an *inner* forme. This hardly looks like the hand of chance incarnate in a careless compositor.

The headlines are also worthy of some attention. On the versos they read "Liber"; on the rectos, "Primus," "Secundus," and so on, as appropriate to the matter. It can be demonstrated from typographical irregularities that basically only one set of headlines was used throughout, on both inner and outer formes of every sheet, the only modification being in the book-numbers. Even here a certain consistency is to be seen: in quires S through Y, the "Q" of "Quartus" is damaged in a distinctive manner in the setting printed regularly on the third and fourth rectos. From Z to the end of the volume, the same damaged "Q" appears in "Quintus" and is still on the third and fourth rectos of every quire. It is evident that even when forced to change his headlines, Marshe changed them as little as possible.

Since one set of headlines was used throughout, it follows that there was never more than one forme imposed at a time. Perhaps there was never more than one forme *ready for imposition—i.e.,* completely in type—at a time, although this is not a necessary conclusion. A consideration of the linear irregularities will now carry us a long step forward. Why should the pages of the outer formes be generally correct, while the pages of the inner formes are frequently incorrect?

[4] A list of all irregular pages (italicized figures represent pages of the outer forme; all others are inner forme): B1^v,2; C2,3^v,4; D2,6,8; E1^v,2,6,7^v,8; F1^v,2,4,5^v,6,8; G3^v,4,6,8; H2,4,5^v,6; *I4^v,5,6^v,7*; L1^v,2,4,5^v,6,8; M7^v,8; N5^v,8; O1^v,4,5^v,6,7^v,8; P1^v,2,4,6,7^v,8; Q1^v,3^v,4,5^v,6,7^v,8; R1^v,2,3^v,4,7^v,8; *S2^v,3,4^v,5,6^v*; T5^v,6,7^v,8; X3^v,7^v,8; Y2^v; Z6,7^v,8; A4, *4^v,5,7*; C8; *D6^v*; E3^v,4,5^v,6. The following pages were excepted from consideration: ¶1-8^v; B1; I1,1^v; K1^v-4^v; M8^v; N1; S1,1^v; Y6,6^v; E6^v-8^v. For an explanation of apparent inconsistencies, see note 7 below.

Let us suppose that the compositor set the first page of his quire
to the standard number of lines, *cast off* an estimated two pages, set
two more pages, cast off two more, and so on until the outer forme
was completely in type, its pages all perfectly regular. The text
of the inner forme would still be in manuscript. He then imposed
the outer forme, complete with headlines, and turned it over to
the pressman. Casting off is a difficult task; a prose manuscript,[5]
especially if written in a crabbed hand or heavily corrected and
interlined, would be hard to cast off accurately. In the case of
Dolman's Cicero, we may suppose that the compositor's estimates
were frequently at fault, with the result already observed: in
many quires that forme which had been cast off (usually the inner forme) was either overset or underset. This is hypothesis, but
I believe it would be difficult or impossible to account in any other
reasonable way for the phenomenon.[6]

It is not clear from Dolman's Cicero which portion of the copy
next engaged the compositor's attention. He may have set the
inner forme of each quire while its outer forme was printing, or
he may have gone on to the outer forme of the next quire. A third
possibility is that he may have waited until the outer forme was
printed off and distributed before composing any more of the text.
If his supply of type were really limited, such a measure might be
necessary to avoid running out of sorts.[7]

[5] It need scarcely be pointed out that a poetical manuscript, dramatic or otherwise, would present little difficulty in casting off, being already divided into lines;
therefore we need not expect to find evidence of the type here discussed in other than
prose works.

[6] It is worth noting that, in Dolman's Cicero as well as in the other books which
will be discussed, overset pages frequently present a crowded appearance and often
lack catchwords. This suggests that there was *no room* for the extra line which the
catchword occupied, which in turn indicates that the printer's error was in his estimate of the amount of text required to fill the pages, and not in his counting of lines
of type. Conversely, underset pages generally exhibit large white areas and other text-
stretching devices.

[7] Before leaving the evidence presented by the Cicero it might be observed that
several of its apparent inconsistencies are capable of plausible explanation. In sigs. I,
S, and Y new sections begin in the inner formes; it is therefore not altogether surprising to find the compositor reversing his usual procedure in those quires by setting
up the inner forme first and casting off the outer.

An example which introduces new complications is the first edition of Nicholas Haward's translation of *A briefe Chronicle* by Eutropius, printed by Marshe in 1564.[8] This is an octavo of 136 leaves, signed A⁸, B⁴, C-R⁸, S⁴; B4 is a blank. Fifteen pages (again excluding the preliminaries and the endings and beginnings of sections) vary from the norm of 24 lines to the page; in no case do these errors occur in both formes of the same gathering; and all but one occur in the inner formes of the several sheets.[9] Ten of the 15½ sheets of text contain at least one irregular page. As in the Cicero, a single set of headlines is used throughout on both formes of every sheet. But in this volume foliation numbers are printed with the headlines, and these tell us a little more of the progress of the book through the press. The inner forme of sheet C repeats the numerals printed on and proper to outer C.[10] The foliation of outer I reappears on inner I and again on outer K. Inner K bears the foliation numbers proper to outer L; while inner N bears the numerals of inner M with some transposition.[11] Inner O bears the numerals proper to outer P, and inner R the numerals of inner Q.

Now it is surely safe to assume that these errors of foliation indicate, as far as they go, the order through the press of the formes in which they occur; that a compositor would be likely to set up the foliation numbers correctly for the pages at hand, and then mistakenly permit them to remain standing for another set of

[8] *S.T.C.* 10579. I have examined the Folger copy, in which leaves S3 and S4 and the blank B4 are supplied from another copy, and the perfect Harvard copy which is in contemporary vellum wrappers.

[9] Irregular pages (outer forme in italics): C4; *D7*; F4; I4; K8; L1ᵛ, *5ᵛ, 6*; M*3ᵛ,4,5ᵛ,7ᵛ*; O4; P4; Q6. Excluded: A1-B4ᵛ; C1; D2, 2ᵛ; E8, 8ᵛ; G3ᵛ,4; H7, 7ᵛ; I5ᵛ,6; L4,4ᵛ; N3ᵛ,4; P1, 1ᵛ; Q8, 8ᵛ; S4ᵛ. It should be noted that Book II begins on D2ᵛ of the inner forme, possibly accounting for the linear error in D7 of the outer; see note 7, above.

[10] This discussion disregards the fact that towards the end of the book all the numerals are more or less in error. It is the printer's intention, not his accuracy, which bears on the point at hand.

[11] This transposition would automatically take place if the wrought-off forme, inner M, was accidentally reversed when placed on the letter-board for stripping, and its furniture and headlines then transferred to inner N, the forme next made up.

pages, rather than the reverse. Thus, while the evidence of the number of lines per page (as I have interpreted it) indicates that outer formes were almost invariably in type and printed before their respective inner formes, it is clear from the erroneous repetition of the foliation numerals that in a number of instances the sheets were not perfected one by one. Instead, the printing of a forme of *another* sheet intervened between the printing of the two formes of a given sheet. Perhaps this was true of all the sheets, but again this is not a necessary conclusion.

One more example may be worth citing in some detail. This is *A briefe treatise concerning the burnynge of Bucer and Phagius*, an octavo printed by Marshe in 1562.[12] It contains 96 leaves, signed ¶[4], A-L[8], M[4], and has normally 23 lines to the page. Twenty-three pages are overset or underset, of which all but one occur in an inner forme; and again errors never occur in both formes of any one gathering.[13] In this book two separate sets of headlines were used, and they were employed in this manner: the first set appear in both inner and outer A, the second in inner and outer B, the first again in inner and outer C, and so on alternately through the book except for the last two gatherings (a sheet and a half).[14] This demonstrates once again that the inner and outer formes of any one gathering were never imposed concurrently. It would also appear probable in this case that the printing of a forme from another sheet (or even several formes from other sheets) intervened between the printings of the two formes of any given sheet.

An undated book by Marshe, probably printed in 1562, contains similar evidence. This is Jean Veron's *A stronge Defence of the*

---

[12] *S.T.C.* 3966. I have used the Farmer-Heber-Britwell copy at the Folger, and checked it against a microfilm of the Huntington copy (University Microfilm series, case 31, reel 181).

[13] Irregular pages (outer forme in italics): A2,3^v,4,6; B1^v,2,5^v,6; C8; D7^v; E2,6,7^v; F5^v,6,7^v; G4,8; H2; K2,4,8; M1. Excluded: ¶1-4^v; A1; M4^v.

[14] Among other features, the following most readily distinguishes the two sets of headlines: set i reads "Martin Bucer. &c." on the first and second rectos of each gathering in which it appears, and set ii reads "Of martin Bucer. &c." on the first and second rectos. These headlines appear as follows:

maryage of Pryestes, an octavo of 89 leaves having normally 27 lines to the page.[15] Excluding preliminaries, there are 11 exceptions to this standard, all but one in inner formes; one sheet has errors in both formes.[16] It is possible to trace the headlines through the eight gatherings of text, and show once more that two skeletons were used, each appearing in both inner and outer formes of alternate sheets.

I shall cite only one more example from Marshe's press: Laurence Humphrey's *The Nobles or of Nobilitye,* an octavo of 1563.[17] It contains 208 leaves, of which the first 20 are preliminary matter and the last eight a separate and appended work; the remaining 180 leaves are set 27 lines to the page, with the exception of 77 pages, of which all but 14 are in inner formes.[18]

So far all have been octavos, a format much employed by Marshe. Appian's *An Auncient Historie and exquisite Chronicle of the Romanes warres,* published by Ralph Newberry and Henry Bynne-

Quire	Inner Forme	Outer Forme
A	i	i
B	ii	ii
C	i	i
D	ii	ii
E	i	i
F	ii	ii
G	i	i
H	ii	ii
I	i	i
K	ii	ii
L	i	ii

M (a half-sheet: all headlines from set i)

[15] *S.T.C.* 24687. I have seen only the Herbert-Huth-Harmsworth-Folger copy. Its collation is A-C⁸ (C7 and C8 both blank and genuine), a-h⁸ (h4+"H.v.").

[16] Irregular pages (outer forme in italics): a4; c8; d1^v, 3^v, 6, 7^v, 8; e1^v, *4^v*; g6; h2. Excluded: A1-C8ᵛ, a1, h8-8ᵛ.

[17] *S.T.C.* 13964. I have examined the two copies (one imperfect) in the Folger Library, as well as a microfilm of the Huntington copy (University Microfilm series, case 42, reel 249). The book collates A-B⁸, C⁴, a-y⁸, Aa⁸ (Aa8 blank).

[18] Irregular pages (outer forme in italics): a5,6ᵛ; b2,3ᵛ,4,7ᵛ,8; c1ᵛ,2,3ᵛ,4,5ᵛ, 6; *d4ᵛ*, 6; *e4ᵛ*, 5, 8; f1ᵛ, 7ᵛ, 8; g1ᵛ, 2; h7ᵛ; i1ᵛ; k2, 4; *l1*, 1ᵛ, *2ᵛ*, 3, *4ᵛ*, 8; m1ᵛ, 5ᵛ; n4, *4ᵛ*,5, 6; o4, 5ᵛ, 6; *p3*, 8; q1ᵛ, 2, 4, 5ᵛ, 6, 8; r2, 8; s1ᵛ, 2, 3ᵛ, 6, 7ᵛ, 8; *t1*, 2, 3, 3ᵛ, 4, 5ᵛ, 6; v3ᵛ, 4, 5ᵛ, 6, 7ᵛ, 8; x1ᵛ, 2, 8; y1ᵛ, 4, 6. Excluded: A1-C4ᵛ; a1; k3, 3ᵛ; q7, 7ᵛ; z4, 4ᵛ; Aa1-8ᵛ. It will be noted that six gatherings violate the rule that errors should occur in only one forme of a gathering. Yet the preponderance of errors in inner formes remains great and, I think, convincing.

man in 1578,[19] is a quarto of 370 leaves. About 85 pages are taken up with title-pages, preliminaries, and other matter which naturally does not conform to a set standard; the remaining pages are set 36 lines to the page, but 95 contain more or fewer lines, 83 of these exceptions appearing in inner-forme pages. In six gatherings irregularities appear in both inner and outer formes, and here the element of careless error must be admitted.[20]

The last example which I shall cite is the most important of all, at least in a literary sense. It is Thomas Creede's printing for William Ponsonby of Sir Philip Sidney's *The Defence of Poesie*, 1595, a quarto of 35 leaves having normally 32 lines to the page.[21] Eight of its pages, every one of which is in an inner forme, are either overset or underset.[22] This book may be examined in almost any library in the excellent Noel Douglas facsimile. It is instructive to note that the pages which are underset appear to be padded with spaces, giving a much lighter effect than the normal page. Evidently there was need to stretch the matter: in other words, the mistake was not in the compositor's having set the

[19] *S.T.C.* 713. I have examined only the Eames-Harvard copy. This agrees with the description of the second-issue copy in the Pforzheimer collection (W. A. Jackson, *The Carl H. Pforzheimer Library*, New York, 1940, I: 13; full collation given under the preceding number in the catalogue, pp. 11-12), except that in the Harvard copy leaf **2 is misbound before leaf *1. Although Newberry and Bynneman received equal prominence on the title-page, the ornaments and initials in the book indicate that Bynneman alone was responsible for the typography.

[20] Irregular pages (outer forme in italics): E4; I4; K1^v,2,4; L1^v,2,4; O1^v; Q3^v,4; R4; X2; *Y1, 1^v, 2*; Aa3^v,4; Bb4; Cc1^v, 2, 4; Dd1^v, 2, 2^v, 4; Ee3^v, 4; Ff1^v, 2, 4; Hh1^v,2; Kk1^v, 2, 3^v, 4; Oo4; Qq1^v, 2; *Rr2^v*; Ss4; Tt3^v, 4; Vv1^v, 2; Xx3^v, 4; *Yy2^v, 4*; *Eee1, 1^v, 2, 2^v, 3^v, 4*; b2; *c3, 3^v,4, 4^v*; e2; g3^v, 4; h3^v, 4; m2; p4; q4; r2; *t1, 1^v, 2*; v2; x2, 4, *4^v*; bb2, 3^v, 4; cc1^v, 2, 3^v, 4; ee1^v, 2, 4; ii2, 3^v, 4; ll1^v; mm3^v, 4; *nn2^v*; *oo1*. Excluded: A1-B4^v; C2^v; K4^v; L1; Y2^v, 3; Gg2, 2^v; Hh4^v; Rr1, 1^v; Vv1; Bbb1-Ccc1; Fff2^v-a1; k1, 1^v; q4^v; r1; y3, 3^v; ii1; nn1, 1^v; oo4^v-Qq2^v. I have also excluded all of signature hh, where the standard has evidently been increased to 37 lines per page in order to end the section in the Carthaginian wars on hh4^v. Granting that to be the case, we find hh3 of the outer forme to have only 36 lines, but hh1^v and 3^v of the inner forme each contain 38 lines.

[21] *S.T.C.* 22535. I have used the White-Harvard copy (title-page in facsimile), and the Noel Douglas facsimile of the Locker-British Museum copy. The book collates [-]^1, B-I^4, K^2.

[22] Irregular pages: E2; F1^v, 2; G2, H2, 4; I1^v, 2. I do not find the headlines susceptible of satisfactory identification and analysis in this book.

wrong number of lines for his page of type, but in his having counted off the wrong amount of text to fill his pages. Once again we have presumptive evidence for the alternate setting and casting-off process which I have hypothecated.

We may imagine various reasons why a printer might adopt this process. If his shop were small and his equipment scanty, he would avoid the danger of running out of sorts. A possible mode of procedure is as follows: he might set up the outer forme of gathering A and send it to the press. While it was printing, outer B could be set up. While outer B was printing, inner A could be set up from the counted-off copy; meanwhile the printed sheets of outer A would be drying; and so on. All the while the printer would need but two to three formes standing in type at a time — an important consideration if his founts were limited. Some interval of drying seems to have been necessary to minimize the possibility of offset; in no other reasonable way could he have obtained that interval without either interrupting the printing process or having at least three to four formes in type at a time. In a larger shop the method might be adopted when only a portion of the facilities could be devoted to a given book: for example, when it was necessary to push through a rush job in addition to a normal printing schedule which could not be interrupted.[23] Other reasons may suggest themselves, but limitations of personnel and equipment seem the most likely motivations.

I should like to emphasize once more the point made in the title of this paper: that all this is merely theory. At this stage of

---

[23] On this point it is interesting to refer once more to the problem of Sidney's *Defence*. Both A. W. Pollard (*The Rowfant Library. A Catalogue*, London, 1886, p. 116) and W. A. Jackson (*The Carl H. Pforzheimer Library*, III: 963-964) conclude from a variety of circumstantial evidence that Olney's edition of 1595, titled *An Apologie for Poetrie*, preceded Ponsonby's edition, *The Defence of Poesie*, of the same date. Olney's edition, printed by James Roberts, is regular in lineation throughout; Ponsonby's, printed by Thomas Creede, has the variations already noted. Textual evidence indicates that the two versions were printed from different manuscripts. Might not these linear variations in Creede's printing of the *Defence* be taken as evidence of a hurried job, hurried in order to replace the Olney edition on the bookstalls? The irregularity might thus serve as some slight corroboration of the conclusion reached by Pollard and Jackson.

the investigation we have a certain number of books (a number which I am confident can be greatly enlarged) all of which exhibit an irregularity in the number of lines to the page; this irregularity occurs in pages of the inner forme in the vast preponderance of cases, and seldom in both formes of any one gathering. Furthermore in several of the books it can be demonstrated that the two formes of any one gathering cannot have been imposed concurrently. Various explanations of these basic facts might be advanced, but I believe that the simplest and most satisfactory is the hypothesis of the alternate setting and casting-off of copy. If this hypothesis is borne out by subsequent investigation, we shall have to revise some of our bibliographical rules of thumb; for example, no longer will the appearance of the same ornament in both formes of the same sheet be the nearly-infallible sign of a reprint. We shall also have a new means of tracing the progress of certain books through the press.

Some Bibliographical Adventures in Americana*

By Clifton Waller Barrett

ERHAPS you may be wondering why an obscure individual such as I should be here today addressing the pundits and experts of the bibliographical world. If any of you may be racking your brains to remember some of the weighty and authoritative articles and books I have contributed to the literature of bibliography or some of the points or issues, burning or otherwise, that I have discovered, and in so doing forced from their pinnacles hitherto well-regarded folios, quartos and broadsides, let me set your minds at rest. The record is almost completely barren. My sole attempt at bookish literature has been a pamphlet entitled *Blueprint For a Basic Library*, which attained the impressive circulation of twenty-nine copies—including members of the family.

Now that I have dispelled any mysterious aura of scholarly achievement that might have floated about my name, some of you may still be seeking the reason for my presence. My own solution of this apparent enigma is that your president felt that it might be of interest to you practitioners of the sweet science of bibliography to see a specimen of the Collector, *Homo Americanus*, late, transfixed on a pin and wriggling before you. I think that he felt, too, that the papers we have enjoyed here for years past have been of so distinguished a character that a little dilution of this kind would not be a serious matter.

Now that I stand before you shorn of all distinction and revealed as one of the mere common bricks that go to make up the

* Read at the meeting of the Society in New York, January 20, 1950.

bibliographical castle, you may permit me to indulge in some introspection as to the characteristics that are to be found in the strange class of which I may be considered a representative member, if so strongly individualistic a group as collectors may be believed to have any traits in common. Nevertheless let me draw you a sort of composite picture of the true *genus Collector*.

First of all, he must be distinguished by his rapacity. If he does not covet and is not prepared to seize and fight for every binding, every issue and every state of every book that falls even remotely within the range of his particular bibliomania, treat him as the lawful fisherman treats a nine-inch bass; throw him back—he is only an insignificant and colorless offshoot of the true parent stock.

Then, he must have the proper attitude towards money. He must continually wonder what the booksellers buy half so precious as what they sell. Francis Taylor of the Metropolitan Museum said some years ago in an address at the Grolier Club that "the history of collecting is the history of money." This statement, I believe, is demonstrably true, and important periods of collecting must indeed be accompanied by an easy supply of money. Your real collector will have no difficulty in determining the proper uses for his available cash. After spending $5,000 for a coveted manuscript, he will be properly aghast at the demand of his wife for $100 to buy a new coat and overshoes for the children.

Again, he must be the type which will not permit his mundane pursuits to interfere with his true vocation. Any merchant who will not desert his biggest buyer, any lawyer who will not leave his best client, any doctor who will not incontinently flee from his best-paying neurotic old lady in quest of the perfect book is not worthy of the name of collector.

Now that I have made a rough sketch of the typical hoarder of rare books, perhaps you will be kind enough to allow me to tell you something about my own experiences in collecting.

In 1938 a book was published by Jacob Blanck entitled *Peter Parley to Penrod*. My collecting career of ten years has been just the opposite. I have gone from Tarkington to Tamerlane. The first edition I purchased, consciously at least, was Booth Tarkington's *Cherry*, in the bookshop of Thoms and Eron in the last days of 1939; and in 1949, I achieved the collector's Nirvana by acquiring a *Tamerlane* in the original wrappers from James F. Drake.

For a year or so after 1939, my collecting continued with the buying of first editions of the books I had read and liked, whether English or American or otherwise. But as time went on, I was introduced to American authors I had never heard of before. The courses in literature I had taken in school and college had been heavily weighted with the English writers, with perfunctory obeisances to the New England group, Edgar Allan Poe, Fenimore Cooper and Washington Irving. They completely neglected such writers as Charles Brockden Brown, John Neal, William Gilmore Simms, Robert Montgomery Bird, John Pendleton Kennedy and James K. Paulding. As I gradually became acquainted with their works and lives, I became fired with the ambition to collect complete sets of their original editions so that this authentic American literature might be preserved for posterity. In time I learned that they had not been completely neglected, and I also discovered the great difficulty of securing complete runs of their books including the scarcest items and ephemeral publications.

Now that I had my feet wet in the limpid waters of American literature, the English and other books went by the board and those I had acquired departed from my shelves for other destinations. By degrees a plan unfolded of trying to put together a comprehensive collection of all worth-while American creative or imaginative literature from the beginning of the republic to the present day. This, of course, would include fiction, poetry, and essays of enduring merit or historical or regional significance.

History of high literary worth would be included, as well as juveniles and works of humor.

In formulating this plan, I was not unmindful of the collections that had been previously assembled. However, a survey going back to the Foote sale in the 1890's failed to reveal anyone which had really covered the entire field. Chamberlin, Maier, Bemis, Arnold, Howe and others had concentrated heavily on the New England authors. Not even Huntington or Clements had covered the whole canvas. Aldis and Foley in their pioneering work had stopped at 1895, and had overlooked many writers of great importance. Hogan and Braislin had been extremely selective. Although many of the tributaries of the main stream of American Literature had been well traversed, there seemed to be a connecting and unifying work to be done in order that American life as portrayed by the foremost American thinkers and writers, the creative artists of the pen, could be viewed in its entire development throughout the life of the republic, a period of approximately 175 years.

And so the long hunt commenced and has continued for ten years through bookshops, auction rooms and the parlors of private sellers. Dealers' and auction catalogues have been painstakingly perused, and orders have been placed from London to California. Fortunately, in the very beginning of this activity, I moved with my family into a larger house and was able to set aside two rooms for the assembling of these literary treasures. Although now quite inadequate in space, they met a pressing necessity in the early stages, as packages of books began to arrive with monotonous and—to my wife—irritating regularity. You can appreciate this when I tell you that in ten years the collection has grown to a total of about 10,000 pieces of printed material, manuscripts and letters, an average of about 20 per week. The important works of over 600 American authors are included. Every important author is represented by a virtually complete collection. With extremely few exceptions, the books are all in the earliest state and binding. Wherever possible, author's presentation or association copies have been procured. Autograph letters referring to the books are present in considerable volume.

As have many others, I have devoted long thought to the question of who are the greatest American writers, and have come to the conclusion (subject to change, of course) that there are eleven who, through the years, have grown in critical appreciation and public favor, and have shown a quality of timelessness in their works which indicates permanent survival. I call them the Redwoods of American Literature because they continue to grow and flourish while the lesser trees and bushes die away and indeed form a sort of compost for their massive roots. These Redwoods are Washington Irving, Edgar Allan Poe, Fenimore Cooper, Emerson, Longfellow, Herman Melville, Nathaniel Hawthorne, Thoreau, Mark Twain, Walt Whitman and Henry James.

With this belief in mind, it seemed quite essential to make an exhaustive collection of all of the books of these writers with as much of the ephemeral material, letters and manuscripts as might be available. This part of the task is substantially near accomplishment. The Washington Irving collection, for one, contains a unique set of *Salmagundi* in parts, all first issue in the original wrappers; a *Sketch Book* in parts and the only known presentation copy of Knickerbocker's *History of New York*. There are original manuscripts of the *Sketch Book, History of New York* and *Bracebridge Hall*, as well as a portion of *Salmagundi* and other lesser ones.

The Poe collection contains all the major works, including the *Tamerlane* previously referred to, a *Murders in the Rue Morgue* lacking (alas) the original wrappers, and a *Tales* of 1845 in wrappers, which in correct form is one of Poe's rarest books. There is a presentation of *Eureka* to Mrs. Osborne, a close friend of Poe and Mrs. Clemm. Perhaps the most interesting piece is

the only known letter from Poe to Washington Irving, proposing a new magazine, reading in part:

> The chief feature in the literary department will be that of the contributions
> from the most distinguished pens (of Americans) exclusively; or, if this plan
> cannot be wholly carried out, we propose, at least, to procure the aid of some
> five or six of the most distinguished, and to admit a few articles from other
> sources—none of which are not of a very high order of merit. We shall en-
> deavor to engage the permanent services of yourself, Mr. Cooper, Mr. Paulding,
> Mr. Kennedy, Mr. Longfellow, Mr. Bryant, Mr. Halleck, Mr. Willis, and,
> perhaps, one or two others. In fact, as before said, our ability to make these ar-
> rangements is a condition without which the magazine will not go into opera-
> tion; and my immediate object in addressing you now, is to ascertain how far
> we may look to you for aid.

The similar letters which he wrote at this time to Paulding,
Bryant and Willis are unlocated. The Cooper letter was mentioned in a sale at Libbie's, April 24, 1898. The Kennedy letter
is in the Peabody Institute, the one to Longfellow at Craigie
House, and that to Halleck in the Huntington Library.

The James Fenimore Cooper group contains an almost complete run of firsts in boards, uncut, wrappers or other original
bindings together with many of the actual first printings in London, Paris and Dresden. There is a copy of *The Spy* presented by
Cooper to his wife, *Precaution* in original leather and a fine *Last
of the Mohicans* in boards, uncut. There are complete manuscripts
of *The Two Admirals* and *Mercedes of Castile* as well as portions
of *The Prairie*, *The Water-Witch*, *Afloat and Ashore*, and *Naval
History of the United States*.

The Emerson collection embraces presentation copies of all of
his books to members of his immediate family as well as to Lowell, Bronson Alcott and Charles Eliot Norton, together with
various manuscripts of his poetry.

With regard to the Longfellow collection, I departed from a
sort of unwritten rule and purchased the entire Carroll Wilson
collection. My reason for doing this was the fact that the Wilson
lot was to be sold only as a unit, which decision was undoubtedly

the proper one, and the realization that probably never again would I have the opportunity to secure a half-dozen of the privately printed pieces, some of which are in unique state.

My own collection of some sixty items contained—*mirabile dictu*—two pieces that were not present in this incomparable Wilson collection, which, incidentally, I believe (with the possible exception of Carroll's own Whittiers) is the greatest collection ever made of an American author. At this point, I pay tribute to the inspiration of that indefatigable bibliographer, literary historian and prince of good fellows, Carroll Atwood Wilson.

The great mystic Herman Melville is represented by a complete group of firsts, including both English and American editions, and a unique *White Jacket* in wrappers. It has six books in presentation state or of intimate association interest, and the last letter written by Melville in autograph.

Of all the great Americans, one of the greatest is Nathaniel Hawthorne. His masterpiece, *The Scarlet Letter,* is present in this collection in a pristine copy containing a contemporary autograph letter from Hawthorne to the Collector of Customs in Salem, and three documents signed by Hawthorne as surveyor at the very time he was writing the introductory part, *The Custom House.* In the copy of *The House of the Seven Gables* there is a letter from Hawthorne to his doctor, which reads in part: "I send a draft on my publishers, as above, and trust, in the course of the present year, to wipe off my pecuniary indebtedness to you —I have a new book nearly ready for the press. I am afraid it won't make such a stir in Salem as the former one; although the scene is laid there."

There are also nine presentation copies from Hawthorne to Longfellow, Franklin Pierce and others. A variety of letters refer to the books. One of the features of the collection is the comprehensive group of early magazines and gift annuals containing the earliest stories of Hawthorne.

Henry David Thoreau, whose light has been gaining in intensity, is represented by the copy of *A Week on the Concord and Merrimack Rivers,* presented to Tennyson, and of *Walden,* given to his mother. The collection also contains the original map drawn by Thoreau of the territory covered in the *Week* and his original compositions at Harvard on Chaucer, Shakespeare and Jonson, etc., as well as many letters.

The run of firsts written by Mark Twain includes presentation copies of *The Jumping Frog, Huckleberry Finn, The Prince and the Pauper* and *A Connecticut Yankee* presented to Charles Dudley Warner's niece. One of the most appealing items is *The Gilded Age* presented by Olivia Clemens to Mark Twain's mother, on Christmas 1873 (the book was published early in 1874), together with an original manuscript chapter of the book in Twain's autograph and one in the hand of his collaborator, Charles Dudley Warner. There is a gilt-edged *Tom Sawyer* and the large part of the original manuscript of *A Tramp Abroad.*

The collection of the good gray poet Walt Whitman includes a fine copy of his first publication, *Franklin Evans, the Inebriate,* in wrappers, a very rare book indeed. There are seven editions of *Leaves of Grass* including a first edition, first issue, which contains Emerson's letter, itself a great rarity. His later works are all present, inscribed, and in some cases presented to Louisa Whitman, E. C. Stedman, etc., as well as a long manuscript of factual autobiography sent to his publisher, David McKay.

An exhaustive gathering of the first editions, English and American, of the old master Henry James, is apt to exhaust the collector. Here we find nearly 200 volumes of which nineteen are presented to Edmund Gosse, Mrs. Humphry Ward, Evelyn Smalley and others. Numerous letters and a few manuscripts accompany the books.

Naturally, in addition to these so-called Redwoods, there are other important writers where the aim has been completeness. For example, the great Southern novelist, William Gilmore

Simms, whose pictures of frontier life and the Revolution rank with Cooper's. I have over 200 items.

The first professional American novelist, Charles Brockden Brown. When that fabulously rare book *Alcuin* came up at auction, I missed it and was saved from despair by David Randall, who was kind enough to turn it over to me.

Susanna Haswell Rowson, famous author of *Charlotte Temple*. The Frank Hogan sale gave me my opportunity to buy this one. There are about 60 items here, including the copies of her books owned by her husband and son.

The novelist-historian of early Virginia and the Civil War—John Esten Cooke. A few months ago, Michael Papantonio helped me complete this group with a copy of *The Virginia Bohemians*, the only one lacking of all his books.

The Apostle of the West—Bret Harte—250 items, including 12 manuscripts.

The pioneer realist Stephen Crane; numerous books, letters and the original manuscript of *The Red Badge of Courage*.

Writers of the New England school, other than those mentioned—Whittier, Lowell and Holmes—are represented by a copy of Whittier's *Moll Pitcher* with the original front wrapper; the original manuscript of *Lowell's Class Poem*, and privately printed lectures of Holmes, together with long runs of first editions.

Oscar Wegelin, Lillie Losche and Lyle Wright are pioneers in classifying and describing American fiction to 1850. With their work as a guide, I have tried to secure every piece of American fiction to the date mentioned. The collection presently contains over 1,000 titles, including, I believe, every one published by 1800. Aside from their importance in literary history, these books are tremendously appealing. They form a great variety of intriguing imprints, in every conceivable style of binding—leather, wrappers, boards, cloth and some that are merely stitched.

They are written in every style from the epistolary to the early forms of realism. Didactic, sentimental, high-blown description or simple narrative, they treat of seductions, Gothic castles, the Revolutionary War and the frontier. It is amazing how many of them offer absorbing reading to this day. Two of the earliest examples, *Charlotte Temple* and *The Coquette*, tell their simple stories of betrayal in a manner calculated to wring tears from a basilisk.

Although I have spoken for the most part of books of the 1800's, the literature of the present century has not been neglected. Dreiser, O. Henry, Ellen Glasgow, Hemingway, Sinclair Lewis, Kenneth Roberts, Steinbeck and others, are present in full measure. If I had to pick out the one writer of the twentieth century most certain of immortality the choice would be impossible, as I could never make up my mind between Willa Cather and Robert Frost. To play it safe, I have gathered together all of their firsts of which, I believe, nearly all are in very interesting presentation state.

Mentioning Robert Frost reminds me that my remarks have been principally directed to prose works. This does not mean that poetry has been unduly overlooked. In addition to the works of the well-known poets previously secured, the location of all first editions of American poetry to 1850 is now in progress, and many items have been acquired.

American humor might be the subject of a new bibliography. There is an excellent chapter on this subject in Spiller's recently published *Literary History of the United States* (New York, The Macmillan Co.). The collection contains numerous books in this category.

The aforementioned *Peter Parley to Penrod* is an indispensable tool for the collector of juveniles, and many of these titles have been procured in addition to earlier examples before 1827 and other later ones.

In general the guiding principle has been to amass the basic and background materials which might be used by the historian, literary or otherwise, or the writer of fiction or poetry concerned with American life, character, history and customs. Any collateral material relating to the inspiration, the method and the purpose of the various books has been eagerly sought after.

At this point, I should like to emphasize that this collection has been in no sense of the word assembled by my unaided efforts. In fact, I have been to a great degree only the gathering point, the receptacle, for this rain of great American original editions. The brains and the bibliographical knowledge of many others have been utilized in fullest measure.

I remember with the keenest pleasure the many fine source books of literary history and bibliography which fired me with the original enthusiasm and desire to make the attempt; the old ones by Tyler, Allibone, Duyckinck and Stedman, and even the Poe-hating Griswold. Then came the pioneering bibliographies of Stone, Foley and Wegelin, later on Merle Johnson and Lyle Wright. One of the great studies of the subject is Arthur Hobson Quinn's *American Fiction, an Historical and Critical Survey*. This has been for me a constant source of guidance and information. *The Flowering of New England*, by Van Wyck Brooks, together with his later studies are rich in suggestion and enjoyment for the collector. The insidious works of A. Edward Newton, John Winterich and John Carter are like sparks to the dry tinder in the mind of the budding bibliophile.

In truth, one of the important dividends of an activity of this kind is the fact that one encounters many personalities of a different type with different ideas and aspirations. I can solemnly say that I would not give up the friends I have made among bookmen for a mint copy of *The Bay Psalm Book*. Can one go further? Seriously, my many friendships in this Society, the Grolier Club, in the libraries and universities, and among booksellers are most prized possessions. May this collection never find its way to the auction room.

My early steps in the game were guided by the genial Charles Vanover of Thoms and Eron. Among the co-architects of this edifice of books, I must own a tremendous debt to David Randall, John Kohn and Michael Papantonio, not to mention Howard Mott. If there is anything these four don't know about American firsts, I would despair of finding out. I am grateful to Marston and James Drake and to John Fleming for some of my prize pieces. I sit at the feet of Jacob Blanck and wonder at his encyclopaedic knowledge and its instant accessibility. And George Goodspeed, pre-eminent in New England.

And to speak of librarians, could there be three more different people in the world than Frederick B. Adams, Jr., James Babb and William A. Jackson? Yet are they not all shining examples of the knowledgeable, inspiring, conscientious and sympathetic bookman?

But let me check myself before I become quite maudlin either about books or persons. Let me thank you for your patience in listening to this catalogue and these opinions, and in conclusion may I say that the game is wonderful and the players even more so.

The Making of the
Short-Title Catalogue, 1641-1700
By Donald G. Wing*

I HAD thought of two possible sub-titles to this paper, one on "the length of a short-title catalogue" and the other, simply "a million slips." The almost inevitable misinterpretation of the word "slips" seemed too risky as a drawing-card to this meeting. Errors there are but, I am sure, not that many. The length of the work is the one factor which seems to interest everyone. Let us begin by agreeing that only a fool would undertake such a project. But he has to be a particularly persevering fool to finish. I don't feel that much time has gone by since I began in 1933, partly because it has, except for one year, been an extra with evenings and week-ends only available. But also at Yale I am surrounded by other fools even more persevering, when we consider the programs of the Walpole and Boswell factories. Their slips will run into the millions but, again, they are each groups of scholars. It may be that I am here today because I am not a group. You will remember the roster of names on the title-page of the first S.T.C. Some had died and their places were taken by others with different ideas and methods; the Bodleian entries all too frequently showing the change, with the same book appearing in more than one place. While I have had lots of help—good, bad, and worse—there can be no other editor to blame.

I should like today to tell you something of the kinds of help I have had and also some of the pitfalls to be avoided by anyone

* Read at the meeting of the Society in New York, January 26, 1951.

rash enough to contemplate a continuation of my continuation. My help has come very largely from this country, and from many members of this society. Except for private collectors my friends in England have been quite naturally unable to offer much in either time or labor. I remember with horror a fat letter from the Librarian of the National Library of Scotland who, in all kindness, enclosed a list of their holdings, giving only the Aldis numbers. These were all additions to the printed book, acquired since its publication. This list of Scottish printed books is arranged chronologically, so that before using the new information I had to look up each number in the bibliography, make slips, alphabet them and compare with my manuscript. It seemed quicker to go back to Edinburgh.

I spoke of private collectors, and they are several different kinds of headaches—as many kinds as you have collectors. In England, thanks to letters from Dr. Harvey Cushing and Dr. John Fulton, I was able to list the private libraries of Sir D'Arcy Power and Geoffrey Keynes. I have since learned that Baron Keynes had a much larger seventeenth-century library than his brother. This is now in King's College, Cambridge, but his former Librarian has not been able to give me a list for even the third volume. I comfort myself with the thought that had I failed to note anything in the collection I should certainly have heard of it promptly. Two other English collectors opened wide their bookcases: Arnold Muirhead, then a schoolmaster and now associated with Peter Murray Hill; and F. S. Ferguson, then of Quaritch's, who collects Scottish imprints. After a fine Sunday dinner we got to work, lasting through a fine tea and a fine supper until I had to run for the last subway back to town. One other enthusiastic Englishman must be mentioned, John Johnson, long printer to Oxford University. We spent several Sunday mornings together in his most extraordinary collection of examples of job printing. It was difficult to keep my eyes away from his luscious labels from tomato cans to concentrate on tiny scraps printed on the frozen Thames and book prospectuses.

In America I had in New Haven the two outstanding medical collections for the later seventeenth century—Cushing and Fulton—both now at Yale. Dr. Cushing also asked me to be on the lookout, in England, for books he lacked, which gave me a wonderful excuse to browse in many book-shops. One Connecticut collector gave me notes of the books in his library. Trying to save private owners from unnecessary correspondence, I gave private locations only when there were less than five public copies located. The collector, I am afraid, felt that his copies were neglected. However, in the second volume he was credited with a rare volume. A letter to him from an Australian scholar asking for a transcript of the title-page went unanswered. I was challenged and had to have the book brought to New Haven. How does one please collectors, I ask you?

Another scholar wrote about locating Miltons in the Middle West before the second volume had appeared. I told him the nearest to him were at Urbana, Illinois. He went there and was turned away. Again I was challenged. The books were there all right, but the Reference Department had not been told what was in the English Department's office.

How I came to start work on the book is briefly told in the Preface to Volume One, but I seldom find evidence of that having been read. In 1933 when Yale had been in its new library building for three years, a last attempt to recover all books at Yale in 1742 was to be made. The manuscript catalogue was more complete than the printed version of the following year, but there were still too many unidentified entries like "Smith's Sermons in Quarto" and "a dirty Old Testament." Random searches in the stacks had turned up over a thousand volumes (of the 2600), but a systematic trip through the card catalogue was desirable. We had also just acquired Falconer Madan's library of Oxford books, and, while his printed catalogue came through 1680, he had collected avidly for the next twenty years. And there were no bibliographical tools to aid in their cataloguing. These two very different crises crystallized into the S.T.C. continuation, but permission was still needed to read the card catalogue. Mr. Keogh, then Librarian, agreed that I might do it in library time, while assigned to a public Reference Librarian desk, if I could think of two more reasons for the project. I suggested listing Connecticut imprints before 1851 (later used by the W.P.A.) and also following up all temporary cards in the catalogue which were ten years old or older. (That, I may remark in passing, is a sure-fire way to alienate the affections of the maturer cataloguers.) In the case of the missing 1742 Library books the majority were religious, so I put the catalogue of the new McAlpin Collection at Union Theological Seminary on slips. And so began my evening, week-end labors. McAlpin was followed by Trinity College, Dublin; the Inns of Court; Advocates; John Carter Brown; Dr. Williams' Library in London; Smith's Catalogue of Friends' Books; Madan; the beginning of Evans, and more than a dozen author bibliographies.

By 1935, when I applied for a Guggenheim grant to search British libraries, I had twenty-five shoeboxes full of slips. When I came back to America I had the present fifty-one. Evenings in England were frequently spent making the cross-references from anonymous works and initials to the final headings. This I had purposely delayed to keep the bulk of the manuscript down.

My first job in England was handling the 26,000 Thomason tracts (which by their size alone had stopped the parent volume with 1640). The temporary North Library of the British Museum agreed to a modified form of endless chain delivery, whereby I received twenty volumes an hour, each with about twenty tracts. When I got ahead of this schedule—as I did each day—I read the British Museum catalogue, sending for all volumes not previously seen elsewhere. By the time I moved on to Oxford seven months later, and to Cambridge, three more months later, I had fewer and fewer titles to examine. At each of the universities I was able to include two college libraries—at Oxford getting locked into Magdalen and Balliol, and at Cambridge listing Magdalene and Trinity. I had difficulty with the last, since its hours were even shorter than the University Library, but when it was remembered that I was a member of the College I was allowed to take the catalogue to my hotel, a tray at a time. What American library would do as much? (In fairness I must record that the University of Texas library loaned me their Rare Book Room card catalogue for a month, and Rutgers and Cincinnati copied their cards for me.) Christmas vacation allowed me to do Scottish libraries, and in the spring I visited a few libraries in Holland and France.

Most American libraries which are included have checked my galleys with their holdings, the most scholarly work being done at the largest collections, Huntington and Harvard. At Columbia we worked out a coöperative exchange that was mutually beneficial. When it was decided that I was to be printed at the Columbia University Press, their officers asked how well Columbia was represented. Well, it wasn't. The Plimpton collection was new and unlisted, I believe, and the Seligman tracts were old but only partly owned and arranged chronologically in two places. It was finally agreed that I should list all uncatalogued material (and this was a lever used to acquire the rest of Seligman) while the Library staff would check my galleys against the card catalogue. Obviously I could have gone on checking new collections forever, but that is no way to be useful. The first S.T.C. thought they had omitted less than ten per cent and I hope I have done as well. There is one kind of material consciously avoided in my list, and that is periodical publications. Almanacs are included, but I have always thought the countless news sheets, especially those beginning with the word *Mercurius*, will need a separate volume—and a different editor. Titles were copied and even stolen, and a proper job can only be done by giving collations and, possibly, even catch-words. This will interest fewer purchasers and appeals to me not at all.

It may be of interest to describe just what was put on each slip. Author, if on the title-page; enough title to distinguish this particular title from any other, keeping the first few words sacred; place, by, for, to be sold by, and date. So much is elementary and all was published except the place "London," which was assumed. Then comes size, and here I followed the gatherings of the book. Only a few times was it necessary to expand into "12° in sixes," etc. Term Catalogue reference if found. Some people have been unhappy because I have called all single sheets "bds." whether printed on one side or two. A clue as to which it is can usually be found, because if printed on two sides the imprint ordinarily appears as a colophon and follows the abbreviation "colop." In tracts without title-pages but dropped headings, again the imprint usually appears as a colophon and the notation "cap. title" for caption-title precedes the size symbol. Size is followed by references to a few standard bibliographies, such as Evans, Madan, Steele on royal proclamations, etc., and, finally, symbols of location. Here a perfect score for a perfectly common book would be British Museum, Oxford, Cambridge, one in Scotland, and one in Ireland. So much for Great Britain. For America, one in California, one in the Mid-West, Library of Congress or nearby, Texas, New England.

There is certain other information set down on the manuscript slips which was not considered suitable for printing. Some of this is incomplete, some irregular, some relating only to individual copies, but it seemed wise with the copy in hand to put it down somewhere. This includes the purchaser if known of copies sold at auction together with the prices fetched. (This is usually of more advantage to me as Order Librarian than as Bibliographer.) The fact that the title-page is in black and red, or that the text is wholly or largely in black-letter also appears only in my manuscript. The pagination is given, if under fifty pages, but this is translated into the printed version by an asterisk. Only in manuscript are other attributed authors, with their sources, whether Halkett and Laing, the DNB or a manuscript notation on an individual copy; and, finally, references to other bibliographies, such as the Grolier Club's *Wither to Prior*, Smith's Quaker lists, county bibliographies, papers of the various bibliographical societies, the *TLS*, *Notes and Queries*, and certain subject bibliographies such as those on engravings, herbals, tobacco, poetical miscellanies, tales and romances, character books, fencing, and fishing. Usually with author bibliographies I have given the reference in the printed book.

The hardest part of the book to write was, as is so often the case, the preface. It was also the hardest to proofread. There I had the help of three friends, all of whom passed the page proof as correct. But by great good fortune one of these friends had a friend who picked up a page and almost immediately found two horrible mistakes just in time. For some reason, instead of saying "i.e." I had written out "id est," and the compositor, with considerable pains inserted a period after each word. The other mistake was one of type-founts. I requested permission to quote this passage from the late D. B. Updike's *Printing Types*, as it seemed to me exactly what I wanted to say. ". . . now that my task is finished, I realize that further emendations could be continued with profit almost indefinitely. But while such a book can never, in any strict sense, be complete, it must be completed, though even the measure of perfection hoped for may not have been reached. It has been written in town and in country, amid the interruptions of business and in intervals of leisure—and 'in time of war and tumults' that at moments made its subject, and all like subjects, seem trivial and valueless." The miserable compositor had contrived to use an entirely new type for Mr. Updike's middle initial. I can think of no place where I should less like to make that kind of error. If a preface is hard to write, there is a wonderful compensation when volumes two and three come along. I only wanted to say "Reread the preface in Volume One."

I should like here and now to disclaim any responsibility or even knowledge of the caption-letters at the head of each page. They were not on any page proof I ever saw. The idea of guiding users more quickly to the wanted page is usually excellent, but here, by limiting them to the first three letters, the result is forty-nine pages (nearly a hundred columns) reading Cha-Cha, when it would have been just as easy and brief to have said Charles I, Charles II; and eight pages of Chu-Chu for both the Churches of England and Scotland. Except for these blemishes, I have nothing but praise for Mr. Loos and his printers. I hope he believes I am improving. On Volume One I had five sets of galleys and one of page proof. For Volume Two, two galleys and one of page proof, and for Volume Three only one of each. I was also very fortunate to be in at the birth of the Index Society, my publishers.

Several interesting observations may be made from the results thus far. A most peculiar geographical idiosyncrasy turns up regarding Oxford and Cambridge. Oxford, it appears, has a better collection of books printed in Scotland than its more northerly sister; while Cambridge, though further away, with its Bradshaw Collection is far stronger in Irish materials. When I visited the Union Catalogue in Philadelphia for books in that general locality I was shocked to find no seventeenth-century editions of any of William Penn's works. In fact, it seems as though Harvard and Yale both had as good early Quaker collections as are to be found anywhere. I also believe it is safe to say that since the publication of Woodward and McManaway's *Check-list of English Plays, 1641-1700*, in 1945, there are more of these plays in this country than in England.

One of the most intense pains of my searching relates to broadsides. At the Bodleian there is a huge volume of the catalogue so called. As I opened it, however, my heart sank. Page after page and entry after entry had the truthful if infuriating notation "no place, no date." It meant handling every one and trying to justi- fy an approximate date by means of types and printers' names— when they existed. A trick I learned early in my stay at the British Museum was to look at everything in a bound collection when it came to hand, rather than run the chance of needing it again for another pamphlet bound with the first. All too often this is a pro- cedure omitted by cataloguers, for many times I have seen titles which did not occur in the Library's catalogue. Sometimes several pieces belong together: they may be called for on the title-page or they may have continuous signature or pagination. Only when none of these was true did I list the succeeding titles. This exami- nation may be less valuable for later periods. I only know that very often all the pieces in a bound collection were all printed within a five-year period. If nine of ten are dated then you have good reason to suspect that the tenth is a contemporary.

We come now to the final section of this paper. The rest is in- tended for that single crazy member of the audience who is still toying with the idea of continuing beyond 1700. Until when? The answer to that question is entirely answered by the counter ques- tion: How many volumes do you propose to compile? Had I been more modest—not to say wiser—I might have done a single volume from 1641-1660, but that is so largely covered by the Thomason Catalogue that I even considered limiting it to books and tracts *not in* Thomason. But the year 1660 is not sacred to any but a king hater or a student of Restoration drama—and there is good sense in completing a century. Something died with Dryden, and the following decades have always been less sympathetic to me. The quantity of anonymous tracts continues after 1700 at much the same high rate, and I suggest to my follower the com- mon sense of putting them all under Daniel Defoe. If we keep adding twenty or thirty a year to his *corpus*, wouldn't it be time- saving to admit now that probably he wrote them all?

A start was made on a continuation by James Tobin, then of

Fordham University. He used to bring a class to New Haven every Friday and make notes from all our chronologically arranged files. But the end date started to shrink; from 1750 to 1735 to 1730 and finally, I believe, to 1725. Without having made any experimental soundings myself, I should think 1750 the next stopping place; to be followed by the final S.T.C. to 1800. After that another notation might properly be evolved, or, what would please me much more, a return to the sixteenth century on the European continent. It all needs doing, and I testify that, granted the proper degree of insanity and a temperament which does not set one dreaming of falling boxes of slips, it is *fun*. It is difficult for me to say what kind of temperament could think it fun, but I have two clues. In the first place I enjoyed being a Reference Librarian for ten years, and that means constant interruption, and variety. It precludes pondering anything. Reader A wants statistics; Reader B wants a trot for his Spanish course but won't say why; Reader C wants to illustrate his new book on metallurgy among the Incas; Reader D wants the sub-plots in Shakespeare in a thousand words—and, what is worse, they are always in a hurry. My second clue goes back to my childhood, and my movie period.

Sometime about the age of ten I started a notebook alphabetically arranged by actors and actresses of all their movie parts. The first notebook was soon filled, thanks to regular purchases of at least three monthly magazines. It was simple to get a larger notebook and fun to copy it all over leaving room for additions —for at least six months. This complete recopying went on at least four more times until either I began to grow up or went to college or rightly or wrongly thought myself too busy. It was fun, and so is an S.T.C.

One of the silliest questions I have been asked since the publication of the second volume is, "When are you going to begin Volume Three?" It is all one alphabet, so obviously it was all equally finished before any of it got printed. The difference is in the checking of galley-sheets for American locations. This has been done in three installments, and is now completed. I am now awaiting page proof from P-Z. Then there will be a question whether or not supplements will be necessary. In the five years since the first volume was published eleven additions have been reported, nine of which are now at Yale. These were largely intermediate editions where I had located, say, the first, second, and fourth editions. Now a third comes along. It is no surprise; it only means that it was not present in the 180-odd libraries searched. More of these will doubtless turn up when the English cathedral libraries are listed, but I expect few entirely new titles. I had heard that Lambeth Palace acted as a deposit for books refused licenses by the censor, but two weeks' search failed to turn up anything new. A supplement may be useful for noting copies now in this country, previously found only in Great Britain. I shouldn't dare print such a list today because it would be a long, long string of Y's. Nor should I dare to ask libraries to recheck and submit their additions. The first job is to produce Volume Three and then let any supplement wait for a demand.

I am not interested in the next half-century myself. I prefer to keep the new four-letter adjective pure. When booksellers offer Wing-period books I don't want to wonder which period.

The History of the Johnson Papers

By Mary C. Hyde*

THE story of the Johnson papers is unlike the story of the Boswell papers, which is a record of extraordinary self-preservation. It follows the opposite and more usual pattern of a famous man's papers, preserved by his contemporary admirers despite his own actions, for throughout his life Johnson was notoriously indifferent to the fate of his manuscripts, and in his last illness he burned "large masses" of them. He spared only a few, though his servant, Francis Barber, was able to rescue a few more from the flames. The only others known to remain were those which Johnson gave away before the conflagration, and the many letters which were in the possession of his correspondents. A thousand and forty-three letters was Birkbeck Hill's count in his edition of the correspondence; in R. W. Chapman's forthcoming edition the number approximates thirteen hundred.

The history of the surviving papers, who owned them first, and through what hands they passed, is filled with interest, for from the beginning Johnson manuscripts have been the subject of cupidity, curiosity and study. "It is wonderful," Boswell wrote Percy in 1788, "what avidity there still is for everything

* Read at the meeting of the Society in New York, January 26, 1951.

relative to Johnson." He referred in particular to Mrs. Piozzi. This close friend of Johnson had carefully preserved her letters from him for a period of twenty years, intending to publish them after his death. When this event occurred, however, she was in Italy on an extended wedding trip, and Johnson's correspondence was in a locked box in her London bank. She was not able to proceed with the project until she returned to England, and at that time discovered that she did not possess enough material herself to fill her second volume to the desired length. She was forced, therefore, to collect additional letters. Her eldest daughter, Queeney Thrale, had sufficient correspondence from Johnson to serve the purpose, but Queeney disapproved of her mother's venture and refused assistance. Queeney was the type of collector who, though withholding material, never destroys it, and her letters from Johnson were eventually published in 1932 by the Marquis of Lansdowne, who had inherited her collection. Although Mrs. Piozzi was wholly unsuccessful with Queeney, she was more fortunate in her pursuit of other correspondents, her persistence being rewarded in the end with the publishing rights of Johnson's letters to Hill Boothby, Joseph Simpson, and Sastres.

Boswell himself was casting a wide net at the same time, applying to some of Mrs. Piozzi's prospects and to many others. He had been engaged on his *Life of Johnson* for several years, and at the time of his subject's death was also at a disadvantage. Boswell was far from London, and had failed to secure from Johnson much material which he needed. Sir John Hawkins, as one of the literary executors, had carried off the papers which Johnson had spared from the fire, and was using them in the preparation of *his* biography of Johnson, an action wholly within his rights. Upon completion of this work, Hawkins was obliged to turn the manuscripts back to Francis Barber, Johnson's residuary legatee, but for the moment he was in the happy position of having the most important Johnson collection on loan.

Boswell, of course, owned certain important material: voluminous correspondence, invaluable notes about Johnson, a few transcripts, and part of the original manuscript and proof sheets of the *Lives of the Poets*, about which Johnson had written him on March 14, 1781, saying, "I have at last finished my *Lives* and have laid up for you a load of copy, all out of order, so that it will amuse you a long time to set it right." Yet Boswell needed more material, and he vigorously set out in pursuit of it.

As usual, certain owners were coöperative and others were wholly unresponsive. Bennet Langton and Edmund Hector gave liberally to Boswell, but Elizabeth Aston, Robert Chambers, George Strahan, and Dr. Taylor firmly refused him. It is interesting to follow up the latter list. The Aston letters were finally given to Pembroke College, Oxford. A few of Chambers' letters made their first appearance in the auction market in 1901, the property of General Macdonald; and a considerably larger group appeared in 1922, the property of Mrs. Flower, the great-great-granddaughter of Chambers.

George Strahan, who resisted Boswell's approach, was vicar of Islington, the son of Johnson's friend, William Strahan. This young man had always been a favorite of Johnson and attended him during his last illness. In the final days, when Johnson was too ill to revise the manuscript of *Prayers and Meditations*, he gave it to Strahan with instructions for committing it to the press, and with a promise, never fulfilled, to prepare a sketch of his life to accompany the text. When Strahan published the book he presented the manuscript to Pembroke College, Oxford, where it can be seen today in two cardboard letter file boxes.

Johnson's old friend, Dr. Taylor, who lived so well at Ashebourne, owned many of the sermons which Johnson had written for him and an important docket of a hundred and eight letters, according to Birkbeck Hill, although R. W. Chapman states it is a hundred and two. A large group of these letters which Taylor carefully preserved but determinedly withheld, are now ac-

A Short Scheme for compiling a new Dictionary of the English Language

Johnson's "Plan of the Dictionary," First Draft

Boswell Sale 1825 — Skegg Sale 1842 —
Pocock Sale 1875 — R. B. Adam — Hyde

cessible in the Berg Collection of the New York Public Library, purchased in 1945 from A. T. Loyd, after they had been through the hands of Lord Wantage, Lord Overstone, Sir John Simeon, and the Pierpont family.

To return to owners who were more obliging to Boswell; Edmund Hector, Johnson's schoolfellow, offered considerable help. He was one of the last people outside of London to see Johnson, for on the final trip from Lichfield to London, a month before his death, Johnson visited Hector in Birmingham, and discussed with him at length the early events of his life. Hector, besides having an intimate knowledge of Johnson over a long period of time, had important letters from him. He also had wide and valuable connections with other holders of manuscripts. It was, for instance, through Hector that Boswell was able to obtain his "little collection" of early poems written by Johnson when at school in Stourbridge.

Another responsive to Boswell's appeal was Bennet Langton, the worthy, learned friend of Johnson, some twenty-eight years his junior. Langton had a number of letters and several manuscripts which were given to him by Johnson a few days before he died. Of these, a manuscript catalogue of *Projected Works*, a *List of Designs*, and the original, unformed sketch of *Irene*, Langton presented to the King, who in turn gave the last to the British Museum. Langton sold Johnson's Latin poems to the booksellers for a small sum to benefit Johnson's relations, and through the booksellers these poems started their progress toward the auction market.

After Hawkins' death in 1789 Boswell came into possession of the bulk of the residue papers through their owner, Francis Barber, and late though it was, Boswell's exultation can be imagined. Barber for some reason withheld two items from both Hawkins and Boswell. One was the *Account of the Life of Dr. Samuel Johnson, from his Birth to his Eleventh Year* which was printed in 1805 for Richard Phillips. The editor in the preface to the little book said that "by purchase from Barber's widow" it came into his possession. The other was the journal of Johnson's *Welsh Tour*.

James Boswell Jr. had knowledge of both these manuscripts and wrote in angry comment to a friend:

Dear Sir,

I hope I shall be always considered in the number of those who are most anxious to show their veneration for the memory of Johnson, but I am sorry to say that I cannot think any one is entitled to much attention on that ground from being the son of Francis Barber who I think was an ungrateful scoundrel. You may recollect the manuscript of Johnson's early life most unfit for publication which he stole & which was afterwards sold to Sir Richard Phillips. We have lately had a tour in Wales which I believe him to have stolen also, out of which Mr. Duppa with the aid of Pattersons road book made an octavo volume. I should not wish to visit all this upon the son but he seems to me to tell a very lame story about his wandering from one trade to another. . . .

From the more important early locations, the story now follows the subsequent fate of Johnson's papers. In 1823 a few Johnson letters made their appearance in the auction sale of Mrs. Piozzi's library at Brynbella. Item 645 was:

A few interesting ORIGINAL LETTERS, (some in French) in the handwriting of Dr. Johnson. Independent of their intrinsic worth—viewed as literary morceaus to illustrate his and Mrs. Piozzi's works, they are invaluable—as Autographs, impossible elsewhere to be procured—as acquisitions to Albums, desirable, and—after this period, in all probability never again obtainable—of so much importance indeed are they, that it will be a matter of national regret if these Johnsonian Relics are not purchased for the British or other public or private museum.

The indication of national pride in Johnson at this date is significant, as is the comment that a Johnson letter is eminently desirable for insertion in an autograph album. With the passing of Johnson's contemporaries, and the coming of another generation, this new trend in the collection of Johnson manuscripts as autographs began. Descendants of former owners were no longer troubled by prospective authors; they were harassed by autograph hunters.

Mrs. Piozzi's adopted son, Sir John Salusbury, wrote to a Miss Lloyd in Anglesey, that he could not resist her second attack upon his gallantry, for he knew that "when a lady sets her mind upon obtaining any object, she never rests till she succeeds." He, therefore, surrendered and wished to present her with "a note from the great Dr. Johnson." In return, Sir John, who fortunately shared the same interest, wondered if Miss Lloyd would send him an autograph of the Duke of Wellington, Melbourne, or Lord Byron, though "he would very much prefer [he said] a letter from Pitt, Fox, Canning, or from some celebrated author of bygone days, such as Cowper, Gray, Young— or even Sir Walter Scott."

For the many collectors who could not establish a personal contact as Miss Lloyd had done, there remained the chance of securing a Johnson autograph at auction, where Johnson letters appeared with increasing frequency throughout the nineteenth century. Johnson's popularity as a literary autograph accounts in some measure for the wide distribution of his letters today, and for the difficulty in establishing their location. Even if located, there is often a further difficulty of approach. More than one Johnson letter, kept in an album alongside letters of Wellington and Gladstone, is known to be considered by the family too personal a possession to admit inspection by an outsider.

The first important dispersal of Johnson manuscripts was the sale of the library of James Boswell Jr. in May 1825. Among the outstanding papers catalogued were: the *Plan of the Dictionary*, first draft, *Plan of the Dictionary*, second draft, the *Life of Pope*, the *Life of Rowe*, the *French Journal*, the *Diary for 1781 and 1783*, and a small paper book, *Repertorium*. All these items went to a single agent, Thorpe. Thorpe was a remarkably shrewd and active dealer, at one time commissioned by Sir Thomas Phillipps to search for manuscripts, later becoming the agent and librarian of William Henry Miller, founder of the Britwell Court library.

Of the items bought by Thorpe at the Boswell sale, the *French Journal* passed through the hands of the Earl of Guilford and of the poet, Samuel Rogers, whose great-nieces gave it to the British Museum. *Repertorium* appeared at Sotheby's again in 1904, and its recent course has been from Colonel Isham to Professor Tinker. The other manuscripts, the *Plan of the Dictionary*, first and second draft, the *Life of Rowe*, the *Life of Pope*, and the *Diary for 1781 and 1783* appeared together again in the important sale of Edward Skegg in June 1842.

Another buyer at the Boswell sale was William Upcott, who secured "Various Proof Sheets of Dr. Johnson's Lives of the Poets, corrected in his own hand-writing," and six of the prayers. Upcott, a natural son of Johnson's friend Ozias Humphry, was an outstanding nineteenth-century collector. He achieved marked success as a bookseller, and in 1806 was appointed assistant librarian of the London Institution. Here, in his office, and in the rooms of his house, every wall was covered with paintings, drawings, and prints. All his drawers and cupboards were crammed, and he had specially fitted shelves and a hundred receptacles into which he dropped a quantity of cuttings on various subjects. He boasted the ownership of thirty-two thousand letters.

At the Upcott sale in June 1846 his purchases from the Boswell library doubtless reappeared, though they are hard to particularize, for example, "seven hundred and fifty two letters of literary men including Johnson, in five volumes." There were also extra-illustrated copies of *The Life of Johnson* containing such material as a catalogue of the sale of books, Worcester, 1718, which was distributed by Johnson's father; a catalogue of the sale of Johnson's library; and several long letters of Boswell and Johnson. It would appear that grangerizing had become an outgrowth of the autograph album.

Throughout the fifties and sixties, Johnson letters were conspicuous in sales, though his manuscripts other than letters were

not frequently seen. Two exceptions to this were Johnson's prayer for September eighteenth 1784 in the George Linnacer auction in March 1850, an item which had passed from Boswell to
Upcott previously, and the manuscript poem "The snow dis-
solv'd . . ." at Puttick and Simpson's on the second of May 1861.

There were also Johnson items in July 1864, at the sale of
George Daniel, a topical writer of the day, a critic and chronicler
of the theatre, and a book collector. His main collecting interest
was in the drama, but he had sufficient enthusiasm for Johnson to
write a reply to Macaulay's essay, and to own several fine manuscripts: the memorandum fragment dated Heale, 1783; Johnson's last prayer, December fifth 1784; and some of the proof-
sheets of the *Lives of the Poets* with the author's corrections. The
last two items had passed through the Boswell and Upcott sales;
the prayer has recently gone from A. Edward Newton to Prof.
Tinker; and the proof-sheets, presumably those Johnson sent
to Boswell ill-assorted, are now partly in the Forster Collection
of the South Kensington Museum, and partly in the British
Museum.

There was an important Johnson manuscript auctioned in the
last year of the sixties, in the John Dillon sale, June 1869. The
catalogue title page bore the usual words, "A Collection of Autograph Letters, Manuscripts, and Historical Documents," and
among these was Lot 574, Johnson's *Life of Pope*, which Thorpe
had bought at the Boswell sale and Holloway at the Skegg
sale. This time it was again purchased by Holloway, and in
1896 came to the Pierpont Morgan Library from the dealer
Henry Sotheran.

The most important sale of Johnson material since the Boswell auction was held in May 1875, the collection of Lewis
Pocock, art amateur and collector. Though Pocock's interest was
primarily in art, he had formed an extensive enough collection
of Johnsoniana to warrant a separate catalogue containing five
hundred and eighty-six items. There were many Johnson letters

in this sale, including the famous retort to Macpherson, which Pocock had bought at the George Linnacer sale in 1850. These familiar manuscripts appeared together once more: the *Plan of the Dictionary*, draft one and two; the *Life of Rowe*; and the *Diary for 1781 and 1783*, all of which had been bought by Pocock at the Skegg sale. They now went to the dealer, Harvey, who sold the *Diary for 1781 and 1783* to Locker-Lampson, from whom it passed to W. K. Bixby of St. Louis, and from thence to the Huntington Library. The other manuscripts were sold to R. B. Adam of Buffalo.

Adam purchased additional lots at the Pocock sale: Johnson's *Considerations on Corn, Note on Mr. Poore to the Club, Diary Record for the 8, 9, 10 June, 1784*, and the poem to Miss Hickman playing on the spinet. From the Pocock source alone, this collector laid a firm foundation for his Johnsonian library, many of the items stemming back to Boswell.

In the next important auction, the Ross sale at Christie's in June 1888, not so much came to Adam. Considerably more items were bought by the dealer Pearson and sold to the Pierpont Morgan Library, and more as well were bought for the great autograph collector, Alfred Morrison. Morrison's purchases included several early letters to Cave, and the important letter to Goldsmith, both of which R. B. Adam II was able to buy at Morrison's sale in 1918. Sometimes, but not often, there is a second chance.

In the eighties and nineties new trends in collecting were apparent. The concentration upon Johnson as a single figure was noticeable in the Pocock and Ross sales and in such libraries as that being gathered by R. B. Adam. There was also noticeable, among such collectors, an increased interest in the study of the subject collected, a search beyond acquisition itself. Collectors sought the aid of scholars, and scholars in turn became collectors.

The influence in the nineties of the great Johnsonian scholar, George Birkbeck Hill, over dealers and collectors was profound.

Auction catalogues of that period frequently recorded "ALS of Samuel Johnson, accompanied by a note of George Birkbeck Hill." In this connection there is an amusing instance to prove the great are not infallible. In the George Manners' sale in November 1890, Item 209 was one of the few letters of Johnson to Mrs. Thrale which up to this time had come to auction. In the catalogue Hill records, "I have seen only three or four at most of Johnson's letters to Mrs. Thrale, perhaps all of them have been destroyed." Hill was still alive in 1901 when these letters began to stream into the market from the descendants of Sir John Salusbury, Mrs. Piozzi's adopted son. As the Salusbury family became progressively impoverished, they disposed of more and more letters, culminating in the spectacular sale of January 1918, which offered "a magnificent series of over two hundred letters from Dr. Johnson to Mrs. Thrale." The owner then was the great-granddaughter of John Salusbury, Mrs. Colman, the same person who sold to the Rylands Library in the nineteen thirties the final, large and breathtaking residue of the Thrale collection.

When R. B. Adam died in 1904, his nephew and adopted son inherited the library, and what is perhaps more remarkable, his uncle's love for it. R. B. Adam II continued collecting in the same manner, but even more extensively. He increased and strengthened the friendly association with other Johnsonian collectors, and with outstanding eighteenth-century scholars, whom he treated with such graciousness that some wrote to him, not about "your" collection but "our" collection. He added greatly to his Johnson material—not many manuscripts, but a vast number of letters. When Birkbeck Hill saw the Adam Collection in 1893 it had only ten letters from Johnson and Boswell combined; by 1921 the number of Johnson letters alone was more than a hundred; and by 1929 more than two hundred and thirty. There were many unpublished letters of importance, notably several to Mrs. Thrale from the Salusbury sales, and the long series to

Chambers which had been denied to Boswell many years before.

A great friend and rival of Adam in the Johnson field was A. Edward Newton of Philadelphia, a man of engaging personality who collected Johnson and advertised him with what is sometimes called fanaticism. His collection was not so large as Adam's, but it was choice. His collecting was a matter of personal excitement about which he was delightfully articulate, and accounts of his adventures served to spread his enthusiasm a great distance.

To imply that R. B. Adam and A. Edward Newton had a free field for their collecting of Johnson would be untrue, because in the twenties the whole field of the eighteenth century, both in England and America, was discovered belatedly and with violence. Many bookshops specialized in it, such as Elkin Mathews, where, it has been said, the eighteenth century was the sole reality. Catalogues were brought out by this firm which were easy and provocative reading and productive of remarkable interest. This shop and others reflected the increasing influence of dealers, many of whom were well versed in the century, and able to act as shrewd and knowledgeable mentors for the collector.

In the twenties the circle of Johnsonians widened and collectors showed a deepening interest in the study of their material. In several libraries the three-part ideal established by the period reached fulfillment, that of acquisition, research, and publication. The activity of scholars in the Johnson field was marked: Nichol Smith, R. W. Chapman, S. C. Roberts, L. F. Powell, A. L. Reade, Charles G. Osgood, and—as has often been pointed out, sometimes in the most extraordinary places—there is a close affiliation between the Age of Johnson and the Age of Tinker.

In the thirties and early forties there was a reaction to the overwhelming popularity which the eighteenth century had enjoyed in the twenties, the cause mainly economic, though in part a matter of taste. The important sale of A. Edward Newton's library came during this time. Beginning in April 1941, his collection was sold, according to his wish, as expressed by de Goncourt, that his library be dispersed under the hammer of an auctioneer, so that each item which had given him pleasure to acquire, could be given again to some inheritor of his taste.

At the Newton sale the Johnson manuscripts and letters were widely dispersed. A few items, including Johnson's *Considerations on Trapp's Sermons* and his efforts in behalf of William Dodd, were bought by the Donald Hydes, and with these purchases their activity began. Their library, which is devoted to Johnson, has had much added through the forties from other auctions, and from the stock of patient and helpful book dealers in America and England. The extensive Johnson manuscripts and letters have been added from both Malahide Castle and Fettercairn House, much of the material Boswell had from Hawkins which did not appear in the Boswell sale. The latest addition has been the R. B. Adam Collection.

The remainder of the history, the present location of other manuscripts, has been indicated at many points. A few are not traced. The *Account of the Life of Dr. Samuel Johnson, from his Birth to his Eleventh Year*, the curious manuscript offered to public view by its editor in 1805, has disappeared, though it would be foolhardy to say that it has been destroyed. Johnson's *List of Designs* and *Projected Works* given to Langton, and by him to the King, are no longer located. The diary fragment for 1783 and *Rules for School* are also elusive. The most obvious and celebrated blank is that of Johnson's correspondence with Boswell, increasingly strange in the light of present discoveries. Only three letters are at present known to survive: the letter from Johnson to Boswell, in an album owned by Lord Clinton of Fettercairn House; the Ashebourne fragment at Yale University; and the fragment sold by R. W. Chapman in 1944. All these manuscripts have once been seen but are at the moment obscured from view. That they may be seen again is a hope inspiring vigilance.

Some of Johnson's papers have met with violence. Many were burned in his conflagration. And the rumor persists in Wales, among the descendants of Dr. Pearson, Lucy Porter's heir, that the manuscript of the *Dictionary* was used to cover jelly jars in a Lichfield attic, the portion of it surviving this treatment later being eaten by rats. A more unusual case is the Latin prose exercise of Johnson, eaten by a baby, a tragedy prompting an eminent British Johnsonian to write that this was added testimony to the danger of such things going to America.

The four perils noted by Agard, the archivist: fire, water, rats, and misplacing, have continued to exact their toll. But despite these casualties, the remarkable conclusion of the story is the known preservation of so much of the material which survived at the time of Johnson's death. It is now widespread in important collections: in England, the British Museum, the South Kensington Museum, the Rylands Library, the Bodleian, Pembroke and Trinity Colleges, Oxford, Lord Rothschild and the Marquis of Lansdowne; in this country, the Pierpont Morgan Library, the New York Public Library, Yale University, the Huntington Library, Arthur A. Houghton, Jr., Prof. Tinker, Herman W. Liebert, and the Hyde Collection.

There is still as much avidity for everything relative to Johnson as when Boswell remarked it. Johnson, if he knew, or knows, could not fail to be touched by the interest, amused, perhaps outraged, by the splitting of hairs, nevertheless, exhilarated by his defeat of oblivion.

The Printing of Shakespeare's *Troilus and Cressida* in the First Folio

By W. W. Greg

THE acute observation and reasoning of three scholars whose names are associated with the Folger Library have placed Shakespearian bibliographers in possession of the facts concerning the printing of *Troilus and Cressida* in the First Folio of 1623.[1] We know that the play was originally intended to follow *Romeo and Juliet* and to occupy pages 78 and following in the section of Tragedies, for several copies of the Folio survive containing the cancelled leaf (sig. gg3) bearing on the recto the last page of *Romeo* and on the verso the first page of the text of *Troilus*.[2]

What happened was this. The compositor ended *Romeo* on the recto of gg3 and at once began to set up the text of *Troilus* on the verso, continuing the composition of this play on gg4 with pages

---

[1] J. Q. Adams, "*Timon of Athens* and the Irregularities of the First Folio," in: *The Journal of English and Germanic Philology*, VII: 53-63 (Jan. 1908); E. E. Willoughby, *The Printing of the First Folio of Shakespeare* (London, The Bibliographical Society, 1932), pp. 46-50; G. E. Dawson, "A Bibliographical Problem in the First Folio of Shakespeare," in: *The Library*, XXII: 25-33 (June, 1941).

[2] Notably the Burdett-Coutts copy now in the Folger Library and the Toovey copy in the Pierpont Morgan Library. Three others are in the Folger collection.

79 and 80. As soon as the four formes of gg3-4 were ready they were printed off as the inner sheet of a normal gathering of three: this was the regular procedure. But at this point something happened that made it impossible, or undesirable, to proceed immediately with the composition of *Troilus*. No doubt it was hoped that the impediment would soon be removed, for a calculation was made of the space needed to complete the play, and printing was continued with *Julius Caesar* on kk1. This left the printer with gg1 and gg2, containing four pages of *Romeo* on his hands, pages which but for the interruption would have been imposed along with those of gg6 and gg5 of *Troilus*. Rather than keep the type of these four pages standing, it was decided to print them off on a single sheet which could stand as a quire gg² by itself.[3]

When the hope of resuming work on *Troilus* was disappointed, it was decided to substitute *Timon*. The last page of *Romeo*, originally printed on gg3 was reset on the recto of the first leaf, signed "Gg", of a new quire, and *Timon* was begun on the verso of the same. But *Timon* is a shorter play than *Troilus* and it failed to fill the allotted space, so that there is a gap in the signatures and pagination between it and *Julius Caesar*. All hope of including *Troilus* having been abandoned, the colophon was duly printed at the end of *Cymbeline* (which had somehow strayed among the Tragedies) and in the preliminaries the title of *Troilus* was omitted from the catalogue of contents. Then, just as the volume was ready for publication, *Troilus* at last became available. The

---

[3] I do not understand the reason for Dawson's statement (p. 33) that "While the inner sheet [gg3-4] was passing through the press the composition of pages 81-4 of *Troilus* had probably been completed." His discovery that gg1-2 were printed as a separate sheet proves that when the order came to stay composition the machining of the sheet gg3-4 had already been at least begun, for otherwise the eight pages of gg1-4 would have been printed as a short gathering of two sheets (as Willoughby supposed); but it surely also proves that the composition of gg5-6 (pages 81-4) had *not* been completed, for in that case they too would have been printed off as a separate sheet (indeed, had the order to stay composition been delayed till that of gg5-6 was complete, there would have been no reason why a normal gathering of three sheets should not have been printed). That composition continued while gg3-4 were on the press is probable, but the order to stay was presumably received soon after machining had begun and when little progress had been made with composition, since the type was distributed again.

last page of *Romeo* and the first three of *Troilus* had, it will be
remembered, been already printed off on the original gg3-4. The
first of these leaves had of course to be scrapped: a fresh leaf
(unsigned) was substituted, bearing on the recto a hitherto unprinted Prologue to *Troilus* and on the verso a close reprint of
the first page.[4] The second leaf was retained with its original
pagination 79-80 (being the fourth leaf of the projected quire,
it bore no signature). Then the play was completed, with a series of arbitrary signatures but without pagination, and the whole
inserted in the only possible place, namely at the head of the section of Tragedies to which it had originally been assigned.

All this is now established fact to the Shakespearian bibliographer. The cause of the trouble is admittedly a more speculative
matter, but it has been plausibly referred to a dispute over the
copyright. On 28 January, 1609, two young stationers, Richard
Bonian and Henry Walley, had entered the play at Stationers'
Hall, and this entrance they followed up the same year with an
edition, in a rather flamboyant preface to which they went out of
their way to proclaim that they were printing the play against the
wishes of "the grand possessors", by which they can have meant
none other than his Majesty's players. We do not know how they
came by their copy of the play, which was certainly a sound one
in the main, but they clearly regarded it as something of a
"scoop." What more likely than that fourteen years later, when
the same company wished to include the play in their collection
of the author's works, Walley, the surviving member of the
partnership, should stand upon his rights and refuse them permission to make free with his "copy," or that the Court of the
Stationers' Company, had the dispute come before them, would
have upheld his action? It is, therefore, quite reasonable to assume that this was the cause of the withdrawal of *Troilus* from

---

[4] There are some 65 differences of one sort and another, but only three that can
be called variant readings. In I. i. 25 "the heating the Ouen" was altered to "the
heating of the Ouen"; in l. 74 "and she were Kinne to me" was corrected to "and
she were not kin to me"; and in l. 79 the prefix *"Pan."* was misprinted *"Troy."*. All
references in this article are to the Cambridge Shakespeare, 1892.

its original position in the First Folio. Bibliographers, however, have further assumed that the eventual inclusion of the piece was due to a last-moment relenting on Walley's part; and it is here that fresh evidence has come to light, which enables us, I think, to put a different construction on the facts.

The truth is that Walley's position was not quite as certain as has been assumed or as he himself perhaps believed. For when he and his colleague registered the play an earlier entrance already stood in the Hall Book. Six years before, on 7 February, 1603, James Roberts had caused the following memorandum to be made: "Entred for his copie in Full Court holden this day. to print when he hath gotten sufficient aucthority for yt. The booke of Troilus and Cresseda as yt is acted by my lo: Chamberlens Men". The Chamberlain's company was, of course, the predecessor of the King's, and the entrance was most likely made with their authority, since the mention of "The booke" suggests, if it does not actually imply, that it was the prompt-book itself that was submitted to the Clerk for registration. By 1623 Roberts, it is true, was dead, but he had, about 1608, sold his business to William Jaggard, so that the publisher of the First Folio had acquired a claim to his copies. Jaggard could have argued that Walley's edition of *Troilus* itself infringed rights he had acquired from Roberts and that the joint entrance of 1609 ought indeed never to have been allowed; and had he chosen to take his case to the Court of Assistants, it is at least possible that they would have revoked Walley's rights in the copy. But this would not, in fact, have helped Jaggard and the King's men, for though it would have prevented Walley from reprinting the play (which he probably had no intention of doing) there is no reason to suppose that it would have allowed Jaggard to appropriate Walley's text.

This limitation may be inferred from two cases that had come before the Court a generation earlier. It appears that early, probably, in 1592 Abel Jeffes printed what seems to have been a gar-

bled edition of *The Spanish Tragedy* (now lost) and he entered it
on 6 October, perhaps on learning that Edward White was about
to replace it by the extant edition, which contains an excellent
text "Newly corrected and amended of such grosse faults as
passed in the first impression." On 18 December Jeffes protested
to the Court, which upheld his copyright and fined White ten
shillings. In 1594 Jeffes reprinted White's text, but in order to do
so he evidently had to come to terms with his opponent and allow
him an interest in the new edition, for this bears the legend
"Printed by Abell Ieffes, and are to be sold by Edward White."[5]
It was also in 1592 that Thomas Orwin printed an edition of *The
Damnable Life and Deserved Death of Doctor Faustus*, "newly im-
printed, and in conuenient places imperfect matter amended", to
replace a lost and presumably defective edition, to which again
Abel Jeffes laid claim. Jeffes's complaint was heard by the Court
the same day as the other, and judgment again went in his fa-
vour, though in this case no entrance had been made by either
claimant. On this occasion Jeffes made no attempt to reprint the
book, but when on 5 April 1596 it was at length entered in the
Register, "havinge thinterest of abell Ieffes thereto", it was once
more by Edward White, who had acted as bookseller for Orwin's edition four years previously, and who doubtless bargained
for the rights of both parties.[6]

We may assume, therefore, that while Jaggard might have
been able to substantiate a claim to the "copy" of *Troilus*, he
would still have had no right to reproduce Walley's text, but
would have had to print it, if at all, from some other source, that
is, from a manuscript. It is at this point that the new evidence
comes in. In the course of a recent article on "The Textual Problem of *Troilus and Cressida*"[7] Dr. Alice Walker remarks that "had

[5] See *The Spanish Tragedy (1592)*, Malone Society Reprint, 1948, introduction,
pp. vi-xiii.
[6] See Marlowe's *Doctor Faustus* (parallel texts), (Oxford, 1950), Introduction,
pp. 1-4.
[7] *The Modern Language Review*, XLV: 459-64 (October, 1950).

the original intention of printing the play immediately after
Romeo and Juliet been adhered to, we should have had in the Folio
text a mere reprint of the Quarto," whereas it is well known that
for the bulk of the text recourse was had to a manuscript. What
she had observed, and was so far as I am aware the first to point
out, was that in the three pages originally set up (pp. 78-80)
the variants between the Quarto and Folio texts are such as any
compositor may be expected to produce when reprinting another
text,[8] while as soon as we reach the first page set up for the first
time after the interruption (that is, the recto of sig. ¶1) variants
appear that can only be accounted for by the use of some independent source, and that these persist throughout the rest of the
play.

Miss Walker gave (on pp. 463-4) a list of readings from the
three pages originally printed and from the following three set
up after the interruption, sufficient, she thought, to establish her
contention. Probably they are, but since the question has now
assumed an importance greater than she at the moment realized,
it may be desirable to print here a more extended collation.[9] Here
first are the readings of pages 78-80.[10]

	QUARTO	FOLIO
Page [78]		
I.i 15	must tarry	must ‡needes tarrie
26	yea may chance burne	*you may chaunce ‡to burne
44	I would not as they tearme it praise her,	I would not (as they terme it) praise †it,

---

[8] The only variant not immediately referable to the compositor is the insertion
of an entrance at I. ii. 35, but this is obviously called for by the text.

[9] Since we have already seen that the differences between the original setting
of page 78 and the reprint are insignificant, I take no notice of the latter.

[10] In the list of Folio readings a * marks the correction of obvious errors, a †
errors committed by the compositor, and ‡ variants that do not evidently fall into
either class. The Folio compositor, beginning work on a play in the section of
Tragedies, naturally altered the "history" of the Quarto head-title to "TRAGEDIE"
and he made a like change in the running title. After the interruption he adopted
the simple and, as Miss Walker calls it, non-committal head-line "*Troylus and
Cressida.*" This, she suggests (p. 462), was due to the anomalous position of the
play between the Histories and Tragedies. But the play was always regarded as belonging to the latter.

70	ill thought on of her, and ill thought of you,	ill thought on of her, and ill thought *on of you:
75	as faire a Friday as *Hellen*, is on Sunday,	as faire ‡on Friday, as *Helen* is on Sunday,
76	but what I? I care not	But what *care I? I care not
87s.d.	*Exit.*	*Exit* ‡*Panda.*

Page 79

100	reides	*recides (*for* resides)
ii.6	Hee chid	He †chides
17	vnlesse the are dronke,	vnlesse *they are drunke,
29	purblinde *Argus*,	‡purblinded *Argus*,
33	the disdaine and shame	the †disdaind & shame
35s.d.	[absent]	*Enter Pandarus.*
43	Illum?	*Illium?
67	nor *Hector* is not *Troylus*	†not *Hector* is not *Troylus*
97	praizd	†prasi'd

Page 80

112	Is he so yong a man,	Is he †is so young a man,
118	valianty.	*valiantly.
120	clowd	†clow'd (*i.e.* cloud)
140-1	But there was a more temperate fire vnder the por	But there was ‡ more temperate fire vnder the *pot
166	So I doe.	So I †does.
172	Ilion,	‡Illium,
184	hee's man good enough,	hee's ‡a man good inough,
185	hees one o'th soundest iudgements in Troy	hee's one o'th soundest ‡iudgement in Troy
187	see him nod at mee.	see him †him nod at me.
195	O a braue man.	O † braue man!
196	it dooes a man heart good,	It dooes a *mans heart good,
198-9	thers no iesting, thers laying on, takt off, who will as they say,	There's no iesting, † laying on, tak't off, who †ill as they say,
209	you shall see *Troylus* anon.	you shall † *Troylus* anon.
216	doe you not here the people	do you not †haere the people
219s.d.	*Troylus.*	†*Trylus.*
223	Marke him, note him:	Marke him, †not him:

Variants of this sort persist throughout the play. But as soon as we reach the first of the pages set up for the first time after the interruption, variants of a different type begin to appear. The following is a fairly exhaustive list of variants of the new type found in the next three pages (pages [81-3]). Opinion will naturally differ respecting what is significant and what is not, and I do not pretend that all the Folio variants in the list necessarily imply resort to a source independent of the Quarto.[11] But even the less significant reinforce the evidence of the more striking and conclusive.[12]

QUARTO	FOLIO
Page [81]	
I.ii.231 *Hellen* to change would giue **an eye** to boote.	*Helen* to change, would giue **money** to boot.
232s.d. [absent]	*Enter common Souldiers.*
246 liberallity and **such like,**	liberality, and **so forth:**
250 You are such **a** woman **a man** knowes not at what ward you lie:	You are such **another** woman, **one** knowes not at what ward you lye.
266 At your owne house **there he vn-armes him:**	At your owne house.
273s.d. [absent]	*Exit Pand.*
286 Then though my hearts **content**	That though my hearts **Contents**
iii.2 hath set **these** Iaundies **ore** your cheekes?	hath set **the** Iaundies **on** your cheekes?
19 And **call** them **shames**	And **thinke** them **shame,**
27 with a **broad** and powerfull fan,	with a **lowd** and powrefull fan,
36 Vpon her **ancient** brest,	Vpon her **patient** brest,
Page [82]	
67 **(On** which **heauen rides)** knit all **the Greekish** eares	**In** which **the Heauens ride,** knit all **Greekes** ears
70-4 [absent]	[a five-line speech]
92 Corrects the **influence** of euill **Planets,**	Corrects the **ill Aspects** of **Planets** euill,
102 Which is the ladder **of** all high designes,	(Which is the Ladder **to** all high designes)
110 each thing **melts** | In meere oppugnancie:	each thing **meetes** | In meere oppugnancie.

[11] For example, the added entry at I. iii. 215 can be inferred from the text just as easily as that at I. ii. 35 (but the accompanying "*Tucket*" cannot): the omission at I. ii. 266 may be accidental (but why should Troilus go to Pandarus' house to unarm?): at I. iii. 219 the correction is obvious and may be conjectural: the variant at I. iii. 228 may be a mere misprint: the omission at I. iii. 238 would probably have been made irrespective of authority: and so on.

[12] In the list relevant differences in the readings are indicated by heavy type.

128 by a pace goes backward **with a** **purpose** | It hath to clime.

137 Troy in our weaknesse **stands** not in her strength.

149 with ridiculous and **sillie** action,

159 with termes **vnsquare,**

164 'tis *Agamemnon* **right,**

Page [83]

212s.d. [absent]

215s.d. [absent]

219 Do a faire message to his Kingly **eyes?**

228 And **bid** the cheeke be ready with a blush,

238 Good armes, strong ioints, true **sword** ,& **great** *Ioues* accord

250 to whisper **with** him,

252 To set his **seat** on **that** attentiue bent,

259s.d. *Sound trumpet.*

262-3 Who in **his** dull and long contin-ued truce, | Is **restie** growne:

267 **And feeds** his praise, more then he feares his perill,

276 a Lady, wiser, fairer, truer, | Then euer Greeke did **couple** in his armes,

289-90 If then one is, or hath **a** meanes to be, | That one meetes *Hec-tor:* if none else **I am** he.

293-4 if there be not in our Grecian **hoste,** | **A** noble man that hath **no** sparke of fire

297-8 in my **vambrace** put **my** withered **braunes** | And meeting him tell him that my Lady,

301 Ile **proue** this troth with my three drops of bloud,

302 heauens **for-fend** such scarcity of **men.**

303-4 *Vlis.* Amen: faire Lord *Æneas*

---

by a pace goes backward **in** a pur-pose | It hath to climbe.

Troy in our weaknesse **liues,** not in her strength.

with ridiculous and **aukward** ac-tion,

With tearmes **vnsquar'd,**

'tis *Agamemnon* **iust.**

Tucket

Enter Æneas.

Do a faire message to his Kingly **eares?**

And **on** the cheeke be ready with a blush

Good armes, strong ioynts, true **swords,** & *Ioues* accord,

to whisper him,

To set his **sence** on **the** attentiue bent,

The Trumpets sound.

Who in **this** dull and long-contin-ew'd Truce | Is **rusty** growne.

That seekes his praise, more then he feares his perill,

a Lady, wiser, fairer, truer, | Then euer Greeke did **compasse** in his armes,

If then one is, or hath, **or** meanes to be, | That one meets *Hec-tor;* if none else, **Ile be** he.

if there be not in our Grecian **mould,** | **One** Noble man, that hath **one** spark of fire

in my **Vantbrace** put **this** wither'd **brawne,** | And meeting him, **wil** tell him, that my Lady

Ile **pawne** this truth with my three drops of blood.

heauens **forbid** such scarsitie of **youth.**

Vlys. Amen. | *Aga.* Faire Lord *Æneas,*

305 To our pauilion shall I leade you sir;	To our Pauillion shal I leade you **first:**
309s.d. [absent]	*Exeunt.* | *Manet Vlysses, and Nestor.*
314-6 *Nest.* What ist? | *Vlis:* Blunt wedges riue hard knots,	*Nest.* What is't? | *Vlysses.* **This 'tis:** | Blunt wedges riue hard knots:

There is, I think, no escaping the conclusion that when work was resumed on *Troilus* a manuscript of the play was available that had not been available, or at any rate was not used, when the first three pages of the text were set up. Incidentally it supplied the Prologue originally wanting.[13] But we earlier saw reason to believe that when the printing of the play was interrupted, Walley's intransigence presented an insuperable obstacle only because his was the one text available to print from; and I suggest that when at the last moment a manuscript turned up (whence we can hardly, in the present state of our knowledge, conjecture) Jaggard felt in a position to snap his fingers in Walley's face. It is immaterial that in fact he printed the play, not from the manuscript, but from the Quarto altered in accordance with it, for if challenged he could produce the manuscript, draw attention to the numerous differences between the texts and the presence in his own of some forty or fifty lines missing in Walley's, and point triumphantly to the Prologue displayed in large type upon the first page. His case was complete, and in fact it was not till a few months ago that the patience and ingenuity of an American professor finally settled the vexed question of the actual copy used.[14]

[13] The manuscript must, of course, have been available when the first page of text was reprinted, and it may be asked why the reprint shows no evidence of this fact. The answer is that since the original leaf bearing pages 79 and 80 was to be used, the reprint of page 78 had to end at the same point as the original, and this would have been difficult if not impossible to achieve unless that original had been used as copy.

[14] Philip Williams, "Shakespeare's *Troilus and Cressida:* The Relationship of Quarto and Folio," in: *Studies in Bibliography,* III: 131-143 (1950).

Concurrent Printing:
An Analysis of Dodsley's *Collection of Poems by Several Hands*

By WILLIAM B. TODD

IMPLICIT in most accounts of presswork on hand-printed books is the convenient assumption that, at a given time, the entire resources of the shop are devoted to the production of a single work. Not infrequently, of course, evidence such as that provided by headlines may indicate a disruption or distribution of labor, but even this fails to identify the occasion or extent of the disarrangement. Since it is, therefore, indeterminate, all activity other than that relating to the book under investigation is generally discounted in our speculations. A certain discretion common to most authorities, including bibliographers, moves us to view the unknown as unmentionable.

Yet we may suppose that other work is engaged, and occasionally to such an extent that it should be regarded as concurrent printing. In the larger establishments of the eighteenth century, particularly, the facilities were certainly adequate for simultaneous work on several projects, involving, in some instances, independent groups of compositors and pressmen, in others, the same group intermittently employed, first on a few sheets of one book, then on a few of another. Under the first circumstance each book would constitute a separate venture, though produced concurrently with others, and thus contain, insofar as this can be ascertained, all the evidence of its manufacture. In effect, then, books of this sort are no different from others produced in the usual manner and need not concern us further. Under the second condition, on the other hand, the book is only one of several components in a more extensive enterprise, and thus exhibits only a portion of the information necessary for its analysis. Until the other portions have been located and the various pieces reassembled in the pattern originally devised the puzzle will remain insolvable.

Fortunately, for our purpose, where the latter condition most often prevails—in the eighteenth century—the means for its solution may often be found in the press figures. These convenient indices, if properly interpreted,[1] not only identify the number of pressmen employed in the shop but usually account for their activities. The figures, though, are not entirely reliable. Sometimes, when the work has been prearranged, the men operate without numbers. On other occasions, so far as we know, several of the men may be temporarily unemployed. Moreover, there is also the difficulty of identifying all the books concurrently printed at a certain time and place. Nevertheless, despite these handicaps, any extension of the investigation beyond the confines of a single work may lead to an approximation which, though still removed from the facts, represents an advance in that direction. The approach to be made in the first section, below, allows us to interpret, in the second, a remarkable event in publishing history which has, thus far, escaped the attention of bibliographers.

I

To exemplify what may be adduced from a correlation of the press figures in several books I have selected the 1758 series of octavo volumes titled *A Collection of Poems By Several Hands*, all printed by John Hughs for publication by Robert Dodsley.[2]

[1] The hypothesis advanced in this paper evolves from the theories discussed in my "Observations on the Incidence and Interpretation of Press Figures," in: *Studies in Bibliography*, III (1950), 171-205.

[2] Hughs is one of the very few 18th century printers who identifies his work. That of the others can only be determined through the several printers' registers now extant or through the use of certain ornaments. For an interesting application of the latter method see William Merritt Sale's *Samuel Richardson: Master Printer* (Ithaca, Cornell University Press, 1950).

This comprises the fifth edition of volumes I-III, the second edition of IV, and—as the figures disclose—two previously undifferentiated "first editions" of V-VI.[3] All eight volumes are interrelated, either as double or triple productions; but none, separately or in combination, fully account for the available labor in Hugh's establishment. Thus, as always in bibliographical discussions, the evidence is incomplete. What there is, however, allows a division of the recorded labor into six phases, of which the last, as the most obvious instance of concurrent printing, may be presented first.

Table I

Phase 6.   Presswork on "B" edition
[To facilitate comparison I have reversed
the sequence of data in the third column]

Volume V		Volume VI	
$A1^{v}(i)4$	$A3^{v}(i)3$	$1(i)A5^{v}$	
	$B8^{r}(i)1$ =	$1(i)B7^{v}$	
	$C8^{v}(o)3$ =	$3(i)C8^{r}$	
$D7^{r}(o)1$	$D5^{v}(i)2$ ~	$2(i)D7^{v}$	$D8^{v}(o)3$
	$E8^{v}(o)1$ =	$1(i)E7^{v}$	
	$F1^{v}(i)4$ =	$4(i)F8^{r}$	
	$G2^{v}(o)1$		$2(i)G6^{r}$	
	$H4^{v}(o)1$		$2(o)H5^{r}$	
$I1^{v}(i)3$	$I2^{v}(o)4$	$1(i)I7^{v}$	
	$K5^{v}(i)4$ ~	$4(i)K7^{v}$	$K8^{v}(o)1$
	$L3^{v}(i)3$		$1(i)L1^{v}$	
	$M7^{v}(i)3$		$2(i)M6^{r}$	
	$N5^{v}(i)4$		$2(i)N6^{r}$	
	$O1^{v}(i)3$ =	$3(i)O8^{r}$	

[3] These may be distinguished by the figures to be reported or, more conveniently, by the presence of an errata list on V, 332, in the actual first edition. I have belatedly discovered that the first four volumes also exist in two editions: one, as described in the text, with chainlines running horizontally throughout and with points generally corresponding to those reported by R. W. Chapman (in *Oxford Biblio. Soc. Proceedings and Papers*, III [1931-33], 272); the other, also designated for I-III as a "fifth" and for IV as a "second" edition, but with a variant set of figures, chainlines running vertically throughout, and points usually differing from those cited by Chapman. This other set, represented by copies at the Duke Library, was, I surmise, printed at some later time when (as observed in the discussion of "A" edition V-VI) the vertical paper replaced the horizontal variety. Unlike the original 1758 set, this reveals no indication of concurrent printing.

$$P8^r(i)4 \quad \Big| \quad \Big| \quad 3(i)P1^v$$
$$Q7^v(i)4 \quad \Big| \quad \Big| \quad 3(i)Q5^v$$
$$R6^v(o)1 \qquad R3^v(i)3 \quad \sim \quad 3(o)R2^v$$
$$S2^v(o)3 \qquad S7^v(i)2 \quad \sim \quad 2(o)S5^r$$
$$T1^v(i)1 \qquad 3(i)T7^v$$
$$U5^v(i)2 \quad = \quad 2(i)U1^v$$
$$X \; none \qquad 3(i)X3^v$$

This concerns edition "B" of the fifth and sixth volumes, both produced by four pressmen whose work on this assignment, as the first table shows, is only incidental.[4] Generally only one man can be spared from some other job, and this individual successively prints and perfects, as illustrated by the equation signs, first a certain signature in one volume, then the corresponding signature in the other.[5] For this, and for a similar practice in the "A" edition, the only explanation seems to be that, whenever practicable, the sheets were passed through the press in parallel order so that both volumes could be completed and published at the same time.[6] On four occasions, those denoted by the equivalent symbol, the one individual has, in conformity with this practice, done most of the work before another (in D, two others) arrives to finish off an outer forme. At other times, as marked by parallels, two men are available from the beginning, 1-2 in the first instance, 2-3 in the second, and 3-4 in the third. Though the assignment for each is four formes, equal to that for one man

[4] For this and later tabulations the entries refer, in order, to page (forme) press figure. In this list two entries, both for the fifth volume, require notation. One relates to the double figure in the inner forme of A, not evidence of cancellation, apparently, but of some mixup in the assignments prior to impression. The other pertains to C, which, in what I believe to be its original state (copy NN), bears only the one figure, as cited, but later (in copies DLC and NcU) also registers $C1^v(i)1$ —presumably an indication that 1 finishes up the remaining sheets of this forme.

[5] From the evidence of other books (cf. my study, *op. cit.*) it appears that the register of one figure to a sheet marks sequential work (one forme after another at the same press), the register of two, simultaneous work (the two formes laid on different presses).

[6] Volumes V and VI edition "A" were, in fact, published together (cf. fn. 18). Both in this and in the "B" edition the volume reference on $1 of each set would prevent an intermixture and enable the binder to arrange the piles for collation.

operating independently, the work in this case extends sequential-
ly through two signatures of the same volume. Except for the
occasional employment of a third man, which serves to lower the
average, the assignment suggests that this is the labor performed
each week, the normal pay period. If so, the number of copies
applied to each forme, and thus the size of the issue, totals 3000.[7]

While incidental work of the order evident in "B" volumes
V and VI would necessitate figuring as a means of checking labor
other than that regularly assigned, such a practice would not be
required for predetermined work. Volumes I and II, constitut-
ing the first phase, represent such an assignment. Since each volume is unfigured, both were probably impressed concurrently
according to some schedule known to the overseer, but not revealed to the bibliographer.

Beginning with the second phase, concerning the work on signatures A-P of volume III, the figures reappear, but in such a
manner as to be completely uninformative:

$$E7^r(o)2 \quad G4^v(o)3 \quad H8^v(o)2 \quad K5^r(o)3 \quad M5^r(o)3 \quad P4^v(o)3$$

From this the only conclusion to be drawn is that we are again
dealing with piecework and that the major project, at this time,
is to be discovered either in I and II (where nothing can be determined) or outside the present series of volumes.

In the third phase, however, a pattern emerges of a kind quite
similar to that previously described. This operation concerns the
remaining signatures of the third volume and the first eleven of
the fourth, two sequences machined concurrently and, on this
occasion, alternately, by the pressmen designated as 2 and 5.

III $Q5^v(i)5$ $R2^v(o)2$ $S8^v(o)5$ $T8^r(i)2$ $U7^v(i)5$ $X4^v(o)2$ $Y7^r(o)2$
IV $A4^v(o)5$ BC *none* $D1^v(i)5$ $E6^v(o)2$ $F4^v(o)5$ $I6^r(i)2$ $L7^r(o)2$
                                              GH *none* K *none*

---

[7] This calculation is based on Stower's estimate that a man at "full press" (with
an assistant) can print 2000 copies a day. If six days are allowed for four formes,
one and one-half days are required for each. *The Printer's Grammar* (London,
1808), p. 527.

As we see, the correspondence between the two sets of figures is almost perfect.[8] Here, as before, the men are simultaneously working the sheets of two volumes. But again, as before, the greater amount of labor among the five men known to be in Hugh's employ is expended elsewhere.

It is only when we come to the fourth phase that we find the majority of the pressmen continually, if erratically, at work. At this time three sequences are going through the presses, the remaining signatures for the fourth volume, and all except a few of those for the "A" edition of the fifth and sixth. As three men were now engaged, numbers 2, 3, and 5, one would suppose that each should be assigned to a different volume. But for some reason—perhaps because of a discrepancy in the size of the issues[9]—some other arrangement was devised which, after certain preliminary adjustments, permitted a rotation among the three men, with two always at work on V-VI and one on IV.[10] The two men are identified as 2 and 3 in the first week, 3 and 5 in the second (occasionally assisted by 2), 2 and 5 in the third, 2 and 3 in the fourth, and so on. The one disengaged, and available for other work, is thus recognized as 5, 2, 3, 5, 2, 3, and on, an order which corresponds, with two exceptions (in gatherings P and Y), with that evident in the presswork on the remainder of IV. All work therefore dovetails in the pattern represented by the second table.

[8] Apart from the "lateral" alternation of 5-2-5-2 there is also a "vertical" one in the register of figures in an inner and outer forme within the same assignment. Possibly this indicates, for each man, the inception of work upon the inner forme of a sheet in one volume and the conclusion of work upon the outer forme of a sheet in the other. The work for 5, then, would progress from III Q(i) Q(o) through IV A(i) A(o), and, on his next assignment, from IV D(i) D(o) through III S(i) S(o). Note that the only departure from pattern occurs in the last sheet of each volume (in this phase), where there is also a departure from the order of assignments.

[9] A larger supply of volumes V and VI, first edition, would be required in order to supplement the several editions of the preceding volumes.

[10] Since there is never more than one man casually employed on the IV sequence, there is never more than one figure to each sheet. The two on the other volumes, however, occasionally assist each other.

Table II

Phase 4.   Presswork from 10 October through 31 December 1757

Week	Date	Volume IV	Volume V		Volume VI
1	Oct. 10	$M8^v(o)5$	[A-C composed but presswork delayed. Cf. Table III]		A[assigned: unfigured] *B *none or* $B6^r(i)3$ *and/or* $B6^v(o)2$
2	Oct. 17	$N8^v(o)2$	$D1^v(i)3$ $D7^r(o)2$ $E4^v(o)5$ $E5^v(i)2$ $F5^v(i)5$ $F8^v(o)2$		$C3^v(i)5$ $D6^v(o)3$ $E6^r(i)3$
3	Oct. 24	$O7^v(i)3$ $†P1^v(i)2$	$*G7^v(i)5$ $H5^v(i)2$		$F2^v(o)5$ $F5^v(i)2$ $G5^v(i)5$ $G6^v(o)5$
4	Oct. 31	$Q4^v(o)5$	$I8^r(i)2$ $*K5^v(i)2$ $*K5^r(o)3$		$H7^v(i)3$ $I3^v(i)3$
5	Nov. 7	$R8^r(i)2$	$L3^v(i)3$ $M1^v(i)3$		$K8^v(o)5$ $L7^r(o)5$
6-7	Nov. 14-26	$S3^v(i)3$	$N1^v(i)5$ $O8^r(i)2$		$M2^v(o)2$
8	Nov. 28	$T8^r(i)5$	$*P8^v(o)3$ $Q6^r(i)2$		$N7^v(i)3$ $N8^v(o)2$
9		Delay for return of proof for Volume VI, sheet O			
10	Dec. 12	$U6^r(i)2$	$*R5^v(i)3$		$O5^v(i)5$ $‡P7^v(i)2$ $P8^v(o)3$
11	Dec. 19	$X6^r(i)3$	$S5^r(o)5$ $S5^v(i)2$		$Q3^v(i)2$ $Q8^v(o)5$
12	Dec. 26	$†Y5^v(i)3$	$T1^v(i)2$ $U2^v(o)2$		$R5^v(i)3$ S *none* [3?]

* Figures for sheets so marked vary during course of impression. Except for VI B I have indicated only what I believe to be the first state.

† The two signatures identified represent departures from the 5-2-3 pattern.

‡ The return of 2 marks the only deviation from the schedule of rotation among the men at work on V-VI.

II

For the impression of the "A" issue of V and VI, the volumes to which we shall now confine our attention, external evidence provides a revelation of the confusion attending the preparation of an edition. Whatever the original plan, this soon went awry as a consequence of several delays in the correction of the proof which Dodsley had dispatched to the principal contributors. Chief among these procrastinators was William Shenstone, who received his copies of the first three sheets, fifth volume,[11] as early as September 1757, but neglected to return them, despite repeated requests from the publisher, until January of the following year. Then, as the paper illustrates, these sheets were finally processed with the concluding sheet of the fifth volume and the last three sheets of the sixth. With this group segregated and set aside for later comment, we may now proceed with an account of the remaining signatures, as specified by the figures cited in Table II.

Printing began, I conjecture, about the 10th of October, several weeks after the copy had been sent to Shenstone and shortly after the more conscientious contributors had returned the proofs for VI A-B. At first, it would seem, the work was rather desultory, requiring at the outset (VI A) the services of only one man, who did not figure, and later (VI B) incidental efforts from two, both of whom then figured to distinguish their work. In the second week, apparently, the three men now on the job experienced some difficulty in keeping up with the compositors. To remove the accumulation of formes two of the men therefore simultaneously machined D and E of the fifth volume, and, in the next week, F and G of the sixth. Thereafter, with few excep-

[11] In the fifth volume Shenstone's poems cover only sheets A-C, only three are differentiated in the paper, only three are identified in later correspondence; yet Dodsley, in his letter of transmittal, mentions that four had been struck off. Ralph Straus, *Robert Dodsley; Poet, Publisher & Playwright* (London, John Lane, 1910), p. 137. Possibly the fourth represents the work of another poet for whom Shenstone had assumed the office of editor.

tions, the work proceeded in an orderly fashion, with numbers 3 and 5 averaging four or five formes a week on the V-VI sequence, and number 2 about three. Thus the issue for this edition, like that for the "B" reprint, was 3000 copies.

Since, in any given time, 2 averages no more than three formes a week, and 5 no less than four, some explanation is required for a reversal in the performance of each during the sixth period. Very likely, if their previous record is any criterion, the work of the less efficient man here extends beyond a week and that of the others—5 in this period, 3 in the next—represents only occasional assistance. This would indicate a deliberate slow-down; and that, I believe, is what has occurred, for at VI signature O the printer was again awaiting proof from Shenstone. As proof was not forthcoming, however, he eventually decided to print the uncorrected formes,[12] and then hurried his men along with the others until, on the last day of the year, they had entirely finished with IV and completed the last of the sheets for signature U in V and S in VI.

Now that the occasional work on IV had been brought to a conclusion, the overseer was able to prearrange that for the remaining sheets of V-VI. Hence, as we might expect, the figures are dropped in this, the fifth phase of operations, to be replaced, however, with evidence of another sort. The last seven signatures of V-VI were machined during a period when a depletion in the stock of paper used prior to this time—paper with turned chainlines running, in octavo format, horizontally across the page[13]—necessitated an intermixture with the ordinary variety.

---

[12] It is to this signature, apparently, that Shenstone refers, first in a letter to Dodsley (21 December 1757) to the effect that "another Sheet is gone to the Press" without his intervention, and later in one to Richard Graves (30 May 1758) where he observes that the improved copy for his verses in the sixth volume (occupying pages $O2^r$-$O4^v$) "arrived a good deal too late" for correction. Marjorie Williams (ed.), *The Letters of William Shenstone* (Oxford, B. Blackwell, 1939), pp. 475-77, 482.

[13] Messrs. K. Povey and I. J. C. Foster have demonstrated that, with few exceptions, these are sheets of normal size with longitudinal lines (before folding) and not, as had been formerly supposed, half-sheets of double-sized paper. *The Library,*

When the original supply began to run out this other paper was introduced in ever-increasing proportions which serve to distinguish the three separate operations reported in Table III: the

Table III

Phase 5. Presswork from 2 January through 18 February 1758

Week	Date	Copy* / Location	1 ICU	2 TxU	3 HWL	4 HWL	5 NNC	6 CtY	7 JLC	8 NcD	9 MH	10 MH
13	Jan. 2	Unfigured. Paper ratio, 70% horizontal, 30% vertical.										
		VI T	H	H	H	H	H	V	V	V	H	H
		VI U	H	H	H	V	V	H	H	H	V	H
		V B	H	H	H	H	H	V	V	H	H	V
14-15	Delay of two weeks											
16	Jan. 23	Unfigured. 50% horizontal, 50% vertical.										
		VI X	V	V	V	H	V	H	H	H	V	H
		V X	H	V	V	H	H	H	V	V	V	H
17	Delay of one week											
18	Feb. 6	Unfigured, 1st printing. Paper vertical.										
		V A	V	V	V							
		V C	V	V	V							
19	Feb. 13	Figured, 2d printing. Paper vertical [2 figured outer forme of both sheets] [Mixed sheets / only 1 figure]										
		V A				fV	fV	fV	fV	fV	fV	V
		V C				fV	fV	fV	fV	V	V	fV
		[Final print: $V\pi^2$; $VI\pi^2$ and cancels A3, P1]										

first including signature B of the fifth volume, along with T and U of the sixth, all machined on a mixture of 70% horizontal and 30% vertical paper; the second involving the final signature X of each volume, both impressed on an equal mixture of both varieties; and the third representing the long overdue A and C of the fifth volume, produced at a time when the vertical stock had completely replaced the other. With these facts in mind we return to the chronology of the remaining signatures.

5th ser., V (1950), 184-200. In the reprint of Volumes V and VI, already described, this paper is again used throughout, except for a few sheets of the other which occasionally appear (as in the NcU copy) in the final signature of the fifth volume. Once again the original allotment did not suffice.

* Copies 3 and 4, Herman W. Liebert; copy 7, James L. Clifford.

Toward the end of December, as the correspondence attests,[14] Dodsley managed to recover sheet V B, one of the several proofs Shenstone had been withholding, and forwarded this revised version to Hugh's office, where, in the first week of the new year, the type was then corrected and the formes laid on press, together with those for VI T and U. After this material had been cleared away there was another exasperating delay while Dodsley once again tried to extract the proof for V A and C from his reluctant contributor. Until this was forthcoming the printer could not go on with X, for the latter contained an index subject to change in view of anticipated substitutions in sheet C. When C, with the substitutions, was eventually returned on Saturday, January 21,[15] the necessary alterations in the index were promptly made and, we may suppose, the X formes for both volumes sent to press the following Monday. Ten days later, on February 2, Dodsley notified Shenstone that the final corrections had been entered for A and C.[16] The printing of these formes was therefore underway about February 6, and soon followed, presumably, by several cancels and the preliminary fold ²for both volumes.

Just when the printing was concluded, however, is another matter. From the evidence given in Table III it would appear that a certain portion of the issue (represented by copies 1-3) was rushed through the press ahead of the remainder. This portion is remarkably uniform, consisting of horizontally lined paper in the first operation, vertically lined paper in the second (with the exception of one sheet in one copy), and unfigured sheets in the third. The remainder, on the other hand, is mixed throughout in the first two sections and figured in the third. Perhaps the distinction marks an intentional underprinting of 1000

[14] Williams, *op. cit.*, pp. 475-77.

[15] Straus, *op. cit.*, p. 148. Dodsley's earnest "Pray send the *Rural Elegance*, & let me finish" indicates that A was still reserved.

[16] *Ibid.*, p. 149.

copies[17] to expedite the issuance of these at the earliest practicable date.[18] Then, as time allowed, the remaining 2000 copies were processed, and partially figured to differentiate this lot from the other. Whatever the procedure, this "disagreeable business," as Dodsley put it, had in one way or another finally come to an end. In all, to recapitulate, the presswork had by then advanced through the five phases represented, along with the sixth, in this summary form:

Time	Before 10 October 1757			Through 18 February 1878		Later
Phase	1.	2.	3.	4. :	5.	6.
Pressmen	??	2,3	2,5	2,3,5	?? (later, 2)	1,2,3,4
Volumes	I A—X II A—X	III A—P	III Q—Y IV A—L	IV M—Y V D—U VI A—S	V A—C,X VI T—X	"B" I A—X "B" II A—X

The bibliographer may very well reëcho Dodsley's comment on his own publication, for the account of it enforces certain disagreeable considerations which, if they hold for this, may have application elsewhere. One is that in instances of concurrent printing the bibliographer must examine all the books so related before attempting the analysis of any. To do less than this, as our experience with phase 2 has shown, is to learn little or nothing at all. The second is that whenever books contain press figures their very presence implies unsystematic piecework engaged in conjunction with other miscellaneous endeavors. For labor which is predetermined, controlled, and properly recorded by the overseer—as in phases 1 and 5—the figures become superfluous

[17] For another probable instance of underprinting see my description of edition "B2" in "The Bibliographical History of Burke's *Reflections on the Revolution in France*," in: *The Library*, 5th Ser., VI (1951), 100-108.

[18] The two volumes were privately distributed on Monday, March 13 (Straus, *op. cit.*, p. 149), and announced five days later, in the *Daily Advertiser*, as published.

and accordingly disappear. Thus as a preliminary to a solution
for the problem at hand the figures serve, first, to introduce us to
the complexities of many others beyond our present concern.

All of this reaffirms my earlier conviction that while the figures are indeed a useful tool, their application may at times involve an effort far exceeding the importance of the investigation.
Moreover, as the eighteenth-century bibliographer will realize,
even if he has the time and patience to put forth this effort, he
may soon reach an impasse; for, unlike his more favored colleagues, with their short-title catalogues, indexes, and colophons,
he has no convenient register of what has been printed, when
and where. He may then admit that, ideally, one should look at
other books, but he may also be excused for occasionally declining
to perform the impossible.

The Forms of
Twentieth-Century Cancels

By JOHN COOK WYLLIE*

"Except for a couple of references to cancelled title-leaves . . . Chapman's monograph on *Cancels* deals with no example later than 1825. . .

"Have we any such guidance for the post-mechanization types of cancel?" John Carter, in "Some Bibliographical Agenda," *Third Annual Windsor Lectures in Librarianship* (Urbana, University of Illinois, 1952), p. 69.

IT is one of the peculiarities of the expanding book market that a successful literary work sometimes starts being successful in terms of numbers sold before the author can read a completed copy of the first impression, and by the time he may want a page, a plate, or a signature cancelled, an entire impression may have been scattered, if not to the winds, at least to the members of a book club. Revision aside, therefore, the efforts of an editor to select a copytext will often in the future involve the use of more than one impression of a first edition.

* The author wishes to record not only his indebtedness for helpful suggestions from Messrs. Jacob Blanck, Fredson Bowers, and Earle Walbridge, but also the fact that this paper had its origin as one of a series of talks on twentieth-century bibliographical problems prepared at the request of the student seminar of the Bibliographical Society of the University of Virginia.

In dealing with cancels, an editor of a twentieth-century work may depend in part only on the classical bibliographer's methods and terminology. R. W. Chapman's *Cancels* (1930) will, of course, serve as his main guide, but he will need to add to Chapman's considerations the concept of cancelled plates. Plates which have been emended without replating are sometimes easy to detect, but present-day re-electrotyping of individual plates is not easy to spot, and as we begin the second half of the twentieth century, we shall doubtless become more and more dependent on mechanized collation for the discovery of cancelled passages. (Details of this procedure are outlined by Charlton Hinman in his "Mechanized Collation: A Preliminary Report," PAPERS, 41 [1947], 99-106.)

Meanwhile, in order that the problems of cancelled leaves, cancelled gatherings, and cancelled plates may be properly placed before the bibliographers who are beginning to be interested in the books of the first half of this century, the following catalogue of varieties is offered.

PART I

Substituted Leaves

The standard twentieth-century example of the classical leaf-substitution cancel is Somerset Maugham's *Painted Veil* (1925), which, besides cancel gatherings, has in one state or issue fifteen single-leaf cancels, inserted in an effort to remove references to Hong Kong as the setting of the novel. For details of these cancels, see Fredson Bowers, *Principles of Bibliographical Description* (Princeton, 1949), p. 419, citing Percy Muir, *Points: Second Series* (London, 1934), p. 132-4; and F. T. Bason, *Bibliography of ... Maugham* (London, 1931), p. 38-9. The more recent Maugham bibliographies also deal with the cancels. (For the titles of these, see PAPERS, 44 (1950), 293-5.)

A less usual substitution, in that a quarto signature is pasted

to the stubs of two cancelled leaves, the two leaves having been
extended to four by leaving the versos blank, is

Louis Charlanne, *L'Influence française en Angleterre au xviie Siècle* ...
Paris, Société Française d'Imprimerie et de Librairie, 1906. xix, 614 p.

Pages ix-xii have been cancelled, and 4 leaves (rectos only printed), signed
a' on the first leaf, have been substituted.

I have heard the objection of bibliographers to the presentation
of evidence from French printing that "French printing is peculiar anyway," but in fact it is not the French, but the printers
and authors who are peculiar; not to speak of those who (like the
present writer) refer to themselves as bibliographers by reason
of their being able to detect and classify certain peculiarities of
printers and authors.

Substituted Gatherings

The detection of substituted gatherings is one of the cruces of
twentieth-century cancels. John Carter, in his "Some Bibliographical Agenda" in *Third Annual Windsor Lectures in Librarianship* (1952), p. 69, cautiously supposed that "none of [the bib-
liographers] seems to have faced the fact that a substitute gathering does not differ in essentials ... from a single substitute
leaf." But the truth is that Fredson Bowers (*Principles of Bibliographical Description*, p. 419) faced the fact squarely enough in
dealing with the "cancellans gatherings" of D. H. Lawrence's
The White Peacock (1911), and the "complete cancellans gatherings" in Maugham's *Painted Veil* (1925). Nor was Bowers any
pioneer in this recognition, as will be seen by looking at John A.
Holden's *The Bookman's Glossary* (New York, R. R. Bowker,
1925), p. 27. It is worth noting that the Lawrence and Maugham
cancel gatherings were discovered by the signposts of cancel
leaves, which are not likely always to precede or follow other such cancel gatherings. Skeletons, press figures, and chainline
patterns may be used as aids to detection in some eighteenth- and

nineteenth-century books, but if anyone wants an example of the difficulty of detecting twentieth-century sheet cancels, let him try to identify one in Franklin D. Roosevelt's *On Our Way* (N. Y., 1934), before looking up the notes on the subject by Frederick B. Adams, Jr., in PAPERS, 37 (1943), 227.

Excised Leaves

The excision of leaves without substitution of others must be extremely unusual, but an example is nevertheless offered:

Association of Tile Manufacturers. *Glazed Tiles and Trimmers . . .* , Beaver Falls, Penna., Published by the Association, [Copyright, 1921]. 86 p. Publication No. K-400.

"Pages 79-84 have been removed because of a ruling of the U. S. Department of Justice which restrains this association from compiling and publishing any tabulations of list prices of tiles. The mailing of the book was delayed for two years awaiting a decision on this point. . . ." (From a leaf pasted to the stubs.)

The explanation for an excision does not always so handily accompany the phenomenon. Howard Mott reported (PAPERS, 35 [1941], 207) that "for some unknown reason the frontispieces were cancelled out of the bound copies" of William Beebe's *Edge of the Jungle* (N. Y., 1921). The only copy of this book that I have seen has no clear indication of its ever having had a frontispiece.

Paste-overs

Paste-over cancels are not uncommon on the covers of twentieth-century European price-tagged books. William Heinemann's paper-bound plays issued before 1920, for example, carried a printed price notice just above the cover imprint. About the time of World War I, this price annotation was cancelled with a series of paste-on slips, one of which read, "To meet the increased cost of binding and overhead charges, the price of Heinemann's paper-covered plays is temporarily raised from 1/6 to 2/-." A later slip in another setting is identical in wording except for the final price figure, which reads "2/6."

The first variety may be seen on the University of Virginia copy of Arthur Wing Pinero's *Preserving Mr. Panmure* (London, 1912); and the second on the same library's copy of the same author's *The Times, A Comedy* (London [1915; i.e., the third impression]).

A less common but more interesting type of paste-on cancel may be seen in Louis Barthou's *Italy's Effort* (Paris, 1917), and Edouard Herriot's *Russia's Effort* (Paris, 1917). When these two pamphlets were printed, the publishers, Bloud & Gay, got mixed up on the covers, so that Herriot's work originally carried Barthou's name and *vice versa*. Paste-over cancels were applied to make the covers conform to the correct authorship assignments on the title pages.

A more common type of paste-over cancel is produced by a change in publisher. Examples could be multiplied, but one from Germany will suffice:

The imprints in Vol. 1 of Leonardo Olschki's *Geschichte der Neusprachlichen Wissenschaftlichen Literatur* (the first volume was entitled *Die Literatur der Technik und der Angewandten Wissenschaften* . . .) originally read "Heidelberg | Carl Winter's Universitätsbuchhandlung | 1919." The facing imprints were cancelled by paste-ons, presumably after the publication of the first volume and before the publication of the second. The paste-on wording is: "Leipzig—Firenze—Roma—Genève | Leo S. Olschki | 1919." Wording of the imprints in Vol. 2 is identical with the cancel except for the date line, which in Vol. 2 reads "1922."

Sometimes, of course, the change-of-publisher paste-overs are not really cancels at all. The American copies of John Holloway's *The Victorian Sage* (1953) are a case in point. The book was printed in London with the normal London Macmillan imprint. Since 1952, however, the London and New York Macmillans have become completely independent firms, and the London publisher's books are distributed in this country by the St. Martin's Press. The label pasted over the imprint in *The Victorian Sage* (it reads: St. Martin's Press | New York) was, therefore, only tipped over the imprint, with no effort at obliterating the original imprint. Indeed, the object of the paste-over seems not only to have been to supply information concerning the American distributor, but also to show who the original publisher was. This can hardly be called a cancel, because nothing was cancelled.

Another such change-of-publisher addition (this time a full leaf) is cited by Paul Dunkin in *How to Catalog a Rare Book* (Chicago, 1951), p. 65, from Percy Muir's *Points* (London, 1931), p. 95. It is in Gordon Bottomley's *The Gate of Smaragdus* (1904), but is again no cancel.

Obliteration, Overwriting and Overprinting

Hand obliteration without access to multiple copies of a work is difficult to distinguish from individual blotting, and overprinting is difficult to spot if it is done on a printing press. The following examples will serve to show something of the possible variety under this heading:

Arthur D. Howden Smith, *Mr. House of Texas* (New York and London, Funk & Wagnalls, 1940).

On page 54, third line of the second paragraph, the sentence "He had a talent for intrigue." has been struck through with India (?) ink. One supposes that a threat of libel suit may have been involved here. Both the cancelled form and an advance reviewer's copy without it, are in the University of Virginia collections. Attention was called to this cancel by a letter to the University of Virginia Librarian from a reader in another city, with another cancelled copy, who wanted to know how the obliterated sentence read.

Titian, Paintings, and Drawings. Vienna, Phaidon Press; London, George Allen & Unwin, Ltd., [1937].

On the verso of the title page, the line "Printed in Austria" was obliterated by a rubber stamp, which also substituted another line "Printed in Germany." The book was printed in Innsbruck, and the stamp obviously postdates the annexation of Austria by Hitler in 1938 in the *Drang nach Osten.*

Mrs. James Joyce Arthur (Glenn Dora Fowler), *Annals of the Fowler Family.* Austin, Texas, 1901.

The original imprint read "Ben C. Jones & Co., Printers and Publishers." A rubber stamp was used to obliterate the printer's name and also (or perhaps another stamp) was used to substitute a line reading "Published by the Author."

Plate Substitution Within an Impression

The essential bibliographical difference between a plate substitution in the middle of a self-perfecting machine run and the resetting of a page in the middle of a handpress machining of a forme must be immediately apparent to the serious student. There are some phenomena arising from the distribution practices made possible by machine printing, however, that are not so immediately apparent, though they have a direct bearing on cancels. The "date of publication" of a handpress book has a reasonably specific meaning that is not altogether applicable to some modern, long-run, chain-line production jobs of this century. To take an exaggerated case of this, consider *Life*, a weekly news-picture magazine, which has a nominal and largely fictitious publication date on Thursday. (The publication date is not of course any more nominal or fictitious in quite another way than that of many present-day novels. Lella Warren's *Whetstone Walls* [New York, 1952], was published in several Southern states on November 7th, in the rest of the United States on the 14th.) As each parcel of copies of *Life* comes off the assembly line, that particular parcel escapes permanently and irrevocably into the public domain and is not retrievable for purposes of cancelling a leaf. In one sense at least the handpress's moment of publication of an edition becomes with some modern productions an immeasurable succession of moments of publication. A cancel in such printing jobs must, therefore, if the term is to be used at all, become a cancelled plate rather than a cancelled leaf. A specific example in *Life* may be offered in Vol. 8, No. 25, the issue dated July 17, 1940, where the original plate for page 83 was captioned "In his latest movie Charlie Chaplin plays a Dictator of the Double Cross." Chaplin, on June 13th, when the press run

was more than half done, obtained an injunction from the federal
courts forcing the deletion of the picture, and claiming damages
of a million dollars (see *New York Times*, June 13, 1940, p. 21).
Later copies from the same impressions have a different picture
on page 83, captioned "Henry Ford inspects an Army pursuit
plane and ponders mass military production." The Chaplin picture was in 1,600,000 copies; the Ford picture in 1,000,000. The
relevance of this example to a literary student's interests will be
more apparent if one remembers that *Life*, though a news-picture
magazine, published an entire Hemingway novel in its issue for
September 1, 1952.

Plate Emendation Between Impressions

Hervey Allen's *Anthony Adverse* (1933) is a good example of
plate-emendation because it offers clear specimens of two different kinds of changes. There are the simple corrections of misprints (as *Xavier* for *Xaxier* on p. 352 in the second or later impression; *ship* for *shop* on p. 1086 in the third or later impression), all obviously efforts to arrive at a correct copy of the original text. And then there is the post-publication textual revision
of a mistranslation (*Fountain* for *Flame* on p. 494 of the fourth or
later impression). Since these are all apparently replatings, the
use of the expression "cancelled plates" in referring to them
seems proper, though plate-cancellation is not always easily distinguished from the technically different word-cancellation within a plate, a phenomenon so common as not to need further illustration.

Whether the bibliographical purist will want to use the term
"cancel" either for a plate cancelled between impressions or for
a word cancelled in a plate between impressions remains to be
seen. It is suggested here that the word should be so used for the
sake of convenience wherever the intent of the author or publisher is rather more clearly to cancel than to correct back to an
original text. Thus it is proposed that plate 352 in *Anthony Ad-*

verse be called a corrected or uncorrected plate, but that plate 494 be called cancelled or uncancelled.

The convenience and usefulness of such terminological use will become immediately apparent to the bibliographer dealing with twentieth-century printing if he will consider Chapter XXVIII in Vol. 4 of *The Cambridge History of American Literature* (N. Y., 1921). The chapter ("Popular Bibles") as originally written was by [Isaac] Woodbridge Riley, but pressure from the Christian Science Church (see *The Nation*, 112 [1921], 641) quickly caused the suppression of the original chapter, and a totally different one written by Lyman P. Powell appeared in all impressions after the first. There was apparently some signature-cancelling in copies of the first impression, which (if it did occur) involved not only pp. 517-32, but also the Contents sheet.

It is submitted that without an elaborate bibliographical investigation, the undertaking of which in this instance seems an idle way to squander time, it is not easy to determine which of the 1921 printed copies (there were impressions in February and October) were original impressions with cancelled signatures, and which were second impressions using new plates for pp. 517-32. The cancels (if there were any) may, for example, have been run on the same stock of Warren Olde Style wove paper as the original impression. For most purposes of bibliographical description of this particular work, it seems easy, accurate, and adequate to say that ViU copy 59199 has the uncancelled plates 517-32 and that ViU copy 289030 has the cancel plates.

For those who search for terminological difficulties, however, it may be well to record that plate 420 in Maurice Thompson's *Alice of Old Vincennes* (Indianapolis, 1900) did not appear in the first five impressions, but ran in several after it was added to the sixth impression. It was finally cancelled. This is a detail that is not fully or correctly described (perhaps because of terminological difficulties) in the fine book by Dorothy Russo and Thelma Sullivan, *Bibliographical Studies of Seven Authors of Crawfordsville*

(Indianapolis, 1952), p. 222. Whether a textual intrusion may properly be said to have been cancelled can be left to the future usage of bibliographers.

Cancelled Bindings

It is not uncommon for small-edition publishers even in the twentieth century to bind only part of an edition on publication, holding a portion of the sewed sheets to reduce the capital outlay. Isaac Jefferson's *Memoirs of a Monticello Slave* (Charlottesville, Va., 1951) is a case in point. A thousand copies were printed, 500 of them bound in 1951 in red cloth, 500 in 1952 in blue cloth. This should not of course be regarded as "cancellation." The expression "cancelled binding" might, however, conceivably be used in referring to such a book as the Varner translation of Garcilaso de la Vega's *Florida of the Inca* (Austin, Texas, 1951). The Kingsport Press in Tennessee did the binding. The original front-cover binding stamp was a mailed fist squeezing Christ on a crucifix. This was withdrawn from fear of offense, and only a few copies for the translator and publisher were stamped with the cancelled stamp. These were never placed on sale. The published copies carried a stamp showing a mailed fist holding an empty wooden cross.

If the suggested terminology for plates is paralleled in this instance for bindings, it should be remembered that it is the stamp and not the binding that has been cancelled. Thus it would be correct to refer to the uncancelled stamp (or to-be-cancelled or cancelled—they would be one and the same; i.e., the one with Christ, as in ViU copy 293180) or to the cancel stamp, as used on most copies (the one with no Christ; e.g., ViU copy 292393).

Cancelled Dust Jackets

Although there are few likely instances in which a dust jacket can have much more bearing on a bibliographer's interest in the text of a book than he might have in the kind of postage stamp used by a publisher to mail a volume, a few examples of cancelled dust jackets are offered.

Thomas Jefferson, *Papers*, edited by Julian Boyd (Princeton, 1950), Vol. I.

Advance copies of the first volume were sent out with a dust jacket which had a misprint "by him" for "to him" in line 8 of the text on the front flap. The jacket was rerun, substituted on "copies distributed to the general public," and separately mailed to the recipients of the advance copies with a slip requesting "Will you please substitute it for the one you have."

Roger Vercel, *Tides of Mont St.-Michel* (New York, 1938).

There were two quite different dust jackets issued with this book before publication. One (a) had a blurb for the book itself on the front flap only, with a Modern Library advertisement on the back flap. On the other (b), the blurb was rewritten and extended, so that it was continued on the back flap, and there was no Modern Library advertisement. The (a) form was on white paper with a gray tint block. The (b) was on yellow paper without a tint block.

The only instance that has come to my attention in which a cancelled dust jacket has any sort of textual interest is Barnaby Dogbolt's [pseud. of Herbert Silvette] *Eve's Second Apple* (N. Y., 1946). The novel, through galley proof, was called *Bomb of Gilead*. In page proof the title was changed to *Eve's Second Apple* because of the appearance of Agnes Edwards Rothery's [i.e., Mrs. Harry Rogers Pratt's] *Balm of Gilead*, 1946. Both authors in 1946 were part of the Charlottesville, Va., community, and since Silvette's novel was a satire on certain aspects of Charlottesville life not connected with Mrs. Pratt, the coincidence of titles would presumably have introduced a confusing misconception of the intended satire.

Although the original title was changed on the title page of the page proof, "Bomb of Gilead" still survived at this stage on the running titles, though these too were finally changed before the press run of the published work.

Meanwhile, however, the dust jacket had proceeded as an independent operation, and at least some jackets were fully printed with the original title. The eventual appearance, therefore, of the work with the corrected "Eve's Second Apple" on title page, running titles, and dust jacket, involved only one cancel, namely the dust jacket; all other changes were proof changes. Thus the survival of a copy with an uncancelled dust jacket would (without access to the proof sheets) be the only strictly bibliographical clue to the novel's original title from any completed copy of the work. I am not sure that any such copy ever existed, or if it did, whether it has survived.

Normally dust jackets are considered the publisher's province, so that even when the author writes glowingly about himself and his work for use on the jacket, he does so in the third person. The probability that authors seldom do see final proofs of the jacket, however, must be the major cause for jacket cancellation. The first impression of the jacket of Francis Coleman Rosenberger's *Jefferson Reader* (New York, 1953) described the editor as a "graduate of" the University of Virginia. Mr. Rosenberger felt that since his University does not award honorary degrees, his publisher shouldn't. In the second impression of the jacket, therefore, the word "attended" was substituted for "a graduate of." If this was a between-press alteration, should it be called a cancel? The remarkable and untidy fact is that it should be, because even the reviewers' advance copies reaching Virginia had the corrected jackets. The probability that the earlier impressed jackets were later used elsewhere can hardly displace the original fact of cancellation.

With the precedent before him of the Modern Library's misstatement on the dust jacket of *Barren Ground* that Ellen Glasgow took a degree and won a Phi Beta Kappa key at the University of Virginia, Mr. Rosenberger need not have been quite so punctilious. At least he had attended the University, which was more than Miss Glasgow had done. At any rate, the *Jefferson Reader* jacket was cancelled, and the *Barren Ground* jacket was not.

The covers of literary journals sometimes suffer from much the same vicissitudes as dust jackets. The April 1929 number of the *Virginia Quarterly Review*, with the exception of two or three copies (one of which I have carefully preserved for posterity), had its original cover ripped off and a new one installed with a corrected spelling in the title of an article, which originally appeared as "The Uncultered South."

Last year's pre-election issue of *Time* which escaped with the wrong cover may also have been an accident.

PART II

It is not to be supposed that textual changes are confined by any means to cancels. When it is thought necessary to change something in a printing surface from which post-proof impressions have already been taken, the alteration or alterations may take quite a wide variety of forms, which may be roughly outlined under the following heads:

In-Press Alterations

(a) *Substituted Type*. Substituted type may be introduced into an unlocked forme if errors are noticed during the press run. The process, common enough in hand-press printing, can occur (and doubtless has occurred many times) in machine printing. It is presumably easier to accomplish such a substitution with linotype-set text than with monotype, but there is no reason to suppose that it has not occurred with both.

(b) *Amended Plates*. The mortising of new type into a plate is not something that can be suddenly done, and since the process of plate emendation carried on within an impression would idle a machine unless another made-up forme were ready at hand for substitution while the emendation is in process, this kind of correction seems unlikely to occur often. No example of it has been found, although plate emendation between impressions is common enough.

It is not surprising that plate emendations should often precede the first plate impression. Casting defects and handling damage are presumably the cause of most of these. Other such emendations, however, come about as the result of access to impressions from the type used for the plate making. Even though these are plate emendations preceding the first plate impression, I deal with them below as "Between-Press Alterations" because two impressions from the same setting are involved, and the changes are made between the two impressions.

Edith Lewis, in her *Willa Cather Living* (New York, Knopf, 1953), p. 161, says of plate proofs, "I believe it is not customary to send the author foundry proofs." While this may, to the best of my knowledge, be taken as a general rule, Miss Lewis goes on to point out that Willa Cather herself "always asked to see them," and in the case of *Shadows on the Rock* had the plates altered at the last minute to change two Archbishops into Bishops. Interesting as this kind of change may be to the textual student, it need not concern the student of cancels because it is clearly a *bona fide* instance of proof alteration. On the other hand, such Willa Cather alterations as from the "transit of Venus" to the "occlusion of Venus" in "Two Friends," or the adjustment that kept water from running up-hill in the Arroyo Hondo troughs in *Death Comes for the Archbishop* (Lewis, *op. cit.*, p. 161) are, under the present proposals, cancels proper and will be found to fall into one of the categories enumerated in this article.

(c) *Plate Substitution.* It takes long enough to make a new plate to rule out plate substitution within an impression as a likelihood except in the very longest runs. In the case of stopped impressions, plate substitution is of course not much less likely than plate emendation; but on long runs, the involvement of two plates means that a cancel plate may be substituted with small loss in press time. The only instance of plate substitution within an impression that has been found was on a press run of more than two and a half million copies. Plate substitution is, however, like plate emendation, common between impressions.

If an example of either plate emendation or plate substitution is found within the impression from a press in which each successive sheet is perfected before the printing of the next sheet (where, in short, there is a time lag between the printing of two states of one sheet), it would clarify the terminology if the word "impression" were reserved for an entire book. Such an occurrence with a one-sheet book would thus produce two impressions if the suggestion of cancelled plates advanced here is unacceptable. But in a multiple-sheet book, the single impression aspect of the majority of the sheets should be adhered to, and the odd re-impressed sheet might most conveniently be referred to as having two impositions within the book's single impression. The terminological problem would not arise with machine presses which print only one side of a sheet in one operation.

Between-Press Alterations

(a) *Amended Standing Type*. With the availability of stereotype and electrotype processes, the preservation of standing type for later impressions must be extremely rare in machine printing except under unusual conditions. Among the unusual conditions should be mentioned the "special editions," where the life of the standing type is short, and the products of the small nonmetropolitan shop.

"Special editions" such as reviewers' copies in page-galley-form (i.e., paged, but run through the proof press in the galley, generally three pages to the galley) from type that has just been returned by the electrotyping department are unlikely to have changes introduced into them intentionally, and thus would not ordinarily be relevant to the present discussion. The reason for printing from such type is that impressions from the plates have not yet been produced and advance copies are needed. The production of such copies from the standing type results in several anomalies. If a change is made as the result of an accident, the first and correct form of the text is in the later impression from the earlier made plates. If a change is made intentionally, the uncorrected form may appear in the later printing (i.e., from the plates). If the copies printed from the type happen to call attention to errors escaped in proofing, then plates may be emended or cancelled even before the first impression has been worked off from them. In this case, the uncorrected text would appear only on the reviewer-copies. Mr. Earle F. Walbridge has kindly supplied me with an example: from a reviewer's galley copy, he himself called the publishers' attention to the fact that Van Wyck Brooks in *The Confident Years* (1952) miscalled Orison Swett Marden "Oliver." The name appeared correctly printed in the first impression from plates.[1]

Another kind of "special edition" in which changes (although generally of a nontextual nature) appear to be likely are those "from type before it is distributed," "on rag paper," "for subscribers only," etc. Where this kind of "special edition" is from type and the trade edition is from plates, it may again be assumed that the type is first used by the electrotyper for his mold, even though the impressions from the type are earlier than the impressions from the electrotyper's plates. Some rearrangement of the type for artistic effect might be assumed to be usual, but if it produces textual differences, the differences are not likely to have textual value and should be referred to the plate impressions.

Standing type in the small nonmetropolitan shop needs no special comment. It is obvious that in a suburban or rural shop which produces a large proportion of job printing and publishes only one or two books a year, the access to stereotype or electrotype facilities might be sufficiently inconvenient, and the holding of standing type so relatively easy, that a second or even a

---

[1] *Post hoc, ergo propter hoc?* No acknowledgment was received from the publishers, who may have detected the error themselves. Or Mr. Brooks may have done so. E.F.W.

third small impression might be cautiously run from the same type. Each of these impressions might have between-press corrections.

(b) The subject of amended or cancelled plates between impressions needs no further elaboration except to repeat that both are extremely common. The textual student need only concern himself with distinguishing between those that result from accidental plate damage and those that are the result of intentional textual change.

After-Press Changes

We come finally to the area of changes in which cancels are necessarily relevant, though there are other ways than by cancellation that after-press changes can be made; namely, the Errata list (printed as part of a late sheet) and the Errata slip. Neither of these can properly be called a cancel when nothing has been cancelled. On the other hand, when there is an effort to remove part of a text, whether to replace it with a correct form or simply to remove it, then a cancel results.

By the same token, an inserted leaf is not properly a cancel unless something is intended to come out when the revision goes in. James Lindsay Gordon's *Ballads of the Sunlit Years* (New York, North American Press, 1904) will serve as an example of the non-cancel insert. The author died "while this volume was going through the press." A leaf with a biographical sketch of the author and some details concerning the production of the volume ("The edition is limited to 990 copies") was separately printed and inserted in front of the half-title.

The 35 x 75 mm. slip reading "Corrigendum Page 76, line 5: *for* card *read* cord" pasted to p. 76 of Hilary Jenkinson's *A Manual of Archive Administration* (London, 1937) is a typical example of the errata slip. This is taken to be a non-cancel form, because while the direction to cancel is there, the erroneous form remains in fact uncancelled.

In a letter to the London *Times Literary Supplement* for October 10, 1952, p. 661, Hugh MacDonald, referring to his book about Andrew Marvell, wrote: "As errata-leaves are practically impossible nowadays, I had to content myself with making manuscript corrections in what copies I could."

Even if "errata-leaves" were "practically impossible" in England, however, a book was to appear in America with an errata slip within a month of MacDonald's letter to the editor: on November 4th, to be exact, Mary Alden Hopkins' *Dr. Johnson's Lichfield* (New York, Hastings House, 1952) carried (even on advance reviewers' copies) a paste-in slip following the list of illustrations, correcting the captions on two of the plates.[2]

An extreme case of peripheral errata slips may be found in reviewers' copies of Denning Miller's *Wind, Storm and Rain, The Story of Weather* (New York, 1952). The book was published by Coward-McCann, but when the printers mailed out the review copies, the insert slip announcing the date of publication, price, etc., was signed G. P. Putnam's Sons. A postcard followed quickly in the wake of the book correcting the error.

An example of the non-cancel form of over-printing is the last sentence of two lines on the bottom of the verso of the title page of *Studies in Bibliography*, III (1950).

The forms of the cancel proper in the twentieth century are sufficiently detailed in Part I of this article, and require no further discussion here. It is hoped, however, that others writing in English on twentieth-century cancels will eschew the Latin form of "cancellans" and stick to the plainer English of "cancel."

[2] Since the Acknowledgments page contained still a third error, love's labor was lost. (Tennant—as the captions read—was changed to Pennant, *but* it is spelled Pennent [*sic*] on this page.) *Editor.*

Bibliography and the Rare Book Trade*

By JOHN CARTER

I THINK myself very fortunate in being, as I believe I am, the only Englishman present on this historic occasion. And if the President's invitation to take part in your jubilee meeting owed something to the fact that Washington is (geographically, if not spiritually) closer to Hartford than London is, the honor conferred on me is none the less for that. It is a further pleasure to me, as it obviously is to all of you, that we should be gathered here in the new home provided by Trinity College, with the munificent aid of the Old Dominion Foundation, for the library founded almost a hundred years ago by a fellow-countryman of mine, David Watkinson. We salute today not only the founding fathers of the Bibliographical Society of America, but also those devoted and distinguished librarians who have added prestige as well as books to the Watkinson Library, and through it, prestige to Hartford itself.

Yet it is, after all, the fiftieth anniversary of the B.S.A. which we are here to celebrate. It is a celebration of no mean signifi-

*Read before the Bibliographical Society of America, Trinity College, Hartford, Connecticut, May 22, 1954.

cance. And when, three or four weeks ago, I was instructed to telegraph immediately, for inclusion in the announcement of this meeting, some title or description to follow my name, a sense of diffidence intensified my usual difficulty in answering this question. For years I have never known, when filling up forms, quite what to call myself. "Bookseller" was inaccurate, for though I have bought a good many books in my time, I have hardly ever actually sold one. "Publisher" was for some years partially true in London, but thoroughly misleading just the same. "Bibliographer" always sounded rather pretentious for an occasional compiler of technical memoranda and commentary; and it is anyway quite meaningless—and therefore suspicious—to most of those who read the forms we fill in. "Professeur de Bibliographie" does very well for French hotels and gets one called Doctor, which gives harmless pleasure to those few of us who have never achieved a Ph.D. But its usefulness is severely limited. At the moment it would, indeed, be strictly accurate to label me as a member of Her Britannic Majesty's Foreign Service. But in the present context, strict accuracy would be (as it so often is) much more misleading than mere imprecision; for a professional in the rare book business does not change his spots just because, for a sabbatical year or so, he has hidden them under a pair of striped pants.

In the event, you may have observed that my name stands naked and unadorned. And lest anyone should have inferred arrogance rather than humility from this, let me say that there simply was not room for all my qualifications to address you today. For I stand before you as a member of the Edinburgh Bibliographical Society, of the Oxford Bibliographical Society, of the Cambridge Bibliographical Society, and a member of the Council of *the* Bibliographical Society (of London).

To the formal messages which have reached you from these bodies, I take leave to add, as a self-appointed delegate from all four of them, fraternal greetings to the B.S.A., congratulations on the achievement of its golden jubilee, and the warmest of good wishes for its prosperity during the second half-century. You may be younger than Edinburgh or London, but you are older than Oxford and much older than my own University's society, to celebrate whose fiftieth anniversary I shall have to survive well into my nineties.

As I descend, however, from the rostrum of salutation to the forum of exposition, I realise that the ambiguity of my status has certain advantages in terms of my assigned topic: bibliography and the rare book trade. In the first place, I have published a certain amount of work in this field, as a by-product of my business activities; I have also had to criticise a good deal of other people's published work, in my spare-time capacity as a reviewer; and I have been for twenty-five years a regular user of, and a constant debtor to, the bibliographical labors of our own as well as of previous generations, since they are the tools of my trade. No rare book dealer could stay in business for a week without bibliographical reference books; and no dealer worth his salt grudges the time and trouble now and again exacted from him by bibliographers at work. (As an author, I sometimes wish the rare book trade was a little more enterprising in promoting current bibliographical and bibliophilic publications among collectors, but perhaps that is a biased view.)

In the second place, ambiguities in the status of your speaker, or of anyone else, are as nothing by comparison with the ambiguities in the connotation of the two units of my title. In the present company, certainly, the difficulty of defining "the rare book trade" is of minor, if not minimal, consequence. We all know roughly what we mean by the term. But "bibliography" is another matter. And I must make it clear that, though I do not need to go as far as Humpty Dumpty, I propose to use the word this morning in its broadest sense: a sense recently defined by the President of the Bibliographical Society in his annual ad-

dress, entitled *Religio Bibliographici.* "For me," said Geoffrey
Keynes, "bibliography must be a fundamentally humane pursuit, shedding light not only on an author's printed texts, but
also on his literary history, his life in general, his personality,
and should often have as its main objective the establishment of
the basic and final text of all his writings."

Sir Walter Greg was undoubtedly right, as he usually is, when
he said, in the fiftieth-anniversary survey published by the same
Society, that we need some more comprehensive term to describe
the study of books, which would leave bibliography free for its
various specialized meanings. But the fact is that we haven't
one, and words cannot be ordered about. So for my present purpose, bibliography must be understood as reaching all the way
across from Fredson Bowers—and even William B. Todd—to
Holbrook Jackson—and even A. Edward Newton.

The relation between bibliography and the rare book trade
has always been, and must always be, an intimate one. It goes
much deeper, I believe, than the simple dependence of dealers
on bibliographers, influential as that is on both parties. Professor
Pottle once said: "Our science of bibliography would be sadly
hampered indeed were it not for the generous and largely disinterested service which private collectors perform by buying,
and putting freely at our disposal, books which our public libraries cannot or will not purchase." I would push that contention one stage further: for where, except from booksellers and
the auction room, would those private collectors get the books
on which the bibliographer proclaims his dependence? It is true,
of course, that this function is seldom entirely disinterested,
since booksellers are not in business for their health, and what
they sell is not primarily conceived of as raw material for bibliographical study. But the good ones are fully aware of its secondary purpose.

In fact, however, I have in mind quite a different factor when
I contend that bibliography and the rare book trade are more

closely interdependent than we sometimes realize. I am thinking rather of that cross-fertilization between these two departments of bibliophily, that constant enlargement of scope and enrichment of texture which each derives from the enlightened practitioners of the other. And since the services of bibliographers are both more readily acknowledged by the trade and more generally recognized by collectors than the services to bibliography performed by booksellers, I should like to take advantage of my temporarily anonymous position to examine the other side of the medal.

The contributions made by members of the rare book trade to bibliography may be divided into three categories. The first is oral, seldom ponderable, and sometimes ephemeral: it is the information and advice which the dealer puts at the disposal of the collector who is thinking of buying, or has bought, or even has decided not to buy, a book. The collector may not choose to note what he hears. He may note it, but decline to be guided by it. He may even prejudge it as a blurb rather than a footnote— and sometimes of course his prejudice will be well founded. But for what it is worth, he gets it as part of the service supplied by booksellers to his bibliographical education.

The second category includes those direct contributions made by members of the trade to the general body of published bibliographical work: whether books, articles, correspondence in the learned periodicals, or a one-line question or answer in *Bibliographical Notes and Queries*—that excellent publication which was initiated, edited, sustained and largely written by professionals (I think I myself was using eight pen-names in the end); which died for lack of outside support, and has now been revived as a department in the London quarterly, *The Book Collector*.

In my country at any rate it has often been noted, and sometimes not without a touch of complacency, that antiquarian booksellers, though articulate enough in discussion or reminiscence, develop a marked diffidence when it comes to putting pen to paper. A minority, of course, subscribe to the theory that the less collectors know about what they call "points," the better for the book trade. But even among the majority, I believe the idea that there is something inappropriate, or even pretentious, about getting into print, has been losing ground in the past few decades.

The author-bibliographies compiled by professional book-sellers have been, it is true, of uneven merit, so that one prefers to remember only the good ones, like Jane Norton's *Gibbon* or Greville Worthington's *Scott* or David Randall's *Frank Forester*. But author-bibliographies form a much smaller proportion of the annual output of bibliographical studies than the average collector is apt to realize. And even if we classify Seymour de Ricci as a bibliographer who did some book dealing rather than as a dealer who made striking contributions to bibliography, the antiquarian trade may well take pride in the fact that the two most important books on old bindings published during our generation—Hobson's *Maioli, Canevari and Others* (1926) and Gold-schmidt's *Gothic and Renaissance Bookbindings* (1928)—were both the work of professionals; and the next generation will know, what we today can only surmise, how much the revision of *S.T.C.* owes to the learning and devotion of Mr. F. S. Ferguson, for many years director of the illustrious firm of Quaritch.

Among the juniors—by which, of course, I really mean my own middle-aged contemporaries—it would be invidious to single out individuals. But I cannot omit mention of Cecil Hopkin-son's *Bibliography of the Musical Compositions of Hector Berlioz*, a frontal attack on a sector of what is bibliographically a veritable *bocage*. And I must unquestionably salute the English book trade's most prolific and most vigorous bibliographical musketeer, my old friend and mentor, Percy H. Muir.

Striking and distinguished indeed have been the considered contributions of antiquarian booksellers to the lists of those few publishers who will risk their money on bibliography: the uni-

versity presses (some of them), the R. R. Bowker Company of
New York, Constable of London in the thirties, Rupert Hart-
Davis today. They have held their own in the pages of the transactions of the learned societies, not least in the B.S.A. PAPERS;
in *The Colophon* and *The Book Collector*; in *Publishers' Weekly* in
earlier times and in *Antiquarian Bookman* today. The Antiquarian
Booksellers' Association of London is now producing an annual
miscellany. The International League of Antiquarian Booksellers is about to produce a multilingual glossary of bibliographical
and bibliopolic terminology.

Yet, in the judgment of history, on that bibliophile Parnassus where Poggio and Edward Johnson discuss the set of capitals
and lower case in a manuscript, where Aldus exchanges views
with William Morris on the merits of Jenson's roman, where
De Thou laments his anachronism with Roger Payne, where
Grolier and Roxburghe and Heber have kept comfortable seats
for Lenox and Beraldi and Gordon Duff—in that select company, all of whom know how much they owed to their booksellers, the verdict might well be that the most important, most
pervasive, and most enduring contributions made to bibliographical studies by the antiquarian trade were to be found in the pages
of the bookseller's readiest and most natural medium of expression: namely, in his catalogues.

We recall the honoured names of the scholarly booksellers
of the past: Obadiah Rich and William Pickering and Henry
Stevens; Baer and Hiersemann, Rosenthal and Breslauer and
Olschki; Luther Livingston and Edgar Wells, Charles Goodspeed and James F. Drake, A. S. W. Rosenbach and Lathrop
Harper; Bernard Quaritch and Charles Massey, R. A. Peddie
and James Tregaskis, Francis Edwards and A. W. Evans. We
salute, as senior representatives of their successors today, such
men as Mr. Percy Dobell, Signor De Marinis and Dr. Ernst
Weil. And we recognize that their scholarship was commonly

applied at the most practical point for its purpose—to the catalogue notes attached to books or manuscripts they were offering for sale. When all is said and done, I suppose that this is the logical medium for the deployment of such bibliographical gifts as a bookseller may possess, whatever he may put together in more formal style in his spare time. And the proof of it may be found in the respectable showing made by booksellers' catalogues on the reference shelves of the more discriminating librarians and collectors.

It would be easy to multiply examples, but I must content myself with a handful: Gumuchian's *Livres d'Enfance*; the *Catalogue of Typefounders' Specimens*, etc., prepared by Graham Pollard for Messrs. Birrell and Garnett in 1928, correctly described in a recent manual for collectors as "one of the standard reference books in its field"; the *Catalogue of Books by or relating to Dr. Johnson and members of his Circle*, prepared by A. W. Evans for Elkin Mathews Limited in 1925, which has been designated by a distinguished member of this audience as "a milestone in the history of bookselling"; that pioneer omnibus for collectors of scientific books, the *Bibliotheca Chemico-Mathematica*, prepared for Henry Sotheran by Mr. Zeitlinger; and finally the catalogue issued by Bernard Quaritch in 1889 of *Fifteen Hundred Books remarkable for the Beauty or the Age of their Binding*, a production illustrated by over a hundred plates, of which E. P. Goldschmidt, than whom there could be no better judge, wrote that it "is as indispensable in a library as any handbook or treatise on the subject."

A good catalogue note can do more than summarize the pertinent information, biographical, literary and bibliographical. It can add to our knowledge of the author, the subject, or the book described. Whether it should or should not be used as a springboard for bibliographical speculation is a moot point, and one which I should like to commend to the attention of an audience such as this. In his contribution to the Bibliographical Society's jubilee volume, *Studies in Retrospect*, Goldschmidt maintained that "it is the privilege of the bookseller to advance a bold hypothesis that will enhance the interest of his books, as long as it is plausible. Not on him, but on the coolly sceptical historian rests the duty to demolish what can not be strictly demonstrated." Commenting on this two years later, the then Sandars Reader in Bibliography in the University of Cambridge observed that "this would be all very well if all booksellers were as learned and as responsible as Mr. Goldschmidt himself. But they are not, and it would be an invitation to abuse by the least, rather than the most, responsible of them if such a principle were generally accepted. Yet," he admitted, "a number of bibliographical discoveries are in fact announced, and a much greater number of bibliographical theories are aired, in booksellers' catalogues every year." The propensity to think the best of one's own property is not confined to antiquarian booksellers: witness the attitude of the late Herr Otto Hupp, and of a certain famous New York library, towards the attribution of the book known as *The Constance Missal*. It is, indeed, a very natural one; and I assume that the reaction of a collector or a librarian to a bibliographical hypothesis advanced by a bookseller in respect of some volume he is offering for sale will mainly depend, first on the evidence adduced for the hypothesis, and secondly on his estimate of the perspicacity and judgment of him who advances it.

I suppose I must have written several thousand catalogue notes in the past twenty-five years, of which perhaps one per cent may have contained some purported addition to the common stock of bibliographical knowledge. I have often, but not always, resisted the temptation to air an hypothesis which seemed to me plausible; and before I resume the writing of catalogue notes, which is a much more delicate species of composition than most people realize, I wish Dr. Gallup (or Dr. S. M. Malkin) would conduct a poll among collectors and librarians, and tell

us professionals whether the intrusion of hypothesis wins friends
and influences customers, or whether it has, as I have sometimes
suspected, the opposite effect.

I have reserved for my conclusion a few words about a scholar-
bookseller whom I have several times had occasion to mention
already in this brief survey and who summed up in himself most
of what I have been trying to say: Ernst Philip Goldschmidt,
whose death has deprived his friends of a companion at once humane and cynical, gay and melancholy; *un ésprit original* who
epitomised the ancient and graceful culture of his native Vienna.

To the book world, Goldschmidt is an irreplaceable loss, in
the sense that there was, and is, and perhaps will be, no one quite
like him. For he was not simply a bookseller with scholarly instincts, aptitudes and training: he was a scholar who adopted the
rare book business as his means of livelihood and as the platform
from which to develop and deploy his scholarship. He combined,
in a degree which I think both his customers and his colleagues
would agree was unique, those two methods of contributing to
bibliographical studies which I have earlier distinguished. His
published works—*Gothic and Renaissance Bookbindings, Medieval
Texts and their First Appearance in Print, The Printed Book of the
Renaissance*—are full of original material and ingenious conjecture, constructed with style and expressed with grace. And we
shall doubtless find the same qualities in his Sandars Lectures,
proofs of which he had just finished correcting when he died.
These are not the *parerga* of a bookseller, to be judged by the
lenient standards which the learned are, mercifully, wont to apply to most of our productions. They are works of scholarship in
their own right.

And yet it may be that Goldschmidt's achievement in the
strictly professional medium will prove to have been, in sum,
even more remarkable. "No bookseller's catalogues," said his
obituarist in the London *Times*, "were given more care than

Goldschmidt's. His learned annotations contributed much to the education of librarians all over the world." They contributed much, also, to the education of collectors all over the world, not to mention those of his colleagues and competitors who knew a good footstep to follow when they saw one. For of Goldschmidt's catalogues it is fair to say, as his old friend Stanley Morison said at his funeral, that "the series as a whole, written as they were over a period of thirty years, amount to an encyclopaedia— written by one man."

To those whose minds were open, Goldschmidt was as prodigal of ideas in talk as he was stimulating and informative in print; and no one whom he admitted to his friendship will find it easy to fill the gap his death has left. Yet both his friends and his more distant debtors and admirers may perhaps console themselves with the reflection that Goldschmidt not only left a substantial body of learned and imaginative work to posterity; he also exerted a widespread influence, which, we may surely hope, will continue to bear fruit in the work of others. We have lost the man who made E. P. Goldschmidt Ltd., of London, what it is today: one of the most highly and widely respected firms in the business among those whose respect is worth having. But we may be confident that the spirit of its founder survives him, and that his successors, at 45 Old Bond Street and elsewhere, will be true to the distinguished tradition he represented: a tradition of imagination and expert knowledge and sound judgment, of honorable dealing, of dedication to scholarship and to the humanities.

Bibliothecohimatiourgomachia[*]

By ROBERT H. TAYLOR

OUR esteemed president should accept responsibility for
this title; after all, he is an accomplished Grecian,
which I am not. However, I will make a stab at trans-
lating it. We all remember Mr. Herman Liebert's stimulating
paper at the January meeting, and with a bow in his direction I
will render this majestic word in English as: "The importance
of *not* having multiple copies."[1]

When Dr. Bühler trapped me into agreeing to make this talk
I experienced the customary sinking sensation which overcomes
me on such occasions. This time it was stronger than usual, because it recalled my first contact with the Bibliographical Society
of America. Some years ago I mentioned to Carroll Wilson that
I was collating the MS of a Trollope novel with the printed text.
"Fine," he said, "will you let me have the result for the B.S.A.
PAPERS?" The offer of so meteoric a rise to fame could not be
rejected, and I hastened home to lard the article with footnotes
and such scholarly apparatus as might render it fit for this Society. A week or two later I again encountered Carroll, who inquired about my progress. "Oh, I've nearly finished," I replied.
Once more he said "Fine!" and then added the paralyzing injunction: "Make it funny." This appalling order produced in
me a cataleptic condition from which I am still suffering.

And since I was reminded of Carroll, let me begin my talk by
describing two of his books that are now in my possession. One
is a copy of Trollope's *North America* presented by the author to

---

[*] Read at the meeting of the Society at Hartford, Conn., May 22, 1954.

[1] It may also be translated as "The Battle Between Libraries and Taylor." *Editor.*

an American friend. It had somehow strayed into a New Hampshire public library, but had found its way out again, ending up in the hands of the bookseller who offered it to Carroll. Being a lawyer, he was not content until he had received from the librarian a quitclaim deed and a statement that the authorities were fully satisfied. This correspondence remains with the book, and shows clearly that because of the transaction the library was able to purchase material it greatly preferred. The second item is Hardy's *Dynasts*, including a copy of Part II with the 1905 title-page. This volume was found in the school library of Phillips Exeter Academy, and Carroll bought it from the trustees.

One other volume of mine that I wish to mention is a superb copy of Vaughan's *Silex Scintillans*, which was a Harvard duplicate. Here, then, are three books that I prize, and which I possess only because three very different libraries were willing and able to part with items which they did not really want. This behavior is not as common as you might think; and it is my contention that unless it becomes more general, the thwarted book collector of the next generation will be found amassing buttons or match-folders.

For desirable old books are disappearing from the market, and almost no collector is content merely to gather new books as they fall from the press. In all civilized ages the interest in collecting, whether of books or of other things, has been intensified by a desire to establish links with what has gone before. Books represent part of our inheritance of wisdom and beauty, and our ownership of them helps to assert our continuity with the past that produced them. No matter how modestly the collector starts, eventually he will come to seek some elusive rarity which by its age and perhaps by its association will communicate intimacy with some period or personality he admires. This same sentiment is shown by the pleasure most bookmen take in a volume with a distinguished provenance. I recently examined a book with an almost epic history: it was the Luttrell-Wynne-

Heber-Utterson-Halliwell-Daniel-Huth-Clawson-Rosenbach
copy. It has now found a good home—I know because I helped
to send it there—but its provenance has ended. At no time in
the foreseeable future will any individual add his name to that
impressive list.

Now the scholar will not regret this; in *Collector's Progress*[2]
Mr. Wilmarth Lewis has admirably depicted the pitying scorn
felt by a bibliographer for anyone who thought that a copy of
Bentley's Designs for Gray's Poems could have any interest merely
because it once belonged to Mrs. Vesey. Just the same, collectors
do feel this way, and no amount of rational argument is going to
change them. It must be clearly understood that, generally
speaking, the collector is sentimental, illogical, selfish, romantic,
extravagant, capricious; all the things, in fact, which the other
three estates of the rare book world—scholars, dealers and librarians—cannot afford to be. It is true that these groups overlap. We all know people who belong in two, perhaps three, of
these categories; but even so, their interest or career identifies
them predominantly with only one. Our question at the moment
is the importance of the collector to the other groups and to what
extent they should pander to his vices.

He is by no means as necessary to the dealer as he once was;
yet I submit that few dealers as yet would care to get along without him altogether. His relations with scholars are happier than
they used to be. The old gibes on the one hand that the collector
never read his books and on the other that the scholar did not
know how to handle a fragile rarity are no longer heard. Each
benefits freely from the other's activity. And as far as librarians
are concerned, let me quote a sentence from *Lock, Stock and Bar-
rel,* that history of collecting, by Douglas and Elizabeth Rigby.[3]
". . . it is a fact worthy of homage that most of the great libraries
in the world, and most of the museums, were born in the homes

[2] New York, Alfred A. Knopf, 1951, p. 91.
[3] Philadelphia, J. B. Lippincott Company, [1941], p. 82.

of private collectors or have battened at the same source." That's
the word they use: "battened." And Mr. John Carter has made
some incisive observations on this point in his *Taste and Technique
in Book-Collecting*.[4] I quote him with especial pleasure, since you
will all be glad to hear from him twice in one morning.

In America, the public-spirited tradition of Lenox and Brown has never died; and the impulse which moved Huntington and Folger, Clements
and Chapin, to dignify their country, their state or their university with
a monument worthily honoring their own names has of recent years been
fortified by the activity of the tax-collector. Even of those many great
collections which have been . . . dispersed by sale, some portions are always bought by or for institutional libraries. The number of desirable
books, therefore, that are withdrawn from any reasonable possibility of
further circulation becomes continually greater every year . . ."

And from the same volume:

There are more American critics than English of some of the present
tendencies in American university library policy towards rare book-collecting . . . What is their concern is the growing volume of university
buying in the rare book market, both public and private, which is the
direct outcome of the greatly increased attention being paid to the rare
book rooms on a hundred American campuses . . . Competition is a good
thing in itself. But whether in the long run the rare book men in the university libraries can have it both ways is another matter. Bread sown on
the waters in the shape of a liberal education in book-collecting to under-
graduates may often return . . . But if the libraries all over a huge and
wealthy continent are also going themselves to invade the auction rooms,
the neglected parlors of stately homes, the file sets and MS cupboards of
living writers and the various other sources normally tapped by collectors
and the trade, it is conceivable that the time may come when they will
drive their own pupils out of the market . . . Unless there is plenty of circulation bibliophily cannot thrive; and the ultimate value of the bibliophile
to pure scholarship as well as to the humanities of scholarship depends on
his recognition as an active entity, not as a mere appendix.

A single instance will suffice to show what has been happening.

[4] New York, R. R. Bowker Company, 1948.

I suppose no group of books is considered more generally desirable than the first editions of Shakespeare quartos. There are very few extant, as everyone knows; yet, between 1900 and 1939, fifty of them passed from private hands into American institutional libraries. It is likely that in the last fifteen years others have traveled the same road. Remember, I am speaking only of the first editions of the quartos—and I have not included any which were first published after 1622. These mournful statistics will not unduly depress realistic collectors; for a century it has been seldom that any individual aspired to collect Shakespeare in that manner, and now of course it is impossible. Not only is this true because there are practically no copies available, but because the price mounts with their scarcity. And the double effect on scarcity and price is symptomatic of what is happening to all rare books.

This, from the collector's point of view, is bad enough; but even worse is the duplication of holdings to be found in many institutions. These are generally the result of gifts or bequests —bequests so hedged about with threats and penalties, if any volume should be disposed of, that the librarian cannot release the duplicates. At least, not until a decent interval of time has elapsed. I have heard it said that in matters of testamentary disposition the word "forever" means "two years"; and I commend this idea to the study of librarians and their lawyers.

It is doubtless invidious to name any of these repositories of duplicates, but, as you would recognize them anyway, I may as well get on with it. Indeed, it is possible that all of our older libraries have duplicates which they may not part with, though I will limit myself to a few instances in the field of English literature. The New York Public Library, for example, has five copies of the First Folio. I don't know that the trustees would be especially eager to get rid of any of them, even if they could; still, once in a while those same trustees do try to raise money. And the Berg Collection in the same institution has two copies of

Tamerlane, two of Bryant's *Embargo* in the original binding, two of Browning's *Pauline,* three of the Kilmarnock Burns, and six Pickwicks in parts. (The seventh copy lacks one part, so I pass over that.) Of course, unless work has been done on all these duplicates, it would be foolish to sell them; but after a careful examination has proved the extra copies to be identical, it would be equally foolish to keep them.

The Folger Library, as all the world knows, has a great number of Shakespeare Folios, which, with magnificent planning, were gathered together for the purpose of scholarship. At some time or other, all of them will have been collated and some will be found to be exact duplicates. It will be interesting to observe whether they will remain together just because it was once desirable to have them under one roof.

I do not know how many copies of *Paradise Lost* are essential to an institution's well-being; but the library of the University of Illinois has numerous copies of each issue, assembled for Professor Fletcher's monumental work.[5] Now that his work is published, the reason for that concentration has vanished—but there has been no rush to put any of the Illinois copies on the market. It is enough to make one question the value of state-supported education.

Let us turn to happier thoughts: the Huntington sales of duplicates, for instance. And of course even in these degenerate days there are occasional bright spots, as witness the three books with which I began this talk. And we must not forget the Pierpont Morgan Library, whose trustees have decided against the purchase of any printed rarity a copy of which is available in some other New York City institution. This decision, I feel, is splendid. It comes a little late, perhaps, but there is more rejoicing in the collector's heaven over one sinner that repenteth than over

[5] Harris Francis Fletcher, *ed., John Milton's Complete Poetical Works Reproduced in Photographic Facsimile, A Critical Text Edition. . . .* Urbana, The University of Illinois Press, 1943-1948. 4 vols.

the ninety-and-nine libraries that don't buy rare books. Such a policy will not enlarge the circulation which Mr. Carter mentions as necessary to bibliophily, but at any rate it will not decrease it.

To be sure, there exists a minimal circulation out of libraries: a book that seems to have found its final resting place *may* be moved. Very occasionally, a librarian will admit that a book under his charge might have a more suitable home elsewhere; and, less often, steps are actually taken to see that it does go elsewhere, rather like the bones of Napoleon being transferred from St. Helena to the Invalides. Under the circumstances, it is perhaps not surprising that "elsewhere" invariably means another institution.

But this is not constructive. Instead, let me urge on rare-book librarians, especially those whose institutions are comparative newcomers in the field, the following considerations:

1. That they make sure every item has a good reason for remaining on their shelves.
2. That all of them do not try to accumulate everything. Even Huntington limited himself to three areas, and it is no longer possible to collect on the scale that he did.
3. That when their fields are decided on, they make the library's aims known to present and potential benefactors.
4. That they explain to such benefactors the hampering nature of gifts or bequests with elaborate restrictions—and, if needful, have the courage to refuse them. It might be useful to suggest to some donors that their books could be sold for the benefit of the library; and, if they are seeking some form of immortality, to remind them that the names of Britwell, Huth and Clawson are probably better known in the book world than those of Spencer, Coe and Parrish. Often the name on an auction catalogue endures as well as though it were carved on a lintel; and the sale price of a collection would benefit many a library more than would the collection itself.
5. And finally, that each librarian whose institution is in any way dependent upon individual benefactors ask himself whether those individuals would be as helpful if none of them were collectors.

It is the libraries who now have the whip hand, and who can

determine, in these days of increasing socialism, how far private enterprise in this field is to be encouraged. For the collecting streams are being fished out, and they will have to be restocked somehow if collecting is to continue as it has in the past. I am well aware that this is a venerable complaint. Nearly every collector has at some point moaned that he will never be able to get any really important books. Certainly we need go back no further than Harry Elkins Widener, who, according to A. E. Newton, lamented, "Mr. Morgan and Mr. Huntington are buying up all the books, and Mr. Bixby is getting the manuscripts. When my time comes—if it ever does—there will be nothing left for me —everything will be gone!"[6] Our grief at this outcry can be mitigated by recalling that he did manage to secure the Van Antwerp First Folio, the Countess of Pembroke's copy of the *Arcadia*, the dedication copy of Boswell's *Life of Johnson*, and many similar items.

Nevertheless, I repeat that wail, familiar as it may be. Books are being absorbed by institutions at a greater rate than ever before, and the pace seems always to accelerate. Mr. Wilmarth Lewis does not think that the Farmington Plan will be used in this field. "It is too much to expect," he says, "that libraries will transfer their rariora in any wholesale manner." Yet eventually what other solution will there be? The number of demands continues to increase. In the last three years the Davison books have gone to Wesleyan, the Lewis to Texas Christian, and the Philips —or perhaps I should say the Wilmerding—to Haverford. In at least two of these places accommodation had to be built especially to receive the collections, showing that these colleges had not previously contemplated this type of acquisition. And at least two of them have promised that their new rare bookrooms will not be mere showcases, but will be centers for study as well as for further accumulation. Truly, of buying many books there is

[6] A. Edward Newton, *The Amenities of Book-Collecting and Kindred Affections* (Boston, The Atlantic Monthly Press, [c1918]), p. 352.

no end—or of plans for buying them, anyway. Robert Hoe's query has more significance for these times than it did for his own: "If the great libraries of the past had not been sold, where would I have found my books?" And where will the libraries find them now? But answer, as the poet observes, came there none; and this was scarcely odd, because they'd eaten every one.

If by any chance anyone present should think that this disquisition has appeared slightly biased, that it has not seemed purely objective, he would be quite right. But do not think that I contemplate spoiling the Egyptians. It is impossible to overestimate the value of the great institutional libraries that enrich this country; and the fact that many of them were created in the last fifty years is a tribute to the foresight and generosity of the past generation, and to the energy and skill of those who have followed. I myself shall always be grateful for the many kindnesses shown me by librarians and for the friendships I have made among them. At least, they were my friends up till now. But whether or not they have begun to regard me with suspicion, I am certain they will agree with a dealer who was irritated by some remark I once made in the course of an argument. "The trouble with you," he said, turning on me bitterly, "the trouble with you is that you're just like every other God-damned collector." And, ladies and gentlemen, I don't ask for any better tribute.

A Doctor's Benefaction:
The Berg Collection
at The New York Public Library[*]

By JOHN D. GORDAN

NEW York City has been unusually fortunate in the number of rare books and important manuscripts which generous citizens have given to the public. Few institutions
have been more handsomely treated over the years than The
New York Public Library. Since the library of James Lenox became part of the original incorporation, the Library has received
no gifts of books and manuscripts richer than those of Dr. Albert
Ashton Berg. It was during Harry Miller Lydenberg's time as
Director that Dr. Berg made his three great benefactions. If it
had not been for H. M. L., for his enthusiasm and for his di-
plomacy, the Library might not today house the Henry W. and
Albert A. Berg Collection in Memory of Henry W. Berg.

Though the Collection reflects the interests of two medical
men, it was not medical material that attracted Dr. Henry W.
and Dr. A. A. Berg. Their interest was in English and American
literature. During his lifetime Dr. A. A. gave approximately

* Read at the meeting of the Society in New York, January 29, 1954.

40,000 items to the Library. Half of these, roughly, were printed material, and half manuscript. The printed items, be they
broadside, pamphlet in soft covers or book in hard, are generally
first editions. Occasionally there will be a later printing with
significant changes of text. Among the printed material should
be included various kinds of proof sheets; much of this proof is
corrected in longhand. There are no manuscripts of the period
before printing. The manuscript material comprises authors'
manuscripts and letters, as well as authors' typescripts, generally
corrected by hand, and typewritten letters.

The Berg Collection is essentially an author collection. It is
not a collection devoted to a subject, like drama or poetry or the
novel, or to a type, like incunabula or broadsides. It has been
built up by collectors who were interested in the great figures of
English and American literature and in many of lesser rank.
These collectors gathered together as much printed and manuscript material by each writer as opportunity, their interest and
their pocketbooks allowed—and there have been some deep
pocketbooks connected with the formation of the Berg Collection.

The formation of the Collection makes a dramatic story. In
the first fifteen months of its life as part of The New York Public Library, it grew from about three thousand to some thirty
thousand items. This was an increase not only in quantity, but in
quality. No such staggering rate of growth could have been
achieved without massive additions, and the Berg Collection
grew, as have almost all the great libraries of the world, by the
acquisition of other entire collections as well as of single pieces.
Dr. Berg added two famous collections to his original gift of his
own. We at the Library have a keen interest in the development
of these two collections when they were in private hands, and in
the collectors whose tastes shaped this development. Our chief
interest is, naturally, in Dr. Berg, as the benefactor responsible

for the final deposit at Fifth Avenue and Forty-Second Street of all this material.

The first gift which Dr. A. A. made to the Library was the 3,000 or so items which he and his brother Dr. Henry W. had assembled over three decades. The brothers had been wide readers in English and American literature. As boys they had worked in the library of Cooper Union, where they had plenty of time for browsing. There was a family tradition that Henry had recited the closing lines of "Thanatopsis" to Bryant when the poet visited the institute one day. Another tradition was that Albert had developed a taste for Dickens at the age of five or six. Ultimately this fondness led him into collecting first editions, as distinguished from a reading library. In all likelihood it was their early reading which turned two doctors—the elder a specialist in the treatment of smallpox and diphtheria, the younger a world authority on the treatment of cancer and ulcers of the stomach and of cancer of the gastrointestinal tract—away from a "shop collection" of medical books to a collection of literary material.

Dr. A. A. began the collecting. His first purchase of a rare book was of a Dickens novel in parts; just which novel, unhappily, he could never remember. This was around 1910, and since the brothers shared their interests, Dr. Henry W. was soon an enthusiast. As a curb on their enthusiasm, they set themselves a limit of $100 an item. The curb did not hold for long, or the collection which they had built up by the time of Doctor Henry W.'s death in December, 1938, would not have been so good as it was.

A year or so before the elder Doctor's death, the brothers approached The New York Public Library to discuss presenting their collection to the Library. They stipulated that they wanted a separate room for their books and would provide a fund for its upkeep. This generous offer put the Board of Trustees in a quandary, because space is almost the most precious thing in a great library today. The Board's acceptance of the Berg Collection turned out, however, to be one of its wisest decisions. It took some time to work out details to the satisfaction of the Doctors, and before final arrangements were made Dr. Henry W. died. Dr. A. A. desired to carry through the gift as a memorial to his brother. In 1939 the remaining details were settled, and on February 6, 1940, the Doctor made a formal offer which the Trustees accepted on February 14.

Once the memorial to Dr. Henry W. had been established and their private collection turned over to the public, Dr. A. A. found his desire to build up the Collection strengthened. Quite possibly, since he would now be buying material for an institution instead of for his own library, his dislike of self-indulgence was no longer a deterrent to large expenditure. His native shrewdness, furthermore, prompted him to take advantage of opportunities to purchase two great collections *en bloc*. Though the amounts paid were too large for the purchases to be classed as bargains, they were small in comparison with the sums that had been put into building up these same collections in a time of mounting prices.

The first opportunity came after the death of William Thomas Hildrup Howe of Cincinnati. A New Englander by birth and a graduate of Yale, Mr. Howe had been for many years President of the American Book Company. He, too, was a bachelor, and for some forty years he had pursued the hobby of collecting— old American glass as well as books and manuscripts—with even more ardor than the Doctors. His interest was also in English and American literature, particularly of the nineteenth and early twentieth centuries. Some of the authors whom he collected, like John Galsworthy and James Stephens, had been his friends, had visited him and had written to him frequently. Most of Howe's library was in Kentucky, at "Freelands," the house which he named after Galsworthy's novel and which appears on his bookplate. In its particular field the Howe collection was known to be one of the richest in private hands, and after Mr. Howe died intestate in August, 1939, several institutions began angling for it.

Dr. Berg's attention was first directed to the collection in August, 1940, by one of the most interesting personalities in the rare book world, the late Mitchell Kennerley. As his success with the Anderson Galleries indicated, Kennerley was a showman of charm and persuasion. He was acting for a well-known Chicago dealer, Walter M. Hill, who represented the Howe estate. The man who really heated to incandescence Dr. Berg's desire to have the Howe collection was Robert M. Lingel, then Chief of the Library's Acquisition Division. Lingel was a master salesman, and he knew how to reconcile interests that were apparently in hopeless conflict: the seller, the buyer, the agent— even two agents! Kennerley and Lingel are both now dead, and it is genuinely distressing to remember that their latter days were not happy. The Berg Collection would not be the outstanding collection that it is today had it not been for these two men.

Negotiations were carried on, at whirlwind speed for such a sizable transaction, during late August and early September, 1940. Lingel and Kennerley made a flying trip to Chicago and Cincinnati; Lingel flew back to Cincinnati for a few hours to obtain an option; and on September 12 the sale was clinched in Philadelphia, where the attorney for the estate happened to be at the moment. The sixteen thousand or so books and manuscripts which made up the Howe collection arrived at The New York Public Library on September 24 to be checked off by library officials, by Miss Edith Tranter (the executor of Mr. Howe's estate), by Walter Hill, and by Mitchell Kennerley. On November 13, the Howe library became officially a part of the Berg Collection.

A few months later, Kennerley came to Dr. Berg with another project. Mr. Owen D. Young, the retired head of the General Electric Company, was anxious to dispose of the collection of more than 10,000 English and American literary first editions and manuscripts which he had been building up for thirty years. This hobby Mr. Young had been able to pursue despite the fact that, unlike the other collectors about whom we have been talking, he was not a bachelor. Born in Van Hornesville, New York, in 1874, the same year as W. T. H. Howe, he has been twice married. It is a pleasure to be able to say that—again unlike so many of the other figures in this story—he is still hale and hearty. It was in order to provide for benefactions of his own in the neighborhood of Van Hornesville that he decided to sell his library. Apparently he had thought of offering several institutions an opportunity to make purchases and had even placed some items with a well-known rare book firm in New York. He had retained Mitchell Kennerley as appraiser and, presumably, as agent.

Once again it was Robert Lingel who fired Dr. Berg with the desire to add the Young collection to his other gifts to the Library. The situation also called for the miraculous ability of the Chief of the Acquisition Division to reconcile apparent irreconcilables. By refusing to take "No" for an answer, by traveling back and forth between New York and Florida, Lingel brought about an acceptable arrangement. Dr. Berg purchased an undivided half-interest in the Young collection for the Library, and Mr. Young presented the remainder. The whole was to become a part of the Berg Collection. This magnificent joint gift was announced on the front pages of the New York papers on May 5, 1941. Thus the tenfold growth of the Berg Collection came about within fifteen months of the Doctor's original gift.

By the spring of 1941, the Berg Collection had reached the same general proportions that it will have for many years to come, even though it steadily increases in size. In range, it extends from the end of the fifteenth century to the early twentieth. Practically, this means that it has a handful of English incunables, and that the most recent of its authors had attained some reputation by the time of the First World War. The strength of the Collection varies greatly over the range of four or more centuries. It is hardly surprising that it contains no material of the Anglo-Saxon period. It is scarcely more surprising that there is no medieval material, except two chronicles printed by Caxton and one by Wynkyn de Worde. There is little of the early Renaissance, but that little is choice. It has, among other first printings, a perfect copy of John Foxe's *Actes and Monuments,* or *Book of Martyrs;* the sixth edition of *Songes and Sonnets,* better known as *Tottel's Miscellany;* a perfect copy of the first English comedy, *Gammer Gurton's Needle;* two titles by John Shelton, and two by John Heywood.

It is only with the late Elizabethan period that the Collection begins to achieve any wide coverage, any density. Over the next two hundred years of English literature it gradually increases in strength until by the eighteenth century it can be said to have excellent but not exhaustive runs of books by the important authors. For the period up to 1641 covered by *A Short-Title Catalogue,* there are in the Berg Collection only 319 titles, some of which are present in more than one copy. It should be borne in mind that these are works of literature, not the religious or governmental publications that so enormously swell the number of entries in STC. There are, for instance, half a dozen Edmund Spensers, including several variants of *The Faerie Queene,* two copies of *Colin Clout,* and two of the *Complaints,* as well as *Fowre Hymnes* and *Prothalamion.* Sidney is represented by *An Apologie for Poetrie* and *The Countesse of Pembrokes Arcadia,* perfect except for a missing blank leaf. There are half a dozen Ben Jonson firsts in addition to the *Workes,* and a dozen and a half of George

Chapman's, with all his translations of Homer. Other Stuart dramatists—Beaumont and Fletcher, Dekker, John Ford, Heywood, Middleton, Shirley, Webster—are well represented. The Collection, however, has only one manuscript of the period before 1641, but an important one: John Donne's poems dating from 1619, formerly in the possession of the Earls of Westmorland.

No attempt has yet been made to check off Berg holdings in Donald Wing's helpful extension of the Pollard and Redgrave *Short-Title Catalogue*. The Collection has reasonably good resources for the major figure of the mid-century, John Milton—twenty-seven titles, including "Lycidas," "Comus," and all six title-pages of the first printings of *Paradise Lost*. The Cavalier poets, the metaphysical poets, the great prose writers like Browne and Burton and Walton are well accounted for, the first four editions of *The Compleat Angler* being present. Dryden, the great figure of the latter half of the seventeenth century, is represented by thirty-five titles. There is only a weak collection of late seventeenth-century dramatists, though there are four original letters of William Congreve's, whose letters are notably scarce. There are few other autograph letters by seventeenth-century figures.

The strength of the Berg Collection is greater in the eighteenth than in the seventeenth century, and it waxes with the century. There are fair to good collections of the important figures of the earlier half—Defoe, Swift, Addison, Steele, Edward Young, Gay, Pope, Richardson, Fielding, William Collins, Thomas Gray; and of the latter half—Dr. Johnson, Sterne, Smollett, Goldsmith, Cowper, Sheridan, Crabbe, Burns, Blake, Jane Austen, and lesser figures. In the eighteenth century the Collection increases in interest for the manuscript material and autograph letters it contains. Of the twenty-one writers just mentioned, all but three (Collins, Fielding and Gay) are at least represented by autograph letters, and all but Addison, Defoe, Blake and Young by manuscript material as well as by letters. The most important of the manuscript material is a rough draft of the first three books of Pope's *Essay on Man*. Two of the collections of letters are sizable; there are fifty by Thomas Gray, and fifty-three by Dr. Johnson. These holdings, however, are small indeed by comparison with the Burney papers belonging to the latter half of the century. In the Collection are the manuscripts of Fanny Burney's *Evelina, Cecilia, Camilla,* and of her *Diary and Letters* as prepared for the press. There are manuscripts of seventeen additional diaries, nine unpublished plays, and twenty notebooks. In addition, Berg has 900 autograph letters of Fanny Burney's as well as several hundred of other members of the Burney family.

It must be remembered that the material in the Berg Collection from 1500 to 1800 has come almost entirely from the joining together of what Mr. Young and the Doctors had collected, and that these collectors had large nineteenth-century holdings as well. Considerably less than half the thirty thousand items of the combined Berg, Howe and Young collections are reflected in these three centuries. It is not surprising, therefore, to find that its nineteenth-century material, English and American, is Berg's strength and its treasure. The collections of books by the principal authors of the century are gratifyingly close to completion, even including two of such rarities as the Bristol edition of Wordsworth and Coleridge's *Lyrical Ballads,* Browning's *Pauline,* Bryant's *Embargo,* and Poe's *Tamerlane,* to mention only the more spectacular.

It is the manuscript material that makes the Collection particularly interesting to scholars of this period. It is tempting to adduce a host of examples, but a half dozen or so must represent the rest. Take, for instance, the Coleridge material: there are thirty manuscripts, three notebooks, and over one hundred autograph letters. There are some 300 Thackeray autograph letters and 500 Dickens autograph letters, as well as minor manuscripts by both men. The turn of the century is well exemplified by Kipling, of whom we have two dozen manuscripts (including a manuscript of *Departmental Ditties*), 125 drawings, and over one hundred letters. In American literature Berg contains interesting Hawthorne material: some dozen minor manuscripts, an Italian diary and notebook, and 220 letters. This is backed up by a massive collection of a dozen or so diaries and several hundred letters of Sophia Hawthorne's and her sisters'. There are better than 1,700 pages of Thoreau's nature studies, and fifty of his letters. Whitman is represented by twenty manuscripts and 385 autograph letters. Clemens, at the turn of the century, can be studied in fifty manuscripts, including *A Connecticut Yankee*, *Following the Equator*, and *Tom Sawyer Abroad*, and 400 autograph letters.

The Berg Collection is unusually rich in association volumes among its nineteenth-century holdings. There are, for instance, five presentation copies of *A Week on the Concord and Merrimack Rivers*—those given by Thoreau to William Cullen Bryant, Ellery Channing, Ralph Waldo Emerson, James Anthony Froude, and Nathaniel Hawthorne. On the more sentimental side, Berg has some fascinating dedication copies. It has, for example, the copy of *The Raven and Other Poems* (New York, 1845) sent by Poe to Elizabeth Barrett, later Mrs. Robert Browning, and the letter she wrote thanking Poe for the dedication and the book. It has the copy of *Vanity Fair* given by Thackeray to Bryan Waller Procter, who wrote poetry under the name of Barry Cornwall, and the copy of *The History of Pendennis* given Dr. John Elliotson, the physician who pulled Thackeray through a desperate illness. For sentimental interest few books can surpass the copy of *Alice's Adventures in Wonderland* which Dodgson gave Alice Pleasance Liddell, or the copy of *A Child's Garden of Verses* which

Stevenson sent Alison Cunningham. Both are in the Berg Collection.

There is one aspect of the Collection which makes it of unusual usefulness, especially to bibliographers. It so often contains two or more copies of the first edition of a title. This situation has come about from the merging of three private libraries. It has already been pointed out that even in the period prior to 1800, where repetition would occur only between the smaller Berg and Young libraries, there is often more than one copy of a book. In the nineteenth century, when the Howe library, larger than both the others put together, enters the picture, the duplication of title becomes heavy. Mr. Howe, furthermore, understood the value of comparing copies of a title, and he often deliberately bought more than one copy.

The value of such multiplicity to the scholar, of course, lies in the variants, states and issues of the text and binding of a first edition which can be brought to light by comparison. Berg has, for example, four copies of the Aylott and Jones, 1846, edition of the Brontës' *Poems*, and among these are three variant bindings. In the investigations carried on by Mr. Jacob Blanck for the forthcoming *Bibliography of American Literature*, under the auspices of this Society, it was a considerable advantage to find in the Berg Collection, for instance, nine copies of *The Scarlet Letter* and eleven copies of *The House of the Seven Gables*. When a careful bibliography on Dickens is made, it will be useful to have in the Collection seven copies of *The Posthumous Papers of the Pickwick Club* in parts.

In closing, I should like to say something about the probable future growth of the Collection. The direction of this growth was taken, with the Doctor's approval, in the dozen years between the gift of Mr. Young's library and the present, during which roughly 10,000 items have been added. Emphasis has been laid upon the acquisition of manuscript material, because scholars have shown themselves on the whole more interested in the written than in the printed word. Income for new acquisitions is not yet available from the munificent legacy the Doctor left the Collection, because of plans for a new stack. When the Collection has this income to spend, the acquisition of manuscripts will doubtless still be the primary interest. Close to that aim will be the completing, insofar as possible, of the runs of printed material and the strengthening of the periods in which this review has shown the Collection to be weak. The Collection has always been considered part of The New York Public Library and not a separate entity in itself, and consequently the building-up of its printed sources will not, except for a special purpose, duplicate what is elsewhere in the Library. In his own lifetime, Dr. Berg carried his benefaction to eminence, and by his princely bequest he made it possible for the growth and usefulness of the Collection to continue. All of us at the Library will do our best to see that his wishes are carried out.

Thomas Jefferson and His Library*

By E. MILLICENT SOWERBY

IT is now almost fourteen years that I have been associated with Thomas Jefferson, for I first made his acquaintance in July 1942. I think I cannot pay him greater tribute than to say that during all this time I have never been bored with him for a single moment. He has roused other emotions, quite a variety of them, but never for an instant has he inspired boredom. He has grown upon me—for I knew absolutely nothing about him to start with—as one of the greatest men of his own, or perhaps of any age. If I may say so, I think that one of his really outstanding achievements and contributions to humanity is the number of people, including of course myself, whom he has helped to support since his death.

Jefferson's stature is such, and so much could be said about him, that it will be difficult to do him any justice in the short space of time allowed. I shall have to confine my remarks solely to him in connection with his books and the *Catalogue* of them, and not allow myself digressions.

Jefferson was a book collector all his life, and ranks as one of the great book collectors of his age. He assembled three libraries altogether. The first was housed in his mother's home at Shad-

* Read at the meeting of the Society at the Library of Congress, Washington, D. C., May 4, 1956.

well, and the greater part was lost when Shadwell was burned down in 1770. The last was started in 1815, when he was 72 years old, and was intended by him for the University of Virginia. It was sold at auction in 1829, three years after his death. The second, and most important library which he collected during the greater part of his life, and which he sold, or, as he himself put it, ceded or relinquished, to Congress in 1815, is the one with which we are concerned this morning.

These books, such as are left of them, are now in the Rare Books Division in the Library of Congress. The original number was around 6,500 (although I have never known whether that meant books or volumes), of which there are now scarcely 2,500 left—and that number does refer to books. This is due in part to the 1851 fire in the Capitol, where the books were housed, and in part to reasons which may reveal themselves as we go along. We all know who are the first enemies of books.

At the time of the sale to Congress, Jefferson's library was probably the finest in the United States. That was certainly his own opinion of it, and he was probably quite right. As early as 1794, in inviting George Wythe to see it, he wrote that it is "now certainly the best in America." Twenty years later, in 1814, during the negotiations for the sale to Congress, he wrote to Samuel Harrison Smith, who was acting as his agent, that such a collection could "probably never again be affected, because it is hardly probable that the same opportunities, the same time, industry, perseverance, and expense, with the same knowledge of the bibliography of the subject would again happen to be in concurrence."

Jefferson, as you see, did not underrate himself, but there is no question that he did succeed in assembling an extremely fine library. It was scientifically collected, and Jefferson himself explained that he based his ideas on the concepts of human knowledge as classified by Sir Francis Bacon in the *Advancement of Learning*. A comparison between Bacon's scheme in tabular form, and

Jefferson's, similarly written at the beginning of each of his manuscript catalogues, is extremely interesting.

The result of this systematic collecting was a comprehensive library containing books on every possible subject from ancient history and literature to modern inventions. It is absolutely staggering to find a man with a mind capable of absorbing and understanding such a variety of subjects, and his letters to his various expert correspondents in different fields show that he really did absorb and understand. Naturally he acquired more books on subjects in which he was deeply interested. The sale to Congress included, for example, more than thirteen hundred books and pamphlets on politics, which was only natural, and his collection of books of travel and geography, especially those which relate to America, including Spanish South America, is particularly fine and comprehensive.

Not that Jefferson admitted any interest in politics, in fact, quite the reverse. "The truth is," he once wrote to Caspar Wistar, "that I have been drawn by the history of the times from Physical & mathematical sciences, which were my passion, to those of politics & government towards which I had naturally no inclination." On surgery, which he described as "a comfortable art because it's operations are freed from those doubts which must forever haunt the mind of a conscientious practitioner of the equivocal art of medicine," he collected only five books.

Jefferson was a book buyer throughout his life. All collections of his manuscripts have book bills from the principal cities of Europe and the United States. His methods of buying, when in Paris as Minister Plenipotentiary, were thus described by him in a letter to Samuel Harrison Smith: "While residing in Paris" he wrote, "I devoted every afternoon I was disengaged for a summer or two, in examining all the principal bookstores, turning over every book with my own hand, and putting by everything which related to America, and indeed that was rare and valuable in every science. Besides this, I had standing orders during the whole time I was in Europe, on it's principal book-marts, particularly Amsterdam, Frankfort, Madrid and London, for such works relating to America as could not be found in Paris." In this letter Jefferson was trying to sell his books to Congress and therefore stressed the Americana, though actually his purchases covered a much wider range. No man ever had greater appreciation of the fact that history was being made in his time, and he seized the opportunity when in France to collect quantities of pamphlets on the French Revolution, the Diamond Necklace, and other matters. He collected also many English and American political pamphlets, always on both sides of the argument, and thus his library contains rich material for the historian scarcely to be found elsewhere. For the same reason he collected newspapers, both Federalist and Republican. Not that he had any faith in the facts printed by newspapers: "Nothing," he once wrote, "can be believed which is seen in a newspaper. Truth itself becomes suspicious by being put into that polluted vehicle. I really look with commiseration over the great body of my fellow-citizens, who, reading newspapers, live & die in the belief that they have known something of what has been passing in the world in their time."

Jefferson did not buy all his books singly from dealers; he sometimes bought private libraries either wholly or in part. After the death of Peyton Randolph he bought the magnificent library which Peyton had inherited from his father, Sir John Randolph, and his cousin William Stith the historian. This purchase included a number of early and irreplaceable Virginia historical and legal manuscripts, which fortunately survived the fire of 1851 and are now in the Library of Congress. He bought books from the estate of Richard Bland, the Virginia statesman and orator, and a large portion of the library of his old friend Samuel Henley, one-time Professor at William and Mary College. In his purchases Jefferson was never averse to second-hand copies, many of which, with the bookplates or autograph signatures of former owners, would be valuable association copies today, even if not from the library of the third President of the United States. There are, for example, books from the library of Benjamin Franklin, some with Franklin's autograph notes, of William Byrd, Robert Proud, Robert Beverley, Lord Dunmore (the Colonial Governor at the time of the Revolution), and a number of others. In addition to the books he bought Jefferson's library contained a large number of gift copies. He numbered among his friends some of the greatest men of the day, both in the United States and in Europe, men of the calibre of Joseph Priestley, Richard Baxter, Sir John Sinclair, Dupont de Nemours, Thomas Paine (that Quisling), Joel Barlow, Abiel Holmes, Benjamin Waterhouse (the first to vaccinate in the United States), and numerous others, all of whom sent him copies of their works as they wrote them. Numerous minor authors too sent him copies of *their* works, especially during his Presidential years, anxious to win a commendation signed by the President of the United States. In addition George Wythe bequeathed to him his fine library, and Martha Wayles Jefferson brought with her a number of books from the library of her father and of her brother-in-law, Reuben Skelton.

Jefferson described himself as a bibliomaniac, which was probably correct, but he was certainly no bibliophile. Not for him the first place in the Ship of Fools. He made this quite clear in a letter to Lucy Ludwell Paradise, who had refrained from buying for him at the Pinelli sale in London a book which exceeded his commission. "Sensible that I labour grievously under the malady of Bibliomania" (he wrote), "I submit to the rule of buying only at reasonable prices, as to a regimen necessary to that disease."

He certainly never spent money unnecessarily on a book, and a first edition meant nothing to him. Eager as he might be to obtain a forthcoming publication, he was always content to wait until a second and cheaper edition had been published, and if a pirated edition of an English book printed in Dublin or Paris could be obtained, so much the cheaper and therefore the better. In 1788 he was actually helping Pissot, a Paris publisher, to get out cheap pirated editions of English books, and in buying his law books he instructed his agent to get them whenever possible from Dublin, as "the Irish 8vos are preferred to the English because cheaper."

Within his price limit, Jefferson was definitely on the fussy side. He hated large books: folios and quartos were anathema to him. He wanted only books in octavo format or smaller, with good clear print, and in nice bindings. He was particularly fond, for example, of the Foulis press editions of the classics in duodecimo and collected a large number of them. These were recommended to him by George Wythe, who wrote to him on March 9, 1770, just a month after the Shadwell fire: "I send you some nectarine and apricot graffs and grapevines, the best I had; and have directed your messenger to call upon Major Taliaferro for some of his. You will also receive two of Foulis's catalogues. Mrs Wythe will send you some garden peas." In addition to the duodecimos he had, I am happy to say, the Foulis Homer's *Iliad* in folio, one of the most beautiful books ever printed, so beautiful that it makes you think you can read Greek even if you can't. His shelves had to look neat, with "good bindings and handsome, without being over elegant for use." His favorite binder was Joseph Milligan, an Englishman who had settled in Georgetown. "For elegant bindings there is no one in America comparable to him. His bindings are so tasty, so solid, and as heavy as blocks of metal." Fortunately a number of Milligan's bindings are still in the collection in the Library of Congress, and prove Jefferson's taste to be excellent. They are usually in tree calf, with gilt-tooled backs and marbled endpapers, though personally I should not describe them as being as heavy as blocks of metal.

So long as the outside of a book was "tasty and handsome," Jefferson was strangely unparticular about the inside. To him libraries were not, as they were to his mentor, Sir Francis Bacon, the shrines where the bones of old saints full of virtue lie buried, or if they were, he felt no need to treat the bones with any particular respect. He seems to have been absolutely without feeling for a book as a work of art, and was ruthless in his treatment of them if the need, for him, should arise. Pamphlets, broadsides, atlases of plates or other publications, issued as quartos or folios but destined by him to be bound in octavo volumes, had perforce to become octavos; their margins were cut to the quick if necessary and the leaves folded to fit into the smaller covers. Binders were instructed to divide volumes into two parts if too large for Jefferson to hold comfortably, and to bind the two parts separately; engraved portrait frontispieces were torn out and lent to borrowers; editions of the classics were cut up, rearranged, and interleaved with translations, and thus conflated, rebound in an increased number of volumes. Jefferson's much admired *Morals of Jesus* is sufficient to prove my point, for it required the destruction of I don't know how many copies of the Bible for its compilation.

It is impossible to do justice to Jefferson as a book collector in a quarter of an hour, but before I begin to talk about the *Catalogue* I want to stress one of his great contributions, not to book-collecting, but to librarianship, and what is now called Library Science. I am referring to his system of classification, which was used by George Watterston in compiling the Catalogue of 1815, and was copied by other libraries. It remained in use, just as is, in the Library of Congress until 1900, when the present building was completed and the books moved into it. By this time the number of volumes in the Library had increased to such an extent that some modification of the system was found necessary. Even so, the new system was founded on Jefferson's, so that not only is his library the nucleus of the present Library of Congress, his system of classification is the basis for the present satisfactory arrangement.

Now for the *Catalogue*. The bicentennial of the birth of Thomas Jefferson was celebrated in April, 1943, and the Library of Congress very properly decided that a *Catalogue* of the books he had sold to Congress in 1815, the aforementioned nucleus, should form part of the celebration. Jefferson's books were not separated from the other books since acquired by the Library of Congress until 1900, and, apart from the very uninformative list compiled by George Watterston in 1815, with which Jefferson himself was far from satisfied, no definitive catalogue of them had ever been made. The early Library of Congress catalogues were compiled strictly according to his classification scheme, and the entries for his copies were marked by a capital J or an asterisk. In 1864 the first catalogue with the books in alphabetical order was printed, and the Jefferson copies remained unmarked.

In July 1942 I had the honor of being appointed to make the catalogue, to be ready in April 1943! I accepted gaily, not having the slightest idea of what I was in for. I imagine the reason that I was honored with the appointment was that I had been in the rare-book world all my life, and the authorities probably thought it would need a rare-book person to cope with Jefferson's library. Had this been the case the work might possibly have been done by April 1943, as most rare books have already been described and catalogued. But, as we have seen, Jefferson's major interests were not rare editions, and any rarity now in his library is there by accident rather than by design on his part. His Williamsburg imprints, for example, now great rarities, were not so when he bought them. The most valuable part of his library from the commercial point of view I should imagine to be the Spanish and other early Americana, in which he had some extremely fine books, none of which, unfortunately, has survived. Actually I was rather thankful that his copies of the first eleven parts of De Bry were not there, so there was no question of bothering with the various issues, either of text or plates.

The idea of the Library officials, as explained to me when I came, was an alphabetical catalogue, which was perfectly all

right with me until I saw Jefferson's manuscript catalogue of his
books, which the Massachusetts Historical Society kindly allowed us to use as the basis of the new Catalogue. The books in
this catalogue are not only classified by subject, but are obviously
entered in the order in which they should be studied, and to lose
that into an alphabetical catalogue would be to lose Jefferson.
The result would have merely looked like a secondhand dealer's
list. Moreover, I had been looking at his printed writings and
had discovered what a lot he had to say about his books and their
authors. Knowing that the Library of Congress owned a large
quantity of Jefferson's manuscripts, though evacuated at the time,
as were also the books, I thought what a wonderful historical
document it would make to have him annotate the book entries
himself, by quoting from his manuscripts. I suggested this plan
to Authority, who agreed with my ideas, but probably still expected the finished work by April 1943. When the books and
manuscripts were returned from evacuation I realized for the
first time what I had let myself in for. However, I was not down-
hearted; that the Library of Congress should have difficulty in
finding money never occurred to me. The Library of Congress
has 42,426 numbered sheets of Jefferson's correspondence, and
I had the privilege of using in microfilm the Jefferson papers in
a number of other libraries, public and private. All these had to
be read and the necessary extracts made. Jefferson kept a copy of
every letter he wrote, either by means of the polygraph, or a
copying press (in which he frequently used too much water and
made the copy illegible), or a recently invented piece of black
paper, apparently resembling our carbon paper. He kept also the
letters written to him, and, apparently for the benefit of posterity
as well as for his own convenience, he made an alphabetical and
a chronological Index of all the letters written and received. I
think that he knew he was making history, and was big enough to
want posterity to know the whole story. The copies of his own
letters include a number which show his political subterfuges,

and those written to him are sometimes far from complimentary. (I recall letters beginning "You red-headed son of a bitch.") It seems to me that only a really great man would keep such letters for posterity to read. In view of all this correspondence, the job I had in mind might have taken anything from five to ten years with an adequate staff, but with one bibliographer and one assistant, both apt to be put on part-time or fired when funds ran out—though thanks to the kindness of the Library that did not happen so very often—it has taken the time it has.

Jefferson's handwriting is fortunately very legible, though that of some of his correspondents, particularly the foreign ones, sometimes presented grave difficulties. The worst of a job of that sort is that one does not know what one may be going to need until one has become really acquainted with Jefferson, and that takes time. I was particularly fortunate in one respect. I was under the erroneous impression that he had not sold a copy of the *Notes on Virginia* to Congress. Therefore I did not list the references to that work at first. I shudder when I think what I should have missed. I should never have suspected that references to *my few poor worthless notes*, or *the few poor crudities I have thrown together*, were references to his beloved *Notes on Virginia*. Fortunately, by the time I did the *Notes* I knew him fairly well, but even so I nearly missed a gem. The *Notes* were actually in galley proof, and I was reading a long letter from Jefferson to John Trumbull on some other matter altogether, when I noticed the name *Stockdale* in the last sentence. Jefferson was at the time negotiating with Stockdale for a London edition of the *Notes*, and I read: "No news from Stockdale. I am done with him irrevocably." I need hardly say that it was inserted in the galleys immediately.

Apart from the correspondence, the books themselves were not without their problems when returned from evacuation. They numbered something over 2,000 and were placed in the stacks of the Rare Books Division. Since then I have found between three and four hundred more in the general or the Rare Book stacks, and I am quite certain that there are a great many more of Jefferson's copies which are now unrecognizable as such, owing to the ways of librarians and the destruction of marks of provenance. I always remember going to the Binding Division when I was quite new to show them the 1815 bookplate and to request to be informed if such a bookplate should come in. They promised to do this, but at the same time informed me cheerfully that they had had for rebinding lots of books with that plate. (Probably Milligan or John March bindings!)

Finding a book in the stacks was always a triumph. I remember well Jefferson's entry for the first book in his American History chapter, "Vater on the peopling of America." This title was similarly entered, and checked as having been received, in the 1815 Catalogue. I could not find an English translation of Vater's book in any catalogue or bibliography. Eventually I went down to examine the German edition in the Library stacks, in case it might have an advertisement or some other announcement of an English edition. The moment I saw the book I knew it was Jeffy's. It was in a John March binding, with Jefferson's original shelf mark, initialled by Jefferson at signatures I and T, and had the 1815 bookplate. Jefferson had merely entered it in English because he did not know a word of German. Jefferson's entries were quite apt on occasion to cause a waste of time. I remember very well his "Meditazione sulla oeconomia politica dal Beccaria." This entry, calling for an edition of 1771, was repeated in all the catalogues which distinguish the Jefferson copies. I hunted high and low without result. I went through Beccaria's *Opere*, as Jefferson sometimes entered a portion of a book as though it were a whole one. I even read a life of Beccaria, all without result. These researches had brought to my attention the fact that a man named Verri had written a book with a similar title, so in despair I decided to see if it could give me any help. To my surprise Verri's card in the General Catalogue had the information that the copy was Jefferson's. I dashed to his stacks, and there was the very book I had been hunting for. It was an anonymous publication, and on the title-page some previous owner had written "Dal Beccaria" copied by Jefferson and the early Library of Congress catalogues. The most delightful story in this connection resulted from a very misleading statement by Jefferson. Jefferson's manuscript catalogue, followed by the 1815 Catalogue, Chapter 4, no. 24, call for "Tracts relating to New England by Cotton Mather, small 4to." In the later catalogues, still ascribed to Mather, the title was changed to "Tracts relating to Witchcraft in New England," with the addition of the date and place of printing: Boston, 1697. The only book by Mather which came anywhere near to fitting the description was his *Memorable Providences relating to Witchcraft and Possessions* of which, although no edition was printed in Boston in 1697, an edition was printed in Edinburgh in that year, with the imprint: Printed at Boston in New England, and reprinted in Edinburgh, 1697. This was not too satisfactory, but was the best that could be done. It was duly described therefore under the Jefferson and 1815 catalogue headings for no. 24, and with a tentative note explaining that it might not be the right book, but that early cataloguers *had* been known to ignore the reprinted phrase, which in this case would leave us with Boston, 1697. Not satisfactory, but there was nothing else to be done. Volume I, including this number, was in corrected page proof when Mr. Langone, then of the Rare Books Division staff, brought me a book which had been called for by a reader, and in which he recognized the 1815 bookplate. This was Robert Calef's *More Wonders of the Invisible World*, printed in London in 1700. It was in a John March binding, and had Jefferson's own shelf mark, chapter 4, no. 24, and the 1815 bookplate with the same data. I immediately checked no. 24 in the 1815 catalogue, and found of course that it was "Tracts relating to New England by Cotton Mather." Calef's book, an attack on Mather and witchcraft, had lost its title-page (which has since been supplied in manuscript), and opened with the Epistle to the

Reader, dated from Boston in New England, August 11, 1697. Moreover, the first thirteen pages contain an extract from Cotton Mather with a preface signed by him. Jefferson must have looked at the book very superficially, but his entry was accounted for. I could have embraced Mr. Langone, but I doubt if the Government Printing Office proof reader had any kindly feelings towards me when I insisted on changing the entry in the page-proof, and I was by no means pleased at the small space into which I had to cram the description. I was delighted to find only a short time ago that George Watterston had also been deceived by Jefferson's and his own catalogue entries. On April 28, 1821, Watterston, signing himself Librarian U. S. Library, advertised in the *National Intelligencer* for some books which had been secretly taken out of the Library of Congress. His list included "a work in p. 4to by Cotton Mather, of some antiquity and great rarity." Watterston knew the book in 1815, but by 1821 had forgotten, for Calef's book was not missing. I was delighted to know about the Watterston slip, which I owe to Mr. Clapp's habit of cleaning out his desk drawers and sending anything that relates to Jefferson down to me.

Speaking of the Government Printing Office, which has done a most remarkable job, I was frequently at odds with them on account of their zeal for accuracy being as great as my own. For instance, I placed a large J before the entries to denote that Jefferson's copy was still extant. The absence of a J, which meant of course that there was no Jefferson copy, was taken by the GPO to mean careless work on my part, and they kindly filled the gaps for me and placed a J before every entry. I regret to state that one or two of these extraneous Js have been overlooked and are still in the catalogue. You can imagine too what difficulties we have had with Jeffy's spelling and capitalization.

Another source of trouble was caused not by the GPO but by early librarians, whose ideas of the classification of pamphlets were at variance with Jefferson's. Jefferson had his pamphlets bound together in volumes, according to subject, and always wrote a list of the contents of the volumes on the fly-leaves. The pamphlets were not as a rule initialled by him, but his handwriting on the fly-leaves gave all the information required. A large number of these pamphlet volumes have been torn apart, the contents bound separately in buckram, and reclassified. Jefferson's fly-leaf of course was lost with the rebinding. In such cases it is impossible to know the contents of the volumes, or to recognize Jefferson's copies. I remember finding one little pamphlet bound in buckram, with Jefferson's list bound in at the end. That was a wonderful stroke of luck.

I have good reason to believe that more Jefferson copies will turn up, because they are still turning up. For instance, Mr. Thomen of the Library staff found some time ago among the discarded duplicates a set of *The History and Proceedings of the House of Lords* in 7 volumes. Each volume had the Library of Congress 1815 bookplate and the bookplate of Reuben Skelton, Martha Jefferson's brother-in-law. Each volume was initialled by Jefferson at signatures I and T; each had a J on the back and a J for Jefferson pencilled on the 1815 bookplate. Yet so small was the interest in Jefferson in 1909, the book was discarded as a duplicate, and the discarder signed her name! This find came too late for Volume III where it belonged, and has had to go into the Addenda in Volume V. Here will be found other discoveries, including a set of pamphlets, obviously Jefferson's, discovered by Miss Mildred Louden in doing her "Not in Evans"—a list (as yet unpublished) of all the books in the Library of Congress not recorded in Charles Evans's *American Bibliography*.

The bibliographical information supplied by Jefferson and his correspondents in this *Catalogue* is quite remarkable. (They are listed in the Index in Volume V.) It is entirely owing to Jefferson that we know that the Farmer of New Jersey who wrote *Observations on Government* in 1787 was John Stevens of New Jersey, and not William Livingston, to whom it has always been ascribed; that William Beverley, not his brother Robert, was the author of the *Abridgment of the Public Laws of Virginia*; and that the pamphlet entitled *Colony Commerce* by Alexander Campbell Brown, and so entered by Sabin and other bibliographers, was actually by Mark Leavenworth of Connecticut, who himself wrote to Jefferson to inform him of the facts. An anonymous and extremely rare pamphlet bound by Jefferson in a volume with others has been torn out and lost, but fortunately not before it was seen by Sabin, whose note reads: "Attributed to Carter Braxton, in Jefferson's handwriting in the copy in the Library of Congress." Two extremely subversive pamphlets were printed without name of place, printer or date. It is thanks to Jefferson that we know that these were by Genêt, the Minister Plenipotentiary from France; Jefferson has not only written *par Genet* on one of them, but has given an account of both in the *Anas*.

I should like to close with a mention of two of the many humorous incidents in Jefferson's library. The first is the set of volumes entitled by Jefferson himself, "The Book of Kings." This consisted of four separate books of European scandals which, until October 1814, when the negotiations for the sale were in progress, were in their proper places on Jefferson's shelves, two in foreign and two in British History. On October 17, Jefferson wrote to instruct his binder, Joseph Milligan, that he was sending

a packet of 6 vols, which though made up of 4. different works, I wish to have bound as one work in 6. vols. to be labelled on the back "the Book of Kings." the 1st and 2nd vols will be composed of the Memoirs of Bareuth, the binding to remain as it is, only changing the label. The Memoirs of Mad. La Motte will make the 3d and 4th vols. pared down to the size of the first & bound uniform with them. Mrs Clarke's will be the 5th vol. pared & bound as before, and 'the Book' will make the 6th which to be uniform in size with the rest must perhaps be left with it's present rough edges. pray do it immediately and return it by the stage that they may be replaced on their shelves should Congress take my library.

It is most unfortunate that these books are no longer extant. However, a delightful touch has been added by George Ticknor, who visited Jefferson in February 1815, before the library had left Monticello, and wrote a descriptive account. "Perhaps the most curious single specimen, or, at least the most characteristic of the man and expressive of his hatred of royalty was a collection which he had bound up in six volumes, and lettered The Book of Kings." After listing the volumes, Ticknor went on: "These documents of regal scandal seemed to be favorites with the philosopher, who pointed them out with a satisfaction somewhat inconsistent with the measured gravity he claims in relation to such subjects generally."

The second story concerns the reconciliation arranged by Benjamin Rush between Jefferson and John Adams. The quarrel, which separated them for years, took place at Jefferson's dinner table, and I recall that Mrs. Adams was "sensibly flushed." It worried their friend Rush, who eventually succeeded in bringing about a reconciliation. To show his pleasure Adams immediately sent Jefferson a gift. On New Year's Day, 1812, he wrote to him: "As you are a Friend to American Manufactures under proper restrictions, especially Manufactures of the domestic kind, I take the Liberty of sending you by the Post a Packett containing two Pieces of Homespun, lately produced in this quarter by one who was honoured in his youth with some of your attention and much of your Kindness." Jefferson was delighted and immediately wrote to Adams a long letter of thanks, beginning: "I thank you before hand (for they are not yet arrived) for the specimens of homespun you have been so kind as to forward me by post." The letter then goes on with a long dissertation on homespun, and a comparison of that produced in the north, the south, and abroad. He made a copy of his own letter and of that of Adams to him, and sent them both, with another long letter, to Benjamin Rush. The man who took these letters to the post brought back with him the parcel of Homespun, which was a domestic manufacture indeed, and consisted of the two volumes of a book by John Adams' son, John Quincy Adams. Poor Jeffy; if only he had waited!

Variant Entry Fees
of the Stationers' Company

By W. A. Jackson

IN his Lyell Lectures[1] Sir Walter Greg has provided students of English publishing practises of the century following 1550 with much that is new and far more that is for the first time accurately set forth, written with the clarity and precision which are to be found in all his work. So inevitable is it that this small volume will become the main guide to future students of the subject, that when, very occasionally, some of the statements in it may seem rather less than final it is more important than is usually the case to call attention to them.

When discussing the fees paid at the time of entrance of a book in the Stationers' Register,[2] Sir Walter, after citing fees ranging from fourpence to twenty shillings, and considering several explanations for this variation, finally concludes, "But there are seemingly insuperable objections to any explanations on these lines [such as size, importance of the book, or fees to outside licensers], and since I have no satisfactory solution to offer, I will

---

[1] W. W. Greg, *Some Aspects and Problems of London Publishing Between 1550 and 1650* (Oxford, 1956).

[2] *Op. laud.*, pp. 38-39. The manner of entry in the various record books is admirably described, pp. 21-38.

refrain from further conjecture." It is probably true that no
"satisfactory" explanation can be set forth for all the recorded
variant fees before 1582, when apparently they were fixed at
fourpence for a ballad and sixpence for a book. However, besides
the minimum fee of fourpence for small books and ballads, it
can be demonstrated that during this period the normal fee for
books of twelve sheets and over was one penny for three sheets.
Sir Walter refers to an entry[3] by John Wight in 1559 of John
Ferrarius's *A woorke touchynge the good orderynge of a common weale,*
for which he paid fourpence with the added note "And at the
fynysshynge of the sayde boke he shall paye for euery iij leves a
pannye." To this note Arber has a misleading gloss: "4*d.* would
at this rate, be the fee for 24 pages," for the word "leaf" was used
by the stationers of that day interchangeably for "sheet," as, for
example, in *Court-Book C,* p. 15, 6 August 1605: "Thoms Pur-
foote thelder Shall haue the woorkmanship of printinge one
leafe of the prymers for the company," i.e. one sheet of a two-
sheet *The A.B.C. with the catechisme.*[4]

It seems probable that other factors than the number of sheets
contained in the books were at times involved in the calculation
of the fees. We must remember that the men who set these fees
were professional printers and would be aware of the various
means by which these charges could be circumvented, as for example by using paper of a larger size.[5] It seems also probable
that allowance was made for the use of large type for the text as
well as for the use of "white" letter, as roman type was usually

[3] Arber I.97.

[4] An edition dated 1605, collating A[8], B[4], with an unrecorded "TP" device of
Purfoot on the title is in the Harvard Library. This division of work was often employed by the warehouse keepers of the English Stock to prevent a printer from over-
printing, and keeping for his own profit, copies of almanacs and other patented
books belonging to the Stock.

[5] In this they were probably wiser than the Commissioners of Stamp Duties who
introduced in 1712 a tax per sheet on newspapers without specifying the size of the
sheet; cf. *The Library,* 4th Series, XXII (1942), pp. 126-137. A postal rate based
on the sheet, established in the United States in the middle of the nineteenth century,
produced newspapers almost the size of bed-sheets.

called at that time, presumably because size for size more text could be set in a given area in roman type than in black-letter. In some instances the variant fees recorded present bibliographical evidence that is of utility if only in confirming hypotheses otherwise established.

The fees for nine books are cited by Sir Walter as illustrating the diversity of the charges. Let us examine them one by one, but, for reasons which may become apparent, in the reverse order of his listing. First, Sir Geoffrey Fenton's *Certaine tragicall discourses*, 1567 (STC 10791), for which Thomas Marsh paid, at two different times, fees totalling two shillings fourpence.[6] It is a quarto in eights collating *[8], **[2], A-Pp[8], Qq[2], or a total of seventy-nine sheets, which at the rate of three sheets per penny leaves one sheet over. The next example is the second edition of *A myrrour for magistrates*, 1563, for which Sir Walter cites only the fee of fourpence paid[7] for "the ij[de] parte of [the] myrror of magestrates." Thomas Marsh had, however, a few days or weeks before paid[8] another fee of fourpence for "the myrror of magestrates," and in 1559 he had paid[9] sixpence for his original entry for the first edition published that same year. The first edition is a quarto of twenty and a half sheets, and so the original fee was apparently at the usual rate of three sheets per penny with two and a half sheets over. The 1563 edition is not a mere reprint of the first edition for it contains a new "second part" with eight new tragedies as well as Sackville's "Induction." The new material occupies just twenty-four sheets for which the two 1563 fees, totalling eightpence, work out at exactly three sheets per penny. Had no copy of the 1559 edition of this book survived, it would have been possible from an examination of the 1563 edition to deduce from the fees paid for it what was contained in the earlier

---

[6] Arber I.343 and 356.
[7] Arber I.208.
[8] Arber I.207.
[9] Arber I.97.

edition. The next book listed is an edition of Thomas Tusser's
A hundreth good poyntes of husbandry entered by Richard Tottell in
1561-1562,[10] of which no copy can now be traced unless it be the
copy in the Eton College Library lacking its title. W. C. Hazlitt, however, described[11] a copy of a 1562 Tottell edition as being
a quarto of forty-eight leaves. Tottell paid a fee of fourpence
which is exactly three sheets per penny.[12]

The identification of the next book, cited by Greg as "a translation of Josephus," is obviously wrong: though the entry reads
"this boke of Josephus," it actually refers to Peter Morwyng's
translation of Joseph Ben Gorion's *A compendious history of the
Jewes commune weale*, 1558, which is an octavo of thirty-six
sheets for which Jugge paid only fourpence.[13] On the same day
that Jugge entered this book he made two other entries, one for
two unidentified books which Arber conjectures were parts of
the same book, for which he likewise paid only fourpence, and
also for Joannes ab Indagine's *Briefe introductions vnto the art of
chiromancy*, 1558, an octavo of sixteen sheets, for which he paid
the same fee. On the grounds that the same fee was exacted for
books of sixteen and thirty-six sheets, that the titles are given
in the vaguest possible way—the Indagine is "the boke of palmes-
trye"—it would seem possible that the entry was made before
these books were printed and that Jugge would be required to
pay the rest of his fee when the number of sheets could be calculated, as in the case of John Wight cited above, but no second payment is recorded.

The next book is Raphael Holinshed's *Chronicles of England*,
1577, two huge folio volumes which after much effort were

[10] Arber I.179.

[11] *Handbook* (1867), p. 618. Owen Rogers was fined two shillings in 1562 (Arber I.184) for printing an edition of this book, "beynge master Totteles," and
the Eton copy might be his.

[12] John Day had entered the book in 1557-1558 (Arber I.78) and so Tottell
must have acquired his rights from Day.

[13] Arber I.77.

finally issued by a family syndicate. John Harrison and George Bishop, his partner, paid a fee of one pound for the entry,[14] the largest fee recorded anywhere in the Register. The two volumes, with certain cancelled leaves, contain 741 sheets, which at three sheets per penny accounts for all but twenty-one sheets. It is possible that the clerk compounded for a round figure in the case of this enormous publication. On the other hand, it may be that the syndicate produced for inspection and gift to the Company (a copy was demanded, as was customary, in addition to the fee) a copy which lacked the table: A-M⁴, N² of the second volume, or twenty-three sheets, either because the table was not yet printed or else in order to save the sevenpence involved. In this connection one should remember both the casual reasonableness of the stationers' "baker's dozens" and "extra copies," and the fact that a sixpence then would purchase a very good dinner.

The four remaining books do not fit the pattern of a normal fee of three sheets per penny (although one of them comes very near to it), but it is possible to suggest reasons why they should be charged more or less than the normal fee. For example, the next two books are both printed in roman type. The first of these is Thomas North's translation of Plutarch's *The lives of the noble Grecians and Romanes*, 1579, which is a large folio—copies are known nearly thirteen inches tall—printed in a pica roman letter which obviously contains many more ems to the sheet than most books of the period. It consists of 298 sheets for which Thomas Vautrollier and John Wight paid a fee[15] of fifteen shillings or about one and two-thirds sheets per penny. On the same day the Plutarch was entered Thomas Norton and Thomas Vautrollier paid a fee of thirteen shillings for the next book, Geoffrey Fenton's translation of *The historie of [Francesco] Guicciardini*, 1579, a folio of 303 sheets, printed in roman letter, which is very slightly less than two sheets per penny. The difference between the charge for

[14] Arber II.329.
[15] Arber II.351.

the Plutarch and that for the Guicciardini may be due to the size of the paper, and consequently of the type page, in the two works.[16] There are very few books of this period for which large fees are recorded which were printed in roman type[17] so that one cannot be certain that the type was a factor in the fee charged.

The next book is John Calvin's *The institution of christian religion*, 1561, a folio of one hundred and thirty-seven sheets for which Reginald Wolfe and Richard Harrison paid three shillings and fourpence[18] which at the rate of three sheets per penny leaves an overplus of seventeen sheets. The collation of this book is somewhat complicated, there being five alphabets of which two only are nearly complete, with several different sized quires, and this might just be a case of miscalculation. The last book, Greg's first, is the 1570 edition of Alexander Barclay's translation of Brant's *The ship of fooles*, a small folio of one hundred and seventy sheets for which John Cawood paid a fee of half a crown[19] or a rate of more than five sheets per penny. An examination of the book, however, suggests a possible explanation of this anomalous rate, for most of the text is verse printed in great primer black-letter with a very large amount of white paper, so that if the normal charge was based on a sheet of solid pica type then this book was properly given a lower rate.

It may well seem that if one has the temerity to suggest an explanation of a phenomenon such as these variable charges for entries one should at least produce an hypothesis which explains most, if not all, the examples, and yet, as we have seen, five out of the nine instances so far discussed do not conform to the normal

[16] The type-page in the Plutarch covers an area of 455 sq. cm. whereas in the Guicciardini it covers 364 sq. cm. or a difference of 25%.

[17] The only example that has been found on a cursory examination of these records is the entry for Edward Dering's *XXVII. lectures, or readings, vpon part of the epistle to the Hebrues*, 1576 (Arber II.302), a quarto in eights printed in roman type and containing sixty-three and a half sheets for which Luke Harrison paid two shillings fourpence, or a rate of two and a quarter sheets per penny.

[18] Arber I.153.

[19] Arber I.360.

and can only be explained by what may well be regarded as ingenious, though reasonable, guesses. However, if we take not a
random sampling but every title listed on a given page of the
Stationers' Register, for example Arber II.329, the page which
contains the Holinshed discussed above, for which a variety of
fees ranging from fourpence to the twenty shillings of the *Chronicles* were paid, we shall find rather more reassuring results. Of
the nine books entered there, one, John Bradford's *Godly meditations*, 1578, has no fee recorded, and two were charged the minimum fee of fourpence because in the case of the Luther (STC
16989) it consists of only six sheets, and in the case of the Nausea
(STC 18413) of only five.

The others, however, all conform reasonably closely to the
norm, if we may include the Holinshed: the Grange (STC
12174) has eighteen sheets for which sixpence was paid; the
Keltridge (STC 14920) has thirty-seven sheets for which
twelvepence was paid, leaving an extra sheet; the Wotton (STC
5647) has forty-four sheets for which sixteenpence was paid
which amounts to two and three-fourths sheets per penny[20]; and
the Bourne (STC 3432) has thirty-five sheets for which twelvepence was paid which is again one sheet off. The only remaining
book entered on that page is the Appian (STC 713) which has
ninety-two and a half sheets for which a half crown was paid, or
an overplus of two and a half sheets. This fee is of some bibliographical significance because in the beginning Henry Bynneman by himself apparently intended to publish merely the first

[20] The number of sheets in this book was taken from Hazlitt's *Handbook*, p. 679,
which gives 176 leaves, information evidently derived from J. P. Collier. However,
since the above was set up, it has been possible to see a microfilm of the Sion College
copy, a quarto collating A-Y⁴, Z², Aa-Qp⁴, or 38½ sheets, which amounts to less
than two and a half sheets a penny. More than an eighth of the book is set in roman
with a small quantity of two column verse in italic. The book was divided between
two compositors or presses, and it is possible that an error in casting-off gave the
impression that the last two of the five histories into which the book is divided would
occupy as many sheets as the first three, which would have given a total of at least
45 sheets, and that the fee was paid before the book was completed. The Sion College does not appear to belong to a condensed second edition.

part of the book, "the Romaine Ciuill warres," and a copy in the Carl H. Pforzheimer Library has an otherwise unknown cancellandum title with only Bynneman's name in the imprint referring solely to the first part which ends with the death of Sextus Pompeius. Bynneman's plans, however, were altered and a second part containing the civil wars to the death of Antony and "the Romanes expeditions against forraine Nations," published by Ralph Newberry in partnership with Bynneman, was added. The first part contains fifty-two and a half sheets, whereas the second part contains just forty. From the fee charged it is apparent that the change of plan was made before the Clerk of the Company recorded the payment of the half crown and therefore it is not surprising that only one copy has so far been traced with the uncancelled original title.

Random checking of the fees recorded in these early years confirms the probability that the normal fee was calculated at the rate of three sheets per penny. It is not unlikely that should someone have the leisure to compare all the entries of these early years with such of the books then entered as can now be traced he would be able to be much more categorical about such matters as whether the entries were often made before the books were in print, and whether leading, size, or kind of type were factors in the calculations of the fees, as well as many other particulars of entry-practises concerning which we have too little evidence as yet even to speculate.

Literary Research and
Bibliographical Training

By CURT F. BÜHLER

I T appears both strange and unhappy that, despite the tremendous progress made in bibliographical knowledge and practices since the middle of the last century, it should still be necessary to plead for a greater understanding, by the practitioners of sister disciplines, of the functions and possibilities in the study of books *per se*. It would seem self-evident to some of us that an acquaintanceship with bibliographical methods was a necessity for the literary student even as a knowledge of palaeography or handwriting must be for the historian, at least for the student of original documents. This is not to argue that every investigator of literary material should be equipped with the full panoply of bibliographical technique or that it be necessary for such a scholar to have mastered the intricacies of the *Principles of Bibliographical Description* so brilliantly set forth by Professor Fredson Bowers.[1] But one should at least expect that those scholars who conduct investigations in the history of literature would know a good deal about the book as the "material vehicle of the living word."[2] In short, and as a minimum requirement, a literary investigator ought to have some knowledge of the works listing the editions pertinent to his research and should know in what bibliographies to seek information covering the field of his interest. Unfortunately, this does not always seem to be the case. Two articles—excellent in themselves, but not so complete and accurate as they might have been if the proper bibliographical

[1] Princeton University Press, 1949.

[2] [Sir] Walter W. Greg, "Bibliography—a Retrospect," *The Bibliographical Society, 1892-1942, Studies in Retrospect* (London, 1945), p. 27.

tools had been employed—illustrate the point I wish to make; these are found in the current number of *Medievalia et Humanistica* (Volume XI, 1957).

I

In his article "The Manuscript Tradition of the *De vita et moribus philosophorum* of Walter Burley" (pp. 44-57), Mr. John O. Stigall includes, as Appendix II, a list of early printed editions of his text. Selecting only the items listed as incunabula from this list, we obtain the following twenty entries:

1. Köln: Ulrich Zell, c. 1470
2. — G. B., 1472
3. Köln: Arnold ter Hoernen, 1472[3]
4. Köln: Printer of the "Flores Sancti Augustini," 1473
5. Köln: Conrad de Homborch, 1475
6. — G. B., 1477 (?)
7. — W. B., 1477
8. Louvain: Johannes de Westfalia, c. 1477
9. Nürnberg: Anton Koberger, 1477
10. Nürnberg: Friedrich Creussner, 1479
11. Louvain: Johann de Paderborn, 1479-82
12. Köln: Konrad Winters de Homborch, 1479
13. — G. B., 1479
14. Toulouse: J. Parix, c. 1480
15. Speier: Johann and Conrad Hist, 1483
16. Köln: Johann Koelhoff, the Elder, c. 1486
17. Augsburg: Anton Sorg, 1490 [in German]
18. France: ———, 1495
19. Paris: Georg Mittelhaus, 1496[4]
20. Eustadt: Reyser, [without date]

On the one hand, the compiler does not explain whence he

[3] Apparently as the result of a misprint, Mr. Stigall gives the name as Arnold ter Hoeren. For this printer, see Ernst Voulliéme, *Die deutschen Drucker des fünfzehnten Jahrhunderts* (Berlin, 1922), pp. 42-43.

[4] This printer, an Alsatian, usually signed his name Mittelhus, occasionally Mittelhuss. Compare Konrad Haebler, *Die deutschen Buchdrucker des XV. Jahrhunderts im Auslande* (München, 1924), pp. 191-192, and Anatole Claudin, *Histoire de l'imprimerie en France* (Paris, 1900-1914), II, 5-12.

obtained his list; on the other, the standard bibliography of incunabula (the *Gesamtkatalog der Wiegendrucke*)[5] lists a total of
only thirteen such editions. Let us consider Mr. Stigall's entries
seriatim.

No. 1: this is GW 5781. No. 2: no printer with the initials
G. B. used in a colophon and no printer identifiable only by these
initials is known to me. Konrad Burger knew of two printers
identified by these initials in the reverse order (B. G.—Bartholomaeus Girardinus of Venice and Bartholomaeus Guldinbeck of
Rome), neither of whom published an edition of the *De vita et
moribus philosophorum*.[6] This entry quite baffled me until I turned
to the old "general catalogue" of the British Museum, where
several editions of the work are briefly listed under Burleus,
Gualterus as "[By G. B.]". This seems to be the ultimate source
for the entry in Mr. Stigall's list. The G. B., of course, stands
for the author and not for the printer. The British Museum's
press-mark (C. 14. b. 7/2) indicates that this edition corresponds
to GW 5785 and the book should be assigned thus: [Nürnberg:
Anton Koberger, c. 1472].[7] No. 3 = GW 5783. No. 4 = GW
5784. No. 5 = GW 5782. No. 6: see also remarks under no. 2.
The incipit, according to the BM general catalogue, suggests
that this edition is the same as no. 8 (see GW 5788). No. 7: no
printer W. B. (or B., W.) is listed by Burger. This entry too
seems to stem from the old BM catalogue, where the incipit suggests that this is the same as no. 9, the only one dated 1477. The
W. B., of course, represents Walterus Burlaeus (or Walter Burley). No. 8 = GW 5788. No. 9 = GW 5786. No. 10 = GW 5787
No. 11: this is the same edition as the one listed under no. 8.[8] No

[5] Leipzig, 1925-1938, V, 681-689, nos. 5781-93.

[6] *The Printers and Publishers of the XV. Century with Lists of their Works*,
(London, 1902), p. 32.

[7] *Catalogue of Books Printed in the XVth Century now in the British Museum*
(BMC), (London, 1908-1949), II:411 (IB. 7140).

[8] John of Westphalia was a native of Paderborn and was known both as Johannes
de Westfalia and as Johannes de Paderborn. Two editions were listed by Marinus
F. A. G. Campbell, *Annales de la typographie néerlandaise au XVe siècle* (La Haye,

12: this is the identical edition as that listed under no. 5.⁹ No. 13: see also remarks under no. 2. The incipit as cited by the BM general catalogue indicates that this is the same edition as no. 10, the only one dated 1479 (compare GW 5787). No. 14 = GW 5789. No. 15 = GW 5790. No. 16 = GW 5791. No. 17 = GW 5793. Nos. 18 and 19: the *Gesamtkatalog* asserts that no edition was printed in France before the sixteenth century.¹⁰ Accordingly, these two editions should be dated *post* 1500. No. 20: noted by Mr. Stigall on p. 57 as "printed by *Reyser* at Eustadt, but without date." Apparently, this entry comes from Hain 4117¹¹ or Brunet I:1407¹² (both assign the edition to: Eustadii, Reyser). The press of Michael Reyser at Eichstätt is not known to have produced such a work.¹³ Hain 4117, according to GW 5790, corresponds to no. 15. One edition not listed by Mr. Stigall is described by the *Gesamtkatalog* under no. 5792.¹⁴

In revised form, and with the usual practice of placing all inferred information into square brackets, the fifteenth-century

---

1874), p. 106, nos. 387 and 388, though no. 387 has since been rejected as a separate edition by several authorities (cf. Maria E. Kronenberg, *Campbell's Annales de la typographie néerlandaise au XVᵉ siècle, Contributions to a new Edition* (The Hague, 1956), p. 71).

⁹ GW 5782 is signed by "Conradus de Homborch," who is identical with Konrad Winters de Homborch (see Voulliéme, *op. cit.*, p. 48). Only one edition of Burley's *De vita et moribus philosophorum* is credited to his press by the standard bibliography of Cologne incunabula (Ernst Voulliéme, *Der Buchdruck Kölns bis zum Ende des fünfzehnten Jahrhunderts* (Bonn, 1903), p. 135, no. 297).

¹⁰ Compare GW V:col. 688. Four editions are here relegated to the sixteenth century which were listed as incunabula by Marie Pellechet, *Catalogue général des incunables des bibliothèques publiques de France* (Paris, 1897-1909), nos. 3089 and 3091-93. Some of these also appear in Mr. Stigall's list of XVIc editions, although there may well be some duplication here. Thus, Joh. Parvus (Jean Petit) printed an edition of which some copies have the device of De Marnef as publisher. The two editions credited to Mittelhus may also represent a single original, since no incunable edition by him is known.

¹¹ Ludwig Hain, *Repertorium bibliographicum* (Stuttgart, 1826-1838).

¹² Jacques-Charles Brunet, *Manuel du libraire et de l'amateur de livres* (Paris, 1860-1880).

¹³ See Voulliéme, *Die deutschen Drucker*, p. 58, and Burger, *op. cit.*, p. 245.

¹⁴ Listed as: [Südliche Niederlande? Drucker der Mensa philosophica (Hain 11076), um 1486/90].

editions of the *De vita et moribus philosophorum* may be chronologically listed thus:

GW	Imprint	Stigall
5781	[Köln: Ulrich Zell, c. 1470]	1
5783	[Köln]: Arnold ter Hoernen, 1472	3
5785	[Nürnberg: Anton Koberger, c. 1472]	2
5784	[Köln: Printer of Flores S. Augustini, n.a. 1473]	4
5786	Nürnberg: Anton Koberger, 6 May 1477	7,9
5782	[Köln]: Konrad Winters, [a. 18 Mar. 1479]	5,12
5787	Nürnberg: Friedrich Creussner, 30 June 1479	10,13
5788	Louvain: Johann de Paderborn, [c. 1479/82]	6,8,11
5789	[Toulouse: Johann Parix, c. 1480]	14
5790	[Speier]: Johann and Conrad Hist, [c. 1483]	15,20
5791	[Köln: Johann Koelhoff, the Elder, c. 1486]	16
5792	[Belgium: Printer of Mensa philosophica, 1486/90]	-
5793	Augsburg: Anton Sorg, 31 August 1490. [German]	17

II

The article by Mr. John N. Hough, "Plautus, Student of Cicero, and Walter Burley," follows next in the journal (pp. 58-68). In the course of his analysis, Mr. Hough cites the *Mer des histoires*, quoting from the edition printed at Lyons by Jean Dupré in 1491. He there observes that this work was certainly descended from Burley's treatise but that, in regard to the added material, "*La Mer* evidently expanded at whim. Whether these are original or not is not possible to determine, but some are certainly Gallic in nature."[15] It should have been relatively easy to determine the true extent and the exact nature of the expansions.

Such reference books as the BMC,[16] Polain,[17] Oates,[18] and

[15] P. 61, note 18.

[16] In the comment on the first edition (VIII:109), it is stated that "Le Rouge had before him the editio princeps of the Rudimentum nouitiorum . . . but decorated his own book more effectively." Compare also the note in Robert Proctor, *An Index to the Early Printed Books in the British Museum* (London, 1898-1903), p. 579, no. 8092.

others[19] plainly state that the *Mer des histoires* is an adaptation of a work first published in Northern Germany,[20] the *Rudimentum novitiorum* printed by Lucas Brandis at Lübeck on 5 August 1475. The first edition of the French text was issued in Paris from the press of Pierre Le Rouge in 1488. In the prefatory matter, the author himself states:

Par quoy en ce present liure qui peult estre nomme La fleur ou la mer des histoires: & en latin est appelle Rudimentum nouiciorum | Cest adire en francois le Rudiment des nouices | ou lenseignement des nouueaulx. Nous raconterons par ordre. de degre en degre la greigneur partie des hystoires & des grandes choses dignes de memoire | qui sont aduenues depuis la creation du monde iusques a present.

Thus it would have been possible to determine exactly the part contributed by the French compiler through a comparison of copies of the two editions,[21] such as are to be found, for example, in the library with which the present writer is connected.[22]

---

[17] M.-Louis Polain, *Catalogue des livres imprimés au quinzième siècle des bibliothèques de Belgique* (Bruxelles, 1932), III, 169-171, no. 2673, and 640-642, no. 3404.

[18] J. C. T. Oates, *A Catalogue of the Fifteenth-Century Printed Books in the University Library Cambridge* (Cambridge, 1954), p. 504, no. 3007, and p. 538, no. 3207.

[19] Margaret B. Stillwell, *Incunabula in American Libraries* (New York, 1940), p. 439; [Sir Henry Thomas], *Short-title Catalogue of Books Printed in France and of French Books Printed in Other Countries from 1470 to 1600 now in the British Museum* (London, 1924), p. 83; Alfred W. Pollard, *Early Illustrated Books* (London, 1893), p. 162; etc.

[20] It is interesting to recall Mr. Stigall's comment (p. 50) to the effect that "no MSS of the *De vita* have as yet been traced in north Germany." Burley's treatise was, in any case, known there. Similarly, Mr. Stigall (p. 49) knew of only one manuscript (Trinity College, Cambridge, MS O. 2. 50) of English origin though written in a Flemish hand (in his catalogue, Dr. Montague Rhodes James merely states "clearly written, perhaps in Flanders"), and not a single English edition of the Latin text is listed by the *Short-Title Catalogue of Books Printed in England, Scotland, & Ireland and of English Books Printed Abroad 1475-1640* (London, 1926). Nevertheless, so fastidious a scholar as Sir Thomas Elyot (1490?-1546) knew and quoted Burley's work; on this point, see my note "Diogenes and *The Boke named The Governour*," *Modern Language Notes*, LXIX (1954), 481-484.

[21] The French sentences cited at the foot of p. 61 and in note 21 (p. 62) have no counterparts in the *Rudimentum novitiorum*.

Mr. Hough also makes the following observation in connection with the account of Plautus (pp. 67-68):

La Mer offers still another, perhaps supplementary, hint as to the origin of the connection [of Plautus] with Cicero. The entry following *Plautus* in *La Mer* is: Plaucius armacius disciple de Ciceron fut grand orateur, etc. and notes his foundation of Lyons (with pardonable Gallic addition of explanation as to why *Gallia comata* is so called). This is identical with Burley (ch. 100, only two "lives" totalling six lines intervene between this and Plautus, ch. 103).

The *Mer des histoires* is here simply following the arrangement in the *Rudimentum novitiorum* (f. 270), where "Plaucius armacius" (in the identical words as in Burley)[23] follows Plautus and is separated from it by this short passage not found at this place in the French text: "Item hoc anno. plaucius apud tharentum. seipsum interfecit."

Still another bibliographical handbook might have suggested a further additional note of considerable interest.[24] Although not a single printed edition of the *De vita et moribus philosophorum* was produced by Italian presses in the fifteenth century, the work was not without influence on Italian literary history. As I pointed out in the reference just cited, the Italian version of the *Vitae et sententiae philosophorum* claiming to be a translation of the work of Diogenes Laertius is nothing of the sort.[25] To a remarkable extent, it is little more than a translation into Italian of Burley's text.[26] One may best illustrate this by quoting the passage on

---

[22] Listed in Ada Thurston and Curt F. Bühler, *Check List of Fifteenth Century Printing in the Pierpont Morgan Library,* (New York, 1939), nos. 507 and 1458; see also the listing on p. 326.

[23] Without the full explanation for *Gallia comata*, which is, therefore, a French addition (as Mr. Hough thought probable).

[24] Curt F. Bühler, James G. McManaway and Lawrence C. Wroth, *Standards of Bibliographical Description* (Philadelphia, 1949), p. 36, n. 34.

[25] The *Gesamtkatalog der Wiegendrucke* lists ten editions (GW 8385-8394) under Diogenes Laertius, with the note "ist eine gekürzte, freie Bearbeitung der lat[einischen] Vorlage."

[26] This was pointed out in my article "Greek Philosophers in the Literature of

Plautus (not to be found at all, of course, in the Greek original of Diogenes Laertius)[27] which may then be conveniently compared with the Latin passage from Burley as printed by Mr. Hough (p. 58):

Plauto poeta fu gran maestro di comedie o uer tragedie: & discipulo di Tullo. Fu eloquentissimo & per po[u]erta[28] scriuea historie & fauole & uendeuale & per sustentar la uita non si uergogno far el mestier del pistor Soleua dir chi non crede esser meritato del ben che fa ad altri singana lui stesso Non torre amicitia de pazzi Con gli huomini peruersi e piu facil cosa hauer odio che familiarita Non si debe far lhuomo troppo amico daltri Diceua ancora lhuomo esser el piu fiero animale & el piu nuouo del mondo imperoche chi gli e alpari di se non lo puo soffrir: se gli e minore elo spreza: se e magiore li ha inuidia: se gli e equale non si concorda seco. Vixe a Roma al tempo di Pompeio.[29]

This, one might suggest, is about as "unhumanistic" a volume as the Italian Quattrocento produced; it is entirely in the mediaeval tradition!

A few literary points might also be raised. In the ter Hoernen edition of Burley (GW 5783), the description of Plautus opens with the words: "Plautus Poeta Comicus Tulij discipulus Rome claruit." This is the precise wording also found in the *Rudimentum novitiorum*, the *Mer des histoires*, the German translation,[30] and the Italian "Diogenes" (with very minor changes). The Koberger (GW 5785) and Winters (GW 5782) editions have the

---

the Later Middle Ages," *Speculum*, XII (1937), 440-455 (especially pp. 451-452). In the same study (pp. 440-445), the textual relationship of the *De vita et moribus philosophorum* to the *Rudimentum novitiorum* and the *Mer des histoires* is also discussed at length.

[27] Nor was an account of Plautus added to the Latin version (by Ambrosius Traversarius), at least in the edition of Venice: Nicolas Jenson, 14 August 1475 (PML 309).

[28] The original has the misprint "ponerta."

[29] Quoted from the first edition, Venice: Bernardinus Celerius, 9 December 1480 (GW 8385; PML 36049), sign. h3, cap. CI. With very minor differences, the same text is found in the edition, Florence: Francesco Bonaccorsi and Antonius Francisci, 5 July 1488 (GW 8387).

[30] "Plautus der poet Comicus tulius junger ist zů Rom erschÿnen" (Sorg, f. 132ᵛ).

text as given by Mr. Hough: "Plautus, comicus, philosophus, Tullii discipulus, Rome claruit." Again, the first group, which refers to Plautus as a poet, sets forth a section "De sentencijs eius moralibus," while the texts which describe Plautus as a philosopher refer to his sayings as being notable rather than moral. These details, as presented above, once more emphasize the fact that it is not only the words as written by the author (the "official" text) that have value; just as often the altered (even corrupt) version is more important in the development of a literary tradition than that authenticated by the writer himself.[31]

These, then, are some details which might have been set forth more accurately or more fully in the two articles under discussion. The present study was not undertaken with the purpose of casting aspersions on either of the studies. Both are extremely interesting and useful contributions to scholarship. It is equally true, however, that a greater acquaintance with bibliographical reference works would have made both essays even more interesting and more useful.

[31] On this point, see also the conclusions reached in my article "Studies in the Early Editions of the *Fiore di virtù*," *PBSA*, XLIX (1955), 315-339.

Lathrop Colgate Harper:
A Happy Memory*

By LAWRENCE C. WROTH

LIFE as Mr. Harper lived it was, intensively, life with books. Very often the books were great books; always they were good books; usually, but not invariably, they were books of rarity. But whether or not they possessed this final added grace, they were in all cases books distinguished by quality. There never lived a man, I believe, more completely absorbed than he was in books, in finding out what they were about, in buying and selling them, in studying the lore and procedures of his bookseller's trade. With persistence one might occasionally divert his mind from its preoccupation by a direct question as to what he thought of some event of transitory importance like the attack upon Pearl Harbor, but after a shrewd, concise, and unarguable affirmation in reply he would take up again the one great subject at the point of interruption.

It was not only in his shop that this continuous thinking and brooding and talking about books went on. It was the same on the bus or in the cab, at dinner in one of his cherished Italian restaurants, or at his home afterwards waiting for the night to pass

* Read at the meeting of the Society at the Sterling Memorial Library, Yale University, New Haven, Conn., May 16, 1958.

so that he could get back to 8 West 40th Street. As horses and dogs were to the character on the Dover coach, books were to him more than a fancy; they were life itself. And as he loved above all else significant books, great and small, to be with him was to share in one of the great spiritual adventures, the search for quality.

My own acquaintance with the world of great Americana began in Mr. Harper's shop at Fifth Avenue and Thirty-Seventh Street. How many are here who remember him in that location? If Mr. Streeter were here he would remember. Miss Stillwell and Mr. Vail remember. Mr. Parsonage remembers better than anyone because it was there that, a boy from London, he went to work at his first American job, and if we may think of Lathrop C. Harper, Inc. as carrying on the old business, his only American job. It was in that shop that one day in 1923 on my way to take up the librarianship of the John Carter Brown, I learned what life was like in the areas which until then had been for me the outer space of the book world. That day Mr. John B. Stetson came in and in the course of his visit found himself pleased with a copy of the Varthema *Itinerario* of Venice, 1520. When in reply to his question Mr. Harper told him the price was "twelve fifty," he slipped the book, unwrapped, into the patch pocket of his tweed jacket and walked out into the crowded New York streets. Misled by this offhandedness, I asked Mr. Harper the foolish question which I am sure you have anticipated. When he replied without any perceptible evidence of surprise at my innocence that the price had been not twelve dollars and fifty cents but twelve hundred and fifty dollars, I realized that I had entered a new world of values. It was not until I got to Providence and made a study of this edition of the Varthema with the Juan Diaz relation appended that I began to see that except in rare instances values in books are fundamentally a measure of esteem for contents. Here in this book was the earliest report in print of the Córdoba and Grijalva discoveries and explorations of Yucatán and Mexico, and therefore the first news carried to Europeans of the revolution, the new era in the economic, political, and so-cial life of mankind, which through these events was about to be inaugurated. Mr. Harper had introduced me impressively to the great books.

From now on throughout this brief address I shall be speak-ing of two concepts which soon became one in my mind—Lathrop Harper and the great books of Americana and incunabula. Not many months had passed after this introduction when I found myself buying from him that very important first printed report upon the fortunes of the Plymouth colony, the Cushman *Sermon* of 1622, the E. A. Crowninshield-Charles Deane-A. T. White-Thomas W. Streeter copy. At the same time he sold us four Ital-ian and French news relations concerning Sir Francis Drake, three of them printed in the lifetime of "il Drago" and the other recounting the freshly received news of his death. So far as I recall, no copy of the Cushman sermon has since been sold in this country, certainly not at auction, and no copy of any one of the four Drake pieces.

These were quiet transactions. Later on drama was occasion-ally to ensue when the book and the dealer and the purchaser came together. Once when I was saying good-bye to him just before he left upon his annual European trip, he spoke to me in the manner of a departing father to his child: "What," said he, "shall I bring you from Europe?" And I, in the same spirit, re-plied, "Bring me a Thorne map for our Hakluyt *Divers Voyages* and a Wright-Molyneux map for our Hakluyt *Principall Navi-gations*." Many weeks later he called me one day and with the most elaborate casualness of manner (in later years I learned to sit up and take notice when he put on that air) asked me when I was coming to New York. I named a day and hour. When I reached 8 West 40th Street at the time appointed I realized that something was about to occur. The stage was set and an audience gathered in the persons of Mr. Grenville Kane, then a member of the John Carter Brown Visiting Committee, Mr. Parsonage, and Miss Lone. "Here," said Mr. Harper, "is something I have brought you." I need not carry on with this. You know that I am leading up to one of those mysterious coincidences which are the salt of the book collector's repast. The "something" he had brought me was two books—one, a fragment of the *Divers Voyages* containing a Thorne map in perfect condition, the other a tall, virtually uncut Hakluyt of 1598-1600 in two volumes, complete with the Wright-Molyneux map. In my agitation I fumbled, and—I continue the baseball lingo—bobbled the volumes and dropped all three of them to the floor. I didn't believe it had happened, and I still think it a sort of miracle that both those monuments of cartography should have come to a library at the same time in the same package. I believe that no more than one of each of these maps has come upon the market in the intervening years. The Wright-Molyneux map, significant in world history as the first practical application of the Mercator projection, was an extraordinary copy—two separate sheets, each with its original untrimmed margins on all four sides just as it came from the press. I love recalling that moment, the smile of Mr. Kane, the surrounding atmosphere of friendliness, the exultation.

If anyone pressed Mr. Harper on the subject of maps, he would be likely to say that he didn't know anything about them and wasn't particularly interested. Indeed, one of his tersely expressed generalizations, born of exasperation with certain enthusiasts I could name, was, "All map men are crazy." But he, too, could be crazy when it was a question of a celebrated map or of a map not at all celebrated in which he had recognized with quick and instinctive reaction the element of historic importance. One day I walked into 8 West 40th, where I found Mr. Harper and Douglas Parsonage in the act of unwrapping a parcel just arrived from England. I must tell those of you who did not know him that in moments of excitement Mr. Harper's mind might run ahead of his tongue, leaving enunciation and pronunciation to take care of themselves. "What do you think I've got?" he asked. "I can't guess," I replied. "I've got a Stavnova with the map," he said in what fiction writers call "hushed tones." In equally hushed tones I said, "I will buy it." And so was consummated, sight unseen, the purchase of a book of very large price, without mention of title, place, or date of publication, designated only by a name which never was on land or sea. But none of that mattered. I knew with complete certainty that by Stavnova he meant Stobnicza and that the book was the *Introductio in Ptholomei Cosmographiam* of Cracow, 1512, and he knew that I knew and that I would go all out to secure for the Library this copy of the book, one of three known with the map. And who, if he had the chance and could beg or borrow the money, wouldn't buy the book which probably more than any other except the *Paesi* of 1507 carried to European readers because of its map a revealing picture of the New World? That map popularized the cartographical concept of the large Waldseemüller map, of 1507. It was, in fact, a plagiarism of the two inset hemispheres found at the top of the Waldseemüller map, printed in the Stobnicza book back to back on either side of a single sheet. The Waldseemüller map came and mysteriously passed beyond the ken of scholars except for a few traces which continued to puzzle them until its rediscovery four centuries later in the year 1901. The Stobnicza hemispheres, specifically the western hemisphere, remained to tell the world that to the westward between Europe and Asia lay two north and south-running continents joined by an isthmus, and that between these continents and Asia lay a vast ocean, as yet undiscovered, in the midst of which lay Marco Polo's Japan. Here was probably the most learned and the most successful conjecture ever made by mapmaker or geographer. "All map men are crazy," but this time Mr. Harper was as crazy as the craziest.

I have already suggested that Mr. Harper had the gift of sententious expression, that he was a maker of the well-packed apophthegm. It was sometime in the late twenties, I think, that one whom we may describe as a fly-by-night Roman bookseller offered a young American librarian a copy of the non-existent, that is to say, the never-existent, printed edition of the lost Cortés First Letter. The terms were enticingly moderate, but cash in advance. Appealed to for advice by the librarian, Mr. Harper brought that negotiation quickly to an end. Not long afterwards a collector came back from Rome boasting a purchase of unusual importance made by what used to be called "private treaty," made in this instance from an individual who had claimed to be the father confessor or devoted old chaplain of a princely but impoverished Roman family. Mr. Eames, Miss Belle Greene, and one or two others pronounced the book a counterfeit. For the moment, certainly, Rome was not appreciated by American booksellers and collectors. Mr. Harper spoke for all of them with the warning, expressed in a sort of "House that Jack Built" progression, "Never buy a book in Rome; especially never buy a book in Rome up an alley; and never under any circumstances buy a book in Rome up an alley from a priest."

The mention of Rome takes me in this unorganized discourse to Paris, where one day my wife and I found ourselves by pure chance, when entering a hotel, occupying the opposite sides of a revolving door with Mr. and Mrs. Harper, and thereafter spent many interesting hours with them. One day I went with Mr. Harper to visit the establishment of Mr. Charles Chadenat, that most gentlemanly of booksellers, dwelling in an ancient house, tall and narrow, set in its own courtyard on one of the quais, house and book room no less cool, spare, and immaculate than their owner. My spoken French is a sad example of wasted opportunity in youth overlaid by the carefree character of AEF communications. Mr. Harper, however, had no French at all and Mr. Chadenat no English, and as negotiations went on I found myself a self-appointed interpreter. Some business was done and as we left the old gentleman's house I felt quite high in my own esteem, so high, indeed, that I said to Mr. Harper, "What do you do in your dealings with European booksellers when there is no one at hand to interpret?" "Oh," he replied, "it doesn't really matter. I know the word for 'imperfect' in every language in Europe."

A few days later we met the Harpers for luncheon at a restaurant behind the Madeleine, one of the many tried and tested by Mrs. Harper and given place in her wonderful little guide to the exceptional but unpretentious restaurants of Europe. As we sat down at a table not yet cleared of puddles of red wine left by the departing customers I asked Mr. Harper if he had bought anything that morning. "Oh," he said, "just one little thing," and as he spoke took from his pocket an ordinary envelope and sailed it across the table to me. I mean "sailed it" literally, because it came skimming lightly through the puddles of wine into my lap. I wiped it off and removed its contents, a perfect, uncut copy, crisp as the day it was printed, of the Father Charles Lallemant *Lettre*, of 1627, the report from the field which began the great series of Jesuit Relations from New France but is separated from it by the years of isolation of Canada from France caused by the English capture of Quebec in 1629. "This, of course, is for the John Carter Brown," I said when I realized what I had in my hand. I think the Lallemant *Lettre* was probably the only book he regretted selling us. When I returned to Providence I found that the Depression had reached a new depth. There was almost no money then or for a good many years afterwards. It took us ten years to pay for that book. Nobody could have been kinder than Mr. Harper. In the course of those years we bought many other things from him and paid for them promptly, but somehow never were able to pay for the Lallemant book. He never said a word about it to me in all that time. What he may have been saying about me to others I don't want to know.

In speaking of book prices it is to be made clear that nobody ever got a bargain from Mr. Harper, but then neither did any-

body ever buy from him an inferior or a shoddy book, or, differences in tastes taken into account, an uninteresting book. We
were among those willing to pay good prices for quality goods,
knowing that only in that way are great libraries made. This
philosophical attitude on our part was put to the test several
times, notably when we bought from him a copy of John Smith's
True Relation of 1608. I think he dealt a shade too strictly with
us on that one, but his bookseller's pride, his prestige even, made
it inevitable that he should demand a large profit on one of the
two or three greatest American books in a fine and most interesting copy. Neither he nor anyone else in New York had ever
handled a work of Americana of much larger significance. As for
us, though we paid well for it, we acquired in that transaction the
Earl of Leconfield-Wizard Earl of Northumberland copy of
the book, presumably a copy which came to the Wizard Earl from
his brother, George Percy, John Smith's successor in the gover-
norship of Virginia. I don't know when another copy of equally
interesting provenance, perfect, with blank leaf A and with the
introduction complete, will come upon the market. It was particularly important that we should have the book for the reason
that already we had upon our shelves two copies of it, one with
blank leaf A and a variant title-page, but both in varying degrees
imperfect. We could, it seemed to us, no longer put off acquiring a
perfect copy of this particular one of the four pillars of American
history north of Mexico, that is, the Cabeza de Vaca *Relacion* of
1542; the Gentleman of Elvas *Relaçam* of 1557; the John Smith
True Relation of 1608; and the Champlain *Des Sauvages*, of 1603,
basic supports, respectively, of the Southwest of the United
States, the Southeast, the English colonies, and New France. It
is possible that if the John Carter Brown owned the Hariot *Briefe
and true Reporte* in the quarto of 1588, I would call that book the
Virginia pillar instead of the John Smith *True Relation*, but the
JCB doesn't own the Hariot, and, anyhow, who is to make the
decision? I wish, however, that the Clements Library custodians

wouldn't show me that book every time I visit their building. I know exactly what it looks like, and I am tired of it.

Our last business with Mr. Harper was in connection with another of the four pillars of which I have spoken. This was a purchase made not from him but through his agency. I refer to the copy of the *Relaçam* of the Gentleman of Elvas in its original edition of Evora, 1557, bought for us in 1950 at the thirteenth sale of the late Mr. Charles Chadenat's surprising stock. That narrative, the first account in print of the De Soto expedition, is known by four copies only, one of them the Colbert copy in the New York Public Library. Encouraged by Mr. Harper and strongly supported by President Wriston of Brown University, we put in a very substantial bid, so substantial, indeed, that Mr. Goldschmidt, who was acting for Mr. Harper, cabled back to him, "Do you mean dollars or francs?" The actual sum at which the auctioneer awarded the book to us went through a quick enlargement when certain booksellers met afterwards at the round table for the *revision* of the price. But the book came to us in the end. It is pleasant to think that our last experience with Mr. Harper after nearly thirty years of association was in connection with one of the greatest of American historical documents. Here was the end of our search together for quality, for documents important in the record of human destiny.

I have been compelled to weave my story around my own experiences with Mr. Harper, but I ask you to remember that similar stories could have been told by Mr. William L. Clements and Randolph Adams, even more piquant stories, perhaps, because his services to the Clements Library had to do with the actual creation of that institution. In the Preface to his book about the Library Mr. Clements estimated that a third of his collection had passed through Mr. Harper's hands, and Mr. Thomas Adams, formerly librarian of the Chapin Library at Williams College, tells me that virtually the whole of the Americana and incunabula in that notably fine collection, made by Mr. Alfred Clark Chapin, was acquired from Mr. Harper or through his agency. The Grenville Kane books at Princeton show his influence, as does the collection of Mr. Streeter. The Library of Congress, the Morgan Library, and the New York Public all contain items sold by him to which they refer with satisfaction.

I have left to the end a too brief reference to Mr. Harper's interest in fifteenth-century books, the slowly growing interest which led him to the position of preëminence among American dealers in incunabula. I was about to say that there have been more spectacular dealers in incunabula noted for occasional sales of single books of extraordinary importance, but even in the realm of the spectacular a bookseller who could offer in the same catalogue, as Mr. Harper did, copies of the *Catholicon* and the Bible of 1462 hasn't much to apologize for in anybody's presence.

Anyone now or in the future interested in the American book trade must turn with admiration to the five catalogues listing 1,000 incunabula issued by Mr. Harper in the period 1928-1930, and in the latter year gathered into a single indexed volume with the unassuming title, *A Selection of Incunabula.* This is one of the memorable American catalogues. Edited jointly by Mr. Harper and his assistants, Miss Lone and Mr. Parsonage, its collations and descriptive notes are concise, comprehensive, and illuminating. It is printed as soberly as a library catalogue, and it is as austere in contents as in form. It is without scareheads or hurrahs; it refrains from touting the second-rate and gives rarity its due weight and no more. It remains a tribute to the intelligence and integrity of its maker and, in addition to that, a reference work of permanent value in the world of letters.

The assembling of so large and varied a stock was in itself an unusual feat. Going into that branch of the business without previous training, he knew by instinct, it seems, the books which had significance beyond the fact of their early date. He successfully avoided buying *en bloc* the slow-moving stocks which had been standing for years upon the shelves of European booksellers. That same instinct for individual quality when employed in the positive sense led him to the purchase of illustrated incunabula, of books in the vernaculars—the true wine of the country—of books in which were expressed the contemporary interests of the communities in which they were produced. A brief analysis of one part only of that catalogue showed me at the time of its publication that it contained verse, fables and jocose tales, current and recent history, schoolbooks, hagiography, biography, language, military art, cosmography, and always, of course, theology and ecclesiology. Many of the books offered had also the interests traditional among collectors of incunabula, especially in the matter of new or little-known presses, of unusual bindings, or unusual typographical excellence. But as a whole the 1,000 titles were dominated or at least strongly tinctured by books of "subject" interest. I can't do better than quote from George Parker Winship's introduction to one of the parts of the catalogue. "Mr. Harper," he wrote, "combining the wisdom of his years in the book-marts with an undimmed freshness of vision, saw the way in which scholarship ought to go, long before the professional plodders knew that there was ever to be any turning."

We may think of Lathrop Harper as a builder of libraries in his lifetime who after his death continues to build libraries. In the last full years of his life his own thrift and industry and the thrift and industry of his family and forbears had combined to make him a man of wealth. In those years he was cherishing in mind and heart, unknown to all of us, the vision of the continuing service his fortune might perform for long generations to the libraries and institutions he loved, enabling them to carry on the tradition of scholarly study which he revered and assuring them of the ability to continue the quest for excellence. As the result of the perfect and beautiful understanding between him

and Mrs. Harper, she became so impressed by the earnestness
of his belief and purpose that she gladly carried out his wishes
and went beyond that to double the effectiveness of his legacy by
the addition to it of her own considerable fortune, laboriously
earned through a lifetime of writing. Lathrop Colgate Harper
and Mabel Herbert Harper are names we must remember.

The Acquisition of Manuscripts by Institutional Libraries*

By A. N. L. MUNBY

I T was explained to me that what was required as an address at the annual meeting was not so much a set paper as some introductory remarks to which a reply could be made, and which might perhaps lead to some discussion. It happened that I had been reading the article in the *Dictionary of National Biography* on Sir Frederic Madden, probably the ablest, and almost certainly the most disagreeable, Keeper of the Department of Manuscripts at the British Museum. Madden died in 1873 and the D.N.B. account of him was written by Richard Garnett, who had been his colleague at the Museum. In general the notice seems to me to be a fair appraisal of Madden's achievements, but I was particularly struck by one phrase in it. "He was indefatigable," wrote Garnett, "in amassing manuscript material, much of which remains unused." It seems to me that there is a note of implied criticism here, although it is difficult to be sure; and indeed if there is a criticism, we need not make too much of it. Garnett was Superintendent of the Museum's Reading Room, where every book had to justify by use the inches of shelfroom allotted to it; and Madden had in his lifetime been sufficiently critical of the workings of the Department of Printed Books to invite some mild riposte. But Garnett's phrase does, I think, suggest consideration of what sort of poli-

* An address delivered at the annual meeting of the Society in New York City, 22 Jan. 1960.

cies, if any, should dictate the acquisition of manuscripts by institutional libraries, and especially of what are the most sensible fields for librarians, and indeed private collectors as well, to operate in today. I am very conscious of raising many more questions than I answer and of producing an untidy tangle of loose ends.

The briefest reflection on the history of institutional collections of manuscripts will confirm the fact that the great majority of libraries, even ones which have a lively tradition of purchasing printed books, expected to be *given* manuscripts. Of course the great blocks of manuscripts in the British Museum which bear the honorable names of Cotton, Harley, and Sloane were bought for the British nation and at Oxford the Bodleian Library has had from the seventeenth century onwards a proud record of self-help in the matter of manuscript acquisitions. But these are exceptions. At my own University, Cambridge, which has a more than respectable collection of medieval manuscripts, nearly all the most famous of them have been gifts. In fact my friend, Mr. J. C. T. Oates, who is at present writing the history of the University Library, tells me that it seems doubtful whether Cambridge actually paid good money for a manuscript until 1785, when the University Librarian, Richard Farmer, better known as a Shakespearian scholar, attended Leigh and Sotheby's sale of the manuscripts of Anthony Askew and bought a number of them, mostly Greek, for the University's collection. This episode, however, cannot be said to have initiated any consistent buying policy, since it was nearly another hundred years before Cambridge University Library, under the direction of Henry Bradshaw, began to make modest but regular purchases in this field. It is interesting, but to me rather painful, to contrast this apathy with the policy of the Bodleian, admittedly very much better endowed, where for example in 1817 the then unprecedented sum of £5,444 was laid out on the Canonici manuscripts. The fact remains that most of the groups of manuscripts in institutional hands, many bearing world-famous names—Archbishop Parker, Samuel Pepys, Tanner, Rawlinson, Gale, and so on—were given or bequeathed by private collectors. And this is natural enough. A collection of manuscripts is unique in a sense which no collection of printed books, however complete or rare, can ever be; and therefore it is especially likely that the collector will take measures to safeguard it from dispersal. But what seems to me unnatural, or at any rate disappointing, is the small extent to which institutions founded for and dedicated to the encouragement of learning should have taken active steps (the wooing of benefactors apart) to amass what by general consensus of opinion must be considered as the highest source of scholarly advancement. Scholars, however, as the late E. P. Goldschmidt used to remark more in sorrow than in anger, have no money; and librarians, who sometimes have a little, though not of course their own, tend to be shy about the purchase of manuscripts. In a characteristically cynical and witty passage in one of his lectures Goldschmidt attributed this shyness to the fact that manuscripts, unlike *incunabula*, editions of Boyle, and so on, had no reassuring reference numbers; and it is certainly easier for a librarian to fill known gaps in a series than to chance his arm on the probably less familiar ground of paleography or text criticism. But if Goldschmidt thought that paleographers and other scholars concerned with manuscripts were immune from the hypnotic effect of reference numbers he was mistaken. I well recall a visit from Mrs. Silva Lake, who made some notes on a Greek lectionary of mine. "What is its number?" she asked. When I said it hadn't got one her face fell. "How can I describe it if it hasn't got a number?" she said. "Please give it one straight away." I explained that I only owned half a dozen manuscripts and that it really seemed absurdly pretentious to label my book "Munby MS 3," but it was only with the greatest reluctance that she acquiesced in my refusal. Her attitude sprang, I think, partly from a point of view which I have observed with interest in scholars, in English scholars especially. This is a kind of reluctance to concede that books and manuscripts in private hands, and not tidily garnered into an institution, really exist at all; and I quite see that the fact of my numberless manuscript being in the private possession of a librarian must have tried Mrs. Lake pretty hard. But I am straying from my point, which is that in general most libraries do not acquire manuscripts as energetically as printed books.

In the remarks which follow I am thinking primarily of the smaller institution or the private collector whose purse is not bottomless. A library such as the British Museum or that of one of the greatest British or American Universities has of necessity a staff of trained paleographers and established collections upon which to build. And if, as they probably do, they follow strength and reinforce holdings which are already distinguished, this at least makes sense. But the problem of the smaller institutions is very different. If they are ancient they may have miscellaneous inherited collections; are these to remain static? And if they are modern, should they not systematically acquire at least some of the materials of original research according to their means, or even a series of exhibits in the field of medieval manuscripts or literary autographs to inculcate some sense of the past into their arts men?

Let me deal with an older institution first, and because I naturally know it best I hope you will forgive me if I take as an example the library of which I happen to be in charge, that of King's College, Cambridge. We have about thirty miscellaneous medieval manuscripts, one textually and one calligraphically distinguished, but otherwise a scratch lot. Our medieval library, like that of nearly all Oxford and Cambridge colleges, melted away in the middle of the sixteenth century and we have had no Parker or Pepys to make good the deficiency. We have, however, a group of over two hundred and fifty Persian and Arabic manuscripts given by a Fellow of the College in 1788, a slight embarrassment to us as we have no orientalist on our very small library staff, a deficiency we have sought to make good by electing to membership of our High Table the University Lecturer in Persian. In the literary field we own nearly all the poetical manuscripts of Rupert Brooke, another Fellow; we naturally have much material concerned with the history of the College during the last five hundred years; we have several blocks of modern papers, the most interesting perhaps being those of Roger Fry, the art critic; and in the Keynes bequest of 1945 we received a really important and substantial collection of the papers of Sir Isaac Newton. And we have, what a surprising number of libraries also have, one of those tantalizing crates of papers to be opened about the year 2000. What are we consciously seeking to add to this very mixed bag? The answer, to our shame, is almost nothing except some modest purchases of autograph material of our own distinguished *alumni*, a task not made easier by the fact that one of the most distinguished of them all was Horace Walpole. And yet—with staggering generosity—Mr. Lewis has sent me a Walpole manuscript for King's. I don't suppose he likes to be reminded of it (he remarked at the time that it was like having a tooth drawn); but I almost feel, to paraphrase a speech of Churchill's—"if the library of King's endures a thousand years, men will still say—that was its finest hour."

Luckily this regrettable picture of our sloth and apathy in the acquisition of manuscripts has one ameliorating aspect. There are in the University of Cambridge about eighty other libraries, and in the aggregate they can offer its own graduate research students, and indeed visiting scholars, a reasonably rich field of material both medieval and modern. But if we were, let us suppose, a recently founded University, remote from other great libraries, how could we spend money on manuscripts advantageously today? And if we were going to encourage a benefactor to build a collection on our behalf, what sort of gift would we hope ultimately to receive?

There are three groups of manuscripts which I propose very briefly to discuss—medieval; collections of historical papers, both ancient and modern; and a few words on literary manuscripts. All three of course overlap, but my main divisions will, I hope, be plain.

Given the means—and nowadays they must be really substantial—it is still just possible to form a first-class collection of medieval illuminated manuscripts today: but I am bold enough to prophesy that some unforeseen catalysm apart which might put onto the market institutional possessions, this is the last generation for which this will be possible, at any price at all. The recent dispersal of Sir Sydney Cockerell's manuscripts, the rich treasures, with more to come, from Mr. Dyson Perrins's collection, the question mark which hangs over the still very rich residue of the Phillipps collection, the noble stocks at present in the hands of two or three of the greatest dealers—all these will indicate that, if money were no object, one or two institutions or collectors, with bottomless purses, could by resolute action still acquire a significant holding of the most aristocratic possession to which a library can aspire, the picture books of the middle ages; and the same could not be said today of Caxtons or Shakespeare quartos. But very recently (really only in the last three or four years) the cost of fine medieval manuscripts decorated with first-class miniatures has moved out of the world of book prices into the quite different scale of values which prevails in the picture market.

This was well exemplified in the Dyson Perrins sale of 1958 when

£39,000 was cheerfully paid for the Helmerhausen Gospels, a twelfth-century manuscript with four large miniatures and other decoration. As recently as 1948 I would have valued this book, perhaps wrongly, at between £5,000 and £10,000. This sharp rise in price should not occasion any great astonishment. In fact, on reflection, the surprising aspect of the matter is the extraordinary difference in value which has prevailed in the past between the most modest piece of medieval easel-painting and the often far finer treasures of book-painting. For example, looking back on it, it was really ludicrous that a manuscript of such caliber as the Evesham Psalter, sold at Sotheby's in 1936, containing a full-page miniature of the Crucifixion which all authorities agreed was one of the masterpieces of thirteenth-century painting, should have realized so modest a sum as £2,400. Some time ago I was going through M. R. James's papers and I found a telegram from Dr. Eric Millar, announcing its acquisition at that price by the British Museum—a triumphant telegram, and no wonder.

But these days have gone for good and the new assessment—and perhaps, as I say, a far truer one—of the value of such books makes it seem to me doubtful whether the libraries of institutions dedicated to learning ought to buy them, even if the funds were available. For I believe that for £39,000 could be bought material of infinitely greater scholarly significance.

It seems to me that, works of art apart, medieval manuscripts are still not expensive, and that, seen in retrospect, twenty years ago they were very cheap indeed. There are few more refined forms of self-torture than the reading of old priced sale catalogues, not of the remote past but of a period when one could have attended the sale in question. As recently as the Phillipps sale of 1935 a fifteenth-century text of Martial on vellum, signed by its Italian scribe, realized £18. The textual or calligraphic manuscripts of the Renaissance have shot upwards in value, and if the matter is viewed dispassionately it was high time. For their value had hardly increased to any significant degree over the previous century and a half. I had occasion recently in connection with some work on Sir Thomas Phillipps to trace the sale-room history of a fifteenth-century text on vellum of the *De gestis Romanorum* of Hercules Brunus. In 1785 Michael Wodhull bought it for sixteen shillings at the sale of Anthony Askew's manuscripts; when

Wodhull discarded it in 1803 Heber bought it for six shillings and sixpence; at his sale in 1836 Phillipps acquired it for ten shillings; in 1899 Phillipps's grandson, Thomas FitzRoy Fenwick, put it into Sotheby's but bought it in for fourteen shillings; he included it, however, in the next Phillipps sale of 1903 when Sir Sydney Cockerell ventured twenty-seven shillings on it, only eleven shillings more than it realized in the Askew sale one hundred and sixteen years before. This was the class of manuscript which was still to be bought on occasion for under, sometimes considerably under, £100 between the wars; and if it now costs nearer £500, who is to say that this is unreasonable?

If I were responsible today for building up a small collection of medieval manuscripts to serve the needs of a young University, I would first assemble a group of single leaves and fragments of as many styles and periods of writing that I could, including papyri, many of which seem to me to be very cheap indeed. There is, however, one exception. In the last year or two single leaves of vellum manuscripts of the sixth to the eighth centuries have become very expensive but by diligence and a reasonable share of good luck it would not be impossible to build a series of say one hundred leaves and fragments of MSS from the ninth century onwards, illustrating the development of the national scripts, of book, diplomatic, and legal hands, which would be of the greatest value to anyone concerned with the teaching of paleography. For although of course facsimiles must always be the main source of paleographical instruction, the handling of originals can give rise to excitement in certain pupils, which no photographs, however excellent, can provide. To reinforce this collection I would try to acquire a dozen or so typical complete medieval books from the twelfth century onwards, mainly for their interest as physical objects upon which could be demonstrated format, the gathering of quires, ruling, signatures, catchwords, foliation, interlinear glossing, rubrication, sewing, binding, press-marking, and the other attributes which a young medievalist should, but so often does not, have brought to his attention. If a benefactor came forward with a few examples of fine illumination and miniature painting, so much the better; but in the present state of the market I do not think that I should spend my library grant on them. If, on top of this, funds were available to add a handful of medieval manuscripts to the collection each year I should unhesitatingly go for *texts*, and texts if possible which still offered some potentialities for research.

I turned up a year or two ago in the Bodleian Library a memorandum drawn up by the Biblical scholar, William Sanday, in 1891. The occasion was a joint attempt (which came to nothing) by Oxford, Cambridge, and the British Museum to buy £25,000 worth of manuscripts by private treaty from the Phillipps collection. In both Universities various experts prepared lists of those manuscripts which it seemed desirable to them to attempt to purchase, and Sanday's task was to make a selection in the field of Biblical and Patristic literature. He interwove into his list, however, some general reflections on the principles which should underlie the acquisition of manuscripts, and though most of them are generally accepted today, they seem to me to be so sound as to be worth repeating. He began by stating that the University should not confine its purchase to a few choice manuscripts, but that "money would be better expended in a quantity of comparatively low-priced MSS than in the purchase of a few at higher prices." Sanday went on to point to what he called "work which is likely to receive the greatest development in the near future, the defining more clearly than has hitherto been done the character and extent of local schools of writing." Having given some examples of current work in this field both in Greek and Latin paleography he added, "I submit therefore that the value of a MS is greatly enhanced if it bears a signature which may serve in any way to fix either the date or place of origin. I believe that this fact alone would make a MS worth possessing if it were older than the 14th century." Today we should obviously extend Sanday's terminal date by a couple of centuries. The importance of signed, dated, and localized manuscripts has of course been widely appreciated during the last fifty years. Sir Sydney Cockerell in England and the late Grenville Kane in the United States are typical of collectors who were swift to grasp this important point. Many fifteenth-century examples, however, are still not at all expensive, and seem to me to be very well worth buying.

Sanday's next point is really a corollary of the above. "It is a characteristic feature of the Phillipps Collection," he wrote, "that it includes portions of a number of monastic libraries, especially Flemish, which can be traced to their origin. I think that the Bodleian should aim at possessing some representative volumes from each of these libraries." Then he goes on to deal with textual matters, pointing out first that the works of the greater Latin fathers and schoolmen are in general so common that their purchase is hardly to be recommended, except where they precede the tenth century in date or have some special feature of interest. He continued:

In regard to the other literature, I suppose it will be agreed that those works are most valuable which are most likely to contain grains of historical fact or at least illustrations of social life at the period to which they belong. For this reason I have paid special attention to *Vitae, Vitae Sanctorum, Passiones, Martyrologia.* I have set down these without very much regard to date, as the later collections often make up for their inferior date by the number of their biographies; and though all doubtless contain a very large proportion of chaff, it is difficult to tell beforehand where the really historical material will be found. Any purchases in literature of this kind must be a matter of speculation; and it would therefore not be worth while to give high prices; at the same time if the prices are not high, valuable material may be obtained for the criticism of the future to exercise itself upon. The Bollandists have shown what may be done; and there are in this collection, as well as I can judge, MSS quite on a par with those of the Bollandists.

And then he goes on to recommend especially the purchase on speculative grounds of manuscripts with miscellaneous contents.

Sanday was of course trying to pick out of some fifty thousand manuscripts a selection which would be of value to an institution which already owned many thousands; but I think that his principles were, and still are, perfectly sound and of wide application. From a paleographical standpoint, go if possible for manuscripts which have named scribes, dates, and places, and from a textual standpoint avoid the standard works and concentrate on the lesser known writings. This may seem to be a crashing platitude to have crossed the Atlantic to deliver, but the odd thing is that sale-room prices seldom appear to reflect much awareness of the textual value of a manuscript, and in fact the booksellers who know or care much about such things are comparatively few; but, one should add, they are increasing in number fast.

The most common, and to me the dullest, medieval manuscripts on the market are the third-rate Books of Hours mass-produced in a commercial scriptorium during the fifteenth century, their miniatures and decoration slavishly copied from originals of a low order of artistic merit. Some of them have a certain gaudy appeal, which normally inflates their value to sums, in my opinion, far in excess of their real worth; and unless they have some feature of unusual interest, liturgical let us say, then I do not think they merit buying—except perhaps one or two purely as specimens of what were the most widely used secular devotional books of the late middle ages.

Medieval manuscripts in general however still provide a field in which a scholarly librarian, well advised by specialists in the faculties of history, classics, and modern languages, can lay out money to excellent advantage. He must remember of course, that the full value of a manuscript may well not emerge until a scholar has worked for a considerable period upon it; and from this point of view his purchases, as Sanday said, must often be "speculations"; and none the worse for that.

Let us now turn to collections of historical papers. Any institution concerned with historical research needs such material, and moreover as its older deposits become mined out by the picks of successive Ph.D. candidates it is important that fresh strata should be laid down as occasion arises. Some of the most rewarding purchases which have been made in the auction room have been made in this field. Let me give an example. In 1939 Lord Brougham and Vaux consigned the papers of his famous ancestor the first Lord Brougham to Messrs. Sotheby for sale. I am painfully well qualified to speak of their extent and interest because amid constant interruptions from the increasingly insistent demands of Territorial military service I struggled to catalogue the contents of the twenty great crates. Trestle-tables covered with papers entirely filled Sotheby's large gallery in Bond Street. There were at least fifty thousand letters addressed to Lord Brougham, as well as great masses of other material, and their value for historians seemed to me to be enormous, since Brougham played a leading part in all the great issues of his day, the trial of Queen Caroline, the antislavery legislation, the Reform Bill, the foundation of the University of London, the growth of the Mechanics' Institutes, popular education, and a score of other themes. Here, I thought, even in these unpropitious times is an archive which will prove irresistible to half a dozen institutions: this is the material out of which the reputations of Faculties of History can be made—a definitive biography of Brougham (for none existed) by the Professor and a dozen really rewarding Ph.D. subjects for his most able research students. My promotional efforts were a total fiasco, and that exceptionally discriminating collector, the late C. K. Ogden, was able to buy the whole lot for what I still think was the derisory sum of £205. They are now, thanks to the generosity of the Nuffield Foundation, at University College, London.

Various factors in Great Britain have made it likely that in the future fewer of such archives will be exposed to the hazards of the auction room. The British Records Association, the National Register of Archives, and similar bodies exist for the purpose of aiding owners embarrassed by family papers to place them on deposit in Record Offices where they will be properly cared for and made available for scholarly consultation; and many owners have shown great public spirit in making such deposits and thereby accepting the financial sacrifices which this policy entails. I need only instance the exceptionally important and valuable Fitzwilliam papers deposited by the family in Sheffield City Libraries in 1949. But sufficient of such material passes through the dealers' hands to justify one comment. One should always buy, if possible, items which are entities and have some cohesion in themselves. It is deceptively easy to fritter away money on superficially attractive fragments of archives, which divorced from the main body of the collection have little potentialities for research. One certainly cannot blame auctioneers for fulfilling their duty to their clients by seeking to make their property fetch as much money as possible; and if a collection of family papers is likely to sell better when broken into a hundred lots then the chances are that they will be catalogued thus for sale. In nine cases out of ten however the results, from a historical standpoint, are to be deplored. There was some very interesting correspondence on this subject in *The Times* in March 1947. Lord Greene, the Master of the Rolls, wrote to deplore the breaking up for auction into forty-five different lots of the three volumes of Braye Stuart papers which had been arranged and calendared by the Historical Manuscripts Commission in 1887. His main point was to underline the historical damage of such dispersal and to express the hope, in his own words, "that owners would regard the break-up of their collections as an extreme step only to be taken in cases of absolute necessity." To this letter the late G. D. Hobson, as Chairman of Sotheby's, wrote a reply. Hobson was an exceptionally able and honorable man but by implication Sotheby's had come under criticism, and he felt it his duty to make as convincing a reply as he could. His main point, which seemed to me insupportable, was that whereas dispersal might prove what he called "a short-term handicap to students" in the long run this "temporary disturbance" would lead to a "more logical distribution and a full publication of records." The late Sir Edmund Craster took him up sharply on this point in a further letter. "Mr. Hobson," he wrote, "talks of a more logical distribution; but it is precisely the fact that the chances of purchases (that is of the sale-room) sever natural affiliations, that produces a grouping far less logical and far less intelligible. What is more, they actually destroy historical evidence; for documents taken out of their original setting because of their saleable value—or even more because of the want of it—lose their significance when taken in isolation. It is not the difficulty in tracing individual items which is so much in question, but the fact that, until the scattered elements are reconstituted, the organism to which they belonged remains imperfect and so can be but imperfectly understood."

It seems to me that a complete archive should be worth the value of the sum of its components, plus a substantial bonus for its completeness; and that this consideration ought to be reflected in the prices which collections of papers realize under the hammer. And, moreover, by scaling up our bids for complete collections and scaling them down pretty drastically for the *disjecta membra* of historical archives we should be applying a forcible argument to auctioneers and owners for their sale as entities. Where such collections are catalogued for sale in a number of lots it is perfectly possible to instruct one's agent to ask the auctioneer if he will sell the collection *en bloc*; and, in the event of a refusal, to bid sparingly or not at all for the components. The owner can after all put a reserve on the complete collection and only if it fails to fetch this figure need the desperate recourse to dispersal be made. I am not so otherworldly as to think that the education of auctioneers on this subject will be speedy or ever complete; but by offering more for completeness and less for fragments we can perhaps in time do our part in reversing what all historians will agree is a distressing trend in modern sale-room practice.

There are, of course, many exceptions to the above remarks. It could be argued for instance, that if an historical figure was ambassador both to China and to Peru, two completely different institutions in different countries would derive the maximum of historical benefit from the ownership of parts of his papers; and librarians can satisfy their collecting instincts very advantageously by the rebuilding of archives which have already been dispersed or by the creation of new *fonds* by the intelligent purchasing of small groups of miscellaneous material. There seems indeed to me to be one significant trend in mid-twentieth-century collecting; I mean the emergence of a few collectors, such as Mr. James M. Osborn, to whom period, subject matter, and many other attributes are subordinated to the potential research value of their purchases, and we owe so much to these collectors and institutions which by piecemeal purchases have built up magnificent quarries of specialized research material that it is difficult wholly to deplore some of the dispersals of the past. All I ask is that we should be chary about being accessories to *unnecessary* dispersals in the future.

And what of modern historical papers? We live today in an age when statesmen, politicians, and military commanders seem to be acutely conscious of their potential interest to posterity. With the aid of an orderly secretary it is possible for any man on the very fringes of affairs of state to accumulate a mass of material which few executors are brave enough to destroy, even if they have been given no specific testamentary instructions on its disposal; and there are of course many blocks of papers of the highest importance for the historiography of the future. My own feeling about the acquisition of such material, by purchase or by gift, is that this function is best fulfilled by the greatest institutional libraries, and in general not by those of the smaller universities and colleges. I base this view not on the fact that such modern archives are often formidably bulky, nor on the grounds that the work involved in processing such papers and making them fit for use by readers is often a very heavy burden on a library with a comparatively small staff. These two factors, however, should be given more consideration before acceptance or purchase than they often seem to receive today. My main reason for wishing such burdens onto the largest libraries is the problem involved over access. In Great Britain a large collection of recent military or political papers will probably contain material to which public access is denied under the Official Secrets Act of 1911. They will certainly have in them much material to which the Government would wish to apply what is known as the "Foreign Office Rule," an arrangement whereby official papers are not open for general inspection until the lapse of fifty years; and they will also certainly contain a mass of correspondence the copyright of which is still vested in the individual writers of letters, many of whom are probably living. The responsibility of the custodian of such papers is ill-defined in English law, but their ownership may well involve time-consuming perplexities. In a large department of manuscripts, where much similar material is housed, an elaborate code of conduct for the use of such papers can be evolved and perhaps responsibility for its enforcement delegated to a particular member of the staff. To a private owner, or to the librarian of an institution not geared to the handling of such material, a single group of official papers can be something of an embarrassment: I can think, for example, of the Milner papers at New College, Oxford.

The papers of eminent men of letters, recently dead, often present comparable difficulties, and I was particularly interested to see that an American scholar, Mr. Norman Holmes Pearson, addressed the English Institute on the *Problems of Literary Executorship* in 1951. Many of you will doubtless be familiar with his lecture printed in Vol. V of *Studies in Bibliography*. For the British librarian the question of copyright is the main problem. His institution often holds the physical ownership of manuscript material which can only be published and occasionally only be consulted by permission of some outside depositor, an arrangement which can work excellently but nevertheless is inherently unsatisfactory. "Living as I do in charge of a large library," wrote Henry Bradshaw to Halliwell in 1869, "all I find is instantly at the service of my neighbours." This is just what many librarians cannot say today. Ideally all material in all libraries should be freely available to all scholars; and it is in my view axiomatic that a librarian should never put himself into the position of having to adjudicate upon visiting scholars' credentials and decide that whereas Professor X *can* be allowed access, Professor *Y* must be denied. The recently dead evoke in their surviving friends and disciples passionate loyalties and intensely proprietary attitudes; and the librarian round whose papers the battles ebb and surge must do his best to remain aloof. I hope I do not betray too shamefully my preference for a quiet life when I confess that on several occasions recently I have opened the *Times Literary Supplement* and thanked my stars that I am *not* the custodian of A. E. Housman's manuscripts.

From time to time some heart-searching on the aims and achievements of our institutional collecting of manuscripts is salutary. Opportunity, funds, benefactions, pressure from one or other of the faculties or from a member of the staff with special enthusiasms—all these factors can play their part in determining how our collections of manuscripts expand. Their expansion on sound and scholarly lines, however, cannot be achieved without a good deal of thought from us all.

The Reconstruction of Benjamin Franklin's Library: An Unorthodox Jigsaw Puzzle*

By Edwin Wolf 2nd

"AFTER it was dark," Manasseh Cutler wrote in his diary on 13 July 1787, describing a visit to Benjamin Franklin, "we went into the house, and the Doctor invited me into his library, which is likewise his study. It is a very large chamber, and high studded. The walls were covered with book-shelves filled with books; besides there are four large alcoves, extending two-thirds of the length of the chamber, filled in the same manner. I presume this is the largest, and by far the best, private library in America." After Franklin's death in 1790 his executors obtained an appraisal of the library which listed 351 folio volumes, 150 topographical pamphlets, 767 quartos, 1,548 octavos, 1,260 duodecimos, and 200 duodecimos stitched, for a total of 4,276 volumes, which were valued at £184.7.10. In his will, written in 1788, the old bookman spoke of a catalogue made of his books. That catalogue has not been found.

What we have, therefore, in attempting to reconstruct Franklin's

* Mr. Wolf's paper was read at the annual meeting of the Society, held at The Grolier Club in New York City on 26 Jan. 1962.

library and to locate the books which he owned is an unorthodox jig-saw puzzle. All we know is that it had 4,276 pieces, and that, put to-gether, the completed picture should look like what the finest private library in 1787 ought to have looked like. It is as though a child had thrown his puzzle into a trashcan, illustrated box and all. We do not know where the pieces are, nor are we sure, when we find a likely one, if it belongs. Franklin used no bookplate, rarely signed his name in a volume, only occasionally annotated, had no secret mark like Jeffer-son's, but did put in a penciled shelf mark the significance of which has only recently been recognized (see Plate I). The pencil mark was frequently rubbed out by a neat owner, more frequently thrown away with the old covers and flyleaves when a volume was rebound.

The problem as presented is not so hopeless as I make it sound. Perfection is unqualifiedly hopeless. Yet, it is surprising how many pieces can be described with a reasonable degree of accuracy, how many large segments of the puzzle can be fitted together. On the basis of various kinds of evidence hundreds of titles can be placed in Franklin's library and hundreds have been located and identified.

The story of Franklin's steady accumulation of a library begins with the account of his youth in the Autobiography: "From a child I was fond of reading, and all the little money that came into my hands was ever laid out in books." One of the books he mentioned as having owned as a teenager, Nicole's *Logic; or, the Art of Thinking*, has been found at the Library Company, to which institution he gave it in 1733. The child became a successful printer; the little money became a com-fortable income. Books were always at the center of his existence, print-ing them, publishing them, selling them, buying them, reading them, and—as the Philadelphia printer became first a colonial and then an international figure of importance—receiving them as gifts.

Franklin's library as it existed in 1776, with the acquisitions of over half a century in America, vastly supplemented by those of his resi-dence in London, was left in his house at Philadelphia when he went on his mission to France. When the British threatened Philadelphia, his son-in-law Bache packed up the books and had them carted to Lan-caster for safekeeping. Meanwhile, the most popular American ever to hold a diplomatic post abroad like a magnet attracted books to his house at Passy. Some of the latest works he bought; learned societies *henry Anderson ex dono ~~Tho: Holland~~*

Πατηγυρις

D. Elizabethæ, Dei gratiâ Angliæ, Franciæ, &
Hiberniæ Reginæ.

A

SERMON PREACHED AT PAVLS

in London the 17. of November Ann. Dom. 1599. the
one and fortieth yeare of her Maiesties raigne, and augmented in those places wherein, for the shortnes of the
time, it could not there be then delivered.

VVhereunto is adioyned an Apologeticall discourse,
whereby all such sclanderous Accusations are fully
and faithfully confuted, wherewith the Honour of
this Realme hath beene vncharitably traduced by
some of our adversaries in forraine nations, and at
home, for observing the 17. of November yeerely in
the forme of an Holy-day, and for the ioifull exerci-
ses, and Courtly triumphes on that day in the honour
of her Maiestie exhibited.

By THOMAS HOLLAND, Doctor of Divinity,
& her Highnes Professor thereof in her Vni-
versity of Oxford.

A great character of
this Holland in wood.
Vol. I. ~~Fol.~~ ∧320.

AT OXFORD,

Printed by JOSEPH BARNES, and are to be solde in
Pauls Church-yard at the signe of the Bible.
Ann. Dom. 1601.

PLATE I

elected him to membership and sent him their journals; schoolbooks and handbooks in the French language he secured for himself and his secretary-grandson Temple Franklin; many more were sent to him by scientists, economists, writers on government and politics, even poets and novelists, all seeking to honor Franklin with their works, and themselves by the great man's acceptance of them. When the tired old diplomat left France to return home, among his vast and varied baggage were scores of boxes of books.

As to all good bookmen so to Franklin was presented the problem of space. The old library, possibly still in its Revolutionary boxes, the French additions crated for transatlantic shipment, and a house full of little Baches! Franklin, as all good bookmen, solved his problem positively. He built a wing to his house, the second floor of which was the library seen by Manasseh Cutler. There, on shelves made of the neatly constructed boxes—or so, at least, I believe—books lined the walls and made alcoves. Being of a utilitarian nature, Franklin knew that books on shelves, without any way of knowing where what was, were but chaotic bits of a valuable machine. So, he did what any sensible man would do under like conditions; he had them numbered and catalogued. In each book was placed—by his grandsons Temple Franklin and Benny Bache we may be sure, for gout and age would have prevented Dr. Franklin from scrambling up ladders—a shelf number locating each volume in its case and in its position in that case. And opposite the title of the work in the catalogue was placed the shelf mark, for example, C47 N4, so that it could be found, taken out and replaced quickly and simply. The catalogue was also used by the old bookman to designate those books which he wanted to go to his two Bache grandsons and to his nephew Jonathan Williams. In his will he mentioned that they were to get such books as he had marked with their names on his catalogue. All the rest and it was apparently the bulk of the library, after a few specific bequests to institutions and other individuals, were to go to Temple Franklin.

It is strange that so fine a judge of books should have been so poor a judge of grandsons. We are not sure that Jonathan Williams ever received his share. In a number of surviving angry letters he complained that he had not. Among a group of books which Williams gave a philosophical society at the Military Academy at West Point in

1810 none can be identified as having come from Franklin's library. Both Benjamin Franklin Bache and his brother William apparently got those volumes which their grandfather had destined for them. A few volumes went to William and Thomas Hewson, the children of Franklin's old London friend Polly Stevenson. Three large sets of scientific works went to the American Philosophical Society, the American Academy of Arts and Sciences in Boston, and the Library Company of Philadelphia, where they still are. The rest were Temple Franklin's, and he apparently did not set great store by them.

Temple left for England in 1790 a few months after his grandfather's death, and never returned to Philadelphia. A few authorities, without giving substantiating evidence, said that Temple took all or part of the books with him. He did take some of Franklin's papers; these are the lot discovered by Henry Stevens and sold to the Library of Congress. No similar cache of books has ever turned up, and I doubt very much that Temple encumbered himself with cases of books. I believe it much more likely that he left them, as he did the major portion of the papers, in the care of his Philadelphia friend George Fox.

In a business deal with Robert Morris, Jr., the details of which are not too clear, Temple pledged or sold his grandfather's library to Morris. At this point, no documentation carries the story over a lacuna of several years. Either Robert Morris, Jr., decided to liquidate this asset, or the creditors of the Morris family made that decision. In any event, on 14 Oct. 1801 the French bookseller N. G. Dufief informed the readers of the *Aurora*, "That he had just added to his numerous collection of books in various languages, a considerable part of the select and valuable Library of the celebrated Philosopher and Statesman, the late Dr. Benjamin Franklin." And so, without great fanfare, the fragmentation of the library of one of the country's greatest bookmen was begun. Coincidentally, in Dufief's hands at exactly the same time was the remnant of a great, somewhat earlier American library, that of William Byrd of Westover.

Let it be recorded in the annals of American book collecting that the early years of the nineteenth century might have broken even the ebullient confidence of a Rosenbach. Poor Dufief, with one of the most unusual collections ever gathered by an American bookman, found that he was offering in a stagnant market. A series of letters from the French bookseller in Philadelphia to President Jefferson spell out his situation in dreary words. There was, to be sure, a flurry of interest after Dufief's public announcement in the newspapers. He told Jefferson a week after it appeared that the enthusiasm of their fellow citizens to acquire the books had prevented him from making a catalogue of them. A few days later William Duane editorially in the *Aurora* bemoaned the fact that the volumes were being scattered over different parts of the continent. We know some of the major purchasers—Zachariah Poulson, Jr., Philadelphia printer and publisher, then Librarian of the Library Company, the American Philosophical Society and its alert secretary John Vaughan, and William Mackenzie, Philadelphia merchant and bibliophile—and no others that we have been able to discover who bought more than a volume or two. The flurry was a nine day's wonder.

In November, 1802, Dufief wrote Jefferson that William Duane was interested in buying the approximately two thousand volumes still left of Franklin's library. Should he not buy them, Dufief would send Jefferson a catalogue of what he had on hand. Duane was hesitating. On the last day of January, 1803, the imaginative bookseller veered on a new tack. With the catalogue of the remaining books (alas, returned by Jefferson and now disappeared) he sent a suggestion that the Library of Congress buy the collection in whole or in part. "What more worthy use of the money," he told the President, "than to employ it to buy the books of one of the Founders of the American Republic and of a great man!" "It is not a spirit of speculation," he continued, "which makes me use such language, for, apart from the fact that these books belong in a national library, being for the large part on the politics, legislation and affairs of America, I would put such a low price on them that no one could accuse me of such a thing." Perhaps, if Congress would not buy them as a lot he would have to break it up and sell them as best he could. "No, Sir," he answered himself in his letter, "although a bookseller I would never sell except in spite of myself the books of Galileo, Newton and Franklin."

To titillate Jefferson's interest he sent on a few books with copious notes by Franklin. Jefferson from the catalogue ordered a handful more for himself. He told Senator Baldwin that the offer had been made and patted Dufief on the back with the statement, "My dealings with him give me confidence that his prices would be moderate." It was theoretically unfortunate that Congress did not have the imagination to buy Dufief's collection; in retrospect it has enabled me to hope that other pieces to the puzzle may be found somewhere sometime. Two thousand volumes from Franklin's library would have been burned in 1814.

The negotiation ended with a note from Jefferson to Dufief on 1 Mar. 1803, telling him that the congressional committee had returned the catalogue to him with the information "that they had already exhausted their funds, and that therefore it was unnecessary for them to take the subject into consideration." Jefferson bought a 1556 edition of Athenaeus, *The First Two Books, of Philostratus*, London, 1680 (lacking the title and last leaf), and the Logographic Press printing of Derham's long-popular *Physico and Astro Theology*, and was given three volumes of Revolutionary tracts which Dufief sent with his compliments "in spite of the religious desire to keep them which they have inspired."

I wish this were a fairy tale and I could now end my story with an account of a knight-in-armor and "they lived happily ever after." Shortly after Jefferson's last letter Dufief had to act, in spite of himself. "Dr. Franklin's Library" was announced for sale by Shannon and Poalk at public auction on 12 Mar. 1803. "This collection, besides a variety of excellent and scarce works in English, French, Italian, German, Greek, Latin, &c., contains several manuscripts, all of which will be sold without reserve. It may with propriety be observed that there never yet was sold at public sale, the library of a man so illustrious, both in the annals of America, and in those of the Arts and Sciences, which he so much aggrandized." This ends the account of the major dispersal of Franklin's library. Although Franklin made or had made a catalogue of his books which was mentioned in his will, although Dufief sent a smaller one to Jefferson, and although one was announced as available at the auction sale, none has survived. The top of the box in which the puzzle came is lost. We have no picture to guide us.

Almost all this information was known to and printed by George Simpson Eddy, whose account of Franklin's library, appeared in the

Proceedings of the American Antiquarian Society in 1925. He was the first to try to put the jigsaw puzzle together. He continued for a number of years to gather information and track down volumes with a Franklin provenance. His catalogue in its final form with notes—sometimes detailed, sometimes speculative—of approximately 1,500 volumes located or supposed to have been in the Doctor's collection is now at Princeton, where its custodians have been most kind in lending it to me for a time span exceeding that of the usual interlibrary loan. Mr. Eddy was on the verge of the breakthrough which has enabled me to go beyond his findings.

The breakthrough was the identification of the shelf mark which was put in Franklin's books, presumably when the catalogue mentioned in his will was made. It is simple; a C denoting case followed by a number, and an N denoting the location in that case also followed by a number, for example, C38 N7, which would mean the seventh book in case 38. If my premise is accepted, that Franklin's bookshelves were the boxes in which the books had been packed, or similar neat boxes which could be placed on one another to make shelves, this becomes perfectly clear. A case was the equivalent of a shelf.

But now, we must go back and work along another spoor, so that the evidence which led to this discovery becomes clear. We know how and when Franklin's library was broken up, but we still do not know what books were in it. Our knowledge of that, a knowledge of what a single piece of the puzzle looked like, comes from various sources. First, we have Franklin's correspondence and the letters written to him. When he wrote to Peter Collinson on 19 Dec. 1756: "I have received Messrs. Hoadly and Wilson on Electricity," it may be assumed that he had obtained those gentlemen's *Observations on a Series of Electrical Experiments*, London, 1756. When Crevecoeur wrote to Franklin in 1787 that he had entrusted to John Paul Jones a copy of "the Second Edition of the American Farmer's Letters, with the addition of a 3d Volume, which please to accept," it may be assumed that the three-volume edition of 1787 of the *Lettres d'un cultivateur Americain* was delivered to Franklin Court. But this is evidence of a sometimes deceptive nature. Franklin did not keep in his library every book he cited, thanked for, or received. It must be remembered that during the first half of his life he was a secondhand bookseller as well as a printer—

most of the books ordered from his London colleague Strahan would seem to have been bought for resale. Yet, even this cannot be relied upon. Bower's history of the Popes, an unlikely work for his personal shelves, did apparently remain there until presented a few years after its purchase to Yale. On the other hand, in 1747, when Franklin was busy forming a militia company, he asked Strahan to send him "Folard's Polybius, in French; it is in 6 Vols. 4to. printed at Paris, and costs about 3 Guineas." Since the editor added a body of material on military science, it might have been reasonable to assume that Franklin wanted it for himself. Almost a year later, however, he wrote to Strahan that he was glad the Polybius had not come, as he had wanted it for his son who had been considering a military career, but had given up the idea. The cancellation of the order apparently arrived too late; the set was delivered in Philadelphia. But, as a letter from James Logan in October, 1749, indicates, it was sold to him, and is now in the Loganian Library.

The letters, filled as they are with citations from books, and statements of books sent and received, must be used eclectically. Some works Franklin lent to friends were the Library Company's and not his own. Some books, the receipt of which he acknowledged, were merely on loan. A folio volume of bird plates which Franklin himself inscribed on the front end paper: "From the Count de Buffon to the Society," never reached the American Philosophical Society during his lifetime. John Bayne saw it at Passy in 1783; Franklin sent it to Aitken to be bound or rebound in 1786; it bears the Franklin shelf mark; and it did not end up in the Society's collection until some later, unknown date. One does now know whether to describe the eighteenth-century practice of borrowing books permanently and shortstopping them on the way to their destination as charming informality or mere irresponsibility. Franklin's library was both enriched and impoverished by the practice. (As a footnote, I would add that he was not alone. In the library of Allegheny College I found the massive tables of longitude which the English commissioners had compiled, with an inscription in Franklin's hand from the University of Cambridge to the Philosophical Society, sent to John Winthrop for, charitably, inspection and transmission. Winthrop kept it, the inscription denying his title and, since it was not crossed through or erased, not bothering his conscience.)

Other major sources for the reconstruction of Franklin's library are various lists. The earliest of these is the catalogue of the sale of the books of Franklin's early friend James Ralph, which took place on 5-6 Apr. 1762. John B. Shipley found a copy in the British Museum with the purchasers' names added, and from that compiled a list of the items bought by Franklin. My count of his purchases comes to 141 volumes plus a rather indefinite lot described as "A Parcel of Waste." Some of these titles I found with the Franklin shelf mark in the Library Company. The next is a list of 23 titles in 37 volumes bought by Franklin on 13 May 1769 from the booksellers D. Wilson and G. Nicol. So far I have been able to identify only one volume from this list as Franklin's copy, but this list I turned up only late in the summer, and hence there is still hope.

One of the richest harvest of titles came through the discovery of a collection of fifty-one volumes of seventeenth- and early eighteenth-century tracts which the librarian Zachariah Poulson, Jr., presented to the Library Company on 3 Dec. 1801, at which time it will be remembered that Dufief was doing his best to sell the Franklin books. The discovery of the Franklin shelf mark in many of these and of further evidence from a letter from the Doctor to his cousin Samuel Franklin in July, 1771, established the Franklin provenance without question. The Philadelphian told his English kinsman that he had just bought "A curious Collection of Pamphlets bound in 8 vols. Folio, and 24 Vols 4to, & 8vo." in which he found tables of contents and notes in a hand which he identified as that of his uncle Benjamin Franklin, Samuel's grandfather. As an autograph expert the all-embracing Franklin left something to be desired. A comparison of the handwriting in the pamphlet volumes with that in commonplace books known to have been kept by uncle Benjamin shows Benjamin II was mistaken. It would have been a nice story if true, but at least the handwriting permitted me to bring together the "uncle Benjamin" volumes, the shelf marks still remaining in some to establish their Franklin origin, and others from a different original source also with shelf marks to make it certain that all fifty-one volumes of the lot came together from Dufief's hands directly to Poulson's and thence to the shelves of the Library Company.

Among the Franklin Papers at the University of Pennsylvania is a list in the hand of Temple Franklin. It is headed in French: "List of the Books of Mr. Franklin taken from his room in the office, December 31, 1781," with a subheading: "List of the Books taken to the Office, January 8, 1782." Here we find binder's titles for 71 works in 65 volumes. A similar list, in the Franklin Papers at the American Philosophical Society, certainly also made at Passy is headed succinctly: "List of Books." It contains 121 titles in 160 volumes. These two lists are similar, and present similar and tantalizing problems. There are annoying titles, such as "English Cookery," "Essay on Punctuation," "Le Babillard," "Instructions sur les Muriers," and "Quinti Horatii Flacci," in 2 vols. In some cases I have been able to identify the work without question and to pinpoint Franklin's copy; in a score of instances I am still trying to find out what "Coup d'Etat" or "Consultations pour M. Alexandre" are; in others it has been impossible to ascertain which of dozens of editions of La Fontaine's *Fables* and *Contes* Franklin owned, which Caesar, Virgil, or Juvenal. These lists present a further problem. Some of the volumes which I have been able to trace in a direct line through the hands of Franklin descendants turn out to bear Temple Franklin's signature on the titles. Reluctantly but ineluctably, I have come to the conclusion that Temple's books were intermingled with his grandfather's at Passy and never sorted out in Philadelphia, so that Manassah Cutler by chance might have pulled a book from the shelves he saw in the library and found it to be young Franklin's. I believe they were included in the 1790 count, and hence I am including them in my reconstruction.

No other lists made during Franklin's lifetime are known, or at the present are known to have survived. Chronologically, the next which has been found is a list of books marked with Benjamin Franklin Bache's name in the catalogue according to the will, and delivered to him by Temple Franklin. The original of this document has not been located; a typescript obtained by George Simpson Eddy from Franklin Bache about thirty years ago is our sole record. And this is a key document. It lists 74 titles in 217 volumes, and preceding the titles is a column listing numbers for Case and Number and a letter for a

Panel, which last I assume to be a section of the library or group of shelves. It was the discovery of books with shelf marks matching those on the list which enabled me to prove that this particular shelf mark was Franklin's. Benny Bache died in the yellow fever epidemic of 1798, and his widow married William Duane. I am now working on the theory that Duane took over most, if not all the Franklin books. A number which I have traced were sold at his sale in 1836, and I have noticed a great number of other titles common to the Bache list and the Duane sale, although I have not yet completed my analysis of them.

Second only to Duane, the American Philosophical Society was alert to the opportunities offered by Dufief. On 2 Oct. 1801, the committee appointed "to examine Dr. Franklin's Library" reported that they had spent $107.62. On 16 Oct. they reported the outlay of an additional $91.50, at which time they were told to go ahead and buy another twenty dollars worth. The 69 titles in 175 volumes, which included runs of European learned society transactions, were listed in full in the minutes. At the auction sale in 1803 the Society again returned as a purchaser, this time securing 62 works in 54 volumes, plus 76 volumes of bound almanacs. With the exception of a few volumes later disposed of as duplicates (one has turned up at Princeton) the Society still possesses its rich haul of 1801-3. George Simpson Eddy listed the works from the titles given in the minutes and in the original bills from the bookseller Dufief and the auctioneers Shannon and Poalk which are in the Society's archives, but he was not able to examine all the books. They have now been segregated, described, and held in proper veneration. For those looking for a bargain, it is safe to say no more will be sold as duplicates.

I have noted the purchase by Zachariah Poulson in 1801 of the English tract volumes now in the Library Company. Another major earlier purchaser recognized the worth of the wares being so forlornly cried by Dufief. It was natural that he should, for the wise bibliophile was William Mackenzie, a wealthy Philadelphia merchant and the first American who we know collected rare books as rare books. How much he bought from Franklin's library we do not know. But in the course of my recent enthusiasm we began turning up in the Library Company dozens of volumes with the Franklin shelf mark, all originating in the lot bequeathed by Mackenzie or sold to the library by his executors on favorable terms stipulated by him. With excitement we went through every Mackenzie book printed before the date of Franklin's death. Many of them had been rebacked and had old end papers covered. These had to be uncovered. Enough marks were found to make this one of the prime sources for books from Franklin's library, and to deliver me into the hands of frustration. For every volume we found with old end papers intact, there were half a dozen volumes completely rebound with all original end papers gone and no sign left, except a gnawing between intuitive certainty and the uncertainty of evidence, that these had been Franklin's. I found many titles, which from other sources I knew had been his, but the Mackenzie copy told me nothing. In the case, for instance, of a set of Chinese history complete in thirteen volumes, of which the rebound Mackenzie set had only twelve, and we have a record of only twelve into Franklin's hands, where my intuitive certainty overbears my innate desire for proof, I have included those tantalizingly unmarked Mackenzie books in my list of located Franklin volumes, with the knowledge that my honest statement of the weakness of my position will be sympathized with by my friends and attacked by my critics.

The third chief repository of Franklin books, the Historical Society of Pennsylvania, came by its treasures indirectly. William Duane, who more than any other individual was conscious of the importance of the provenance, bought a considerable number of volumes from Dufief after Jefferson had turned them down, or at the auction. Among these were 148 tract volumes, several of the political ones of the pre-Revolutionary period with extensive notes in Franklin's hand. In 1822 Duane sold them to the Athenaeum of Philadelphia, together with a run of the *Pennsylvania Gazette* from 1729 to 1747, said by an old history of the institution to contain notes by Franklin giving the names of the contributors of articles. Alas, the Athenaeum was a lending library. How any one could "borrow" and not return a dozen and a half folio volumes of a newspaper is not known. The run of the *Pennsylvania Gazette* is gone, and no set with Franklin annotations has been found even by so keen a Franklin bloodhound as the persistent, scholarly Dr. Whitfield J. Bell, Jr. Gone, too, before authorities at the Athenaeum became aware of the value of their holdings were twenty-seven

of the tract volumes. Broken out of their bindings and separately rebound, usually in morocco, by dealers who knew a good thing when
they saw it, and may or may not have known their origin, many of
the pamphlets, dripping with Franklin marginal comment and frequently not a little of his biting pen, turned up in such distinguished
sales as those of Menzies and Brinley. Not bearing a sign of their
previous ownership (the Athenaeum did not use defacing rubber
stamps until after the thefts became known) some of these thin precious volumes are in the Boston Public, New York Public, Morgan,
Antiquarian Society, and the collection of Boies Penrose. I am not suggesting that we enter into a Texas-British Museum debate or that a
hundred-year-old theft now be atoned for by innocent possessors, but
I would like to discover where the rest of the twenty-seven volumes
went. The Athenaeum in 1888, aware that historical treasures should
be in a historical library, turned over the remaining 121 volumes to
the Historical Society where they now are. Although Eddy made a
rough list of the pamphlets in the collection, the titles do not appear
in the card catalogue of the Historical Society, and the tract volumes
—of supreme importance to the Franklin scholar—have been little
used and are little known.

This brings us down almost to the day before yesterday. Occasionally books which bore unmistakable signs of a Franklin provenance
were sold at auction sales or were discovered in libraries. It is amazing
how difficult it is to trace a book sold or seen fifty years ago, or even
twenty-five. These scattered volumes would, however, barely fill a
shelf. But there did remain unscattered another major cache of Franklin books. I do not think Jonathan Williams ever received his share of
the library. Temple Franklin's we have traced in dispersal. Bennie
Bache's ended up, I believe, in the hands of Duane and were sold at
his sale. That leaves us with Billy Bache's book legacy from his grandfather. These, I am convinced, were passed down in the family and
ended up in the hands of Franklin Bache. This lineal descendant was
a friend of Eddy and sent him not only a copy of the document listing
Benny Bache's share—none of which he owned—but another list of
books in his own possession compiled some time before 1914. This
list has been another of my major sources.

After the death of Franklin Bache's widow, almost all these books were sold at Freeman's in 1947. Franklin Bache had carefully put cloth wrappers around many of the volumes on which he had typed "From Benjamin Franklin's Library." Some of the volumes bore presentation inscriptions, others had the shelf mark, a number the signature of Temple Franklin, a few that of his father William. It was at this sale that I first noticed the shelf mark and called it to the attention of Dr. William E. Lingelbach of the Philosophical Society. He and Mrs. Gertrude D. Hess had already noticed it in some of the Society's books, and conspiratorially before the sale we came to the conclusion that it had been put in by Dufief. We were interested in it, but not fully convinced of its Franklin importance. I could not speak so feelingly of this sale had not I been one of those blind to its opportunity. For the Philosophical Society, Percy Lawler, who attended the sale, bought a number of lots. The rest were scattered among other successful bidders, who found themselves declared the winner after a bid of three or five dollars a lot. Even the volumes with presentation inscriptions to Franklin or bearing his name in a contemporary hand on a cover went for prices which can only be described as dwarf low. What mass psychology convinced the audience at the sale that, in spite of evidence to the contrary, none of the books had really belonged to Franklin I do not know. Perhaps, it was Franklin Bache's amateurish attempt to establish the pedigree by putting wrappers on all the books which shrieked the fact. Three volumes of Priestley's scientific works, presentation copies delivered to Franklin by the scientist Magellan, went to the astute Dr. John Fulton for only $90. Seven volumes of Rozier's work on agriculture with a long inscription hailing Franklin as the Aristotle of America was bought for the Philosophical Society for $30. Journals of Congress, in original boards, some with Franklin's name on the front cover, went for from $3.50 to $16.00. Volumes with Temple Franklin's signature went for even less.

I am now convinced that all these books came from the house on Franklin Court after its owner's death, and were all part of Franklin's library. Since some of them, including a good many with definite indications that they were the Doctor's, do not have the shelf mark, I can only assume that either the task of marking the books was not completed before Franklin's death or that books shelved in rooms other

than the library were not marked (4,276 volumes are a great many to
have been squeezed in a room 17 by 33 feet which also served as an
office). It would seem that the task of tracing books sold as recently
as 1947 would be a comparatively easy one. It has not been. Many of
the purchasers set so little store by their cheaply bought acquisitions
that they discarded them. Others sold them or put them away and do
not now know where. I am still looking for scores of volumes from the
Bache sale, for many of which I have found supporting evidence of
Franklin's ownership in the letters and the lists.

    This brings me to the end of my story. By all the means described,
in the American Philosophical Society I have identified as Franklin's
426 titles in 457 volumes, plus 76 volumes of almanacs; in the Library
Company 1,293 titles in 223 volumes; in the Historical Society 861
titles in 121 volumes. These are where most of Franklin's books ended
up. Scattered in twenty-five other collections are some more. By looking in many libraries at copies of books I know Franklin owned I have
been able to locate additional volumes. In the Library of Congress by
this method I found Franklin's copy of Fournier's history of printing, recently rebound in library buckram but fortunately still with the
original flyleaf bearing the shelf mark which matched that on the list
of books delivered to B. F. Bache. At Princeton I found a ten-volume
set on Chinese history, a record of which existed in a letter. It too had
the shelf mark in some volumes. Searching haphazardly through a
shelf of pamphlets at the American Antiquarian Society I found one
with a table of contents in Franklin's hand. Now separated from its
fellow pamphlets and bound in morocco, it is probably one of the lost
Duane-Athenaeum volumes, and was sold at the Brinley sale for $10
to the Society unaware until this summer of its Franklin provenance.
From the list of books once owned by Franklin Bache, I found twenty-
six volumes at the Free Library of Philadelphia, given it by Bache
in 1914. Another work, once there, was discarded as "used" in 1919,
for the Franklin connection of none of the volumes had been recognized. In the Franklin Institute I found the Philadelphia printer's
copy of Moxon, identifiable only by a single brief note in Franklin's
hand, but presumably the B. F. Bache copy sold at the Duane sale,
bought by the press manufacturer Adam Ramage and given by him to
the Institute. By pure chance I discovered on the shelves of the Patent

Office Library a seven-volume set of inventions and machines approved by the Académie Royale des Sciences. I took it off the shelf, opened it and saw the telling shelf mark. These are but needles in haystacks. There are lots of similar haystacks still to be searched in the country, and probably some needles yet to be found. I have identified and located a total of 2,981 titles in 1,020 volumes, plus the hundreds of individual almanacs in the 76 volumes. I have records of, but have not located or identified, an additional 640 titles in 1,106 volumes, and I have not yet finished working through the Franklin Papers. Since Mr. Eddy spoke of having discovered 1,350 "volumes," which I gather from his lists was a combination of volumes and titles, all of which he had not located or identified, I believe that I am fair in saying that I have doubled his results. To return to my original metaphor, about one-quarter of the puzzle in terms of volumes has been put in place. I know what another quarter looks like, but I have not found the pieces. I am still hunting, piecing together, and praying for a major stroke of serendipity.

The Changing World of Rare Books

By GORDON N. RAY*

AS it appears from the outside, the rare book world is perhaps best symbolized by the great shrines of the book—the Folger, the Houghton, the Huntington, the Morgan, and latterly the Beinecke and the Lilly. In these sumptuous buildings are preserved the greatest triumphs of the mind of man in literature, in science, and in many other fields, as they became part of the printed record. Here are treasured as well the masterpieces of printing, illustration, and binding which five centuries of the book have left behind. And this is only the apex of the pyramid. There are many other institutional libraries, hardly less dignified and opulent. There are princely private collectors, whose hoards derive a further fascination from their very inaccessibility. Supporting all these collections is a massive apparatus of dealers, auction houses, and collectors' clubs. Moreover, the whole enterprise is carried on to the accompaniment of a constant flow of monographs, bibliographies, and articles from scholars of the book, whose precise and loving erudition is as impressive in its way as the objects to which it is devoted.

Of course these great shrines of the book are better envisioned as

* This paper was delivered in part at the Mississippi Valley Regional Meeting of the Bibliographical Society of America held in Lexington, Kentucky, on 5 April 1965 in conjunction with the celebration of the centennial of the founding of the University of Kentucky.

fortress-cathedrals on the pattern of that at Albi, than as open temples on the pattern of the Parthenon. When Carlyle read the file of her letters which his wife left behind at her death in 1866, he asked himself: "Can nothing of it be saved, then, for the worthy that still remain among these roaring myriads of unworthy?"[1] It was in this spirit, certainly, that many of the country's earlier rare book collections were established; and though different assumptions lie behind those created in recent years, there is an inescapable element of exclusiveness in the very idea of a rare book collection. Perhaps this is not altogether to be regretted in an age in which the sense of the past has declined as literacy has increased. Indeed, "to the happy few," the epigraph which Stendhal chose for the second volume of his *Histoire de la Peinture en Italie* (1817), seems now to apply not merely to Stendhal's readers but to all those who concern themselves with preserving the monuments of mankind's history.

The conception of great libraries as fortress-cathedrals gains additional validity from the recent emergence not merely of non-bookmen but of no-bookmen. With non-bookmen, who advocate so strenuously the various forms of photographic reproduction, accommodation if not fellow-feeling is possible. At least they still take books as their starting point. But what of the no-bookmen, the scientists who hold that in their fields knowledge is developing so rapidly that books, scientific papers, and even duplicated memoranda are too quickly superseded to be of use? Only the latest words dropped at a conference in Berkeley, Gif-sur-Yvette, or Tel Aviv will serve. "If that hypothesis of theirs be sound," the book seems destined to pass into history as an outmoded artifact, like armor or the longbow, which can claim only an archaeological interest.

Thus from the outside the world of rare books appears to be a remote and godlike realm over which a *Götterdämmerung* may possibly impend. It will be my endeavor to describe the world of rare books as it appears from the inside. In this perspective the splendor quickly fades. Seen in their day to day operations, the inhabitants of this world emerge as harassed men with mundane worries, very much like the

[1] Charles Richard Sanders, "Carlyle as Editor and Critic of Literary Letters," *Emory University Quarterly*, Summer, 1964, p. 109.

rest of us, whose appropriate laureate would be Balzac or Dreiser, not Wagner. But it also becomes apparent that they serve serious purposes worthily, and this may enhance their interest for those who have hitherto regarded what they do as esoteric and marginal.

Since my experience of the rare book world is limited, if reasonably protracted, I sent brief sets of questions to collectors, librarians, and dealers among my friends and acquaintances in preparation for my task. My inquiry, or "inquisition" as one restive respondent termed it, apparently came at a lucky time. I received 49 replies, most of them of considerable length, and many expressing strong convictions. My questions were too brief and undifferentiated to permit a statistical summary of answers, but their very breadth proved provocative of wide-ranging discussion. As a result of these replies, some of the assumptions on which my questions were based have been modified, and many important considerations to which I had given no thought now have their proper place in my argument. Though only one respondent specifically asked that his anonymity be preserved, I have refrained from identifying individual witnesses in order to leave myself a free hand in pungent quotation. A list of all who answered is given in Appendix I. Anyone who amuses himself by guessing the authors of quotations, a game which in a few cases at least should not prove difficult, will presumably not assign my occasional echoes of the Bible, Dickens, Milton, Shakespeare, and Tennyson even to Mr. Hayward or Mr. Powell.

I shall first describe the great forces for change in today's rare book world: affluence, institutional involvement, and the knowledge explosion. I shall go on to consider the situation and prospects of the principal groups which make up the rare book world: collectors, libraries, and dealers. My coda will concern the inescapable subject of prices. I should also specify at this point that the "world" of rare books with which I shall be dealing is the United States, with occasional glances at England; that the examples which I have used in discussing prices are chiefly first editions of nineteenth- and twentieth-century English and American literature, a familiar and reasonably representative field, which is also the one I know best; and that I have avoided all consideration of manuscripts and autograph letters.

II

The rare book world, like every other aspect of contemporary life, is profoundly affected by present-day prosperity. Our society is an easy-money society. Our markets, except for mass-produced items, are sellers' markets. With regard to what are sometimes called "cultural artifacts," the picture is uniformly one of "too many buyers chasing too few goods."

It must be granted, of course, that among cultural artifacts, rare books are only on the outer fringes of affluence. In comparison with the demand for collectors' pieces in painting and sculpture, old furniture, porcelain, silver, and above all coins, the demand for rare books is modest indeed. The reason for their relatively disfavored status is no doubt the absence in them of any broad and simple ground of appeal. Unlike the collector of paintings, the bibliophile cannot hang his precious possessions on the wall for every visitor to admire. For most people the visual attraction of books is summed up in the old-time cataloguer's term "bookcase furniture." Rare books are too bulky and cumbersome to be regarded as "portable property," a phrase that conveys at least part of the attraction which rare coins have for several million Americans. Rare book collecting, then, is a pursuit which commands powerful loyalties, but only among a small minority. A degree of learning and sophistication is required even to see the point of it. One respondent, after noting how signally the prices of rare books have failed to keep pace with the prices of rare coins and paintings, proposed this disheartening principle: "The increase in the monetary value of cultural artifacts is in inverse proportion to their research value for institutions of higher learning!"

As we shall see, it is indeed the institutional libraries, with their paramount concern for the research value of acquisitions, which have chiefly altered the rare book world. But at the same time prosperity has also stepped up sharply the activity of collectors. There are dedicated bibliophiles who will sacrifice almost anything to obtain the books which they desire, but in the case of most collectors books are bought from what margin remains after the necessities of life have been provided for. With easy money this margin has become wider and wider for more and more collectors.

Moreover, other encouraging factors have come into play. In

France, for example, rare books have been favored as a hedge against inflation. They represent "valeur or" to French bibliophiles, as French currency decidedly does not. In the United States the 30 per cent federal income tax deduction allowed for gifts to libraries acts as a potent stimulus to private collecting. This regulation provides the collector in a reasonably high income bracket with the assurance that the rare books which he purchases will be readily disposable at little or no loss to himself. No longer is he confronted with the doubtful prospect of sale to a dealer, who has his own profit to think about, or by an auction house, which charges a substantial fee for the service and takes only a moderate interest in anything except "high spots." The collector can count on having everything which he offers gratefully received by a worthy institution at a fair, sometimes a generous, valuation.

The importance of this assurance is substantial, for it is still not possible to recommend rare books as a preferential investment. Though prices for books have risen over the years, they have not risen as rapidly as the Dow-Jones Average, and their market performance has been quite as erratic and unpredictable as that of common stocks. A bookseller among my respondents pointed out that an alert buyer could have bought first editions of Ackermann's *History of Cambridge*, Boswell's *Johnson, Tom Jones*, Gould's *Birds of Australia*, Johnson's *Dictionary*, and *The Wealth of Nations* in 1938 and 1939 for £210, and an alert seller could have sold the same books in 1963 and 1964 for £4,135. An increase in value of nearly 2,000 per cent during twenty-five years is eminently satisfactory. But it is given to few people to pick nothing but winners, either in the book or the stock market. I shall later describe an inquiry into current prices based on those achieved in 1964-65 by 49 English and American first editions of the last two centuries. When it turned out that the Lilly Library had copies of 48 of these, Mr. David Randall sent me a list of the prices at which they had been acquired by Mr. Lilly, chiefly during the nineteen-thirties. Eliminating the one missing item, Mr. Lilly's costs totaled $11,585; the near-record prices of the last year totaled $11,905.40. Admittedly Mr. Lilly's copies met his high standard of condition, while the general level of the 1964-65 copies was merely good. Nonetheless, the case for rare books as an investment hardly seems demonstrated.

The second great change in the rare book world since 1945 is that what was once largely the preserve of private collectors is now largely the preserve of institutional libraries. Indeed, the increase of institutional rare book collections has proceeded with startling rapidity. The first annual conference of the Rare Books Section of the American Library Association was held at the University of Virginia in 1959. Amid general amazement, it was discovered that 187 individuals were on hand, representing 97 institutions, 57 of them college or university libraries, the rest national libraries, historical society libraries, private libraries, and municipal public libraries. The Rare Book Section of the A. L. A. now includes 453 individuals representing 180 institutions, a remarkable increase in less than six years.

Seeking to interpret this efflorescence, I asked the librarians to whom I sent my questions: how many significant rare book libraries does the United States have? how many did it have in 1945? how many will it have in 1985? I received two kinds of replies, set apart by the meaning given the word "significant." A representative statement in the first group ran:

> If you define a significant rare book library in classical terms, that is, one whose collections range all the way from medieval manuscripts to modern literature, there are perhaps a dozen or fifteen in the United States. Not many of these have achieved this status since 1945, and there are not likely to be many future additions. I need not stress the obvious reason: that the foundation collections in many fields simply cannot be assembled today.

Other respondents with comparably austere standards thought respectively that there are 10, 11, 21, and 25 significant rare book libraries in the United States. Two of these respondents expected an additional nine or ten libraries to be added to the list by 1985.

Most of the librarians who answered took a broader view of what constitutes significance in rare book libraries. In 1942 Mr. Robert B. Downs drew up a list of about 75 subjects and asked some 500 authorities to state which libraries held the best collections in these subjects. Some 32 libraries were named for ten or more subjects, and of course this tabulation by its very nature excluded libraries like the Folger and the Morgan which at that time at least were strictly limited in range.[2] Among the librarians who accepted something like Mr. Downs's criteria, the number of significant rare book libraries was estimated at 20 to 45 in 1945 and 35 to 50 in 1965, and was projected to 45 to 100 by 1985.

From any perspective, then, there has been a spectacular expansion of institutional concern for rare books. This expansion has been reflected most dramatically, perhaps, in expenditures in this area by libraries which previously made only modest and sporadic purchases. The University of Texas and the Friends of the University Library have spent over $12,500,000 for rare books in the past eight years. Indiana University has spent over $5,000,000 in the past ten years. In 1964 the Newberry Library acquired the Louis J. Silver collection for more than $2,500,000. During one euphoric period of twelve months, Cornell University added collections worth $600,000 to its shelves. Such a list could be extended almost indefinitely. Though it is true that even Texas' expenditures do not approach the sums spent either by Henry Huntington or by J. P. Morgan in comparable periods during the first two decades of this century, the cumulative effect of all this new money has been formidable.

One of the questions which I put to the dealers among my respondents concerned the proportion of business which they do with institutions as opposed to collectors. Not all dealers answered this question, and a sportive inquiry was made by one as to whether or not Mr. C. Waller Barrett was to be regarded as an institution. But of the eleven who provided estimates, only two pegged the figure below 50 per cent and one put it as high as 85 per cent. The mean figure was 60 per cent. All agreed that there had been a very marked increase in the proportion of buying done by institutions during the last two decades, and most expected this proportion to go on increasing. Obviously today's picture differs greatly from that which prevailed as late as 1945, when libraries in this country with substantial rare book purchase programs could still be numbered on the fingers of two hands.

It has taken more than "a fugitive and cloistered virtue" to win these "immortal garlands" for Texas, Indiana, and the rest. A university's clientele, and even its staff, will always include a good many

[2] "Leading American Library Collections," *Library Quarterly* XII (July 1942), 457-73.

persons who object to rare book purchases on the ground that there are more pressing needs for the institution's funds. But the time has long since passed when the president of a great university could permit himself to include among his "Ten Commandments for College Presidents" the fatuous admonition: "Thou shalt not covet . . . to have the largest number of unused books in your library."[3] For many years now institutional libraries have had supporters in high places eager to compete in a race which is not to be run "without dust and heat." Mr. Harry Ransom, for example, was once addressed by a Texas legislator as the "Chancellor of Second Hand Books." No one who has heard Mr. Ransom develop his comparison of obsolescence in books and in scientific equipment will doubt his ability to meet this sort of critic on his own ground. A great book, his argument goes, is an investment in perpetuity, which will outlast fifty successive buildings housing it. A new piece of scientific equipment is typically outmoded in five years. When the initial cost of a great book is divided by its anticipated useful life, its price comes to seem low indeed.

Of course this remarkable expansion of rare book libraries has not been without its follies and excesses. From time to time an institution has rushed into the field without adequate consideration or planning because its authorities have heard that a rare book library is now one of the "maturity symbols" of the American university. Where status rather than need has been the predominant motive, the results are sometimes ludicrous. A paneled "treasure room" with locked cases and carpeting on the floor; scattered collections and star pieces which have been assembled without regard to the special interests of the faculty; a curator converted from a librarian past her work or the feeblest member of the English department—all this may amount to no more than window dressing of the most expensive and useless kind. Nor should we underestimate the harm which the multiplication of such pointless manifestations might do to the cause of scholarship. An English bibliographical scholar who knows the United States well writes: "My concern is how thin the jam gets spread as more libraries try to compete. I would estimate the median number of copies of my eighteenth-century verse in libraries at just over three: to see all the works of Nahum Tate (or almost any other minor poet) you have to

[3] *Newsweek*, 20 Aug. 1951, p. 84.

go from London to California. This isn't going to get any better. Would it have been a good thing if all the Shakespeare quartos at Folger had been scattered one to each university library across the states?"

I pass now to the third principal factor that is changing the rare book world, the knowledge explosion of the last twenty years. All of the "knowledge-producing industries and occupations," as Professor Machlup calls them, are booming. Higher education, research and development, the communication media, and information machines and services are alike experiencing unprecedented growth.[4] The rapid expansion of higher education is particularly relevant to our concerns. America's higher educational establishment has tripled in size since 1940 and will again increase by a factor of two and one-half by 1980. Many colleges have become universities, and many universities where graduate work used to be rudimentary are now major centers for granting advanced degrees.

But just as significant as the growth in number of faculty members and students is the higher level at which they are working. Throughout our educational system the pace of instruction is being stepped up. It is often true that students now learn in grade school what they used to learn in high school, in high school what they used to learn in college, and in college what they used to learn in graduate school. And with the increasing specialization that has resulted from these advances, there has been an increasing ramification of subjects to which serious study is devoted.

In only a fraction of our universities is there now a full-scale research library, yet most of them realize that they will need such facilities to achieve their aims. Research libraries are consequently multiplying, and so is the range of subjects which each seeks to cover with thoroughness. The reverberations of these developments have created a situation of increasing confusion in which the sedate rare book world of the past has in effect become a province of the out-of-print book world. The traditional stand-bys of rare book collecting— first editions of literary classics, early printing, books remarkable for typography, illustration, and binding, and the rest—are now almost

---

[4] Fritz Machlup, *The Production and Distribution of Knowledge in the United States* (Princeton, 1962).

submerged among dozens of other areas. Each year brings its standard histories and bibliographies, and with the aid of these maps librarians are zestfully homesteading the newly opened country. In
such fields it is almost impossible to draw a line between antiquarian
books of research interest and rare books proper. Conscious that any
book generally sought by medium-size American libraries which has
been out of print for at least twenty-five years is now probably very
scarce, one respondent suggested this working definition: "a rare book
is one which it is more efficient to preserve than to replace." This
formula, which is certainly a better test for inclusion in a library's
reserve stack than is the conventional touchstone of price, nicely illustrates how greatly the territory of the rare book world has expanded.

III

I move next to a discussion of the essential human elements of the
rare book world: dealers, librarians, and collectors. All three must
now reconcile themselves to a milieu in which the pace has been greatly
quickened, in which there is an increasing premium on alertness,
flexibility, and resilience. With regard to dealers, this means that
familiar stereotypes drawn from the classics, from Lamb's essays, let's
say, or the novels of Anatole France, no longer apply. At a book-trade
dinner in London recently, Mr. David Daiches expressed a wonder
which was in itself surprising that those present "were not all funny
old gentlemen with whiskers and skull-caps, shaky in the joints but
strong on the points."[5] When I spoke at the annual meeting of the
Antiquarian Booksellers of America a couple of years ago, I found
little quaintness among the brisk, well-dressed, and businesslike persons in attendance, though still a blessed tolerance of eccentricity.

This change in the personal characteristics of dealers in antiquarian
books, for I take it that there clearly has been a change, reflects a
change in the conditions of the trade. A veteran of the nineteen-
twenties in New York has described to me how dealers in those days
could confidently depend for their supply on a constant flow of libraries from private houses. Every mansion on Long Island seemed
to have its collection, and enough of these came up for disposal to

[5] Raymond Kilgariff, "Not So Much a Trade, More of a Closed Shop," *A. B. A. News
Letter*, Winter, 1964, p. 4.

enable the firm with which he was associated to acquire on the average a new library a week. In the small apartments of today few New Yorkers attempt significant collections, and the occasional private library that does become available as often as not is sold or given *en bloc* to an institution.

In consequence, the general secondhand bookshops, which were once the happy hunting grounds of collectors, are now denounced by them as "whited sepulchres." These dusty caverns, where the bemused slovenliness of the proprietor used to be cheerfully accepted as a sign that the prospect of "finds" was good, today offer chiefly review copies of books which are selling poorly, recent novels that nobody wants, battered examples of standard works, and paperbacks, paperbacks, paperbacks. Even in England the picture is not much more encouraging. A dealer writes:

> Bookshops in Great Britain have been diminishing rapidly since 1939. At one time there was at least one antiquarian bookshop of some standing in every major town and smaller shops at which one would expect to find something in many minor towns. Now, often there are none at all, and those that there are contain mostly overpriced leather bound sets and second-hand and paperback editions of no collecting value.

A door seems to be closing forever on what for some at least was the most exciting part of book collecting.

Sharply dwindling supply, coupled in recent years with sharply rising demand, has turned the antiquarian book trade decisively towards specialization. Only by concentrating on a limited area in which his special knowledge gives him particular advantages can a dealer hope to prosper under present-day conditions. Here some notice must be taken of a development which is related to my topic, though not strictly part of it, the burgeoning of the already mentioned out-of-print (or "O. P.") book trade. Among specialist bookdealers, indeed, those who concern themselves with rare books may be compared to the one-tenth of the iceberg which is visible above the water, for as a glance at any issue of the *Antiquarian Bookman* will demonstrate, "O. P." dealers are far more numerous today than rare bookdealers. They have multiplied because they sell service quite as much as they do books, and service has become the scarcest commodity on the market. An overworked acquisition librarian cannot spend her time leafing through catalogues in search of thousands of items which rarely appear and which probably will be pre-empted by prior orders even on the occasions when she manages to find them. She willingly pays a substantial increase over catalogue prices to the "O. P." dealer who will assume this burden for her. The somewhat anomalous result is that when an "O. P." firm and a rare bookdealer both offer an item, the former's price may be twice the latter's. It is for the same reasons that publishers of photo-offset reprints of out-of-print books are apt to set the price of their offerings not at the level at which copies have recently changed hands but well above it. The convenience of being able to order the item from a list is worth the premium.

Everyone agrees that the supply of books is declining, particularly in traditionally collected fields. One English dealer writes:

> Books that one bought quite often in, say, 1945, and even in 1955, now seldom turn up. I find it almost impossible to replace the key books in education, philosophy and literature of the 17th and 18th centuries. 17th century poetry has virtually disappeared, 18th century poetry is fast following suit. Bound volumes of quarto or folio miscellaneous verse of the 18th century turn up far less frequently. It is awful to think that at Murray Hill's we practically threw away uninteresting late quartos! There has been a marked increase in interest in the poetry of the 19th century. I imagine that a great deal of the latter was destroyed in the salvage drives of the last war, and good copies of even obscure poets are becoming harder and harder to find.

And another English dealer offers this confirmation:

> When I began to form the Ian Fleming collection some thirty years ago, I was able to find a very large number of extremely rare items, none of which has appeared on the market at all in recent years despite the greatly increased interest in the subject. For my own amusement and eventually as a business proposition, I completed a collection of contributions which won the Nobel Prize in the various departments of science and medicine. Five years ago I was asked to repeat this and had to give it up, simply because the material was quite unfindable.

Yet despite such declarations, most dealers sturdily maintain that their stocks have been steadily improving since 1945. This is not the impression of collectors, who speak sorrowfully of the scarcity of interesting items on dealers' shelves. It is maintained, indeed, by an English collector who speaks with particular authority that if the index number 100 is assigned to dealers' stocks in 1945, today's index number should be 20. These divergent views may perhaps be reconciled by taking into account the factor of turnover. Sales records for 1945 and 1965 would in the cases of most dealers show a greater number of interesting books sold per month in the latter year. The difficulty is that these books don't remain on the shelves very long; indeed many of them never get there at all, since the dealer has an immediate purchaser for them.

The current sellers' market has not only made dealers prosperous, it has also played its part in greatly enhancing their status in the rare book world. One of the most successful writes:

> We are at the point where we are able to decide who shall have first refusal of any really fine or important book that we have. The customers who have consistently patronized us and have allowed us to participate in the development of their collections in such a way that we have a personal interest and pride, are the ones we favor. Quite naturally we incline towards the ones who exhibit the friendliest attitude toward us and who have not objected to our taking a reasonable profit. More and more, the rare bookseller today is closely involved with the collector and the institution, almost to the extent of being an authorized agent. He very often exerts himself to bring important gifts of collections and individual items to institutions and concerns himself to see that the collections he assists in forming shall be outstanding and that the cost shall be advantageous to the customer wherever possible. Such close relationships are the outstanding new development, in my estimation, in the field of rare book collecting.

No one who remembers what rare bookdealers had to endure in the quarter of a century following 1929 will begrudge them today's prosperity and enhanced status. But like most good things, these have their undesirable by-products. Dealers no longer have the leisure which was once theirs for gaining a scholarly mastery of the books in which they specialize. Moreover, dwindling supplies may mean that they see fewer copies of these books, though their diminished oppor-

tunities in this respect are probably more than compensated for by
the greatly increased availability of authoritative bibliographies.
Several collectors commented that today's dealers, with a number of
admired exceptions, seem disinclined to help the beginner or indeed
the small collector generally. They are not so willing as they once were
to take pains in finding cheaper and less significant books. It seems
unlikely that today's younger generation of collectors is receiving the
careful nurture from dealers that luckier collectors of the past have
received.

A charitable explanation of this seeming aloofness is offered by the
critical shortage of staff in the rare book business. To the question:
"how are recruits found for the rare book business," most dealers re-
sponded that they wished they knew. Reporting that untrained young-
sters were of little value to them, they saw the best prospects in knowledgeable collectors becoming booksellers. I also asked the dealers
among my respondents if they would advise a young friend to enter
the trade. Most replied in the affirmative, but with many qualifications. Some said that dealers are born, not made; if a young man has
to ask for advice, he probably lacks the necessary dedication. Others
stipulated that he should love books, have a flair for bibliographical
detail, and display marked business acumen. Most pointed out that
unless he had the very considerable capital now required to strike out
on his own, he would have to reconcile himself to several years of
apprenticeship on a low salary. Not a few were haunted on his behalf by the specter of 1929. He would be at a disadvantage, thought
one old hand, "because everything inclines him to the view that the
prices of books move only upwards and that all you have to do is to
buy a book, mark it at any margin of profit that you think fit, and wait
until that margin is arrived at." Another added: "I would warn him
that while money is loose at the present, there is no tougher game than
the rare book one during a depression."

Since the prospects thus sketched hardly suffice to guarantee a supply of new dealers, perhaps there should be joint action on the part
of existing dealers to remedy this staff shortage. Mr. Raymond Kilgariff has recently written in an English book-trade journal:

> Is it not time to consider the introduction of a concerted apprentice
> scheme? Each year one or two selected trainees could be engaged

and given the opportunity of working for a year or two at a time in
some four or five different and diverse businesses. They could be
given just the kind of thorough grounding it is impossible to get at
present. Surely it is not beyond the capacity or will of most firms to
join in initiating such a programme. And surely it would not put at
hazard the security of any to make this modest contribution to the
common good.[6]

With their vastly greater numbers and resources, American rare bookdealers would presumably find such a scheme even easier to imple-
ment.

IV

The fundamental condition of life for rare book librarians has already been suggested in section II: an immensely increased concern
for rare books on the part of the institutions for which they work.
Theirs has become very much a scarcity field. Many rare book librari-
anships are unfilled, some in major institutions; and a number of re-
tirements are impending. The backlog of rare book or "special collections" cataloguing in some libraries can only be computed in terms of
years. A decade with the present staff is the estimate at the University
of Texas, where Mr. Ransom has recently appealed for recruits between the ages of 21 and 35. There is a scarcity even of personnel
competent to supervise the use of rare books. The rare book librarian
of a great eastern university writes as follows of his campaign to add
a trained assistant to his staff:

> There does not seem to be any supply of rare book librarians. We
> have a good one, new this year. But we fought and kicked and
> screamed and bled and died in order to get him. He had nine offers
> other than this one, and all of them were good. And we were com-
> pelled to move into a very high salary bracket in order to get a satis-
> factory man.

It was inevitable that this shortage should develop once the need
for rare book personnel became widespread, since there is no organized
system for recruiting such individuals and no established pattern for
training them once they have been recruited. A casual observer might
assume that this was the proper business of the country's numerous

[6] *Ibid.*, p. 6.

and thriving Schools of Library Science. But in point of fact only marginal attention is paid to such training in these schools, the students in which are for the most part not the sort to have much inclination towards rare books. A leading advocate of keeping rare book librarians firmly within the frame of the library profession offers this candid summary of the situation:

> The recruitment and training of rare book personnel is generally as satisfactory, or perhaps I should say as unsatisfactory, as is the situation for medical library personnel, law library personnel, and other library specialists. It's a tough business, and one that we share with other learned professions these days. Competition for the best young people is extremely keen at the point of pulling them into graduate training programs whether for medieval studies or for rare book librarianship. And the more exacting you make the requirements, the more vexing you make the recruitment program.

My respondents, who were mostly librarian-administrators rather than administrator-librarians, tended to favor the recruitment and training of rare book librarians outside of library schools, though none of them doubted that along the way the student should pick up some familiarity with the sort of information which library schools provide. "A good man can be made better by education in a bibliographically oriented library school," was the summary of a veteran in the field, "but I must say that most of the American library schools are not such." It was the general belief that the best foundation for a career as a rare book librarian is a B.A. degree in the humanities, preferably in literature or history. This should be accompanied or followed by immersion in books, either through book trade or library work experience. A respondent wrote:

> I am old-fashioned enough to think that you should work for your Leah to get your Rachel. There is nothing that makes one more book-wise than handling, cataloguing, leafing through, feeling, and smelling books. The more books you have seen and can remember, the better bookman you are. And then there is learning where to get a piece of information you need. Next to knowing something, knowing where to find it out is paramount. All this takes time, and can't be taught in so many courses a week in library school.

As much graduate work as possible in the fields of scholarship which particularly interest the trainee was also advocated. "It is from an atmosphere of learning and of bookish interests, and from a milieu in which there is respect for knowledge for its own sake, that we will get bookmen and rare book librarians. . . . We do not need any more people than we have already who may know how to hold a book without cracking it but who do not know how to read."

Considerable doubt was expressed as to whether a formal graduate program appropriate to the needs of rare book librarians could be developed, since course work in the eyes of most observers is not the answer. Frequently mentioned as the most promising development in the field was the "internship" provided for three years at the Lilly Library for two library school graduates each year. Those who completed this program had their choice among excellent and well-paid jobs. Funding for it was private, however; and when the money ran out, Indiana University did not transfer the program to its own budget. There is some hope that it may be revived, perhaps without the stipulation that recruits should have library school degrees.

Even if programs on this pattern were put into operation at several major rare book libraries, however, they would supply only a trickle of trained librarians. Moreover, these would be persons whose unusual background justified fairly exalted expectations. There would still be no provision for the hewers of wood and drawers of water who are now needed in large numbers. Unless this demand subsides, which is unlikely, something like mass production methods appear to be required, and we would accordingly seem to be driven back to the library schools as the only educational organizations equipped to provide training on so large a scale. This may explain in part why a library school cadre for training in rare book librarianship was insisted upon by those among my respondents who are administrator-librarians rather than librarian-administrators.[7] The subject is on the agenda of the Rare Book Section of the A. L. A. for its meeting in July 1965. It should be an interesting session.

To what sort of career can a recruit to rare book librarianship look

[7] On the whole subject of rare books in libraries, see Robert Vosper, "A Rare Book is a Rare Book," *University of Tennessee Library Lectures: Numbers Seven, Eight, and Nine* (Knoxville, 1957), pp. 43-62.

forward? What are his prospects with regard to salary, status, and a chance to move up the ladder? There is general agreement that the head of a major rare book collection should experience little difficulty in making his mark. He stands for his library, which after a time is usually envisioned in his image, and in any event he is often a considerable person in his own right. Such talents do not go unrewarded in our society. Admittedly he is viewed as a staff rather than a line officer, who is not usually thought of in connection with top administrative posts in general libraries, but then he is rarely the sort of person who would be interested in such posts.

Rare book cataloguers also enjoy a favored position. Whether or not they have the doctorate, the knowledge that they need to perform their tasks competently often extends well beyond Ph.D. requirements, and they have clearly earned their place in the community of scholars. Indeed, it is often a problem to provide adequate remuneration for them within the existing hierarchy of library salaries. Comparing them to the technicians without whom scientific work could not proceed, Mr. Ransom has recently asked whether the $17,000 a year expert glassblower in the laboratory should not have his counterpart among cataloguers in the library.

The position and prospects of other subordinate librarians in major collections and principal librarians in minor collections are far less certain. Salaries vary greatly, and it was suggested that in particular "the old, old institutions pay very badly." Since rare book librarians are not fully assimilated in the library profession, their status is apt to be, not exactly inferior, but peripheral. In provincial institutions some prejudice may even linger on against them as odd persons engaged in precious pursuits. It was pointed out, however, that outside the profession the rare book librarian enjoys compensations for his ambiguous rank within it.

> This may be true because of the more glamorous aspects of rare book librarianship, because of the greater opportunities to be closer to the scholarly and academic worlds, because of the greater intimacy with the book trade, the bibliophilic world, the philanthropic world; it may be because a great many rare book librarians are not professional librarians; it may even be because most rare book librarians are men and not women.

There was sharp difference of opinion as to whether a rare book librarian is better off when his department is an integral part of the general library or when it is virtually an *imperium in imperio*. On the one hand it was argued that "enhanced status for rare book librarians will come most effectively through continued programs to improve the general status of librarians within the academic community." They would then be part of a substantial and well-organized group to which university administrators listen attentively. On the other hand it was maintained that rare book librarians should make common cause with faculty members. There should be provision for them to teach part time, and they should be encouraged to devote themselves to research. Their salaries should be competitive with those of faculty members of equivalent experience and accomplishments. Only in this manner, some respondents felt, could the best qualified persons be attracted to rare book librarianship.

It may be so, but a number of the librarians responding regretfully reported their inability to interest many faculty members in what they are doing. Rare books as rare books do not usually fire the academic imagination. I once took a friend of graduate school days who has become a famous literary scholar around my own collection. I produced first editions of the books about which he had written, sometimes in presentation form. I showed him autograph letters and occasional manuscripts. I brought out bindings by Marius Michel and others with inlaid covers, doublures, and gauffered edges. I displayed volumes with engravings by Blake and lithographs by Daumier. But no spark was struck. Just before he departed, obviously feeling that it was only polite to show a somewhat livelier concern than he had thus far manifested, he asked: "May I see that book with the badgered edges again?"

Accommodations for rare book collections differ greatly. The great unaffiliated libraries like the Pierpont Morgan are still *hors concours*; all of their resources can be directed to a single purpose. Among university libraries, the size and standing of an institution offer uncertain guidance to its provisions for rare books. A number of Ivy League and Big Ten universities have splendid rare book buildings; others have arrangements of varying meagerness and inadequacy. With one or two exceptions the south and the west coast offer nothing comparable to the best in the east and middle west. A visiting librarian provides these snapshots of the rare book rooms in the three ranking California universities:

> (1) unbelievable, no room, and no staff, (2) the room is big, but one can't work there with all those undergraduates lying around on the rugs doing their calculus, and the staff seems to consist of one overworked librarian, (3) well lighted, but cramped, and there just isn't room for any staff.

Even the largest and most luxurious rare book libraries, moreover, are rapidly running out of space. If they are in big universities, of course, this does not necessarily mean that they are neglected. They may merely be sharing the common fate at a time when resources are so limited in comparison with needs that new quarters are almost always too small by the time they are ready for occupancy. In any event, as one librarian remarked not without irony, they can always console themselves with the thought that unmet needs in housing "are a sign of health and strength, not weakness."

The work of a rare book librarian consists of acquiring materials, cataloguing them, seeing that they are properly taken care of, and supervising their use. Something must be said about at least the first of these activities. The emergence of a distinct rare book acquisition program has come late in the day in many libraries. A librarian who has guided his institution towards such a policy sums up the arrangements formerly prevailing as follows:

> Of course some libraries say they don't *want* a budget for rare books, that such a budget introduces a false category. Allocate funds, they say, for history or for literature; for the classics, or the middle ages; for poetry or for chemistry; but not for "rare" books. Build up your holdings, they say, in your various subject fields. Some of these holdings, a few of them, will turn out to be costly, scarce, or irreplaceable. Put these in your rare book room. Regard them as high quality parts of your general collection. But acquire them because they are parts of your collections, not just because they happen to be expensive. This notion, I believe, is gradually disappearing.

When a rare book library is established as a separate activity, there remains the question of where funds can be found for its acquisition budget. In many private universities the conviction still prevails that this kind of purchase cannot be justified out of the income of endowed funds. Such institutions must rely on gifts, even if these gifts are closely guided by the library staff. Thus Harvard and Yale may be said to lead a hand-to-mouth existence with respect to rare book acquisitions, though it must be admitted that in these instances at least the hand is never far from the mouth. In an increasing number of state universities there is substantial provision for rare book purchases in the general library budget. Gifts are welcome, of course, but in many state universities they have not been forthcoming. Hence other arrangements had to be made.

Opinions differed greatly as to the wisdom of current rare book acquisition policies. No one questioned the desirability of building up rare book collections in the country's major research libraries, but considerable doubt was expressed as to whether the many would-be imitators of these libraries which have emerged in recent years could succeed or indeed ought to succeed. Some of these late comers were accused of muddying the waters by their intense competitiveness, their preoccupation with public relations rather than scholarship, and their indiscriminate purchases of inferior material at excessive prices. A recent English visitor to most of the larger rare book collections in the United States offered these observations:

> Leaving aside the very proper functions of a library of having enough books of various periods accessible to stimulate interest, and dealing with gifts of special collections which need proper handling and backing-up with reference material, we come to the rare book library as a serious scholarly organization. In this respect, a collection of first editions is of very little value these days. Anyone who considers editing a text now will start with a Xerox master copy and collate that with as many copies as he can find or thinks worth while: so, while the presence of an original on the spot is useful, it's by no means essential. And when one comes to putting a work in context, what one needs is a really big collection which will include a lot of contemporary material (often rarer than the "rare books," but not usually housed in rare book collections) and modern journals and critical works. On this basis, I would say that the only really fruitful rare book collections in the U. S. A. are at the Library of Congress and the New York Public Library; Folger, Huntington,

and Newberry; Harvard and Yale; U. C. L. A., Illinois, and
Texas. I think that's about all. I well remember asking a rather
distinguished professor at a university which you might expect to see
on my list how he found its rare book collection. "Never use the library here," he said. "Always save up my problems for Harvard or
the B. M. It's much quicker and less frustrating."

An answer to this indictment, I suppose, would be that rare book libraries, like every other element in our universities, are going through
a process of upgrading imposed upon them by powerful and irrevers-
ible forces. A number of American libraries have become "serious
scholarly organizations" only in the last twenty years. Presumably a
good many more will reach that status during the next twenty. Who
can prophesy with any certainty today which ones they will be?

V

We have seen that, though rare book dealers and librarians have
their irritations, these irritations are for the most part growing pains
which can be cheerfully borne. Unhappily this is not true of collectors.
The majority of those responding felt that their opportunities had
contracted sharply during the past twenty years. Ground by the upper
millstone of a diminishing supply of books and the nether millstone
of overwhelming institutional buying, today's collector is apt to think
of himself as the forgotten man.

The decline of the private collector has been most marked in England, the very country which was once his particular preserve. Consider, for example, these reflections on past and present:

> I was brought up in a collecting atmosphere where the collector was
> first and foremost a university scholar and teacher in English litera-
> ture who collected on the side in his particular specialty or specialties.
> He probably was not a rich man, and he might be a very poor one,
> but he was still able to collect since supply was ample and price mod-
> est, and his specialist knowledge and interest gave him certain ad-
> vantages. Oxford was full of such people—H. F. B. Brett-Smith,
> Colonel Wilkinson, Hugh McDonald, Percy Simpson, and a host
> of others. The previous generation had been even richer in such men.
> They still exist today, and I can think of half a dozen spread out
> amongst English universities, but every one is aged at least 55. The

opportunity for the current young English don has almost disappeared, at least for the period up to 1750. Cost and availability are so forbidding that most people would be put off from even trying.

Taxation, the high cost of living, the need to provide for the education of one's children—all this has left most potential English collectors with little money for the purchase of rare books. Two respondents among English collectors were particularly trenchant on this point. One remarked flatly that "institutions will end by buying out collectors." The other was convinced that "the ordinary collector is being priced out of the market," though he at least was able to add, "Luckily I've got most of the books I want!"

Things are not yet so desperate in the United States, where collectors continue to offer effective opposition to institutional buyers in certain areas. Several dealers insisted that, if they now look to institutions for bread and butter, they still rely on collectors for caviar and champagne. For books of association interest, copies in extraordinarily fine condition, and "high spots" generally, collectors remain their best market. Indeed, most collectors of considerable means were reasonably sanguine about prospects for the future. Some of them even find present difficulties exhilarating. When one road is blocked, they take another, broadening their interests as circumstances make necessary. One such collector asserted: "I continue to find enough material each year to exceed any reasonable budget I might set myself."

The most plaintive collectors were those who specialize in early books. They have found themselves virtually driven into retirement because the material in which they are interested comes into the market so seldom and is so expensive when it does appear. One of these unfortunates, who now finds himself pretty well restricted to binding up disbound quartos which he had once expected to replace with better copies, sees his only hope for the future in the widespread adoption by libraries of a policy of selling their duplicates,[8] and he doesn't think this is likely to happen.

Most concern was expressed, however, about the young man of

[8] On this controversial topic, see Robert H. Taylor, "Bibliothecohimatiourgomachia," *Papers of the Bibliographical Society of America* XLVIII (1954), 230-38.

modest resources who has the desire and the knowledge to collect. In the past he was able to make his way by zealously searching the shelves of general antiquarian bookstores, using time to supply the place of means. We have already seen what these establishments have become. How many young collectors of the present generation will be able twenty years hence to match the following history provided by a recruit of the last generation?

> My own collecting activities, if I may dignify so smallscale an operation by so flattering a name, have taken place almost entirely during the fifteen years that began in 1949 with my entering graduate school a short hour's train-ride from the second-hand bookshops of New York. There I spent my spare change (mostly appropriated from the food budget; I can remember often a whole day spent on 4th avenue, spending 8 or 10 dollars on books, and a few pennies for chocolate from the subway vending machines) for three years, mostly buying English and American fiction of the last 100 years, mostly in poor condition, mostly from the "special" sale tables, 10 and 25 and 35 cents apiece. Suddenly, after about three years, I had everything that could be obtained from such sources, that I wanted. Fortunately I entered the army about then and spent three years at Fort Devens, Mass. On weekends I dealt handsomely with the Boston bookshops, the low-priced ones like Starr's, and spent the vast sums of a private's and corporal's monthly pay on books that cost a dollar, a dollar and a quarter, a dollar and a half. Back in graduate school, between 1956 and 1958, with GI bill, a good fellowship, and my newly acquired wife's pay (or a portion of them) at my disposal, I filled out my author-collections by paying a little more at places like Seven Gables, and began ordering a great many more books from catalogues. I suppose that I had bought around 15 of Ellen Glasgow's 23 books at an average of a dollar apiece, by the time I left service in early 1956. Two years later I had bought all but two (the collections of verse and stories) at prices up to $3.50, I should guess. To duplicate this modest achievement now would require a lot of time and, I should think, three times the money that I spent.
>
> My two best collections are Faulkner and Churchill. I should think that the Faulkner is probably one of the 10 or 12 best in the country, though I am not sure; the Churchill perhaps one of the half-dozen best, though I'm much less confident of this. I could not even contemplate making a real Faulkner collection today, though I began this one in 1956, well after the palmy, pre-Nobel Prize days. (If, in

1949, I had just spent my money on Faulkner instead of Hemingway, Dreiser, Hawthorne, and so on!) I spent $70 for my *Marble
Faun* in 1958; $22.50 for my limited, signed *The Unvanquished* in
1960; and nothing more than $12.50, so far as I recall, on any of
the others. It would probably take $3,500, judiciously spent, to re-
place my "prime" items—the first editions and limited signed issues,
and I might spend a decade, and three or four times the very modest
sum originally spent, in building up my important working collection of second and subsequent printings of the books. With Churchill
the market rise has been even more recent and spectacular. I began it
only five years ago, substantially completed it by two years ago, and
I could not think of starting such a collection today.

Young collectors of this sort have thus far provided the continuity of
book collecting. It would be distressing to think that their day is over.

Under the circumstances which I have described it is only natural
that collectors should allow themselves an occasional quip about the
institutions and the dealers who make the pursuit of their avocation
so difficult for them. One collector, for example, offers the following
proposal for rectifying matters as far as libraries are concerned:

> First, that all rare booksellers give private collectors first offers of
> all books, and for a 10% discount on price; second, that all libraries
> should pay a surcharge of at least 10% on list prices; third, that those
> libraries which have sold duplicates to an adequate degree should be
> exempted from any surcharge and may even be allowed a discount:
> fourth, that those libraries which refuse to disgorge duplicates pay
> an extra surcharge ranging between 25% and 50% depending on
> the proportion of their duplicates which remains undisgorged.

Another collector finds an epitome of the stoic resolution with which
he and his fellows are facing their unhappy fate in W. E. Henley's
"Invictus." He suggests applying the second stanza of that poem to
the most price-happy dealers:

> In the fell clutch of [*name of dealer to be supplied*]
>   I have not winced or cried aloud.
> Under the bludgeonings of [*name of second dealer to be supplied*]
>   My head is bloody but unbowed.

Another source of complaint concerned a side effect of the very
federal income tax provision which has proved so powerful an in-

centive to American private collecting. As gifts have become a major source of institutional acquisitions, librarians have grown more and more aggressive in seeking them. After a particularly blatant approach, from which anxiety not to be forestalled by a competitor has banished all delicacy and restraint, the harassed collector may long to refer his tormentor to Hamlet's remarks to Rosencrantz and Guildenstern in the passage beginning: "Will you play upon this pipe?" (III, iii) But the collector restrains himself. He knows that the library's emissary is not really a Rosencrantz or Guildenstern, that he is acting indeed from the most commendable and disinterested of motives. The collector only wishes it were more generally realized that "Ask, and it shall be given you" is a text to be used with the most careful discretion.

All of the collectors whom I questioned were veterans. They had little consciousness of young collectors as individuals, but expressed a general sense that such persons must be around. They agreed that the young collector could still make his way, even under current conditions, if he would act as a trail blazer and let institutional buyers come plodding after him. For the most part he should avoid fields covered by standard histories and authoritative bibliographies, though it might from time to time be worth his while to go back to a field once fashionable but now fallen into neglect. Books that illustrate the history of a significant subject were particularly recommended. Here is how one experienced collector developed this theme:

> I started collecting Panama Canal material a few years ago, and without even trying I've accumulated quite a bit of excellent material at extremely modest prices. Yet I feel that this is just as much a part of Americana as any other, and in some ways more exciting. Business Americana is another field. The origin and rise of the computer is another. Space exploration another. Civil rights provide a new and vital field of interest.

It was suggested that young collectors back their hunches with regard to contemporary authors of substance (Louis Auchincloss, Saul Bellow, Anthony Powell) or presently unappreciated authors of the past (Cabell, Carlyle, Ruskin, Stevenson, Edith Wharton). But there were also warnings against modish writers (Salinger, "the Beats," "the Angries"). Finally, the futility of attempting the impossible was neatly brought home by a respondent who advised against collecting "Anglo-Saxon manuscripts, Chaucer letters, presentation copies of Elizabethan plays in original stitched condition, and proof sheets corrected by Milton in his later years."

VI

I come at last to prices, a dangerous but inescapable subject. They constitute the tension point at which all the conflicting interests which have been described meet head on. When a key book changes hands at an announced figure, a moment of truth has occurred, and slight adjustments are required throughout the rare book world. Price can determine profit or loss for the dealer, success or failure for the librarian in charge of an institution's acquisition program, and satisfaction or frustration for the collector. It is not surprising that they sometimes generate heat.

Three years ago Mr. William Rees-Mogg, City Editor (in American parlance, Financial Editor) of the London *Sunday Times*, offered a price index for his field of collecting, English literature of the eighteenth century. Taking 1945 as his base of 100, he claimed "a rise to 135 by 1950, to about 250 by 1958 and to about 400 by 1961."[9] During this period eighteenth-century English literature moved from a neglected to an actively cultivated area, and its curve presumably showed a sharper rise than that for rare books generally; but their movement as well has undoubtedly been upward.

In the three years since the appearance of Mr. Rees-Mogg's calculations, a much more rapid escalation of the general price index has occurred. Indeed, we seem to be moving towards a new way of regarding prices, at least for books of unusual interest. The traditional conception of a prevailing market price, or "prix honnête" as the French call it, is disappearing. Only in such areas as private press books, where examples come along with some frequency and don't differ much from copy to copy, can it be said to survive. The acquisition of a volume of particular interest by a dealer is apt instead to become the occasion for negotiation between him and a favored customer. A growing recognition of this situation has led with increasing frequency to sudden spurts in the prices realized at auction or proposed in dealers'

[9] "A Collection of 18th-Century Literature," *Book Collector* x (Winter, 1961), 423.

catalogues. This is sufficiently disorienting when books are known to be rare and desirable, but it is even more disturbing when books of far more dubious claims are caught in the same upward spiral. Such seemingly arbitrary pricing has given rise to a widespread sense of uneasiness among collectors and librarians alike.

A dealer of long experience suggested another way of viewing this development. As he sees it, the conception of a standard market price has never been appropriate for rare books. By their very nature rare books are a scarcity field in which the supply of goods is unpredictable. They cannot be manufactured to meet increasing demand, unless indeed one adopts the methods of T. J. Wise, which in any event are presumably not susceptible to routine application. In the depression decade from 1929 to 1939 and during the unsettled fifteen years between 1939 and 1954 a special situation prevailed. For the time being the supply of desirable books exceeded the demand. Under these exceptional circumstances something like standard prices established themselves for titles which frequently changed hands. But as the world's economy readjusted itself after the Korean War, demand once again came greatly to exceed supply. Thus we have simply returned to normal with regard to the pricing of rare books. Some confirmation of this theory is offered by the speculations of a collector who is also a publisher.

> The glut of books upon the market in the 1930's combined with lack of financial resources on the part of libraries and collectors alike gave the impression of ample supply. It only needed a relatively small increase in demand to tip the scale from "ample supply" to "extreme unavailability." The same thing can be seen in the case of new books published in the 1930's. Many of the most important collected works and editions then published sold scarcely at all for years and were eventually remaindered. They are now so scarce that they fetch extraordinary prices; yet if they were reprinted today it is quite possible that relatively few copies or sets would be bought of the reprint. This not only illustrates the narrow margin between glut and scarcity, but also the contradictory psychological impact on buying habits of availability and non-availability.

Whatever the merits of this theory, there can be no doubt that many collectors and librarians regard the spurts in price of the last few years as leaps into the wild blue yonder. To test opinion on this subject I

listed the prices at which 49 first or significant later editions in English
and American literature of the last two centuries had been offered by
dealers or had sold at auction during 1964 and 1965. In each case I
had selected the price because it seemed high to me, but I did not tell
this to the collectors, librarians, and dealers whom I asked to assign
these prices to four categories: high, reasonable, low, and no opinion.
Thirty-two of my questionnaires were completed, 16 by collectors
and librarians and 16 by dealers. I shall shortly comment on the results, which are tabulated in Appendix II, but first I shall cite some
of the general reflections offered by my respondents.

A collector who saw, but did not complete, the questionnaire found
"the prices uniformly high, some of them shockingly so." A librarian
wondered if "what almost seems like mad money has not wiped out
the meaning of value and substituted price." Another librarian offered
the "forlorn contention" that buyers should decline to pay extremely
high prices. "Enough rejections will make dealers refuse to pay high
prices to their sources, and the sources will cease to expect the kind of
profit that now dazzles everyone. Otherwise, I see no solution except
paying more and more for less and less." Still another librarian wrote:
"All you can be sure of with regard to prices is that you are going to
be shocked. You read a catalogue, you laugh helplessly, you call in
your friends and ask them to share your incredulity; you say 'never
me,' and then, maybe a few weeks later, you buy the book, recognizing that if you want it, you have to pay the dealer's price." This conclusion was confirmed by a library administrator, who wrote: "The
prices for individual book titles on your list are realistic in today's
market. Whether we think they are low, reasonable, or high, these
are the kinds of prices we will have to pay if we want the books."

As was to be expected, dealers took a more measured view of the
subject, though even they on occasion expressed indignation at the
overpricing of certain categories of books. Faulkner's works were the
target of two veteran dealers. "I have, against *The Marble Faun* at
$1,000 entered no opinion," wrote one. "This is not honest because I
think the price is a lunacy so great that I cannot trust myself to comment on it." The other developed the same theme in these terms:

> I think the prices paid for men like Faulkner, Hemingway, and
> Fitzgerald are outrageous. Last year the limited edition of *Go Down,
> Moses* [100 copies, 1942] fetched $600. I can remember only three

or four years ago marking the book $27.50, with no wild scramble for it. I think you will see the day when the book will once more be marked $27.50. Again last year I watched a *Marble Faun*—a lousy book of verse, so admitted by the author—fetch $1,700. A month later I purchased the *editio princeps* of Aristophanes (1498) for $900. Something is wrong with this picture.

Two English respondents offered contrasting comments on the rationale of pricing.

> I find your list difficult to complete, [wrote one,] because I am a cagey old bookseller who, on seeing that another dealer asks £245 for *Pride and Prejudice*, at once thinks it is bloody dear, and then wonders whether it is the copy he was underbidder on at £160, and finally feels that if it is very fine he would probably price it higher. I hope you see my difficulty. Perhaps a book is worth what you ask for it if you can sell it.

For the second dealer, however, another consideration was important: "I still rather like a book to go where I feel it belongs and would rather offer it to my customer at the price I think reasonable than, perhaps, catalogue it at a very much higher price and leave a free for all."

To show concretely the situation which faces today's dealers, I persuaded the proprietors of the Seven Gables Bookshop to provide me with an analysis of the response to their recent catalogue *First Books by American Authors*. This was by no means a run-of-the-mill catalogue. Starting with what the Seven Gables Bookshop had in stock, perhaps 15 per cent to 20 per cent of the eventual total, Mr. John Kohn for two and a half years sought out additional material. The whole assemblage was then meticulously described and attractively presented. When 1,500 copies of the catalogue went out to potential customers, there was good reason to expect a satisfactory response.

In the event the response was better than satisfactory. The catalogue contained 324 items. In the month following its appearance 985 orders were received, including at least one order for all except 14 items. A table analyzing these orders by source and price range appears on the opposite page. Mr. Kohn had not intended to offer bargains, yet for 12 of these books there were eight or more orders apiece. Even for the most expensive items, those offered at $250 or

TABLE

An Analysis of Orders for Items in *First Books by American Authors*
Seven Gables Bookshop, 1965

Price Range	Number of Items	Number and Percentage of Orders from						
		Collectors		Libraries		Dealers		Total
— $15	103	92	25%	249	67%	26	8%	367
$16 – $34	86	52	24%	152	71%	11	5%	215
$35 – $74	67	53	26%	128	62%	26	12%	207
$75 – $249	46	41	31%	75	55%	19	14%	135
$250 – ———	22	23	38%	27	44%	11	18%	61
Totals	324	261	27%	631	64%	93	9%	985

more each, there was an average of nearly three orders per item. What is Mr. Kohn to do when he gets his next copy of Saul Bellow's *The Dangling Man* (c. 1944) for which there were 17 orders at $12.50, of Hart Crane's *White Buildings* (1926) for which there were 13 orders at $30, of Gertrude Stein's *Three Lives* (1909) for which there were 11 orders at $60, of Tom Wolfe's undergraduate essay *The Crisis in Industry* (1919) for which there were 8 orders at $350, or even of *The Marble Faun* for which there were 3 orders at $1,000? He will have to reflect that if 17 people want a book at $12.50, there may well be two or three of them who will pay several times that sum for it. If three people want a book at $1,000, at least one of them may still be interested at $1,500.

The analysis of orders is revealing in other ways. Though libraries accounted for 64 per cent of the orders, a figure which should not surprise us in view of the dealers' estimates recorded earlier in this paper, collectors came increasingly into play as prices rose, until in the category of items priced at $250 and up 38 per cent of the orders came from them. Nor were orders from other dealers negligible. They accounted for 9 per cent of the total, and for 18 per cent in the most expensive category.

With this background we are better prepared to understand the response to the questionnaire on prices which I have already described. I have quoted the critical remarks of collectors and librarians about the general level that they exemplify. Yet when these 16 collectors and librarians set down their opinions about the 49 individual prices listed, 37 per cent were judged reasonable or low and only 49 per cent high. Concerning the remaining 14 per cent the respondents recorded no opinion. These percentages differ substantially from those for the 16 dealers who filled out the questionnaire: 44 per cent reasonable or low, 36 per cent high, and 20 per cent no opinion. But they do not support any contention of overwhelming skepticism.

Various explanations of this discrepancy suggest themselves. To an experienced buyer judging a price is an eminently practical operation. What he is willing to pay is based on his estimate not only of the absolute importance and scarcity of the book, but also of the intensity of current demand for it. Moreover, both collectors and librarians are typically in the process of completing collections that are already well begun. Satisfaction at high prices for books in hand to a certain extent

mitigates dissatisfaction with high prices for books still to seek. It is
perhaps significant, however, that only 3 per cent of all prices listed
were considered low.

The books covered by the inquiry fell into three groups: nineteenth
century, transitional, and modern. Certain broad discriminations were
made by dealers, collectors, and librarians alike in their evaluation of
current price levels in these three categories. Relative confidence was
expressed in 20 nineteenth-century books by such authors as Jane
Austen, Coleridge, Dickens, Hardy, Melville, Thoreau, Whitman,
and Wordsworth. Percentages in this category were 35 per cent high,
45 per cent reasonable or low, and 20 per cent no opinion. Stronger
faith was manifested in the nine books in the transitional group. These
included *The Old Wives' Tale*, *A Shropshire Lad*, *Of Human Bondage*,
and *Look Homeward, Angel*, the prices of which have for the most part
declined since their heyday 30 or 40 years ago. Percentages in this
category were 36 per cent high, 54 per cent reasonable or low, and 10
per cent no opinion. Doubt was most pronounced concerning 20 titles
by such leaders of the modern literary revolution as Eliot, Faulkner,
Hemingway, Joyce, Dylan Thomas, and Yeats. Percentages in this
category were 53 per cent high, 31 per cent reasonable or low, and
16 per cent no opinion.

A few responses to individual titles deserve comment. At least
three-fourths of those who expressed opinions concerning *Lamia* in
boards at $1,000, *Leaves of Grass* at $1,500, *Of Human Bondage* at
$125, and *Look Homeward, Angel* at $100 thought these prices reasonable or low. At the other end of the scale were Richard Hengist
Horne's "farthing epic" *Orion*, an unquestionably rare book which
was almost forgotten until Mr. Hayward included it in his catalogue
of *English Poetry*, at $150; *The Marble Faun* at $1,000; Graham
Greene's ineffable first book of verse, *Babbling April*, at £42; the
Limited Editions Club *Ulysses*, a book issued in an edition of 1,500
copies, nearly all of which have certainly been preserved, at £265;
and two publications by Yeats, *Eight Poems* (1916) at £75 and *Poems*
(1949) at $170, issued in editions of 200 and 375 copies respectively.
No more than six of the 32 respondents thought the prices for any one
of these reasonable or low. Indeed, everyone who expressed himself
concerning *Babbling April* found its price high.

What conclusion can be offered concerning the vexed subject of prices? In his *Essay on the Principle of Population as it Affects the Future Improvement of Society* (1798) the Rev. Thomas Robert Malthus proposed to maintain population in equilibrium with food supply by persuading mankind to observe the preventive check, deferral of marriage until the achievement of economic independence, in order to avoid the operation of the positive checks, disease, war, famine, and vice. As the world's present dilemma sufficiently demonstrates, neither the one check nor the others have operated with much efficiency. Yet somehow mankind has muddled through. Since the acquisitive instinct is certainly as strong as "the passion between the sexes," which was Malthus' decorous way of referring to the reproductive instinct, I suspect that anyone setting himself up as the Malthus of bibliophily would find his fulminations, too, falling on deaf ears. The preventive check of refusing to buy at excessive prices is beyond weak collecting nature, and the positive checks of a collapse of values on the pattern of 1929, the elimination of tax deductions for contributions to libraries, and so on, are unlikely to occur. But once again we shall probably muddle through.

*   *   *

The prosperous and exciting rare book world which I have described does not need a declaration of independence, which it already enjoys, but a declaration of interdependence. If I were asked to summarize the points of danger within it which promise trouble for the future, I would emphasize the following addition to excessive prices: that there is no satisfactory system for recruiting and training either rare book librarians or dealers; that the prospects facing young and impecunious collectors are discouraging; and that the acquisition policies of a good many institutional libraries are naïve in conception and inept in execution. But I would do this without much belief that these trouble spots could be cleaned up, except perhaps the recruitment and training of rare book librarians and dealers, because in so incoherent a situation, where so many conflicting interests are at play, there is no way of organizing effective action.

Yet at the same time I would also call attention to some sentences in Tocqueville's *Democracy in America*. Though they were written nearly 130 years ago, they remain applicable to the problems just mentioned as well as to more important dilemmas of modern American life. "Democratic liberty is far from accomplishing all the projects it undertakes with the skill of an intelligent despotism. It frequently abandons them before they have borne their fruits, or risks them when the consequences may prove dangerous; but in the end it produces greater results than does any absolute government. It does fewer things well, but it does a greater number of things."[10] So it is possible to look forward with some confidence to what will emerge from the vital if wasteful profusion of today's rare book world.

APPENDIX I.

Names of Respondents

The persons listed below sent answers to my inquiry. Those whose names are marked with asterisks also received and completed my questionnaire concerning prices. Messrs. Kohn and Papantonio collaborated in filling out a single questionnaire.

Abbey, Major J. R.	*Gordan, John D.	*Nowell-Smith, Simon
*Adams, F. B., Jr.	*Graves, Harold E.	Osborn, James M.
*Austin, Gabriel	*Hayward, John	*Papantonio, Michael
*Barrett, C. Waller	*Healey, George H.	*Powell, Lawrence Clark
Bond, William H.	Horblit, Harrison D.	*Randall, David
Brett-Smith, J. R. B.	*Howell, Warren R.	*Smith, Wilbur J.
*Cahoon, Herbert	Keynes, Sir Geoffrey	Strouse, Norman H.
*Carter, John	*Kohn, John S.	Taylor, Robert H.
*Colbeck, Norman	*Lazare, Edward	*Todd, William
Downs, Robert B.	*Magee, David	*Tolley, William P.
*Duschnes, Philip C.	*Massey, Dudley	Vosper, Robert
*Edelstein, J. M.	*Meriwether, James	Wainwright, Alexander D.
Fleming, John	*Metzdorf, Robert F.	Wolf, Edwin, II
Foxon, David	*Miller, A. T.	Wolff, Robert Lee
*Gallup, Donald	*Muir, Percy	*Wreden, William P.
*Goodspeed, George T.	*Muirhead, Arnold	*Zeitlin, Jacob
	Murphy, Franklin D.	

[10] Quoted by John Stuart Mill, *Dissertations and Discussions*, 2 volumes (London, 1869), II, 29.

APPENDIX II.

Opinions concerning Recent Prices

(The prices below were taken from dealers' catalogues or auction sale records during 1964 and early 1965. They were for good copies, in original condition except where noted.)
(H—High, R—Reasonable, L—Low, NO—No Opinion)

Title	Price	Opinions of Dealers				Opinions of Librarians and Collectors				Totals			
		H	R	L	NO	H	R	L	NO	H	R	L	NO
I. 19th Century													
Austen, *Pride and Prejudice*, 3 vols., 1813, contemporary calf	£245	5	10	1	–	7	6	–	3	12	16	1	3
Coleridge, *Poems*, 1796, contemporary calf	£85	4	9	2	1	7	6	–	3	11	15	2	4
Dickens, *A Christmas Carol*, 1843, first issue	$350	5	5	2	4	4	8	–	4	9	13	2	8
——, *David Copperfield*, 20 as 19 parts, 1848-1850	$425	5	6	2	3	7	4	–	5	12	10	2	8
Godwin, *Caleb William*, 3 vols., 1794, contemporary calf	£95	8	6	–	2	4	6	1	5	12	12	1	7
Hardy, *The Trumpet Major*, 3 vols., 1880	£45	5	8	1	2	6	7	1	2	11	15	2	4
G. M. Hopkins, *Poems*, 1918	£30	2	9	1	4	4	8	–	4	6	17	1	8
Richard Hengist Horne, *Orion*, 1843	$150	10	2	–	4	9	2	–	5	19	4	–	9
Keats, *Lamia*, 1820	$1000	1	11	–	4	5	7	1	3	6	18	1	7

Title	Price	Opinions of Dealers				Opinions of Librarians and Collectors				Totals			
		H	R	L	NO	H	R	L	NO	H	R	L	NO
Melville, *Narrative of a Four Months' Residence among the Natives of a Valley of the Marquesa Islands*, London, 1846 [the first edition of *Typee*]	$275	3	8	1	4	10	4	1	1	13	12	2	5
Meredith, *The Egoist*, 3 vols., 1879	£50	4	9	–	3	5	8	1	2	9	17	1	5
Southey ed., *The Annual Anthology*, 2 vols., 1799-1800	£66-10	8	5	–	3	8	4	–	4	16	9	–	7
Stevenson, *New Arabian Nights*, 2 vols., 1882	$200	7	6	1	2	9	4	–	3	16	10	1	5
Surtees, *Handley Cross*, 17 parts, 1853-1854	£140	7	6	–	3	7	2	–	7	14	8	–	10
Thoreau, *A Week on the Concord and Merrimac Rivers*, 1849	$450	3	7	–	6	7	6	–	3	10	13	–	9
Trollope, *Orley Farm*, 2 vols., 1862	$250	8	4	–	4	9	3	–	4	17	7	–	8
Twain, *Huckleberry Finn*, London, 1884	$85	2	10	3	1	5	10	–	1	7	20	3	2
Whitman, *Leaves of Grass*, 1855	$1500	–	11	1	4	4	10	–	2	4	21	1	6
———, *Leaves of Grass*, 1860/1	$75	4	7	1	4	4	5	2	5	8	12	3	9
Wordsworth, *The Prelude*, 1850, ½ mor.	$75	8	4	2	2	5	8	1	1	13	12	3	4
Totals		99	143	18	60	126	118	8	68	225	261	26	128
Percentages		31	45	6	18	39	37	3	21	35	41	4	20

Title	Price	Opinions of Dealers				Opinions of Librarians and Collectors				Totals			
		H	R	L	NO	H	R	L	NO	H	R	L	NO
II. Transitional													
Bennett, *The Old Wives' Tale*, 1908	$175	5	7	1	3	9	6	–	1	14	13	1	4
Conrad, *Almayer's Folly*, 1895	$125	4	10	–	2	11	5	–	–	15	15	–	2
Galsworthy, *Jocelyn*, 1898	$175	10	5	1	–	9	5	1	2	19	10	1	2
Housman, *A Shropshire Lad*, 1896	£85	3	12	1	–	7	7	1	1	10	19	2	1
Masefield, *Salt Water Ballads*, 1902	£48	6	8	–	2	10	6	–	–	16	14	–	2
Maugham, *Of Human Bondage*, 1915	$125	2	11	2	1	5	7	1	3	7	18	3	4
Shaw, *Cashel Byron's Profession*, 1888	$125	6	9	–	1	3	10	–	3	9	19	–	4
Synge, *The Playboy of the Western World*, 1907	$50	2	11	–	3	5	6	3	2	7	17	3	5
Wolfe, *Look Homeward, Angel*, 1929	$100	1	10	–	5	5	9	–	2	6	19	–	7
Totals		*39*	*83*	*5*	*17*	*64*	*61*	*5*	*14*	*103*	*144*	*10*	*31*
Percentages		27	58	3	12	45	42	3	12	36	50	4	10
III. Modern													
W. H. Auden, *Poems*, 1930	$75	5	6	–	5	6	8	–	2	11	14	–	7
Eliot, *Prufrock*, 1917	£80	7	9	–	–	8	7	1	1	15	16	1	1
——, *Ara Vus Prec*, 1919	£65	7	7	1	2	7	5	1	3	14	12	1	5
Faulkner, *The Marble Faun*, 1924	$1000	7	2	1	6	13	–	1	2	20	2	2	8
——, *The Mansion*, 1959, one of 500 signed copies	$50	6	4	–	6	13	–	2	1	19	4	2	7

Title	Price	Opinions of Dealers				Opinions of Librarians and Collectors				Totals			
		H	R	L	NO	H	R	L	NO	H	R	L	NO
Frost, *A Boy's Will*, 1913	$500	3	11	1	1	11	4	1	–	14	15	2	1
Graham Greene, *Babbling April*, 1925	£42	12	–	1	4	13	–	–	3	25	–	1	7
Hemingway, *In Our Time*, Paris, 1924	$650	5	6	1	4	8	7	–	1	13	13	1	5
——, *Three Stories and Ten Poems*, Dijon, 1923	$500	5	5	2	4	10	4	1	1	15	9	3	5
Joyce, *Dubliners*, 1914	$130	7	5	–	4	5	9	2	–	12	14	2	4
——, *Ulysses*, Paris, 1922	$425	8	5	1	2	8	6	1	1	16	11	2	3
——, *Ulysses*, 1935, illustrated and signed by Matisse	£265	10	2	–	4	10	3	1	2	20	5	1	6
Salinger, *The Catcher in the Rye*, 1951	$75	6	5	–	5	13	2	–	1	19	7	–	6
Thomas, *18 Poems*, 1934	$185	5	6	1	4	9	4	1	2	14	10	2	6
Williams, *A Streetcar Named Desire*, 1947	$50	4	2	–	10	10	5	–	1	14	7	–	11
Yeats, *The Secret Rose*, 1897	£22-10	9	3	1	3	9	7	–	–	18	10	1	3
——, *In the Seven Woods*, 1903	£24	9	4	–	3	9	6	–	1	18	10	–	4
——, *Eight Poems*, 1916	£75	10	1	1	5	11	3	1	2	21	4	–	7
——, *New Poems*, 1938	$35	7	4	–	5	8	7	–	1	15	11	–	6
——, *Poems*, 2 vols., 1949	$170	10	2	–	4	12	3	1	–	22	5	1	4
Totals		142	89	8	81	193	90	13	24	335	179	21	105
Percentages		44	28	3	25	60	28	4	8	53	28	3	16
Cumulative Totals		280	315	31	158	383	269	26	106	663	584	57	264
Percentages		36	40	4	20	49	34	3	14	42	37	4	17

The Serpentine Progress of the STC Revision

By KATHARINE F. PANTZER*

BEFORE I wind into my subject, here are a few preliminaries. The STC revision has been under way for about eighteen years, having been officially started by William A. Jackson and F. S. Ferguson sometime in 1949. I joined the staff in September 1962 toward the end of the letter *L*. Professor Jackson died in October 1964 when *Q* was finished, and I have been in charge since. The revision has now reached nearly a quarter of the way through the letter *T*. Recently I checked the work my part-time assistant, Mrs. John C. Critics, had done on John Taylor, the Water Poet. The last Taylor number is 23817, and with the last number in STC being 26143, we have revised 91 percent of the entries.[1] We have 2,326 entries left to do—approximately two years' work at our present rate.

My other assistant, Miss Suellen Mutchow, who works full time, has just finished going over the Almanac section in detail. The final draft was very complicated for this section, the typescript having been finished in 1950 and numerous manuscript additions arrowed-in since. We decided an extensive reëxamination was necessary. One of the results was that separate Prognostications, which had been scattered throughout the regular run of STC entries, have now been moved to

---

* Read at a meeting of the Society at The Pierpont Morgan Library, New York City, 26 Jan. 1968.

[1] This was on 26 Jan. 1968. We are now, in early June, at 24055 and 92 percent complete.

the Almanac section. This has made coping with "title page only" Prognostication fragments simpler, and you will find the section altogether easier to use (although I doubt that the pages of the Almanac section will ever be well thumbed!) Now Miss Mutchow is starting to look into the rest of letters *A-C* to find out what amount of retouching is necessary to make it legible printer's copy. We hope that most of this can be done by xeroxing and pasting.

Right away one of the more trying problems of the revision crops up: the problem of consistency. Professor Jackson's conception of methods sharpened over the years. The title transcriptions became fuller. We started describing format more accurately, distinguishing, for example, between ordinary 4°, 4° in 2s, 4° in 6s, 4° in 8s, 4° in alternate quires of 8s and 4s, 4° with perpendicular chainlines. I think it interesting to see what information this kind of format description reveals. 4° in 2s suggests the products of a physically small-sized press, and occasionally Scottish publications will have this format. 4° in 6s suggests incunables or very early sixteenth-century books. 4° in alternate 8s and 4s suggests slightly later sixteenth-century books— about 1505 to 1535, and particularly from the press of Wynkyn de Worde. 4° in 8s suggests a reprint of a popular standard item such as romances, navigation manuals, sermon collections, and so on. 4° with perpendicular chainlines suggests the period circa 1605-15 when a few printers like Edward Allde and William White printed a few editions or parts of editions of popular items, like plays or Samuel Rowlands' poems, on halfsheets of double-sized paper.[2] The result is occasionally called 8° in 4s, but since the result is like ordinary 4° in size, design, and proportions, Professor Jackson decided to call it 4° with perpendicular chainlines. The real 8° in 4s, that is, usual 8° size, design, and proportions but printed in halfsheets, seems to have been used from about 1530 to 1580, and even then it is relatively rare for normal publications. Some of the Marprelate and John Penry tracts of the late 1580s are probably in this format because amount of type and size of press were limited by the necessity of traveling light to keep ahead of the authorities. Although what I have just said about

---

[2] I have since noticed Allde using this format as early as 1592 (STC 22894) and Thomas Cotes as late as 1635 (STC 22339), but the bulk of its use is quite early in the seventeenth century.

format is not based on any statistics, I think my observations are fairly accurate.

Indeed, no sooner had I finished writing this section of my talk than Miss Mutchow brought to my attention Laurence Anderton's "Progenie of Catholics and Protestants," 4°, *Rouen, the widow of Nicolas Courant*, 1633 (STC 579). Professor Jackson had altered the format from 4° to 4° in 2s. Now this struck me as interesting, as I am unfamiliar with Continental printing in general and have not examined much recusant printing, so I looked at the film of the Bodleian copy which Miss Mutchow had on the reader. What was immediately noticeable was that the page and type-area proportions (fairly tall and relatively slender) were those of folio rather than 4°. By using the measurement gauge at the beginning of the film and comparing the results with the measurements for the McAlpine copy at Union Theological Seminary, I found the copies measured a little over 9 x 6½ inches or 23½ x 16½ cm. This is smaller than the average folio but taller than the average 4°. The film was too beautifully made, alas, to show any chainlines in the paper, and I have not yet had a chance to make personal examination of a copy. If the chainlines are perpendicular, there is no question that the book is a folio. If the chainlines are horizontal, that is, normal for a 4°, as I think they must be from Professor Jackson's examination,[3] I wonder if this is not another case of double-sized paper cut in halfsheets and ought not be called folio with horizontal chainlines rather than 4° in 2s. If the printer approached the design and execution of his work in terms of folio in every detail except that of his paper stock, I think an annotated folio designation would be more appropriate. I should be interested to hear your comments.

To return to the improvements in STC technique: we began putting subtitle or colophon imprints in parentheses, leaving only the first or general title-page imprint and/or date plain in the entry. We started making more of an effort to track down printers where their names do not appear, and assigning particular sections of the text when two or more printers were involved. I shall be saying more about this later on. We are also trying to make our occasional notes about variations

[3] The Folger copy, described by Dorothy E. Mason, and the Sion College copy examined by me this spring have horizontal chainlines.

among copies more intelligible. For example, instead of saying copies vary in the dedication and leaving it at that, we now give the name of the dedicatees and the location of at least one copy of each variant. This will help those who can't tote around a copy of F. B. Williams, Jr.'s, *Index to Dedications* as well as the STC.

The early letters in the revision cannot be totally gone over again and brought up to the current standard, but we hope that in the process of copyediting we can incorporate some of the improvements. However, do not rely on there being uniform improvement from *A-Z*: too many different persons with various amounts of bibliographical training have helped so that the entry for a unique sermon by Zumelius at Whatnot Cathedral which neither Professor Jackson, nor F. S. Ferguson, nor I had a chance to examine personally, though it is described to us in a letter by a most willing Canon-Librarian, may not be as accurate as that for a sermon by Ahazuerus of which Harvard has a copy or film. The Anderton item I mentioned in terms of format is another example. So farewell consistency! I hope, however, that the revision will always be intelligible. And I have come to the conclusion that the problems presented by the revision are so various that a totally consistent solution for all of them is impossible.

Now it will be fun for me to give a few illustrations of what I mean by the "serpentine progress" of the STC revision—or possibly it could better be called the "tangled web" of the revision.

I was working my way through the John Taylor entries recently when I came to an unrecorded prose broadside at the Society of Antiquaries in London (number 233 in Robert Lemon's catalogue of the collection, STC 23741+) "Christian admonitions, against the two fearefull sinnes of cursing and swearing," *Eliz. Allde for Henry Gosson*, [n.d.]. Since Professor Jackson had acquired for the STC office at Houghton Library negative photostats of all the STC period broadsides in the Lemon catalogue, I went over to look up number 233 to check the transcription. The looseleaf binder opened at number 234, an unrecorded Church of England Visitation Articles for the Archdeaconry of London, without imprint or date, but with a woodcut initial letter *I* which I had noticed quite recently when looking up something else. I couldn't remember who the printer was, so I looked to see what we had in the revision. All we had supplied was [*London*, n.d.], and the item was added between a broadside Visitation Articles at the British Museum printed by John Windet in 1585 (STC 10268) and another unrecorded broadside in the Lemon catalogue printed by the Royal Printing Office and dated 1617 in manuscript. Since I knew the printer was identifiable, I tried to remember where I had seen the initial and was able fairly soon to find it again in a book printed by Thomas Purfoot in 1636 (STC 15099) which showed a crack in the bottom of the *I* in a more damaged state than in the Visitation Articles. Then I noticed that Archdeaconry of London Articles from 1620 to 1631 were printed by Purfoot, though they were all in 4°, but that there was a broadside without imprint and dated in manuscript 1634 at Marsh's Library in Dublin (STC 10271). We had entered the two Lemon broadsides next to one another and distinguished between them, but we had not noted a method of distinguishing them from the Marsh copy. I looked back in the Marsh correspondence and found a letter of October 1958 in which Miss Mary Pollard gave a description of the Marsh copy which tallied closely with the Lemon Purfoot broadside, but the Lemon Articles ended with the instructions: "You shall bring your Presentment into Mr Hulets Office at the west end of old Fish street" while the Marsh copy stipulated "M^r. Dawsons office in Carter-Lane."[4] Now I had a printer and a means of distinguishing the text; what remained was supplying a date. The Lemon broadside was 1636 or before because of the state of the woodcut initial. Later I found the same initial in F. S. Ferguson's collection of initial-letter facsimiles of which Professor Jackson obtained a copy for the STC office, where the example was dated 1606 and had no damage to the *I*. The Lemon broadside was so close to Marsh's in wording and so different from the 1617 broadside that a date fairly close to the Marsh manuscript 1634 seemed reasonable. I have, therefore, supplied the date [c. 1630], which roughly covers the time 1625-35. It should be possible for someone to find out when Mr. Hulet was in office and so date the Articles more exactly, but I feel I have come close enough.

Having finished making a new entry for the Visitation Articles, I wound back to Lemon 233 and continued with John Taylor. After verifying the title transcription, I altered Mrs. Critics' suggested date of "after 1628" to "c. 1630." 1628 is the year Edward Allde died and his widow Elizabeth, whose name was in the Taylor imprint, took

---

[4] I have since examined the Marsh copy and believe it to be printed by Thomas Harper, though this will need checking.

KEY TO THE FIGURES

1621-32 the Eliot's Court Press had as partners: J. Haviland, G. Purslowe, and E. Griffin

fig. 1 Apostle *A*

> 6272+ A. Darcie, "Theatre de la gloire," 4°, [*London,* 1626] L. WAJ suggests W. Stansby. KFP inclines to Ed. Allde.

*C3^r 23725 [Eliz. Allde] 1630

fig. 2 Small Arabesque *T*

A3^r 23574 Eliz. Allde, 1630

*B5^r 23725 [Eliz. Allde] 1630

p.1 5850 E[liz.] A[llde] 1631

fig. 3 Large Factotum

A1^r 24058 [Eliot's Court Press] 1629

*E2^v 23725 [Eliz. Allde] 1630

fig. 4 Small Factotum

I4^r 4277 [G. Purslowe] 1628

B1^r 4279 E[liz.] A[llde] 1630

*F5^r 23725 [Eliz. Allde] 1630

fig. 5 Criblé *I*

*H3^v 23725 [Eliz. Allde] 1630

A4^r 17712 [?] 1633

> FSF attributes to J. Beale. KFP attributes quires B to the end to T. Cotes; quire A unattributed.

fig. 6 *I* with cornucopias

*A4^r 23762 [Ed. Allde] 1622

B1^r 18631 E[liz.] A[llde] 1631

D11^v 24398 [G. Purslowe] 1631

Ddd2^v 21094 [This part by Eliot's Court Press? or R. Oulton?] 1638

O4^r 10078 [This part by Eliot's Court Press? or R. Oulton, c. 1640]

fig. 7 Large Arabesque *T* with dents

A1^v 18454 [Ed. Allde] 1599 (with top dent but not the diagonal one)

B1^r 18532 [Ed. Allde] 1607

B3^r 23763 [Ed. Allde] 1613

*A3^r 24058 [Eliot's Court Press] 1629

fig. 8 Large Ship Cut

A2^v 23763 [Ed. Allde] 1613

*A1^v 23753 J. Haviland, 1627

A1^r 23734 E. P[urslowe] 1640

fig. 9 Small Ship Cut

tp 22795 [Ed. Allde] 1608

tp 21005 Ed. Allde, 1610

*tp 23753 J. Haviland, 1627 (the Harvard copy has the date cropped and clumsily added in ink)

---

* = example illustrated from Harvard copy

WAJ = W. A. Jackson

FSF = F. S. Ferguson

KFP = K. F. Pantzer

FIG. 1

FIG. 2

FIG. 4

FIG. 3

FIG. 5

FIG. 6

FIG. 7

over his shop. Because medial *u* as in "haue" and "giue" is used in the
Taylor broadside, and because medial *v* began coming into use around
1635, it seemed to me that the circa date was more informative than
the "after" date and certainly easier to put in an index.

As I mentioned earlier, one of the very recent improvements in
STC is to indicate what portions of a text are the work of each printer
where two or more are involved. John Taylor's folio *Works* of 1630
is a case in point. Although the imprint states only "I. B. [that is, John
Beale] for James Boler, 1630," Elizabeth Allde and the two partners
Bernard Alsop and Thomas Fawcet also shared in the printing. We
had a collation by F. S. Ferguson in which he assigned the various
portions: quires A, Aa-Ss, and 1st Aaa-Kkk to Beale; quires B-O to
Elizabeth Allde; and 2nd Aaa-Mmm to Alsop and Fawcet. The Beale
and the Alsop and Fawcet sections had recognizable and characteristic
ornaments and initials, but the section Dr. Ferguson attributed to
Elizabeth Allde had a rather shabby assortment of initial letters—
certainly not what I normally think of as Allde initials. Consequently
I looked some of them up in Dr. Ferguson's facsimiles, which I have
occasionally annotated and added to. Of about six initials that I looked
up, I found examples of only two. One was an "apostle" *A* with twelve
circles in the top border (fig. 1). Many printers had "apostle" alphabets, usually distinguished by their borders. John Beale had an *A*
with eleven circles in the top, and the Eliot's Court Press had one with
thirteen circles, but I had never been aware of one with twelve circles,
nor did I associate "apostle" initials with Allde at all. Dr. Ferguson's
example was from an unrecorded STC 6272+ Abraham Darcie's
"Theatre de la gloire et noblesse d'Albion," 4°, [*London*, 1626],
unique at the British Museum. Dr. Ferguson had not ventured to
make a printer attribution. Professor Jackson had been bolder, as I discovered in checking the revision, and had suggested William Stansby.
Now, as will appear shortly, I have no confidence that anything used
by Elizabeth Allde in 1630 was in her shop before or after 1630. But
Stansby did not have an "apostle" alphabet either, and I can't tell
what it was that suggested Stansby to Professor Jackson.[5] The second

---

[5] There is no microfilm of this item yet available, and regrettably I forgot to examine
it this spring when I was at the B.M. The item may have a headpiece with a woman's
head, cornucopias, and snakes—a cast-metal ornament which both Stansby and Allde had.

initial I found was a small T with diagonally shaded arabesques (fig. 2), which I had added to Dr. Ferguson's collection because it resembled in general character other specimens of T with which I had had trouble. The example I had noted was in a book printed by Elizabeth Allde in 1630, so that it confirmed Dr. Ferguson's attribution. I then got xeroxes of most of the initials in the Allde section of Taylor's *Works*, snipped them out, and continued examining other Taylor items. I noticed that some of the woodcuts of sailing ships which Edward Allde had used to illustrate books around 1610 turned up in a different Taylor item with imprint *John Haviland for Henry Gosson*, 1627 (STC 23753; figs. 8 and 9). The large factotum (fig. 3) I had noticed at the Folger last November when I was looking ahead at the STC books there. It was in a copy of Hobbes's translation of Thucydides, folio, [*Eliot's Court Press*] *for Henry Seile*, 1629 (STC 24058). The same first quire of the Thucydides with the factotum also had a T (fig. 7) which I had always associated with Allde, but it was used again in quire Pp, and since the whole of the Thucydides seemed to be the product of one press, I was a good deal puzzled. This T has a dent in the cross bar. I call it a "dent" because it is virtually certain that this was a cast-metal letter since several other printers had identical specimens. Allde himself had a second, and they both appear in the outer forme of quire B in STC 23763, Allde 1613. This particular one, however, received a "dent" first in the cross bar and then a diagonal one on the right-hand side extending through the stem of the T (this last portion not visible in the reproduction).

Then I went looking for the small factotum (fig. 4) and found it, to my dismay, in a book printed by George Purslowe in 1628, as well as in another book by Elizabeth Allde in 1630. The criblé I (fig. 5) was found in a book the printing of which Dr. Ferguson attributed entirely to John Beale, but after examination, I believe quires B to the end to have been printed by Thomas Cotes, though I am unsure whether to attribute the first quire to Elizabeth Allde.[6] The first quire, however, is very probably by a printer different from that of quires B to the end. Finally I remembered an I (fig. 6) which had passed from

[6] I have since come across this I in two books: STC 10752, *John Waley*, 1557, and STC 22159 *John Waley*, n.d. but probably close to 1557. Unfortunately Waley was a publisher rather than a printer, and I have so far been frustrated in my attempts to identify the printer. Whether, if I identified the 1557 printer, I would be able to trace how the I crept into Elizabeth Allde's hands is another matter.

Fig. 9

Fig. 8

the Allde shop to Eliot's Court Press sometime in 1631. Confusion! I was not then and am not now able to make any satisfying sense out of these demonstrable movements of initials, cuts, and factotums. It is not as if in a single year Mrs. Allde had sold a certain part of her stock to the Eliot's Court Press, for the years differ, and at least the two factotums seem to move from Eliot's Court Press to the Allde shop. I can summon up the vision of an aspiring journeyman printer who was buying worn-out stock to have something for starting out in business by himself and who worked both for Mrs. Allde and for the Eliot's Court Press, but this solution leaves me acutely unhappy as there is not much one can learn about anonymous journeymen. It may be that an exhaustive examination of all the books printed by the Alldes from 1625 to 1635 and all the books in the same time span put out by the Eliot's Court Press as a group and by its members individually would yield some sort of rational explanation. But I do not have the time to make that kind of study. If anyone here wishes to take up the problem, he may do so with my blessing, if only he will send me a copy of the results.[7]

A different kind of confrontation, this time primarily with dates, arose out of my meeting in London in June of 1966 Miss Leba Goldstein, who was working on cataloguing the ballads in the Pepys Library at Magdalene College, Cambridge. I asked her if she had seen the ballads in Manchester Free Reference Library, of which Professor Jackson acquired photostats for the STC office. When Miss Goldstein answered no I offered to send her a xerox of our typed list of contents.

When I returned to Houghton, I xeroxed the list, and then when I saw that it gave only titles, I started to leaf through the photostats, adding imprints and dates to the list where they were present. While most of the ballads were after 1640, there were several that qualified for STC, and I began trying to estimate dates. I mentioned before that around 1635 printers began to use medial v instead of medial u. About this time also type ornaments (printers' "flowers") changed from large and relatively lacy designs to blacker, blunter, and usually

---

[7] In proofing the galleys for this article and verifying references, I took a closer look at STC 21094, R. O[ulton] 1638. In addition to fig. 6 this book also has fig. 2 (G4^v) and fig. 4 (I2^v) along with a number of Eliot's Court Press initials and ornaments. I do not know what the nature of the collaboration was, but Oulton, the son of Elizabeth Allde by a former marriage, is surely the culprit I was looking for.

smaller designs. My general impression is that in ballads these new styles were late to be introduced because the broadsides were popular items aimed at a lower-class audience which wanted its ballads to look the way they had always looked. Besides, there was not much incentive to use fresh new stock on things as ephemeral as ballads. I should, in any case, be glad to allot to Mr. Wing all black-letter ballads with medial *v* and the heavy type ornaments that are not definitely 1640 or before from the imprint, contents, dated heading, or other verifiable factors. I don't think STC would be cheated of many items, and at least we would have a definite set of criteria for parceling out ballads between us.

A case in point is the *Ballad of Chevy Chase*, of which the original STC listed no editions. There are two editions of it among the Manchester Ballads. One is nearly complete, has medial *v*, small dense type ornaments, and the imprint: *Printed for E. Wright dwelling in Gilt-spurstreet*, [n.d.]. This edition had been added to STC with the supplied date [c. 1625] since the ballad had been entered to the Ballad Partners, including Edward Wright, on 14 December 1624. The other Manchester edition was more damaged, having only three out of the five columns of text. Its imprint was gone and there were no type ornaments, but it had medial *u*. This edition had not been added to STC.

There was a third edition of the ballad in Volume I of the Pepys Ballads, of which we have negative photostats in the STC office thanks to Hyder Rollins, who acquired them for his edition of the Pepys Ballads. This edition had *Printed for H. G.*, that is, Henry Gosson, who was also one of the Ballad Partners and who died in 1641. This edition had the lacy kind of type ornament and medial *u*, and it had been entered in the STC revision with the date [c. 1630].

Being able to compare the texts of the three editions, I noticed that the Pepys and the Manchester "Wright" editions shared readings which differed from those in the Manchester defective copy. Since the Wright edition was the latest of the three with its medial *v*, I drew the conclusion that the defective copy was the earliest. I have given it the [c. 1625] date though it could well be earlier than that. As for the Wright edition, I checked in Professor Jackson's annotated *Printers' Dictionaries* (Edward Wright was unfortunately omitted from the

printed text of both the McKerrow and Plomer dictionaries) and discovered that Edward Wright's address was given as "near Christ
Church Gate" in 1615-21. It so happens that Edward Wright sold
many of John Taylor's works, and Mrs. Critics recently added a note
that Wright's address in 1640 (STC 23809) was still "near Christ
Church Gate." While it is *possible* that Edward Wright had two shops
at the same time before 1640, I am not going to believe it unless someone can show me a book dated 1640 or before with the Giltspur Street
address. And in the meantime I am happy to hand over to Mr. Wing
all Edward Wright ballads with the Giltspur Street address which I
can find lurking in the revision.

I suppose some of you may be wondering whether all this fuss over
printers and publishers is worthwhile. It certainly is one of the major
reasons why the revision snakes back and forth as I have shown by
winding in and out of John Taylor. I can only answer that for me it is
a kind of compulsion—I like to catch the printers with their ornaments and initials showing: a bibliographical Peeping Tom, so to
speak. And the justification for it is twofold. First, the revision will
be a more accurate tool; and second, the results will be made available
in a new Printers' Index on the same plan as Paul Morrison's for the
old STC, and the new Index will be ready at approximately the same
time that the revision itself is published. Mrs. Critics, who is doing the
main work for the Index, and I had a short-lived flirtation with a
7094 computer before deciding to make the Index manually, that is,
on handwritten slips of carbonized NCR paper to be sorted by hand.
You might enjoy a short account of our experiences.

Harvard seems to have computers spattered around most of the
streets of Cambridge, and it was not until the third address Mrs.
Critics and I visited that we found someone who was neither horrified
by the tremendous number of variables that would have to be pro-
grammed nor desirous of initiating us into the full complexities of
how a computer could work on a hundred other projects in addition to
ours. But at last we did find some meeting of the minds and began de-
vising a pattern whereby the necessary information could fit into a
scheme of 80 characters on a punch card: 15 characters for the STC
number, 30 for the printer's or publisher's name, 6 for the date, 14

for a place of printing other than London, 13 for a category indication (verse, play, sermon, catechism, law, history, etc.) and 2 for a code symbol indicating a forged, false, or quixotic imprint. (For a forged imprint see STC 20304, of which there are now two editions, one genuine, printed by Joseph Barnes at Oxford and having the device McKerrow 336 on all title pages—at L³, O, F, HN, HD—the other forged by George Eld, though with the same imprint, and with McKerrow 338 on all title pages— L, O¹⁰. STC 22897 *Basle, T. Emlos* has a false imprint, as the "printer's" name is the "author's" name backwards. The Marprelate tracts offer a number of quixotic imprints, e.g. STC 17456 *Printed in Europe, not farre from some of the bounsing priestes.*)

I think that most of you can see already that the greatest obstacle to computerizing STC whether one thinks of titles or only of printers' and publishers' names, is that everything in the entry is transcribed in "yᵉ olde spellynge" (except for the i, j, u, v nightmare). This meant that the poor old computer would have frightful indigestion coping with, say, Richard JONES, JOHNES, or JHONES, unless we fed it gold-plated pills in the form of a very expensive and complex program, or unless we standardized the spelling of each name before it was punched on the card. Mrs. Critics and I had foreseen this problem and thought we could xerox the typescript of the revision, annotate it, and color-code it: printers' names in red, dates in blue, and so on. So Mrs. Critics selected fifty STC entries from the draft to cover a number of typical problems, color-coded them, standardized the spelling, and we handed the pages over to the computer people.

The first results were rather exhilarating. We could actually ask for a printer's name and a particular year and end up with a group of STC numbers. However, when we began to be more exacting in our requests, particularly in the matter of supplied printers or circa dates, we found that we had not provided accurately enough for the complexities. Though it would have been possible to overcome the difficulties, by that time we had spent $400 in programming charges, $34 in key-punching charges for the fifty items, and $62 in charges for computer time in producing the trial printouts.

At that point we decided to cut our losses and settle for handwritten slips. They take very little more time to prepare than color-coding and standardizing the typescript, and when they are done and sorted, we have something we ourselves can read and use and correct as we continue to compile information, and we have it right in the STC office rather than half a mile away. For the time being Mrs. Critics is sorting slips only for printers and publishers. She may have time at the end to sort for places of printing other than London. When that is complete and typed up like Morrison's index, it can be published immediately. We shall then decide if there is enough interest to make worthwhile sorting and typing a second index according to date, that is, all books printed within a given year, and a third index by category. I hope there will be a demand, but that lies beyond the immediate effort of the STC revision.

I hope I have given you a fair idea of the type of work that goes on in the office. It is really exciting and challenging. While I have held the main stage this afternoon, I wish to make clear that the work of the revision is possible only through the unstinting cooperation we receive from librarians, private owners, book dealers, and scholars all over the world. But the largest indebtedness of the revision, both for supplying about 98 percent of the grist for its mill and for initiating me into the delights of STC research, is to that great scholar and former president of the BSA: William A. Jackson.

Bibliotheca Americana

By C. K. SHIPTON*

THE project of a Bibliotheca Americana exercised a very definite prenatal influence on the American Antiquarian Society. Isaiah Thomas had begun a list of imprints in connection with his *History of Printing,* and in his files of newspapers his pencil marks can still be seen beside booksellers' advertisements. He projected a list of significant books and pamphlets, deliberately omitting such ephemera as his own delightful little volumes of children's literature. Not long after his death there came to the desk of the librarian of the Society, Christopher Columbus Baldwin, the volumes of Robert Watts's *Bibliotheca Britannica.* The sight of these inspired the librarian to carry on Thomas' bibliography, which he said would not be a difficult matter because America had such a short history. Two years later Baldwin was killed in a stagecoach accident in Ohio, and work on the project ceased. It was resumed twenty years later by Dr. Samuel Foster Haven, Jr., son of the then librarian of the Society, and ceased again when he died at the Battle of Chancellorsville. The list was finally published, without having had more critical work done on it, with the second edition of Thomas' *History of Printing.*

There the Bibliotheca Americana rested until 1901, when Charles Evans began anew. He soon found that the American Antiquarian Society was the most helpful of institutions, but our involvement really began in 1908 when Clarence Brigham became librarian. He at once began a systematic campaign of seeking out and buying, wherever possible, every item which would be described in Evans. As a foundation upon which to build he had the strongest collection of early American printing, and by fifty years of work he increased that collection elevenfold. He set up our imprint catalogue to do the preliminary work for Evans and he found the means to finance the later volumes of the bibliography. When Evans died, his work had been carried through the letter O in the year 1799, and I compiled Volume 13, which carried the work through the year 1800. For that volume we saw most of the items we described, but we did not seek

---

* Read at a meeting of the Society at The Pierpont Morgan Library, New York City, 26 Jan. 1968.

470

out others which had been described by careful bibliographers. This proved to be a mistake, not because the other bibliographers were inaccurate, but because their interpretations were sometimes unexpected.

By this time it was apparent that the next step ought to be a revision of the Evans volumes. We were still acquiring not-in-Evans items at an average of one a week. His bibliographical achievements were miraculous for his day, but modern tools made it possible for us to do better. He was, his experience had proved, too trusting. If a bookseller issued a list of books "this day published" Evans assumed the existence of editions of those works with that bookseller's imprint. In the course of the revision of Evans we had to go through most of the newspapers printed in the United States between 1704 and 1800 looking for advertisements which might have been the origin of the ghosts in his work. Frequently his entries are misleading because he loved to reconstruct titles. From nothing more than an advertisement of "Ready Reckoners for sale" he would sometimes create a title with line ends indicated and capitalization and suitable pagination provided.

But how to finance such a revision of Evans? Microfilm of the titles not in the American Antiquarian Society would be prohibitively expensive, slow, and often unobtainable. This was our situation in 1954 when Albert Boni walked into my office with the proposal that the American Antiquarian Society and the Readex Microprint Corporation produce a microprint edition of the full text of everything listed by Evans. He assumed that all of these items existed, and could be located and reproduced without much editing; I saw in his proposal the opportunity to finance a thorough revision of the bibliography. We began work at once, with a promise to the subscribers that it would be completed within ten years with a letterpress, short-title guide or index.

You who have worked with the Early American Imprints sides have been puzzled by some of our methods and inconsistencies, so I would like to make your work easier by taking this opportunity to explain them. When writing for a microfilm, we sent along a target, showing the Evans description of the item, to be filmed in the first frame. When we received the film, we checked the item against the target, and made a new target when corrections were necessary. The revised target was then filmed and sent to the Readex people to be substituted for the original one on the reel, before the microprint was made from it. Because of various accidents, which I shall not stop to explain here, some of these substitutions were not made, so the target and the microprint sometimes do not agree.

At the outset we decided that the purpose of target cards and catalogue cards was quite different, so we designed a form for our purpose. Then it occurred to us, after the printing of the microcards had begun, that the easiest way to make the short-title revision of Evans would be to run the target cards into a single alphabetical order and print an offset volume like the Library of Congress catalogue series. But the format of the Library of Congress cards, particularly as regards corporate authors, was not particularly suitable to eighteenth-century material, so we made our improvements. Then our microprint subscribers began to call for reference cards which could be dropped into their catalogues informing readers that titles were to be had in the microprint series. Thus we had to redesign our targets again so that they could be interfiled with Library of Congress cards.

In the original Evans volumes there are hundreds of errors as to the identity of authors, the commonest one being assigning an item to a man of the same name but different dates. In our revision we have looked at every imputed author, made certain that there was such a man, and that he could have written such a book. At first we quietly revised these author attributions, but as soon as the microprints began to appear, librarians began to write us questioning these changes, so we began the practice of entering on the targets a parenthetical biographical reference under the author's name. Halfway through the project the questioning letters ceased, so we thereafter gave these biographical references only when we were correcting errors in modern bibliographical works, such as the Library of Congress cards.

Taking the 39,000 items of the original Evans as a whole, about one in ten is a ghost or contains a serious bibliographical error. For the period of the 1790s, when he was working against time, one item in three is bad. For each ghost we have placed on the microprints a parenthetical statement explaining the source of Evans' error, and these corrections will appear in the short-title revision. Some of these targets on the microprints have returned to haunt me. In several instances I have traced the source of Evans' entry to a newspaper item of the "just published" sort, have assured myself that there is no other record of such an item, and have printed a target saying the item is a ghost arising from an advertisement in such and such a newspaper, only to have a copy of the alleged ghost materialize and appear on the market after the publication of the microprint. In several instances institutions have assured me that they never had a particular and unique item attributed to them by Evans, and I have written it off as a ghost on the microprint target, only to have it turn up later. We shall catch all of these changes in the revised short-title list.

In the course of the revision we have looked at every item carefully, making sure, for example, that it is a separate work and not a part of a larger one. Evans was misled by the habit of many nineteenth-century librarians, like ours at the Antiquarian Society, of making catalogue cards for articles printed in historical society publications. He was misled by nineteenth-century printed catalogues which sometimes listed items under the half title, the running title, or even the backstrip title. Some are descriptive titles for tract volumes. In the revision we have looked at every title carefully, making certain that such a book could have been written at that time, published in that city by such a printer on that date. Sometimes I have looked at a title many times before I detected the false note. Thus Evans lists a sermon on St. John by one Samuel Gilman, published in 1728. I was aware of that entry for years before it suddenly occurred to me that there was no American minister by that name in 1728, and that few of them would have referred to "Saint" John. There was, of course, Samuel Gilman, the author of "Fair Harvard" who, it turned out on investigation, did publish a sermon on St. John in the year 1828. Evans had been misled by a printer's error in the Antiquarian Society catalogue of 1837. Similarly I was troubled by one "Stephen Seward" of Salem, Massachusetts, when it occurred to me there was no such name in that town. The individual was "Stephen Sewall" of course, the error having originated in a slip of Sam Haven's pen in Civil War days.

Published with Haven's bibliography in the second edition of Thomas' History is a list of "errata" consisting of items which young Sam Haven had set aside as probably ghosts, as indeed most of them turned out to be. Evans could hardly be blamed for accepting them on what appeared to be the authority of Isaiah Thomas. On the other hand, he was too trusting when he assumed in the case of almanacs which were printed occasionally that there were issues for all the intervening years, and when he assumed that a legislature having once started to issue session laws had continued to do so from year to year, although he could find no copies. These ghosts are all the more convincing in that for the almanacs Evans supplied an assumed pagination, and for the session laws he supplied an appropriate imprint.

Evans disliked entering anonymous works under title, so he reached far for authors, and the fact that he did not bracket the names which he supplied has caused trouble. In the revised bibliography we are listing all anonymous works under title as well as under author. This habit of Evans is the largest single cause of what my office called the false-not-in-Evanses, although simple typographical errors in dealers' catalogues provide nearly as many. Over the years, the staff at the Society has decided that nine tenths of the so-called not-in-Evans items which they are called upon to check are simply misdescriptions of this kind.

This will give you an idea of the enormous task of sifting which our associate, Roger Bristol, faced in the preparation of his supplement to the Evans bibliography. Soon after our revision and the Early American Imprints project was announced, John Wyllie called me up and asked what the Bibliographical Society of Virginia could do to help. I suggested the supplement, and he offered to give Roger time to work on it. Our intention was to take Bristol's supplement and continue the Evans numbers through it, revising the targets, and placing them in the alphabetical sequence of the revision. Unfortunately this did not work out. We had, in general, followed Evans' practices, thus placing almanacs under author, whereas, it turned out, the Bristol supplement placed them under title. This and many like differences made it impossible for us to use the Bristol list as it stands, or to file his entries into our already existing alphabetical list without a general revision. Equally serious was the question of inclusion and exclusion. Evans deliberately omitted tickets and printed forms which were intended to be filled out in manuscript. Roger has attempted to include every scrap of print in his supplement. For a while we tried to play along with him on this, since he was doing the work, and as a result our bibliography will contain for the earlier years of American printing ephemera of a type which we had to omit from the later years. Roger's list includes one lottery ticket of a series of which we have thirty; he includes one of a score of varieties or Massachusetts treasurers' notes, and the like. An hour spent in any collection of the manuscripts of a merchant will produce many printed forms and trade cards not described in any bibliography. Bristol's supplement, in short, includes a thin sampling of a vast mass of hitherto unrecorded ephemera.

The question of time also made it impossible for us to wait for the finishing of the Bristol supplement. We had promised our two-hundred-odd microprint subscribers that we would in 1964 place in their hands a bound short-title list which would serve as the index to their boxes, and they had paid their money. As of today, the short-title revision is completed and alphabetized through the number 46,000, and the completion awaits only the receipt of certain film from which we can revise the targets and run them in. Hopefully we shall before spring begin the printing of the revised Bibliotheca Americana; it will fill two volumes the size of the Library of Congress catalogue volumes.

While waiting for film of the Evans supplement items, we have issued in microprint the material listed in the Shaw-Shoemaker bibliography through the year 1805. As Mr. Shaw and Mr. Shoemaker explained when they proposed this work, it is a preliminary bibliography because only a preliminary list could be made now and in the time allotted. It will be invaluable to the people who do the definitive bibliographical work. In editing the entries for microprinting we have found the inevitable errors, and have corrected them on the targets of the Early American Imprints, Second Series. We have found as many as five successive items which were ghosts, many of them simple errors in transcribing dates or imprints in making up the WPA slips. There are as many omissions, the most important group being the college broadsides, which were on neither the WPA slips nor the American Antiquarian Society imprint cards which we loaned to Shaw and Shoemaker. There is no present plan for the revision of Shaw-Shoemaker like the revised Evans.

Looking back on the dozen years of my life which were taken up chiefly by the revision of Evans, I am overwhelmed with a sense of gratitude for the assistance given by people like Roger Bristol and a thousand other employees of four hundred cooperating libraries. My other vivid impression is the absolutely incredible snafu. My demands were a great burden on cooperating libraries, and were of necessity turned over to uninterested subordinates. The heads of two of the great libraries of the world were distressed to hear that at one time their photoduplication departments were four years behind in filling my orders. The camera operators of one of the great European libraries insisted on filming my orders with the camera head reversed, so the text read from right to left, and the order of the pages was 2-1, 4-3, and so on. When I explained the difficulty and asked to have the material refilmed, the operators refused to do my work, and I got no more help from that library. And this was all too common an experience.

Of the thousands of reels of film made for me in other institutions, one third turned out to be unusable, most of them simply the wrong items. This involved long delays and much correspondence. Evans lists a Cambridge, Massachusetts, printing of the *Isle of Pines*, and when the proofs of the list of Cambridge imprints were circulated, five of the major libraries claimed it. It took considerable filming and correspondence to establish the fact that these five Cambridge imprints were ghosts of the well-known English printing.

Or take the case of the alleged Boston printing of the first map of New Hampshire, which Evans credits to an American library. When the film came to me, it was of the London printing. I replaced the order, with explanation, but the library again filmed the London printing. I took my target in hand and went to the library, where I was informed that they had deliberately filmed the London printing because they did not have the Boston one. Indeed, there was no Boston printing; the entry was a ghost. The same library filmed manuscript copies of items which I ordered.

I allowed a year for the filling of each order, and when that time was up, I wrote asking about it. Time and again I was assured that no such order had been received, so I had typed out another set of targets which I forwarded with the request that the originals be destroyed if they turned up. But all too often, a year or so after I had received the film of the second set of targets, the first turned up, and the items were refilmed, and a second set of films sent to me, after the microcards had been printed. One major library had three sets; apparently its microfilm department thought that I would fade away if ignored long enough.

It proved to be impossible to explain to some State Archives our bibliographical needs. One of them could not be brought to film the items which we needed but time and again sent us instead film of the pages of the standard bibliographies on which those items were described.

Law libraries were obliging but fixed in what were for us bad habits. Frequently they filmed the "best" modern reprints of the laws which we ordered. Regularly they omitted the title pages, which we had to battle to obtain.

We examined the pagination of the film of each item to determine the likelihood that it was issued with a half title, and in our record the pagination we reported such pages if they seemed to be indicated. But we did not attempt to obtain film of such half titles because all too frequently our order was filled by filming the upper half or the lower half of the title page. We did battle to obtain film of back matter, such as publishers' advertisements, which was all too frequently omitted by the camera operator, who assumed that we wanted only the text of an item.

There were certain variants of items of which we did not attempt to obtain film, and which will not be distinguished in the revised Evans. For a time the broadside printing of Acts of Congress appeared in two forms, identical except that on one of them there was a line saying that this was printed for deposit in the archives. We simply did not have the time to conduct all of the correspondence which would have been necessary to locate a copy of each form.

May I stress the fact that none of this snafu was due to ill will. Of the five hundred libraries at one time or another asked to cooperate, only three declined. Most of the private individuals who owned unique items were cooperative; here the typical problem was that the last recorded owner had died.

Complaining to you in this manner I feel like the minister who blasts his congregation for not attending church when, obviously, the sinners are the ones not present. Looking over this gathering, I can see many, many people who labored with the utmost good will, and who shared their bibliographical knowledge, to make the revision of Evans better. Many of the jewels of correction in the short-title list record your knowledge rather than my astute detection. The list of cooperators is too long to print in the revision. At present the best that I can think of to do is to say on the title page, "by C. K. Shipton, etc."

Bibliotheca Americana: A Merry Maze of Changing Concepts

By THOMAS R. ADAMS*

AFTER I selected the title of my talk I began to wonder whether Henry Stevens's term "Bibliographia Americana" rather than "Bibliotheca Americana" wouldn't have been more appropriate. But the more I considered the question the more I realized that it is the formation of libraries and not the making of bibliographies which has determined the underlying concepts of the field.

My thesis is that Americana is the collective result of what the individuals who have formed the collections and libraries on the subject want it to be. Let me give you an example. About a year ago the John Carter Brown Library mounted an exhibition at the Grolier Club in New York of some of its most treasured books and maps. This past spring the American Antiquarian Society did the same thing. Some members of the Club felt that this was an unnecessary duplication. As it turned out just the reverse was true. Only five books were common to both shows. Neither of us could deliberately omit the Bay Psalm Book or the Cambridge Platform. Beyond that the two exhibitions told entirely different stories. The Antiquarian Society, traced through books printed in what is now the United States, the development of a nation from the mid-seventeenth to the mid-nineteenth century. The JCB on the other hand, beginning with the fifteenth century, attempted to show some of the major works that reflected the impact of America on western civilization to the end of the colonial period. Here are two collections begun at almost the same time, yet today they stand not as rivals but as allies. I don't want to mislead. Clarence Brigham on the one hand and George Parker Winship followed by Lawrence Wroth on the other, were perfectly capable of going after the same book at the same time, but it was always for different reasons.

In the beginning America was simply a geographical concept. It

* Read at a combined meeting of The Society and The Association of College and Research Libraries (ALA) at The Historical Society of Pennsylvania, Philadelphia, 19 June 1969.

wasn't until a century later that the "Age of Discovery" began to emerge as an identifiable body of literature. The earliest printed list we have been able to find is in Antonio Possevine's *Apparatus* of 1597 which includes sections on the "Indies" and on the "New World." In the 1621 edition of Georg Darud's *Bibliotheca Classica* the term America is actually used but Leon Pinelo's *Epitome* of 1629 returns to the "Indies." It isn't until the publication of White Kennett's *Bibliotheca Americanae Primordia* in 1713 that the America emerges as the standard way of referring to books about the western hemisphere.

With the nineteenth-century *Bibliotheca Americana* becomes firmly established as the term used by those who collected American books. In one form or another it was employed by David Bailey Warden in his catalogues of 1820 and 1831, by Thomas Aspinwall in 1832, and by Obidiah Rich in his catalogues of 1835 and 1844. Then of course there is Henri Ternaux-Compans catalogue of 1837 which for thirty years was the yardstick by which collectors measured their progress.

With the exception of Rich all the above were private collections. Such collections could not have been formed without that essential element the bookseller. I do not know when the first bookseller's catalogue bearing *Bibliotheca Americana* appeared but I suspect it was either French or English. For present purposes, however, I have turned to George McKay's *American Book Auction Catalogues* to see just when the term emerged in the American auction market. It wasn't until 1841 that a catalogue used the term "American Books." 1844 saw the sale of part of the library of the English historian George Chalmers sold as "American History." Then in the following year Leonard's in Boston issued a catalogue bearing the title *Bibliotheca Americana*. The books came from the stock of the New York firm of Bartlett and Welford. In 1846 there was a sale at Gurley's in New York which used the term "books relating to America." For the next thirty years these four terms, "American Books," "American History," "Bibliotheca Americana," and "books relating to America," were used interchangeably. In 1879 the Brinley Collection was sold as an "American Library" but the term never caught on. Indeed it was just at this time that "Americana" abruptly emerged as the favorite term and steadily increased in popularity right down to the Streeter sales.

Turning from the mere use of the term to the more complex question of its meaning we have a situation in which conceptually it contracted as its popularity increased. All too frequently visitors to the John Carter Brown Library have to be reminded that everything south of the Rio Grande is America also. Despite Wright Howes valiant attempt to introduce the awkward U.S.iana, the term Americana has come to mean to a large number of persons simply books having to do with the history of the United States.

The hard core of the subject has always been the narratives of discovery and exploration. Possevion, in 1578, had entries for Columbus and Vespucci and for standard chronicles such as León's *Historia del Peru* and Acosta's *De Natura Novi Orbia*. Fifty-one years later León Pinelo broadened the concept. Selecting from a much larger list which he had compiled for the purpose of editing and codifying the laws of the Indies, he included books about comparatively recent events which included entries for the French attempt to settle Florida while the English efforts are represented by Thomas Hariot's *Virginia* and Ralph Hamor's *A True Discourse of the Present Estate of Virginia*. Geographically he extended the scope to the Philippines which Spain treated as part of their American Empire. More revealing are some of the subjects which had their own subsections. Indian languages, the history of the church in America, writings of missionaries, collections of laws and natural history suggest that León Pinelo was aware that America was a complex entity that had moved beyond the dramatic events of the first half of the fifteenth century. Even more interesting are the two entirely separate treatments that he gives to works on navigation and works on cosmography and geography. The intellectual and technical problems man was facing in an expanding world were, to him, an integral part of the subject.

Bishop White Kennett's *Bibliothecæ Americanæ Primordia. An Attempt Towards Laying the Foundation of an American Library. In several Books, Papers, and Writings, Humbly given to the Society for the Propagation in Foreign Parts*, published in London in 1713, has been described as the first bibliography devoted exclusively to America. In one sense this is true, but Kennett's purpose was to write a history of the propagation of the Protestant Religion in America, which of course means English America, and the largest part of the books are in English. However, a substantial number of them are on subjects that some today might be surprised to find in an "American Library": voyages and travels to the Near and Far East, the Dutch struggle for independence, anti-Catholic or anti-Spanish works (they were almost the same thing), trade and commerce to all parts of the world, and international law. The title that intrigues me the most is John Wilkin's *The Discovery of a world in the Moon: Or a Discourse tending to prove that 'tis probable there may be another habitable World in that Planet*, London 1638.

Also present are a substantial number of non-English works. Arranged chronologically the first forty-six pages include chroniclers such as Peter Martyr, Castanheda, cosmographical and geographical authors such as Pomponius, Mela, Peter Apian, and Tryco Bray.

Leman Thomas Rede's *Bibliotheca Americana* of 1789 has never enjoyed a very good reputation. This began with its initial reception when he was accused of simply copying titles from the British Museum lists, the *Monthly Review*, and Jefferson's *Notes*. Rede was quite open about this and indeed he also admits to having used Clavigero's *History of Maine*, Robertson's *History of America*, and of course White Kennett. In the "Introductory Discourse on the State of Literature in North and South America" he speaks only briefly of South America as an "Elder sister" and then goes on to deal almost exclusively with books about the original thirteen colonies. He was highly selective in what he copied from his predecessors and omits almost entirely the tangential material that White Kennett collected.

A somewhat less restrictive view was also present in Alcedo's unpublished *Bibliotheca Americana* which was completed about the same time. Just as Rede, as a minimum, included certain basic Latin American works such as Ovalle's *History of Chile*, and Garcilaso de la Vega's *History of the Incas*, so Hakluyt, Purchas, are to be found in Alcedo's list. An interesting point is that he has four of Cotton Mather's works as opposed to only two listed by Rede. However, on balance Alcedo's main concentration is on South America.

Arthur Homer's *Bibliotheca Universales Americana* apparently proposed something more ambitious. I have not seen the original which is a Phillips manuscript or the manuscript copy made in 1841 for Jared Sparks now at Cornell but the printed prospectuses between 1799 and 1803 gives some idea of his coverage. In addition to the usual categories which appeared in earlier compilations he speaks of the Slave

Trade, the African Company, Medicine, Surgery, Poetry, Novels, Agriculture. Under Religion he mentions specifically the Quakers and the United Brethren. Even more interestingly he states that he will include all "books by American Authors, or [which] have proceeded originally from the American press, upon what subjects soever they may treat." This, as far as I have been able to make out is the first mention of American imprints as Americana. He also proposed to pay attention to Latin America by making use of Barcia's revision of Pinelo and Eguira's *Bibliotheca Mexicana*. However, if one reads the Prospectus closely it is clear that Homer's principal reliance was going to be mainly on English materials.

It is to be regretted that neither Alcedo or Homer was ever published. They came at the beginning of the new era in book collecting inaugurated by the Roxborough sale in 1812. To quote Seymour De Ricci "From being the hobby of a scholar or the whim of an eccentric commoner, the collecting of rare books became . . . the favourite pastime of the wealthy nobleman. Fine bindings again became the fashion and everybody knows that if a shoddy tract may be lost or thrown away, a book once handsomely clothed in Morocco is practically safe from destruction." In other words, books became something that were valued for their own sake. As an object to collect they took on an importance which was larger than the text they might contain. Yet as far as collecting of Americana was concerned the most recent work devoted exclusively to the subject was Rede's poor effort. And he, like White Kennett, was primarily concerned with the text, as evidenced by their practice of making separate entries in their appropriate chronological position for the various narratives in Hakluyt, Purchas, Churchill, and the like.

It is difficult to identify all the factors at work in molding the concepts of Americana that emerged in the nineteenth century. Fascination with the new nations arising across the Atlantic, final exploration of the Pacific basin and Polar Regions and national pride all played their roles. It is clear that the initial impulses that created the bibliographical guides came from Europe. The first three citizens of the United States to publish catalogues of collections of Americana—Warden, Aspinwall, and Rich—were Consuls in France, England, and Spain respectively. Warden's two catalogues, 1820 and 1831, are the most useful because they both are arranged topically. After the obvious categories of history and geography he singled out for special treatment Indians, Agriculture, Commerce, Medicine, Politics, Education, Mineralogy, Natural History, and Maps. It is interesting to note that under ecclesiastical works he lumped Roman Catholic and Protestant writers together.

The tradition represented by these men reached its high watermark in the third quarter of the century with the publication of the various editions of the catalogues of the John Carter Brown Library. The four volumes prepared by John Russell Bartlett between 1865 and 1871 became standard reference books. Arranged chronologically they listed 5,600 items printed before 1801. The second edition of the two volumes through 1700 published in 1875 and 1881 almost doubled the number of items for those early years. The collection continued to grow and in 1919 Worthington C. Ford began the publication of the third edition which to date has come down to 1674. Work on the last quarter of the century is going forward and in the near future volumes for 1675-1700 will appear, although their dress will be somewhat less luxurious than that of the earlier volumes which came from the Merrymount Press.

Let me turn now from Americana as seen by collectors to Americana as it is viewed by professional bibliographers. After Leman Thomas Rede's work (the first true bibliography of Americana in the sense that it was prepared for its own sake not as an adjunct to something else) the next notable effort was Hermann E. Ludewig's *Literature of American Local History; a bibliographical essay*, 1846. The work is exactly what its title says it is except that United States should be substituted for American. When he comes to Texas for instance, Spain's 300 years are ignored.

The beginning of the modern period comes in 1866 with Henry Harrisse's *Bibliotheca Americana Vetustissima; A Description of Works Relating to America Published Between the years 1492 and 1551*. Confined chronologically to the age of discovery, conceptually it attempts to include any book printed between those dates which contains the slightest mention of America. Avoiding what he called "inferential Americana" which every one from León Pinelo to Rede included,

Harrisse set out to list all the literature through which the New World made itself known to the Old.

In the same year the *Bibliotheca Americana Vetustissima* appeared a bookseller named Joseph Sabin issued a Prospectus announcing his *Bibliotheca Americana or A Dictionary of Books Relating to America, from its discovery to the present time*. On the face of it he was proposing to do for three hundred and seventy-five years what Harrisse had done for fifty-nine years. I say "on the face of it" because, unlike Harrisse who has an introduction in which he explains at some length his purpose and method, Sabin says simply "The words 'Relating to America' are used with a wide meaning." The only specific statement he makes is to apologize because "serious and proper objection may be taken to some of the titles . . . as for example, the various works by the early New England Divines." Sixty-eight years later when R. W. G. Vail brought the work to completion he wisely followed Sabin's lead in the "Final Statement" and confined his explanation to statements about what had to be left out. With all its shortcomings Sabin is still the most comprehensive bibliography of Americana ever attempted. But what were the criteria that he used? In the last analysis I think that we have to fall back on the fact that Sabin was a bookseller. I believe that his solution to how to handle borderline cases was simply to ask himself whether he could label a book as Americana and sell it as such. In other words he was quite willing to include "inferential Americana" such as imaginary voyages, economic and political pamphlets reflecting the colonial wars—but with no mention of America—and the English and continental aspects of religious controversies which had an American counterpart such as the writings of Quakers and other dissenters. Perhaps his most original extension is to include the writings of authors of American interest even though the work in question had nothing to do with America such as George Sandys's translation of *Ovid* which happens to have been done in Virginia, and Sir Walter Raleigh's *History of the World* which managed to get as far as the history of Rome. Native American authors also appear. Twenty pages are devoted to James Fenimore Cooper, including English, French, German, Dutch, Danish, Swedish, and Italian editions of his works.

There was, however, one area that Sabin clearly did not attempt to include—American imprints. Homer's mention of the concept in his Prospectus was followed by the lists of Stephen Daye and Samuel Green imprints Isaiah Thomas included in his *History of Printing* in 1810. Thomas also referred to "a catalogue of the books printed in the English colonies previous to the revolution" which he hoped to publish at a later date. This did not appear until the second edition of his *History* in 1884 in which he included Samuel Haven's attempt to revise Thomas's notes. Locally the imprint approach was carried on by men like Hildeburn, Roden, and Littlefield. These were of course but preliminaries to the announcement in 1902 by Charles Evans that he was going to start the publication of his *American Bibliography*, which Clifford K. Shipton brought through the year 1800 in 1955. Shaw and Shoemaker and now Shoemaker alone are carrying the work into the nineteenth century, paralleled by special studies such as McCorison's for Vermont and Byrd's for Illinois.

Canadian imprints have been taken care of by Miss Tremaine's fine work which Hare and Wallot have carried through 1840. When we turn to Latin America there is the pioneer work of Icazbalceta which was carried on by that incredible series of bibliographies compiled by José Toribio Medina. That they need further revision goes without saying but, like Evans, they will always be basic. The West Indies have taken their own special set of problems and more work needs to be done in that area. In general I think it may be said that as far as the early products of the American printing press are concerned the bulk of the work has been done.

The interesting thing about almost all the imprint bibliographies is that they came into existence not because of a bookseller or a book collector but rather because of the interest of professional bibliographers and scholars. The collecting of American imprints appears to have been a comparatively late development. Growth of general interest in the field may be judged by the earliest appearance of the term on an auction catalogue, the one for the Pennypacker sale of 1908. Conceptually an imprint bibliography is a fairly easy thing to do. All that has to be determined about a book is date and place of publication.

The development of bibliographies of the works of American authors, as distinct from lists appended and incidental to biographies and the like, is primarily a twentieth-century phenomenon although

P. L. Ford's work on Chauncy, Hamilton and Franklin, and Tomkins' work on Jefferson date from the 1880s. The field of collective bibliographies of American authors which began with P. K. Foley in 1897, is now completely dominated by Jacob Blank. Incidentally, both men came to bibliography from bookselling.

Out of the some four centuries during which attempts have been made to find a way of listing American books, two approaches seem to have emerged as the most effective, the chronological approach and the imprint approach. With American imprints well on their way to being under some kind of control, what we have left are the European imprints.

Back in 1923 when Sabin was still bogged down in the middle of the "Smith's," George Parker Winship wrote, "The fate of Sabin's Dictionary, overloaded with a miscellaneous cargo, much of which seems well nigh worthless while the balance requires highly specialized attention, is both pathetic and instructive. The completion of the work would be a comparatively simple matter ... but it is by no means certain that it is worth the cost and trouble of putting it through the printing press ... it is now well started on the path to oblivion to join works looked at when there is nothing else at hand." Yet Sabin was taken in hand and completed by this Society. In 1962 it was reprinted and I believe has gone through at least another reprinting. In 1963 Frederick R. Goff wrote of it "Scarcely a day passes when I am at my office that I do not have occasion to consult [it]." The reasons for this continued survival in the face of constant criticism lies in Winship's last sentence "works looked at when there is nothing else at hand." Not only that but Winship's "miscellaneous cargo" represents not a hodgepodge of unrelated material but rather an as yet unresolved historical problem—what did the discovery of America mean to Western civilization as a whole and how was that experience communicated?

Yet to be identified is the vast European literature about America from the 1493 Barcelona edition of the Columbus Letter to the most recent book attacking our foreign policy. Academically the earlier period is emerging under the rubric "the Expansion of Europe" and is being formalized in organizations such as the Society for the History of Discoveries."

It is most convenient to divide this material into the colonial and noncolonial periods. However, this does not give us any neat date as a dividing line because, depending on the part of America you are dealing with, one could choose anything from 1776 to the present. As a practical matter, the year 1800 seems to be a reasonable one to use as a starting point.

At the present time there is under consideration a plan to compile and publish a bibliography of eighteenth-century European imprints relating to America. It is a project which goes back to a bookseller whose name can never be omitted in any consideration of Americana— Henry Stevens of Vermont. In 1848, just three years after he had arrived in London to begin his career, he proposed to the Smithsonian Institution the publication of a *Bibliographia Americana* which was to include "all books relating to Americana . . . all books printed in Americana, prior to 1700, which may be found in the principal public and private libraries of Europe and America, or which are described in other works."

I will not attempt to trace the convolutions through which the whole business has gone during the past 120 years except to say that sometime early in this century Winship suggested something similar for the eighteenth century, and in 1938 his idea was taken up by Lawrence Wroth. Meetings with fifteen libraries were held in New York but nothing ever came of it and in 1961 the state of bibliographies of Americana was discussed at a meeting of this society.

You might reasonably ask, however, why at this late date we are trying again. First of all the work that has been done on American imprints makes it unnecessary to include that area, thus cutting down the size of the work (sixty-four per cent of the items in Sabin for 1774 are American imprints). Second, the academic interest in European Americana mentioned earlier has its parallel in library collecting. The Folger Library and the Bell Collection at Minnesota are moving into the area, as are a number of universities who now have faculties interested in the expansion of Europe. Finally, and most important, there appears to be a practical way of financing the project.

In a simplified form this is what is contemplated. Seven libraries, calling themselves "Initiating Libraries," have joined together and this summer are running a pilot study to see how costly it would be to prepare completed descriptions of the books for the first few years

starting with the year 1701. The libraries are: the American Antiquarian Society, the John Carter Brown Library, the Massachusetts
Historical Society, and the Library Company of Philadelphia in conjunction with the Historical Society of Pennsylvania. At some point
arrangements will be made to allow other libraries, which will be
designated "Participating Libraries," to contribute a record of their
holdings if they feel that they can do so. One of the reasons the 1938
proposals failed was that it was not practical to ask places such as the
New York Public Library, the Library of Congress, Harvard, and
Yale to start from scratch and extract from their collections the European books relating to America. The present project includes preliminary short-title lists, year by year, which can be used as point of
departure for checking the holdings of larger libraries.

These preliminary lists will consist of two elements. First, all the
titles as listed in Sabin, and second, the books relating to America not
in Sabin but held by the Initiating Libraries. You may ask what standards are these libraries going to use in making that decision. Well, all
of them, in some way or another, specialize in American History so the
criteria will simply be "does the individual library consider the book
to be Americana?"

In order to gain some idea of the magnitude of this undertaking,
studies were begun last summer. Through data processing all the
Sabin numbers were rearranged chronologically. It turned out that,
counting all the items included in the notes, Sabin lists 140,756 items.
Of these only six per cent or 8,896 were printed before 1701, while
seventy-two per cent or 100,907 were printed after 1800. This leaves
twenty-two per cent or 30,953 eighteenth-century imprints. Using as
a sample the years 1701 and 1751 we found that half of these were
American imprints and, if the sample for 1774 with its sixty-four per
cent is any indication, the total number for the whole century is probably higher. Thus we are left with something under 15,000 European
imprints in Sabin for the years 1701-1800. To this, for the two sample
years of 1701 and 1751, the Initiating Libraries were able to add a
third more items not in Sabin. Thus we ended up with a hard core of
about 21,000 separate entries. Again on the basis of the two sample
years we found that sixty-six per cent of these items were to be found
in one of the seven Initiating Libraries. Through the National Union

Catalogue we tentatively located another nineteen per cent which leaves another fifteen per cent yet to be found. However, we feel that a number of these will turn out to be ghosts or duplicate entries, although others will obviously be troublesome to find.

I now come to the vital question of "who is paying for this ride." Early in our discussions Mr. Albert Boni came to us to explore the possibility of having the Readex Microprint Corporation do for Sabin what they did for Evans. Together we worked out this project. Since then the Readex Microprint Corporation has given us some fiscal guidelines. If we can find a way to do the job within these guidelines, they have said they are prepared to underwrite the editorial costs of preparing the bibliography. The pilot study being carried on this summer will, we hope, determine whether this is possible, but we have every reason to think it will. I should add at this point that for purely technical reasons it was decided to omit all European periodicals and European government documents. The bibliographical problems of controlling this sort of material are quite different from those for individually issued items and should be the subject of another project.

At this point I would like to answer two very obvious questions. What about the period before 1700, and what about the nineteenth century? If the project proves to be successful, work on the earlier periods can be undertaken either concurrently with or after the eighteenth century has been completed. The STC-Wing, and to a certain extent, the John Carter Brown catalogues offer minimal control over the pre-1700 imprints. The eighteenth century, on the other hand, is almost untouched. The nineteenth century presents more complex problems but again, if the initial project proves successful, thought must be given to some way of dealing with it. Perhaps some date like 1835 or 1840 would be a reasonable one to which the work might be carried.

Our final product will consist of three parts: a chronologically arranged bibliography (probably issued in fascicles as each year or group of years is completed) of European imprints relating to America derived from Sabin and from the holdings of the Initiating libraries. To this hopefully will be added locations and additional items from Participating Libraries. Second: microprint reproductions of the items so listed. It should be explained here that Participating Libraries would not commit themselves to allowing their books to be photographed by cooperating in the bibliographical aspect of the project. That would be subject to separate negotiations and would include any fees or other charges each individual library might wish to impose. Thought has been given to being selective so that such things as multiple editions with no important textual changes are not repeated. However, no final decision on that point has been made. Third: the descriptions in the bibliography will be in a form that will make it possible to also issue them separately as catalogue cards.

I would like to comment briefly on the implications of all this, both for the concept of Americana and for the study of history. Our own collecting leads us to believe that the work will probably include most of the works in English about America. However, when it comes to the continental material, existing bibliographies, except for Medina's *Biblioteca Hispano-Americana*, have just scratched the surface. A member of the French Department at Brown has for the past few years been compiling a bibliography of French books about the British colonies of North America. The number of hitherto unidentified Americana books he has found is substantial. We hesitate to make any firm statement but right now it is our impression that in German and Italian books, the number is probably at least twice as large as is currently realized. Thus what would be presented bibliographically would be a point of departure in exploring Americana as it was originally conceived by León Pinelo and which Sabin attempted to carry on. In one sense this would be new because it has been a long time since anyone has actually dealt with the subject in those terms. In another sense it would be old because this is the way men of the fifteenth through the eighteenth centuries conceived of America.

A question that will undoubtedly come up will be how will the micro-reproduction of the books affect both libraries and scholarship. When the Evans project was first announced, there were those who said that a demand for the originals would come to an end. We have found just the reverse to be true. The Evans microprints have served to introduce the subject to many scholars and students all over the country who otherwise would not have had any notion of what the material was like. More people are working in the field and once they have exhausted the reproductions they are finding that they need to come to see not only the originals but the much vaster literature on the subject that surrounds it in libraries whose first responsibility is to build collections of American books.

Once our project is completed, people can start playing the "not in" game. What form future studies will take depends upon how men come to view America. From León Pinelo to White Kennett, anything that seemed to reflect man's experience with the expanding horizons that America represented was appropriate. Then came the eighteenth century with each European nation developing its own views about its overseas possessions. The nineteenth and the first half of the twentieth centuries saw the concept narrow even further. Americans and Europeans, little by little, ceased to feel that they were sharing a common experience. One of the measures of the extent to which we are moving away from that is the emerging realization that for 300 years at least America and Europe had an effect on one another to an extent that we do not yet fully understand.

The Preparation of the *Third Census of Incunabula in American Libraries*

By FREDERICK R. GOFF*

HE publication of a *Third Census of Incunabula in American Libraries* was first suggested to me by my old friend and colleague Curt F. Bühler, who at the time was Curator of Printed Books at the Pierpont Morgan Library. This suggestion took the form of a letter dated 12 January 1957. "This is tentative," he wrote, "but sooner or later the matter will have to be brought before the BSA Council. It concerns the *Census* which is about 'O.P.'" "Should we lay plans for a third Census?" he continued. "Who is to edit it? You are, of course, the obvious choice, but may not want to do it. If you do not, alas, want to be the Editor, would you be willing to head an Advisory Committee to select an editor and to give him the benefit of your great experience?"

The matter did indeed come before the Council of the Bibliographical Society on 25 January 1957, and I was named the editor of the undertaking. Meantime, of course, I had secured the approval of my superiors at the Library of Congress, who were willing for me to devote what free time I had to the proposed project. As for the previous experience mentioned by Dr. Bühler, I had been the close associate and assistant from 1935 to 1940 of Miss Margaret Stillwell, editor of the *Second Census*, which was published late in 1940.

* Read at the Pre-Conference of the Rare Book Section, Association of College and Research Libraries, 26 June 1970, in Detroit.

The first order of business for the new *Census* was naming the Committee on Publication. Dr. Bühler agreed to serve as chairman of this committee which was composed of the late William A. Jackson, Miss Dorothy M. Schullian, and Rudolf Hirsch. As a committee they functioned with the utmost efficiency and scarcely ever bothered the editor who was left with a free hand to proceed with the work. As Bill Jackson wrote me, "I think the committee should be whatever you want—you're the one who has to do the work—and the rest of us I'm sure will agree with anything that you would prefer." And in the main so it was.

In due time a prospectus was drafted, approved, and printed during the spring of 1957. It was issued by the Bibliographical Society of America over the signatures of the late John Gordan as president and Curt F. Bühler as chairman of the Society's Publications Committee. A deadline of 1 January 1959, was established for reporting to Census headquarters. The prospectus, rather sanguine in its expectations, stated that the *Census* would be ready for publication in 1960—an error in calculation of about two years.

Miss Stillwell in her characteristic cooperative spirit forwarded to me her files of the correspondence dealing with supplementary reports to the registrations recorded in the *Second Census* that had reached her. Much useful information was extracted from these files and transcribed into my well-annotated personal copy of the *Second Census*, which not only contained the complete and revised records of the Library of Congress' holdings but pertinent information as well that had come to my attention from various sources such as the Houghton Library annual reports, the BSA *Papers, The Library,* catalogues of individual collections, and occasional catalogues of exhibitions.

This annotated copy served as the working text, and the extensive marginalia in various colored inks as well as pencil provided a colorful commentary to this master copy. As the reports from the contributing libraries trickled in, all new information was properly recorded except for entirely new entries. These were transcribed onto individual cards in the same fashion as those devised for the *Second Census,* verified as to bibliographical details and references, and filed by an appropriate number based on its proper interpolation in the *Second Census* scheme of arrangement.

Two members of the Advisory Committee—our only major difference by the way—took violent exception to the new numbering scheme which I proposed to use in the *Third Census*. Both Bill Jackson and Curt Bühler felt that the Stillwell enumerations should remain inviolate for entries common to both Censuses with a decimal point kind of interpolation for new entries. I argued that the *Second Census* was quite different from the *Short Title Catalogue,* which Bill Jackson used as a model in presenting his argument, and further that canceled and inaccurate entries in the earlier *Census* would cause additional confusion. I insisted on a new enumeration with a dash between the letter and the number (Miss Stillwell's suggestion by the way) with the *Second Census* number in a subsidiary position and with a concordance indicating the canceled and transferred entries of the earlier compilation. In practice the new Census enumeration has worked quite well, and there seems to be no evident confusion between the two systems. Certainly most citations appearing in bibliographies and dealers' catalogues that have come to my attention have been correct.

To return for a moment to the details of compilation, the prospectus was mailed during August of 1957 to 600 possible contributors derived in the main from the list of owners in the 1940 *Census* with obvious deletions and additions. By January of 1958, 83 owners had reported their holdings; by May of that year, 122 had done so, and by 1 January 1959, the deadline, some 417 owners had submitted their reports. We did not hold to this deadline too rigidly, and by the time the *Census* was published the holdings of 760 institutions and private collectors had been incorporated.

By the spring of 1959 the compilation had reached the stage where final editing and the typing could begin. The entries were typed in duplicate on regular-size paper, measuring 8 x 10½ inches, in the form as they appear in the *Census* with a wide margin at the right for later corrections, revisions, and interpolations. The methodology followed is carefully described in the introduction to the *Third Census* and need not be repeated here. Suffice to say that virtually no entry as it appeared in the 1940 *Census* remained entirely unaltered. Important new bibliographies had appeared in the twenty-year interval and proper citations in the reference section were added for J. C. T. Oates' *Catalogue* of the incunabula at Cambridge, volumes VIII and IX of the continuation of the British Museum Catalogue of their fifteenth-century books, covering France and the Low Countries; Dr. Francisco Vindel's *El arte tipográfico en España,* and the Italian *Indice* through the letter R, the four volumes available at that time, with volume 4 existing only in page proofs which I brought back from Rome in September of 1962. The fifth and final volume of this invaluable record of the incunabula available in Italian libraries has only recently reached my hands. It currently exists only as a set of the page proofs without the final enumeration.

Each entry was revised regarding the ownership of copies, many privately owned ones recorded in 1940 having been given to or purchased by institutions. The new entries—some 1,500 in number—were interpolated after final checking. By the end of July of 1960, the final editing had reached the end of letter E, but two more years elapsed before the typescript of the text proper was finished on 30 July 1962. The entire manuscript was typed by the editor on a thirty-year-old Remington noiseless typewriter that I am happy to say is still going strong. The typescript itself ran to 2,224 pages. This was exclusive of five springback notebooks for the concordances, the cross-references, and the printers' and publishers' indices which were typewritten on cards which occupied two standard size boxes.

As the compilation neared completion negotiations were conducted with a number of printers. The final contract was awarded to the Anthoensen Press, a most fortuitous coincidence, since that press had printed the earlier *Census,* and Mr. Warren F. Skillings, the compositor, who single-handedly set the 1940 *Census* in type, was able to oversee the printing. Copy was exceedingly clean and virtually free from error. Those who have had experience with the Anthoensen Press know that this praise is well deserved.

The first of the original printer's copy was mailed to the press early in October of 1962. As the typescript was passing through the press, and during the interval when proofs were received, read single-handedly, and returned, both the concordances to the references to the *Gesamtkatalog,* Hain, and Proctor, and the cross-references were prepared, as well as the index to the printers and publishers which was a new feature of the *Third Census.* The introductory material was also composed, including the owners' names and symbols, the references cited, the abbreviations appearing in the entries, and the introduction itself. The first copy from the bindery reached my hands on 3 December 1964, nearly seven years after Curt Bühler's short note arrived on my desk.

The *Third Census* records some 47,188 incunabula in American ownership. Of this total less than 10 percent, or 3,864, were held in private collections. As we pointed out in the introduction the term "census" is somewhat misleading since more than 90 percent of the total is held by institutions whose holdings may be regarded as more or less permanent. The role of the American collector in assembling personal collections and leaving them to institutions is too well known to be repeated here, but public acknowledgment of this inspired tradition which has done so much to enrich American libraries seems very much in order. The American collector deserves great praise for recognizing his responsibilities and for the taste and acumen he has demonstrated in building many of the important collections which serve today as the basis of so many of our great research libraries.

Nor is the work finished. Not by any means. Since the *Third Census* was published in 1964, the supplementary records which we maintain on a current basis record the acquisition of 2,024 additional titles including 166 new entries, increasing the 1964 total, 12,599, to 12,765 distinct editions which are available in American collections. It must be admitted that this increase is due in large measure to the activities of a number of libraries rather than the private collectors, although much of the support for this activity comes from private funds and endowment. In these cases the collector has ceased to perform his traditional function, but the necessary wherewithal which makes these acquisitions possible is in large measure due to the private factor. The dealer's role, too, in making these books available should also be acknowledged. He seeks them out, knowing the tastes of his clientele, and offers them either through a personal approach or through his catalogues. A most exceptional example of the way a dealer's stock can become a part of an institutional collection is furnished through the recent wholesale transfer of the incunabula available in the stock of Lathrop C. Harper, Inc., some three hundred or more volumes, to the Lilly Library in Bloomington, Indiana. More recently Yale University has acquired a fine collection of early Dutch books, including two hundred or more incunabula, the majority of which are not recorded as entries in the last *Census*. Full details are promised in a forthcoming report from Dr. Thomas Marston, my faithful reporter from the Beinecke Library.

Before many more months elapse it is anticipated that the total of the incunabula in American libraries will reach 50,000. When one recalls that the first census of 1919 included only 13,200 copies it is at once evident that the American libraries have been quite busy during the fifty years' interval. Before too long we expect to commence the editorial work on the supplement itself. This will include not only the new acquisitions never before reported, and the new entries, but will record the many transfers of ownership which have taken place during the intervening six years and will correct many inaccuracies and not a few errors. These I humbly acknowledge. As a one-man operation the *Census* is bound to reflect the inadequacies of the one individual responsible, and he can hardly claim infallibility. Additional references to the fourth volume of the Italian *Indice*, published in 1965, are now available and will appear in the supplement together with the changes that have occurred among the owners including the fifty new names of both public and private collectors, who have joined the roster.

The private collectors of incunabula while less numerous today than they were thirty years ago, about one hundred fewer in fact, should be encouraged to form well-integrated collections which like many of the collections of their predecessors, will one day become part of the fabric, and indeed the basic underpinning, of some of our finest American research libraries. As the earliest printed books incunabula remain in a class by themselves, and from the many facets of their interest they will always occupy an exalted and exceptional position in the history of printing, bibliography, and bibliopegy.

One might add a final word about the librarians, and by this term I refer almost exclusively to the rare book librarian, who in collaboration with the collectors have made the three Censuses possible. These librarians are sophisticated ladies and gentlemen who are talented through their bibliographical skills. They know what fifteenth-century books are available in their libraries, and what is more they know how to take care of them and how to exploit them in numberless ways. There is no question that the three Censuses have helped them to acquire this sophistication, but I doubt that any country in the world has such expertise so generally available. I am grateful to all of you who have assisted my labors in the past and who will continue to co-operate in keeping me informed of your current acquisitions. I hope that those of you within the range of my voice will report to me any additional information useful to the supplement I have in hand, once you have returned to your respective libraries. And if you will be so kind as to pass this request to others who also can help in this endeavor, I shall continue to remain in your debt.

Thomas W. Streeter, Collector,
1883-1965

By HOWELL J. HEANEY*

OME months ago I visited one of the libraries of which
Thomas W. Streeter was a benefactor, and turning a corner
came suddenly on a portrait of him with a feeling at once of
pleasure, and disappointment until I remembered that the artist could
no more set down the whole man on his canvas than I can hope to here,
though warmth, generosity, determination, and principle were all
suggested in his painting. Here we must concentrate on Mr. Streeter's
career as a book collector. To it he brought the same energy and purpose he devoted to business, and the same breadth of vision, accepting
as part of the title "collector" not only the pleasures of acquisition, but
also the obligation to study and explain what he had gathered together,
and to play his full part in the community of bookmen.

It was natural that Mr. Streeter should collect Americana, for he
was born to a sense of the past. His forebears had been settled in New
England from the 1630s. His maternal grandfather, Alonzo P. Car-
penter, was Chief Justice of New Hampshire, and his father, Frank
Sherwin Streeter, was the leading lawyer of the state in his own time,
its attorney general, and, by the way, attorney for Mary Baker Eddy,
for whom he had the greatest respect.

Born in 1883, Thomas Winthrop Streeter was educated at St. Paul's
School and Dartmouth College, from which he was graduated in 1904.
His first published work as a bibliographer and historian appeared in
1905, "Stark's Independent Command at Bennington," by Herbert
D. Foster with the collaboration of Thomas W. Streeter, a substantial
monograph of seventy pages.[1] At that point a promising historian
seemed to have been lost in his going to the law school at Harvard, but

---

* Read at the Pre-Conference of the Rare Book Section, Association of College and
Research Libraries, 26 June 1970, in Detroit.

[1] *Proceedings of the New York State Historical Association*, 5 (1905), 23-96.

fifty years later, with the publication of his *Bibliography of Texas*,[2] it became evident that legal training and a career devoted to the law, to the affairs of a number of major corporations, and to banking, had served to refine his talent for exact and cogent statement. At the end of 1939 Mr. Streeter retired from business to devote himself to his books and writing, and to service the libraries and historical societies in whose work he had such faith.

His career as a collector had, of course, begun much earlier, almost casually. As Mr. Wroth tells us in his admirable introduction to the Streeter catalogue,[3] Mr. Streeter's first purchases were of "the interesting editions of English and American works of various sorts which he called 'after dinner' books, show pieces for the delectation of guests. Along with this tentative venture in collecting, he had carried on with one of the main interests of his college days at Dartmouth, the reading and study of American history. Soon he began the purchase of early books in that field. He attended his first auction sale—*Historical Nuggets*—at the Anderson Galleries in 1920. About this time he began to realize that his slowly forming determination was to collect books on 'beginnings,' books relating to first explorations of states and areas, first settlements, and cultural foundations in the form of first and significant issues of the press in the individual colonies or states."

Although this pursuit was begun in New York, it was carried on with increasing vigor in the big, comfortable house in Morristown, New Jersey, familiar to three generations of booksellers, fellow collectors, scholars and librarians, with its wide porch looking out over woods to the hills beyond, and its large, quiet library, shelved to the ceiling on two sides, the lower shelves projecting to provide a convenient surface for consulting reference works. In one wall a door led to the vault. The shelves there and those in the library must once have been adequate for the collection and Mr. Streeter's reference books, but as time went on, and both collections grew, they began to invade the living room, where the writings of Henry Wagner occupied a

---

[2] *Bibliography of Texas, 1795-1845* (Cambridge: Harvard University Press, 1955-60), 5 vols.

[3] *The Celebrated Collection of Americana Formed by the Late Thomas Winthrop Streeter* (New York: Parke-Bernet Galleries, 1966-70), 8 vols., 1 [5-8] at pp. [5-6]. Reprinted in *The 1970 AB*, Part Two, 3-4.

place of convenience near the door to the library, and all but the rarest Wagner-Camp items took over glass-fronted bookcases, no doubt intended by the architect of the house for a "gentleman's library." Reference books infrequently used were stored in a room on the third floor, and long runs of government documents were shelved in the basement. The breakfast room was largely abandoned to canals and railroads, with certain periodicals added, and here, in piles of books and pamphlets, the practiced eye could trace, in almost geological drifts, the results of periodic "orderings" of the library proper in preparation for visits of distinguished groups—the Hroswitha Club, the Walpole Society, the booksellers and collectors attending some major sale.[4] There were even books on the great chest beside the front door, generally on their way to the public library in Morristown, but these, as Mrs. Streeter observed, were more likely to be her books than Mr. Streeter's.

The size of his collection and the bibliographies and catalogues he undertook called for the help of a librarian, and in 1936 Miss Elizabeth G. Greene, who had been an assistant editor of Sabin, came to Mr. Streeter as his first librarian. I followed Miss Greene in 1947, and was succeeded in 1955 by Joseph G. Roberts, and then, in 1958, by Miss Marian Griffin, who had been Mr. Streeter's secretary from 1947. They say that a man is never a hero to his valet. I cannot imagine Mr. Streeter with a valet, but he was certainly a hero to his librarian. His attitude toward the term librarian was a curious one, born I think of impatience with a word that lumped clerks and the learned together. If a man was really distinguished—Lawrence C. Wroth, Keyes D. Metcalf, William A. Jackson—he was not to be counted as a librarian. I am not myself given to arguing the point as to whether librarianship is a profession. That discussion seems to me to have all the grace of a woman arguing the question as to whether or not she is a lady, but I did hate to see the best men barred because they had been effective. I ought perhaps to admit that our discussions on this subject often arose when I had tried to carry a point of descriptive cataloguing

---

[4] For a delightful account of Mr. Streeter by his daughter, now Mrs. Britton Chance, see Lilian C. Streeter's "Father's Occupation—Book Collector," *The Atlantic: Prize Papers—1944-1945 Atlantic Contests for High School and Private School Students* (Boston 1945), pp. 9-10.

by citing some library code. Such points I sometimes carried, and sometimes lost to the remark that "a foolish consistency is the hobgoblin of little minds." Mrs. Streeter's opinion of librarians was, as all her opinions, direct. Like plumbers or bank presidents, they were worthy of respect if they did what they set out to do well. If she was inclined to think of some librarians as removed from practical affairs, that view was reinforced by experience, for coming home one afternoon she found her youngest on the sofa in the living room trying, unsuccessfully, to stanch a violent nosebleed, and my predecessor, true to her training, on the third floor consulting the *Encyclopaedia Britannica* to see what ought to be done.

Although Mr. Streeter's early collecting of Americana centered on his native New England, it soon broadened in both time and area, backward to include an edition of Pomponius Mela that laid the groundwork for the discoveries of Columbus, and forward to the guidebooks for the emigrants to the homesteads and mining fields of the West. His interest in the West was given impetus by the publication of Henry R. Wagner's *The Plains and the Rockies* in 1920, and *The Spanish Southwest* in 1924, and fed by Edward Eberstadt's three auction sales of "A Great Collection of Original Source Material relating to the Early West and the Far West," beginning at the Anderson Galleries in November 1922, which ushered in a new era in collecting. The growth of Mr. Streeter's collection can be traced in the provenance lines in the entries in the catalogue of its sale, for here, with the sense of justice characteristic of him, the booksellers are given their place with the other collectors on whose shelves each volume once stood. The progress of his collecting, as Mr. Wroth has said, was one in which book opened book. The principle which guided it was that of a search for distinction, not equating Ninian Edwards's message of 1814, the first imprint of Illinois, with the Cambridge Platform of 1649, but recognizing the importance of each to its own time and place. Added to this was an abhorrence of imperfection in any book which could be had in fine condition, absolute fairness and dispatch in coming to a decision on purchases, and in paying for them (qualities some librarians might cultivate to their advantage), and respect for the knowledge of the booksellers, so many of whom he counted amongst his friends.

I remember one notable gathering of booksellers at a dinner party at Morristown, before the Auerbach Sale in October of 1947, at which the guests included Mike Walsh, Ed Eberstadt, Rollie Tree, Peter Decker, Glen Dawson, Charlie Everitt, Warren Howell, and Dave Randall (I name them with familiarity because they are so well known, certainly not as I knew them then), and one man whom I thought by his dress to be less prosperous than his fellow dealers, only to find that he was William J. Holliday, whose collection on Arizona and New Mexico rivalled those of Mr. Streeter and William R. Coe. If Charlie Everitt did not tell the two stories that follow that evening it was because the competition was too keen to allow him space. He did put them in his *Adventures of a Treasure Hunter*, and I repeat them here because they illustrate the advantage Mr. Streeter's attention to detail gave him over more casual collectors.

Everitt went to an American Art Association sale prepared to bid up to $250 for a copy of John H. Robinson's map of Mexico, Louisiana, and the Missouri Territory, published at Philadelphia in 1819. As he tells it: "At the sale somebody yelled ten dollars, and I said twelve and a half, and down came the hammer. Eberstadt and half the other bright lights of Americana were in the room watching, but this distinguished company was supplied to me at no extra cost. The map meant nothing to them, and they were thinking about something else. When I got the map back to the store, where I was by then in very cramped quarters (having discovered that the fat books just fill shelves and the thin ones bring you the money), I tried to open the map, but since it was over five and a half feet square, all I could look at was one uninteresting corner.

I was contemplating this without enthusiasm when Ed Eberstadt came in.

'What you got there, Charlie?'

'Oh, I don't know. I can't get the damn thing open.'

'What'll you take for it?'

'Well, I was going up to two hundred and fifty. It's yours for seventy-five.'

Ed paid and departed. Ed's office was even smaller than mine. He too was just trying to inform himself when Philip Ashton Rollins, a truly great collector of Western Americana . . . came into the store.

'Ed, what was that thing Charlie bought yesterday?'

'Don't know; I'm just trying to find out.'

'What will you sell it to me for?'

'I gave Charlie seventy-five dollars; take it for a hundred.'

Shortly after this, word of the transaction got around, as word always does. My friend and customer Tom Streeter called up and said, 'Charlie, I kind of think you made a mistake on that map. There are only two other copies in existence, and the Library of Congress has both.'

Tom promptly went down and traded some of his duplicates to the Library of Congress for their spare."[5]

The other story concerns one of the great Texas broadsides. Everitt had just bought some volumes of Texas newspapers in a Henkels's auction for $14, plus ten percent, and was in the act of collating them when Mr. Streeter came in. "As he was looking over my shoulder, a volume fell open to a broadside from the period of Texas independence.

'How much?' said Streeter, eagerly.

'Oh, a hundred and fifty.'

Three or four pages further on, another broadside.

'How much?'

'A hundred and fifty.'

A few pages further on, the rarest Texas broadside in the world. The bottom had been torn off. It was one of Stephen Austin's pronouncements, no copy of which had ever been seen before.

'How much for that, Charlie?'

'With my compliments, Tom; you'll never complete it.'

The next time I was in London I had a letter from Streeter saying: 'Here are the last seven lines of that broadside; I found them in a Missouri newspaper. See what you can do with it.'"

The broadside was completed in pen-and-ink facsimile, and as Everitt concludes, "This is one occasion when the discovery of a unique item has not lured out any further copies."[6] It should be added that this address of Austin's of 1823 is the first Texas imprint which

[5] Charles P. Everitt, *The Adventures of a Treasure Hunter* (Boston: Little, Brown and Company, 1951), pp. 165-66.

[6] Everitt, pp. 201-02.

has survived, and that Mr. Streeter's copy, a proof, had numerous corrections in Austin's hand.

One dealer with whom Mr. Streeter had a special relationship was Lathrop C. Harper. Mr. Streeter wrote of him: "My own dealings with Lathrop Harper began with some small purchases of New England books in the spring of 1920. I soon grasped every opportunity to steal away from my job to go uptown for a little visit with him, for I was fascinated by his knowledge of books and quickly learned to have complete confidence in his judgment and integrity. It did not take me long to learn that he had very definite ideas as to where certain books should go. . . . When Lathrop Harper really approved of [you], he would . . . practically order you to buy a book or map he thought belonged in your collection. On one occasion he had a copy of the rare and important Costansó map of California, published at Madrid in 1771, which he showed to me marked at what I thought was a pretty stiff price. For years I had followed what I think is a pretty good rule, of never dickering on the price of a book. I did not then fully realize the importance of the Costansó map and so, thinking the price was out of line, I made some noncommittal comment and tried as tactfully as possible to get on some other subject. As I got to know more about the beginnings of the Spanish settlement in what is now the State of California I realized that I had made a bad mistake in not snapping up the Costansó when I had a chance and it was a great relief when I went back to Mr. Harper some months afterwards to learn that the map was still available. I did not learn the whole story until after Mr. Harper's death when Lawrence Wroth told me that when he heard I had turned down the Costansó he inquired whether it could be bought for the John Carter Brown Library and was told by Mr. Harper that he thought 'the map belonged in Streeter's collection and that he was going to hold it for him a while longer.'"

In the same sketch[7] Mr. Streeter writes that if he may be pardoned a somewhat personal reference he can add his own testimony to that of other booksellers and collectors illustrating Mr. Harper's quiet acts of generosity and kindness. "The financial going was pretty rough

[7] "Lathrop C. Harper, 1867-1950," The *News Sheet* of the Bibliographical Society of America, No. 71, 15 May 1951, pp. 4-5.

for me after the 1929 crash. We were such friends that he was cognizant of the tough time I was having and he readily agreed to pay me a large sum, much more than I had any right to expect, for the greater part of my then collection of Colonial Americana. It was due in part to this purchase that I was able to weather the storm and I have always been grateful to him for the friendly way he handled the whole transaction. I should add that for a long time Mr. Harper had in his office what he used to call 'The Streeter Shelf' from which I bought back some of the books from time to time, and I was glad to hear from Douglas Parsonage not long ago that 'they had really done well on the entire purchase and that the "Streeter Shelf" is now a thing of the past.

"I might remark that one of the happy outcomes of that Harper purchase from me concerns the Cambridge Platform of 1649. Mr. Harper allowed me, as I recollect, the generous price of $7,000 for my copy and some years later when my financial skies had cleared he bought for me the only remaining copy of the Platform not in an institution, and this copy, due to the researches of George P. Winship, later turned out to be one of the two known copies of the first issue." (This second copy brought $80,000 at the Streeter sale, and is now at Harvard.)

The same adversity which forced the sale of his Colonial Americana turned Mr. Streeter's attention to the development of canals and railroads in the United States. Their reports and surveys being then available at modest prices, he devoted the early thirties to assembling fine runs on both subjects. His collection of railroad pamphlets published before 1841 was second only to that of the New York Public Library. These collections he gave away, largely to the American Antiquarian Society, although material on European railroads was given to the Baker Library of the Graduate School of Business Administration at Harvard,[8] that on certain Southern railroads to the University of Virginia, and on certain New England railroads to Dartmouth College.

[8] For a description of this gift see *The Pioneer Period of European Railroads: A Tribute to Mr. Thomas W. Streeter* (Boston 1946), vi, 71 pp. (Publication Number 3 of The Kress Library of Business and Economics), with its appreciation of Mr. Streeter by Arthur H. Cole at pp. v-vi.

If the earliest material on the discovery and exploration of America and the establishment of the colonies and territories which became the United States formed a major portion of Mr. Streeter's library, his interest in collecting material on one of those areas, Texas, was equally strong. Early in 1927 he embarked "lightheartedly and almost casually on the project of compiling a critical bibliography of books, broadsides, and maps relating to Texas, 1795-1845." As Mr. Streeter tells us, "I did not know then what Dr. Paltsits had said many years before, 'Anyone can compile a list, many can make a catalogue, but few can agonize to bring forth a bibliography.' In my state of complete bibliographical innocence, it appeared to be a comparatively simple task, for the spare time of a busy life, to assemble the material of that half century printed in or relating to Texas and describe it with critical notes."[9] Some twenty-seven years were to pass before the publication of the first part of the bibliography, listing Texas imprints, and five more during the publication of the volumes on Mexican and United States and European imprints relating to Texas. The magnitude of the work can be judged not just from the fact that there are 1,661 main entries in its five volumes and an appendix on Texas newspapers, but also from the fact that each entry has a note which characterizes the piece and sets it in its place in the story of Texas as a province and republic. The five volumes are, by the way, a bibliography not a catalogue of Mr. Streeter's collection—though I have known the point to be missed—and the search for material to be included was very wide, even extending to the state libraries of Mexico, where chickens were sometimes found roosting all unaware amongst the bombast of military proclamations against Texas, and the process of finding books was on at least one occasion complicated by the precision of a retired Colonel who had rearranged the collection in his care by size to within a quarter of an inch, leaving the catalogue almost useless.

The sketch of Mr. Streeter which serves as the frontispiece to the first volume of the catalogue of the sale of his library catches him in a characteristic posture, sitting erect on the straight, hard chair at the table in his library, at work on one of his notes. Long hours were com-

[9] *Bibliography of Texas,* i, p. xi.

monplace to him, but long notes were to be avoided. The point was not to tell all one knew, but to tell what mattered, and that meant drafting and redrafting. Mr. Streeter agreed heartily with Theodore Roosevelt's remark that the revolt of the new historians of the turn of the century against superficiality and lack of research was justified, but that their belief "that the ideal history of the future [would] consist not even of the work of one huge pedant, but of a multitude of small pedants" was noxious.[10] Useful though the descriptions, references, and locations of copies in the *Bibliography* are, it is Mr. Streeter's notes and introductions that raise the finished work to the level of literature.

Mr. Streeter's success in collecting Texas material was remarkable. In roughly thirty years he was able to gather more than half of the items located in the *Bibliography*, and more by 108 than were to be found in the next largest collection, that at the University of Texas. His collection covering the entire range of Texas history ran to more than 2,000 items. Following talks initiated in 1956 by James T. Babb, Librarian of Yale University, that entire collection was sold to Yale, thus solving for Mr. Streeter's executors what would otherwise have been the difficult problem of disposing of a large group which by its nature required sale as a whole.[11]

Mr. Streeter's sense of relative importance prompted him to include in the introductions to the successive parts of the *Bibliography* lists of the items he considered of greatest significance. As Anthony Trollope, socially, preferred the company of distinguished men, so Mr. Streeter, bibliographically, preferred the company of distinguished books. He speaks with feeling of the fascination, and the pitfalls, of making such lists. His earliest major effort was as a member of the committee of the Grolier Club that selected *One Hundred Influential American Books Printed before 1900*—here the word "America" means the United States—published by the Club in 1947. Thirty-two of the notes were Mr. Streeter's. This task of choice and annotation

---

[10] Quoted in Howard K. Beale's "The Professional Historian, His Theory and His Practice," *Pacific Historical Review*, 22 (1953), pp. 227-55 at p. 228.

[11] A catalogue of *The Only Located Copies of One Hundred Forty Texas Pamphlets and Broadsides* drawn largely from this collection and marking its gift by friends of the Yale University Library was published by the Library in Feb. 1957.

was a congenial one, and led Mr. Streeter to the publication of his own
broader *Americana—Beginnings* in 1952,[12] a selection of seventy-nine
major items from his collection shown in honor of a visit of the Hroswitha Club in May of 1951. Included were the stars of the seven parts
of the Streeter sale, taking them in order of magnitude: the Cambridge
Platform, Pigafetta's *Voyage,* the Lewis and Clark in printed boards,
the second Plannck edition of the Columbus letter, the Northwest
Ordinance, and Ninian Edwards's message to the Illinois legislature,
of 1814. In an exhibition at the Grolier Club in 1959[13] these were
joined by others from the Hroswitha list, and by additions to Mr.
Streeter's collection in the interval, notably: the first edition in English of Cartier's account of his four voyages to Canada, the first separate printing of the Gettysburg Address, James Van Horne's account
of the Chicago Massacre during the War of 1812, and one of the two
known perfect copies of *The Declaration of the American Citizens on the
Mobile* (1807), the first imprint of Alabama. It is interesting to speculate on the choices Mr. Streeter might have made for such an exhibition from the acquisitions of his last six years of collecting. The jury
in the salesroom, if prices are an indication, voted for: Smith's *Generall
Historie of Virginia* (1624), Alexandre O'Reilly's proclamation of August 1769 as Governor of Louisiana, either the first or second example
of printing in New Orleans, Hartshorne's *Further Account of New
Jersey* (1676), the first separate account of New Jersey, and the Arthur
Swann copy of the first issue of the first edition of *Leaves of Grass.*

The seven volumes prepared for the sale of Mr. Streeter's collection,[14] which took place between October of 1966 and October of 1969,
stand as a record of his collecting and study for a period of more than
forty-five years. Here the whole sweep of discovery and exploration,
of the development of the United States and the influences on that
development are traced by region and subject, the entries for each sec-

[12] Issued at Morristown, New Jersey, in July 1952, in an edition of 325 copies, of which
fifty were for sale.

[13] Recorded in its *Catalogue of an Exhibition of Historical and Literary Americana*
(New York: The Grolier Club, 1960). Mr. Streeter's books and annotations appear as
Nos. 1-50, pp. 7-30.

[14] Described in Note 3 above. Vol. 8, the index, was compiled by Edward J. Lazare.
An illustrated brochure listing the major items to be sold in each of the seven parts of the
sale was issued by Parke-Bernet in the spring of 1966.

tion arranged in chronological order. Here the principles of unity and significance set down in Mr. Streeter's "Notes on North American Regional Bibliographies"[15] are applied, and in the descriptions the emphasis he placed on the importance of maps given scope. If we might wish for more of the notes to be found in the eighty-seven loose-leaf notebooks of his original catalogue, now deposited at the American Antiquarian Society, we must remember that this is a sale catalogue, and be grateful for its fullness and for the hundreds of quotations from those notes signed with the initials "TWS". The parallels between this and the Brinley sale have been drawn, and the results of the sale ably summarized by Kenneth Nebenzahl in the *Papers of the Bibliographical Society of America*.[16] There is no occasion to regret the dispersal of Mr. Streeter's books, for, as Archibald Hannah has pointed out, his collections which covered a single subject in depth—Texas, canals, railroads—had already gone to research libraries, and this was a collector's collection whose dispersal strengthened many libraries.[17] In their efforts to fill important gaps a number of those libraries had the help of bequests provided for in Mr. Streeter's will. It should, by the way, be remembered that these bequests, unlike Brinley's, were outright gifts for the purchase of books, not credits to be used at the sale.

Mr. Streeter's interest in his sale, running back at least twenty years

[15] *PBSA*, 36 (1942), 171-86. For a reply see Charles F. Heartman's *Thoughts Upon Reading Thomas W. Streeter's Essay "North American Regional Bibliographies"* (Hattiesburg, Mississippi: The Book Farm, 1943).

[16] "Reflections on Brinley and Streeter," *PBSA*, 64 (1970), 165-75. A total of $3,104,982.50 was realized from the 4,421 lots sold from 25 Oct. 1966 to 22 Oct. 1969. Excellent listings by Sol. M. Malkin of the highlights of the successive parts of the sale appeared in *AB*, 7 Nov. 1966, pp. 1802-10 (for Vol. I), 15 May 1967, pp. 1939-44 (Vol. II), 13 Nov. 1967, pp. 1787-94 (Vol. III), 6-13 May 1968, pp. 1758-60 (Vol. IV), 11 Nov. 1968, pp. 1651-54 (Vol. V), 19 May 1969, pp. 1812-16 (Vol. VI), and 17-24 Nov. 1969, pp. 1651-56 (Vol. VII). These lists were reprinted, with the omission of the names of successful bidders originally given for Vol. I, in *The 1970 AB*, Part Two, pp. 10-28. Summaries by John R. Payne were published in *The American Book Collector* 18 (1967-68), No. 9, pp. 27-28, No. 10, pp. 25-28 (Vol. I); 19 (1968-69), No. 1, pp. 10-16 (Vol. II); No. 2, pp. 18-24 (Vol. III); No. 3, pp. 30-32, No. 4, pp. 28-32 (Vol. IV); No. 5, pp. 23-27, No. 6, pp. 19-27 (Vol. V); No. 10, pp. 23-28; 20 (1969-70), No. 1, pp. 12-15 (Vol. VI); No. 4, pp. 13-16, No. 5, pp. 23-25 (Vol. VII).

[17] "A Memoir of T. W. S.," *The 1970 AB*, Part Two, pp. 7-8 at p. 7. Part Two also includes "A Personal Appreciation of T. W. S.," by John Carter, pp. 5-6; "A Memorial to T. W. S.," by Lindley Eberstadt, pp. 6-7; and "A Few Recollections," by Michael J. Walsh, pp. 8-9.

before it occurred, was never morbid. He would often remark of some new arrival, "Now here's a book you'll want to watch at my sale," explaining its significance, and perhaps why it had been undervalued by earlier collectors. I like to think that he was, himself, watching the sessions at the Parke-Bernet galleries, and relishing the contests there. Surely price is as interesting a feature of a book as provenance or rarity, and a certain test of current opinion. Generally, as the old Scots preacher observed, a man will put his hand twice to his bonnet for once to his pouch. If rarity is a grace added to distinction, price is a compliment paid to both. It has been said that as a result of the pursuits of the ordinary collector, in the matter of old books nothing is so common as rarities. Mr. Streeter, as these catalogues and his *Bibliography of Texas* show, was an extraordinary collector, on whose shelves the great books familiar to generations of Americanists were joined, in every area and period of American history, by scores of distinguished imprints theretofore unknown.

A listing of Mr. Streeter's major services to libraries and historical societies can do no more than suggest the part he played in their affairs: as chairman of the Friends of the Dartmouth College Library, of the Associates of the John Carter Brown Library, and of the Council of the Fellows of the Pierpont Morgan Library; as a director of the Friends of the Huntington Library; as a member of the visiting committees of the libraries at Yale, Princeton, and Harvard, and the Mc-Gregor Library of the University of Virginia; as a fellow of the California Historical Society; as a member of the council of the Grolier Club, as a member of the council and president of the Bibliographical Society of America, as a trustee and treasurer of the New-York Historical Society, and a councillor and president of the American Antiquarian Society. To them he contributed not only his experience in finance (the portfolio of the New-York Historical Society almost tripled under his care), and in building collections, but also that most precious commodity, time from his own studies toward the writing of papers: amongst others, his presidential address "Notes on North American Regional Bibliographies," which appeared in the *Papers of the Bibliographical Society of America* in 1942,[18] "The Rollins

---

[18] *PBSA*, 36 (1942), 171-86.

Collection of Western Americana" in the *Princeton University Library Chronicle* in 1948,[19] and sketches of Henry R. Wagner in the *California Historical Society Quarterly* in March 1957,[20] in the *Yale University Library Gazette* in October of that year,[21] and in *Grolier 75: A Biographical Retrospective to Celebrate the Seventy-Fifth Anniversary of the Grolier Club in New York* published by the Club in 1958.[22] His "Notes on North American Regional Bibliographies" had a direct influence on the formation of the Bibliographical Society's Committee on Bibliographies of American Imprints, of which Mr. Streeter became the chairman, and he contributed the appendices on Federal and Confederate Army Orders to Albert H. Allen's *Arkansas Imprints, 1821-1876*, published in 1947,[23] the second in the series sponsored by the Committee. These services brought him the honorary degree of Doctor of Letters from Dartmouth in 1946, the gold medal of the New-York Historical Society in 1957, and, for his *Bibliography of Texas*, the Wagner Memorial Award of the California Historical Society in 1962.

Mr. Streeter's own compliment to achievement was to call a man a useful citizen, a compliment he fully merited himself. On his eightieth birthday, a little less than two years before his death, one of his daughters-in-law described him as:

> . . . the Patriarch, the Sage
> A person from a finer age
> When many talents, many árts
> Combined to make the man of parts;
> Beloved by all, and all-discerning
> In law, in finance, and in learning.

Surely he earned his place in each of those fields, and will be remembered, with respect and affection, as long as the books he loved.

[19] 9 (1947-48), 191-204.

[20] "Henry R. Wagner, Collector, Bibliographer, Cartographer and Historian," 36 (1957), 165-75. Reprinted in *Henry Raup Wagner, 1862-1957* (San Francisco 1957), pp. 1-11.

[21] "Henry R. Wagner and The Yale Library," 32 (1957-58), 71-76.

[22] "Henry Raup Wagner, 1862-1957," pp. 118-20.

[23] At pp. 183-205.

Scholarship and Editing

By FREDSON BOWERS*

W HEN the history of scholarship in the twentieth century comes to be written, a very good case should be made for calling it the age of editing. The second half of the nineteenth century saw a wave of editing of our earlier literature, Medieval and Renaissance. I cannot speak for the Medieval, but at least in the Renaissance and later I do not recall a single text, except perhaps for versions of the Globe edition of Shakespeare, that has survived in common use today save for lack of competition. The fading of these nineteenth-century editions raises the question whether the same fate will overtake those of the twentieth century that, especially in our second half, are being produced in considerable numbers for scholarly use. Despite the fact that history generally shows human optimism to be excessive, I rather think that the situation is in process of changing and that something of a case can be made for the relative permanence of a certain school of editions that are now being produced.

In an ideal world excellence would be the sole criterion for survival, but these days the matter is by no means so simple. The competition for public response possible for paperbacks is scarcely feasible for weighty editions of standard authors, each volume quite possibly costing thirty to fifty dollars. Even libraries that pride themselves on

* An abridged version of this paper was read before the annual meeting of the Bibliographical Society of America in New York City 23 Jan. 1976.

completeness may revolt if asked to purchase two competing editions, each replete with commentary and elaborate textual apparatus, of authors like George Peele, John Dryden, Henry Fielding, Dr. Johnson, Charles Dickens, or Nathaniel Hawthorne, at a price far above that for ordinary commercial publications.[1] Thus the mere fact that some editor or group of editors, and a compliant university press, have engaged themselves to a massive editorial project discourages competition not only in the present but for many years afterward since any full-fig scholarly edition will saturate the limited market for such productions.[2] If the edition is a good one—an edition that may properly be called 'definitive'—no great harm may be done by this automatic preëmption. However, even if an edition has serious faults in its methodology and thus in its attempt at definitiveness, few publishers are likely to encourage another editor to attempt to replace it within the same generation by a superior form when the challenge will often be to a highly regarded press and the market disastrously limited for the recovery of heavy costs. This is as true in times of ease as in the present years of financial restriction.

As a consequence, I take it that a moral obligation should rest upon both editor and publisher to insure that their present-day editions do indeed conform to what may be described as definitive standards and hence that the longevity of these editions will be merited in a permanently satisfying manner by their usefulness first to scholars and

1. Indeed, one publisher gave it as his opinion to me that even for Shakespeare there would be no market for two competing old-spelling editions. He was certainly right if the two editions were contrived in the same pattern. However, possibly two editions could survive if one concentrated only on the text and its elaborate apparatus, whereas the other provided an excellent commentary as its chief attraction and was content with minimal textual apparatus. Each would then appeal to a different market.

2. The market is greatly limited by price. Few individual scholars (not so fortunate as to receive review copies) are likely to feel they can afford to put on their shelves multivolume definitive editions of authors in whom they are interested but are not in process of making special studies for publication. These large-scale editions are chiefly bought by libraries and are consulted there. Their chief impact, therefore, may be described as for reference. At a minimum an editor hopes that scholars will use his edition as the standard for page reference and quotation in articles and books. Some few specialists, of course, are bound to study the editions more deeply and to find new critical material in the collational records of the development of various texts; but if the shallow quality of the average review of these editions is any criterion, there will be few such studies by more general scholars in the period. This is a pity since the close critical analysis of the growth of a work through different forms, as well as from manuscript to print, can reveal an author's intentions and methods of working as can no other evidence.

then to the widest spectrum of readers, and not by the mundane fact that their expensive existence stifles all competition for years after their publication. I cite the moral obligation because no extraordinary financial pressure exists. Publishers have experienced the paradox that a preëmptive edition will sell just about as well whether or not it meets the highest standards for textual authority that should be expected. I am far from suggesting that the publishers of scholarly editions are cynical men who deliberately issue faulty works. I merely point out that few directors of presses or their boards have the technical knowledge to approve the textual methodology of an edition proposed to them in the manner in which they are equipped to judge a critical or historical work. Various directors with whom I have talked remark that they have little option but to place their faith in the standing of the scholar who suggests an edition. As a result, reputable literary scholars but inexperienced firsthand in bibliographical and textual techniques may set themselves with a publisher's approval to large editorial projects when their chief interest lies in the critical commentary and introductions. And since a completed volume is very rarely submitted by the publisher to a competent reader before publication, as are the manuscripts for all other books before acceptance, the usual scholarly edition is published almost exclusively on its prospectus and the hope of the press that the editor knows his business.[3]

A discouraging aspect of textual scholarship is the general indifference of those to whom it should matter most to have properly edited texts. I recently dined with a philosopher and raised the question of Professor Nidditch's new edition of Locke's *Human Understanding*. He was a specialist in the philosophy of the period, but he said that fifteen pounds (or its equivalent in dollars) simply was too much for him to pay for a new edition. He was confident that the old edition got Locke's sense sufficiently right and was reasonably satisfactory to use for study and reference. It did not seem to him that the refinements no doubt introduced in the new text would be worth his while to study. If he had been curious enough to examine this new and

---

3. In England, where no organization like the Center for Editions of American Authors exists (soon to be expanded into a Center for Scholarly Editions under the guidance of the Modern Language Association of America), this informal system of acceptance with little or no prior scrutiny has resulted in quite uneven editorial standards even within the editions published by a single press.

bibliographically motivated edition in his university library and had read Professor Nidditch's analysis of the deficiencies of the older standard text, he might have felt differently—but possibly not. Here was a specialist in the field, who perhaps never will hold the new edition in his hand. I still recall and refer to the occasion when I and my ilk were belabored by a prominent scholar of English literature for wasting our time on nonessential things like texts. It made no difference to him, or in his opinion to any fundamental value in the play, whether Hamlet's flesh was solid or sullied. We should be devoting our talents to more important matters, he advised us. This is not the only example in my experience to indicate that students of literature—although generally more sensitive to the problem of the texts they read than their colleagues in other humanities or in the social sciences—are by no means paragons of enlightenment.[4]

I recognize that I am preaching to the converted—at least I hope I am!—and so will not elaborate this all too familiar theme. Instead I shall take it that we are genuinely interested in the quality of the texts of the editions we read, as well as in their surrounding critical matter; and believe that if we are to pay our dollars at a high rate (or to persuade our libraries to spend theirs so that we may utilize the texts) we have a right to expect an attempt at definitiveness in a preemptive scholarly edition. Just as war is said to be too important to be left to the generals, so textual scholarship is too important to be left to the publishers, or to purely critical scholars.

In certain basics no difference should exist between a scholarly and a popular text except that of old-spelling versus modernization for our earlier literature. Whether modernized or unmodernized, however, both should attempt to get right what the author has written, according to the most refined principles and techniques for determining this all-important consideration. There is little point in rehearsing at length the dismal story of the sloppiness of most popular texts,

4. It is something of a contemporary phenomenon that starting with Edmund Wilson but carried on from the sidelines by American-literature academics of varying experience, an extremely contentious defense of the status quo and the familiar has been characteristic of many reviews of the volumes issued through the Center for Editions of American Authors. However, the low water mark to date comes from a young student of American history (printed, oddly enough, by the *American Scholar*), whose deliberate use of the Big Lie technique passes all bounds of decency.

particularly in their common paperback reprint form. Even their
pretensions to authority may be false. I cite the case in England of a
paperback edition of Mrs. Gaskell's *Wives and Daughters* that alleged it was a reprint of the original serialization of 1864-66 in the
Cornhill Magazine whereas a concerned scholar showed that instead
it was only the latest in a line of reprints deriving from a highly
corrupt form of the text dating from 1891. British reviewers lately
have come to be more than a little concerned about the faulty basis
for various other of these popular Penguin texts, as well as the numerous misprints and corruptions in their production. In this country I am
minded of a popular edition of Hawthorne's *Scarlet Letter* alleging
that it was based on the third edition of 1850, corrected by the author
—a double falsehood, for Hawthorne never revised any edition and
instead this paperback was a reprint of an 1884 series offering the
most corrupt text ever to see print. Such carelessness of standards in
popular editions with their texts progressively degenerating from
cumulative reprinting of the last one to be issued has led the National Endowment for the Humanities to require that every volume
of the Center's funded editions must be made available shortly after
publication to paperback publishers and at a purely nominal fee or
royalty. Some publishers have taken advantage of this remarkable
opportunity to break the chain of textual corruption; but many continue the vicious spiral because they or their 'editors' will not pay the
small sum required to insure a correct text or else will not perform
the special required proofreading.[4a] The conscientious publishers join

4a. When resetting instead of photo-offset of the CEAA edition is in question, the problems of securing accurate texts in paperback reprints or in anthologies increase, and in a
manner of speaking the baby falls between two stools. The Center for Editions of American Authors requires the issuing presses of its approved editions to proofread any reprint
by another house. This idealistic requirement is frequently violated by the university
presses. In fact, normal proofreading—i.e. looking for typos—is not enough, for to insure an accurate reprint text the proofs should be *re-collated* not once but several times. The
presses assert, and with some justice, that their personnel have other things to do, and that
the cost of this operation would exceed the fee for reprinting. On the other hand, commercial publishers are usually adamant. When the house of Macmillan was queried by the
CEAA about substantive errors in the reprints of two Stephen Crane short stories in a new
anthology (the University Press of Virginia having neglected to pass on to Macmillan
the CEAA proofreading requirements, which they were not themselves prepared to enforce),
the following answer was received from Macmillan: "I am very sorry if our interpretation
of our license to reprint 'The Open Boat' and 'The Blue Hotel' does not accord with that
of the CEAA. I should like to point out that in at least three other instances of permission

the Foundation, however, in accepting the proposition that good scholarly editions must precede good popular texts, and that these editions generate excellence to a far wider public than could be attracted to their original scholarly form of publication. Even an old-spelling Elizabethan text can be made available to a modernizing textbook editor to save him from resorting to some handy but incompetent nineteenth-century text in the public domain.

It is time now to deal, although in necessarily summary fashion, with what is meant by the term 'definitive edition,' which is the ideal of the more thoughtful modern scholarly editors. The initial requirement is that it must be an old-spelling or—a wider term and one more suited to nineteenth-century texts—in unmodernized form. Modernization of early literature is a necessity for popular texts, but the dangers and ambiguities of the constant and unrecorded editorial decisions that must be made cause modernization to be unsuitable for a definitive scholarly basic edition.[5] No modernization can ever be trusted accurately to reflect its original. A scholar cannot view such a text as more than superficially useful for any close analysis of the work.

How is one to treat an unmodernized text? This issue goes deeper than the relatively simple matter of making older typographical con-

---

for *Anthology of American Literature* the CEAA reprint policy was defined as a condition of license, and we immediately sought and obtained substitute texts. In the economics and, more important, scheduling of commercial anthology publishing, compliance with all the CEAA controls is impractical in our view, and we simply could not bind ourselves to a protracted and expensive series of steps (over some of which we should have had no control) to ensure a minutely faithful reproduction of the CEAA editions." In all justice, Macmillan stated that it was not advertising or remarking in any way in the anthology that the two texts were reprints of the CEAA edition. Nevertheless, caveat emptor. Some sympathy may be felt for the trials of commercial publishing, it is true, but sympathy is also due to the readers of texts of anthologies which appear with corruptions not to be detected by ordinary commercial proofreading without collational comparison with the printer's copy and which sometimes make small sense. The road to virtue is indeed a rocky one. It is admirable for an anthology or paperback publisher to have enough conscience to pay a small fee for a license to use a CEAA-approved text; it is then somewhat dashing to know that thereafter no safeguards are applied to insure accuracy, and that any proposal to request the publisher to apply such standards would be met by a transfer to an inferior text as copy, usable without restrictions and therefore economically feasible.

5. The most complete discussion of the virtues and defects of modernization is John Russell Brown, "The Rationale of Old-Spelling Editions of the Plays of Shakespeare and his Contemporaries," and Arthur Brown, "The Rationale of Old-Spelling Editions of the Plays of Shakespeare and his Contemporaries: A Rejoinder," *SB* 13 (1960), 49-76.

ventions palatable for present-day readers without anything that could be called linguistic modernization—mechanical matters like substituting the short 's' for the old long 's', the medial 'v' for 'u', and so on. Again briefly, because I am speaking of familiar discussions, the general trend of scholarship is toward a critically edited text; that is, a text admitting editorial emendation and not therefore an exact reprint in every detail of a normally faulty original. An exact reprint is of course definitive to its original, but that is not necessarily to say that it is definitive to what the author wrote, or intended to write, either in a single edition or a series of revisions. Errors and interpretations of the printing house or of some other transmissional agent intervene between the author's lost original manuscript and its published derivative. Exceptions can be taken in some respects to McKerrow's definition of a critical edition as one that comes as close as the preserved documents permit to a careful authorial fair copy; but this is at least a generally acceptable statement of an *ideal*, attainable in greater or lesser degree according to the nature and amount of the preserved evidence.

Emendation is of two basic varieties. The most common occurs when only a single authority is present for a text. Thus whether an editor cites some reasonably contemporary reprint as the source for an emendation (as he should for the sake of historical accuracy), or credits its initiation to some preceding scholar (again a matter of historical interest), or himself makes a new contribution, the result is the same, for no alteration of a single-authority text *can* have literal 'authority' and so the origin of the alteration is a technicality of little or no critical consequence for the validity of the emendation adopted. The definitiveness of single-text editions is evaluated ordinarily by their accurate reproduction of the readings of the original, by the justness of their emendations, and by the orderliness and completeness of the apparatus that records the original rejected readings as well as the sources for all departures from the copy-text. In my view other sections of a textual apparatus should be required in a definitive edition, but at least the record of emendation is always basic. Unless the reader can determine where and in what exact respects the original has been altered, no edition can pretend to scholarly definitiveness.

Always subject to dispute in its evaluation is the estimate critics will make of the editor's gullibility in accepting frivolous or sophisticating emendations unlikely to represent the lost pure original; or, at the opposite pole, another editor's equally gullible conservatism in retaining and defending what might better be regarded as the errors of the original,[6] a danger more prevalent these days in the name of scholarship than is unprincipled emendation.

Depending upon their date and the history of their transmission, some originals will need considerable attention paid to the editorial correction less of the words themselves than of the presentation of these words, as through punctuation for instance. Elizabethan manuscripts were often notoriously ill punctuated, or scarcely punctuated at all, and thus they were subject to the compositors' attempts at determining not only the syntactical but also the rhetorical relationship between the words. Since these workmen were in a hurry and not always so advised in their decisions as a modern editor can be from his close acquaintance with an author's style, sometimes hundreds of such editorial alterations must be made and—of course—recorded. Whether in older or in modern texts the intention is not to impose an alien system of presentation, as of the substitution of a purely syntactical for the rhetorical punctuation system of the Elizabethans,[7] but instead, to correct the originals as conservatively as will make sense to an informed reader familiar with the period and its conven-

6. Of course, a critic has some responsibility to make certain that a conservative editor is in fact perpetuating an error by his refusal to emend the original. Reviewers do not always consult the *O.E.D.* as carefully as do conservative editors. Recently, the Wesleyan-Clarendon edition of Fielding's *Tom Jones* was reproved for retaining 'I shall plead to their Jurisdiction', alleged to be nonsense and requiring, in context, the editorial addition of 'not', as in the (unauthoritative) Murphy edition. The editors had had no note on this passage since the *O.E.D.* clearly approved the idiom as used in *Tom Jones*; and in fact the very day that Professor Battestin saw the review, he came upon an identical 'plead to the Jurisdiction' in another contemporary document. The idiom is well established and to add 'not' in the common manner would be a philological sophistication, concealing an interesting idiom from future lexicographers. Correspondingly, another reviewer thought to have one's hair 'stand an end' was an obvious error for 'on end'. Again, *O.E.D.* approves this form as completely correct in Shakespeare's day and later.

7. An unsuccessful attempt at this substitution, in reverse, was that made by M. R. Ridley in the New Arden edition of Shakespeare's *Antony and Cleopatra*, who in a modernized text retained the original Folio rhetorical punctuation—a jarring and unhelpful mishmash of two styles.

tions, and in their own terms both for author and for historical period.[8]

I mention just in passing another form of emendation, since its principle is not always accepted. Because consistency is not an Elizabethan virtue, it would be a foolish exercise to attempt to impose very much uniformity on most features of the presentation of a sixteenth- or seventeenth-century text. For example, one cannot ordinarily distinguish compositor from author with any certainty in Elizabethan spelling, and when a book was set by more than one compositor, each with different spelling habits and sometimes different punctuation and capitalization conventions that he imposed on the text, to attempt to produce any serious uniformity would be essentially to modernize, and thus forbidden in an old-spelling text. However, the case may differ in some nineteenth- and twentieth-century texts. I offer only two examples just as an indication of the problems that an editor may face. In his whole lifetime Stephen Crane, on the evidence of his manuscripts, never prefaced dialogue with anything but a colon except for a handful of slips, whereas in published form his writings are highly inconsistent between colons and commas, according to no system except as various compositors followed copy or altered it according to standard rules of styling. Is it of any value to a reader to present him, in late nineteenth-century texts, with such wildly meaningless mixture of compositorial styles when it is very simple to normalize to what one can guarantee would have been the consistency of the manuscript? William James, interested in spelling reform, among various examples liked to write 'tho' for *though*, and, in the British manner, 'connexion' for *connection*. In the French manner he liked to reduce to lower case the capitals of adjectives made from

---

8. One of the most criticized features of the Yale edition of Dr. Johnson, for instance, is the silent alteration to lower case of noun capitals characteristic of the time, a process that makes a mockery of an old-spelling edition. The Yale reviewer of *Tom Jones's* pleading, previously cited, wondered aloud, "what is really gained by preserving the conventions of an eighteenth-century printing house.... The silent change of the letter *s* from old to new style does not alter what the author was saying. Isn't this also true of the old-fashioned capitalization and italicizing? I ask the question innocently" (*Yale Review*, Autumn 1975, p.133). Innocence, indeed, can go no further than to confuse typographical with rhetorical conventions. The Yale Johnson, which obviously feels uneasy with the concept of old spelling in relation to modern readers would have been better advised to have modernized the text completely, instead of halfheartedly. A definitive edition is not constructed on these terms.

proper names, as in 'kantian' and 'hegelian.' His manuscripts are not invariably consistent in these respects, although generally so; but in correcting his typescripts he tried to impose his wishes, even though missing some examples here and there inadvertently. Moreover, even in proof, for certain of these reform or idiosyncratic usages he would change house-styled normalizations to his preferred forms. What he intended to see in print in these matters is in no possible doubt. Hence the preservation in a book copy-text of a few 'though' oversights, for instance, when the majority of the spellings are 'tho'—would not this retention in an edited text of clear-cut authorial oversights be a curious form of pedantry?[9] I myself firmly believe that for nineteenth- and twentieth-century texts we should normalize in a suitably conservative manner, and always with record, such compositorial departures from an author's norm, and especially the author's own inadvertent slips. But I argue for this delicate procedure only when one can establish what the norm was for an author and that it is present among the variations in the work concerned—otherwise I should not touch it. I am inclined to the view that if one facet of the term definitiveness is indeed faithfulness to an author's intention in an attempt to reproduce *so far as the evidence is present in that work* of what he would himself have done in a careful fair copy, then such normalization is not only innocent when conducted with discretion from a solid base of evidence, but is even a tiny contribution to overall definitiveness in an edition.

In the nature of the case, emendation of a single-authority copy-text can represent nothing more than the attempted *correction* of the original. But when more than one text can be shown to possess authority, alteration of the chosen basic text by reference to the other authority may involve more than correction whenever one text represents the original, or something close to it, and the other a revised

9. Moreover, preservation of original anomalies in such matters will never permit a reader to be certain whether he is faced with a faithfully preserved authorial spelling or with a compositorial form. This normalization has no connection with modernization, of course, either in theory or in practice. Indeed, the result is usually to place a writer more firmly in his own period than in ours, where he does not belong. Ordinarily, also, an author's invariable norm is so restricted that an editor can choose not very many of such variants to normalize with any confidence; hence there is little danger that the original will be altered in an unrecognizable manner.

form of the work. Hence in this textual situation the duty of an editor expands to include the evaluation of all variant readings between the two authorities in an attempt to separate normal transmissional corruption from authorial revision. (In one sense this is what Housman recommended for classical manuscript texts.) The aim of a critical edition, in most circumstances, then, is not to print corrected parallel texts of two authorities on facing pages, but instead, whenever practicable, to conflate these two authorities to produce a reading or critical text that corresponds as closely as the evidence of the documents permits to the author's final intentions in all possible respects. These intentions are not always served by simply reprinting the revised edition, even if only the wording were in question and matters of presentation, or styling, were not to be considered. For example, the fourth edition of Fielding's *Tom Jones* was revised by annotating a copy of the unrevised third edition, but in this process Fielding missed practically every printer's change of his wording made in the third, so that this revised fourth not only contains Fielding's final intentions in respect to some readings but also a large number of words that he never wrote at any time and in his revision failed to recognize as not his own.[10] No text could be called definitive that reproduced these demonstrable textual errors. Opposition has been voiced to such eclectic texts by a small group of students of American literature who were not brought up under the discipline of textual criticism as developed for English literature; but the idea of a single composite final text as refined by Greg's theories seems both so practical and so rational a benefit both to author and to reader as to admit of no controversy as a proposition, subject only to the caveat that a few literary texts exist in such special multiple revised forms as to resist conflation and to require either separate publication or the modified form of separate publication represented by parallel texts. The earlier works of Henry James substantially rewritten for the New York Edition furnish the usual modern examples.

Revised texts are most commonly found in linear relation to each other since ordinarily an author will mark up some earlier edition

10. That by inadvertently passing these textual corruptions he 'approved' them is a proposition not worthy of discussion.

with his revisions, interleaved as necessary, and send it to the printer. Another form of multiple authority is created when two or more texts stem independently—or radiate—from some lost original. The simplest example would be a book set up both in England and the United States, one printer using the ribbon and the other the carbon copy of the absolutely identical typescript. Unfortunately, not all examples are so simple, for one line of the text may have been revised and the other not,[11] or both may have been revised independently and thus differently, or both may have been revised in some part in common and in some part independently, as occurs in the journal and book publication of William James's *A Pluralistic Universe* set from the same basic ribbon and carbon typescript. These two copies had been revised together before James sailed to give the lectures in England; thereafter James revised the copy for the journal further and, independently, the galleys of the book proof stemming from the original copy left behind in Cambridge. A method for treating such multiple witnesses to a basic text, whether or not revised, has long since been developed in classical scholarship as well as in the editing of medieval vernacular manuscripts. However, the introduction of printing created special bibliographical relationships between such texts from the fifteenth century to the present that appear only infrequently in manuscript study, so that new principles and new methods are required.

For over two hundred years Shakespearean editors have been accustomed to treating such examples of multiple authority as occur in *Hamlet, Othello,* and *King Lear* by constructing a single conflated text in the classical or medieval manner. But the problems of radiating texts are so different from those with simple linear relationship—to which modern critics have hitherto been accustomed in the usual run of textual affairs with which they have been concerned—that perhaps no other area of editing theory is more in dispute than this. Any confla-

11. An example would be Stephen Crane's *Third Violet,* the typescript of which was revised for the book but not for syndicate newspaper publication. Even though not revised, one line of a text may derive with an intermediate step in the second branch of radiation. For instance, Cora's typescript of Crane's *Active Service* was so badly done that the American publisher had it retyped from the copy sent him, although the English publisher used the other copy of the original. The retyping introduced various corruptions in the American edition not known in the English.

tion is of course anathema to an utterly conservative critic who, like
McKerrow, or Lachmann before him, longs to have his edited text
served up to him as if it were an ideal case of single authority involving only normal editorial intervention, no matter what the transmission. An advance has been made in the last decade or so, however,
in that many conservatives are now prepared to accept Sir Walter
Greg's theory of copy-text (to which I shall come in a moment); but
it has become the new conservatism to elevate these principles, suitable only for textual revision in one stage or in a series of individual
linear edition-stages, into a form of dogma that excludes the possibility of a definitive edition being constructed by the conflation of
texts with multiple radiating authority. A conservative can see and
understand the rigorous limitations placed upon an editor whose sole
task, as in *Tom Jones,* is to distinguish authorial revision on the one
hand from compositorial corruption on the other.[12] But if two texts
have been revised in radiating relationship to each other and thus
with no direct connection between the two sets of revisions, and if no
overriding advantage appears in establishing that one set was later
than another, then what Greg in another connection called 'the
tyranny of the copy-text' takes over.

According to this new tyranny a conservative is bound to hold that
the only possible definitive edition is that one which establishes the
superior authority of a single line of the revision and reprints that
one line with no more reference to the other than is required by correction only. Most modern upholders of this doctrine for printed texts
do not appear to recognize that in so doing they are reverting to the
seriously tarnished Lachmannian procedures for manuscripts. Such a
position distorts not only Housman but also the Greg rationale of
copy-text, suited for linear relationships in a single line, and hence it
excludes the possibility that a definitive edition could ever select
from among the authoritative readings of two competing texts.[13] Such

12. Or, in what is essentially the same problem, to distinguish the revisions that
Hawthorne made in the proofs of his romances from the compositorial departures among
the variants that collation reveals between the printer's copy manuscript and the first editions of *The House of the Seven Gables, The Blithedale Romance,* and *The Marble Faun.*

13. The emphasis is on the word *select* since in such a situation one cannot properly
speak of the 'emendation' of one text by another when the reading that is less preferred
is not an error.

a position is the more untenable when each of two or more related texts represents a revised form of an original and when—after certain bibliographical limitations on choice have been observed—some decisions may remain that can be made only by an editor's judgment that one reading is superior to the other in completing the author's fullest intentions.[14] Pertinently, in their view, critics argue that no edition can be called definitive that depends so much upon variable editorial judgment, not always explicable in precise and convincing terms because in part stemming from an editor's almost unconscious sympathy with or understanding of the author's peculiar ideas and their expression, and hence not subject to rule.[15]

One may grant, of course, that given the same evidence it is theoretically and even practically possible for two editors tackling the same material to vary markedly in the texts they would construct from it; and it would follow that some difficulty might be felt in asserting that each edition was a definitive one. This is a real problem, but the difficulty seems to me to be more apparent than real. Whenever multiple authority is present, even of the linear kind, differences in judgment are inevitable between editors. Even in a single-authority Shakespearean text, conservative or less inhibited emendation of the

14. This seems to be the situation in *Hamlet* even though the question whether the Folio text represents a revision by Shakespeare of any readings in the Second Quarto is moot. The two texts vary, for whatever reasons, in a number of readings in which we cannot demonstrate that F or Q2 is in error. A similar situation, although with almost no chance for authorial revision, occurs in Beaumont and Fletcher's *Beggars' Bush* and in Fletcher's *Woman's Prize*. In both these texts the question of the earliest or latest version (in transmissional terms only) has very little to do with the editorial problem of distinguishing the true authorial readings from the variants caused by other agents such as scribes and compositors and perhaps some other person who had a hand in preparing the text for a performance. In such a confusion between mutual corruption, sometimes indistinguishable from revision, the authority of a copy-text may have little weight and a document farther from the author's manuscript may as readily preserve the good reading as the nearer one. The present-day proponents of 'unified authority', come what will, seem not always to be acquainted with more than a narrow range of nineteenth-century texts which offer insufficient variety for the construction of general textual theory.

15. Also, let us face it even in this egalitarian age, some critics have superior sensibilities to others and hence, by and large, superior judgment when faced with alternative readings. Dame Quickly's description of Falstaff that on his deathbed 'a babbled o' green fields' in Theobald's emendation may not be so demonstrably what Shakespeare wrote as Warburton's 'a god kissing carrion' in *Hamlet* for the texts' 'good kissing'; but the strained arguments begun by Hotson and picked up by a number of critics in defense of the original *a table of green fields* force meaning by such extreme ingenuity as to defeat probability. Yet they were (and perhaps are) seriously held.

original's deficiencies may produce two different results in dealing with the number of cruxes that occur. Editing, it is true, is often a mechanical matter, governed by fairly stringent rules or guidelines that in many texts ought to produce relatively uniform results in the hands of two different editors, subject chiefly to variation in dealing with real textual cruxes on an individual basis. But the more complex the textual problems involving multiple authority, the more editing becomes an art from which will emerge different decisions when more than crucial variants are involved. Only time and the mass weight of critical opinion can make a final decision about the preferential features of such texts, and the resulting definitiveness, in terms of general acceptance and thus of the longevity of one or other edition.

It seems to me that if the three basic requirements of a definitive edition have been satisfied—that is, a rationally principled text constructed by acceptable methodology for dealing with transmissional problems, the full apparatus for this text, and finally the formal analysis of the documents in which the text is preserved, their relationship and relative authority—if these requirements are satisfied, it is sufficient to consider a scholarly edition as provisionally, or attemptedly definitive, the final judgment to be passed on the results by time. This is what has happened in the texts of Shakespeare and I see no alternative. Pragmatic cold comfort of this sort will not satisfy the school of critics that believes that uniform results are the test of definitiveness. In some circumstances they may be, in part, but uniformity is not a criterion to be applied without critical discrimination. It is not absurd to suggest that 'definitive edition' is a comparative that often cannot be applied as an approximately absolute term until the judgment of time has been secured.[16] If so, then it is more important than ever for textual and other critics to agree on the ground

16. Even after the affirmative of time, no edition except the most mechanical can expect to meet universal approbation for every one of the disputed readings in which editorial judgment has had to decide on one or other variant. So many critics, so many differing (and no doubt often conflicting) opinions. But something of a consensus has proved to be possible, and so long as all of the variants in the collated documents are recorded, as they must be, the edition itself can maintain its usefulness and authority if on the whole it seems to have steered a sensible course. From the sidelines critics have had their fun with this proposition, but they offer no alternative except faithful reprints of documents of unified authority, substantially without emendation, whereas I am talking about editions of complex textual documents where unified authority is impossible.

rules, or criteria within which attemptedly definitive editions should operate so that the judgment of time (which begins of course even with the initial reviews of a new edition) can focus on the results of a common methodology and not be diffused by having to deal as well with divergent views on basic textual ideals and procedures.

I have suggested three criteria that can, I think, be established as the framework within which an attemptedly definitive edition should operate. The methodology by which the text is to be constructed is perhaps the most important of the three, and to this question I have already addressed some remarks about the conditions of single or of multiple authority under which texts are found and of the problems of emendation or selection that may follow. Important as questions of emendation are in textual criticism, they are by no means the only or even, on the whole, the most important part of the textual construct. The amount and kind of emendation is much more importantly decided beforehand by the fundamental decision made as to the most appropriate early text chosen as one's copy-text, that is as the true basis for the edition. Certain of the principles of copy-text have been so thoroughly discussed that only a brief account is necessary here.

A quarter of a century ago Sir Walter Greg pointed out that not all textual documents have unified authority, and indeed we now see that ordinarily this unified authority is strictly possible only when a single early edition was printed which was never authorially revised.[17] When more than one authoritative text exists, as when a later edition is a revision of an earlier, the authority of the texts splits into two parts. The first Greg called the *accidents* of a text, or its *accidentals*, these consisting of such details of its presentation as the punctuation, capitalization, word-division, spelling, and methods of emphasis. The

17. For simplicity's sake I do not consider here the special case of a revised edition so controlled in almost every minute detail of the two parts of the text as to qualify as the copy-text instead of earlier forms of the work. Even in the most extreme of such cases, such as I have encountered with William James, the texture of 'accidentals' in the revised text cannot be quite so authoritative, from a purely technical point of view, as when only a single authority is present and we have no choice. Paradoxically, the accidentals of a revised book text, in James, are usually more authoritative in fact than those in a journal source over which he had chosen to exercise less control; but if the journal article were never revised for a book, and if its manuscript is not preserved, it is the only game in town—our only and absolute authority in a technical sense such as McKerrow so logically discussed in *Prolegomena*.

second is the *substantives*, or the words themselves and their forms. Professor Nidditch has recently proposed the use of the term *formal variants* for Greg's not entirely felicitous 'accidentals' and of *material variants* for Greg's 'substantives.'[18] I shall try to use these interchangeably, for convenience.

Greg's main point was that obviously the revised readings of an author reproduce his fullest intentions[19] more accurately than the original readings and hence must be selected when variation in wording occurs, subject only to the effort on the editor's part to identify a variant in the later edition as a true authorial revision and not as a transmissional corruption. Since critical intelligence evaluating meaning can be brought to bear on this verbal problem, an editor's decision can often be justified. But when a decision seems indifferent to critical analysis, Greg suggested that the odds should favor the editorial adoption of the later reading since it appeared in a text that had general authority for its substantives.

On the other hand, critical intelligence is much less capable of appraising the authority of the accidentals or the formal features of a text, especially in Elizabethan times when every reprinting was sub-

18. Greg's terms are not technical jargon, as has been suggested by unfriendly critics, but seem to derive from distinctions in medieval scholasticism. I should welcome Professor Nidditch's terms more warmly if—like Greg's—they were capable of adjectival as well as nominal use; but unfortunately they are not and thus they are the less convenient to employ in all situations. A scrupulous critic might object to *material* variants that exclude *formal* ones which in their sense may become *material*. This objection is as pertinent for Greg's terms, however, and it implies that textual critics use the differentiation in a more absolute sense than they do. An *accidental* can readily become substantive (or, as I prefer to write, *semi-substantive*) when true substantive meaning is involved in its form.

19. One could as easily say 'final intentions' if it is understood that this is no place to venture on the delicate and complex question of true 'final' in a critical sense versus 'final' in a purely chronological sense. A good example may be drawn from Melville's changes in English editions to adjust his language to non-American readers. Chronologically these are final, but not in any critical sense, usually, since we can be certain most would never have entered the text had it not been for the problems posed by English publication. In the journal articles William James made from his *Pluralistic Universe* lectures he was careful to remove the forms of address to a lecture audience that he was at pains to keep in his book. The alterations for the journal forms of the lectures were chronologically later than the main revision given the book text in galley proof, but that fact does not require an editor to go contrary to James's 'final' intentions and invariably to alter the book to agree with the articles. A considerable amount of recent textual discussion is vitiated by critics taking such phrases as 'substantive variants' or 'final intention' in a completely literal manner without recognizing that special senses inhere to textual language when used by working textual critics.

ject to a different view of the matter, and the task of determining which of the formal variants were the result of authorial revision and which of compositorial restyling is generally insuperable. Moreover, experience suggests that most authors—and especially early ones— would concentrate their revision on the material features, that is the words themselves, and less on the formal features which, especially in Elizabethan times, they knew they could scarcely control in the new edition, even if they greatly cared. It follows that the most authoritative accidentals are those of the edition nearest to the author's manuscript, since these have undergone the minimum of compositorial interference. These, then, should be selected as copy-text for a critical edition, and into their texture should be inserted the substantives of the revised edition which have passed the editor's scrutiny as authorial. A synthetic or eclectic text is thus constructed which in each of its two parts—the formal and the material—is within the circumstances of maximum faithfulness to authorial intentions and (whatever its inevitable shortcomings) may be said to come as close as the documents permit to McKerrow's ideal of an authorial fair copy.

Although Greg's rationale of copy-text was constructed only with Elizabethan texts in mind, it is equally applicable in any period whenever the same distinction between the authority of the accidents and substantives of a text, and the author's variable treatment of them, is valid. Thus with Greg a new principle for the selection of a copy-text was born, one now generally accepted, a principle that for all time destroyed the myth that the last edition in an author's lifetime should automatically be taken as the textual basis. A by-product of this rationale has been less well appreciated. McKerrow's struggles to justify the treatment of Shakespeare's plays with multiple-authority texts—plays like *Othello* or *Troilus and Cressida*—by selecting the generally most authoritative edition and reprinting it conservatively with only a minimum of emendation may now be seen historically as the last defense of the concept of unified authority in an edited text that exists in multiple documents other than simple reprints. Instead, Greg's split authority introduced to modern textual scholarship the concept of the eclectic text in unmodernized form, a revolutionary theory which has still not been sufficiently recognized as of wider application than the rather narrow textual situations to which Greg confined himself.

I select two of these broader situations although I can do little more than mention their circumstances without going into such detail as they properly require. Among modern textual critics lip service is paid only to a handful of invariably mentioned exceptions to Greg's rationale, like Ben Jonson's *Every Man in his Humour* where the substantive revision has been so thorough that it would be impracticable to attempt to place the Folio revised wording within the texture of the Quarto accidentals. But the accidentals in a revision are by no means always at the mercy of the substantives, as with Jonson's play, and examples may arise with more frequency than has been recognized, especially in modern times, in which the author can be shown to have devoted as much attention to the formal features of his text as to its material or substantive features. In his Clarendon edition Professor Nidditch makes a good case for this situation as early as 1690 in the progression of Locke's formal alterations through the successive revisions of *Human Understanding*, and he offers his collations as justification for his choice of the fourth edition as copy-text on the grounds that its accidentals represent Locke's consciously imposed intentions as fully as its substantives. These editions are in linear relationship and they appear to call for a relaxation of Greg's principle, not at all for the reasons adduced for Ben Jonson but instead because the author can be shown to have paid such particular care to the essentials of his formal presentation as to make the fourth edition more authoritative in its accidentals on the whole than the first edition despite the first's closer relationship to the holograph. In this case the mechanical and conjectural measurement of authority on the sole basis of transmissional closeness to a lost manuscript must yield to a superior, that is, to evidence of close authorial supervision of the accidentals in a revised edition.

The release offered by Greg's division of authority from the tyranny and the inequities of the concept of unified authority held by McKerrow has been so welcome to recent textual critics that they have had a tendency to overreact against any other rationale and—simply because the problem does not come under the conditions of Greg's destruction of McKerrow's *Prolegomena* propositions—they have been loath to accept any suggestion of a return to unified authority even when the special situation warrants it. We may take as an example William James's *A Pluralistic Universe* (1909), preserved in a heavily revised manuscript, four of the eight lectures in journal publication prior to the issue of the first edition, and then the book itself. References demonstrate that James had a typescript prepared. The textual evidence then indicates that he revised both ribbon and carbon copy of this typescript, left one (let us call it the ribbon) with the book printer in Cambridge, Massachusetts, before he sailed to deliver the lectures at Oxford, but took the carbon with him. This carbon must have been the copy from which he read his lectures, and then four of its parts were further revised and modified for publication in the *Hibbert Journal*. Comparison of the agreements of journal and book against the manuscript provides us with the numerous revisions he made in both typescripts before sailing. Thus the further variation in the journal texts can be identified as revision at a later stage than that found in the typescript for the book, which was set while James was abroad. Yet the book differs from this reconstructed typescript even more frequently than does the journal, and these variants identify the very considerable further revision from the typescript that James characteristically gave in proof to the text of the book.

This evidence concerns the substantives, of course. However, the accidentals of the book, and to a lesser extent those of the journal articles,[20] have been pretty thoroughly reworked from their manuscript form and in favor of greater consistency to James's usual characteristics. In this special case we know from a considerable body of evidence preserved in other books and their antecedent documents that James was likely to write his manuscripts hurriedly and that he considered them in no sense comparable to McKerrow's fair copies

20. Throughout his career James seems generally to have been careful to read proof, and even to demand revises, for his journal articles, but the total evidence shows, also, that in comparison he was a great deal more scrupulous about revising both accidentals and substantives in his books, which he considered the permanent repositories of his philosophical ideas. As a consequence, although he was his own styler in his books, he was mostly content to accept journal styling of his accidentals and hence his control over this feature of his text was looser in the journal texts than in his books. Various of his articles he knew were only way stations to the final collected form, and he treated them accordingly.

but instead as drafts to be typed, revised, set into type-metal, and then thoroughly revised in galley proof. We also know from preserved documents that James was as concerned to refine and alter his accidentals in this process as he was his substantives. The whole evidence in *A Pluralistic Universe* is almost demonstrable in its quantity and quality that the formal presentation of the book coincides in the vast majority of its details a great deal more closely with James's wishes—his final intentions—than does the manuscript. Under these special conditions and with the special evidence that goes well beyond opinion, one may venture to be heretical and to choose the revised book as copy-text despite the fact that it is at two removes from the preserved holograph. The mechanical measurement of authority in the accidentals must give way to the special conditions of an author's revision of these same features on an equal footing with his revision of the substantives. It is obvious from some of his cautionary statements about his own rationale that Greg would have agreed.

Emendation in this text presents an interesting problem that may arise in multiple radiating authority when revision has been present in both of its branches. A chronological reconstruction of events indicates the practical certainty that James had read galley proof for his book and returned it to the United States before he revised at least three of the four articles for the *Hibbert Journal*. Except for the possibility of further alterations in the page proof of the book, it would seem that the journal articles, although published before the book, in at least some respects offer a later even though sketchier range of revision. It is certain, at any rate, that both book and articles were revised without consultation of each other so that each set of revisions is truly independent. The conservative view would certainly argue that the book must invariably supersede the articles and that the article variants must be disregarded in anything but a corrective capacity.[21]

21. This view runs into some theoretical difficulty in that chronologically the revision of the journal text was later than the main revision of the book in galleys. For James I do not myself believe that such questions of early or late have any practical bearing on the problem: given the evidence of quantity and quality one could scarcely on mere chronology reverse the procedure and take the journal as copy-text, with exclusion of the book's revisions. I suggest merely that James was temperamentally incapable of reading over his own material without tinkering with its style; that on the evidence he made no attempt that can be identified to transfer his journal stylistic revisions to the book since he knew he had already thoroughly revised the book's galleys and that he was chiefly touching up

But in the variant revision of articles and book I recognize precisely the same situation as in James's variant independent revision of the preserved ribbon and carbon copies of the typescript for his book *Some Problems of Philosophy*, which he did not live to see finally through the press. Thus not only in critical theory (as in Greg) but in the observed facts of how James was likely to treat the independent revision of two copies of the same document, I hold that an editor will offer to readers of *A Pluralistic Universe*, as well as of *Some Problems of Philosophy*, both treated broadly as *works*, James's full intentions by inserting in the generally authoritative book copy-text those revisions in the radiating article texts that were not clearly made for the special purpose of adapting material to article presentation. This is a controversial editorial procedure but in my view it is a logical extension of the doctrine of eclectic texts that Greg enunciated in his rationale although under conditions that differ. Indeed, I should be prepared to suggest that this procedure scarcely differs from the commonplaces of Shakespearean editing of textually complex plays like *Hamlet* and *Troilus and Cressida* or *King Lear*, and should come as no shock to anyone whose experience with texts of radiating authority precedes those of the nineteenth century.

I can only sketch in the requirements for the apparatus if an edition is to attempt definitive status. The full record of every alteration to the text must be recorded in a list of Emendations with the identification of the most immediate emending agent and the reading of

---

the unrevised journal typescript copy; and finally that no logical reason is apparent why nonconflicting stylistic improvements in the journal should not under these conditions be perpetuated in an edited text of the *work*, if we adopt Professor Tanselle's acute distinction between 'work' and 'book' for textual purposes. That is, an edition of the 'book' *A Pluralistic Universe* obviously would need to exclude the journal revisions; but if an editor takes a broader view and holds that he is editing *A Pluralistic Universe* as a philosophical work, the book is only a single document that joins the other documents of manuscript and journal articles from which the ideal text of the 'work' must derive. That the book turns out to be the most important of these documents, and indeed must be selected as the copy-text, does not mean that the edition is limited to the book and does not extend to the work. Correspondingly, the selection of the manuscript as copy-text for Hawthorne's *House of the Seven Gables* does not mean that the edited text is of that manuscript and not of the work, which includes the first edition as a second authoritative document even though one inferior to the manuscript despite the authorial proof-corrections that appear in it. For this important distinction in concept, although made in another connection, see G. T. Tanselle, "Descriptive Bibliography and Library Cataloguing," forthcoming in *SB* 30 (1977).

the original copy-text. If any apparatus is to be admitted to the foot of the page, in my view it should be confined to the most important class of emendations, that is, to the substantives only, in which case a separate list of emendations to the accidentals can be placed in an appendix. If the record of substantive emendation is transferred from the foot of the text page to the back of the volume in the interests of providing a clean page for future offset printing in a popular edition, the two kinds of emendation may be joined in one list (probably the most convenient method) or separated. Accompanying the record of emendations should be the record of what I call the Historical Collation. This is usually confined to the substantives but in special cases may well include the accidentals. Its purpose is to make available in one list, at a minimum, all substantive departures from the copy-text. These will be of two classes. In the first, the Historical Collation continues the record of the history of the editor's substantive emendations beyond that of the most immediate emending agent (the custom in the Emendations list) so that a full account through all the collated editions is here presented. Second, the Historical Collation contains all rejected substantive variants appearing in the roster of the editions collated for the purpose of the edition.[22] At the least, this must record the variants in every document that can be assessed as possessing some authority. At an intermediate, early editions within the formative history of the text may be included, even though without authority, as in the Second, Third, and Fourth Folios of Shakespeare. At a maximum, it may also include a record of the rejected substantive readings adopted by previous editors, a device to expand the original documentary list to a relatively full conspectus of the critical history of the text up to the new edition.

If a manuscript is preserved, I hold it to be essential to record in a separate list every variant, whether material or formal, created in the

22. In linear editions an editor must decide whether or not the author's concern with the accidentals of a revised edition warrants the space to add a full record of accidentals to that of the substantives in the Historical Collation. For the edition of William James's Works it was felt that James's care in such matters required a full record. Texts with radiating authority such as various of Stephen Crane's newspaper sketches automatically require the addition of the accidentals to the substantives. It would be pointless, however, to include a record of accidental variants in the Historical Collation for linear editions that had not been revised.

course of its inscription and review. This record should be devised so that any reader can reconstruct the manuscript complete in all its features no matter where he is in residence and thus without travel for a firsthand view.[23] A series of Textual Notes may be useful for discussing especially difficult or interesting emendations or refusals to emend. A Textual Introduction at the minimum should offer a physical description of all authoritative documents, analyze their transmission and relative authority, and explain the use to which they have been put in the editorial procedures adopted for the text.

This elaborate apparatus should offer every textual fact that a reader could himself derive from the authoritative documents used in the preparation of the edition. I am scarcely prepared to argue that such an apparatus reduces the importance of the artful construction of the critical text. That line of argument leads on the one hand to the current German tradition of editing, which is basically that of a textual variorum in which the copy-text is substantially unemended and serves chiefly as a peg on which to hang the all-important apparatus.[24] On the other, it could be used to excuse faults in the construction of a balanced critical text suitable whether in modernized or unmodernized form to serve as a standard for all readers. That is, an overconservative editor might be tempted to an extreme of critical inaction on the ground that the apparatus will provide an interested reader with the evidence for emendation if he himself wishes to make it,[25] a fact only if the Historical Collation provides a sufficiently full record of preceding editions, both early and edited. Or an editor might be led in the opposite direction to an extreme of personally idiosyncratic treatment, confident that a dissenting reader could always recover the readings of the original.

I do not take it that the apparatus should be a substitute for good editing of the text, or that it can offer a crutch to support a crippled

23. The problems of notation for such a list of manuscript variants are examined in my "Transcription of Manuscripts: The Record of Variants," *SB* 29 (1976), 212-64.

24. The principles and methodology for this type of editing, largely unfamiliar in the United States and in England, are expounded by Hans Zeller, "A New Approach to the Critical Constitution of Literary Texts," *SB* 28 (1975), 231-64.

25. The concept of every reader his own editor is a peculiar one, however. With Greg I take it that the business of an editor is to edit. If he is unprepared to take the risks of backing his own judgment, he should peddle another line of goods.

job of editing.[26] What I have chiefly in mind is that this apparatus supports in a powerful manner the claims of an edition to definitiveness if its editor has supplied a text with a correctly chosen copy-text foundation and a reasoned system of emendation, or of conflation in the case of multiple authority. Future years, or even generations, may discover small imperfections of judgment in emendation or in some minor matter of methodology, but these need not make an edition out of date as a consequence. The reasoned choice of copy-text is crucial as the foundation of a definitive text, reasoned emendation or conflation is extremely important, the apparatus is an essential. If these parts link together, a modern text will have achieved a new status in editorial design that should lead to a worthwhile longevity—on its merits.

ADDENDUM

With some hesitation I raise one further point that may apply to 'definitive editions.' In brief, if a so-called definitive edition has secured sufficient common acceptance so that it comes to be relied on as the authority in its field and further printings are called for, revisions as well as corrections always need to be made to improve the value to its readers during the course of its useful life. Indeed, publishers of these editions would be advised to order a somewhat smaller first printing than usual in order to allow for the 'improvement' of the edition by further exposure.

This improvement takes two main paths. First, correction. Despite every precaution that a concerned editor can take, even simple misprints are almost impossible to weed out when a succession of proofreaders, though carefully collating the text against its copy, or even against the original documents, see what they expect to see and not what is actually in type. However, the main difficulty lies less in such obvious and isolated misprints as in the variants from copy now produced as an inevitable by-product of the increasingly low technical state of even the best printing both in the United States and in England, in England now being tardily recognized as an unwelcome but inevitable occupational scholarly hazard whether one is printed by Oxford or by Cambridge. As a consequence, an editor must struggle with very incorrect proofs not only in

26. Since one of the important reasons for the construction of large-scale scholarly editions is the basis they supply for reprinting in popular editions without the apparatus and technical textual discourses, it is clear that a good reading text is a desideratum and that the apparatus is no substitute for a faulty text in methodology or in execution.

mechanical matters but in the substitution or omission of words, a general inability of modern compositors to follow copy accurately and of printers' proofreaders to correct more than technical errors, all of which puts a sometimes insupportable burden upon the securing of absolute accuracy. The problem is not confined to the initial proofs but continues throughout the stages of revision, with at least a 25% factor of further error to be expected in any set of revises. Moreover, between each stage of revision in proof it is customary for printers to reset lines for various reasons—accidents, the improvement of spacing, the elimination of faulty letters or alignment, and so on—this resetting being made of lines that were not marked in proof for alteration. Such resettings are supposed to be ticked off in the next proof to warn the editor to recheck lines that he would not otherwise know had been reset; but often either such lines are not marked at all or else they are incompletely noted. Hence the editor has no means of knowing except through re-collation at each stage what has happened in proof beyond what he has ordered.

When corrected galleys are made up into pages, further proofreading is required to correct errors that follow on the paging. In England the common use of monotype creates endless problems for editors. In the last proofs of his play in the third volume of the Beaumont and Fletcher edition, printed by the Cambridge University Press, Professor L. A. Beaurline found seven fresh errors created by types dropping out when page proofs were made up from corrected galleys thought to have been in final corrected form. Linotype slugs can and do get misplaced when galleys are paged in the United States, so that lines are transposed and even whole slugs dropped and lost in the paging of galleys. (Monotype is by no means immune to these errors, either.) After the editor has passed his final proofs and given the order to print, the job printer (uncontrolled by the publisher) may see things that he thinks need correction and, in a desire to be helpful, he may alter readings without consulting editor or publisher, creating errors, of course, from correct approved readings. Even later, if the printing is done from type-metal, type can get mashed in the press and it is a rare pressman who will submit reset lines to a proofreader; naturally, the editor never knows of these accidents and the errors in resetting until he sees the printed book and a reviewer remarks on his amazing carelessness.

The growing use of printing by offset from photographs of the type-pages prevents such accidents in press but poses its own special problems. Final master proofs, called repros, are submitted to the editor and he is assured that these are the identical pages that will be photographed and that the printer can have no more to do with the type to make surreptitious changes. But the repros submitted to the editor by the Harvard University Press for the first two volumes of the edition of William James had been made up not exclusively of the finally revised and approved page proofs: the careless job printer to whom the books had been entrusted made repros of a dozen or more pages from an early, not the final, stage of the proof-corrected pages of *Pragmatism*. It had been proposed to put the repros on the Hinman Collating Machine against the earliest state of the proofs in order to detect unauthorized and unmarked re-setting of lines, certain to have produced unknown errors. Some of these were discovered though few that had not been turned up by previous stages of proof-reading; but this optical collation did not, of course, disclose the wrong source for the repros since the repros and the faulty early proof quite naturally agreed in their common error and nothing showed up on the machine. Fortunately, the facts of the case were discovered by pure accident, and publication of the first volume was delayed by six weeks until correct repros were provided and machined. It was a previously unencountered paradox that the actual type, as corrected, was in fact identical with the finally approved and revised proofs; but since the wrong set of proofs was chosen for repros, this corrected type would never have seen print. This peculiar situation could not happen, of course, if printing had been by type-metal.

Professor Meriwether adopts the desperate expedient of ordering the pub-lishers not to bind the book until he has machined a copy of the actual printed sheets against the final proofs. He reports that on every occasion he has picked up printers' changes made after he had approved the last proofs. Cancels are then printed to perfect the text. But even this extraordinary precaution does not protect against unauthorized variants that could have crept into the proofs in some intermediate state and by accident never been discovered. Some editors take an extra precaution of demanding special proofs of all discarded lines that the printer keeps in special galleys, and so checking these against the final proofs as one means of discovering unauthorized resetting. Of course, this is useful but one cannot trust the printer to have kept every single discarded lino-type slug from all stages of the proofing; and indeed, the printer of the James edition had melted up these types once he thought the pages were corrected, in disregard of precise instructions. In short, desirable as it is as an ideal, perfection in a printed book is, in practice, an almost complete impossibility in these de-generate printing days, even at the level of mechanical error. This is a fact that must be faced as something of a new phenomenon, no matter what the press and printer.

At the level of the editorial staff's own accuracy, despite every possible pre-caution and series of checks in the preparation of copy, it is always a case of to err is human. Reviewers and concerned readers can always be helpful in improving an edition's next printing by notifying the editor of its inevitable slips. Moreover, with the passage of time and the accumulation of experience, the editor's own view of knotty problems he has had to decide may alter about this detail and that; and the suggestions and criticisms he receives may lead him to change his initial position on some vexed reading or other. This accumulation of experience and of information leading to the improvement of editorial work as something of a cooperative enterprise can usefully perfect an edition through its several printings as a natural course and one to be expected by any sensible user. In this view, if a definitive edition is a scholarly public service, as indeed it is, the community which it serves may well feel an obligation to assist in its progress toward even greater usefulness, over the years. It is the author whose work is perpetuated in the edition who is being served, not the greater glory of the editor—for glory does not now seek out an editor.

The State of Bibliography Today

By G. Thomas Tanselle*

THE Bibliographical Society of America celebrates this year its seventy-fifth anniversary. The attainment of that venerable age is a cause both for self-congratulation and for stocktaking, and I propose to engage in a little of both. Since everything in bibliography—including the meaning of the word itself—seems to give rise to controversy, it may be apt to point out that some punctilious historian is likely to ask whether we are not in fact older than seventy-five. For five years, from 1899 until 1904, the Bibliographical Society of Chicago served by default as the American bibliographical society, and the national society that grew out of it inherited its constitution, membership, and interests.[1] Nevertheless, even if the present society's prehistory extends back to 1899, it was not formally organized until 1904, and its fiftieth anniversary was observed in 1954; so we are on firm ground in regarding the present year as the seventy-fifth. We are thus the third oldest bibliographical society in the English-speaking world: as John Carter put it, when he addressed this society twenty-five years ago, calling himself "a self-appointed delegate" from four British societies, "You may be younger than Edinburgh or London, but you are older than Oxford and much older than my own University's society [i.e., Cambridge's]."[2]

---

* Read before the Annual Meeting of the Bibliographical Society of America at the Pierpont Morgan Library, 26 Jan. 1979. Before beginning his paper, Mr. Tanselle said: "It is particularly fitting that Tom Adams should preside over this anniversary year: he is, I believe, the first president of this Society to be the son of a former president. His father, Randolph G. Adams, was president in 1940-41—that is, at about the halfway point of our history up to now. Anniversaries are always occasions that suggest continuity, and the continuity of bibliography from generation to generation is well represented for us today by Tom Adams."

1. The most detailed account of the Society's early years is Henry B. Van Hoesen, "The Bibliographical Society of America—Its Leaders and Activities, 1904-1939," *PBSA,* 35 (1941), 177-202. See also J. M. Edelstein, "Bibliographical Society of America," in *Encyclopedia of Library and Information Science,* ed. Allen Kent and Harold Lancour, 2 (New York: Dekker, 1969), 395-401. The bibliographical history of the first half of this century, with particular reference to the Bibliographical Society of London, has been expertly treated in *The Bibliographical Society 1892-1942: Studies in Retrospect* (London: Bibliographical Society, 1945), which includes a chapter by William A. Jackson on "The Study of Bibliography in America," pp.185-87.

2. "Bibliography and the Rare Book Trade," *PBSA,* 48 (1954), 219-29 (quotation from p.221).

Among the nearly four dozen constituent societies of the American Council of Learned Societies, there are some dozen and a half that antedate the BSA, including the societies devoted to philology, biblical literature, modern languages, history, economics, folklore, psychology, and philosophy—a roll call that suggests the course of development of professional self-awareness among the scholars in various fields in the late nineteenth century. The BSA's origins, therefore, go back to that great period for the formation of learned societies in America, the period from the 1870s through the early years of this century. Organization does not necessarily imply agreement, and bibliographers since then have repeatedly debated the nature of their calling and the definition of their subject; but their field is by no means unique in giving rise to such discussion, which is after all a sign of intellectual vitality. There is in any case an underlying level of agreement that holds us together, a recognition that we are associated in a common undertaking. And we have reason to take pride in the course of development that has led us to our seventy-fifth year and in the state of the intellectual health of our field on this occasion.

In assessing where we now stand, we must take into account work produced outside, as well as inside, the United States. Although Americans have played an important role in modern bibliography, it would be unduly parochial to limit our view to their contributions, or to American bibliography defined in any other way, and would give a false impression of the purview of our Society. BSA members, after all, come from both sides of the Atlantic, and BSA publications—articles in the *Papers* as well as separate monographs—range far beyond American subjects. The present occasion is best observed, then, by looking at the Anglo-American tradition of bibliography as a whole. And this moment is an appropriate one for reflection: the death, just within the last few years, of such figures as John Carter and Graham Pollard, of A. N. L. Munby and Donald G. Wing, of Allan Stevenson and Allen Hazen, of John S. Van E. Kohn and Michael Papantonio, has put us in a retrospective mood and has emphasized how much we owe to the generation of bibliographers who were working in the past quarter century. As if the death of so many prominent figures does not in itself indicate that an era is ending, the feeling has been reinforced by the appearance in recent years of a remarkable number of volumes of collected essays or reminiscences and of *Festschriften*. We have had, for example, in the last decade or so, the collected essays of Victor Scholderer (1966), W. W. Greg (1966), William A. Jackson (1967), A. F. Johnson (1970), and A. N. L. Munby (1977) and the *Festschrift* for Graham Pollard (1975). Happily, however, such occasions are not always valedictory, and we have also had collected volumes from Curt Bühler (1973), Fredson Bowers (1975), and Howard Nixon (1978), who continue to add to their splendid achievements. Their volumes, indeed, could hardly be bettered as symbols of sustained work over the last twenty-five years: Nixon's is particularly symbolic, containing, as it does, his regular contributions on bindings to a quarterly journal founded just before our fiftieth anniversary, contributions which thus reached their hundredth number just before our seventy-fifth. If publications of this kind inevitably cause us to look backward, they also suggest continuity, as we have been particularly reminded by Geoffrey Keynes's *Bibliotheca Bibliographici* (1964), Margaret B. Stillwell's memoirs (1973), and the book of tributes celebrating Percy Muir's eightieth birthday (1974)—for these three figures were already well known by the time of this Society's twenty-fifth year, and their publications have continued from the 1920s to the present. (Keynes's latest bibliography, of Berkeley, appeared in 1976; Miss Stillwell published two books with this Society in the 1970s; and Muir still writes regularly for *The Book Collector* and published a book on *Victorian Illustrated Books* in 1971.) Other volumes could be named, such as the reminiscences of E. Millicent Sowerby (1967), Wilmarth Lewis (1967), David Randall (1969), David Magee (1973), and H. P. Kraus (1978) and the *Festschriften* for Alfred Fairbank (1965), Dorothy Miner (1974), John Sparrow (1977), Harold Hugo (1978), and N. R. Ker (1978). But enough has been said to indicate that a dominant strain in the bibliographical literature of the past decade has been one of nostalgia.

The distance bibliography has traveled since the BSA's fiftieth anniversary can be suggested by recalling that in 1954 *Studies in Bibliography* was a young publication, just five years old, and that Bowers's *Principles of Bibliographical Description* had been available for only five years, Greg's "The Rationale of Copy-Text" for three, and Carter's *ABC for Book Collectors* for two. These now-classic works have formed a good part of the essential equipment that bibliographers of the last twenty-five years have employed. During that period, another half dozen of Greg's books came out, including the last two volumes of his great *Bibliography of the English Printed Drama to the Restoration* (1957, 1959). Bowers, who was emerging as Greg's successor in the early 1950s, became the undoubted leader of the field after Greg's death in 1959 and has remained the dominant force, publishing his Sandars Lectures (*Textual and Literary Criticism,* 1959), his Lyell Lectures (*Bibliography and Textual Criticism,* 1964), and an extraordinary number of editions, ranging from Renaissance drama to twentieth-century American philosophy, in addition to maintaining *Studies in Bibliography* at a high level. These years have also seen many publications from Stanley Morison, including *The Typographic Book 1450-1935* (1963) and the magnificent volume on John Fell (1967); from Allan Stevenson, who in articles, in the Hunt catalogue (1961), and in his study of the Constance missal (1967) greatly advanced the bibliographical analysis of paper; and from William B. Todd, who in his pioneering articles and his bibliography of Burke (1964) brought a new sophistication and rigor to the bibliographical examination of eighteenth-century books. From *The Rothschild Library* (1954) to Elizabeth L. Eisenstein's *The Printing Press as an Agent of Change* (1979), this period has produced more than its share of bibliographical landmarks, such as (to name a few not already mentioned) Jacob Blanck's *Bibliography of American Literature* (1955-   ), Clifford K. Shipton's completion of Evans's *American Bibliography* (1955) and his ensuing work on the microcards of Evans titles (1955-64), Shaw and Shoemaker's extension of the coverage into the nineteenth century (1958-63), the Davis and Carter edition of Moxon (1958), Charlton Hinman's *The Printing and Proof-reading of the First Folio of Shakespeare* (1963), Frederick R. Goff's third census of *Incunabula in American Libraries* (1964), Graham Pollard and Albert Ehrman's *The Distribution of Books by Catalogue* (1965), D. F. McKenzie's *The Cambridge University Press, 1696-1712* (1966), Rudolf Hirsch's *Printing, Selling and Reading, 1450-1550* (1967), Philip Gaskell's *A New Introduction to Bibliography* (1972), C. William Miller's bibliography of Benjamin Franklin's Philadelphia printing (1974), D. F. Foxon's *English Verse, 1701-1750* (1975), Katharine F. Pantzer's completion and publication of one volume (1976) of the revision (begun by W. A. Jackson and F. S. Ferguson) of the Pollard and Redgrave *STC,* and the Munby-Coral list of British book auction catalogues (1977). The list must also include the large series of editions prepared under the auspices of the Center for Editions of American Authors and its successor, the Center for Scholarly Editions; the contributions to collecting history made by Munby in his *Phillipps Studies* (1951-60), Millicent Sowerby in *The Library of Thomas Jefferson* (1952-59), Edwin Wolf 2nd in *The Library of James Logan of Philadelphia, 1674-1751* (1974), Anthony Hobson in *Apollo and Pegasus* (1975), and Nicolas Barker in *Bibliotheca Lindesiana* (1977); and such catalogues as the Walters Art Gallery's on bookbinding (1957) and calligraphy (1965), Harrison D. Horblit's Grolier Club catalogue listing *One Hundred Books Famous in Science* (1964), the Streeter auction catalogue (1966-69), *Printing and the Mind of Man* (1967), Colton Storm's catalogue of the Everett D. Graff collection (1968), and the great series based on exhibitions at the Morgan Library, as well as the new edition of the *General Catalogue* of the British Library (1959-66) and the *National Union Catalog: Pre-1956 Imprints* (1968-   ). The flourishing of bibliography in this period is also reflected in the founding of the Printing Historical Society (1965), the American Printing History Association (1974), the Private Libraries Association (1956), the bibliographical societies of Australia and New Zealand (1969), Northern Illinois (1973), and Birmingham (1978), and the Toronto editorial conferences (1965), and in the establishment of various newsletters on bookish subjects, most notably Terry Belanger's *Bibliography Newsletter* (1973-   ). This list of publications and events is obviously not a systematic one, and it has left out names that deserve a place in even a short list. But I think it demonstrates that bibliography has been an enormously active and productive field in the last quarter century; indeed, the quantity of important work has been greater than anyone could reasonably have predicted in 1954.

This impressive development should not, however, lead to complacency, because it has by no means been free of problems, and many problems of method and approach remain. The four publications I mentioned earlier as immediately preceding our fiftieth anniversary have become basic documents in four different areas of bibliography. I should like to comment briefly on the present situation in these four areas and point out some of the still-unresolved problems that will have to engage the attention of bibliographers in the next quarter century.[3]

The appearance of *Studies in Bibliography* can be seen in retrospect as a manifestation of a new movement in the study of analytical bibliography. McKerrow, Pollard, and Greg had of course already done much work to show the bearing of physical evidence on literary matters. But a series of articles by Bowers, Hinman, and William H. Bond, just before and after the Second World War, on the bibliographical evidence furnished by running titles, half-sheet imposition, cast-off copy, and proof correction, foreshadowed the nature of things to come. An increasing body of scholars launched a new onslaught on the physical evidence furnished by English Renaissance books and, building on one another's work, erected an elaborate superstructure of analysis. In the hands of its best practitioners, such as Hinman and Robert K. Turner, Jr., bibliographical analysis became a much more sophisticated and finely tuned instrument than it had been before. Hinman's two-volume work, indeed, stands as the monument of the method and shows what a remarkable amount it is possible to learn about the printing of a Renaissance book by the patient accumulation and examination of small details; his study demonstrates a wide range of techniques of analysis and should serve as the textbook for anyone wishing to learn to use these techniques with sensitivity and sense.

Unfortunately, however, not all bibliographical analysis has attained this level, for the quantitative aspects of the work sometimes lull the workers into a false sense of the certainty of their conclusions, and the notion that the undertaking is largely mechanical has sometimes attracted the kind of person not inclined to make—or perhaps not capable of making—careful judgments in the weighing of evidence. Certainly the work lends itself to facile parody and ridicule: the vision of a scholar spending months and years tabulating the recurrences of various broken letters in a particular edition conforms all too readily with the popular stereotype of a pedant; and the less accomplished articles, which present statistics unaccompanied by significant analysis (implying that there is a self-evident need to know, for instance, all the locations of a particular

3. I am not taking up the kind of bibliography sometimes called "enumerative." For some useful remarks on the present state of that field, see Jackson R. Bryer, "From Second-Class Citizenship to Respectability: The Odyssey of an Enumerative Bibliographer," *Literary Research Newsletter*, 3 (1978), 55-61.

damaged center rule), play all too easily into the hands of those who want to believe that this kind of investigation has lost sight of priorities or proportions. Unquestionably there has been resistance, or even hostility, to analytical bibliography on the part of some literary critics. Whether the reason has been an ill-founded distrust of all statistics in literary study or a more defensible belief that the results are frequently inconclusive, the fact remains that a gap often exists between the analytical bibliographer and the literary critic. Repairing this rift is an important task for the future; and because neither side is blameless, both will have to mend their ways.

The heart of the problem can be approached through a well-known statement of Fredson Bowers: "When bibliography in its pure state *can* operate at the level of demonstration, and bibliographical and critical judgement clash . . . , the critic must accept the bibliographical findings and somehow come to terms with them."[4] The finality of this pronouncement startled many critics in 1959, and no doubt startles some still. But the justice of it is undeniable, whenever the conditions it describes obtain. The problem is in knowing when a physical analysis is conclusive. Physical facts may not lie, but false generalizations can easily be drawn from them. Precisely this point has been pursued by D. F. McKenzie in the most substantial criticism yet made of analytical bibliography. His essay in *SB* entitled "Printers of the Mind" (1969) is one of the most celebrated of the last twenty-five years. To the extent that it causes bibliographers to be more cautious in drawing generalizations from their evidence, it is a beneficial force. For there is no doubt, as McKenzie effectively shows, that bibliographers have sometimes based conclusions on insufficient evidence or have made unwarranted assumptions about the regularity and efficiency of printing practice in order to reduce the number of variables for analysis. (There is the inevitable line about the compositor with a hangover whose lack of efficiency throws off the bibliographer's careful calculations.) But it would be unfortunate if his article had the effect of discouraging work in analytical bibliography or casting doubt on the importance of examining physical evidence. McKenzie's criticisms of

4. *Bibliography and Textual Criticism* (Oxford: Clarendon Press, 1964), pp.155-56. Cf. his earlier statement in *The Bibliographical Way* (Lawrence: University of Kansas Libraries, 1959): "It cannot be repeated too often that when the evidence of analytical bibliography is available, critical judgment must be limited by bibliographical probabilities and must never run contrary to bibliographical findings" (p.18).

the inductive method seem less convincing than his demonstrations of weaknesses in particular arguments; it is difficult to see how we can hope to make advances without inductive observation. Even granting that hasty generalizations have sometimes resulted, I think it can be said that one of the principal bibliographical accomplishments of the last twenty-five years has been the intensive analysis of the physical evidence preserved in Renaissance books. The evidence of the printed matter itself is, after all, the primary evidence the bibliographer has to work with. External documents, such as printers' ledgers, although they are of great interest in their own right, are secondary to the books themselves as evidence about the books. One could vary Bowers's statement for a different purpose by saying that when the evidence within a book contradicts what is said about its production in some supposedly authoritative document, the latter must yield.

In the years ahead analytical bibliography must not retreat but must build in two ways on the warnings offered by McKenzie. First, it must be integrated into, and expand in conjunction with, the body of work on printing, publishing, and book-trade history. There is too often a lack of communication between historians of printing and those scholars—usually students of literature—who record the typographical details of a particular book. That there is great interest in the serious study of printing and publishing history is illustrated by the appearance of the *Journal of the Printing Historical Society, Publishing History,* and *Printing History* (and we need much more of the kind of work they publish); but it is safe to say that most of those who appear in such journals have little acquaintance with compositor analysis or the examination of headlines as evidence of the deployment of skeleton formes. The generalizations of printing and publishing history must ultimately be based, of course, on the accumulation of facts about individual cases; at the same time, an informed reading of the evidence in a given book can occur only if that evidence is viewed in the context of what is known about the printing practices of the time. The two pursuits are reciprocal. Histories of printing sometimes suffer from too exclusive a reliance on documents external to the books themselves, whereas analytical bibliography frequently is weakened by a narrowness of vision that does not take in anything outside a single book (not even the other jobs under way in the same printing shop). Research in the two areas must go forward jointly, to the benefit of both.[5]

A second way in which analytical bibliography must mature is in developing a more rigorous self-discipline. The framework for such assessment has been provided by Fredson Bowers in his Lyell Lectures, published as *Bibliography and Textual Criticism* (1964). These lectures—which have never received the attention they deserve—address themselves to the inductive nature of bibliographical analysis and define three orders of certainty—the possible, the probable, the demonstrable—to which various analytical conclusions can be assigned. If analytical bibliographers begin to pay more heed to Bowers's observations, and to work together with historians of printing and publishing, there is every reason to hope that this field will expand, not only into further investigation of Renaissance books but into all the other periods where analytical bibliography has barely scratched the surface. Even scholars of the caliber of Foxon, Gaskell, Hazen, and Todd have not been able to solve all the problems of eighteenth-century bibliography, and later periods have attracted still smaller numbers of dedicated workers. Edwin Wolf a few years ago impressively exposed the great lack of bibliographical analysis of early American books.[6] There is an enormous amount to be learned about printing and publishing from the books presently on our shelves, and the responsible development of new or more refined analytical techniques for extracting that information is surely one of the great desiderata in bibliography at present.

Analytical bibliography—it should no longer need to be argued—is not simply an ancillary discipline but is of interest in its own right, by providing statistical evidence about various printing and publishing practices. It does, however, underlie certain other kinds of bibliographical study, one of which is descriptive bibliography: regardless of the amount of detail they contain, bibliographical descriptions must grow out of some confrontation of the physical evidence. Bowers's *Principles of Bibliographical Description* provided at mid-century a rigorous and

5. Some desiderata in American printing history have recently been summed up by Rollo G. Silver in "Writing the History of American Printing," *AB Bookman's Weekly*, 59 (16 May 1977), 3035-43 (also printed separately by Edna Beilenson for the American Printing History Association).

6. "Historical Grist for the Bibliographical Mill," *SB*, 25 (1972), 29-40.

sensitive guide, and because it was firmly based on the standards that had evolved over the previous seventy-five years it was accepted at once as the classic treatment of the subject, and has remained so. Additional statements since then, by Bowers and by others, have revised some details here and there but have left the basic structure unaltered.[7] One might imagine, then, that the general level of the descriptive bibliographies published in the past quarter century would have been higher than what prevailed earlier. There have been, it is true, a number of excellent descriptive bibliographies during this period, but there have been even more inadequate ones, and I am afraid that no dramatic improvement can be discerned.

Why this should be so is a complicated question, but one of the reasons must surely be the state of analytical bibliography: the fact that analytical bibliography has not yet developed to the point where a synthesis and codification, comparable to Bowers's for descriptive bibliography, has appeared. This explanation is only a partial one, of course, for one can gather from many of the less satisfactory bibliographies that their authors would not have been inclined to engage in much bibliographical analysis in any case. If those who are concerned to get their names into print quickly have sometimes been misguided enough to think that an author bibliography is the ideal vehicle for this purpose, they have unfortunately been abetted in this enterprise (or lack of it) by some publishers who are more interested in having another author bibliography to publish than in having a good author bibliography. It used to be said that bibliographies were difficult to get published, because they were expensive to produce and had a small audience. Now, it seems, they are almost eagerly sought, at least by certain publishers. The reason is not simply that they do not have to be expensive to produce (especially if they are reproduced directly from the author's typescript and if that typescript is not given a careful checking); more important is the fact that, being reference books, they can be expected to have a relatively stable and predictable market in a time when libraries are forced to cut back. I would be the first to agree that a good reference department must buy author bibliographies as they come out, whether those bibliographies are praiseworthy or shoddy. But I deplore the exploitation of this situa-

7. See, in particular, Bowers's "Bibliography Revisited," *Library*, 5th ser., 24 (1969), 89-128.

tion by authors and publishers who rush new volumes into print prematurely, with little concern for their quality. Those responsible often defend themselves with some version of another old saying: that a bad bibliography is better than none at all. I am not convinced of this proposition, for errors in print are hard to eradicate, and the difficulties they cause all round are by no means always offset by whatever merits the work may otherwise have. Furthermore, the existence of such a bibliography may cause publishers to feel—whether or not the feeling is actually warranted—that the market will not bear another bibliography of the same writer for some time. It is obviously true that scholarship advances by stages, with defective works being replaced by more reliable ones; but surely there is a point at which lowering one's sights begins to partake less of healthy realism than of sheer irresponsibility. There has been a flurry of unfortunate author bibliographies and checklists lately, and some reviewers are beginning to call attention to the fact.[8] How the trend can be altered is difficult to say; but the problem is one that those seriously interested in bibliography must continue to ponder.

Now some of these so-called bibliographies are intended only as checklists, and the question whether or not they should have been conceived differently leads one into a major issue of methodology that has yet to be satisfactorily addressed. Just how much detail is appropriate for a given bibliography and how (or whether) the amount of detail can be varied within a single bibliography are matters that have been debated for more years than this Society has been in existence, but it is doubtful that we are nearer a solution. The publication of Todd's Burke bibliography provided the occasion for some exchange of views in the columns of the *TLS* on the so-called "degressive principle"—a topic of greater moment than many that have appeared in that space. More recently, the relation between full-dress bibliographical descriptions and less detailed entries—indeed, the relation between bibliographies and catalogues—has been much in the air, largely because of the planning for and work on the eighteenth-century short-title catalogue.[9] As Miss Pantzer's masterly revision of the original *STC* shows, an STC does not necessarily imply brevity of research or shortness of entry. Clearly there will never be uni-

8. See, for example, Eric Korn's review in the *Times Literary Supplement,* 18 Aug. 1978, p.931.

9. Some of this discussion is summarized in my "Descriptive Bibliography and Library Cataloguing," *SB,* 30 (1977), 1-56.

versal agreement on how detailed a particular bibliography or catalogue ought to be or on the extent to which a catalogue should involve research outside the collection being catalogued. But rigid guidelines are not what one wants in any case; what is important is that decisions about the level of detail in a bibliography emerge from the intelligent assessment of various considerations both theoretical and practical, an assessment that would involve the balancing of the potential usefulness of a detail against the time and effort required—given the present state of research—to produce it. Too often, a thoughtlessly restricted view of the purpose of descriptive bibliography results in a narrow conception of potential usefulness: details may be excluded, for instance, simply because they fail to assist in the identification of a first impression. Although it has been more than half a century since Michael Sadleir demonstrated the value of a descriptive bibliography as a segment of printing and publishing history—his Trollope bibliography (1928) is the *locus classicus* for this point of view—many would-be bibliographers have not yet learned the lesson. Too few of those who produce author bibliographies, even now, conceive of a descriptive bibliography as a *history*—as a study of a carefully circumscribed area of printing and publishing history, preserving details about type, paper, binding, and the processes of production and distribution. If descriptive bibliography is to make real progress in the coming years, Sadleir's point must become more widely and thoroughly understood. When it is, questions about quantity of detail, though they will certainly not disappear, will be discussed in a more productive context; and the pointless distinction—now dying but by no means dead—between bibliographies for collectors and bibliographies for scholars will have received its fatal blow.

What underlies this old idea that scholars do not need to know physical details—the collector's "points"—is the failure to recognize the connection between intellectual content and physical form. In recent years this connection has been given increasing prominence by the great amount of activity in editing—which, in turn, has developed from another of those publications that just preceded our fiftieth anniversary, Greg's "The Rationale of Copy-Text,"[10] now surely to be regarded as one of the most influential scholarly essays ever published. As championed by Fredson

10. *SB*, 3 (1950-51), 19-36; reprinted in his *Collected Papers*, ed. J. C. Maxwell (Oxford: Clarendon Press, 1966), pp. 374-91.

Bowers, this essay has become the foundation on which an imposing array of multivolume editions now rests. Anyone surveying the bibliographical scene of the last twenty-five years has to be struck by the tremendous increase in scholarly editing, and in discussions about such editing, that took place in that period. And whatever criticisms one may have of particular policies or volumes, one must admit that these editions as a whole—those produced under the auspices of the CEAA and the CSE, and other editions influenced by them—constitute one of the great bibliographical achievements of our time.[11] They are of course a literary achievement as well, but I wish here to emphasize their bibliographical accomplishment: these volumes form a massive storehouse of data regarding printing and publishing practices and the physical details of books. In most cases they are far more thorough than the existing descriptive bibliographies of the authors concerned and, until fuller bibliographies appear, should routinely be consulted in conjunction with the bibliographies. And collectively they amount to the most comprehensive and detailed survey of nineteenth-century publishing customs available.

All this information, furthermore, is not mere decoration—a lagniappe offered in addition to the main business of editing—but is the result of research that is essential for informed textual decisions. The lesson that these editions teach—or, if that is too optimistic a verb, the lesson to which they expose—a largely nonbibliographical audience is the impossibility of carefully studying the content of a text without knowing the physical history of its transmission. One is constantly astonished by the naïveté with which otherwise sophisticated readers unquestioningly assume that what is in print before them is *the* text of the work they are reading. The current interest in editing, and the resultant outpouring of editions, should eventually produce a more widespread understanding that editing is the point where literary study and the study of the history of books and printing come together. Editing is not solely bibliographical, and bibliographical knowledge does not by itself make a good editor; but an editor cannot be good without taking bibliographical matters into account. Those who think they are concerned only with the intellectual

11. A convenient listing of many of these editions, along with a survey of the editorial literature that has grown up along with them, is in *The Center for Scholarly Editions: An Introductory Statement* (New York: Modern Language Association of America, 1977), pp.4-15 (printed also in *PMLA,* 92 [1977], 586-97).

content of books generally assume that research into the technology of book production has no direct bearing on them as readers and critics; the new editions dramatically demonstrate how wrong that position is, but we have a long way to go before this fact is accepted as common knowledge, even among scholars.

Greg's essay, to which most of these editions are linked in one way or another, has by now been repeatedly and variously analyzed and interpreted. It has its weak points, to be sure, but it has proved itself to contain a particularly generous ration of sound advice and to provide a remarkably flexible approach to editorial problems. Those who criticize the current dominance of Greg as a sign of rigidity and dogmatism in editorial circles fail to understand that the essence of Greg's approach is its adaptability and lack of prescriptiveness. Although a good many of the criticisms of Greg have been misguided, they have probably served a useful purpose in the long run: by making editing the center of a controversy, they have caused more people to be aware of editorial scholarship and the issues it struggles with. There is not yet by any means a consensus among scholars, either within a single field or between fields, regarding the theoretical or the practical aspects of editing; but editorial activity and standards have risen together over the last twenty-five years, partly as a result of the MLA committees on editing and the fact that some of the well-established editions have served as productive training grounds for young editors. One of the important tasks for the future is to encourage an interdisciplinary spread of editorial discussion—so that the editors of the letters of a novelist, of a statesman, of a scientist, or of a sculptor, for example, will not be working in isolation from what their fellow editors in other fields are doing. Of the recent criticisms of Greg that deserve serious consideration, one is that perhaps for some periods the accuracy of compositors was such that the odds shift, making later, rather than earlier, readings the ones to fall back on in the absence of other evidence. Another criticism is that Greg did not adequately consider varying kinds of authorial intention that might modify the concept of "author's final intention" as the goal of editing. It may be that both these points result from an overly narrow interpretation of Greg's essay, but in any case further debate on such matters will strengthen editorial theory.

Another classic work published just over twenty-five years ago, Carter's

ABC for Book Collectors, serves to remind us on this occasion of another important area of bibliographical endeavor. Those who collect books (both for themselves and on behalf of institutions) and those who handle the selling of books (both by auction and through shops and catalogues) contain among their number some of the most learned members of the bibliographical world; and their contributions, both tangible and intangible, to the well-being of the world of books have shown no signs of becoming less plentiful. Carter's book, now in its fifth edition, has been basic reading for a whole generation; and the young collectors and dealers of scholarly bent now entering the scene—of whom there are many—can be expected to be all the more thoughtful in their approach as a result of having been nurtured on Carter. Two of the characteristics of the past twenty-five years have been the founding or increased development of special collections departments in institutional libraries and the decline in the number of general used-book dealers in central-city locations—both tending to restrict the availability of many of the kinds of books that have traditionally been collected. The present widespread interest in book collecting is in part the result of its discovery by investors who had formerly placed their money elsewhere, and their entry into the book market has put even more pressure on the dwindling supply of so-called "collectible books." Unfortunately, many recent guides for collectors, inspired largely by this trend, have been based on an unthinking approach to collecting and have continued to stress the well-trod paths. Instead, collectors should be encouraged to develop new fields: otherwise they will miss the satisfaction of creating unified entities that make contributions to knowledge. Imaginative collectors must be scholars; indeed they become scholars in the process of collecting. For all that has been said about the interdependence of collecting and scholarship, too many people still behave as if these activities can be separated: one still sees bibliographies, for instance, that are claimed to be for collectors rather than scholars, as if the distinction were not artificial and self-defeating. Just as there can never be an end to the search for knowledge, there can never be a shortage of ideas for productive collecting. As the supply of certain classes of books dries up, the importance of previously neglected approaches is gradually discovered; collectors who move in those new directions are pioneer scholars, charting new areas of study. The vitality of collecting depends on the continued emergence of persons with this viewpoint, and the state of collecting today would be healthier if this fact were more widely recognized.

In commenting on some of the problems that exist in these various branches of bibliography, I do not mean to underestimate the great accomplishments that have occurred in the past quarter century. There is no doubt that this period has been an exciting and productive one for those engaged in bibliographical studies. But in any field that is intellectually alive, pride over past achievements will inevitably be tempered by recognition of how much of a basic nature there is yet to think about and to do. What I have been saying about analytical and descriptive bibliography, editing, and collecting will not come as news to members of this Society; but the issues are no less fundamental because they are familiar. I have rehearsed them once again in the hope that we can all agree, whatever our own particular interests, that these matters are indeed crucial and must be addressed in the years immediately ahead. For an essential element in the success of this enterprise—the refrain I have found myself repeating in connection with each area—is cooperation and communication among bibliographers of diverse approaches and concerns. Bibliography, like other fields, is full of specialties; but we must not allow the situation to develop in which these specialties grow in isolation from one another. The historian of printing machinery, the editor of literary texts, the collector of private press books, and the library cataloguer must be able to exchange ideas—must do so, in fact, more than they do now—for their fortunes, and those of all other students of the book, are tied together.[12] John Carter spoke on our fiftieth anniversary of the interdependence of bibliography and the book trade: "I am thinking," he said, "of that cross-fertilization between these two departments of bibliophily, that constant enlargement of scope and enrichment of texture which each derives from the enlightened practitioners of the other" (p.223). If this kind of relationship can be encouraged to grow still stronger among all branches of the book world, we shall have an even larger roster of achievements to celebrate at our centennial.

12. F. N. L. Poynter speaks in similar vein of the unity of the world of bibliography in *Bibliography: Some Achievements & Prospects* (Berkeley and Los Angeles: University of California School of Librarianship, 1961), p.4.